水下考古学研究

Studies of Underwater Archaeology

第二卷 Volume 2

国家文物局水下文化遗产保护中心 编

科学出版社
北京

内容简介

本书为水下考古学及相关研究领域的学术论文集刊，现由国家文物局水下文化遗产保护中心编印，拟不定期出版。本卷为第二卷，刊发18篇论文，内容涉及东南亚海域沉船及出水文物研究、东非水下考古新发现、中国古外销陶瓷与海外贸易史研究、出水文物保护、欧洲船舶考古与历史等方面，是一本以水下考古学研究为主的综合性学术集刊。

图书在版编目（CIP）数据

水下考古学研究. 第2卷 / 国家文物局水下文化遗产保护中心编. —北京：科学出版社，2016
 ISBN 978-7-03-049560-0

Ⅰ.①水… Ⅱ.①国… Ⅲ.①考古技术－水下技术－丛刊 Ⅳ.①K854.1-55

中国版本图书馆CIP数据核字（2016）第189575号

责任编辑：李 茜 ／ 责任校对：张凤琴
责任印制：肖 兴 ／ 装帧设计：北京美光设计制版有限公司

科学出版社 出版
北京东黄城根北街16号
邮政编码：100717
http://www.sciencep.com

北京华联印刷有限公司 印刷
科学出版社发行　各地新华书店经销

*

2016年3月第 一 版　　开本：889×1194 1/16
2016年3月第一次印刷　　印张：25 1/2
字数：734 000

定价：320.00元
（如有印装质量问题，我社负责调换）

编辑委员会

主　　任　　柴晓明

副 主 任　　宋建忠

委　　员　（按姓氏笔画排列）

　　　　　　王大民　权奎山　孙　键　吴春明　宋建忠
　　　　　　张　威　林　果　杭　侃　赵嘉斌　柯　兰（法）
　　　　　　姜　波　栗建安　柴晓明　徐光冀

执行主编　　孟原召

目录

Contents

001 | 记"黑石号"（*Batu Hitam*）沉船中的广东青瓷   谢明良
On the Guangdong Celadon Wares from the Belitung Shipwreck   HSIEH Ming-liang

021 | 关于所谓"的惺号"及其出水文物的一些意见   陈国栋
Some Thoughts on the So-called "Tek Sing" Wreck
and Its Marine Artifacts   CH'EN Kuo-tung

045 | 9~14世纪南海及周边海域沉船的发现与研究   童歆
Findings and Researches of Shipwrecks in South China Sea
and Southeast Asian Waters, 9th to 14th Century   TONG Xin

102 | 关于奥美尼角沉船遗址的初步认识   邓启江 张辉 曾瑾
The Preliminary Research on the Ngomeni Ras Shipwreck Site
   DENG Qi-jiang / ZHANG Hui / ZENG Jin

119 | 景德镇旸府山明代窑址瓷器之考察   陈冲 刘未
Study of Porcelains from Kiln Site of Yangfushan in Jingdezhen of
Ming Dynasty   CHEN Chong / LIU Wei

138 | 肯尼亚蒙巴萨耶稣堡出土克拉克瓷的便携式XRF产地研究
   崔剑锋 徐华烽 秦大树 丁雨
Provenance Study Using Portable XRF Analysis of Kraak Porcelains
Found in Fort Jesus, Mombasa, Kenya
   CUI Jian-feng / XU Hua-feng / QIN Da-shu / DING Yu

150 | 从玲珑瓷看中国与伊斯兰世界的文化交流   林梅村 马丽亚·艾海提 沈骢
Cultural Interaction between China and Islamic World: a Perspective of
Linglong Porcelain   LIN Mei-cun / Maliya AIHAITI / SHEN Xie

158 | 赐赉抑或贩卖？
——关于海外留存元代青花瓷输出性质的一个思考   黄珊
Gift or Exported Porcelain?
—A Study on How Blue and White Spread Overseas in Yuan Dynasty
   HUANG Shan

Contents

171 | 澳门出土明代青花瓷器研究   马锦强
Research on Chinese Ming Dynasty Blue and White Porcelains Found at Macau
    MA Kam-keong

205 | 海洋出水有机质文物的保护
——以木材和谷物为例   〔韩〕车美永
Conservation of Waterlogged Archaeological Organic Objects Excavated Underwater
—Focused on Woods and Grains   CHA Mi-young

227 | The Naval Architecture of Ancient Fujian Style Sailing Junks, an Overview   XU Lu
福建古代造船技术略论   许路

259 | Introduction: Of Ships and Men
    Paola CALANCA / Pierre-Yves MANGUIN / Eric RIETH
"船与人·欧洲船舶考古与历史"专题论文导言   柯兰 莽甘 李特

265 | The Maritime Cultural Landscape: An Introduction to an International
Perspective on Coastal Cultures   Christer WESTERDAHL
海洋文化景观：国际视野下的海岸文化导论   克里斯特·维斯特道尔

288 | Nautical Ethnography as an Aid to Understanding the Maritime Past   Seán McGrail
航海民族志对理解海洋史的作用   肖恩·麦克格雷

304 | Widening the Scope and Refining the Methods of Maritime and
Experimental Archaeology:
The Roskilde Case - Viking Ships from Excavation to Full-size Sea Trials
    Ole CRUMLIN-PEDERSEN / Tinna DAMGÅRD-SØRENSEN
海洋和实验考古学的视野拓展与方法改进：
以罗斯基勒维京船的发掘到原尺寸复原试航为例
    奥勒·克拉姆林–佩德森 汀娜·达姆加德–索伦森

Contents

329 | Determining an Architectural Family and Its Evolution:
The Example of the Greek Tradition of Sewn Shipbuilding
in the Ancient Mediterranean   **Patrice POMEY**

古代地中海希腊缝接造船传统：一种造船体系的确认及其演化的例证

帕特里斯·帕米

341 | Wrecks and Nautical Archaeology of Inland Waters: New Perspectives of Research.
The Example of the 15th Century Wreck EP1-Canche (Pas-de-Calais, France)

Eric RIETH

内陆水域的沉船与船舶考古学研究新视角：
以法国加莱海峡省15世纪沉船康什河EP1为例   埃里克·李特

364 | Crews' Material Culture from the Study of Artefacts Recovered off Historic French
Shipwrecks:Gathering Data, Processing and New Evidence   **Elisabeth VEYRAT**

从法国历史时期沉船文物看船员物质文化：资料收集、整理与新证据

伊丽莎白·维拉

381 | French Seamen and Chinese Commerce at the Beginning of the 18th Century:
The Voyage of La Découverte (1707-1716)   **Michel L'HOUR**

十八世纪初期法国海员与中国贸易："发现号"之旅（1707～1716）

米歇尔·劳尔

393 | 约稿启事

Call for Papers

395 | 编后记

Afterword

记"黑石号"(*Batu Hitam*)沉船中的广东青瓷

On the Guangdong Celadon Wares from the Belitung Shipwreck

谢明良

(台湾大学艺术史研究所)

HSIEH Ming-liang

(Graduate Institute of Art History, Taiwan University)

内容摘要 /

本文主要是考察唐代"黑石号"(*Batu Hitam*)沉船打捞上岸的广东青瓷。经由与窑址和墓葬出土标本的比对,可以大致得知沉船舶载广东青瓷是来自梅县窑系和珠江河口区域等瓷窑所烧制。另一方面,若结合沉船其他遗物以及文献所记载的中国和波斯湾之间的航道,本文认为黑石号沉船这艘由尸罗夫商人所经营的缝合船(Sewn-Plank Ship),有较大可能是由聚积有大量各地物资的扬州出港,在一度停靠广州,后原拟顺季风归航波斯湾,却不幸在印度尼西亚海域触礁沉没。

关键词 /

唐代 黑石号 广东青瓷 扬州

ABSTRACT / This paper investigates the Guangdong celadon wares salvaged from the Belitung shipwreck of Tang dynasty. A comparison with kiln locations and excavated burial objects indicates that the Guangdong celadon wares from the wreck were produced in Meixian kilns and the porcelain kilns in the Pearl River estuary area. On the other hand, taking into account the other remains from the wreck and the recorded navigational routes between China and the Persian Gulf, this paper argues that the Belitung shipwreck, a sewn-plank ship operated by Siraf merchants, was likely to set sail from Yangzhou, a port storing large quantities of goods from various places, but suffered shipwreck in Indonesian waters on the way sailing back with the monsoon to the Gulf after a stopover at Guangzhou.

KEY WORDS / Tang dynasty; Belitung shipwreck; Guangdong celadon wares; Yangzhou

一

前言

1998年，距离印度尼西亚勿里洞岛（Belitung Island）海岸不及1千米，深度约仅17米的海底偶然发现大量成堆的陶瓷等遗物。初勘结果，确认是属于沉船遗留。由于该沉船推测可能是因撞及西北150米处当地人称为"黑石"的黑色大礁岩而失事沉没，因此参与勘查工作的人员遂将之命名为"黑石号"（*Batu Hitam*）。"黑石号"沉船的探勘打捞作业始于1998年9月，之后曾因西北季风一度中断工作，翌年4月重新开工，同年6月基本竣工。

从长约15米的"黑石号"沉船遗骸打捞上岸的遗物种类和数量极为丰富，就其质材而言，至少包括有金、银、铜、铁、铅、骨、木、石、玻璃和各类的香料以及陶瓷器等，而除了植物香料和玻璃等遗物之外，绝大多数的文物均来自中国所制造生产。其中，以陶瓷器的数量最为惊人，估计至少有六万七千余件。依据目前所累积的中国陶瓷史研究成果，人们已可轻易地判明沉船陶瓷主要是属于公元九世纪的产品。特别是沉船中发现的一件器外壁在入窑烧造之前阴刻"宝历二年七月十六日"铭记的长沙窑釉下彩绘碗（图一），而与该纪年铭碗形制相同的长沙窑彩绘瓷碗于沉船中达数万件之多。因此，如果我们相信瓷器从烧成至贩卖之间不至于相距太久，则"黑石号"沉船的绝对年代就有可能是在晚唐宝历二年（826年）或之后不久。

十年前，我受委托调查"黑石号"出水陶瓷，并撰文考察沉船所见中国陶瓷[1]。不过，当时撰文的重点是在越窑青瓷、邢窑白瓷以及河南省巩县窑所谓唐青花和窑口仍待确认的北方窑系铅釉陶器，对于广东青瓷只是轻轻掠过，未能详细介绍。2010年沉船图录正式出版，其中虽亦包括广东青瓷制品，可惜或因受限于篇幅[2]，其内容亦属简介性质。考虑到"黑石号"沉船存在着一些至今未曾披露或者说尚未被辨识出来的广东青瓷，所以我想借由过往调查"黑石号"陶瓷的见闻，结合近年考古发掘数据，尽可能如实地呈现沉船舶载广东青瓷的具体面貌。行文时的原则是：先归纳、梳理沉船中广东青瓷的种类，除了例举中国考古遗迹所见相同器类以便厘测特定器类的相对年代和可能的产地之外，亦将适时指出中国以外消费地同类制品的出土实例。文末再次省思"黑石号"沉船的贸易商圈兼及解缆出航港湾等航路问题。

---

[1] 谢明良：《记"黑石号"（*Batu Hitam*）沉船中的中国陶瓷器》，原载《台湾大学美术史研究集刊》第13期，2002年，后收入《贸易陶瓷与文化史》，台北：允晨文化，2005年，页81～134。

[2] Regina Krahl. Green Wares of Southern China. *Shipwrecked: Tang Treasures and Monsoon Winds*. Washington: Freer Gallery of Art and Arthur M. Sackler Gallery, 2010, pp. 195–199.

  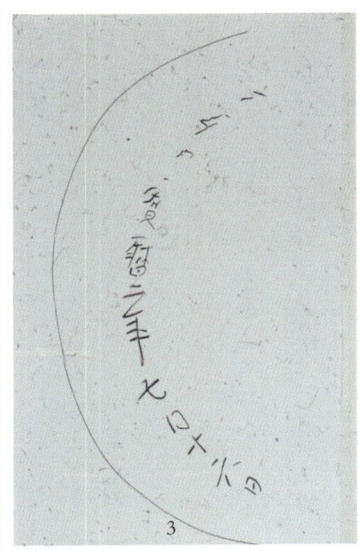

图一 "黑石号"沉船出水长沙窑碗
1.釉下彩绘　2.宝历二年（826年）七月十六日刻铭　3.铭文线描图

二

沉船所见广东青瓷的种类

陶瓷器的分类因人而异，有多种不同的区分方案。就"黑石号"沉船的广东青瓷而言，相对理想的分类方案或许应该是先区分作品的产区而后进行器式排比。不过，就笔者目前所能掌握到的广东地区青瓷窑址调查资料看来，虽有部分窑址出土标本可与沉船作品进行比附，从而得知其确切的产地，但沉船所见推测属广东青瓷当中，事实上还包括许多仅只依据作品的器形和胎釉特征所做的主观判断，而支持此一判断的原因无非是类似器式曾出现于广东地区墓葬或遗址等间接线索罢了。尽管目前窑址调查资料未臻齐备[3]，难以涵盖沉船所见多样的青瓷标本，但似可参酌20世纪80年代后期何翠媚调查广东瓷窑的见闻资料，得以对沉船青瓷标本进行间接的产地厘测。本文以下的分类主要即依据中国考古单位的考古报告书和何翠媚瓷窑田野调查资料，惟其中亦包括部分个人依据胎釉特征所做的产地推测。

1. 梅县青瓷窑系

沉船所见广东窑系青瓷当中，以一类胎骨厚重，整体施罩青色调透明开片亮厚釉的作品最为精良，所见器式多属碗、盘类，亦见少量壶罐。从广东梅县唐墓屡次出现该类青瓷碗[4]，同时梅县水车公社等窑址也出土了造型特征完全一致的标本[5]，可以认为沉船中的该类施罩透明亮厚青绿釉的作品，是来自唐代梅县窑区所生产。

[3] 何翠媚著、土桥理子译：《唐代末期における廣東省の窯業および陶磁貿易について》，《貿易陶磁研究》第12期，1992年，页159～184。

[4] 广东省博物馆（古运泉）：《广东梅县古墓葬和古窑址调查发掘简报》，《考古》1987年第3期，页211图5之一。广东省博物馆等：《广东出土晋至唐文物》，香港：香港中文大学文物馆，1985年，页220所载畲坑3号墓出土品。

[5] 曾广亿：《梅县古窑址调查简记》，原载广东《文博通讯》1978年第3期，收入：广东省博物馆：《广东文物考古资料选辑》第1辑，1989年，页193～195转页188。

计百余件的梅县窑系青瓷碗的造型多呈敞口，斜弧壁，底置宽圈足或璧足。圈足碗口沿切割成四花口，花口以下器身外壁饰凹槽，内壁对称处有出戟，满釉，底有三处团状支烧痕（图二）；璧足碗亦施满釉，仅于足上抹拭出三块团状垫烧时的涩胎，口沿有四花口和平口等二式，前者于内壁于花口下方饰出筋，后于亦于内壁等距饰四道纵向出筋（图三）。应予留意的是，除了广东地区唐墓之外，江苏省扬州文化宫遗址（YWF1）曾经出土类似器式的璧足青瓷碗[6]（图四），但其确实产地还有待查证。另外，东南亚泰国等地亦见类似标本，何翠媚依据其本人所调查的梅县瓦坑口和啰屋坑等窑址数据将称为"梅县瓷"[7]，山本信夫从之，但将其归入"广东青瓷A类"[8]。碗盘类之外，沉船打捞文物中另包括壶罐类，如一件双系带流罐（图五），其胎釉和器形特征均和20世纪80年代梅县墓所出推测是梅县水车窑制品（图六）一致[9]。

[6] 中国社会科学院考古研究所等：《扬州城——1987～1998考古发掘报告》，北京：文物出版社，2010年，页176图147之1；图版123之1。

[7] 何翠媚著、田中和彦译：《タイ南部・コーカオ島とポー岬出土の陶磁器》，《贸易陶磁研究》第11期，1991年，页60、62及页78图15右上。

[8] 山本信夫：《日本、東南アジア海域における9～10世紀の貿易とイスラム陶器》，《國立歷史民俗博物館研究報告》第94集，2002年，页110、111。

[9] 广东省博物馆等：《广东唐宋出土陶瓷》，香港：香港大学冯平山博物馆，1985年，页87图75。

图二　四花口圈足碗
（"黑石号"出水）

图三　四出筋璧足碗
（"黑石号"出水）

图四　敞口璧足碗
（扬州文化宫遗址出土）

图五　双系带流罐　　　　　　　图六　双系带流罐
（"黑石号"出水）　　　　　　　（梅县唐墓出土）

2. 珠江河口区域及其他窑群

沉船所见此类青瓷标本，包括内壁以耐光泥团垫烧而成的粗质青瓷器形计有：

敞口饼足碗　内壁近口沿处阴刻弦纹一周，弦纹下方间隔分布六只垫烧泥团痕。外壁半截釉，釉斑驳不匀（图七）。类似青瓷制品除出土于广东省之外[10]（图八），江苏省扬州文化宫（图YWF2）[11]（图九）、（YWG4mA）[12]，亦曾出土。

圆底碗　口微敛，内壁近口沿处阴刻弦纹一周，弦纹下方留有等距的六个垫烧用砖红色泥团。施青黄薄釉，有剥釉现象，外壁施釉不到底，露胎处可见六只团状垫烧痕迹（图一〇）。属珠江河口区域的高明大岗山窑[13]、新会官冲窑[14]、古劳窑址群、凤岗支群[15]或佛山奇石窑[16]等窑址可见类似标本；广州南越王宫苑遗址也出土了同类青釉制品[17]（图一一）。东南亚亦见出土，相当于山本所谓的"广东青瓷B类"[18]。

折沿盆　折沿带唇，内壁弧度收成大平底，有六只团形垫烧泥痕，釉色青绿，施釉不匀，有明显泪痕。外壁半截釉，下置饼形假圈足，饼足内侧修一道凹痕（图一二），珠江口区域古劳窑群、凤岗支群可见类似标本[19]（图一三）。

平口四系盆　平口以下斜直内收成大平底，外壁近口沿处等距贴置四只横耳（图一四）。青黄釉釉质不匀，泪痕明显。类似标本见于新会官冲窑址[20]（图一五）。

唇口盂　口呈唇口式，大口，斜弧壁，平底。釉色不一，既见施罩青黄色釉者（图一六），亦见青灰色釉制品（图一七），釉带开片。类似作品多次出土

[10] 广东省博物馆等：前引《广东出土晋至唐文物》，页227图上。

[11] 中国社会科学院考古研究所等：前引《扬州城——1987～1998年考古发掘报告》，页147图120之1，图版80之5。

[12] 中国社会科学院考古研究所等：前引《扬州城——1987～1998年考古发掘报告》，页176图147之4，图版123之1。

[13] 广东省文物管理委员会：《佛山专区的几处古窑址调查简报》，《文物参考资料》1959年第12期，页53。

[14] 广东省文物管理委员会：《佛山专区的几处古窑址调查简报》，页54、55。薛剑虹：《新会、鹤山古陶瓷窑址初探》，收入Ho Chumei edited. *Ancient Ceramic Kiln Technology in Asia.* Hong Kong: Centre of Asian Studies University of Hong Kong, 1990, p.27, pl.3-6.

[15] 何翠媚著、土桥理子译：前引《唐代末期における廣東省の窯業および陶磁貿易について》，页177图1、2。

[16] 黄晓蕙：《佛山奇石古窑与相关问题》，《越窑青瓷与邢窑白瓷研究》，北京：故宫出版社，2013年，页450图8。

[17] 南越王宫博物馆筹建处等：《南越宫苑遗址1995、1997考古发掘报告》下，北京：文物出版社，2008年，图版76之5、图版77之1。

[18] 山本信夫：前引《日本、東南アジア海域における9-10世紀の貿易とイスラム陶器》，页111。

[19] 何翠媚著、土桥理子译：前引《唐代末期における廣東省の窯業および陶磁貿易について》，页177图1、2。

图七　敞口碗
（"黑石号"出水）

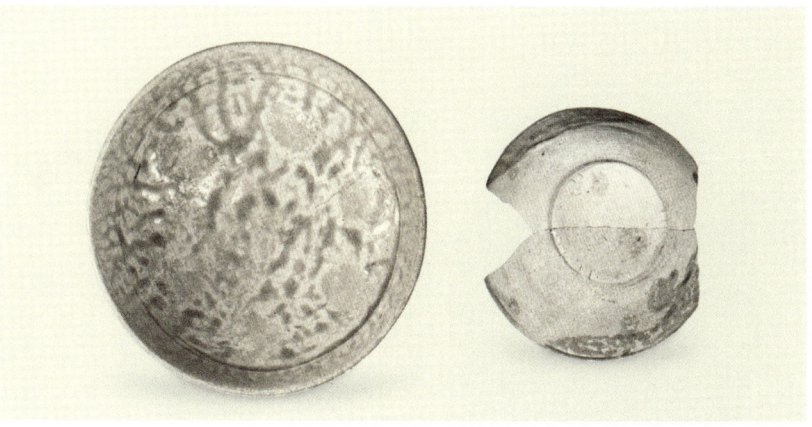

图八　敞口碗
（香港赤腊角深湾村出土）

图九　敞口碗
（扬州文化宫遗址出土）

图一〇　圜底碗
（"黑石号"出水）

图一一　圜底碗
（南越王宫苑遗址出土）

图一三　珠江口区域窑址群出土瓷器标本

图一二　折沿盆
（"黑石号"出水）

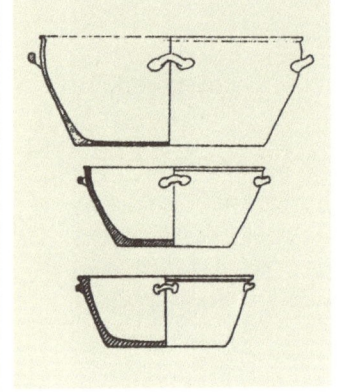

图一四 平口四系盆
（"黑石号"出水）

图一五 平口四系盆
（新会官冲窑址出土）

图一六 唇口盂
（"黑石号"出水）

图一七 唇口盂
（"黑石号"出水）

于广东地区唐墓，如始兴县赤土岭（赤南M13）[21]（图一八）、广州皇沙（M2）[22]、广州市太和岗御龙庭工地（M61）均曾出土[23]。

短颈罐 口沿外翻，束短颈，肩以下弧度内收，平底。施青黄色薄釉（图一九），个别作品釉剥落殆尽（图二〇）。类似作品见广州黄花岗唐墓（M13）[24]（图二一）。

唇口双系大口罐 大口，口沿呈唇状，口以下斜弧内收成平底，整体造型略如前述唇口盂。不同的是另于罐肩置二横系，内外施青绿（图二二）或青黄、黄褐等色釉，外壁施釉不到底（图二三）。20世纪70年代西沙群岛北礁礁盘打捞出类似制品[25]（图二四）；广州南越王宫苑遗址亦曾出土类似作品[26]（图二五）。另外，沉船另见一式肩置二横系及多棱短流的青釉带盖罐（图二六），从胎釉特征看来有可能属广东瓷窑制品。

唇口四系罐 唇口，口沿下方饰数周阴刻弦纹，最大径在肩部，以下斜弧内收成平底，肩置四横系，施淡青釉不到底（图二七）。广东韶关市北郊卒殁于开元二十八年（740年）尚书右丞相张九龄墓曾见类似器式的唇口四系罐[27]（图二八）。

短口溜肩四系罐 短平口，口沿以下斜弧外敞，最大径在器身中部，以下斜弧内收成大平底，器肩部位置四横系，施釉不到底（图二九）。造型相

[20] 广东省文物考古研究所等（刘成基）：《广东新会官冲古窑址》，《文物》2000年第6期，页36及页29图7之12～14。

[21] 广东省博物馆等：前引《广东出土晋至唐文物》，页231图上。

[22] 广东省博物馆（杨式挺等）：《广东始兴晋—唐墓发掘报告》，《考古学集刊》（2），1982年，页130图25之9。

[23] 广州市文物考古研究所：《铢积寸累》，北京：文物出版社，2005年，页158图155。

[24] 广州市文物考古研究所（朱海仁）：《广州黄花岗汉唐墓葬发掘报告》，《考古学报》2004年第4期，页480图27之5。

[25] 广东省文物管理委员会等：《南海丝绸之路文物图集》，广州：广东科技出版社，1991年，页61图上。

[26] 南越王宫博物馆筹建处等：前引《南越宫苑遗址1995、1997考古发掘报告》下，图版76之2。

[27] 广东省文物管理委员会等（杨豪）：《唐代张九龄墓发掘简报》，《文物参考资料》1961年第6期，页50图9左。

图一八 唇口盂
（始兴县赤土岭唐墓赤南M13出土）

图一九 短颈罐
（"黑石号"出水）

图二〇 短颈罐
（"黑石号"出水）

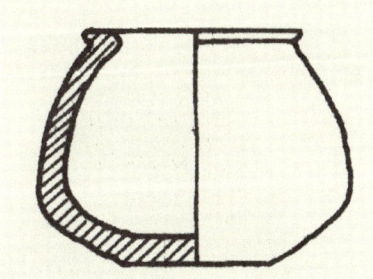
图二一 短颈罐
（黄花岗唐墓M13出土）

图二二 唇口双系大口罐
（"黑石号"出水）

图二三 唇口双系大口罐
（"黑石号"出水）

图二四 唇口双系大口罐
（西沙群岛北礁打捞品）

图二五 唇口双系大口罐
（南越王宫苑遗址出土）

图二六 双系带流盖罐
（"黑石号"出水）

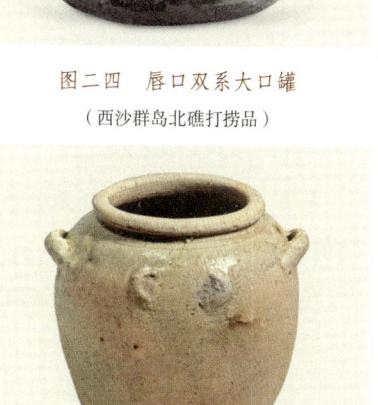
图二七 唇口四系罐
（"黑石号"出水）

图二八 唇口四系罐
（韶关市唐张九龄墓出土）

图二九　短口溜肩四系罐
（"黑石号"出水）

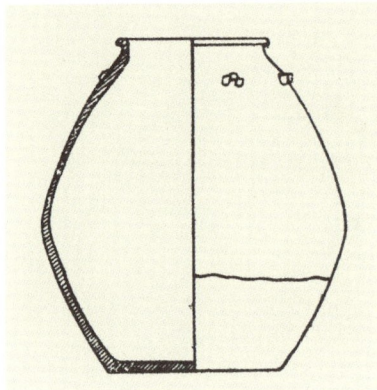
图三〇　短口溜肩四系罐
（始兴县赤土岭唐墓赤南M23出土）

图三二　短口鼓肩四系罐及其墨书
（"黑石号"出水）

图三一　阴刻有阿拉伯文铭文的四系罐残片
（伊朗尸罗夫遗址出土）

似的带系罐曾见于广州唐墓（赤南M23）[28]（图三〇）、20世纪70年代David Whitehouse所报导波斯湾尸罗夫（Siraf）出土的带阴刻阿拉伯文的青釉带系罐残片可能亦属相近罐式[29]（图三一）。后者口肩部位特征与江苏省扬州文化宫遗址出土的所谓宜兴窑青釉四系罐，有类似之处[30]，但还有待日后进一步的验证。

短口鼓肩四系罐　短口，鼓肩，肩腹部位饰阴刻弦纹，上置四横系，最大径肩腹处，以下斜弧内收成大平底。沉船此类罐式青釉色调不一，有呈青绿或青灰者，口部口径也有大小的区别，施釉不到底。其中一件施罩青灰色釉的大口罐，器腹露胎处有墨书[31]（图三二），但内容无法识别。广州唐墓（赤南M13）曾出土相近四系罐[32]（图三三）。另外，广东珠江口地区鹤山县古劳窑址和安铺港地区遂溪县杨柑河窑址曾采集到类似的带系罐残片[33]。

短口鼓肩四系带流罐　短口，鼓肩，肩部阴刻弦纹上置四横系，器形和釉色一如前述短口鼓肩四系罐（图三四）。不同的只是在两只系耳之间另饰注流，注流造型属多棱式，打捞出水时有的内置铅条（图三五）或八角（图三六），另据参与沉船打捞作业的工作人员告诉笔者有的内贮白瓷杯。珠江口区域和雷州半岛西北地区窑址曾见采集到类似标本[34]。这类青釉四系带流罐既见于泰国南部林文波（Laem Pho）遗址[35]，还见于伊朗尸罗夫（Siraf）港湾遗迹[36]。尤可注意的是，扬州汶河路遗迹也出土了笔者推测属于广东窑系的同类四系带流罐[37]（图三七）。

六系橄榄形大罐　唇口，口沿无釉，溜肩以下外弧至器上腹部位而后内

[28] 广东省博物馆（杨式挺等）：前引《广东始兴晋—唐墓发掘报告》，页130图25之5。

[29] David Whitehouse. *Chinese Stoneware from Siraf: the Earliest Finds*. New Jersey: South Asian Archaeology Noyes Press, 1993, p. 245, fig.18.1. J. D. Frierman. T'ang and Sung Ceramics Exported to the West in the Light of Archaeological Discoveries. *Oriental Art,* Summer 1978, p.196, fig. 1, 2.

[30] 中国社会科学院考古研究所等：前引《扬州城——1987～1998年考古发掘报告》，页156图128之4及图版92之2。

[31] 广东省博物馆（杨式挺等）：前引《广东始兴晋—唐墓发掘报告》，页130图25之1、2。

[32] 广东省博物馆（杨式挺等）：前引《广东始兴晋—唐墓发掘报告》，页130图25之4。

[33] 何翠媚著、土桥理子译：前引《唐代末期における廣東省の窯業および陶磁貿易について》，页59~184。

[34] 何翠媚著、土桥理子译：前引《唐代末期における廣東省の窯業および陶磁貿易について》，页2。

[35] 何翠媚著、土桥理子译：前引《唐代末期における廣東省の窯業および陶磁貿易について》，页8图5右上。

[36] Moria Tampoe. *Maritime Trade between China and the West*. B.A.R. International Series 555,1989,p.307,No.1321,1322.

[37] 扬州博物馆等：《扬州古陶瓷》，北京：文物出版社，1996年，图48。

[38] J. D. Frierman. *T'ang and Sung Ceramics Exported to the West in the Light of Archaeological Discoveries*, p.196,fig.1.

[39] *Encyclopaedia of Islam*, New Ed.1965,vol.2, pp.188-189:DAYBUL; Mumtaz Husain Siud, *Arab Period*, Hyderabad, pp.417-427.转引自：家島彦一：《インド洋におけるシーラーフ系商人の交易ネットワークと物品の流通》，收入：田边胜美等：《深井晋司博士追悼シルクロード美術論集》，东京：吉川弘文馆，1987年，页211。

[40] 佐佐木达夫：《バンボール出土の中國陶磁と海上貿易》，收入：田边胜美等：《深井晋司博士追悼シルクロード美術論集》，东京：吉川弘文馆，1987年，页247。

[41] 广东省文物管理委员会等（曾广忆）：《广东新会官冲古代窑址》，《考古》1963年第4期，页222图4之8。薛剑虹：前引《新会、鹤山古陶窑址初探》，p.27,pl.3.

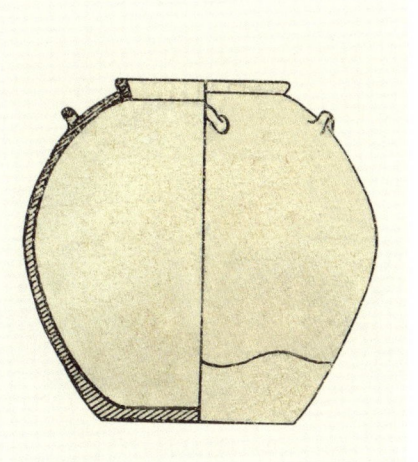

图三三　短口鼓肩四系罐
（始兴县赤土领唐墓赤南M13出土）

图三四　短口鼓肩四系带流罐
（"黑石号"出水）

图三五　短口鼓肩四系带流罐
（内贮铅条，"黑石号"出水）

图三六　短口鼓肩四系带流罐
（内贮八角，"黑石号"出水）

收成平底，肩饰阴刻弦纹一周，上贴置六只横系（图三八），系耳之间偶见"端政"（图三九）、"文"等刻铭。施釉不到底，釉色多呈黄褐色调，釉质不匀，有明显泪痕，造型尺寸较大，通高近80厘米。从打捞出水时罐内摞迭长沙窑碗（图四〇），可知"黑石号"所见此类大量的坛罐是作为陶瓷等物品舶载时的外容器。这类六系大罐除了出土于伊朗尸罗夫遗迹之外[38]，还曾见于巴基斯坦喀拉蚩（Karachi）以东的中世都市遗迹班勃卢（Banbhore）（图四一），该遗迹有可能是九世纪贾耽著《广州通海夷道》所记提䫻国的所在地[39]。虽然此一俗称为Dusun ware的青釉带系大罐有时被视为是9~11世纪时期越窑系作品[40]，不过从"黑石号"沉船彩绘碗多系装盛于该类大罐之中，知其年绝不晚于九世纪前期；另从广东地区部分瓷窑窑址曾经出土造型不完全一致，但胎釉特征则和该类青釉大罐颇为近似的带系罐标本一事看来[41]，不排除这类作为陶瓷等商品外容器的青釉大罐有可能来自广东地区瓷窑所烧造。最

图三七　短口鼓肩四系带流罐
（江苏扬州出土）

图三八　六系橄榄形大罐
（"黑石号"出水）

图三九　六系橄榄形大罐
（肩上部见"端政"铭文，"黑石号"出水）

图四〇　六系橄榄形大罐
（内贮长沙窑彩绘碗）

近，亦有人明确指出此类带系青釉罐乃广东官冲窑所烧造[42]，可惜并未出示窑址相关标本，因此详情依旧不明。

提梁壶　平底，半球形的器身上方置半环式提梁，提梁壶垂直方向侧设短注流，另一侧设一钱币大小的圆孔，圆孔周围明显可见凸圈。由于胎釉结合不佳兼因海水浸泡，釉多已剥落，个别作品釉色呈褐色调（图四二）。广东化州县那京江和广西壮族自治区钦州墓曾出土类似的提梁壶，两者均于提梁一侧置短流，对侧近提梁处穿两小孔与器体相通，但前者无釉，器表磨光（图四三），报告认为其年代在汉代[43]。后者釉脱落殆尽，据称出土墓葬相对年代在隋至初唐[44]。另外，珠江河口地区新会官冲窑也出土了此类提梁壶，提梁对侧设一长一短的注流，原施罩青黄色釉，但多已脱落[45]（图四四）。

小口带流大坛　"黑石号"沉船陶瓷以一件造型呈小口、丰肩、鼓腹内收成平底形似所谓"梅瓶"的大坛尺寸最为巨大，通高逾1米，从近底处设一筒式

[42]　林亦秋：《南青北白长沙彩》，《越窑青瓷与邢窑白瓷研究》，北京：故宫出版社，2013年，页354、355。

[43]　广东省文物管理委员会办公室等：《广东文物普查成果图录》，广州：广东科技出版社，1990年，页69图103。

[44]　广西壮族自治区文物工作队（韦仁义等）：《广西壮族自治区钦州隋唐墓》，《考古》1984年第3期，图版陆之6。

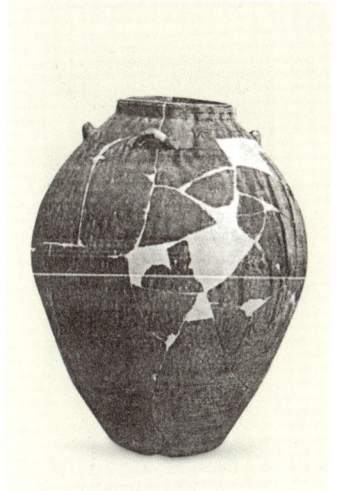

图四一　六系橄榄形大罐
（巴基斯坦班勃卢出土）

图四二　提梁壶
（"黑石号"出水）

 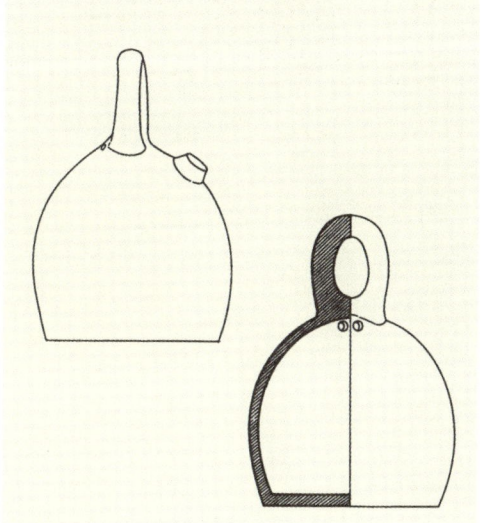

图四三　提梁壶
（化州县出土）

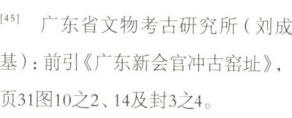

[45] 广东省文物考古研究所（刘成基）：前引《广东新会官冲古窑址》，页31图10之2、14及封3之4。

 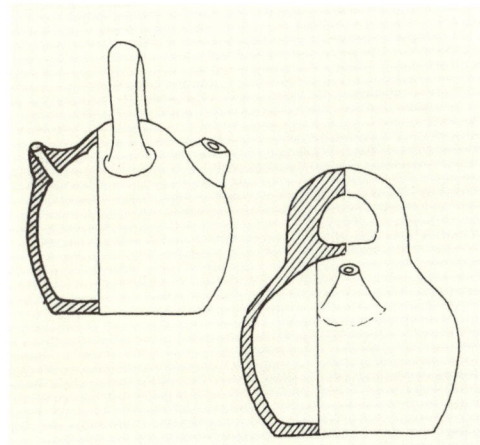

图四四　提梁壶
（新会官冲窑址出土）

图四五　小口带流大坛
（"黑石号"出水）

短流看来，其应是内贮液体的容器，并且可用栓塞控制出水（图四五）。肩上部刻饰稀疏的变形蕉叶、网格斜纹和波纹，施罩青黄釉不到底，有明显泪痕。从胎釉特征和前述推测与广东瓷窑所烧制的四系带流罐（见图三四）等制品较为类似等推测，有较大可能亦属广东瓷窑制品。

三

"黑石号"沉船出港地点的厘测——以沉船中广东青瓷罐为例

笔者以前曾援引唐人贾耽作于贞元年间（785~804年）所谓"广州通海夷道"所记述的航线，比较了航线据点出土唐代陶瓷与"黑石号"沉船陶瓷的种类，试图复原、理解"黑石号"船原本预定的航路和最终的目的地。众所周知，近代学者对于贾耽所记述航线地名有详细考证，但就本文而言，重点是所谓"广州通海夷道"乃是从广州出发这一简单的事实。即自广州赴占不劳山（今越南占婆岛），经新加坡海峡（海峡北岸是罗越国即今马来半岛南端，南岸是室利佛逝国即今苏门答腊东南部），经师子国（斯里兰卡）、没来国（今印度西南Quilon）、提颶国（今巴基斯坦Karachi以东Banbhore）[46]，通过波斯湾抵罗和异国（今波斯湾西阿巴丹附近）[47]。

另一方面，经由船舶史等相关学者对于"黑石号"沉船残骸的船体形状、

[46] 章巽：《我国古代的海上交通》，北京：商务印书馆，1986年，页42、43；陈炎：《海上丝绸之路与中外文化交流》，北京：北京大学出版社，1996年，页84、85。

[47] 家岛彦一：前引〈インド洋におけるシーラーフ系商人の交易ネットワークと物品の流通〉，页211。

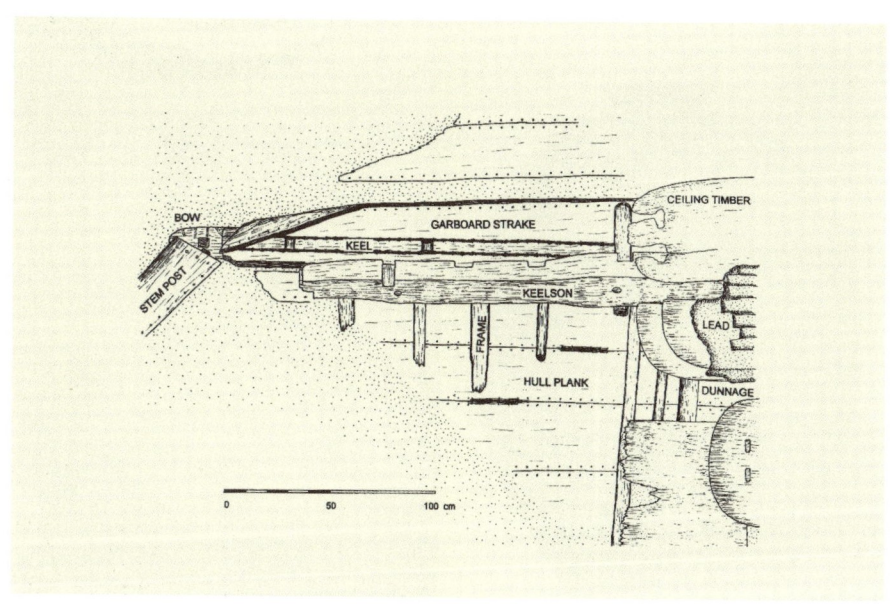

图四六 黑石号沉船船板线绘图

构造方式和建材种类等之分析考察，则沉船船体应是在阿拉伯或印度所建造，船身木料来自印度，同时船体构件连接不用铁钉而是采用穿孔缝合的建造方式，也和中国传统的船体构造大异其趣[48]（图四六）。唐末刘恂《岭表录异》提到"贾人船不用铁钉，只使桄榔须系缚，以橄榄糖泥之，糖干甚坚，入水如漆也"[49]，指的正是这类形态的船舶。这种于舷板穿孔，以椰子壳纤维搓制成的绳索系缚船板，再充填树脂或鱼油使之牢固的所谓缝合船（Sewn-Plank Ship）（图四七、四八），早在纪元前后已出现于印度洋西海域，而9世纪中期的伊斯兰文献则强调指出缝合船是尸罗夫船工擅长建造的构造特殊的船舶，9～10世纪尸罗夫和苏哈拉（Suhar）是缝合船的制造中心[50]。这样看来，"黑石号"沉船不仅有可能是由尸罗夫船工所建造，同时也不排除船东即是活跃于当时海上贸易圈的尸罗夫系商人。就此而言，9世纪中叶阿拉伯商人苏莱曼（Solaiman）著《中国印度见闻录》所记述自尸罗夫以迄中国的航线，对于理解"黑石号"沉船的可能航路无疑亦具重要的参考价值。

依据苏莱曼所记航道，则船自尸罗夫启航经马斯喀特（Musgat，今阿曼首都）、故临（Koulam，今印度半岛西南端，即贾耽所记没来国）、朗迦婆鲁斯岛（Langabalous，今苏门答腊北部西海岸，即贾耽所记婆露国）、个罗国（Kalah，今马来半岛东岸吉打）、满潮岛（Tīyouman，今马来半岛东岸）、奔陀浪山（Pan-do-Uranga，今越南藩朗）、占婆（Tcampa，今越南中南部）、占不牢山（Tchams，占婆岛）、中国门（Bad al-Sīn，今西沙群岛诸暗礁），最终抵达广州。此一航线除了由马斯喀特直接越洋赴故临之行程，与《广州通海夷道》自没来国（故临）驶往波斯湾系采取沿岸停泊的航程有所不同之外，其余航路则大致相同。这样看来，无论是贾耽或苏莱曼都是以广州为航路的起始点或终站，而这是否就意味着"黑石号"沉船是由广州解缆出航的？众所周知，

[48] Michael Flecker. A Ninth-Century AD Abab or Indian Shipwreck in Indonesia: First Evidence of Direct Trade with China. *World Archaeology*, 2001, vol. 32, no. 3, pp. 335-354; A 9th-Century Arab or Indian Shipwreck in Indoesian Waters. *The International Journal of Nautical Archaeology*, 2000 29-2, pp. 199-217; Tom Vosmer. The Jewel of Muscat: Reconstructing A Ninth-Century Sewn-Plank Boat. *Shipwreck Tang Treasures and Monsoon Winds*, Washington: Freer Gallery of Art and Arthur M. Sackler Gallery, 2010, pp. 120-135.

[49] 桑原隲藏：《波斯灣の東洋貿易港に就て》，《史林》1卷3号，1916年，页18。戴开元：《广东缝合木船初探》，《海交史研究》第5期，1983年，页86~89。

[50] 家岛彦一：《アラブ古代型縫合船Sanbuk Zafariについて》，《アジア・アフリカ文化研究》，第13期，1977年，页186~188。家岛彦一译注：《中国とインドの諸情報》1，东京：平凡社，2007年，页91注36。家岛彦一译注：《中国とインドの諸情報》2，东京：平凡社，2007年，页43及页133注112、注113等。

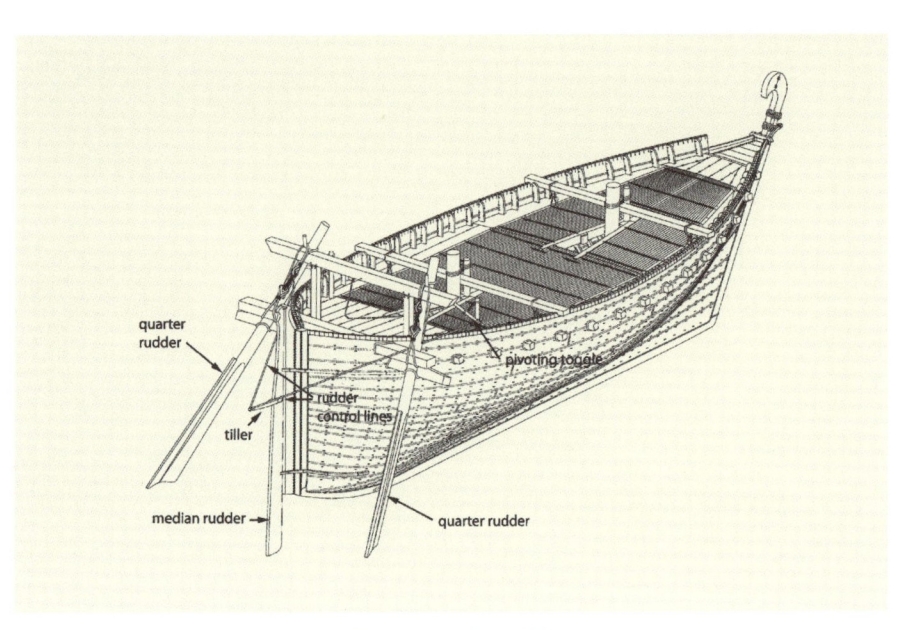

图四七　缝合船示意图

图四八　缝合船示意图

广州是当时与南海通交最为重要的港口，外国商贩云集于称为"蕃坊"的侨居地，朝廷亦设有市舶使掌管对外贸易。更重要的是，"黑石号"沉船不仅出土了数百件的广东瓷窑作品，数以万计的长沙窑彩绘瓷碗和部分北方邢窑系白瓷亦是装盛于推测可能是广东地区瓷窑场所烧造的大型瓮罐之中。因此，若说"黑石号"沉船是由广州起航出海，似乎也言之成理。然而，若从沉船陶瓷的组合情况看来，事实恐怕未必如此地单纯。

由于"黑石号"沉船陶瓷除了有部分来自广东瓷窑所生产的作品之外，主要还包括有长沙窑、越窑、邢窑、巩县窑、北方白釉绿彩陶和数件伊斯兰蓝釉陶器。尽管广东地区墓葬或遗址亦曾发现邢窑白瓷、越窑青瓷和长沙窑彩绘瓷，但其发现频率低、数量小，只有长沙窑的件数相对较多，但估计亦不过十数件[51]，目前尚未见到巩县窑白瓷或白釉绿彩陶的正式考古出土报道，遑论青花瓷器了。另一方面，同为唐代对外贸易据点之一的扬州陶瓷出土组合的情况则颇耐人寻味。姑且不论墓葬的零星出土数据，仅就居住遗址所反映的陶瓷组合而言，如扬州市文化宫唐代建筑基址出土的3万余件陶瓷标本当中即涵盖了长沙窑、越窑、邢窑、巩县窑、青花瓷、白釉绿彩陶和伊斯兰陶器[52]，其种类几乎囊括了"黑石号"沉船广东瓷窑之外的全部品种，类似的出土陶瓷组合也见于三元路唐代罗城范围内遗址，该遗址既出土有长沙窑、越窑、巩县窑、青花瓷和白釉绿彩陶[53]，同时出土了数以百计的波斯釉陶残片[54]。就目前我所掌握的资料看来，伊斯兰釉陶器于浙江宁波、福建福州、广西容县、桂林以及广州南越宫苑等地遗址虽亦曾出土，但均止于个别的少量发现[55]。至于白釉绿彩陶于南方地区除了安徽巢湖唐墓和淮北市柳孜运河遗迹之外[56]，目前也只见于扬州唐代遗址。不仅如此，经常与伊斯兰釉陶、白釉绿彩陶共伴出土的唐代青花瓷更是仅见于扬州遗址的稀有器类。换言之，扬州唐代遗址以长沙窑彩绘瓷、越窑青瓷、邢窑系白瓷、巩

[51] 宋良璧：《长沙铜官窑瓷器在广东》，《中国古代陶瓷的外销》，北京：紫禁城出版社，1988年，页41、42。

[52] 中国社会科学院考古研究所等扬州城考古队（王勤金）：《江苏扬州市文化宫唐代建筑基址发掘简报》，《考古》1994年第5期，页416～419。

[53] 扬州博物馆（马富坤等）：《扬州三元路工地考古调查》，《文物》1985年第10期，页72～76。

[54] 周长源等：《扬州出土的古代波斯釉陶研究》，《文物》1988年第12期，页60。

县窑白瓷、青花瓷、白釉绿彩陶和伊斯兰陶器的陶瓷组合是非比寻常的特殊事例，于中国唐代遗址中显得极为突出，而这样的共伴组合则又与"黑石号"沉船陶瓷完全一致。尤可注意的是，相对于长沙窑瓷于中国境内极少出土，扬州旧城区汶河路发掘的一处范围仅十余米的堆积，出土可复原成完整器的长沙窑瓷达五百件，当中仅盖盒一种即有百件之多，报告者认为该遗址既未见其他瓷窑作品，其发现地点又邻近古河道，很可能是当时卸货清仓时的残器遗留，进而推测唐代扬州设有专营瓷器的店铺[57]。如前所述，"黑石号"沉船即是以长沙窑的数量最多，计六万余件，后者尚包括有狮、鸟等玩具置物，这类小瓷玩偶除曾见于长沙窑窑址之外，目前亦只发现于扬州唐代遗址[58]。

《新唐书·田神功传》载神功兵至扬州，大食、波斯贾胡死者数千人，至8世纪中期扬州已群聚众多的伊斯兰教商人[59]，他们还开设名为"波斯店"的商铺经营珠宝等商货[60]，而扬州文化宫中晚唐遗址则曾发现推测系胡商邸店的建筑遗留，其不仅出土精美的白瓷、青瓷、青花瓷、波斯釉陶和玻璃瓶，屋内地面还散落着金块[61]。有趣的是，"黑石号"沉船的文物当中即包括有少量的玻璃瓶（图四九）和整摞的金箔。因此，笔者认为"黑石号"沉船商货主要应是获自位于大运河和长江天然航道且聚集着南北物资的扬州，并由扬州出港的。问题是我们要如何来面对存在于沉船中的广东瓷窑作品？阿拉伯地理学家伊本·胡尔达兹比赫（Ibn Khordâdhbeh，838～912年）所著《道里邦国志》在记述通往中国之路顺序时提到的港口是鲁金（Lūgin，今越南河内一带）、汉府（Khānfu，今广州）、汉久（Khānju，杭州？）和刚突（Qāntu，江都）[62]，桑原骘藏认为后者之江都即扬州[63]。从沿岸停靠的港口看来，不排除"黑石号"沉船中的广东陶瓷有可能是北上或南下时一度停靠广州之际所取得。

如前所述，20世纪90年代公布扬州市汶河路遗址曾出土笔者推测属广东窑系的四系带流青瓷罐（见图三七）。应予留意的是，这类带系罐打捞上岸时除了可见罐内置放铅条或八角[64]，亦有贮置白瓷杯碗之例。不仅如此，大量的长沙窑彩绘瓷碗也是置放在青瓷六系大口罐当中（见图四〇），后者推测亦属广东瓷窑制品。因此，假若本文对于该类青瓷坛罐的产地推测无误，则可推知作为货物集散地的扬州原本就预留此类贮置外贸物资的外容器，当然也有可能是从事贸易活动的尸罗夫商人购自广东的仓储用器。无论如何，本文想强调指出的是扬州遗迹出土唐代广东青瓷并非孤例，除了前述青瓷四系带流罐和青瓷六系大口罐之外，扬州文化宫遗址所见珠江河口地区所烧制的内底有泥团垫渣的粗制青瓷碗，因其装烧工艺特征明显，可以认为是广东瓷窑制品流散货集结至扬州的考古例证。换言之，"黑石号"沉船出土的大量推测属广东瓷窑所烧造的各类坛罐，并不意味着

[55] 何翠媚：《9-10世紀の東·東南アジアにおける西アジア陶器の意義》，《貿易陶瓷研究》第14期，1994年，页43、44。另外，宁波出土例参见：林士民：《浙江宁波公园路唐宋子城遗址考古发掘获重要成果》，《中国文物报》1998年4月12日第一版。傅亦民：《唐代明州与西亚波斯地区的交往——从出土波斯陶谈起》，《海交史研究》2000年第2期，页66～70。广西出土例参见：李铧等：《广西出土的波斯陶及相关问题探讨》，《文物》2003年第11期，页71～74。广州出土例参见：南越王宫博物馆筹建处等：前引《南越宫苑遗址1995、1997年考古发掘报告》下，彩版7之3、10之5、23之5。

[56] 巢湖地区文物管理所（张宏明）：《安徽巢湖市唐代砖室墓》，《考古》1988年第6期，页575。安徽省文物考古研究所等：《淮北柳孜——运河遗址发掘报告》，北京：科学出版社，2002年。

[57] 周长源：《试论扬州蓝天大厦工地出土的唐代长沙窑瓷器》，《中国古陶瓷研究会1994年会论文集》，《东南文化》增刊，1994年，页65～69。

[58] 南京博物馆等发掘工作小组等：《扬州唐城遗址1975年考古工作简报》，《文物》1977年第9期，页25图20。

[59] 桑原骘藏著，冯攸译：《中国阿拉伯海上交通史》，台北：台湾商务印书馆，1967年史地丛书版，页21。

[60] （明）谢肇淛：《五杂俎》："唐时扬州常有波斯胡店，太平广记往往称之"，（卷12），详见：桑原骘藏：前引《中国阿拉伯海上交通史》，页22。

[61] 蒋忠义：《唐代扬州城遗址》，《中国考古学年鉴1991》，北京：文物出版社，1992年，页178。中国社会科学院考古研究所等扬州城考古队（王勤金）：前引《江苏扬州市文化宫唐代建筑基址发掘简报》，页420。

图四九　伊斯兰玻璃瓶
（"黑石号"出水）

"黑石号"是由广州出航。相对的，从沉船所见陶瓷的组合看来，其有较大可能是由聚积有大量各地物资的扬州出港，在一度停靠广州后原拟顺季风沿贾耽"广州通海夷道"或苏莱曼《中国印度见闻录》所记述的路线归赴波斯湾，却不幸在印度尼西亚海域触礁罹难。

四

小结

从"黑石号"沉船舶载的广东青瓷可知广东陶瓷也是唐代外销货物之一。不过，相对于东南亚泰国或伊朗尸罗夫出土有唐代广东陶瓷，东北亚日本却基本未见广东瓷窑制品，而是以越窑青瓷、长沙窑和北方白瓷为主要的陶瓷输入组合[65]，此说明了中国以外陶瓷消费地的种类其实和贸易船泊出港地点和停靠港湾息息相关。这也就是说，就日本遗迹所见唐代陶瓷的种类组合以及中日交通航线看来，扬州是日方取得陶瓷等物资的重要据点之一，而主要从事南海贸易的广州则和日本关系相对淡薄[66]，致使广东地区瓷窑基本未见于日本考古遗迹。经由"黑石号"沉船所见广东青瓷，可以推估9世纪广东陶瓷输出种类颇为丰富，同时由于沉船陶瓷年代相对明确，因而又可据此验证或修正中国方面出土类似作品的年代。比如说，被定年为汉代的广东化州县出土的提梁壶（见图四三），就可依据"黑石号"沉船出土的类似作品订正为唐代制品。不仅如此，唐代广东青瓷窑制品作风的掌握和再确认一事，还有利于中国其他省区出土类似标本产地的判定，如前述江苏省扬州文化宫出土的报告所称窑口未定的青釉碗（见图九），从烧造技法等特征看来很有可能属广东瓷窑制品。

[62] 宋岘译注：《道里邦国志》，北京：中华书局，1991年，页71、72。

[63] 桑原骘藏著、杨炼译：《唐宋贸易港研究》汉译世界名著甲编488，台北：台湾商务印书馆，1966年，页76。

[64] Michael Flecker. A Ninth-Century Arab Shipwreck in Indonesia: The First Archaeological Evidence of Direct Trade with China. *Shipwreck Tang Treasures and Monsoon Winds*, Washington: Freer Gallery of Art and Arthur M.Sackler Gallery, 2010, p.109, fig.81.

[65] 龟井明德：《贸易陶磁史研究の課題》，《日本贸易陶磁史の研究》，京都：同朋社，1986年，页4。

[66] 谢明良：《日本出土唐宋时代陶瓷及其有关问题》，原载《故宫学术季刊》13卷4期，1996年，后收入前引《贸易陶瓷与文化史》，页58、59。

一个令人稍感意外的事实是，"黑石号"沉船越窑青瓷等瓷窑制品往往因海水浸泡冲刷而致釉面如毛玻璃般失去光泽，甚至露出胎骨，然而广东梅县青瓷窑系所施罩的开片厚釉，其釉表光泽依旧，且无剥釉现象，其于胎釉结合和耐磨抗碱等各方面均优于浙江越窑青瓷。过去由于梅县壁足碗的器式特征酷似越窑制品，因此往往被认为是在越窑青瓷的影响下发展起来的[67]，甚至被纳入所谓"越窑系"。姑且不论这样的论点是否得当，鉴于包括梅县青瓷在内的广东瓷窑制品亦曾外销东南亚和中东，因此似乎不能不考虑以往被视为乃是受到越窑或邢窑等著名瓷窑作品影响的伊斯兰陶器当中，是否也包括了广东青瓷的影响要素在内？

文末，应予说明的是，本文虽勉力介绍"黑石号"沉船所谓广东青瓷，但部分作品的产地判断其实只是依据其胎釉特征和类似标本的出土地点等间接线索所做的主观推测；第三段有关"黑石号"沉船地点的厘测，其内容和2002年发表的讨论"黑石号"中国陶瓷之拙文大致类似，特此说明并请读者指正。另外，本文部分内容曾在International Symposium on Scientific Investigation and Development of Northeastern Asian Celadon for Developing Gangjin Celadon（Gangjin Celadon Museum 2012.8.2）研讨会上宣读。

[67] 广东省博物馆（古运泉）：前引《广东梅县古墓葬和古窑址调查发掘简报》，页215。

引用书目

1. 古代文献

宋岘译注：《道里邦国志》，北京：中华书局，1991年。

2. 近人论著

安徽省文物考古研究所等：《淮北柳孜——运河遗址发掘报告》，北京：科学出版社，2002年。

曾广亿：《梅县古窑址调查简记》，原载《文博通讯（广东）》1978年第3期，收入：广东省博物馆：《广东文物考古资料选辑》第1辑，1989年，页193～195转页188。

巢湖地区文物管理所（张宏明）：《安徽巢湖市唐代砖室墓》，《考古》1988年第6期，页522～527。

陈炎：《海上丝绸之路与中外文化交流》，北京：北京大学出版社，1996年。

戴开元：《广东缝合木船初探》，《海交史研究》第5期，1983年，页86～89。

傅亦民：《唐代明州与西亚波斯地区的交往——从出土波斯陶谈起》，《海交史研究》2000年2期，页66～70。

广东省博物馆（古运泉）：《广东梅县古墓葬和古窑址调查发掘简报》，《考古》1987年第3期，页207～215。

广东省博物馆（杨式挺等）：《广东始兴晋—唐墓发掘报告》，《考古学集刊》（2），1982年，页113～133。

广东省博物馆等：《广东出土晋至唐文物》，香港：香港中文大学文物馆，1985年。

广东省博物馆等：《广东唐宋出土陶瓷》，香港：香港大学冯平山博物馆，1985年。

广东省文物管理委员会：《佛山专区的几处古窑址调查简报》，《文物参考资料》1959年第12

期，页53~57。
广东省文物管理委员会等：《南海丝绸之路文物图集》，广州：广东科技出版社，1991年。
广东省文物考古研究所等（刘成基）：《广东新会官冲古窑址》，《文物》2000年第6期，页25~43。
广东省文物管理委员会等（曾广忆）：《广东新会官冲古代窑址》，《考古》1963年第4期，页221~223转页203。
广东省文物管理委员会等（杨豪）：《唐代张九龄墓发掘简报》，《文物参考资料》1961年第6期，页45~51。
广东省文物管理委员会办公室等：《广东文物普查成果图录》，广州：广东科技出版社，1990年。
广西壮族自治区文物工作队（韦仁义等）：《广西壮族自治区钦州隋唐墓》，《考古》1984年第3期，页249~263。
广州市文物考古研究所：《铢积寸累》，北京：文物出版社，2005年。
广州市文物考古研究所（朱海仁）：《广州黄花岗汉唐墓葬发掘报告》，《考古学报》2004年第4期，页451~484。
〔日〕龟井明德：《貿易陶磁史研究の課題》，《日本貿易陶磁史の研究》，京都：同朋社，1986年。
何翠媚著、田中和彦译：《タイ南部・コーカオ島とポー岬出土の陶磁器》，《貿易陶磁研究》第11期，1991年，页53~80。
何翠媚著、土桥理子译：《唐代末期における廣東省の窯業および陶磁貿易について》，《貿易陶磁研究》第12期，1992年，页159~184。
何翠媚：《9-10世紀の東・東南アジアにおける西アジア陶器の意義》，《貿易陶瓷研究》第14期，1994年，页35~59。
黄晓蕙：《佛山奇石古窑与相关问题》，《越窑青瓷与邢窑白瓷研究》，北京：故宫出版社，2013年，页447~464。
〔日〕家岛彦一：《アラブ古代型縫合船Sanbuk Zafariについて》，《アジア、アフリカ文化研究》第13期，1977年，页181~204。
〔日〕家岛彦一：《インド洋におけるシーラーフ系商人の交易ネットワークと物品の流通》，收入田边胜美等：《深井晋司博士追悼シルクロード美術論集》，东京：吉川弘文館，1987年，页199~224。
〔日〕家岛彦一译注：《中国とインドの諸情報》1，东京：平凡社，2007年。
〔日〕家岛彦一译注：《中国とインドの諸情報》2，东京：平凡社，2007年。
蒋忠义：《唐代扬州城遗址》，《中国考古年鉴1991》，北京：文物出版社，1992年，页178。
李铧等：《广西出土的波斯陶及相关问题探讨》，《文物》2003年第11期，页71~74。
林士民：《浙江宁波公园路唐宋子城遗址考古发掘获重要成果》，《中国文物报》1998年4月12日第一版。
林亦秋：《南青北白长沙彩》，《越窑青瓷与邢窑白瓷研究》，北京：故宫出版社，2013年，页354、355。
南京博物馆等发掘工作小组：《扬州唐城遗址1975年考古工作简报》，《文物》1977年第9期，页16~30。
南越王宫博物馆筹建处等：《南越宫苑遗址1995、1997考古发掘报告》（下），北京：文物出版社，2008年。
〔日〕桑原骘藏：《波斯灣の東洋貿易港に就て》，《史林》1卷3號，1916年，页18。
〔日〕桑原骘藏著、杨炼译：《唐宋贸易港研究》，汉译世界名著甲编488，台北：台湾商务印书馆，1966年。

〔日〕桑原骘藏著、冯攸译：《中国阿拉伯海上交通史》，台北：台湾商务印书馆，1967年史地丛书版。

〔日〕山本信夫：《日本、東南アジア海域における9～10世紀の貿易とイスラム陶器》，《國立歷史民俗博物館研究報告》第94集，2002年，頁85～144。

宋良璧：《长沙铜官窑瓷器在广东》，收入：《中国古代陶瓷的外销》，北京：紫禁城出版社，1988年，页39～44。

谢明良：《日本出土唐宋时代陶瓷及其有关问题》，原载《故宫学术季刊》13卷4期，1996年，后收入前引《贸易陶瓷与文化史》，页37～80。

谢明良：《记"黑石号"（*Batu Hitam*）沉船中的中国陶瓷器》，原载《台湾大学美术史研究集刊》第13期，2002年，后收入《贸易陶瓷与文化史》，台北：允晨文化，2005年，页81～134。

薛剑虹：《新会、鹤山古陶瓷窑址初探》，收入：Ho Chumei edited. *Ancient Ceramic Kiln Technology in Asia*. Hong Kong: Centre of Asian Studies University of Hong Kong, 1990, pp.22-29.

扬州博物馆等：《扬州古陶瓷》，北京：文物出版社，1996年。

扬州博物馆（马富坤等）：《扬州三元路工地考古调查》，《文物》1985年第10期，页72～76。

章巽：《我国古代的海上交通》，北京：商务印书馆，1986年。

中国社会科学院考古研究所等：《扬州城——1987～1998年考古发掘报告》，北京：文物出版社，2010年。

中国社会科学院考古研究所等扬州城考古队（王勤金）：《江苏扬州市文化宫唐代建筑基址发掘简报》，《考古》1994年第5期，页413～420。

周长源等：《扬州出土的古代波斯釉陶研究》，《文物》1988年第12期，页60～65。

周长源：《试论扬州蓝天大厦工地出土的唐代长沙窑瓷器》，收入：《中国古陶瓷研究会1994年会论文集》，《东南文化》增刊1号，1994年，页65～69。

〔日〕佐佐木达夫：《バンボール出土の中國陶磁と海上貿易》，收入：田边胜美等：《深井晋司博士追悼シルクロード美術論集》，东京：吉川弘文館，1987年，頁225～258。

Michael Flecker. A 9th-Century Arab or Indian Shipwreck in Indoesian Waters. *The International Journal of Nautical Archaeology*, 2000, 29-2, pp. 199-217.

Michael Flecker. A Ninth-Century AD Abab or Indian Shipwreck in Indonesia: First Evidence of Direct Trade with China. *World Archaeology*, 2001, vol. 32, no. 3, pp. 335-354.

Michael Flecker. A Ninth-Century Arab Shipwreck in Indonesia: The First Archaeological Evidence of Direct Trade with China. *Shipwreck Tang Treasures and Monsoon Winds,* Washington: Freer Gallery of Art and Arthur M.Sackler Gallery,2010,pp.101-119.

J. D.Frierman.T'ang and Sung Ceramics Exported to the West in the Light of Archaeological Discoveries. *Oriental Art*, Summer 1978, pp. 195-200.

Regina Krahl. Green Wares of Southern China. *Shipwrecked: Tang Treasures and Monsoon Winds*. Washington: Freer Gallery of Art and Arthur M. Sackler Gallery, 2010, pp. 195-199.

Moria Tampoe. *Maritime Trade between China and the West*. B.A.R. International Series 555, 1989, p. 307, No. 1321, 1322.

Tom Vosmer. The Jewel of Muscat: Reconstructing A Ninth-Century Sewn-Plank Boat. *Shipwreck Tang Treasures and Monsoon Winds,* Washington: Freer Gallery of Art and Arthur M. Sackler Gallery, 2010, pp. 120-135.

David Whitehouse. *Chinese Stoneware from Siraf: the Earliest Finds*. New Jersey: South Asian Archaeology Noyes Press, 1993.

关于所谓"的惺号"及其出水文物的一些意见

Some Thoughts on the So-called "Tek Sing" Wreck and Its Marine Artifacts

陈国栋

("中央"研究院历史语言研究所)

CH'EN Kuo-tung

(Institute of History and Philology, Academia Sinica)

内容摘要 /

本文针对2000年进行文物拍卖的所谓"的惺号"沉船与出水文物，提出质疑与探讨。本文从所谓"的惺号"失事的1822年的相关记载加以考证，确认这艘帆船的真名是 Teek Seeun，中文名字不详，但绝对不可能是"的惺"两字，因为与中国船舶命名的法则不符。本文也重建了1822年那艘中国帆船失事的经过，并且对涉及的航道、贸易，以及海事风险作一深入的评述。本文发现中国帆船在东南亚失事的情况颇为常见，而所谓"的惺号"沉船出水地点的加斯帕海峡一带更是海难经常发生的地方。

关键词 /

的惺 蔡峇峇 加斯帕海峡 帆船贸易 船难

ABSTRACT / In 2000 artifacts of the so-called *Tek Sing* wreck were auctioned. This paper makes inquiries into the real facts of the said sea disaster. It is found that the 1822 wreck belongs to a Chinese junk bearing a name as "Teek Seeun" while its characters are not available. Chinese junks follow certain principles of nomenclature, but the Chinese characters given by the excavators are not appropriate. This paper also details the story of that particular accident, discusses shipping routes, overseas junk trade, as well as maritime risks relating to it. It is revealed that junk wrecking was not infrequent and the Gaspar Straits, where the *Teek Seeun* sank, had many shipping disasters in history.

KEY WORDS / Tek Sing; Baba Chy; Gaspar Straits; junk trade; shipwrecks

一

前言

2000年，在德国斯图加特（Stuttgart）的一场拍卖会上，出售了一批被打捞出水的沉船文物。打捞者与拍卖商宣称文物原属一艘称作"Tek Sing"的中式帆船所有[1]。打捞者更在其出版的专书上，把"Tek Sing"两个字的汉字写作"的惺"（图一）。笔者对"Tek Sing"与"的惺"两词的写法有不同的意见。但为了行文方便起见，本文暂时还是将该船称作"Tek Sing"或"的惺号"或"的惺"船[2]。

下文中，笔者将致力于考订打捞者如何制造或变造这艘船的名称，同时对两位打捞者所声称的拍卖会所出现的出水文物都来自同一艘船的说法，提供若干质疑。笔者从事海洋史的研究，但不是水下考古学者，见闻不周，学养不足，错误自所难免。相关刍见，谨权供参考。

[1] 拍卖者为纳高拍卖行（Nagel Auction House）。该行创始于1922年，为德国一家老资格的拍卖公司。其为此次拍卖会出版的目录为Fritz Nagel, *Nagel Auctions: Tek Sing Treasures* (Stuttgart, Germany: Stuttgarter Kunstauktionshaus, 2000)；据该书第10页，提交拍卖的物件有350,000件以上，拍卖的日期从2000年11月17日开始。部分物件的代表性样品从8月起就在斯图加特火车站展出。

[2] 打捞者出版的专书为Nigel Pickford and Michael Hatcher, *The Legacy of the Tek Sing* (Cambridge, U.K.: Granta Editions, 2000)。为了行文方便，以下称为《"的惺号"的遗物》。

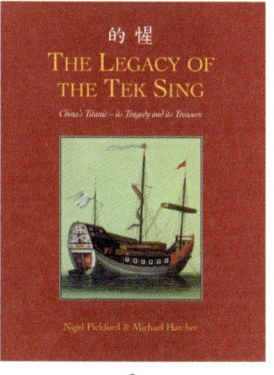

1　　　　　　　　2　　　　　　　　3

图一　Tek Sing号沉船拍卖图录与专书

1、2. 拍卖图录（Fritz Nagel, *Nagel Auctions: Tek Sing Treasures*, Stuttgart, 2000）

3. 专书（Nigel Pickford and Michael Hatcher, *The Legacy of the Tek Sing*, Cambridge, 2000）

二

Hatcher与他们的团队——事先的调查与事后的说明

所谓"的惺号"文物的打捞工作，从资料搜集、分析，一直到打捞完毕，出版专书、进行拍卖，都由Michael Hatcher与Nigel Pickford两人合作完成。

Michael Hatcher于1940年生于英国的约克郡，成长于"巴纳德儿童之家"（Barnardo's children's home）。在澳大利亚历史上所谓的"儿童移民计划"之下，他于1954年被转送到澳大利亚[3]，失去与一切亲友的联系。少年时期的经历，想来对他成年后的思想与行为有所影响。

他到澳大利亚32年之后，1984～1985年，以打捞"南京船货"（the Nanking Cargoes）开始扬名立万。"南京船货"原本归属一艘叫做"赫尔得玛尔森号"（the Geldermalsen）的荷兰船舶所有。"赫尔得玛尔森号"系由荷兰东印度公司热兰省商会（Chamber of Zeeland）在1746年打造，长约45米，载重能力达1100吨，是相当大的一艘船，所载的商品量当然很大[4]。该船于1751年12月8日从广州扬帆，在返回阿姆斯特丹的途中，于1752年1月3日在南中国海盖尔德里亚暗礁（Gelderia Shoals）失事。值得特别重视的是"南京船货"于1986年拍卖时，创造了破纪录的拍卖所得，诱发了一股打捞沉船的热潮[5]。

Michael Hatcher的合伙人Nigel Pickford并不是个名不见经传的人物。照Michael Hatcher的说法，事先的研究都是Nigel Pickford做的。事实上，Nigel Pickford应该也是《"的惺号"的遗物》一书的主稿人。Nigel Pickford的简单经历如下：

Nigel Pickford于1946年出生于伦敦，早先曾在英国剑桥大学就读，读的是英国语文。不过，毕业后，他主要是承袭他的家族传统，从事历史沉船的研究，以提供必要而有用的讯息给有意的打捞者为务。长期从事资料搜集的结果，也为他的家族累聚了汗牛充栋的文献，他人罕可望其项背。据云他的研究至少让70批沉船文物得以重见天日。近年来，他曾在1985年与Michael Hatcher合作，成功打捞起据称属于"赫尔得玛尔森号"文物的"南京船货"；他也曾与Sverker Hallstrom合作，为1991年打捞"头顿（Vung Tau）船货"的工作做准备。他出版过包括《沉船宝物图谱》（The Atlas of Shipwreck Treasure）与《20世纪的沉没船宝藏》（Lost Treasure Ships of the Twentieth Century）在内的沉

[3] 关于澳大利亚的"儿童移民计划"，可参考麦克·莫波格（Michael Morpurgo）著、余沁薇译，《独自一人在大海上》，台北：木马文化，2009。澳大利亚总理陆克文（Kevin Rudd）曾在2009年11月16日，为此事公开表示歉意。20世纪前期的这个计划把一些没有亲人陪伴的英国儿童，强迫移民到澳大利亚。他们当中有些会被当做童工剥削劳力，有些也会被寄养家庭虐待，这是毫无可疑的现象。更惨的是，等到这些儿童或少年年长之后，建立家庭，乃至于事业有成之时，对他们最大的折磨却不是这些被剥削、被虐待的记忆；而是他们能追溯的记忆其实太少！他们被送到澳大利亚之后，被打散分到各地，连一起从英国同船过来、认识也不过几十天的朋友们，也都被强迫打散，真正成为在世界上举目无亲的一种人。

[4] 参考 C. J. A. Jörg, *The Geldermalsen: History and Porcelain* (London: Kimber, 1986).

[5] 见Nigel Pickford与Michael Hatcher合著之《"的惺号"的遗物》一书的作者介绍，以及John Wright, *Encyclopedia of Sunken Treasure* (London: Michael O'Mara Books, 1995), pp. 145–148.

船相关书籍。不过，他另外还有一项嗜好，就是写小说。《党工》(*The Party Agent*)[6]为他的作品之一[7]。

作为一个寻宝人，同时又是一名兼职的小说家，我们可以猜想他的写作态度与历史学家所要求的严谨性一定有相当程度的差距，而不能将宝藏的秘密泄露太多也是势所必然了。更何况，他与他的合作者们还要考虑到出水文物的市场问题。

在《"的惺号"的遗物》一书中，*Tek Sing*一名是突然跳出来的，完全没有交待依据及出处；至于"的惺"两个字则只出现在封面。该书解释说："该船的名称是'的惺'，意思是'真正的星星'，其目的地是爪哇岛上最重要的城镇巴达维亚（现在叫做雅加达）。"[8]

在《"的惺号"的遗物》一书中，这两位具名作者也交待了寻找这项埋藏宝藏的动机。他们说，在1843年出版的Horsburgh著作的第5版第188页出现了以下的信息："在贝尔威得暗礁（The Belvidere Shoals）上翻覆过一艘巨型中式帆船。其一部分的船员去到了加斯帕岛（Gaspar Island），其他人靠着沉船碎片漂浮，而由一艘属于加尔各答的港脚船（country ship）英勇地救起。"[9]紧接着引文之后，这两个人说："就只有这些了！"意味着只有这一点点信息。若说他们只有这项资料，而该资料完全没有提到船名、人名，而该书却有人名、船名乃至于完整到不可思议的细节，为什么呢？

他们所参考Horsburgh的著作，书名为《亚洲指南》。他们用的是1843年的第5版，笔者看到1852年的第6版[10]。无论如何，原编者James Horsburgh在1836年就去世了。同一段描述在第6版中的内容并无实质上的差别，只是数字与符号的写法略有不同而已。两位作者说他们只有这项资料，而该资料完全没有提到船名、人名，而该书却有人名、船名乃至于完整到不可思议的细节，为什么呢？我的看法是他们隐瞒了一部分的资料并且虚构了一些没有确定依据的故事[11]。

三

"的惺号"（Tek Sing）是怎么来的

事实上，James Horsburgh本人更早在1825年就曾经报导过前述发生在贝尔威得暗礁的中国帆船船难[12]。不过，即使他在1825年就写了文章，但他还是没

---

[6] San Francisco: Black Swan Press, 1990.

[7] 见Nigel Pickford所编辑的*Atlas of Ship Wreck Treasure* (London: Dorling Kindersley, 1994)和Nigel Pickford与Michael Hatcher合著之《"的惺号"的遗物》两书的编者介绍。

[8] 《"的惺号"的遗物》，页15。

[9] 《"的惺号"的遗物》，页6。按：18、19世纪时，英国人将亚洲内部的贸易称作"港脚贸易"（the country trade），不过，所谓的"港脚船"通常指在印度的非东印度公司所属之英国人拥有，或者印度本地人拥有的贸易船舶。此处所指之船舶系一名在孟加拉国的英国人的船只。

[10] James Horsburgh, *The India Directory, or Directions for Sailing to and from the East Indies, China, Australia, and the Interjacent Ports of Africa and South America*, 1852年第6版（第2册，页186、187）。按：由于历史的错误，欧洲人长期把亚洲海域称为印度（India）或东印度（East Indies），因此这两个名词都应该正名为亚洲。

[11] 他们有找到一些1822年沉船的资料，也加以利用，但不敢完全公开其资料。他们环绕着那些资料，作了一些附会或比附，好让这些出水物有个著名的身份。他们的说法有些是事实，有些不是。这是历史学家最痛恨的造假。

[12] 见*Asiatic Journal*, vol.20 (1825), pp.419–420。

有拔得头筹。因为有关那艘大型中式帆船船难的报导,更早在1823年就已经在他发表文章的同一个刊物《亚细亚杂志》(*Asiatic Journal*)刊出过了[13]。而《亚细亚杂志》的报导其实是转载自《加尔各答政府公报》(*Calcutta Government Gazette*),最初就刊登在事发的1822年。内容就是出手拯救1822年年初在贝尔威得暗礁沉没的中国船的英国船长所提供的相关资料。

事实上,1822年中国船发生船难时,英国港脚船"印地安娜号"(the *Indiana*)船长James Pearl中尉曾经出手捞救,将救到的受难者送到婆罗洲的坤甸(Pontianak)。他与当地荷属东印度驻在官 J. H. Tobias的通信,当年即于《加尔各答政府公报》刊出,并在次年转载于《亚细亚杂志》。这是为何James Horsburgh能在事件发生后不久就能报导此事的因由;同时也是许多航海指南都记录该次中国船难的原因。

James Pearl船长在该次航行中招致财产损失,原期待中国政府能给予补偿。这当然是空想,当时的清朝官员即便有这方面的讯息恐怕也不会认为有那种必要。1835年,James Pearl递交中国官方一份陈情书;他同时也运动英国外相巴麦尊子爵(Viscount Palmerston, 1784–1865)致函在中国的商务监督,请求协助。结果都石沉大海。其后广州的外国人社群刊物《广州纪要》(*Canton Register*)刊印了一本小册子陈述相关的内容。1836年6月18日,James Pearl再次从英国利物浦致函广州怡和洋行(Jardine Matheson & Co.)。1837年7月,广州、澳门出版的《中国丛报》(*The Chinese Repository*)刊出相关的报导[14]。依据《中国丛报》的叙述,关于1822年年初这次船难经过的大致情形如下:

《中国丛报》说船上乘员有1600人,被英国港脚船*Indiana*船长Pearl救起的有198位。*Indiana*船,368吨,预定航程自孟加拉前往婆罗洲。变更航行计划救人,船长自称损失40 000元。

1822年2月7日(清道光二年正月十六日),清晨7点半钟,自加斯帕岛东面朝西北偏北方向4英里半的地方,*Indiana*船的成员看到一些显然是船只失事的残留物:船板、箱子、成捆的雨伞、竹竿,还有一些其他漂浮着的东西,彼此相去不远。漂浮物上,攀附着一两位到五六位失事的受难者。往后一天多的时间内,船长改变了原先的计划,下令出手搭救眼前的受难者,最终救起了198人。

第一天获救者当中,有一位名叫Baba Chy(蔡峇峇)[15]者,他是巴达维亚的土著,当时系要从中国返回巴达维亚,回到他的父亲身边。之前,他是回到中国接受教育。正因为蔡峇峇兼通汉语与马来语,而英国船上有人懂得马来语,他因此成为双方面的沟通媒介。

[13] 刊登在*Asiatic Journal*,vol.15 (1823), pp.36–39。

[14] *The Chinese Repository*, July 1837,pp.149–153.

[15] "峇峇"系汉人与马来人混写生下的男子的称呼,并不是这个人的名字。

[16] 《中国丛报》刊出的Pearl船长的叙述，离开那次船难已经十多年。因此无法确定船名第二字拼音的首字母。不过，事件发生不久时，那个首字母也写作"N"，而整个船名写作"Teek Necun"。如此说来，要到1837年才排版排成"Teek Seeun"，之前则作"Teek Neeun"。

[17] 原文作"Capella Mera, or Red Head"，都是"红头"之意。"Capella Mera"在现代马来文中，拼作"kepala merah"。"红头船"即广东省的帆船代称。

根据蔡沓沓的陈述，这艘失事的船叫做"Teek Seeun"或者"Teek Neeun"[16]。这是一艘八九百吨级的厦门船，23天前从厦门起航，前往巴达维亚。船上所载除了值钱的商品之外，不算船员在内，还搭载了年龄从6岁到70岁的乘客约1600名。由于走错航道，该船在前一天黄昏时分，在加斯帕岛西北方12英里处的贝尔威得暗礁触礁。

船上的财副（相当于副船长）在经过相当的时间，也从惊吓中回过神来以后，告诉Pearl船长，就在他们失事的当儿，有一艘小型的红头船[17]在他们附近经过，并且了解到他们的不幸，却没有停下来伸手救援。

2月8日深夜，船长召集一些人讨论后，认定除了已经救起的198人外，再也别无指望。考虑到搭载这么多的受难者，有严重的食物及饮水问题，必须立即航向陆地。次日（2月9日）下午就扬帆前往西婆罗洲的坤甸（Pontianak），寻求坤甸的荷兰当局协助。2月22日抵达坤甸。Pearl船长致函荷兰驻在官（Resident）J. H. Tobias，荷兰驻在官也回了信。被Pearl船长救起的198人当中，除了10位原本是巴达维亚城的居民留在*Indiana*船上，另外安排返回巴达维亚外，其他人都在坤甸下船。

在事件发生不久即已刊出的《亚洲杂志》的内容与此相近，并且还将Pearl船长与荷兰驻在官 J. H. Tobias往复的书信也一并刊出。

或许Hatcher与Pickford等人真的没有看到《亚细亚杂志》。但是《亚细亚杂志》（1823年）所刊载的英国船长的相关资料稍早或同时也发表在加尔各答的另一个杂志《加尔各答政府公报》，可是这两位作者也不提这个杂志的刊名。倒是他们略略提到了《中国丛报》，只是没有交待完整的出版信息而已。

这两组文件的信息都直接出自该名英国船长，内容远比James Horsburgh的各种叙述来得详细。这让我们对*Tek Sing*与"的惺"得名的由来有了进一步的了解。

1. 拼音是*Tek Sing*还是*Teek Seeun*呢？

Nigel Pickford将这艘船比定为"*Tek Sing*（的惺号）"，用部分James Pearl的叙述来加强这个故事的内容。就他们打捞的地点来说，与文献所记1822年中国沉船所在位置相近。出水物之一的墓碑也有"道光二年端月"字样，也就是1822年年初的讯息。不过，1822年沉没的那艘中国船，其实并不叫作"Tek Sing"，或者说源自James Pearl的原始报导，其拼音与这样的写法多少有所出入。

一则是，在James Pearl交给坤甸的荷兰驻在官的书信中，该船的船名被拼作Teek Secun。这里有一种可能，就是"c"其实应作"e"，也就是"Teek Seeun"。再则是，《中国丛报》的资料将该船的船名认定为Teek Seeun或（Teek）Neeun，该资料声明不确定第二个字的首字母到底是"S"还是"N"，显然是这两个英文字母的大写颇为近似的缘故。若参考其他信息，显然应以"S"为是。换言之，这艘船的船名应该是"Teek Seeun"。

Nigel Pickford事先获得有关James Pearl捞救沉船人员的资料，进而与Michael Hatcher在勿里洞岛附近打捞，果然发现庞大的沉船遗物。不过，在欠缺合理论证的情形下，他们一口咬定（比附）为1822年沉船的船货。Nigel Pickford说不定只是附会吧！因为那艘1822年中国沉船并不叫作"Tek Sing"，而应该是叫作"Teek Seeun"才对！未知他们为何不依据史料直接称它作"Teek Seeun"，而要去创造一个无中生有的"Tek Sing"。这会不会是因为他们不想让人直接拿1822年沉船Teek Seeun的资料来查证呢？可是依据前述几项原始文献，Teek Seeun是一名来自沉船受难者之一的土生华人蔡荅荅的亲口叙述啊！

Nigel Pickford等人还给了这艘船两个很不恰当的汉字"的惺"。在《"的惺号"的遗物》一书中，Tek Sing一名是突然跳出来的，两位作者完全没有交待依据及出处；至于"的惺"两个字则只出现在封面。仅在内文中用英文解释"的惺"两字的意思是"真正的星星"。虽然该批出水物还是有可能为Teek Seeun的船货，或者包含相当数量的该船承载的物品，不过证据与推理都很欠充分。他们的用意颇令人怀疑。

2. 的惺、得胜，还是其他名字？

Hatcher与Pickford这两个人把他们打捞的那批船货称为"的惺船货"，把那艘船叫做"的惺号"。然而稍稍熟悉中文用法的人，都不免质疑"的惺"这两个字看来颇为碍眼，完全不符合中国帆船的命名习惯。我们不妨推测：他们以相关历史文献为基础，稍稍变化，把那艘船叫做"Tek Sing"，再靠稍稍懂得中文的人把这个拼音写成汉字。可惜这位写下汉字的人中文底子有限，才出现这么奇怪的写法。中国学者显然无法接受"的惺"两个字，纷纷想为它改名，例如改成"泰兴"之类[18]。

1822年沉船的真实名字是Teek Seeun。Teek Seeun一名来自巴达维亚土生华人蔡荅荅的口中，应该近于厦门读音[19]。果真如此，则近于"得顺"或"德顺"，而与"泰兴"两字相去颇远。当然，先前建议使用"泰兴"或其他字眼的作者并不知道"Tek Sing"本来就不是那艘船的真名，因此也不能说他们完全想错了。现在我们知道这艘船的真名是Teek Seeun，可是我们目前没有任何

[18] 例见郑炯鑫：《从"泰兴号"沉船看清代德化青花瓷器的生产与外销》，《文博》2001年第6期，页49、50。柴商之：《"泰兴号"被毁记》，《椰城》2008年第2期，页20。

[19] 关于巴达维亚华人与厦门方言之间的关系，可参考包乐史、吴凤斌：《18世纪末巴达维亚唐人社会》，厦门：厦门大学出版社，2002年。

资料来确认这艘船的中文叫法。这虽然颇为遗憾，但是我们不妨还是可以参考一些中国船舶命名的惯例来想象。以下举若干史料作说明。首先是乾隆十五年（1750年）两广总督的一件奏折提到：

> 广商船户名目，好用合、利、万、顺等字样，盈千累万，大同小异。其船内货色，尤易混杂，大约数日之后，即难问数日以前之诡弊；而对外至之人，断不能知局内之阴私……[20]

提奏人两广总督陈大受强调船户偏好"合、利、万、顺"这类字眼。虽然因其大同小异，容易引起官方困扰，以故不为其所喜，但是无疑地，不外乎是透过命名以祈求合作、和谐、吉祥、顺利之类的意思。此本是人之常情，而海上风险大，命名更重视选用佳字。不过，这里讲的是广东船，那福建船呢？

依据闽浙总督汪志伊的一件题本的报导，在嘉庆（1796～1820年）时期，官兵与东南沿海的大海盗蔡牵争斗期间，为了加强官兵的战力，曾经有几年的时间雇用商船协助作战。根据该项资料所开列的船名，嘉庆十一年（1806年）雇用的三十五艘商船为：

> 陈恒合、陈慎德、洪德兴、陈藏发、金进顺、金正吉、富长春、金万合、纪宝财、金振声、陈瑞亨、纪恒益、金丰昌、金宁顺、周德胜、金万和、林豹良、金进发、林合利、林合美、欧振源、杨发金、金泰来、金万镒、金福春、傅源升、李荣华、金得春、金如发、郑福源、金双合、张达成（即金广春）、蔡双财、傅源裕、纪锦兴。

其后，因原雇商船有遭遇沉没、击碎之事，或者放回经商，因此在嘉庆十三年（1808年）又加雇了九艘，其船名为：

> 金发宝、金联旺、新源成、福隆荣、连捷兴、金振成、林得兴、金顺成、金吉顺。

嘉庆十四年（1809年）又加雇了十二艘，其船名为：

> 刘益成、林德兴、陈丽春、陈允胜（即陈进泰）、金益隆、金得发（即杜荣华）、新源发、新藏春（即李大来）、张和祥、陈和成、陈合利、金源盛。

最后，在嘉庆十五年（1810年）又加雇了五艘，其船名为：

> 叶顺胜（即金万胜）、新荣源、金益全（即连全发）、陈协利、吴得万[21]。

以上，从嘉庆十一年到十五年，曾经受雇于官方的厦门商船总共有61艘，其中6艘另有第二个名称，因此总共有67个船名。

在此先插入说明一船两名的问题，此或者系出于船名、牌名（船名是船只所有人或使用人叫的名字，牌名是在官府登记的名字）不一的缘故。陈支平提

[20] 台北故宫博物院藏军机处档案：录副奏折第006335号，乾隆十五年十二月二十五日两广总督陈大受奏，乾隆十六年正月十五日奉朱批、发抄。

[21] 以上各条船名，见"中央"研究院历史语言研究所：《明清史料·戊编》，台北："中央"研究院历史语言研究所，1994年，页576～584，《闽浙总督汪志伊残题本》。

到晋江陈氏族人合伙从厦门购得一艘被官府没收的海盗船，拿它来从事闽台两地之间的贸易活动。不料同安县的张捷、张园父子出来首告，主张该船只之所有权。张捷的状词云：

> 具呈人嘉禾溪岸商民张捷，年八十六岁，为埋没赂□□思怜开释，勒限究结事。

> 窃捷籍马巷，徙居厦门，汗积建置商船二只：一名长兴，牌名金发号；一名长春，牌名金如意号。辖同安县□□□□□所倚源发行保结，历年各港贸易[22]。

陈支平所引用的档案，进一步还指出以上船只活动的时间在咸丰三年（1853年）前后。一船两名，一名自己叫，一名登记在官府。因此，即使官府登记有资料，不明就里，还是无法弄清楚特定船只的常用名称。值得注意的是，船只所有人（船户、船东）自己使用的名字是简单的两个字而已，但登在官方的船牌名字却都冠了个"金"字。

回来看汪志伊题本所提到的67个船名，首字为"金"字者共出现25次，"福"字及"富"字各1次，"新"字4次；此外有36次皆为一般姓氏。姓氏当然与船只所有人有关；"新"则代表新造或更新的意思；"福"字及"富"字皆为祈愿的表示。至于"金"字，一方面可以想成与祈愿有关，希望利市发财；另一方面则表示一种合伙拥有该船的状况。

道光（1821～1850年）初年，周凯的《厦门志》，说：

> 闽俗……合数人开一店铺或制造一舶，则姓"金"。"金"犹合也。[不]惟厦门，台湾亦然[23]。

提到合伙开店或造船的事，在厦门和台湾都很常见。必须注意的是，合伙有时确实是因为个人资金有限的缘故；但是至少在造船的场合可能也有分摊风险的考虑在内。一个人将他的资金分散投资打造不同的船，万一有一两艘失事，不会损失全部的投资。许多人合造一船，失事时，每位投资者只分摊到一部分的损失。在海事活动上，合伙不仅有扩大资金的功能，而且也能产生分散风险的作用。

以"金"作船名前缀词的习惯，也随着华人侨居海外，而见诸海外华人的船舶。例如19世纪仰光的庆福宫碑文就罗列一些捐款赞助该庙的中式船舶的名称，提到新加坡来的船（叻船）计有：

> 陈金星（声）、陈金钟、杨广昌、蔡福元、蔡福美、洋顺船、金协德、金裕盛、金福泰、金长发、美利船、道利船、振成船、维立船、金丰发、金庆瑞、杨广源、金源隆[24]。

---

[22] 陈支平：《清代闽台商人间经济纠纷的案例分析》，收入其《民间文书与明清东南族商研究》，北京：中华书局，2009年，页263、264。

[23] 周凯：《厦门志》，台北：台湾银行经济研究室，《台湾文献丛刊》第95种，1961年，页649。《福建省例》，台北：台湾银行经济研究室，《台湾文献丛刊》第199种，1968年，页703："白底艍一种船只，尤当加倍严查，并取具连环切结也。大号商船，揽载客货，资本至数千金，多系身家股实之人，且有行保、族邻，连环具结，未必便肯为匪。岛屿穷民，以海为田，造船讨海，或合伙同造一船，名曰十三股艚。"

[24] 见陈荆和、陈育崧：《新加坡华文碑铭集录》，香港：香港中文大学出版部，1972年，陈育崧的《绪言》，页24。陈育崧原注出处为李汉青：《闽侨开发东南亚史略》，《福建文献》（台湾）第4期，1968年，页13、14。

[25] 该文件收录在《福建沿海航务档案（嘉庆朝）》，页151～178，为一甚长的文件，无日期，但为嘉庆年间（可能就是嘉庆十四年）应无问题，因为文件中提到王提督（得禄）相关事迹。本段引文出现在页162。参考陈国栋：《清代中叶厦门的海上贸易，1727～1833》，收入中国海洋发展史论文集编辑委员会：《中国海洋发展史论文集》（第4辑），台北："中央"研究院中山人文社会科学研究所，1991年，页61～100。

[26] Leonard Blussé, "Junks to Java: Chinese Shipping to the Nanyang in the Second Half of the Eighteenth Century," in Eric Tagliacozzo and Wen-chin Chang eds., *Chinese Circulations: Capital, Commodities, and Networks in Southeast Asia* (Durham and London: Duke University Press, 2011), pp. 221-258.

[27] Leonard Blussé, "The Vicissitudes of Maritime Trade: Letters from the Ocean Hang Merchant, Li Kunhe, to the Dutch Authorities in Batavia, 1803-1809," in Anthony Reid ed., *Sojourners and Settlers: Histories of Southeast Asia and the Chinese* (Honolulu: University of Hawai'i Press, 2001), pp. 154-163. 该文经摘要后，改题为"Letters from Chinese Merchants to Batavia"，收入在Tineke Hellwig and Eric Tagliacozzo eds., *The Indonesia Reader: History, Culture, Politics* (Durham and London: Duke University Press, 2009), pp. 165-172。七封中文函件的内容，可参考包乐史著、庄国土等译：《巴达维亚华人与中荷贸易》，南宁：广西人民出版社，1997年，页256～272。

其中以冠姓氏或冠"金"字为常。在船名不冠首字的场合，就将两字船名末尾加上个"船"字，构成三字一组的船名。所谓的"的惺号"依此原则，应该称作"的惺船"。

用"金"字表示合伙关系的用法，《厦门志》说不只用于船只，也用于开店。此处补充下面一个例子。嘉庆年间一份厦门一带的文件提到：

> 遵照宪檄，饬传各行商查询。去后。拠该商金和合、金联成、金广益、金源益、金坤元、金丰美、金瑞安、金和美、金长隆、金振兴、金全胜、金益兴、金众利、金晋祥、金联兴、金丽全等金呈词称：……[25]

这个文件指涉的年代，也在嘉庆中期（1810年左右），当时几乎所有的厦门海事服务的牙行都在行名上冠个"金"字。

除去船名首字的"金"字、吉祥文字、船东姓氏，或者船名末尾的"船"字之外，船名的主体由两个汉字构成，而这两个汉语单字，或由此两个单字构成的单词，也都代表吉祥与致富的意味。"的惺"两个字不但不能说是"真正的星星"，而且也不是隐含船舶命名的基本精神，绝对不会是1822年沉没那艘船只的名称。

四

厦门与巴达维亚之间的中式帆船贸易

据Pickford等人所述，"的惺"船于1822年自厦门启碇扬帆，目的地是巴达维亚。两地之间，早从17世纪初以来，就已存在着一个相对稳定的贸易[26]。对于做这一区段远洋贸易的中国帆船，我们也有幸有一些嘉庆年间的数据可以检视。荷兰学者包乐史（Leonard Blussé）云："近来在莱顿大学图书馆发现了一些未被整理分类的卷宗，内有40封1790～1810年几个中国洋行写的原始信件。"他公布了其中厦门洋行商人李昆和在1803～1809年写的7封信件[27]。

这7封信提到的船名及船主（船上的指挥者，类似西方的船长）递年为：荣发船，船主黄及官（1803年）；荣发船，船主黄及官（1804年）；荣发船，船主黄及官（1805年）；十三万胜船，船主许表官（1806年）；十三万胜船，船主马华官（1807年）；十三万胜船，船主马华官（1808年）；十三万胜船，船主马华官（1809年）。厦门洋行昆和行连续七年都发船前往巴达维亚[28]。

昆和行不只承揽往来巴达维亚的帆船。下面这封出自船难者之手的书信，时间为嘉庆十四年（1809年）文件，显示昆和行也做越南生意。

福建省厦门口昆和行家长李西老整发金顺源船往㟁猊，在厦二月初七日扬帆，驶至十五夜到万里长沙打破。至二十一日，幸有甲板二只

兵船未氏罅时／兵船未氏们二位大船主

二十一日出杉板到沙屿来救命五百六十一人。至二十九日驶到会安港，立刻上关报失水。候至三月初六日，会安官将人众俩入关上。计住甲板船中共十六日。多蒙船主二位十分恭敬，感恩不尽。再蒙厚爱，另借出佛银二百一十大员。约到广省，立即奉还，不感忘恩。此上

船主未罅时、未氏们二位大人尊照

眷弟李宽、财副周沛、伙长江胆

板主罗奎、阮耀[29]

按，未氏罅时和未氏们即Captain Ross和Captain Maugham两人，为救起那五百多位失事者的英国船长；㟁猊也写作仝猊或同猊，高棉语"Dong-dai"的译音，原意为鹿之原野。它也叫做鹿洞或农耐大铺，当时属于越南边和省。该地位于今西贡东北方30~50千米处，是西贡兴起以前南圻的第一大城，为明郑旧部陈上川所建。会安在越南中部，为顺化附近的港口[30]。失事地点的万里长沙相当于西沙群岛。这艘船虽然并不前往巴达维亚，但是其走的航道，与前往巴达维亚之船舶的前半段航道相同；而其失事获救者高达五百余人，可知乘员中不乏偷渡出国，往外移民者。这与"的惺"船的情况虽然人数多寡有别，其性质则颇为类似。

通贩外国的商船在南海遭风的，依据杨国桢与张雅娟两人的研究所见，现存中外记载有：

嘉庆八年（1803年），厦门洋行李昆和发往马六甲、槟榔屿、苏禄三船俱失。九年（1804年），闽船遭风漂至越南；厦门洋行李昆和荣发船自巴达维亚返航，收风粤东。十年（1805年），闽船遭风漂至越南。十一年（1806年），广东官船一只在海遭风，漂荡外洋，8人被英国洋船搭救，载至新埠（新加坡）。厦门洋行李昆和十三万胜船自巴达维亚返航，因风收入羊城。十三年（1808年），台湾船漂至越南；厦门和振万船往把挟，遭风漂到单丹，6人染病身亡。回棹在洋中遭风，漂收广东。十四年（1809年），漳州诏安船户陈泉等39人驾金发兴船自暹罗回国，遭风沉没，27人逃在三板漂流获救，回到澳门。十四年（1809年），厦门金集春船在番仔瓦洋面冲礁击碎。十五年（1810年），厦门昆和洋行金源顺船往㟁猊，到万里长沙打破，561人被英国兵船救起，送至越南会安。福建吴竟船自暹罗回国，在广东洋面遭风漂至福建。

[28] 文献出处见上注。至于所谓"十三万胜船"系指该船的名字为"万胜"或"十三万胜"。"万胜"之前冠以"十三"两字，表是该船亦属多人合伙打造的事实，其用法与"金"字完全相同。周凯：《厦门志》，《船政略·渔船》条，页174云："按《会典》……渔船向止大、小二种，后渐造为中号渔船，有曰'艋艚'、曰'描缯'、曰'虎艚'、曰'十三股艚'、曰'汉洋钓'。甚者曰'草鸟船'，形如劈开鸭蛋式，多桨而能行，不畏风浪；潜赴粤省，私载违禁鸦片土，在洋行劫。……"据此，"十三股艚"应为中型渔船，且系多人合伙同造。至于其他场合，将船名冠以"十三"两字，当然也与合伙造船有关。参考注20。

[29] 英国国家档案馆藏，F.O., 233/189 (no. 220)。未押日期，实际为1809年（嘉庆十四年）。

[30] 参考陈荆和：《清初郑成功残部之移殖南圻（下）》，《新亚学报》第8卷第2期（1968），页424。

二十三年（1815年），闽船一只遭风漂至越南富安[31]。

两位学者所列，虽然不能说是完整，但也清楚呈现中国船舶在东南亚一带航行，意外失事，并不少见。

五

Gaspar Strait（Selat Gaspar）一带的海难

"的惺"船失事的地点在加斯帕海峡（the Gaspar Strait）一带，而该处船难甚多[32]。著名的例子如搭载英国使臣阿美士德（Lord Amherst）出使中国的英国海军舰艇"阿尔赛斯特号"（the H.M.S. *Alceste*），在1817年回程时，就在航向巴达维亚的途中在附近失事[33]。

1862年，日本人也在附近失事。这一年，日本德川幕府请求荷兰总领事J. K. de Wit协助在荷兰打造一艘蒸汽船。同时，日本也派遣留学生（包括后来担任过海军卿与外务大臣等职的榎本武扬在内）前往荷兰学习造船、行船的知识与技术。一行人搭乘荷兰三桅船（bark）*Calypso*号，由船长G. Poolman指挥驾驶。同年11月26日至27日的半夜，该船行至加斯帕海峡时，就在阿尔赛斯特暗礁（Alceste Reef），也就是"阿尔赛斯特号"先前发生船难的同一地点失事。邦加与勿里洞两岛的驻在官派人抢救，领军者为一名华人雷珍兰（荷兰统治者任命华人头人为甲必丹，其副手为雷珍兰）。获救者及其财物先被送到邻近的Liat岛，然后转送Lepar岛。其后被转送到巴达维亚，在12月9日到达。其后成功地前往荷兰学习，并且造成轮船"开阳丸"驾回日本[34]。

以上是特别有名的案例。其他较不为人所知的案例，至少还有：

1789 - *Vansittart*，英国东印度公司船，828吨。

19世纪初期 - Glass Wreck。

1806 - *Forbes*，英国港脚贸易船。

1816 - 一艘来自澳门的葡萄牙船舶。

1816 - *Amelia*，葡萄牙船。

1817 - "阿尔赛斯特号"。

1817 - *Le Minerve*，法国船，805吨。

1824 - *The Severn*，纽约来的船。

1824 - *The Columbian*，纽约来的船[35]。

[31] 杨国桢、张雅娟：《海盗与海洋社会权力——以19世纪初"大海盗"蔡牵为中心的考察》，《云南师范大学学报（哲学社会科学版）》2011年第3期，页4。同页也整理了中国沿海之船难。该文内容不尽然正确，但无碍于说明船难之难以避免。

[32] "黑石号"（*Batu Hitam*）为其中之一。参考*Shipwrecked: Tang Treasures and Monsoon Winds*, 2011. 谢明良，《记黑石号（*Batu Hitam*）沉船中的中国陶瓷器》，《"国立"台湾大学美术史研究集刊》第13期，2002年，页1~60及页277。John Guy（约翰·盖伊）著、王丽明译：《九世纪初连结中国与波斯湾的外销瓷：勿里洞沉船的例证》，《海交史研究》2008年第2期，页14~26。

[33] 可参考阿美士德使团成员的两本作品，这两本书现在皆有中译本。阿裨尔著、刘海岩译：《中国旅行记（1816~1817年）——阿美士德使团医官笔下的清代中国》，上海：上海古籍出版社，2012年。亨利·埃利斯著、刘天路、刘甜甜译：《阿美士德使团出使中国日志》，北京：商务印书馆，2013年。

[34] Anonymous, "Notes on the Japanese Mission which was Shipwrecked between Bangka and Billiton in 1862 on its Way from Japan to Holland via Batavia," *Munumenta Nipponica*, 5:2 (July 1942), pp. 540-550.

六

中国人海难现象与叙述

Pearl船长对"的惺"船船难发生后失事现场一带的描述，令人触目惊心。这反映了两件事情：其一是中国人没有适当的对付船难的做法；其二是中国文献少有船难现场的报导。

中式帆船遭遇灾难的时候，欠缺合乎现代科学意义的紧急处理手段，往往只能诉诸丢包、划水仙与弃船逃命等消极性的作为。若是事态严重，跌落大海，终究人财两失。若是侥幸得免于难，由于遭遇者绝大多数不是文人，因此事后的报导也不多。虽然如此，仔细爬梳史料，还是可以选择几个个案来介绍，借以充实我们对船只遇难状况的想象与理解。

第一个是郁永河的经验与叙述。1645年出生的郁永河，在1697年时，为福州的地方官前往台湾北部的淡水采集硫黄。郁永河在台南登陆之后，选择从陆路前往北台湾；他的同伴王森（字君云）选择继续搭船沿台湾西海岸北上。航程中，遇到不佳的天候，先后失去船碇、折损船舵，也将舟中物件抛弃三分之一，还是风险万分。驾船人说只有举行"划水仙"的仪式，靠天保佑，方能登岸脱困。他们真的就那么做了，也真的幸运地脱离险境[36]。他们的获救其实与"划水仙"没有任何关联。可是有人在船只遇险时，做了"划水仙"的动作，随后转危为安，于是也就有人相信这样做是有益的了。

郁永河之后过了将近两百年，都已经到19世纪末了，还是有人把"划水仙"当成是一种船只遇险时没有办法的自救办法。《点石斋画报》刊登过一幅"划水仙"石印版画（图二），并且为我们解释"划水仙"是怎么一回事：

划水仙：海洋有神焉，曰水仙王，不知祂自何时，亦不详其姓氏。凡海舶在大洋中，或遇飓风忽起，骇浪如山，舵折樯倾，绳断舷裂，技力不得施，智巧无所用，斯时唯有"划水仙"一法能拯救之。"划水仙"者，洋中危急时，近岸不得，则率舟中人相与披发共蹲舷间，以空手作拨棹势，而众口复假为钲鼓声，为五日竞渡状，自能转危为安，顷刻抵岸，一若有人暗中持之者，鬼神之力也。去年有二船舶自台郡开赴鸡笼淡水，忽为大风折舵，船腹中裂。舟中之人皆自分无再生之理。舟师告曰："唯有划水仙可免"，遂依法行之。于是舟之沉者旋复浮出，破浪穿风，疾飞如矢。须臾，即抵彼岸。故虽徒手拨虚棹，而能抗海浪、

[35] Tony Wells, *Shipwrecks & Sunken Treasure in Southeast Asia, with over 450 Wrecks including the FLOR do Mar* (Singapore: Times Editions, 1995), pp. 91-97为Bangka and Gaspar Straits沉船信息；p. 97为Carimata Strait沉船信息。请注意：很多记录其实分不清楚Bangka Straits与Gaspar Straits。简单地说Bangka Straits介于苏门答腊与Bangka之间；而Gaspar Straits则介于Bangka与Billiton两岛之间。

[36] 郁永河著、方豪校：《合校足本裨海纪游》，台北：台湾省文献委员会，1950年，页14，云："五鼓失碇，船无系，复出大洋，浪击舵折，舳首又裂，知不可。舟师告曰：'惟有划水仙，求登岸免死耳！'划水仙者，众口齐作钲鼓声，人各挟一匕箸，虚作棹船势，如午日竞渡状。凡洋中危急，不得近岸，则为之。船果近岸。"

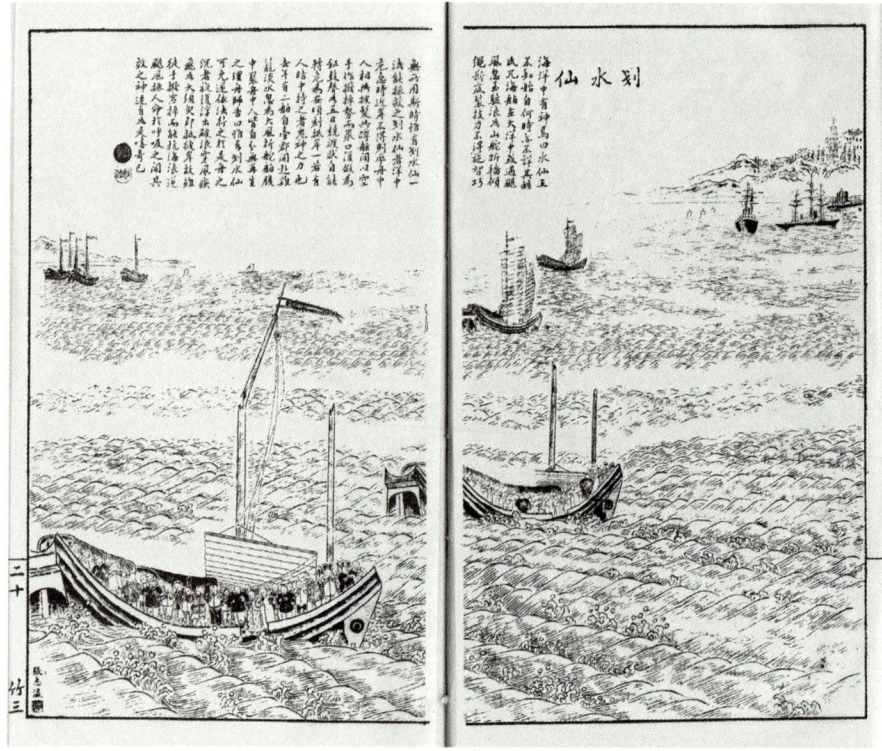

图二 "划水仙"石印版画
（采自《点石斋画报·三集》，竹集，页19、20）

逆飓风，拯人命于呼吸之间。其效之神速，有如是嘻奇已[37]。

至于船毁人亡的情况，报导与记录都很难见到。虽然南宋的洪迈（1123～1202年）说过不少海洋奇遇的故事。不过，大概只有明代的黄衷（1474～1553年）所叙述的海难故事内容最丰富而且真实。黄衷《海语》"铁板沙"条记录说：明宪宗成化二十一年（1485年），给事中林荣、行人黄乾亨两人受命前往占城，执行册封该国国王的任务。由于当时属于海禁时期，只有遇到这种特殊的场合，才能合法地扬帆外国，因此许多商人就设法随行。

使节一行的船队，由一艘大船为主，再由一艘称为"头领"的小艚当导航船走在前头。大船之后，绑了两条小船，用来从事近海樵汲，以补充燃料及饮水，同时也兼充警备之用。两条小船称作"快马"或"脚艇"。事实上，"头领"与"脚艇"都不可能多载人员或货物，因此大船就全面地担当起这样的任务。

报导上说，整艘大船上搭载的军、民总共有千人之谱，而且"货物太重"——显然是超重得太厉害。更糟糕的是，或许是因为长期海禁的缘故，"火长"（驾船的人）不熟航道，于是厄运就降临了。当船只行进到占壁啰[38]时，就不幸触底沉没。两名"天使"当场溺毙，而随船军民十分之九也都葬身鱼腹。不过，黄衷有一位名叫麦福的同乡，他与另外七十几个人抢到一艘脚艇，幸运地划到海岸。黄衷根据麦福事后的描述，转述说：

[37] 《点石斋画报·三集》，竹集，页19、20。

[38] 即尖笔罗，中国史料亦记作占不劳山或占婆岛。位于越南中部，会安东方海中，为东南亚往来中国海岸的重要地标。

回望大舶覆处，近如席前。洪涛澜汗，惟败篚破甑，出没于其间。数百人者，沤灭无迹，众皆长恸[39]。

这样的描述与Pearl船长目睹到的"的惺"船失事现场的景象，至为雷同。可惜很少有与此类似的作品[40]。

中国帆船及其驾驶者似乎没有很理性地对付紧急状况的标准作法，船长也没有绝对的权威。因此，发生船难时的损失必然很大。不过，还是有撑过危急状态而平安抵达目的地者。这中间，往往会为了减轻船舶载重而采用丢包的做法。因此，一艘沉船所在，当然有不属于该沉船的文物。

但是，船沉时，也只有较重的物件会就地下沉。其他物件可能漂流水面一阵子再下沉，或者终究中途消失或被浪头打上海岸。加上盗取等因素，一个沉船遗址出水的东西，顶多也只呈现一艘船舶所载诸物的部分内容。欧洲商船通常会有载货舱单（bill of lading）。然而，从舱单也只能看到主要船货。船舶本身、个人用品以及私人货物，并不见于舱单。至于中国帆船，几乎根本不曾存有这方面的文献。历史学家必须从其他资料来源来补充不足的信息。

[39] 黄衷：《海语》（《岭南遗书》本），卷三，页2ab），"畏途：铁板沙"条。接下去描述他们求生及获救的经过。

[40] 一般船只遇难的描述，以出使琉球的使臣留下的为多。例见全魁、周煌：《请加封号谕祭疏》（乾隆二十二年四月二十一日），收在周煌：《琉球国志略》，台北：台湾银行经济研究室，1971年，页169、170。

[41] 施琅：《海疆底定疏》，（康熙二十四年三月十三日）《靖海纪事》，台北：台湾银行经济研究室，1958年，下卷，页69～71；多种台湾文献题作《论开海禁疏》。

七

移民与船货

成化二十一年（1485年）册封占城国王的天使船因为搭载太多人员与货物，在接近越南时触礁沉没。当时系因为贪图顺便贸易的缘故，所以乘员过多。清代前期，海外贸易合法化了，可是行走东南亚的中国船舶，往往依旧多载人客。

清代中国洋船搭载非法移民，十分普遍。无论是迫于生计或者是追求更美好的明天，只要有机会、有渠道，就有人想移民外国。例如，康熙二十四年（1685年）三月，施琅《海疆底定疏》[41]就有如下的报告：

太子少保、靖海将军、靖海侯、兼管福建水师提督事务、臣施琅谨密题。为船疆底定、更宜加慎、以垂永安事。……

臣以为展禁开海，固以恤民裕课，尤须审弊立规，以垂永久。如今贩洋贸易船只，无分大小，络绎而发，只数繁多，赀本有限，饷税无几，不惟取厌外域，轻慢我非大国之风，且藉公行私，多载人民，深有可虑。

如近者臣在省会议，据中军参将张旺报称：船户刘仕明赶缯船一只，给关票出口往吕宋经纪，其船甚小，所载货无多，附搭人数共一百三十三名。臣据报时即行查，而该船已开去矣。一船如此，余概可知。此时内地人民，奸徒贫乏不少，弗为设法立规，节次搭载而往，恐内地渐见日稀。

施琅在康熙二十三年（1684年）八月才接受台湾的郑克塽政权投降，而在同年底康熙皇帝才同意开海贸易。随即船户刘仕明就请领关票，前往菲律宾的马尼拉，说是要做贸易。然而根据中军参将张旺的观察，该船甚小，载货无多，但是附搭的乘客就多达133人，显然是偷渡移民。

如前所见，清代中叶许多前往东南亚的中国帆船根本是移民船，也就是偷渡船（因为就官府的角度而言，移民不合法）。17、18世纪时，荷兰东印度司接受来自中国的移民，不过定有人数限制。中国方面则禁止移民外居。"的惺"船一次载出那么多人，无论就中国官方的角度，还是就巴达维亚荷兰官方的角度而言，显然都属非法，意图偷渡。潮州人说"无可奈何炊甜粿"（蒸年糕当干粮，以便搭船移民海外）。"的惺"船全船乘员多达1600～1800人之多，考虑到一路伙食与携带少量随身物品的必要性，所剩装载货物的载重能力与空间皆属有限。当其沉没之时，真的会有大量的瓷器吗？可是Hatcher与Pickford在斯图嘉拍卖的文物倒是琳琅满目，数量也相当可观（图三～图六）。把这些文物都说成是"的惺"船的遗物，显然不尽可靠。

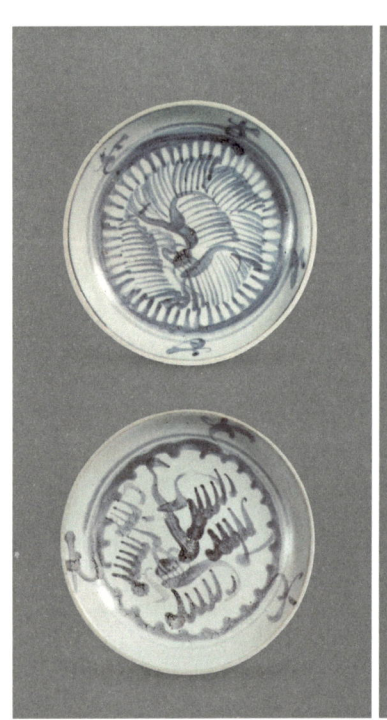

图三　*Tek Sing* 号沉船打捞的青花瓷器

（均采自Fritz Nagel, *Nagel Auctions: Tek Sing Treasures*, Stuttgart, 2000）

图四 Tek Sing 号沉船打捞的青花瓷盘
（采自Fritz Nagel, *Nagel Auctions: Tek Sing Treasures*, Stuttgart, 2000）

图五 Tek Sing 号沉船打捞的陶瓷遗物

1. 青花大盘 2. 青花杯 3. 白釉盏 4. 青花碗 5. 青釉炉 6. 青釉小瓶

(均采自Fritz Nagel, *Nagel Auctions: Tek Sing Treasures*, Stuttgart, 2000)

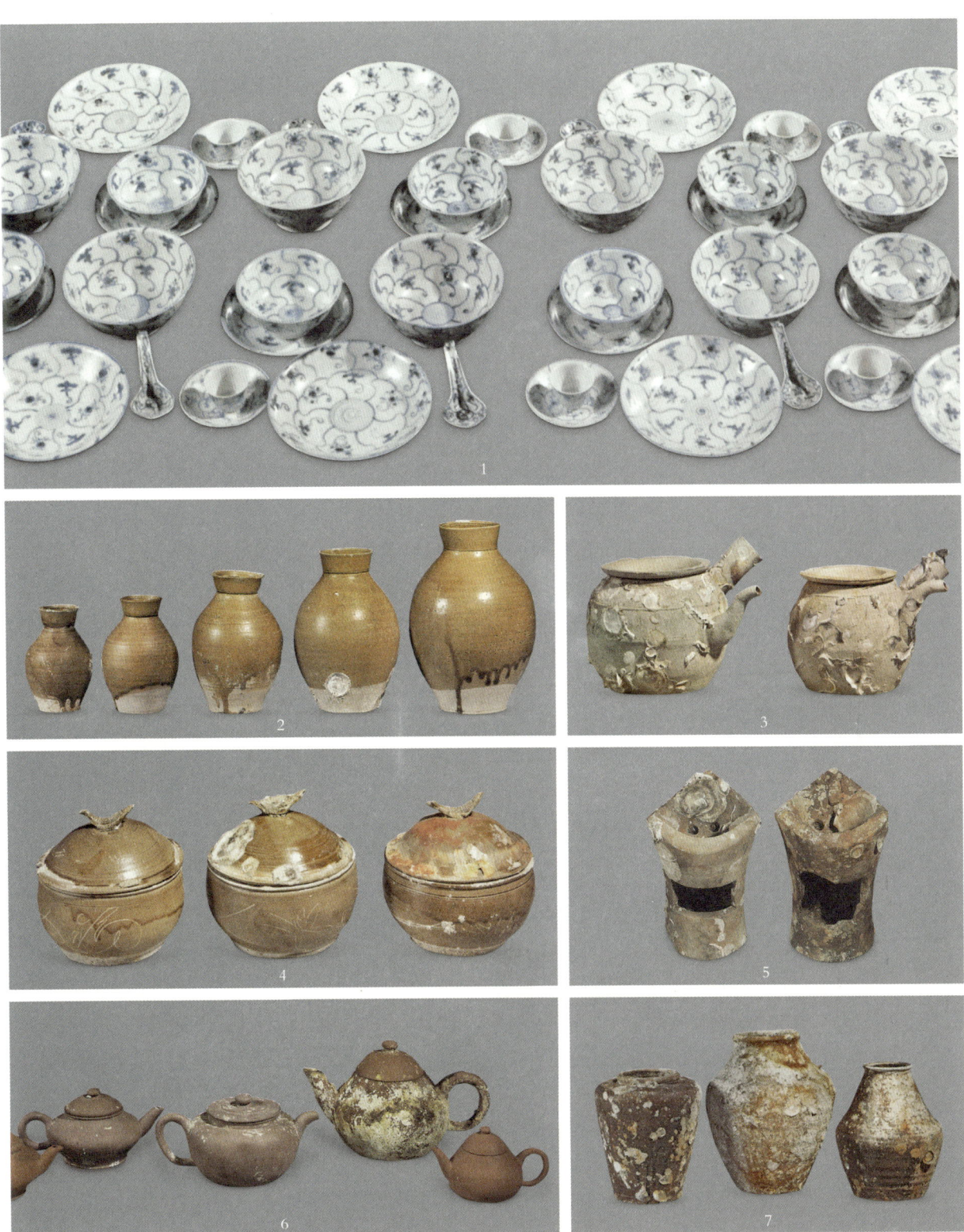

图六 Tek Sing 号沉船打捞的陶瓷遗物

1. 青花瓷器　2. 酱釉罐　3. 陶急须　4. 酱釉罐　5. 陶炉　6. 紫砂壶　7. 陶罐

（均采自Fritz Nagel, *Nagel Auctions: Tek Sing Treasures*, Stuttgart, 2000）

八

学术与商业

Hatcher和他的合伙人们,成功地从大海捞起许多文物,送进拍卖市场。他们缘饰以学术以增加其权威,从而扩大其商业价值。但在信息来源上颇有造假或任意使用的情形,而其打捞过程也不符合水下考古规范。至于针对出水文物的说明,也欠缺学术水平。从人类文化遗产的观点来看,他们其实是打劫者。因为他们使考古学家与历史学者失去可以善加利用的时间胶囊,丧失重建史实的机会。

我们或许可以推测所谓"的惺"船的出水文物恐怕非属同一艘船舶的船货,有可能是先后在同一个地点或同一块海域多次沉船所累积的文物。

可是为了坐实他们的出水物来自所谓的"的惺"船,也就是Pearl船长所搭救的那艘失事船舶。有关Pearl船长义行的报道都指向那是1822年,即道光二年,干支为"壬午"的那一年,为此,Hatcher及Nagel展示了一块墓碑(图七)。墓主名叫杨廷柱;立碑人为其子杨浙江、杨北海与孙子杨振源与杨振漾。碑眉的"赤岭"两字,说明墓主可能来自漳州府漳浦县的赤岭。碑上的日期为道光二年端月,也就是正月。由于时间上的吻合,确实是有可能是在"的惺"船出航时载出的石碑[42]。

[42] 海外华人往往从中国订制墓碑。不过,1819年新加坡开埠之后,新加坡也供应东南亚华人墓碑。例如远在印度尼西亚极东的阿鲁群岛(Aru Archipelago)也是。19世纪中叶,英国的博物学家华莱士(Alfred Russel Wallace, 1823-1913)就观察到:"这里的中国人也像在别处一样,用从新加坡运来的结实的花岗岩作为墓碑,上面深深刻着碑铭,并漆成红字、蓝字和金字,显示着他们过人的财富和文明。"参考华莱士著,彭珍、袁伟亮等译:《马来群岛自然科学考察记》,北京:中国人民大学出版社,2004年,页423。

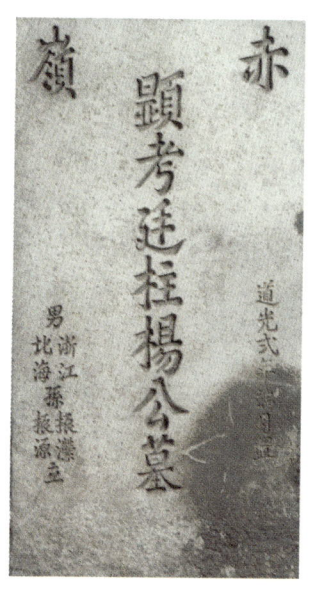

图七 *Tek Sing*号沉船打捞的墓碑

(采自Fritz Nagel, *Nagel Auctions: Tek Sing Treasures*, Stuttgart, 2000)

因此，我们并不否认在该现场的失事船舶包括"的惺"船在内，可是我们要强调的是在同一地点出水的文物，不一定属于"的惺号"所有。例如，Hatcher与Pickford送到斯图嘉拍卖的所谓"的惺"船文物当中，有相当数量的小童瓷偶（seated boys）（图八；图九，1），而在越南金瓯省沉船（1723~1725年）出水的文物当中，也有极其相似的小童瓷偶被发现[43]（图九，2）。金瓯省沉船比所谓的"的惺"沉船的时间早了约100年。这也说明了同一种风格与样式的商品可能流行相当长的一段期间，而当它们在同一沉船所在地点被打捞出来时，并不能一厢情愿地就将它们认定是同一艘船舶的船货。其实，金瓯省沉船之外，Hatcher等人自己也承认，在也是他们在1985年打捞、1986年拍卖的"南京船货"当中也有一模一样的小童瓷偶（图九，3）。

所谓的"的惺"沉船及依附于其名送至斯图加特拍卖的文物，在相关信息的正确性与严谨性上的呈现都不理想。虽然所谓的"的惺船货"名气相当响亮，学者若欲引用来从事论述，务必仔细小心！

[43] 关于越南金瓯省发现的沉船的发掘与研究，参考Nguyen Dinh Chien, *The Ca Mau Shipwreck 1723-1735* (Hanoi: National Museum of Vietnamese History, 2002); Nguyen Dinh Chien, Pham Quoc Quan, *Ceramics of Five Shipwrecks off the Coast of Viet Nam* (Hanoi: National Museum of Vietnamese History, 2008)。拍卖目录见Sotheby's, *Made in Imperial China: 76,000 pieces of Chinese Export Porcelain from the Ca Mau Shipwreck, circa 1725* (Amsterdam: Sotheby's, 2007)。李庆新：《越南海域发现清代广州沉船——金瓯沉船及其初步研究》，上海中国航海博物馆：《国家航海·第六辑》，上海：上海古籍出版社，2014年，页17~43。

图八　*Tek Sing* 号沉船打捞的小童瓷偶

（采自Fritz Nagel, *Nagel Auctions: Tek Sing Treasures*, Stuttgart, 2000）

图九　东南亚海域沉船发现的小童瓷偶
1. Tek Sing号沉船打捞（采自Fritz Nagel, *Nagel Auctions: Tek Sing Treasures*, Stuttgart, 2000）
2. 越南金瓯省沉船出水（1723～1725年，采自*The Ca Mau Shipwreck 1723-25*, Ha Noi: Ca Mau Department of Culture and Information&The National Museum of Vietnamese History, 2002）
3. Geldermalsen号沉船打捞（1752年，采自*The Nanking Cargo*, Christie's Amsterdam, 1986）

引用书目

1. 古代文献

（明）黄衷：《海语》，《岭南遗书》本，卷三，页2ab。

（清）全魁、周煌：《请加封号谕祭疏》（乾隆二十二年四月二十一日），收在周煌：《琉球国志略》，台北：台湾银行经济研究室，1971年，页169、170。

（清）施琅：《海疆底定疏》（康熙二十四年三月十三日），《靖海纪事》，台北：台湾银行经济研究室，1958年，下卷，页69～71。

（清）郁永河著、方豪校：《合校足本裨海纪游》，台北：台湾省文献委员会，1950年。

（清）周凯：《厦门志》，台北：台湾银行经济研究室，《台湾文献丛刊》第95种，1961年。

"中央"研究院历史语言研究所：《明清史料·戊编》，台北："中央"研究院历史语言研究所，1994年，页576～584，《闽浙总督汪志伊残题本》。

台北故宫博物院军机处档案：录副奏折第006335号，乾隆十五年十二月二十五日两广总督陈大受奏，乾隆十六年正月十五日奉朱批、发抄。

英国国家档案馆藏，F.O., 233/189（no. 220）。未押日期，实际为1809年（嘉庆十四年）。

阿裨尔著、刘海岩译：《中国旅行记（1816～1817年）——阿美士德使团医官笔下的清代中国》，上海：上海古籍出版社，2012年。

亨利·埃利斯著，刘天路、刘甜甜译：《阿美士德使团出使中国日志》，北京：商务印书馆，2013年。

华莱士著，彭珍、袁伟亮等译：《马来群岛自然科学考察记》，北京：中国人民大学出版社，2004年，页423。

《点石斋画报·三集》，竹集，19、20页。

James Horsburgh, *The India Directory, or Directions for Sailing to and from the East Indies, China, Australia, and the Interjacent Ports of Africa and South America*, 1852.

Asiatic Journal, vol.20(1825), pp.419-420.

Asiatic Journal, vol.15(1823), pp.36-39.

The Chinese Repository, July 1837, pp.149-153.

2. 近人论著

包乐史著、庄国土等译：《巴达维亚华人与中荷贸易》，南宁：广西人民出版社，1997年，页256～272。

包乐史、吴凤斌：《18世纪末吧达维亚唐人社会》，厦门：厦门大学出版社，2002年。

柴商之：《"泰兴号"被毁记》，《椰城》2008年第2期，页20。

陈国栋：《清代中叶厦门的海上贸易，1727～1833》，收入中国海洋发展史论文集编辑委员会：《中国海洋发展史论文集》，台北："中央"研究院中山人文社会科学研究所，1991年，第4辑，页61～100。

陈荆和：《清初郑成功残部之移殖南圻（下）》，《新亚学报》第8卷第2期，1968年，页424。

陈荆和、陈育崧：《新加坡华文碑铭集录》，香港：香港中文大学出版部，1972年。

陈支平：《清代闽台商人间经济纠纷的案例分析》，《民间文书与明清东南族商研究》，北京：中华书局，2009年，页263、264。

约翰·盖伊（John Guy）著、王丽明译：《九世纪初连结中国与波斯湾的外销瓷：勿里洞沉船的例证》，《海交史研究》2008年第2期，页14～26。

李汉青：《闽侨开发东南亚史略》，《福建文献》（台湾），第4期，1968年，页13、14。

李庆新：《越南海域发现清代广州沉船——金瓯沉船及其初步研究》，上海中国航海博物馆：《国家航海（第六辑）》，上海：上海古籍出版社，2014年，页17～43。

谢明良：《记黑石号（Batu Hitam）沉船中的中国陶瓷器》，《"国立"台湾大学美术史研究集刊》，第13期，2002年，页1～60及页277。

杨国桢、张雅娟：《海盗与海洋社会权力——以19世纪初"大海盗"蔡牵为中心的考察》，《云南师范大学学报（哲学社会科学版）》2011年第3期，页4。

郑炯鑫：《从"泰兴号"沉船看清代德化青花瓷器的生产与外销》，《文博》2001年第6期，页49、50。

Anonymous, "Notes on the Japanese Mission which was Shipwrecked between Bangka and Billiton in 1862 on its Way from Japan to Holland via Batavia," *Munumenta Nipponica,* 5:2 (July 1942), pp. 540-550.

Leonard Blussé, "Junks to Java: Chinese Shipping to the Nanyang in the Second Half of the Eighteenth Century," in Eric Tagliacozzo and Wen-chin Chang eds., *Chinese Circulations: Capital, Commodities, and Networks in Southeast Asia* (Durham and London: Duke University Press, 2011), pp.221-258.

Leonard Blussé, "The Vicissitudes of Maritime Trade: Letters from the Ocean Hang Merchant, Li Kunhe, to the Dutch Authorities in Batavia, 1803-1809," in Anthony Reid ed.,*Sojourners and Settlers: Histories of Southeast Asia and the Chinese*, Honolulu: University of Hawaii Press, 2001, pp.154-163.

Leonard Blussé, "Letters from Chinese Merchants to Batavia", Tineke Hellwig and Eric Tagliacozzo eds.,*The Indonesia Reader:History, Culture,Politics,*Durham and London: Duke University Press, 2009, pp. 165-172.

Nguyen Dinh Chien, *The Ca Mau Shipwreck 1723-1735*, Hanoi: National Museum of Vietnamese History, 2002.

Nguyen Dinh Chien, Pham Quoc Quan,*Ceramics of Five Shipwrecks off the Coast of Viet Nam*, Hanoi: National Museum of Vietnamese History, 2008.

C.J.A. Jörg, *The Geldermalsen: History and Porcelain*,London: Kimber, 1986.

Fritz Nagel, *Nagel Auctions: Tek Sing Treasures,* Stuttgart, Germany: Stuttgarter Kunstauktionshaus, 2000.

Nigel Pickford ed.*Atlas of Ship Wreck Treasure,* London: Dorling Kindersley, 1994.

Nigel Pickford and Michael Hatcher, *The Legacy of the Tek Sing,*Cambridge, U.K.:Granta Editions, 2000.

Sotheby's, *Made in Imperial China:76,000 pieces of Chinese Export Porcelain from the Ca Mau Shipwreck, circa 1725*, Amsterdam: Sotheby's, 2007.

Tony Wells, *Shipwrecks & Sunken Treasure in Southeast Asia, with over 450 Wrecks including the FLOR do Mar,* Singapore:Times Editions,1995, pp. 91-97.

John Wright, *Encyclopedia of Sunken Treasure,*London:Michael O'Mara Books, 1995, pp.145-148.

9~14世纪南海及周边海域沉船的发现与研究

Findings and Researches of Shipwrecks in South China Sea and Southeast Asian Waters, 9th to 14th Century

童 歆

（北京大学考古文博学院）

TONG Xin

(School of Archaeology and Museology, Peking University)

内容摘要 /

中晚唐至宋元是中国对外贸易重心转移、海上贸易勃兴与繁荣的重要阶段，影响深远，不仅直接促进了中国与东南亚及以西地区的经济交往，推动国际贸易体系建立与发展，同时也增进了各地区的文化交流，推进了航海技术等的革新。

然而长期以来，人们这一阶段海外贸易的认识都来自于文献。由于相关记载，特别是东南亚地区史料较为匮乏，加之文献书写本身存有的局限性，使得仅据书面记录的研究无法多层次地展现这段海上贸易史的面貌。

20世纪70年代以来，南海及周边海域陆续发现晚唐至宋元时期的古代沉船。作为直接反映海上贸易过程的证据，沉船船体、沉没地点以及其上运载的船货，为研究跨区域航海贸易，特别是商品构成、贸易规模以及航运线路等提供了新材料与新方法。

关 键 词 /

9~14世纪 南海及东南亚海域 沉船

ABSTRACT / From the middle and late Tang Dynasty to the Song and Yuan Dynasty, there was a shift in the focus of China's foreign trade, which promoted the prosperity of the maritime trade. Along with the establishment and development of the international trading system, the regional political and cultural exchanges, as well as marine technology, were also thriving.

However, for a long time, people's understanding of maritime trade during this period was constrained within the historical texts, which were scarce and incomplete, making the research be unable to go further into details.

Since the 1970s, there have been 30 wrecks dating back to the 9th-14th century discovered in the South China Sea and Southeast Asian waters. As evidences directly reflecting the maritime trades, the hulls, the sites and the cargoes of sunken ships, have provided new materials and new methods for the study of trans-regional maritime trade, especially commodity composition, trade scale and shipping routes.

KEY WORDS / 9th to 14th century; South China Sea and Southeast Asian waters; shipwrecks

一

地理环境与历史背景——亚洲地中海的早期贸易时代

南海及其周边的苏禄海、爪哇海等地处太平洋与印度洋交汇要冲，是联系东亚、东南亚与印度洋沿岸各地的海上通道。在南中国大陆、中南半岛、马来半岛及东南亚诸岛屿的环抱下，这一系列西太平洋的边缘海组成一片半封闭的海域，连同属于今天南中国和东南亚各国的沿岸地区，构成一个相对完整且独立的地理单元，是"名副其实的地中海"[1]。20世纪50年代，凌纯声撰文提出"亚洲地中海"的概念，认为"亚洲地中海的东南西三岸为弧形的岛屿所环绕，自北向南而西，有阿留申弧、千岛弧、日本弧、琉球弧、菲律宾弧、摩鹿加弧……马来弧，再北上有安达曼弧。在这一连串的弧形岛屿中之海，可称为广义的亚洲地中海……亚洲地中海为南北向，可以台湾分开为南北两地中海"[2]。

尽管多有暗礁和台风，这片海域却不失为航海活动的理想场所，特别是一年两度季风吹拂，为航行提供了绝佳的条件。汪洋大海在这里与其说是阻隔，不如说是联系的纽带。就像布罗代尔笔下波澜壮阔的地中海世界，自古以来，这片亚洲地中海的跨区域经济、社会与文化交流从未间断，而在其中扮演关键角色的正是海上贸易。考古证据显示，早在新石器时代，南海及周边海域沿岸各地通过海路开展的商贸活动就已有迹可循[3]。不过区域间真正成规模的海上贸易，则要等到造船与航海技术成熟，并伴随沿岸各地区社会生产与商品经济发展才逐渐成形。

8世纪中期以后，海域北面的中国经历了重大的社会经济变革，促使对外贸易的运输通道由陆路转向海路。一方面唐王朝的势力退出西域，"陆上丝绸之路"阻塞中断。另一方面国内经济重心开始由北向南转移，南方地区的手工业生产和商品经济日益发展成熟。此外，造船与航海技术不断提高，并且相较于陆路转运，海上运输运量更大，成本更低，特别是当陶瓷等较重且易碎的货物成为出口的大宗商品之后。因此，直到明初禁海之前，中国的对外海上贸易蓬勃发展，成为促进整个亚洲地中海乃至印度洋沿岸及欧洲地区贸易网络形成的重要推动力。

在这近6个世纪的时间里，处在东西方交流十字路口的东南亚地区，受内外因素的共同影响，海上贸易也迅速发展。在其区域内部，国家政权不断兴起，

---

[1] G. 赛代斯著，蔡华、杨保筠译：《东南亚的印度化国家》(1944)，北京：商务印书馆，2008年，页14。

[2] 凌纯声：《中国古代海洋文化与亚洲地中海》，《海外杂志》第3卷第10期，页7，1954年；后收入《中国边疆民族与环太平洋文化：凌纯声先生论文集》，台北：联经出版社业公司，1979年，页335。

[3] 洪晓纯：《台湾史前玉器在东南亚的分布及其意义》，中国社会科学院考古研究所：《华南及东南亚地区史前考古：纪念甑皮岩遗址发掘三十周年国际学术研讨会论文集》，北京：文物出版社，2006年，页324～340。

中南半岛上的占婆、高棉，菲律宾群岛的蒲端、麻逸，苏门答腊的三佛齐以及爪哇诸王国，都通过发展手工业，建立新港口等措施推动海外贸易交往，有的甚至将政治中心迁移到沿岸地区以便进行更好地控制[4]。同时，除了来自北面中国的影响外，西边印度乃至阿拉伯地区的跨区域商贸活动不断渗透，特别是泰米尔商团在其中发挥重要作用，极大增强了东南亚地区与周边的海上贸易联系[5]。

可以说，9～14世纪的亚洲地中海，伴随区域内政治、社会、经济的变革与发展，逐步形成专业化和网络化的海上贸易模式，而相较于之后来临的大航海时代，这一时期可以被称作早期贸易时代[6]。

二

海上贸易的直接证据——9～14世纪沉船遗址的发现

长期以来，人们对9～14世纪亚洲地中海早期贸易阶段的认识都来源于文献，特别是记载丰富的中文史籍。利用这些或出自官方或成于民间的记录，中国的历史学者从本国海外贸易的研究视角出发，构建起了亚洲地中海早期海上贸易史的诸多方面[7]。不过，由于东南亚地区史籍相对匮乏，加之文献书写本身存有的局限性，使得仅据书面记载的研究无法多层次地展现这段历史的面貌。20世纪70年代以来，南海及周边海域陆续发现晚唐至宋元时期的古代沉船。作为直接反映海上贸易过程的证据，沉船船体、沉没地点以及其上运载的船货，为研究跨区域航海贸易，特别是商品构成、贸易规模以及航运线路等提供了新材料与新方法。

目前南海及周边海域发现并见诸报道的9～14世纪沉船遗址共有30处[8]（图一），包括中国的平潭分流尾屿沉船、泉州湾海船、泉州法石沉船、白礁一号沉船、平潭大练岛一号沉船、"南海Ⅰ号"沉船、华光礁一号沉船、石屿二号沉船，泰国的"朗坚岛"沉船（Ko Rang Kwien Wreck）、"芭堤雅"沉船（Pattaya Wreck）、"阁西昌Ⅱ号"沉船（Ko Si Chang Ⅱ Wreck），菲律宾的"圣安东尼奥"沉船（San Antonio Wreck）、"锡马纳汉礁"沉船（Simanahan Reef Wreck）、"调查员礁"沉船（Investigator Shoal Wreck）、"碎浪礁"沉船（Breaker Reef Shoal Wreck）、"乌尼桑"沉船（Unisan Wreck），马来西亚的"丹戎新邦"沉船（Tanjung Simpang Wreck）、"玉龙号"沉船（Jade Dragon Wreck）、"图日昂"沉船（Turiang Wreck），印度尼西亚的"黑石

[4] 梁志明等：《东南亚古代史：上古至16世纪初》，北京：北京大学出版社，2013年，页272～517。

[5] G.赛代斯：《东南亚的印度化国家》，页53～67；Hock Guan Lee. Tamil Merchants in India and Abroad (9th–14th Centuries). *The Newsletter of International Institute for Asian Studies*, No.63, 2013, network 39.

[6] Geoff Wade. An Early Age of Commerce in Southeast Asia, 900–1300 CE. *Journal of Southeast Asian Studies*, 2009, No.2, pp. 221–265.

[7] 相关的综合性研究有陈高华、吴泰：《宋元时期的海外贸易》，天津：天津人民出版社，1981年。关履权：《宋代广州的海外贸易》，广州：广东人民出版社，1987年。李金明、廖大珂：《中国古代海外贸易史》，南宁：广西人民出版社，1995年。高荣盛：《元代海外贸易研究》，成都：四川人民出版社，1998年。黄纯艳：《宋代海外贸易》，北京：社会科学文献出版社，2003年。

[8] 由于广东与福建交界处的南澳岛与台湾岛南端的鹅銮鼻连线是南海与东海的分界，福建海域并不属于自然地理意义上的南海范围。然而，本文所讨论的是一个贸易文化区域，包括南部中国的沿海地区。因此，发现于福建海域的沉船也在研究对象范围之内。另外，由于沉没环境的差异，致使沉船船体保存状况不一，没有发现船体遗迹的严格说来应叫做沉船遗址，但为了行文统一及叙述简练，下文提及统一称作某沉船。

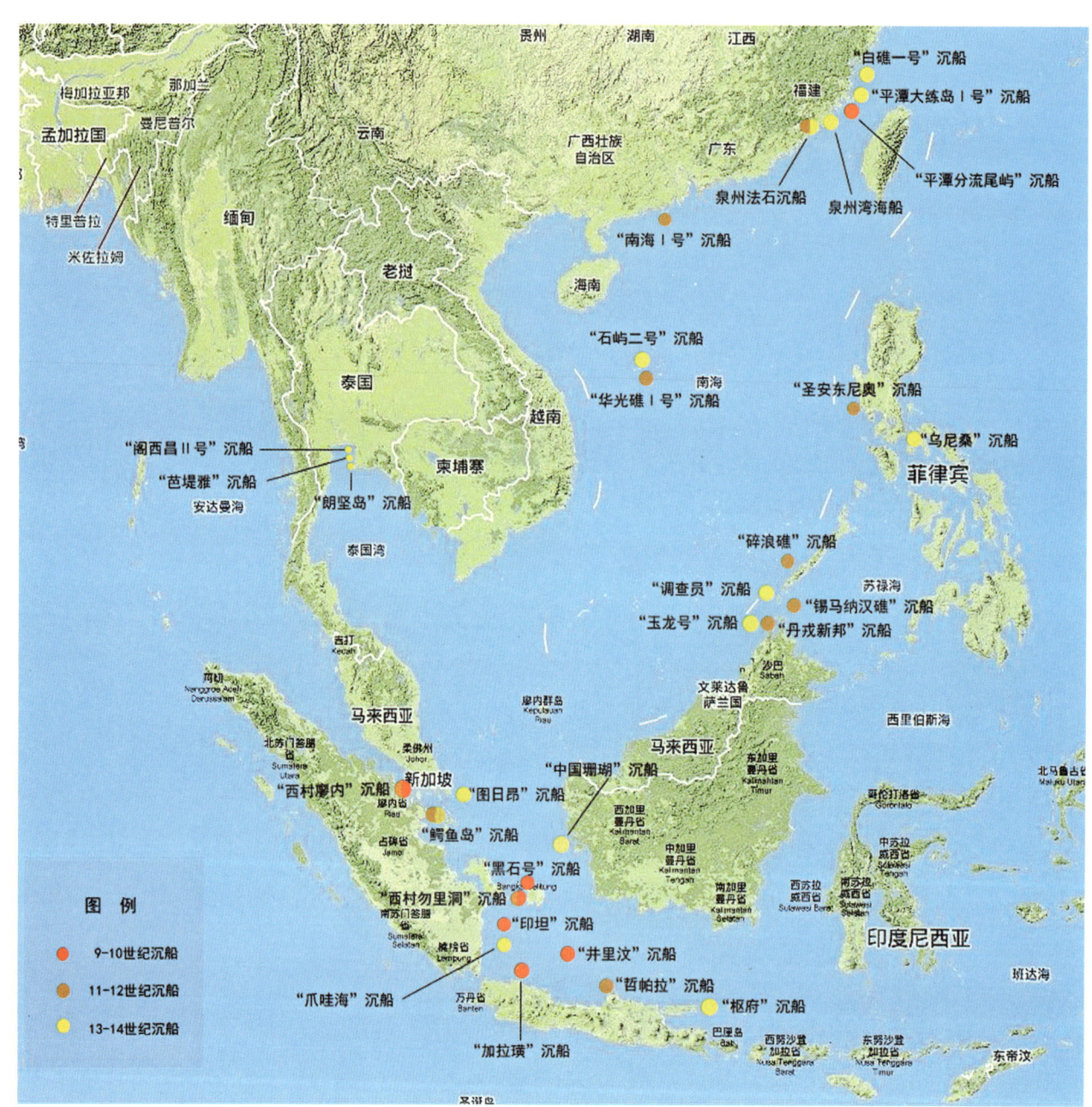

图一 9～14世纪南海及周边海域沉船遗址分布示意图

号"沉船（Belitung Wreck）、"印坦"沉船（Intan Wreck）、"加拉璜"沉船（Karawang Wreck）、"井里汶"沉船（Cirebon Wreck）、"西村廖内"沉船（Xicun Riau Wreck）、"西村勿里洞"沉船（Xicun Belitung Wreck），"哲帕拉"沉船（Jepara Wreck）、"鳄鱼岛"沉船（Pulau Buaya Wreck）、"爪哇海"沉船（Java Sea Wreck）、"中国珊瑚"沉船（Karang Cina Wreck），"枢府"沉船（Shufu Wreck）。

鉴于大部分沉船资料，特别是东南亚地区的沉船在国内尚未有发表，下文就对这30艘沉船进行概要式的介绍。文中所引沉船图片资料均采自相关简报或报告，图中不再一一注明。

（一）中国

1. 平潭分流尾屿沉船[9]

沉船遗址位于福建平潭海域海坛岛西南分流尾屿的北部，水深约10米。2009年因盗捞被发现，2010年福建水下文物调查队对遗址进行了调查，并采集部分标本。

遗址所处海床为泥沙底，遗物较为集中分布的面积约500平方米，遗址表面未发现船体遗迹。调查出水遗物均为青釉瓷器，主要为碗、碟、盏托及少量执壶残片（图二）。器物形制规整，胎体普遍较薄，胎质细密，釉呈青灰、青褐色，部分泛黄。碗、碟、盏托类器物均内外满釉，由装烧痕迹可知其方法为支钉叠烧。

从瓷器的特征来看，应为越窑产品。再通过与纪年墓中的发现相比较，并结合出水遗物的烧造工艺等特征，初步判断该沉船遗址的年代为五代中期。这是目前发现的中国近海海域时代最早的沉船遗址，对研究五代时期海外交通史以及陶瓷贸易史，特别是越窑产品的外销有着重要意义。

[9] 中国国家博物馆水下考古研究中心、福建博物院文物考古研究所：《福建平潭分流尾屿五代沉船遗址调查》，《中国国家博物馆馆刊》2011年第11期，页18～25。

图二　平潭分流尾屿沉船出水瓷器

1. 青瓷碟　2. 青瓷碗

2. 泉州湾海船[10]

[10] 泉州湾宋代海船发掘报告编写组:《泉州湾宋代海船发掘简报》,《文物》1975年第10期,页1~18。福建省泉州海外交通史博物馆:《泉州湾宋代海船发掘与研究》,北京:海洋出版社,1987年。

1974年出土于泉州后渚港的海滩中,东经118°59′,北纬24°91′。遗址区域原为港湾,船体沉没后,由于长期堆积和地壳上升,海岸线外移,形成后来的海滩,故船体以上堆积层和船内均为淤积细密的海泥。经考古发掘,发现船体上部残破,只保存了原来埋于水下的部分。船身残长24.2、残宽9.15、残深1.98米(图三)。船内用十二道隔板将全船分为十三舱,并残存下半部分隔舱板。每舱都保存肋骨,木质虽朽,但仍可辨识。以船中为界,船前半部的肋骨在隔舱板之后,而后半部之肋骨则在隔板之前。在第一与第六舱内有桅杆座。船尾有舵承座,然而未发现船舵残件。

船舱出土遗物丰富,有香料药物,木货牌,木签,陶瓷器,铜钱、铜器,竹、木、棕、麻编织物等,其中香料木占绝大多数,未经脱水时其重量达4700多斤,包括了绛真、沉香、檀香、乳香、龙涎等。船上发现的金属品主要是数量较大的铜钱(图四),以及少量铜器、铜镜、铁质工具以及几枚铁钱。铜钱以北宋钱为主,包括了唐钱和南宋钱,其中两枚"咸淳元宝"背文分别为"五"和"七",可知船上铸造时间最晚的铜钱为咸淳七年(1271年)。沉船还出土近百件的木牌、木签,其上保留着墨书文字,有地名、货名、人名以及其他名称(图五)。船舱发现的陶瓷器数量也不少,多数出土于船头船尾各

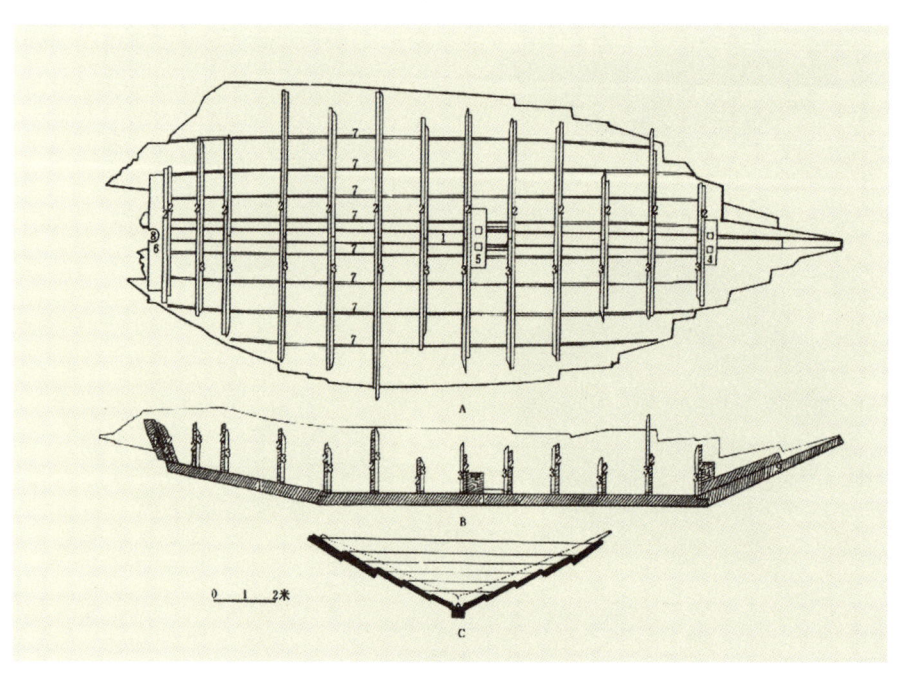

图三 泉州湾海船平、剖面图

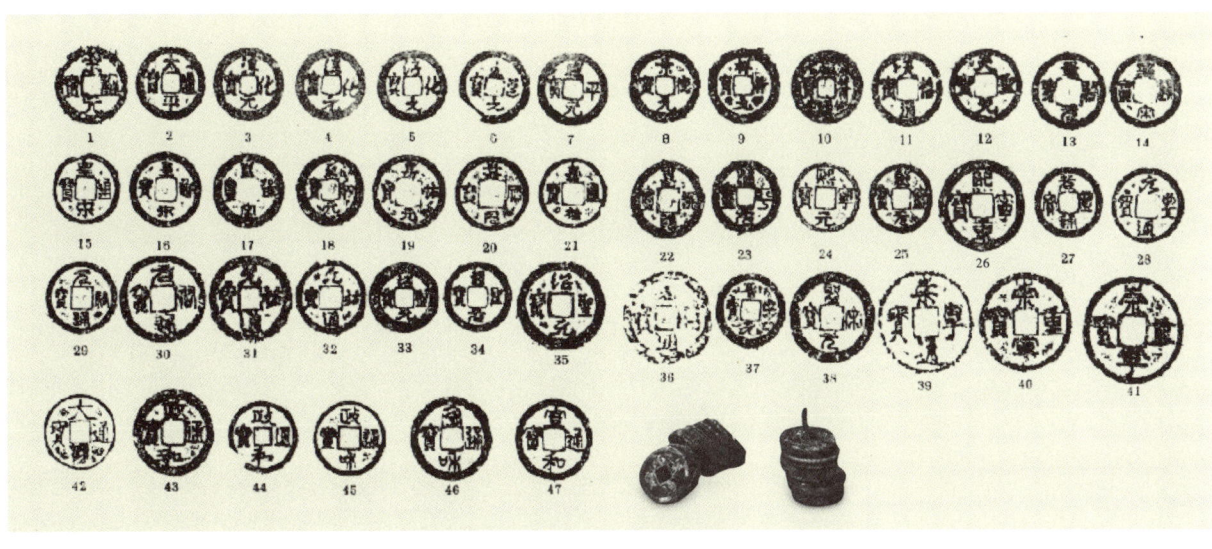

图四 泉州湾海船出土铜钱

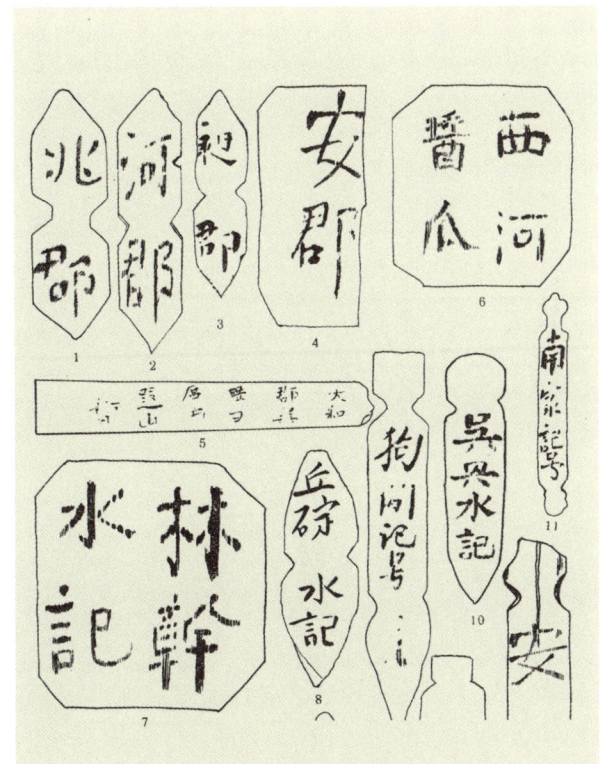

图五 泉州湾海船出土木牌木签

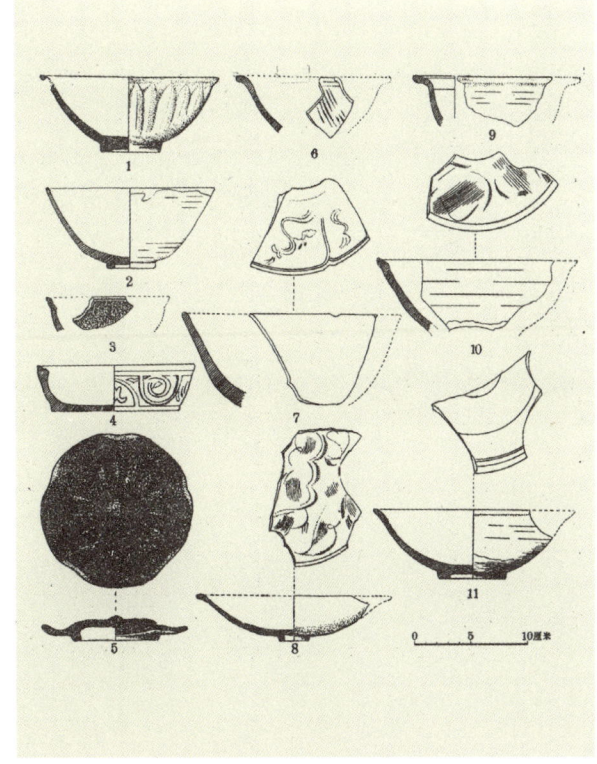

图六 泉州湾海船出土陶瓷器

舱。瓷器釉色有青釉、黑釉、白釉、青白釉等,器型以小碗为主(图六)。陶器釉色有青釉、青黄釉、酱色釉和黑釉等,器型以瓮、罐为多。这些产品来自龙泉窑、建窑以及泉州地区各窑址。

根据出土海船沉积环境的科学分析、船体使用状况、出土铜钱以及木签等,判断该船建造于南宋末年,是一艘远洋贸易返航归国的海船,沉没于咸淳七年(1271年)以后的几年中。

3. 泉州法石沉船[11]

[11] 中国科学院自然科学史研究所、福建省泉州海外交通史博物馆联合试掘组：《泉州法石古船试掘简报和初步探讨》，《自然科学史研究》1983年第2期，页164～172。

沉船1976年发现于福建泉州市东海街道法石社区，属晋江下游交汇海口的冲积平原，遗址区域原为港口。由于船体中部、前部压在现今建筑之下，1982年由中国科学院自然科学史研究所和福建省泉州海外交通史博物馆组成的联合考古队仅试掘了古船后部的四个舱位，出土了部分船舶构件和古代遗物。

从揭露出船体后部的四个舱位的情况来看，船头指向为北偏东20°，船身放置接近水平，船体木料含水较多，船体残破比较严重，上层结构无存，所见的后部船底基本完好（图七）。船为有龙骨的尖底船，且发现有水密舱隔舱板残段，初步判定为一艘福船船型的海船。

试掘过程中，在接近舱底处清理到少量陶瓷片和瓦片、木器件以及动植物遗存等。陶瓷器包括小口瓶、碗、瓮罐等，均为南宋时期产品。木器包括小木桶及雕花木饰件。根据沉船所处地层为南宋文化层以及船舱出土陶瓷器特征，推断该船于南宋时沉没。

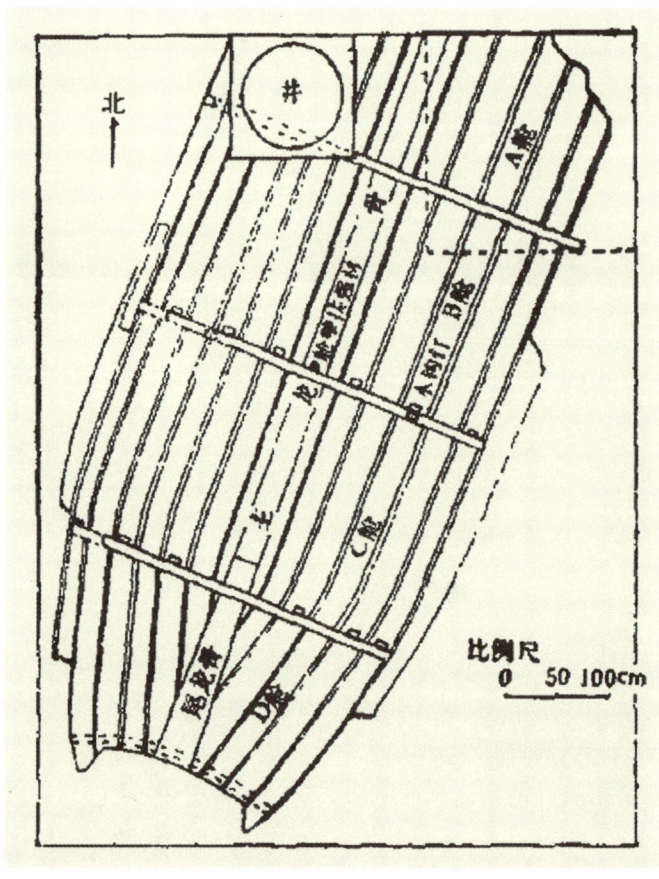

图七　法石沉船后部四个舱位示意图

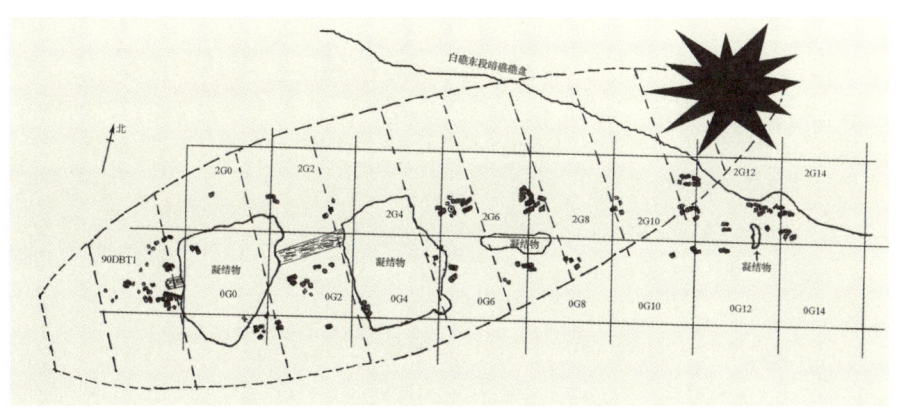

图八　白礁一号沉船遗迹分布与船体平面推测复原示意图

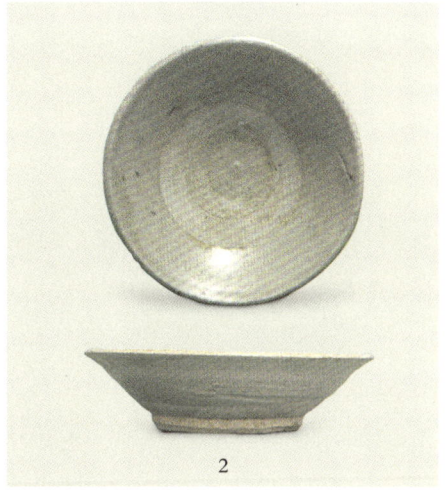

图九　白礁一号出水器物
1. 黑釉盏　2. 青白瓷碗

4. 白礁一号沉船[12]

沉船遗址位于连江县定海湾，闽江入海处北侧，水深约10米左右。1989~2002年，经过多次水下考古调查、勘测和发掘，基本弄清了沉船遗址的分布范围、堆积状况、遗物面貌等问题。该船船体破坏严重，仅大型凝结物底部叠压的疑似龙骨部分残存。根据沉船中心遗迹带的规模和内在结构，推测该船全长19~20、宽5~6米，是一艘具有9~11个隔舱的中型海船（图八）。

沉船出水遗物以瓷器为主，此外遗址上还有多块大型金属凝结物，但具体金属构成并未探明，在采集到的小块凝结物中曾发现条形铁器。历年出水陶瓷器总计2678件（片），类型单纯，主要是建窑系黑釉盏和仿龙泉窑系青瓷，表现出鲜明的船货特征。其中黑釉盏发现数量最多，器形变化很小，总体风格一致，一般口径为10~11、足径3~4、高4~5厘米，胎体为灰色，釉色深浅不一，制作工艺较为粗率；历年采集的青白瓷、青瓷器占出水陶瓷总量的15.5%，基本都是碗类（图九）。

遗址文化层发现的木质遗物取样^{14}C测定数据为距今1000±70年，此外结合瓷器年代特征，推断白礁一号沉船时代约为南宋至元代。

[12] 中澳合作水下考古专业人员培训班定海调查发掘队：《中国福建连江定海1990年度调查、试掘报告》，《中国历史博物馆馆刊》1992年第18~19期，页242~249。中澳联合定海水下考古队：《福建定海沉船遗址1995年度调查与发掘》，《东南考古研究》第二辑，厦门：厦门大学出版社，1999年，页186~198。张威、吴春明、林果：《关于福建定海沉船考古的有关问题》，《东南考古研究》第二辑，厦门：厦门大学出版社，1999年，页199~207。赵嘉斌、吴春明：《福建连江定海湾沉船考古》，北京：科学出版社，2011年。

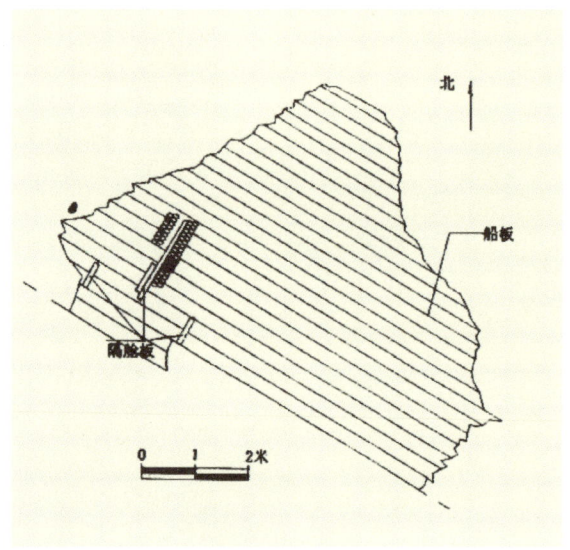

图一〇 平潭大练岛沉船船体平面图

[13] 平潭大练岛元代沉船遗址水下考古队：《平潭大练岛Ⅰ号沉船遗址水下考古发掘收获》，《福建文博》2008年第1期，页21～26。中国国家博物馆水下考古研究中心等：《福建平潭大练岛元代沉船遗址》，北京：科学出版社，2014年。

5. 平潭大练岛沉船[13]

沉船遗址位于福州市平潭县大练岛的西部海域，东距大练岛约200米，西北面为小练岛，水深约18米。2006年遗址遭盗捞，破坏严重，2007年进行抢救性水下考古发掘。

沉船船体破坏严重，首尾均残，仅存部分船体的底部，南侧部分船板露出海床，其余部分埋于沙层中。船体方向300°，呈西北—东南走向，残长约7米，残宽约5.5米。船体西南部残存两道隔舱板和一道隔舱板痕迹（图一〇）。

采集出水可复原瓷器标本300余件，皆为龙泉窑青瓷器，主要器型有盘、洗、罐、碗等，此外还有1件铁锅。出水瓷器以盘的数量最多，胎色灰、灰白，胎质紧密，内外均满施釉，足端或外底面局部无釉。釉色以青绿为主，少量泛黄褐，装饰技法以刻划为主。小罐的数量也较多，均为灰胎，青釉泛黄、灰，内满釉，外施釉至腹底部，装饰方法均为模印，纹饰有卷草、缠枝花卉等，有的口沿外附双系（图一一）。

根据出水瓷器的特征，初步判断其烧造年代为元代晚期，据此推断沉船年代亦为元代晚期。

 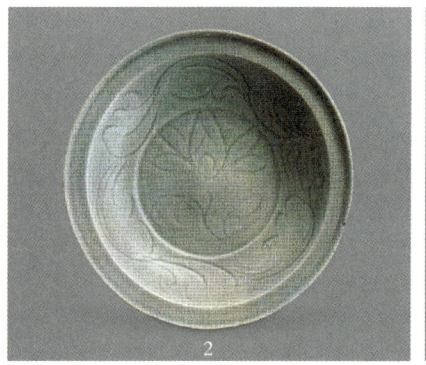 

图一一 大练岛一号沉船出水器物

1. 青瓷洗　2. 青瓷盘　3. 青瓷小罐

6. 南海Ⅰ号沉船[14]

南海Ⅰ号1987年发现于广东阳江海域。1989～2007年，水下考古工作者先后对该船进行了8次考古调查、勘探和试掘，确认其位于海平面以下24米，表面覆盖1～1.5米的淤泥，船体保存较好，现存长度为30.4、宽9.8、型深4.2米，上甲板以下部分结构基本完整，船舱内满载陶瓷、金属器、漆木器和石质器物等（图一二）。2007年4～12月，"南海Ⅰ号"被整体打捞出水，安置于广东海上丝绸之路博物馆，等待进一步考古发掘、保护和研究工作。2009年8～9月以及2011年3～5月，广东省文物考古研究所对沉船进行了两次试掘，采集了沉船相关数据并提取了部分文物。自2013年底开始对沉船进行考古发掘与保护工作。

[14] 崔勇：《"南海Ⅰ号"的发现与调查》，《中国文化遗产》2007年第4期，页12～18。崔勇：《"南海Ⅰ号"发现始末》，《广东艺术》2008年第2期，页17～21。魏峻：《"南海Ⅰ号"2007整体打捞》，《中国文化遗产》2007年第4期，页19～28。魏峻：《"南海Ⅰ号"沉船考古与水下文化遗产保护》，《文化遗产》2008年第1期，页148～153。广东省文物考古研究所：《2011年"南海Ⅰ号"的考古试掘》，北京：科学出版社，2011年。张万星：《广东"南海Ⅰ号"沉船船货的内涵与性质》，《海洋遗产与考古》，北京：科学出版社，2012年，页138～154。

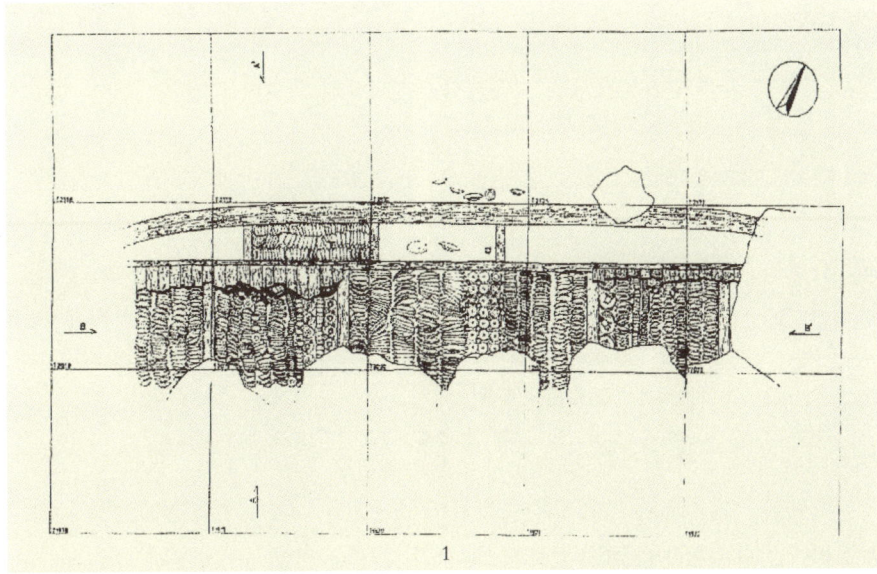

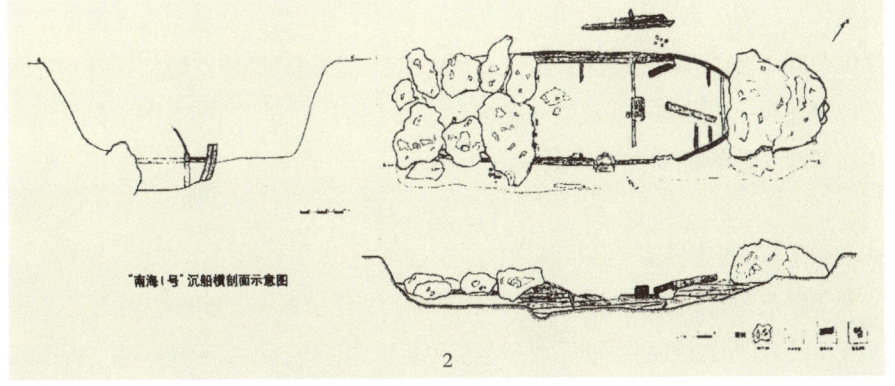

图一二 南海Ⅰ号沉船

1. 纵剖面示意图 2. 平、剖面示意图

图一三 南海Ⅰ号沉船出水器物

1.白釉粉盒 2.白釉四系罐 3.白釉喇叭口瓶 4.白釉碗 5.青白釉花口碗 6.酱釉小口壶 7.青瓷碗 8.白釉执壶

图一四 南海Ⅰ号沉船出水瓷器墨书

据估计，南海Ⅰ号沉船遗物总量有6万~8万件，其中陶瓷器皿为最大宗，主要包含了东南各省外销瓷生产窑口的日用器皿。目前可分辨的窑口包括江西景德镇窑，浙江龙泉窑，福建的德化窑、闽清义窑、晋江磁灶窑和建窑等，这其中又以福建窑产品占船载数量、种类比重最大。这些陶瓷器包括青瓷、青白瓷、白瓷和低温绿釉瓷，器类有碗、盘、碟、壶、粉盒、瓶等（图一三）。出水的部分陶瓷器底部可见清晰的墨书，书体多样，内容有"李大用置""大用置""五""李长保""林上""赐"等。据统计，绝大部分带有墨书的器物来自福建窑口（图一四）。

沉船上还有大量金属船货，包括铁锅、铁钉、银锭、铜环、钱币等（图一五）。其中船载铁器主要存放于上部甲板位置，包括铁锅和铁条材。铁锅依照锅体口径叠套，形成圆柱擞状的凝结物，长度在80~100厘米。铁条材呈扁平状椎体，尖部对交，数十枚以竹篾成捆。截止到2012年，南海Ⅰ号沉船一共发

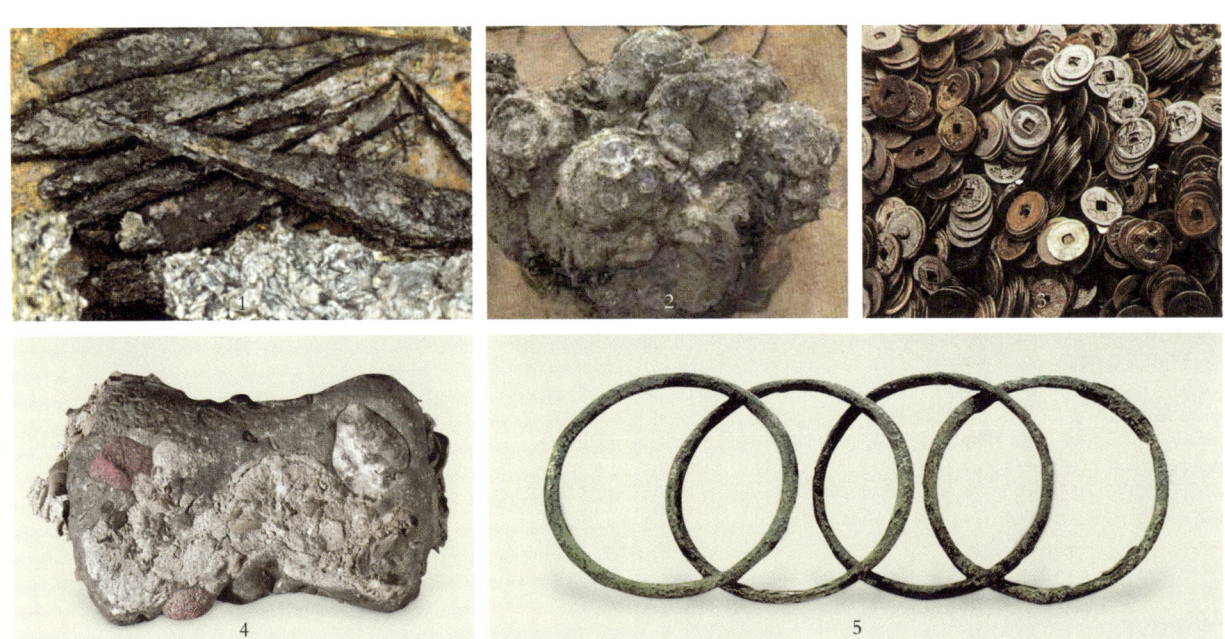

图一五 南海Ⅰ号沉船出水器物
1. 铁条材 2. 铁锅 3. 铜钱 4. 银锭 5. 铜环

 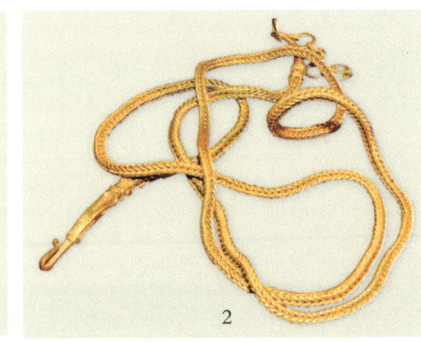 

图一六 南海Ⅰ号沉船出水金器
1. 戒指 2. 腰带 3. 镯子

掘出8000多枚铜钱，其中钱文清晰可辨的有4300余枚。经清理比对，年代最早的为西汉"五铢"（前118年），还有东汉的"货泉"（14～40年）。其次为隋唐时期的"五铢"和"开元通宝"，少部分为五代十国钱币，如后周"周元通宝"（955年）、南唐"唐国通宝"（959年）。钱币绝大部分是北宋时期各年号铜钱，最晚的是南宋的"绍兴元宝"（1131～1162年）。此外还发现有成批的铜环，装于陶瓷粉盒之中，以及数量尚不清楚的银锭。除船货以外，还有私人物品，如鎏金银腰带、鎏金虬龙纹环、金戒指、方楞金环、铜镜、石砚、石雕佛像、石雕观音坐像、朱砂、粉盒、纤细卷曲的金条，亮丽精致的漆器残片、石枕等（图一六）。

南海Ⅰ号瓷器的釉色、胎质以及装饰纹样与德化窑、义窑、磁灶窑以及龙泉窑等窑口北宋中晚期至南宋早期窑址出土遗物相符合。同时，结合该船出水最晚年号的铜钱为"绍兴元宝"，可以初步判断"南海Ⅰ号"为一艘南宋早期的对外出口贸易货船。

7. 华光礁一号沉船[15]

华光礁位于海南省西沙群岛中永乐群岛南部。华光礁一号沉船遗址发现于华光礁环礁内侧，遗址海域水深2~3米。自1996年发现以来，曾遭多次非法盗捞，沉船遗址破坏严重。1998年进行过初步试掘工作，出水文物近1800件，出版《西沙水下考古1998~1999》。2007~2008年，西沙群岛水下考古工作队先后两次对华光礁一号遗址进行了抢救性发掘。

沉船大致呈东南—西北走向，遗址表面存留数处体积较大的凝结物，遗址由船只沉没在坚硬的珊瑚沙上，骨架断裂散落后形成，和船体原始面貌差距甚远。发现的船体已经被破坏了一部分，残存船体覆盖面积约180平方米，船体残长20、宽约6、最宽处9米，型深3~4米，发现11个残留的隔舱，除船体上层建筑外，底层船体保存基本良好，初步估计该船排水量大于60吨（图一七）。

发掘出水文物近万件，陶、瓷器占绝大部分。出水瓷器以青白瓷居多，青瓷次之，酱褐釉器最少。器型主要为碗、盘、碟、盒、壶、盏、瓶、罐、瓮等，装饰技法有刻划、模印、堆贴等（图一八）。在一些器物的底、足内，发

[15] 中国国家博物馆水下考古研究中心、海南省文物保护管理办公室：《西沙水下考古1998~1999》，北京：科学出版社，2006年，页35~48、66~138。孙键、李滨、徐海滨：《揭秘华光礁一号沉船》，《华夏地理》2007年第10期，页158~169。张威：《西沙群岛华光礁Ⅰ号沉船遗址抢救性发掘》，国家文物局：《2007中国重要考古发现》，北京：文物出版社，2008年，页173~176。海南省博物馆：《大海的方向：华光礁Ⅰ号沉船特展》，南京：凤凰出版社，2011年。

图一七　华光礁一号沉船船体遗迹

Findings and Researches of Shipwrecks in South China Sea and Southeast Asian Waters, 9th to 14th Century

图一八 华光礁一号沉船出水器物
1. 青白瓷碗　2. 青瓷碗　3. 青瓷碗　4. 青白瓷执壶　5. 青白瓷瓶　6. 青白瓷盘　7. 酱釉军持　8. 青白瓷碗　9. 青白瓷碗

现有墨书题记，个别器底还有模印铭文、纹样等（图一九）。青白瓷大致可分为两类，一类灰白胎、胎体稍厚，施灰白釉，有刻划、篦划纹装饰，与福建地区宋代窑址产品类似，应来源于此；另一类为白胎、胎体薄，施青白釉，也有刻划、篦划纹装饰，是典型宋代景德镇湖田窑器物。青瓷大部分来自于福建窑口，细分有泉州地区、闽北地区以及晋江磁灶窑产品。酱褐釉器应该来自晋江磁灶窑的宋元窑址。此外，华光礁一号还发现有作为船货的铁条材。截面呈"U"形，长35~50厘米，用两道竹篾捆扎成直径12~15厘米的炮弹头状，椎体中心有填充物胶结（图二〇）。根据出水瓷器墨书及器物形制，判断沉船年代为绍兴年间或之后不久。

图一九　华光礁一号沉船出水器物
1、2. 器底墨书　3. 内底印文

图二〇　华光礁一号沉船出水铁条材

8. 石屿二号沉船[16]

石屿二号沉船遗址位于西沙群岛石屿东侧的珊瑚礁石上，水深1～2米。该遗址表面扰动严重，分布着大小不一的盗坑。由于位于礁盘附近，常年受到海水冲刷侵蚀，导致遗迹堆积较薄，遗物散布范围大，且瓷片大多较为破碎，并未发现原生船板痕迹。

2010年度西沙水下考古调查，在该遗址采集的标本均为瓷器，有青花、卵白釉、白釉、青灰釉、酱釉等几类，器型类别丰富，以日常生活用器为主，有碗、杯、洗、盒、瓶、罐等（图二一）。这些瓷器分别产自江西景德镇窑、福建德化窑、晋江磁灶窑以及福建地区的其他窑场。

出水的青花瓷器，与内蒙古、甘肃、江西等地城址、墓葬以及窑址出土的元代青花瓷器，在胎质、釉色、青花色泽、纹饰内容及绘画风格等方面均十分相似，而出水的元青花瓷器也为中国水下考古工作中的首次发现。此外，卵白釉瓷器也都为元代的典型器类。因该遗址出水遗物的年代一致，分布较为集中，且比较单纯，故可推断石屿二号沉船遗址的年代应属元代。

[16] 中国国家博物馆水下考古研究中心、海南省文物局：《西沙群岛石屿二号沉船遗址调查简报》，《中国国家博物馆馆刊》2011年第11期，页26～46。孟原召：《西沙群岛海域出水元代青花瓷器初探》，《中国国家博物馆馆刊》2011年第11期，页69～82。

图二一（1） 石屿二号沉船出水器物

1. 白釉洗　2. 白釉盒盖　3. 卵白釉杯

图二一（2） 石屿二号沉船出水器物
4.青花杯 5.青花罐盖

（二）泰国

1. 朗坚岛沉船（Ko Rang Kwien Wreck）[17]

沉船位于捆坎水道，西离色桃邑Bang Sare湾约10千米，离朗坚岛仅800米，深约25米，曾遭到严重盗捞。1978~1981年，泰国文化艺术部（Fine Arts Department，TUAD）下属水下考古部（Underwater Archaeology Division）与杰瑞米·格林（Jeremy Green）领导的西澳大利亚海洋博物馆进行合作，对沉船遗址进行了发掘。

船体保存较好，从建造技术来看，判断为一艘东南亚拼板船（图二二）。出水中国铜钱数千枚，仍由丝线串着，其中有开元通宝、圣宋元宝、大定通宝、大宋元宝、洪武通宝等，此外还有陶瓷器、铜锭、铜锣等，共计约200千克（图二三）。船体木质标本^{14}C年代测定为1270±60年，据洪武通宝判断，应为14世纪末明初的沉船。

[17] Karen Atkinson et al. Joint Thai-Australian underwater archaeological project 1987-1988 Part 1: Archaeological survey of wreck sites in the Gulf of Thailand, 1987-1988. *International Journal of Nautical Archaeology*, Volume 18, Issue 4, 1989, p. 307.

图二三 朗坚岛沉船出水瓷器

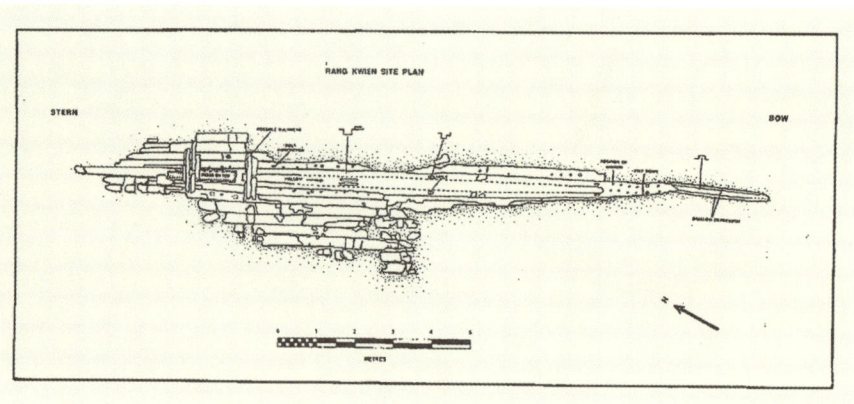

图二二 朗坚岛沉船遗址平面图

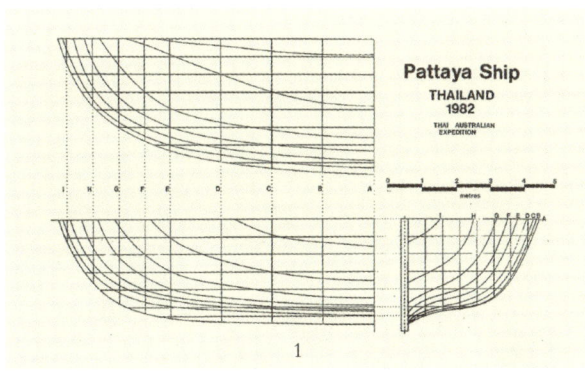
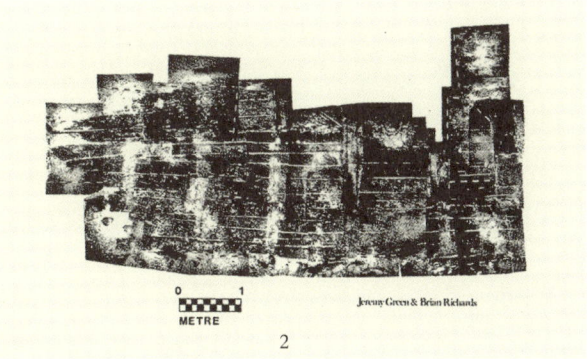

图二四　芭提雅沉船船体
1. 复原图　2. 影像拼接平面图

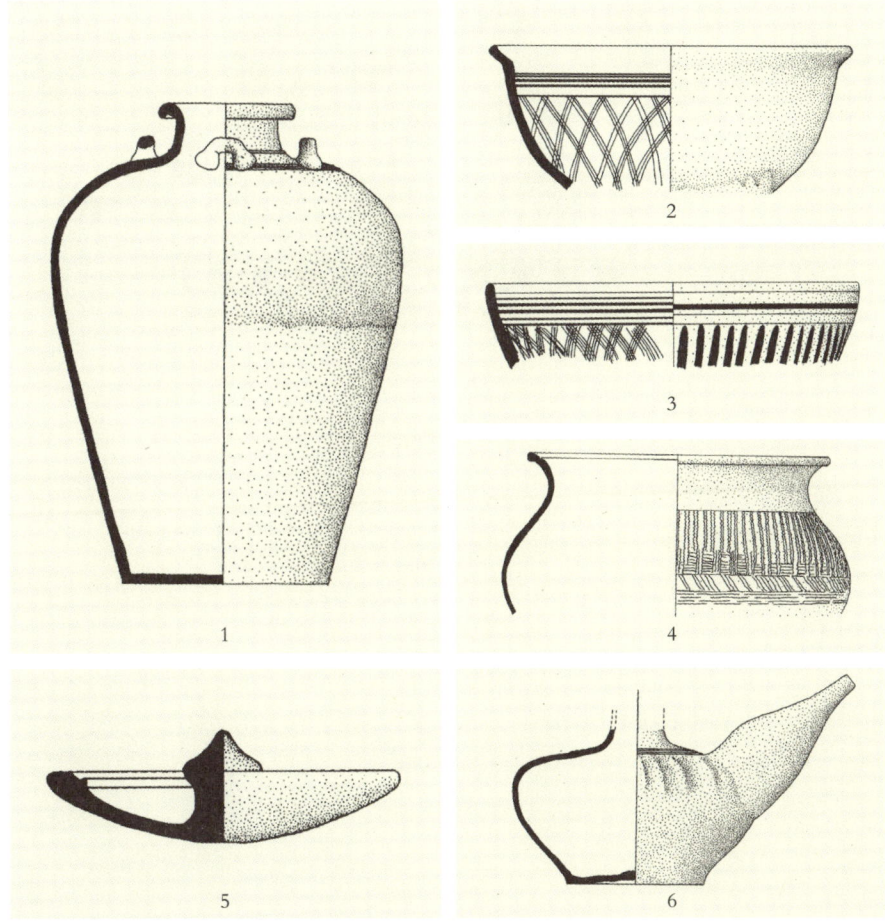

图二五　芭提雅沉船出水器物
1. 瓷罐　2. 青瓷碗　3. 青瓷碗
4. 陶罐　5. 陶罐盖　6. 陶军持

2. 芭堤雅沉船（Pattaya Wreck）[18]

船位于 Ko Lan 岛与芭堤雅间海域，深约90米，1982年泰澳联合考古队进行了发掘。船体保存较好，其结构与泉州湾海船类似（图二四）。

出水了数量较多的泰国和中国陶瓷，包括青瓷、酱釉陶器等，器型多样（图二五）。船上还发现数量较多的金字塔形铅锭以及大型铁质凝结物，其中包含有铁条材等（图二六）。船体木质标本 ^{14}C 年代测定为 1370±50 年，结合出水陶瓷器特征，判断沉船年代为14世纪末。

[18] Jeremy Green and Vidya Intakosai. The Pattaya Wreck Site Excavation, Thailand, an Interim Report. *The International Journal of Nautical Archaeology and Underwater Exploration*, Vol. 12 (1), 1983, pp. 3–13. Jeremy Green and Rosemary Harper. *The Excavation of the Pattaya Wreck Site and Survey of Three Other Sites, Thailand, 1982*, Australian Institute for Maritime Archaeology Special Publication No.1, 1983. Karen Atkinson et al. Joint Thai-Australian underwater archaeological project 1987-1988 Part 1: Archaeological survey of wreck sites in the Gulf of Thailand, 1987-1988, pp. 306–307.

图二六 芭提雅沉船出水铅锭

3. 阁西昌Ⅱ号沉船（Ko Si Chang Ⅱ Wreck）[19]

遗址位于阁西昌岛西约3千米，深约100英尺。1982年泰国—澳大利亚联合考古队对该遗址进行了首次调查，1987年进一步勘察，测量了遗址相关数据。

船体部分保存，船板由铁钉从内侧钉合，不同于一般认为的东南亚船或中国船的接合方式（图二七）。出水有泰国和中国等地的陶瓷器，金属器包括一块方形铅锭和一枚中国铜钱。船体木质标本^{14}C年代测定为1270±60年，研究者推断沉船年代为14世纪。

[19] Jeremy Green. The Ko Si Chang Excavation Report 1983. *Bulletin Australian Institute for Maritime Archaeology*, No.7 (2), 1983, pp. 9-37. Karen Atkinson *et al*. Joint Thai-Australian underwater archaeological project 1987-1988 Part 1: Archaeological survey of wreck sites in the Gulf of Thailand, 1987-1988, pp. 300-306.

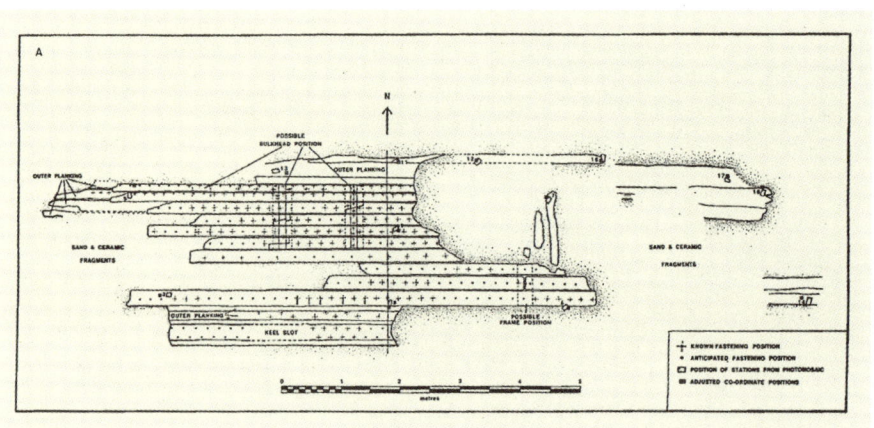

图二七 "阁西昌Ⅱ号"沉船遗址平面图

（三）菲律宾[20]

1. 碎浪礁沉船（Breaker Reef Wreck）[21]

1991年菲律宾国家博物馆从渔民处获悉碎浪礁附近发现陶瓷，之后委托欧洲水下考古研究院确定遗物出水位置，明确遗址位于距菲律宾巴拉望岛西南8英里处的珊瑚礁上，水深约5米，船体则被冲到了更远的位置。同年，由Gilbert Fournier 负责开展了发掘工作。

遗址区域没有发现木质遗存，但发现一块3米长的碇石，两头窄中间宽，形制与泉州湾发现的碇石类似。

出水陶瓷近千件，其中出水龙泉青瓷300余件，另外还有青白瓷、褐釉瓷器、黄釉瓷器、黑釉、白瓷、磁州类型的釉下黑彩等，这些瓷器可能来自福建、浙江、广东等地的窑口，器类多样（图二八）。此外，还出水了铅锭、少量铁锭和铁锅残片。根据分析出水陶瓷特征，研究者判断遗址为北宋晚期，即11世纪末至12世纪初。

[20] "圣安东尼奥"沉船和"锡马纳汉礁"沉船遗址的调查发掘材料目前无法获取，暂不作介绍。

[21] Marie-France Dupoizat. The Ceramic Cargo of a Song Dynasty Junk Found in the Philippines and its Significance in the China-South East Asia Trade. *South East Asia and China: Art, Interaction and Commerce*, eds. Rosemary Scott and John Guy, Percival David Foundation of Chinese Art, 1995; Frank Goddio et al. *Weisses Gold*, pp. 47–68.

图二八（1） 碎浪礁沉船出水器物
1.青瓷铭文碗 2.青瓷盘 3.青白瓷碗 4.青白釉喇叭口瓶 5.青釉平底执壶 6.酱釉军持

图二八（2） 碎浪礁沉船出水器物

7. 黑釉盏 8. 白釉黑彩小口瓶 9. 白釉黑彩执壶 10. 青白瓷八棱炉

2. 调查员沉船（Investigator Wreck）[22]

遗址位于榆亚暗沙东北部，朝向巴拉巴克海峡，水深2~3米。在菲律宾国家博物馆获知消息前已遭盗掘，后由Frank Goddio与欧洲水下考古研究院一道进行抢救性发掘。

遗存散落于海底，未发现木质船体遗存。出水的遗物主要有陶瓷器和金属铜环、铁质凝结物，其中陶瓷器主要来自福建各地的窑口，此外还有景德镇瓷以及龙泉青瓷，又以龙泉青瓷和福建瓷器所占的比例较大，包括碗、罐、军持等（图二九）。这些遗物存放于菲律宾国家博物馆、法国吉美博物馆和远东海洋考古基金会。根据出水瓷器的特征，研究者推断该沉船遗址的年代为13世纪

[22] Frank Goddio et al. *Weisses Gold*, Göttingen: Steidl Verlag, 1997, pp. 69~78; Marie-France Dupoizat. The Ceramics of the Investigator Shipwreck. Paper presented at the Symposium on Chinese Export Ceramics Trade in Southeast Asia, organized by Asian Research Institute, National University of Singapore, 12th~14th, March, 2007.

图二九　调查员礁出水器物

1. 军持和铜环 2. 青瓷碗盘 3. 青白瓷盘 4. 青白瓷执壶

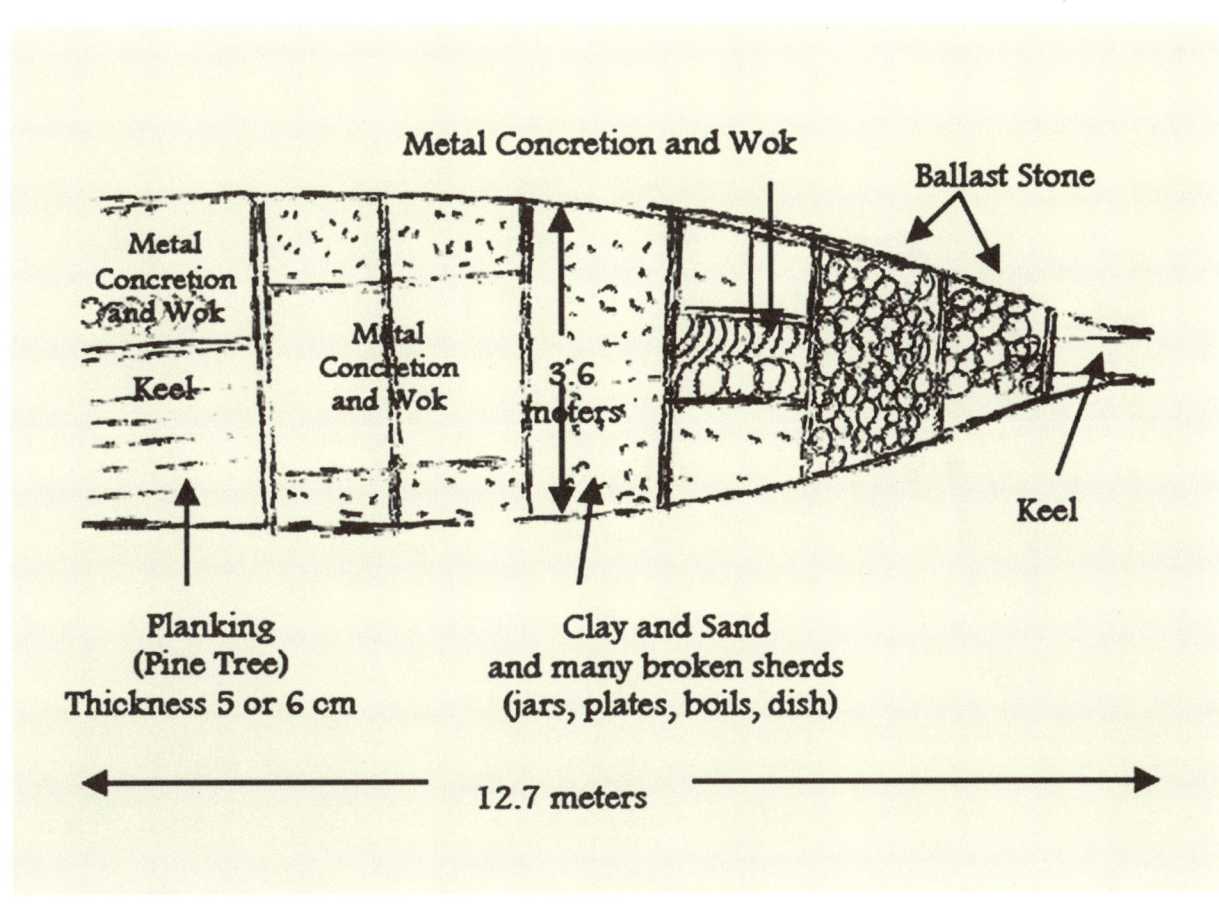

图三〇 乌尼桑沉船平面布局示意图

中期。

3. 乌尼桑沉船（Unisan Wreck）[23]

沉船位于菲律宾吕宋岛南部乌尼桑西南部海域。在2004年菲律宾国家博物馆开始考古调查之前，遗址已遭非法盗捞达两年之久。考古队在遗址表面发现34件瓷器、6个铅块、1个象牙手镯和1个金属块，此外还有数量较多的铁锅，但未采集出水。船体保存状况不清，船板木料被鉴定为松木，结合瓷器特征，研究者认为这是一艘14世纪的中国船（图三〇）。

（四）马来西亚

1. 丹戎新邦沉船（Tanjung Simpang Wreck）[24]

遗址最初于2003年由渔民上报当地博物馆，此前曾遭到严重的盗捞。之后南海海洋考古公司（Nanhai Marine Archaeology）取得搜索许可，并最终确定了遗址的位置在距沙巴州北部丹绒新邦孟阿瑶北面海岸400米的海域中，水深12米。

海底泥沙层上成摞的铜锣揭示了沉船的存在，但遗址区域只留下少量的船

[23] Roxanna Brown and Pariwat Thammapreechakorn eds. Earliest China-built Ship in the Philippines. *Southeast Asian Ceramics Museum Newsletter*, Vol.2, No.2, 2005, pp. 1, 4.

[24] Michael Flecker. The China-Borneo Ceramics Trade Around the 13th Century: The Story of Two Wrecks. 秦大树、袁旔：《2011：古丝绸之路——2011亚洲跨文化交流与文化遗产国际学术研讨会论文集》，新加坡：世纪科技出版公司，2013年，页177~184。The Tanjung Simpang ship: http://www.maritimeasia.ws/tsimpang/.

体结构，散落难辨。取样测定后，初步认为这些船木属于温带树种，并据此推断该沉船为一艘中国船。

出水器物包括303件能复原的瓷器，以及250千克瓷片，产地均为中国（图三一）。另外主要有61件铜锣，以及76件圆形或椭圆形的铜锭和铁锅，且瓷器和铜锣都发现有墨书"郭"等字款（图三二）。根据瓷器特征，判断遗址年代为11～12世纪。

图三一 丹绒新邦沉船出水器物
1. 小口瓶 2. 青白瓷执壶 3. 白瓷执壶 4. 酱釉军持 5. 青白瓷粉盒 6. 青瓷盘 7. 青瓷碗

图三二　丹绒新邦沉船出水器物
1. 铜锭　2. 铜锣　3. 铁锅　4. 铜锣　5. 铜锣及瓷器底部墨书

2. 图日昂沉船（Turiang Wreck）[25]

沉船发现于1998年，西距马来半岛东南端陆地约100海里，水深42米，由Sten Sjostrand 主持调查与发掘工作，并以船货中发现有泰国素可泰时期"图日昂"窑产品为沉船命名。

由于处在捕捞水域，遗址破坏较为严重，约有30%的原初遗物被现代渔网拖离沉船地点。遗址海床表面遗留多件大罐，其余遗物连同船体被掩埋于沙泥之中。船体由铁钉接合软木制造而成，因此被判定为一艘中国船（图三三）。

出水器物有陶瓷器，其中中国陶瓷占35%，包括绿釉、褐釉和青瓷器，越南陶瓷占8%，泰国陶瓷占57%；还发现有多块大型铁质凝结物，据观察其原本个体形制为圆球状，另外还出水了多块锌矿石（图三四）。^{14}C年代测定范围为1305～1440年，结合分析出水中国、越南和泰国陶瓷的特征，判断沉船年代在1370年前后。

[25] Roxanna Brown and Sten Sjostrand. *Turiang: A 14th Century Shipwreck in Southeast Asian Waters*, Pasadena: Pacific Asia Museum, 2000, pp. 11-39; Roxanna Brown and Sten Sjostrand. *Maritime Archaeology and Shipwreck Ceramics in Malaysia*, Kuala Lumpur: Department of Museums and Antiquities, 2002, pp. 43-45.

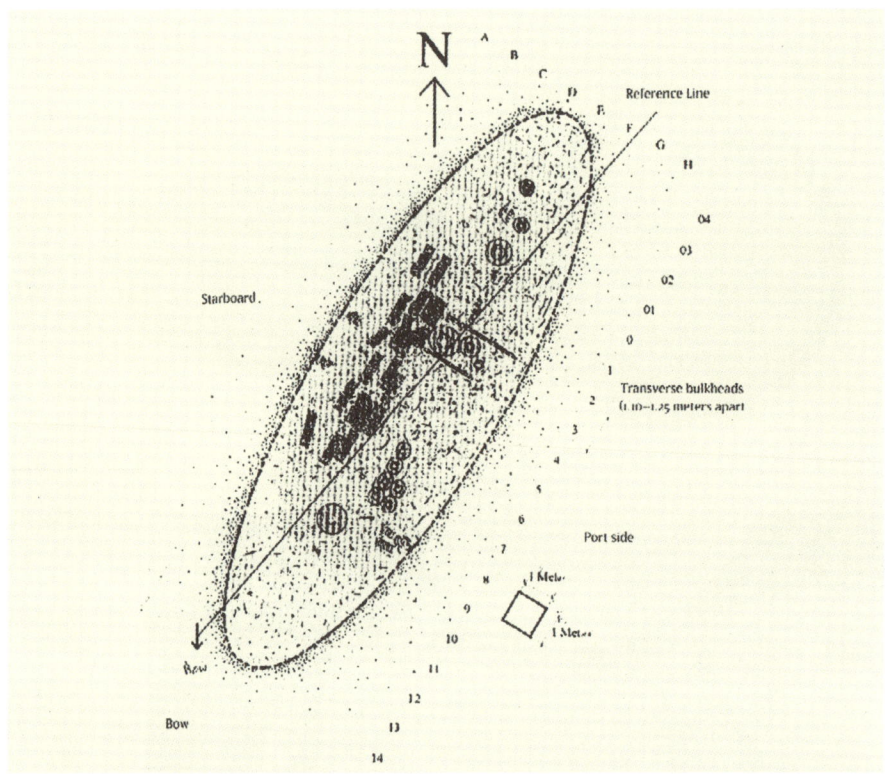

图三三　图日昂沉船遗址平面示意图

图三四（1）　图日昂沉船出水器物
1. 黑釉盒　2. 黑釉盏

图三四（2） 图日昂沉船出水器物
3. 铁质凝块　4. 青瓷盘　5. 褐彩双系罐　6. 褐彩碗　7. 青瓷双系罐　8. 青瓷荷叶盖罐

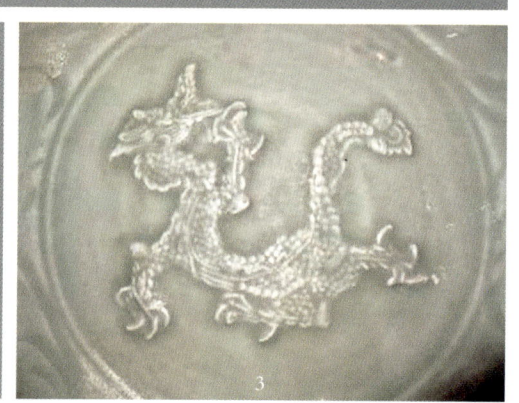

图三五　玉龙号沉船出水器物
1. 青瓷带系罐　2. 青瓷双鱼洗　3. 青瓷盘

3. 玉龙号沉船[26]

沉船遗址发现于沙巴州北部海域，遭到严重盗捞。沙巴州博物馆与海洋探险公司（Maritime Explorations）合作进行了调查发掘工作。船体结构部分保留，通过对造船技术的分析，断定为一艘东南亚的拼板船。出水遗物中的陶瓷器全为龙泉青瓷，此外还发现有铁条材等金属遗物（图三五）。根据陶瓷器类型，初步判断沉船年代为14世纪初。

（五）印度尼西亚[27]

1. 黑石号沉船（Belitung Wreck）[28]

沉船位于距印尼勿里洞邦加港西岸不到2海里的海域中，东经107°35′，南纬2°41′，水深17米。1998年由一家德国打捞公司发现，并以其附近的一块黑色礁石"Batu Hitam"命名，中文译为黑石号。打捞始于1998年9月，至1999年6月基本完成，从2000年开始对打捞文物进行整理。

黑石号船体保存基本完整，底部破损的大洞推测为触礁所致，沉船地点海床结构为黏土而非岩石，因此船体沉没时激起的泥沙就形成了保护层。龙骨长15.3米，船体最宽处为5.1米（图三六）。该船采用绳索缝合捆扎技术建造而成，在对船体木材以及捆扎绳索纤维进行检测之后，研究者推断这是一艘在中东地区建造的缝合帆船，之后在印尼地区用当地材料进行过重新缝合。

船上运载的大部分船货储存在大罐中，因此遗物保存状况也较好。黑石号

[26] Michael Flecker. The China-Borneo Ceramics Trade Around the 13th Century: The Story of Two Wrecks, pp. 162–176.

[27] "中国珊瑚"沉船遗址的调查发掘材料目前无法获取，暂不作介绍。

[28] Michael Flecker. A 9th century Arab or Indian shipwreck in Indonesian Waters. *The International Journal of Nautical Archaeology*, Vol.29(2), 2000, pp.199–217. Michael Flecker. A Ninth Century AD Arab or Indian Shipwreck in Indonesia: First Evidence for Direct Trade with China. *World Archaeology*, Vol.32(3), 2001, pp.335–354. Michael Flecker. A 9th century Arab or Indian shipwreck in Indonesian Waters: Addendum. *The International Journal of Nautical Archaeology*, Vol.37 (2), 2008, pp. 384–386. Krahl, Regina, John Guy, Keith Wilson, and Julian Raby eds. *Shipwrecked: Tang Treasures and Monsoon Winds*, Smithsonian Books, 2011.

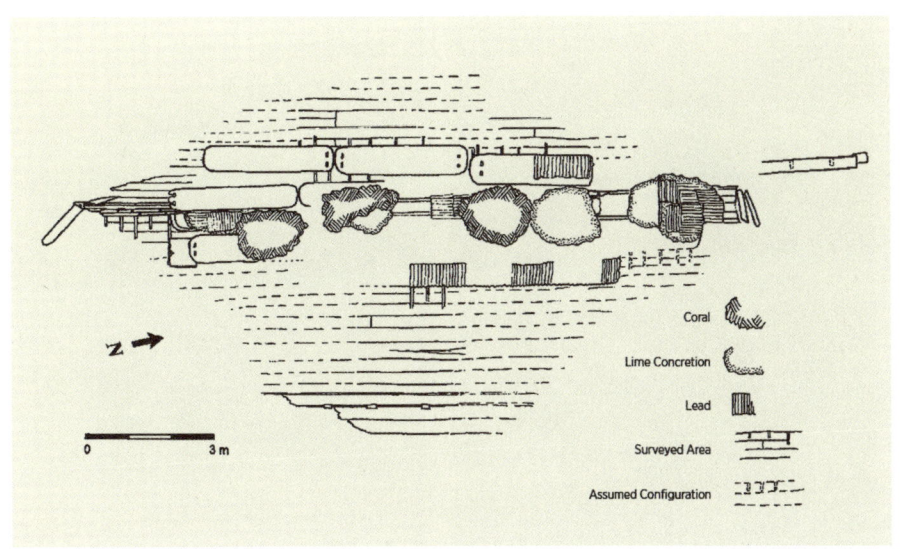

图三六 黑石号沉船结构示意图

打捞出水的陶瓷制品多达6万多件，其中98%是中国陶瓷。长沙窑瓷器有5万多件，器型以碗为主，其次为执壶。其他器型包括杯、盘、盂、盒、罐、熏炉、油灯和少量生肖瓷塑。另外还包括唐青花、越窑青瓷、北方白瓷、北方白釉绿彩陶瓷和广东地方窑口烧造的粗糙青瓷（图三七）。除陶瓷制品之外，打捞出水的船货还包括金银器、银铤、铜镜、铁锅、铅锭和香料等（图三八），其他零星文物可能为船上用品和船员私人物品，其中包括玻璃瓶、象牙制游戏器具、砚和墨等。

对出水香料、八角和船木的^{14}C测定数据分别为680～780年、670～890年以及710～890年。而根据出水长沙窑瓷碗上带有唐宝历二年（826年）铭文，结合对其他器物，特别是越窑青瓷的排年分析，推断沉船的年代为826～850年。

图三七（1） 黑石号沉船出水瓷器
1、2. 白瓷

图三七（2） 黑石号沉船出水瓷器
3. 白釉绿彩高足长柄龙首壶　4~7. 白釉绿彩瓷器　8. 越窑青瓷熏炉

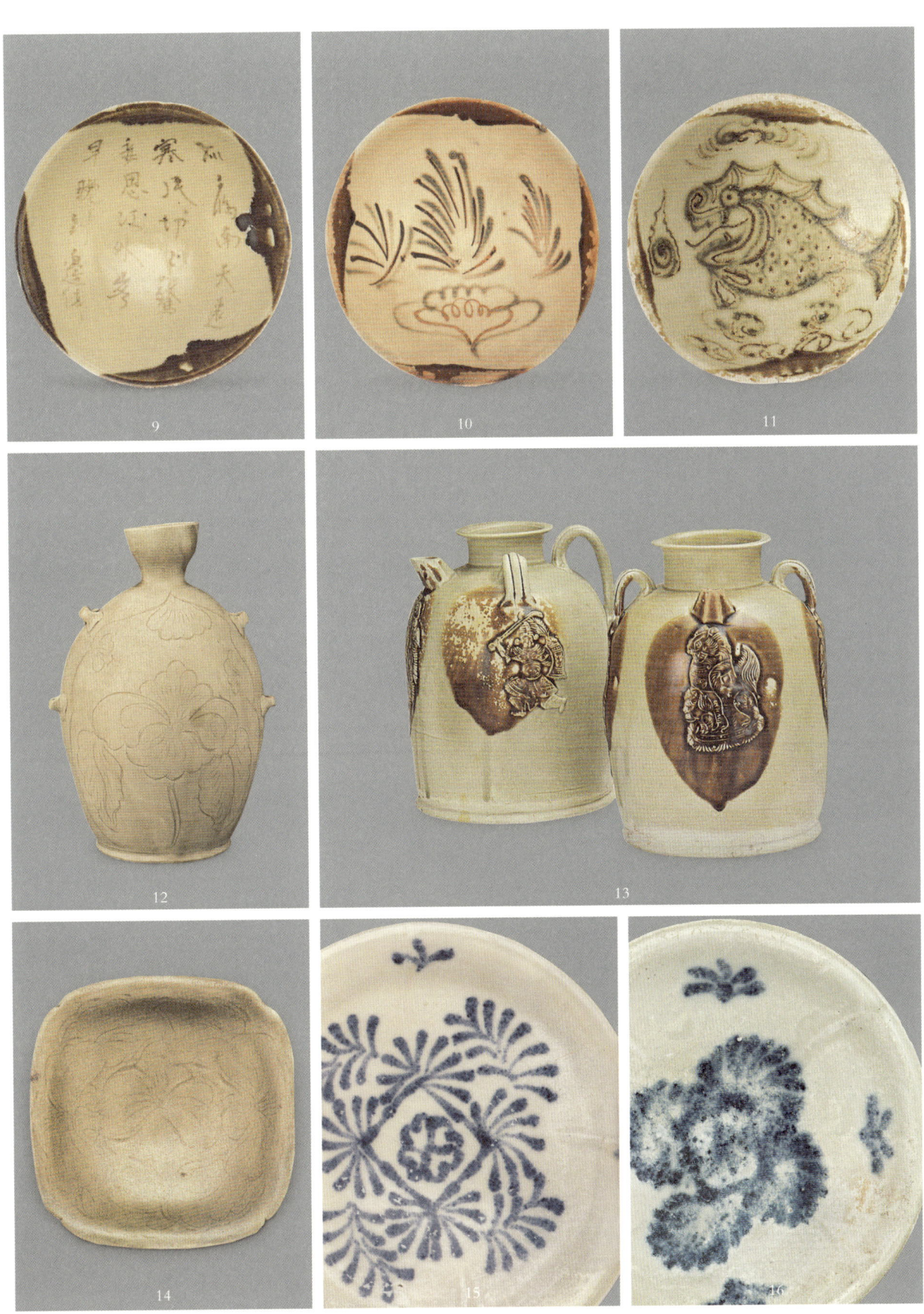

图三七（3） 黑石号沉船出水瓷器

9~11、13. 长沙窑青釉褐彩瓷器　12、14. 越窑青瓷　15、16. 青花瓷盘

图三八（1） 黑石号沉船出水器物

1～5. 金器　6、7. 鎏金银器

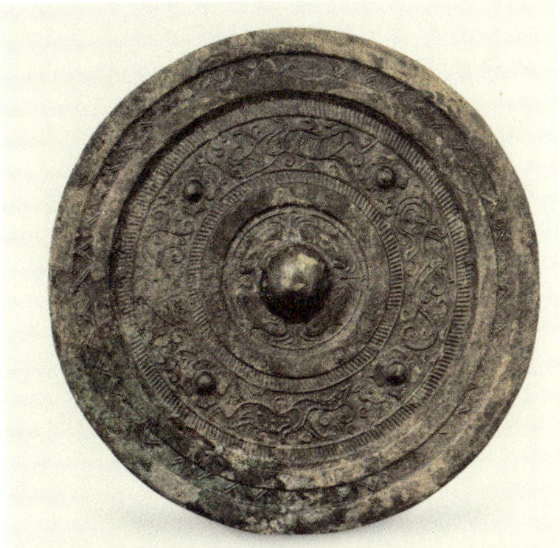
8

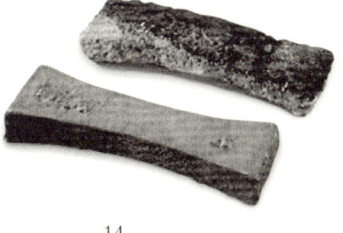

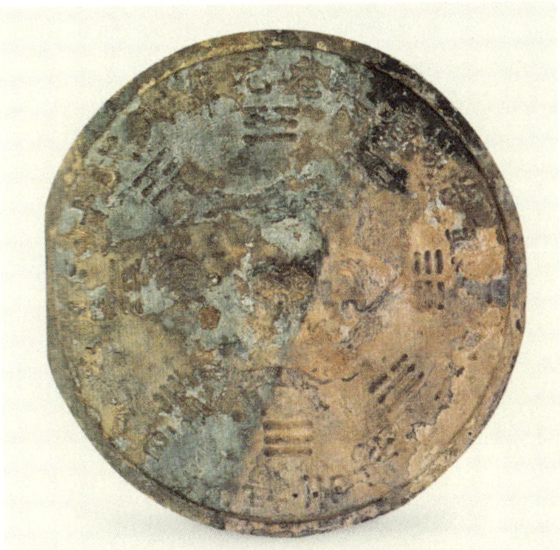
9

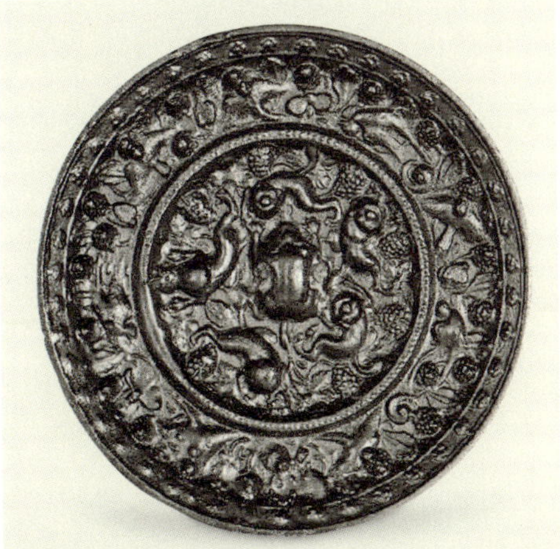
10

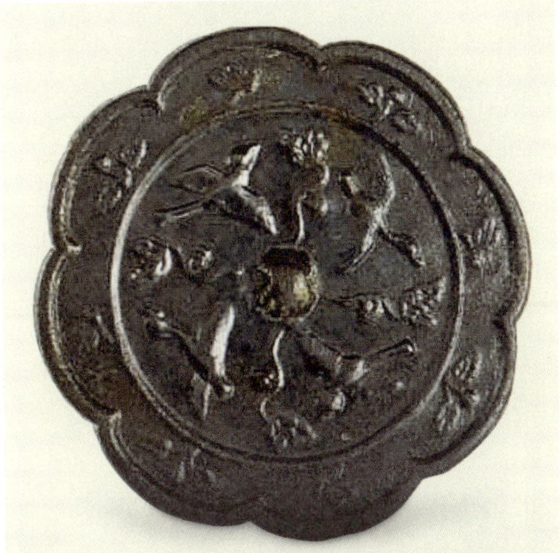
11

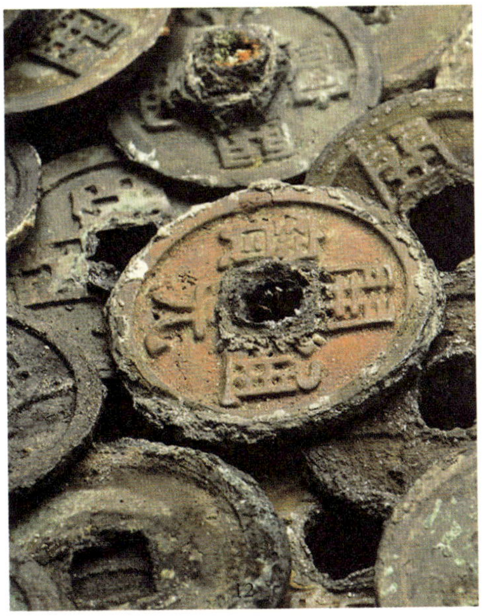
12

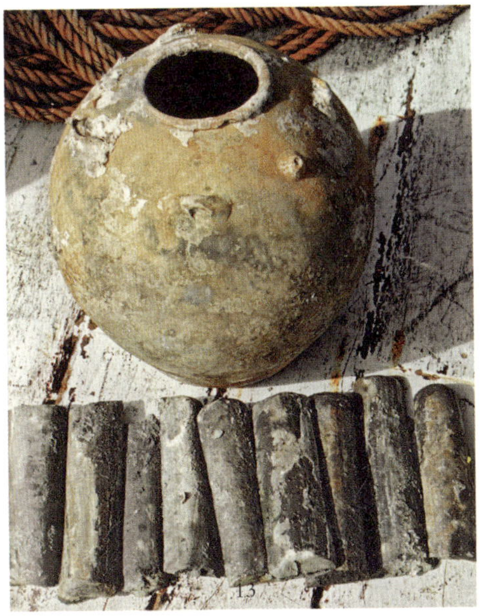
13

14

图三八（2） 黑石号沉船出水器物

8~11. 铜镜 12. 铜钱
13. 铅锭 14. 银锭

2. 印坦沉船（Intan Wreck）[29]

[29] Michael Flecker. *The Archaeological Excavation of the 10th Century Intan Shipwreck* (Ph. D dissertation), National University of Singapore, 2001), Archaeopress, 2002, pp. 18-140. Intan Wreck Details & Photos: http://maritime-explorations.com/intan%20artefacts.htm

沉船位于爪哇海域西北部，西距苏门答腊东岸45海里，南距千岛群岛北端60海里，东经106°41′，南纬4°24′，水深26米，因附近的印坦油田得名。1996年底遭到非法打捞后，引起印尼当局重视。1997年初印尼海军逮捕了盗捞人员并没收文物，之后印尼沉船委员会委托P.T. Sulung Segarajaya（PTSS）公司进行打捞。该公司于1997年6月确定沉船位置，并开展了为期两周的打捞工作，之后又与德国的海底勘探公司（Seabed Explorations）合作，并由Michael Flecker主持发掘。出水文物先在雅加达进行初步处理，然后转运德国进行长期的文物保护工作。

船体结构现已不存，仅有46块残余木片出水，通过检测分析，研究者推断这是一艘属于印尼地区的拼板船，而根据遗物的分布范围，推测船长为25～30米（图三九）。

出水陶瓷7000多件，有中国越窑青瓷、白瓷、青白瓷、褐釉青釉瓷、中东陶瓷、印尼陶瓷等，此外还有6000多件其他文物，包括青铜、铅、银、铁、锡、金、玻璃、石质品、有机物等，来源涵盖中国、马来西亚、泰国、印尼和中东等地（图四〇）。根据^{14}C测年数据，结合分析中国钱币和陶瓷，研究者判断印坦沉船的年代为918～960年。

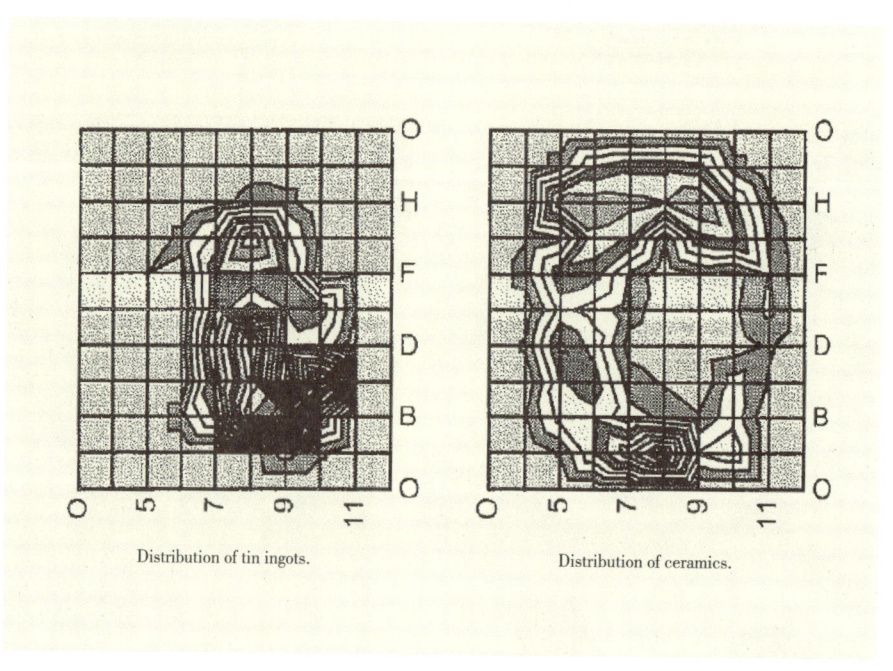

图三九　印坦沉船遗物分布范围

图四〇 印坦沉船出水器物
1. 玻璃瓶 2. 青瓷双鱼瓶 3. 青瓷执壶
4. 黄金饰片 5. 青铜铺首 6. 青铜模具
7. 酱釉小口瓶及军持

3. 井里汶沉船（Cirebon Wreck）[30]

沉船位于爪哇海域、南距爪哇岛井里汶市90海里，水深57米，东经108°58′，南纬5°14′。2001年由渔民发现，之后印尼PT.PPS公司取得发掘许可，调查证实水下沉船遗址保存良好。随后又与比利时Cosmix水下考古与打捞公司合作展开发掘，工作从2004年4月开始至2005年10月结束，共出水495671件（片）文物，其中完整器物155 685件、可复原器物76 987件、瓷片262 999片。

船体结构保存较好，长约31、宽约10、残高1.5米，没有发现铁钉，使用木钉拼合船板，并用绳索绑紧，属于拼板船（图四一）。未见船尾柱、桅柱孔或船舵，但有两件被认为是中国制造的铁锚。发掘者认为这可能是一种南岛船型，即越南南部、马来西亚或印度尼西亚。船木分析测试结构表明其来自苏门答腊和加里曼丹，因此该船应该是在印尼地区制造。

出水遗物种类非常丰富，据统计有近30余万件片，绝大多数为越窑系青瓷，器型多样，另外还有少量质量较高的邢窑白瓷以及可能产于河南安阳一带的相州窑产品（图四二）。金银器、银锭、青铜器、铜镜、铅锭、铅钱、玻璃瓶及玻璃原料、佛教法器、锡刀和棱锥、青金石、大量红宝石、蓝宝石、珊瑚珠、红石等（图四三）。根据遗物特征，推断沉船年代为10世纪中后期。

[30] Adi Agung Tirtamarta撰、辛光灿译：《井里汉海底十世纪沉船打捞纪实》，《故宫博物院院刊》2007年第6期，页151～154。KJPP Abdullah Fitriantoro & Rekan eds. *Katalog Kapal Karam Abad ke-10 di Laut Jawa Utara Cirebon*, Kementerian Kelautan dan Perikanan Direktorat Jenderal Kelautan, Pesisir dan Pulau-pulau Kecil Satuan Kerja Direktorat Pesisir dan Lautan, Jakarta, 2011. The Cargo from Ceribon Shipwreck: http://cirebon.musee-mariemont.be/home-6.htm?lng=en. Horst Liebner.Cargoes for Java: Interpreting Two 10th Century Shipwrecks, pp.1–9.

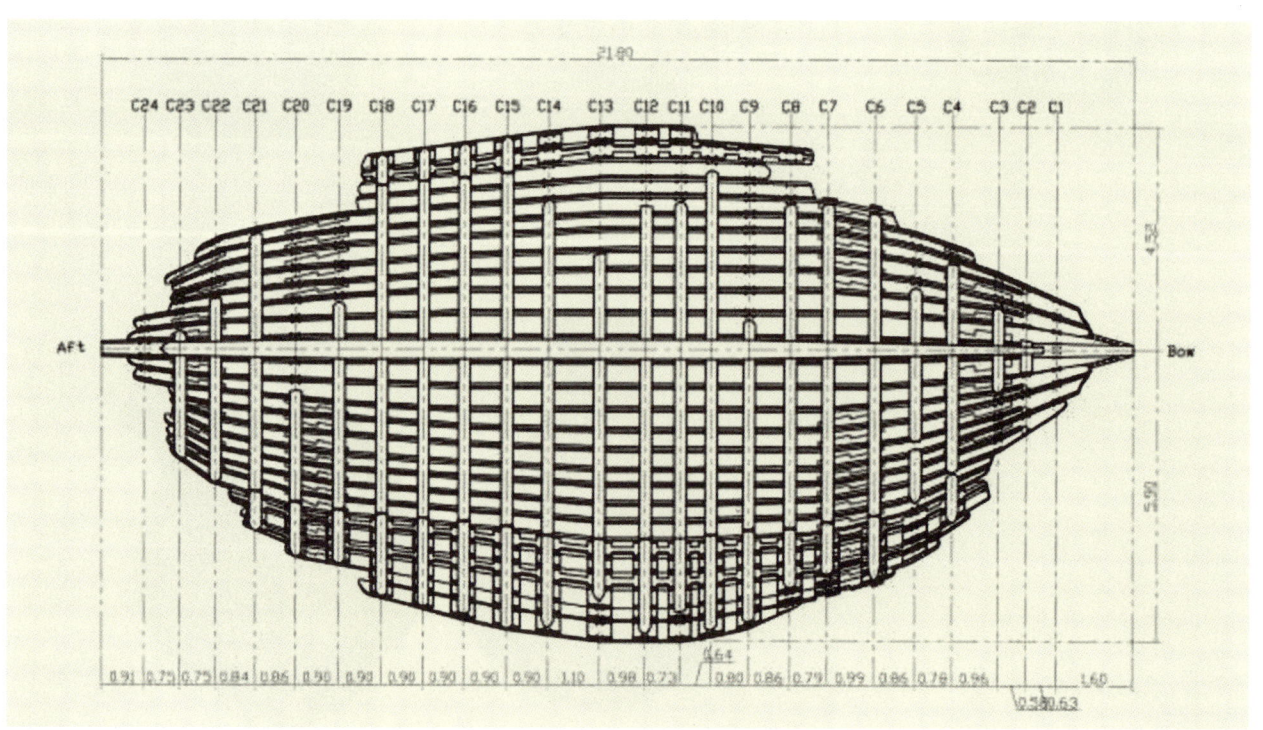

图四一　井里汶沉船船体结构平面示意图

图四二（1） 井里汶沉船出水瓷器
1、2. 白瓷　3～11. 青瓷

12　　　　　　　　　　　　　　13　　　　　　　　　　　　　　14

图四二（2）　井里汶沉船出水瓷器
12~14. 青瓷

1　　　　　　　　　　　　　　2

图四三（1）　井里汶沉船出水器物
1~4. 铜镜　5. 铅钱　6. 铅锡锭

3　　　　　　　　　　　　　　4

5　　　　　　　　　　　　　　6

图四三（2） 井里汶沉船出水器物

7～9. 玻璃器　10. 宝石　11. 金刚杵　12. 金器　13、14、16. 银锭　15. 锡锭

4. 加拉璜沉船（Karawang Wreck）[31]

[31] Horst Liebner. *The 'Karawang' Wreck: A Cargo of 10th Century Trade Ceramics*, Jakarta: PT Putera Paradigma Sejahtera-PT Nautik Recovery Asia, 2009; Horst Liebner. Cargoes for Java: Interpreting Two 10th Century Shipwrecks. Paper for 13th International Conference of the European Association of Southeast Asian Archaeologists (EurASEAA13), Berlin, 2010, pp. 9–16.

沉船位于爪哇海域，东经107°44′，南纬5°30′，水深55米。2007年由渔民首先发现，之后亚洲海洋打捞公司（PT Nautik Recovery Asia）与PT.PPS公司共同申请打捞。获得许可后，调查打捞工作于2008年6月开始，12月中旬因天气原因被迫中止。

船体结构无存，也没有发现任何木构残片。陶瓷器为主要的船货，有青瓷、白瓷以及酱釉陶器，形制有碗、盘、罐、盒、执壶、瓶、军持、器盖等（图四四）。非陶瓷产品则有铜镜、钱币、金属锭、玻璃器等。钱币有"开元通宝"铅钱，背面有"闽""福"字样，这是闽国（909～945年）的铸币，此外还有一枚南汉（917～971年）的"乾亨重宝"铅钱（图四五）。据此并结合陶瓷器特征，打捞者判断沉船年代为10世纪。

图四四（1） 加拉璜沉船出水瓷器
1. 青瓷

图四四（2） 加拉璜沉船出水瓷器
2. 青瓷　3. 酱釉瓷

图四五　加拉璜沉船出水器物
1. 铅钱　2、3. 铜镜

图四六　西村廖内沉船出水瓷器
1、2. 青釉褐彩碗

5. 西村廖内沉船（The Xicun Riau Wreck）[32]

2012年年初，沉船遗址发现于印尼卡里汶岛（Karimun）北部海域，船体长约40米。印尼一家打捞公司随后申请获得了沉船打捞许可，并准备与另一家日本公司合作。沉船遗物基本保留在原址，少有流入市场。目前所见的沉船瓷器包括广东西村窑类型的褐釉印花盆、青釉铁线绘花大碗、白釉厚唇大碗、青白釉碗以及褐釉小口瓶等（图四六）。根据同印坦、加拉璜以及井里汶沉船出水陶瓷器的类比判断，这艘载有西村窑瓷器沉船的年代很可能在960~1020年。

6. 西村勿里洞沉船（The Xicun Belitung Wreck）[33]

2012年印尼雅加达市场上新出现一批瓷器，追溯来源是一艘勿里洞岛海域的沉船。目前可见的器型主要为盘碟（图四七），包括西村窑常见的宽平缘青釉印花盘以及矮足青釉牡丹花纹盘，两者胎质釉色相近，应该是同一时期同一窑场的产品。出水的厚唇白瓷大碗，同10世纪三艘沉船（印坦、加拉璜、井里汶）上发现的繁昌窑瓷碗类似。此外，还有灰釉蕉叶纹鼓腹罐，以及"S"形刻花大碗。根据瓷器类型判断，该沉船的年代也应在10世纪后半叶至11世纪前半叶。

7. 哲帕拉沉船（Jepara Wreck）[34]

沉船位于爪哇海域，南距哲帕拉市45千米，东经110°31′，南纬6°28′，水深54米。船体保存状况不清，遗址地点海床上散落有大量砾石，研究者据此推

---

[32] Roberto Gardellin. Shipwrecks around Indonesia. *The Oriental Ceramic Society Newsletter*, No.21,2013,pp.17–18.童歆编译：《海外陶瓷考古新发现》，《陶瓷考古通讯》2013年第2期，页69。

[33] 童歆编译：《海外陶瓷考古新发现》，《陶瓷考古通讯》2013年第2期，页18、19、69、70。

[34] Atma Djuana and Edmund Edwards McKinnon. The Jepara Wreck. *Proceedings of the International Conference: Chinese Export Ceramics and Maritime Trade, 12th–15th Centuries*, ed.Cheng Pei-Kai,Hong Kong:Chungwa Publishing,2005,pp.126–134.

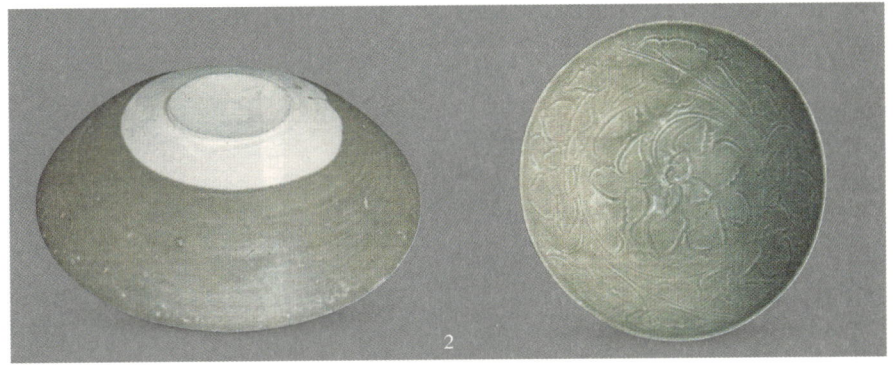

图四七　西村勿里洞沉船出水瓷器
1、2.青瓷盘

测可能是火山爆发导致了该船的沉没。此外，出水一块碇石，其形制两头窄中间宽，与泉州海交史博物馆陈列的类似（图四八），表明该沉船很有可能是一艘中国船。

图四八　哲帕拉沉船出水碇石

20世纪30年代就有遗址出水的陶瓷器在市场上流通。1998年P.T Eka Lingga Adikencana公司获得许可，打捞出水3334件陶瓷。由于渔民炸药捕鱼的破坏，使沉船瓷器受损失去商业价值，打捞公司决定终止打捞。2002年，当地商业潜水员又重新开始打捞，出水器物流入古董市场。陶瓷类型多样，产地包括福建德化、安溪以及浙江龙泉等（图四九）。

除陶瓷外，还发现有铜锣、铜镜、铁锅，以及一个罐子中的3500枚铜钱。这些铜钱约1000枚能够辨识，时代从隋至北宋都有，最迟的年号为北宋重和（1118～1119年）。据此并结合陶瓷分析，研究者判断其为一艘属于12世纪上半叶的南宋早期沉船，年代约在1130年左右。

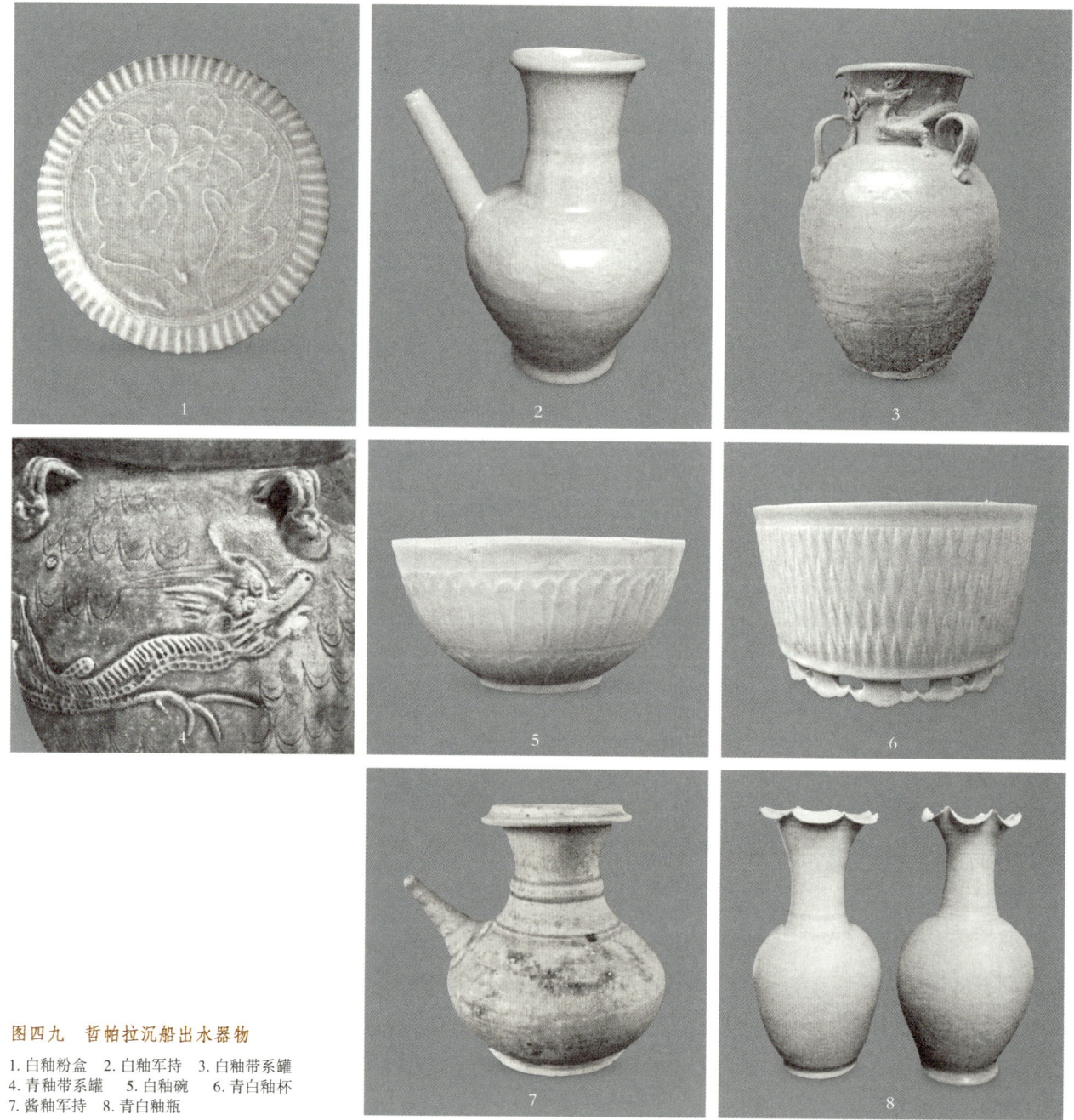

图四九　哲帕拉沉船出水器物
1. 白釉粉盒　2. 白釉军持　3. 白釉带系罐
4. 青釉带系罐　5. 白釉碗　6. 青白釉杯
7. 酱釉军持　8. 青白釉瓶

8. 鳄鱼岛沉船（Pulau Buaya Wreck）[35]

沉船位于印度尼西亚鳄鱼岛附近的林加群岛水域，东经104°13′，北纬0°11′。

遗址发现于1989年，船体保存状况不明。出水了大量陶瓷器，除一部分青白瓷外，主要是烧造于广东窑场的陶瓷（图五〇）。此外，还出水了铜锭、铜环、铅锭、铜钱、铁锅、铁条及玻璃器（图五一）。研究者推断这是一艘12世纪至13世纪初的沉船。

[35] Abu Ridho and E. Edwards McKinnon, edited by Sumarah Adhyatman.*The Pulau Buaya Wreck: Finds from the Song Period*, The Ceramic Society of Indonesia, 1998, pp.1-98.

图五〇（1）　鳄鱼岛沉船出水瓷器
1. 青釉盘　2. 青釉碗　3. 青釉小罐　4. 青釉执壶　5. 青白釉执壶

图五〇（2） 鳄鱼岛沉船出水瓷器
6. 青釉碗　7. 青白釉钵　8. 青白釉瓶　9、10. 青白釉碗

图五一（1） 鳄鱼岛沉船出水器物
1、2. 铅锭　3. 铜锭

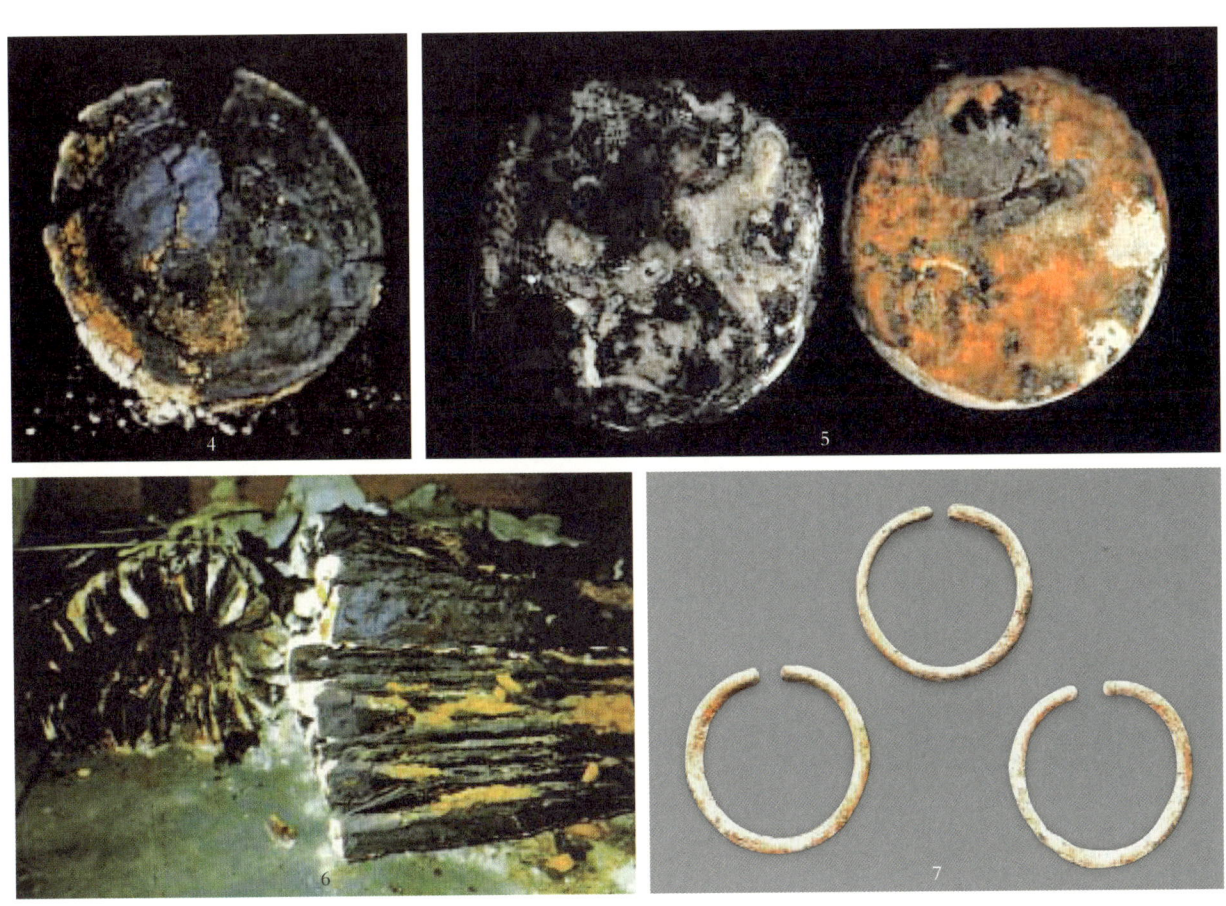

图五一（2） 鳄鱼岛沉船出水器物
4.铁锅 5.铜锣 6.铁条材 7.铜环

9. 爪哇海沉船（Java Sea Wreck）[36]

沉船位于邦加岛和雅加达之间的爪哇海域，东经106°40′，南纬4°14′，水深26米，南距雅加达约110海里，西距苏门答腊东南海岸约50海里。遗址最先由渔民发现，并遭到盗捞。之后当地打捞公司申请并获准进行打捞工作，截至1994年出水8000多件器物，但后因技术和资金问题被迫中止。1996年，太平洋海洋资源公司取得资格开始重新打捞，项目由Michael Flecker负责。

船体木质结构不存，但遗址上的铁凝结物则保留下船舱的布局形态，推测原来船体长28～30、宽约8米（图五二）。发现两片木块有明显的木钉孔，证明造船使用的是拼板技术。另外，船板木料检测为东南亚地区产的马来蔷薇和糖胶树，说明该船很可能是印尼建造的拼板船。然而隔舱的存在又被认为是南中国海传统船型的特征，因此泰国也有可能是该船的建造地。

船货主要是铁器，绝大部分已形成凝结物，估计重达190吨，其中包括铁锅和铁条；其他遗物还有陶瓷器、青铜像、铜镜、玻璃、乳香、砺石、象牙、铜、锡块等（图五三）。根据香料的^{14}C测定并结合陶瓷年代特征，研究者判断其沉没时间为13世纪中后期。

[36] William M. Mathers and Michael Flecker: *Archaeological Recovery of the Java Sea Wreck*, Pacific Sea Resources, 1997, pp.1-94. Michael Flecker. The 13th Century Java Sea Wreck: A Chinese Cargo in an Indonesian Ship. *The Mariner's Mirror*, Vol.89 No.4, November 2003, pp.388-404.

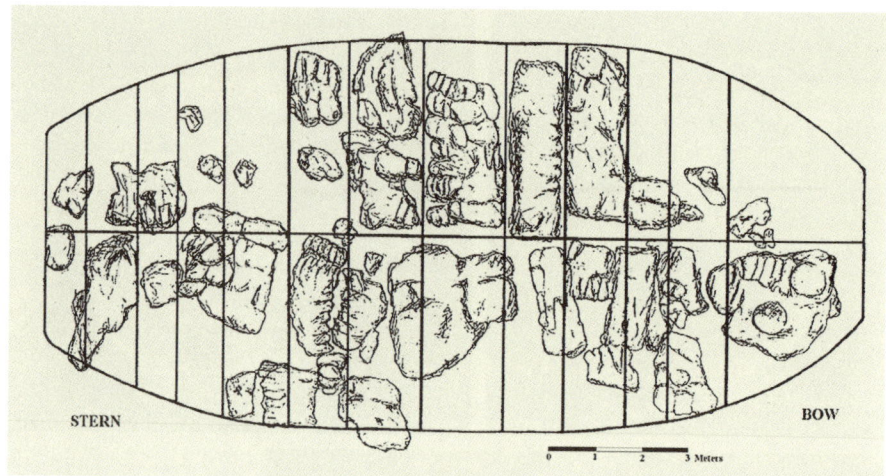

图五二 爪哇海沉船结构平面示意图

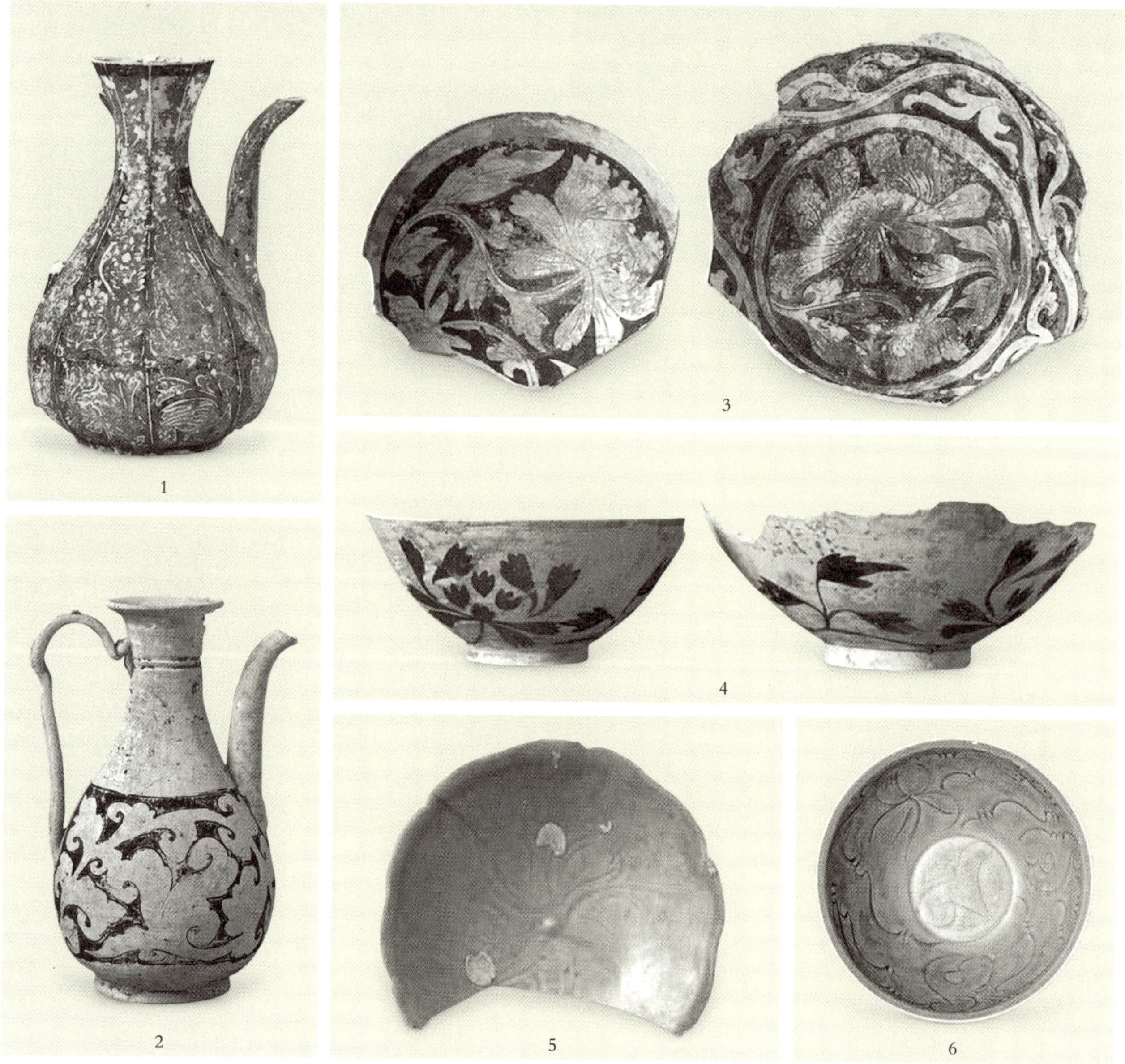

图五三（1） 爪哇海沉船出水器物

1~6. 瓷器

图五三（2） 爪哇海沉船出水器物

7～10. 瓷器　11. 铜锣　12. 铜锭　13. 铁锅　14、15. 铁条材

10. 枢府沉船（Shufu Wreck）[37]

该沉船2005~2006年发现于印尼马都拉岛（Madura）海域，之后并未开展考古工作而是遭到当地渔民盗捞，致使大量出水瓷器被人为损坏并流入古董市场。目前所知，这批瓷器全由敞口式的枢府瓷组成，包括卵白釉印花圆曲腹小碗、侈口花口小碗、印花小盘、侈口印花波浪纹大碗等（图五四）。同国内高安、集宁等地出土的枢府瓷相比，这批沉船瓷器的烧成温度较低，釉质玻璃感不强，多气孔、火刺，施釉不均，且多数有变形。这与东南亚地区发现的德化白瓷情况类似，折射出东南亚陶瓷贸易的一个侧面，即由于缺少本地竞争，中国的次等陶瓷可以畅销无阻。

[37] Roberto Gardellin. Shipwrecks around Indonesia, pp.16-17. 童歆编译：《海外陶瓷考古新发现》，《陶瓷考古通讯》2013年第2期，页70。

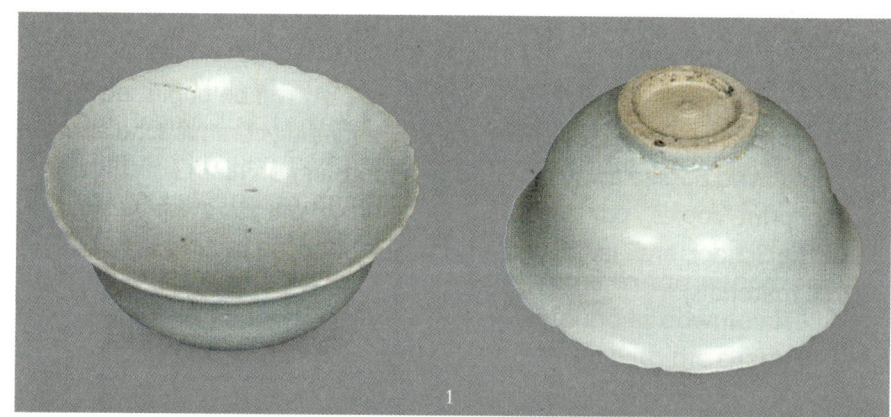

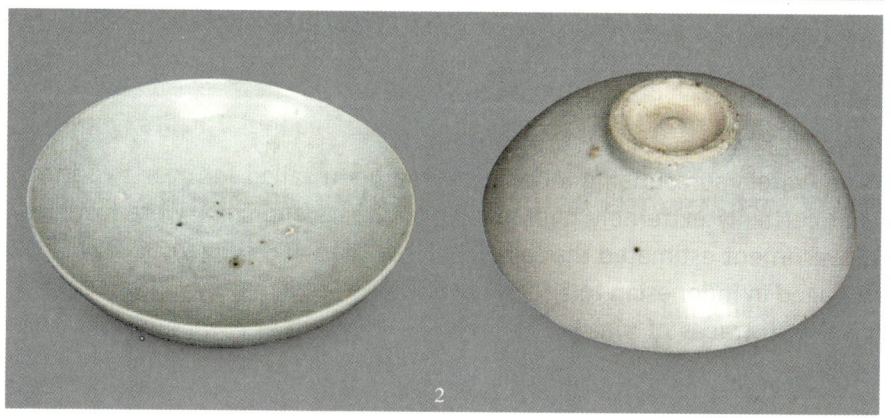

图五四　枢府沉船出水瓷器
1. 卵白釉花口小碗　2. 卵白釉印花盘

三

沉船的研究——以船货为中心

综观上述9～14世纪沉船，陶瓷器和金属器为其运载量最大的货品，反映了早期贸易阶段的商品构成情况，是研究海上贸易史最直观的材料。目前，针对相关陶瓷和金属船货的研究，可分为围绕单艘沉船的讨论以及参考多艘沉船的综合研究。

由于资料发布等多种原因，对泰国、菲律宾、马来西亚地区沉船的研究少见，目前单艘沉船的讨论主要集中于中国和印度尼西亚地区的发现。作为具有重大发现意义且材料发布较为充分的几处沉船遗址，泉州湾海船[38]、"南海Ⅰ号"沉船[39]、华光礁一号沉船[40]、"黑石号"沉船[41]、"井里汶"沉船[42]都有系列研究文章。此外，"印坦"沉船、"爪哇海"沉船及"鳄鱼岛"沉船出版过考古报告或类似的资料汇编，发掘者及研究者对其中出水的船货或多或少都进行了分析和研究[43]。

最早对包括上文大部分9～14世纪沉船在内的南海及东南亚海域沉船进行整理，并利用船货资料开展考古学研究，是美国学者罗珊娜·布朗（Roxanna Brown）。所著《明代间隔期与东南亚沉船陶瓷：对泰国贸易陶瓷的编年研究》[44]一书，以南海和东南亚海域为主，兼及印度洋及以西、东亚与美洲间太平洋海域的沉船，从分区和编年两方面进行列举并附参考文献。在此基础上，选取14世纪晚期至15世纪的东南亚沉船遗址，通过对其中出水陶瓷器的研究，以实物资料论证并展示了"明代间隔期"这一概念。之后又结合陆上发现，对14～16世纪泰国贸易陶瓷进行编年。无论是基础资料整理还是研究思路方法，布朗的工作无疑为其后南海及东南亚海域沉船的考古研究提供了极富价值的参考。

利用本文所论9～14世纪东南亚沉船材料进行的研究，主要有秦大树《试论早期阶段海上贸易的模式——9～10世纪的文献记载及沉船资料》[45]以及戴柔星《东南亚发现的宋元时期沉船出水陶瓷研究》[46]。前文通过9～10世纪东南亚沉船出水材料，分析了当时中国外销瓷贸易的特点，并结合船货的多样性与丰富性，论证了室利佛逝在9～10世纪环印度洋贸易圈中所处的中心位置。戴柔星的研究则是以东南亚发现的10艘宋元时期沉船为对象，通过将其中出水陶瓷与纪

[38] 福建省泉州海外交通史博物馆：《泉州湾宋代海船发掘与研究》下编《泉州湾宋代海船研究论文选》，页75～183。王曾瑜：《宋代的铜钱出口——兼谈泉州发掘的宋船铜钱》，《海交史研究》1978年第1期，页54～57。

[39] 孙键：《南宋沉船与宋代瓷器外销》，《中国文化遗产》2007年第4期，页32～45。李庆新：《南宋海外贸易中的外销瓷、钱币、金属制品及其他问题——基于"南海Ⅰ号"沉船出水遗物的初步考察》，《学术月刊》2012年第9期，页126～129。张万星：《广东"南海Ⅰ号"沉船船货的内涵与性质》，《海洋遗产与考古》，北京：科学出版社，2012年，页138～154。

[40] 海南省博物馆：《大海的方向：华光礁Ⅰ号沉船特展》，南京：凤凰出版社，2011年。孙键：《南宋沉船与宋代瓷器外销》，页32～45。刘薇、张治国、李秀辉、马清林《中国南海三处古代沉船遗址出水铁器凝结物分析》，《中国国家博物馆馆刊》2011年第2期，页145～156。杨传森、王菊琳、张治国：《华光礁出水铁器腐蚀产物及脱盐研究》，《化工学报》2011年第9期，页2582～2587。马丹、郑幼明：《"华光礁一号"南宋沉船船板中硫铁化合物分析》，《文物保护与考古科学》2012年第3期，页84～89。包春磊：《华光礁Ⅰ号出水铁器文物的腐蚀与保护措施》，《腐蚀与防护》2012年第7期，页614～625。

年墓和窑址发现的材料进行比对，并结合船上其他纪年材料与测年数据，讨论了每艘沉船的年代。然后在此基础上，对宋元中国瓷器外销阶段进行分期，并从器物组合、釉类组合、器物类型及形制等方面详细介绍了每一期沉船出水陶瓷的特点。此外，作者还通过沉船位置及船体结构，讨论了宋元时期中国与东南亚海上贸易的航线及船型问题。

除了陶瓷器以外，也已有针对这些沉船金属船货的专门研究。童歆《9至14世纪南海及周边海域沉船出水中国产金属器研究》[47]在全面搜集30艘沉船资料的基础上，分析整理出遗物中的中国产金属器，包括金银器、银锭、铜钱、铜镜、铜铙、铜锣、铁器、铅锭、铅钱等。结合沉船背景，利用考古学方法，对各类遗物进行形制分析，并根据陆上发现与沉船时代，判断制作年代。其中，除略早于沉船时间的情况外，还发现有前代器物存在。考察金属遗物在沉船中的功能性质，确定目前发现的金银器、铁条材、铅锭为贸易船货，而银锭、钱币、铜镜、铜锣、铁锅、铁釜则具有船货与非船货两种属性。文章还进一步结合文献史料，讨论了船货金属器反映的中国金属输出与海上贸易有关问题，同时也涉及非船货金属器所见的船上生活与信仰活动。总结归纳有以下几点：9～14世纪中国外销金属器的生产与输出集中于沿海港口及其内陆腹地，尤以广东、福建为最；中国金属船货销往东南亚大部分地区，其中铜铁制品最具市场，贸易规模庞大；交易方式存在9～10世纪苏门答腊岛至爪哇岛之间的转运贸易，以及从11世纪晚期开始中国商船行至各地的直接贸易；贵金属与贱金属船货分别反映了海外贸易高价商品与平价货物不同的单位价值；官方政策影响下产品的流向，特别是政权对特定金属实施的禁榷，决定了中国金属器外销或官或私的性质；非船货金属器中既有船员物品，也有航海所需的实用器，以及祭神祈福仪式用品。

新加坡学者王添顺（Derek Heng）在其研究10～14世纪中国与马来地区贸易及外交的著作[48]中，用一章讨论中国输入马来地区的产品，其中包括陶瓷器、金属器及丝绸制品等。他利用文献、东南亚陆上考古发现以及泉州湾海船、"图日昂"沉船、"鳄鱼岛"沉船、"黑石号"沉船、"印坦"沉船以及"爪哇海"沉船的实物材料，对贸易品及其背后的区域海上贸易史进行了讨论。虽然不是从专门的考古学角度出发，又限于马来地区，但其对材料的分析以及讨论的有关问题，对讨论南海及东南亚海域沉船金属沉船及其背后的历史意义有着重要的参考价值。

---

[41] Regina Krahl, John Guy, Keith Wilson, and Julian Raby eds., *Shipwrecked: Tang Treasures and Monsoon Winds*, Smithsonian Books, 2011. 谢明良：《记黑石号（Batu Hitam）沉船中的中国陶瓷器》，《"国立"台湾大学美术史研究集刊》第13期，台北：台湾大学艺术史研究所，2002年，页1~60。齐东方：《海底宝藏——黑石号沉船铜镜与瓷器》《黑石号沉船上的中国金银器》《黑石号沉船与扬州的海外贸易》，待刊。

[42] 李旻：《十世纪爪哇海上的世界舞台——对井里汶沉船上金属物资的观察》，页78~90；秦大树：《拾遗南海 补阙中土——谈井里汶沉船的出水瓷器》，页91~101；沈岳明：《越窑的发展及井里汶沉船的越窑瓷器》，页102~106；约翰N·米希著，辛光灿译：《井里汶沉船的精致陶器——始发地、目的地和意义》，页107~114；扬之水：《对沉船中几类器物的初步考订》，页115~124；齐东方：《玻璃料与八卦镜——井里汶沉船文物札记》，页125~135；潘华美著，项坤鹏译：《密宗佛教金刚乘仪式中的青铜器》，页136~140；袁婕：《室利佛逝及沉船出水的密宗法器》，页141~144；马金龙著，项坤鹏译：《中东、南亚、东南亚和中国：早期地区间海上贸易的一个注记》，页145~150，以上均刊于《故宫博物院院刊》2007年第6期。

[43] 参见文章第二部分各沉船引用资料。

[44] Roxanna Brown. *The Ming Gap and Shipwreck Ceramics in Southeast Asia: Towards a Chronology of Thai Trade Ware*, River Books, 2009.

四

结语

同所有考古遗址一样，一艘沉船从沉没事件发生，到遗址形成保存，再到被后世重新发现，都是一系列偶然和随机事件的组成。因此，必须首先认识到沉船资料对于历史研究的局限性。正如本文所论9～14世纪亚洲地中海的沉船，其中属于11世纪的发现就很少。但从大量的史料记载可知，北宋时期，海外贸易蓬勃发展，往来中外的商船应是络绎不绝。不过，另一方面，文献本身也并非包罗万象，甚至存在疏误错漏。每一艘沉船的发现无疑都是历史拼图上重要的一块，除了印证并更直观地呈现文字记载，还往往在文献不及之处补充新材料，提供新认识，其中有的甚至具有颠覆意义。

[45] 秦大树：《试论早期阶段海上贸易的模式——9～10世纪的文献记载及沉船资料》，《徐苹芳先生纪念文集》，上海：上海古籍出版社，2012年，页234～252。

[46] 戴柔星：《东南亚发现的宋元时期沉船出水陶瓷研究》，北京大学博士研究生学位论文，2012年。

[47] 童歆：《9至14世纪南海及周边海域沉船出水中国产金属器研究》，北京大学硕士研究生学位论文，2014年。

[48] Derek Heng, *Sino-Malay Trade and Diplomacy from the Tenth through the Fourteenth Century*, Ohio University Press, 2009.

引用书目

近人论著

包春磊：《华光礁Ⅰ号出水铁器文物的腐蚀与保护措施》，《腐蚀与防护》2012年第7期，页614～625。

崔勇：《"南海Ⅰ号"的发现与调查》，《中国文化遗产》2007年第4期，页12～18。

崔勇：《"南海Ⅰ号"发现始末》，《广东艺术》2008年第2期，页17～21。

戴柔星：《东南亚发现的宋元时期沉船出水陶瓷研究》，北京大学博士研究生学位论文，2012年。

〔英〕杜希德、思鉴：《沉船遗宝：一艘十世纪沉船上的中国银锭》，《唐研究》第十卷，北京：北京大学出版社，2004年，页382～431。

福建省泉州海外交通史博物馆：《泉州湾宋代海船发掘与研究》，北京：海洋出版社，1987年。

广东海上丝绸之路博物馆等：《海上敦煌——探秘"南海Ⅰ号"》，广州：南方日报出版社，2010年。

广东省文物管理委员会等：《南海丝绸之路文物图集》，广州：广东科技出版社，1991年。

广东省文物考古研究所：《2011"南海Ⅰ号"的考古试掘》，北京：科学出版社，2011年。

广州博物馆、广东省博物馆、香港市政局：《南海海上交通二千年》，香港市政局，1996年。

海南省博物馆：《大海的方向：华光礁Ⅰ号沉船特展》，南京：凤凰出版社，2011年。

洪晓纯：《台湾史前玉器在东南亚的分布及其意义》，《华南及东南亚地区史前考古：纪念甑皮岩遗址发掘三十周年国际学术研讨会论文集》，北京：文物出版社，2006年，页324～340。

赖珊珊：《从定海湾沉船看闽江下游的海洋文化》，厦门大学硕士学位论文，2009年5月。

〔泰〕黎道纲:《泰国古代史地丛考》,北京:中华书局,2000年。

李旻:《十世纪爪哇海上的世界舞台——对井里汶沉船上金属物资的观察》,《故宫博物院院刊》2007年第6期,页78~90。

李庆新:《"南海Ⅰ号"与海上丝绸之路》,北京:五洲传播出版社,2010年。

李庆新:《南宋海外贸易中的外销瓷、钱币、金属制品及其他问题——基于"南海Ⅰ号"沉船出水遗物的初步考察》,《学术月刊》2012年第9期,页121~131。

栗建安:《福建水下考古工作回顾》,《福建文博》1997年第2期,页19~22、46。

栗建安:《定海水下文物的发现及其相关问题》,《福建文博》1997年第2期,页31~39。

梁志明、李谋、杨保筠:《东南亚古代史:上古至16世纪初》,北京:北京大学出版社,2013年。

凌纯声:《中国古代海洋文化与亚洲地中海》,《海外杂志》第3卷第10期,页7~10,1954年;后收入《中国边疆民族与环太平洋文化:凌纯声先生论文集》,台北:联经出版社业公司,1979年,页335~344。

刘薇、张治国、李秀辉、马清林:《中国南海三处古代沉船遗址出水铁器凝结物分析》,《中国国家博物馆馆刊》2011年第2期,页145、156。

马丹、郑幼明:《"华光礁一号"南宋沉船船板中硫铁化合物分析》,《文物保护与考古科学》2012年第3期,页84~89。

平潭大练岛元代沉船遗址水下考古队:《平潭大练岛Ⅰ号沉船遗址水下考古发掘收获》,《福建文博》2008年第1期,页21~26。

齐东方:《玻璃料与八卦镜——井里汶沉船文物札记》,《故宫博物院院刊》2007年第6期,页125~135。

齐东方:《海底宝藏——黑石号沉船铜镜与瓷器》《黑石号沉船上的中国金银器》《黑石号沉船与扬州的海外贸易》,待刊。

秦大树:《试论早期阶段海上贸易的模式——9~10世纪的文献记载及沉船资料》,《徐苹芳先生纪念文集》,上海:上海古籍出版社,2012年,页234~252。

秦大树、袁旃:《古丝绸之路:2011亚洲跨文化交流与文化遗产国际学术研讨会论文集》,新加坡:世纪科技出版公司,2013年。

泉州湾宋代海船发掘报告编写组:《泉州湾宋代海船发掘简报》,《文物》1975年第10期,页1~18。

〔法〕G·赛代斯著,蔡华、杨保筠译:《东南亚的印度化国家》,北京:商务印书馆,2008年。

孙键:《南宋沉船与宋代瓷器外销》,《中国文化遗产》2007年第4期,页32~45。

孙键、李滨、徐海滨:《揭秘华光礁一号沉船》,《华夏地理》2007年第10期,页158~169。

Adi Agung Tirtamarta撰、辛光灿译:《井里汶海底十世纪沉船打捞纪实》,《故宫博物院院刊》2007年第6期,页151~154。

童歆:《9至14世纪南海及周边海域沉船出水中国产金属器研究》,北京大学硕士研究生学位论文,2014年6月。

魏峻:《"南海Ⅰ号"2007整体打捞》,《中国文化遗产》2007年第4期,页19~28。

魏峻:《"南海Ⅰ号"沉船考古与水下文化遗产保护》,《文化遗产》2008年第1期,页148~153。

吴春明:《环中国海沉船——古代帆船、船技与船货》,南昌:江西高校出版社,2003年。

谢明良:《记黑石号(Batu Hitam)沉船中的中国陶瓷器》,《"国立"台湾大学美术史研究集刊》第13期,台北:台湾大学艺术史研究所,2002年,页1~60。

杨传森、王菊琳、张治国：《华光礁出水铁器腐蚀产物及脱盐研究》，《化工学报》2011年第9期，页2582~2587。

张万星：《广东"南海Ⅰ号"沉船船货的内涵与性质》，《海洋遗产与考古》，北京：科学出版社，2012年，页138~154。

张威：《西沙群岛华光礁Ⅰ号沉船遗址抢救性发掘》，《2007中国重要考古发现》，北京：文物出版社，2008年，页173~176。

张威、吴春明、林果：《关于福建定海沉船考古的有关问题》，《东南考古研究》第二辑，厦门：厦门大学出版社，1999年，页199~207。

赵嘉斌、吴春明：《福建连江定海湾沉船考古》，北京：科学出版社，2011年。

郑培凯：《十二至十五世纪中国外销瓷与海外贸易国际研讨会论文集》，香港：中华书局，2005年。

中澳合作水下考古专业人员培训班定海调查发掘队：《中国福建连江定海1990年度调查、试掘报告》，《中国历史博物馆馆刊》1992年第18~19期，页242~251。

中澳联合定海水下考古队：《福建定海沉船遗址1995年度调查与发掘》，《东南考古研究》第二辑，厦门：厦门大学出版社，1999年，页186~198。

中国国家博物馆水下考古研究中心、福建博物院文物考古研究所：《福建平潭分流尾屿五代沉船遗址调查》，《中国国家博物馆馆刊》2011年第11期，页18~25。

中国国家博物馆水下考古研究中心、福建博物院文物考古研究所、福州市文物考古工作队编著：《福建平潭大练岛元代沉船遗址》，北京：科学出版社，2014年。

中国国家博物馆水下考古研究中心、海南省文物保护管理办公室：《西沙水下考古1998~1999》，北京：科学出版社，2006年。

中国国家博物馆水下考古研究中心、海南省文物局：《西沙群岛石屿二号沉船遗址调查简报》，《中国国家博物馆馆刊》2011年第11期，页26~46。

中国科学院自然科学史研究所、福建省泉州海外交通史博物馆联合试掘组：《泉州法石古船试掘简报和初步探讨》，《自然科学史研究》1983年第2期，页164~172。

中国社会科学院考古研究所：《华南及东南亚地区史前考古：纪念甑皮岩遗址发掘三十周年国际学术研讨会论文集》，北京：文物出版社，2006年。

Atkinson, Karen, Jeremy Green, Rosemary Harper and Vidya Intakosai. 1989. "Joint Thai-Australian underwater archaeological project 1987−1988 Part 1: Archaeological survey of wreck sites in the Gulf of Thailand, 1987−1988", *International Journal of Nautical Archaeology*, Volume 18, Issue 4, pp. 299−315.

Brown, Roxanna. 2009. *The Ming Gap and Shipwreck Ceramics in Southeast Asia: Towards a Chronology of Thai Trade Ware*, River Books.

Brown, Roxanna and Pariwat Thammapreechakorn eds. 2005. "Earliest China-built Ship in the Philippines", *Southeast Asian Ceramics Museum Newsletter*, Vol.2, No.2, pp. 1, 4.

Brown, Roxanna and Sten Sjostrand. 2000. *Turiang: A Fourteenth-Century Shipwreck in Southeast Asian Waters*, Pasadena: Pacific Asia Museum.

Brown, 2002. *Maritime Archaeology and Shipwreck Ceramics in Malaysia*, Kuala Lumpur: Department of Museums and Antiquities.

Chiew, Lim Yahand and Natalie Ong. 2010. "Five Dynasty Treasures: Chinese Ceramics found in the Indonesian Cirebon Shipwreck", *Southeast Asian Ceramic Society*.

Clark, Paul, Eduardo Conese, Norman Nicolas, Jeremy Green. 1989. "Philippines archaeological

Dizon, Eusebio Z. 2003. "Underwater and Maritime Archaeology in the Philippines", *Philippine Quarterly of Culture and Society*, Vol.31, pp. 1−25.

Djuana, Atma and Edmund Edwards McKinnon.2005. "The Jepara Wreck", *Proceedings of the International Conference: Chinese Export Ceramics and Maritime Trade, 12th−15th Centuries*, ed.Cheng Pei-Kai, Hong Kong: Chungwa Publishing, pp. 126−142.

Dupoizat, Marie-France. 1995. "The Ceramic Cargo of a Song Dynasty Junk Found in the Philippines and its Significance in the China-South East Asia Trade", *South East Asia and China: Art, Interaction and Commerce*, eds. Rosemary Scott and John Guy, Percival David Foundation of Chinese Art.

Dupoizat, Marie-France. 2007. "The Ceramics of the Investigator Shipwreck", Paper presented at the Symposium on Chinese Export Ceramics Trade in Southeast Asia, organized by Asian Research Institute, National University of Singapore, 12th−14th, March.

Flecker, Michael. 2000. "A 9th-century Arab or Indian shipwreck in Indonesian Waters", *The International Journal of Nautical Archaeology*, Vol.29, No.2, pp. 199−217.

Flecker, Michael. 2001. "A Ninth Century AD Arab or Indian Shipwreck in Indonesia: First Evidence for Direct Trade with China", *World Archaeology*, Vol.32, No.3, pp. 335−354.

Flecker, Michael. 2002. *The Archaeological Excavation of the 10th Century Intan Shipwreck*, Ph. D dissertation, National University of Singapore, 2001, Archaeopress.

Flecker, Michael. 2003. "The Thirteenth-Century Java Sea Wreck: A Chinese Cargo in an Indonesian Ship", *The Mariner's Mirror*, Vol.89 No.4, November, pp. 388−404.

Flecker, Michael. 2008. "A 9th-century Arab or Indian shipwreck in Indonesian Waters: Addendum", *The International Journal of Nautical Archaeology*, Vol.37, No.2, pp. 384−386.

Flecker, Michael. 2013. "The China-Borneo Ceramics Trade Around the 13th Century: The Story of Two Wrecks", 2011《古丝绸之路: 亚洲跨文化交流与文化遗产国际学术研讨会论文集》, eds. Qin Dashu and Yuan Jian, Singapore: Global Publishing, pp. 159−186.

Gardellin, Roberto. 2013. "Shipwrecks around Indonesia", *The Oriental Ceramic Society Newsletter*, No.21, pp. 15−19.

Goddio, Frank, et al. 1997. *Weisses Gold*, Göttingen: Steidl Verlag.

Green, Jeremy. 1983. "The Ko Si Chang Excavation Report 1983", *Bulletin Australian Institute for Maritime Archaeology*, No.7(2), pp. 9−37.

Green, Jeremy and Rosemary Harper. 1983. *The Excavation of the Pattaya Wreck Site and Survey of Three Other Sites, Thailand, 1982*, Australian Institute for Maritime Archaeology Special Publication No.1.

Green, Jeremy and Rosemary Harper. 1987. *The Maritime Archaeology of Shipwrecks and Ceramics in Southeast Asia: the Maritime Connection*, Australian Institute for Maritime Archaeology Special Publication No.4.

Green, Jeremy and Vidya Intakosai. 1983. "The Pattaya Wreck Site Excavation, Thailand, an Interim Report", *The International Journal of Nautical Archaeology and Underwater Exploration*, Vol. 12(1), pp. 3−13.

Heng, Derek Thiam Soon. 2009. *Sino-Malay Trade and Diplomacy from the Tenth through the Fourteenth Century*, Ohio University Press.

KJPP Abdullah Fitriantoro and Rekan eds. 2011. *Katalog Kapal Karam Abad ke-10 di Laut Jawa Utara Cirebon*, Kementerian Kelautan dan Perikanan Direktorat Jenderal Kelautan, Pesisir dan Pulau-pulau Kecil Satuan Kerja Direktorat Pesisir dan Lautan, Jakarta.

Krahl, Regina, John Guy, Keith Wilson, and Julian Raby eds. 2011. *Shipwrecked: Tang Treasures and Monsoon Winds*, Smithsonian Books.

Lee, Hock Guan. 2013. "Tamil Merchants in India and Abroad (9th–14th Centuries)", *The Newsletter of International Institute for Asian Studies*, No.63, network 39.

Liebner, Horst. 2009. *The 'Karawang' Wreck: A Cargo of 10th Century Trade Ceramics*, Jakarta: PT Putera Paradigma Sejahtera-PT Nautik Recovery Asia.

Liebner, Horst. 2010. "Cargoes for Java: Interpreting Two 10th Century Shipwrecks", paper for 13th International Conference of the European Association of Southeast Asian Archaeologists (EurASEAA13), Berlin.

Mathers, William M. and Michael Flecker. 1997. *Archaeological Recovery of the Java Sea Wreck*, Pacific Sea Resources.

Ridho, Abu, and E. Edwards McKinnon ed. 1998. *The Pulau Buaya Wreck: Finds from the Song Period*, The Ceramic Society of Indonesia.

Wade, Geoff. 2009. "An Early Age of Commerce in Southeast Asia, 900–1300 CE", *Journal of Southeast Asian Studies*, No.2, pp. 221–265.

http://www.shipwreckasia.org/ ——亚洲各地区沉船信息在建数据库。

http://maritimeasia.ws/index.html ——提供东南亚沉船发现资料与研究成果。

http://cirebon.musee-mariemont.be/home-6.htm?lng=en ——发布井里汶沉船资料与研究成果。

http://www.maritime-explorations.com/ ——由Michael Flecker创建，发布其发掘或正在发掘的沉船信息与研究资料。

http://www.mingwrecks.com/tgsimpang.html；http://www.maritimeasia.ws/tsimpang/ ——"丹绒新邦"沉船资料。

http://www.maritimeasia.ws/turiang/ ——"图日昂"沉船资料。

关于奥美尼角沉船遗址的初步认识

The Preliminary Research on the Ngomeni Ras Shipwreck Site

邓启江[1]　张　辉[2]　曾　瑾[3]

（1.国家文物局水下文化遗产保护中心；2.安徽省文物考古研究所；3.吉安市博物馆）

DENG Qi-jiang[1]　ZHANG Hui[2]　ZENG Jin[3]

(1.National Center of Underwater Cultural Heritage; 2.Anhui Provincial Institute of Cultural Relics and Archaeology; 3.Ji'an Museum)

内容摘要 /

奥美尼角沉船遗址是肯尼亚和东非的一次重大考古新发现，为探讨肯尼亚乃至东非沿海贸易提供了珍贵的资料，也为海上贸易与交流史研究提供了新的实物资料。本文以2013年度奥美尼角沉船遗址水下考古发掘为基础重点探讨了遗址所在海域的水文环境、遗址船体结构和部分出水文物等相关问题，并对奥美尼角沉船遗址的时代和性质进行了初步分析。

关键词 /

奥美尼角沉船遗址　水文环境　船体　出水文物　时代　性质

ABSTRACT / Ngomeni Ras shipwreck site is a new important archaeological discovery in Kenya and East Africa. It supplies valuable document for the research on coast trade around Kenya and East Africa. Even more it supplies some material data for the research on ocean trade and communication history. This article discusses some problems about the hydrology surrounding, ship structure and artifacts basing upon the excavation of Ngomeni Ras shipwreck site in 2013. Further more this article analyses the date and character of Ngomeni Ras shipwreck site.

KEY WORDS / Ngomeni Ras shipwreck site; hydrology surrounding; ship structure; artifacts; date; character

奥美尼角沉船遗址位于肯尼亚马林迪市奥美尼镇东北方向3～4海里的海域，东南距海岸线300米。2013年11月20日至2014年1月8日由中国国家博物馆和肯尼亚国家博物馆组成的中肯联合水下考古工作队对奥美尼角沉船遗址进行了正式的水下考古发掘[1]（图一）。

该遗址凸出于沙质海床之上，呈东北—西南长条状走向，最长处约47、最宽处近17米，总面积500平方米，遗址表面散落有大量的石块和多个高大的凝结物，个别凝结物高度达2米左右。遗址主体为一艘木质沉船残骸，残存船体长约36.4、宽约10米，方向60°，沉船船体边缘之上覆盖有一层厚度不均的黄沙，船体主体部分为凝结物和石块覆盖（图二）。

[1] 中国国家博物馆水下考古研究中心、肯尼亚国家博物馆滨海考古部：《肯尼亚马林迪奥美尼角沉船遗址2013年度水下考古发掘简报》，《中国国家博物馆馆刊》2014年第9期，页6～23。下文奥美尼角沉船遗址的材料皆出自于此文。

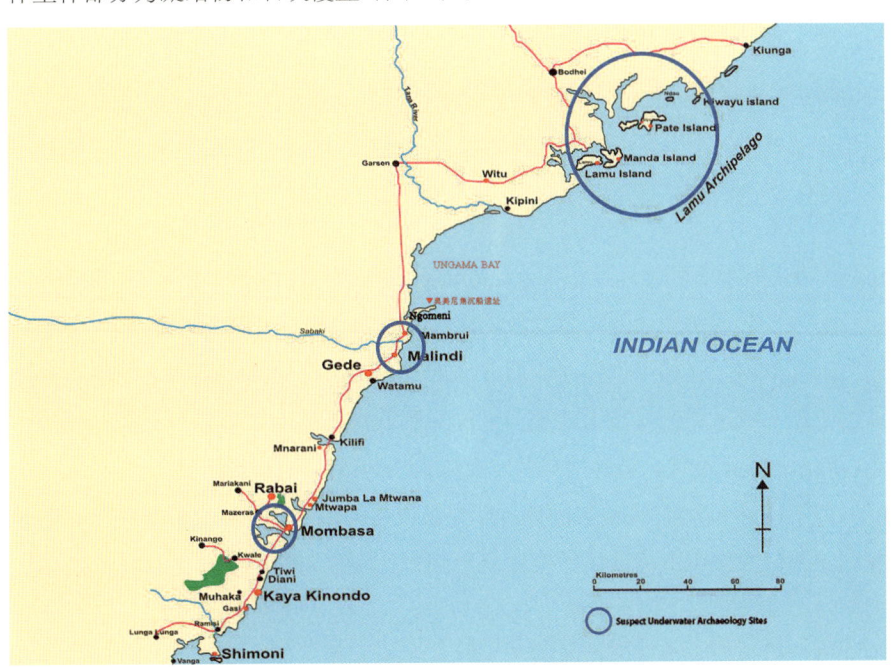

图一　奥美尼角沉船遗址地理位置图
（蓝色圆圈为2010～2013年中肯合作水下考古工作区域）

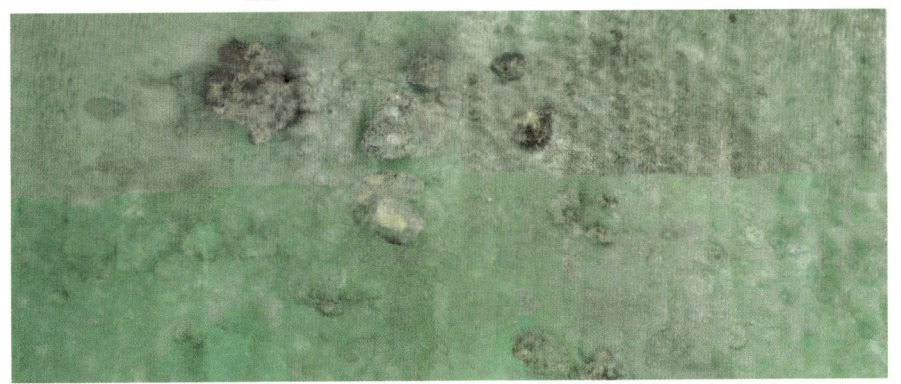

图二　奥美尼角沉船遗址发掘前水下全貌（摄影拼接）

马林迪奥美尼角沉船遗址水下考古发掘是自20世纪70年代蒙巴萨沉船遗址发掘以来，时隔30余年后肯尼亚又一项重要的水下考古发掘工作，该沉船遗址是肯尼亚乃至东非的一次重大考古发现，为探讨肯尼亚乃至东非沿海贸易提供了珍贵的资料，也为海上贸易与交流史研究提供了新的实物资料。

作为此项水下考古工作的参与者，笔者对马林迪奥美尼角沉船遗址有如下初步认识，望各位方家不吝指教。

一

沉船遗址所在海域的水文环境

马林迪奥美尼镇位于肯尼亚中东部、印度洋西海岸，当地气候及生态环境主要受到来自印度洋的热带洋流和季风的影响，同时印度洋的热带洋流和季风也对东非、红海、印度以及东南亚之间的航线和海上贸易产生了重要的影响。

来自马达加斯加北部和科摩罗的印度洋南赤道热带洋流在坦桑尼亚中南部进入东非海岸，这种热带洋流随后分成两支，一支在返回印度洋之前向北经过肯尼亚东北海岸到达索马里南部，被称为东非海岸洋流，另外一支经过莫桑比克后向南返回印度洋，被称为莫桑比克洋流或马达加斯加洋流[2]。

每年11月至次年3月奥美尼角沉船遗址所在的东非海岸盛行东北季风，船舶在东北季风的作用下可以从印度洋航行到东非海岸，并在莫桑比克洋流或马达加斯加洋流的影响下通过莫桑比克海峡向南一直到达刚果的基尔瓦；从5月开始东非海岸转为西南季风，在西南季风和东非海岸洋流的共同作用下船舶可以从南部向北航行至坦桑尼亚中部和肯尼亚，因此船舶如果想要去往更北的地方如印度、中东以及红海，必须要借助于一直持续到10月的西南季风[3]。

奥美尼角沉船遗址凸出于较为平坦的沙质海床表面，水深4～6米，水温常年20°左右。遗址所在海域海平面的起伏、海水流向、流速以及水下能见度等主要受到印度洋北向热带洋流和季风的影响，同时由于遗址所在位置与奥美尼镇码头之间的海域有两道东南—西北走向的沙岗，低平潮时甚至露出海平面，这两道沙岗在潮汐转换时也会影响到遗址所在海域的海况。

通常情况下，奥美尼角沉船遗址所在海域涨潮时水下能见度较好，退潮期水下能见度很差，最差时水下能见度几乎为零，受到东南-西北走向二道沙岗的阻挡影响，海水流速及流向在潮汐转换之间变化不大；西南季风时遗址所在海

[2] Felix A.Chami. *Zanzibar And The Swahili Coast From c30, 000 Years Ago*, E&D Vision Publishing Limited, 2009, p.31-37.

[3] Felix Chami. *The Tanzanian Coast in the First Millennium AD*, Societas Archaeologica Upsaliensis. Uppsala, 1994, p.34-42.

域水质较清，水下能见度较好；东北季风时海面有涌浪，水下也有涌浪，水下能见度不佳。

二

沉船船体结构

由于奥美尼角沉船遗址分布范围较广，囿于工作时间限制，2013年度中肯联合水下考古工作队仅发掘了遗址总体范围的四分之一，但是通过在遗址中发掘纵横两条探沟还是获取了船体的分布范围和基本结构等重要信息。

奥美尼角沉船船体为木质，上层建筑和甲板已不见，残存船体底部；近底部的船壳外板、肋骨、舱底垫板、隔板等主要构件保存较好，清晰可辨且复原性高；船壳外板单层、厚实，肋骨密集、粗壮，舱底垫板单层、轻薄，船材外包铅皮、中缝填塞铅条，造船工艺独特而富有研究价值（图三）。

根据发掘过程中揭露的船体看奥美尼角沉船遗址船体有如下特点：

（1）船壳板只有一层，大多宽15～30厘米，亦有一小部分宽35～40、厚8～10厘米。船壳板外部包裹有一层铅皮，铅皮通过铁钉固定在船壳板之上（图四），相邻的船壳板之间大多数为纵向平接，局部位置受船材的限制也有使用榫卯拼接的情况（图五）。船壳板之间用粗细、长短不一的铅条填塞缝隙（图六）。

图三　奥美尼角沉船遗址2013年度发掘区域水下全貌（摄影拼接）

图四　奥美尼角沉船遗址船壳板外包裹铅皮情况

图五　奥美尼角沉船遗址船壳板拼接情况

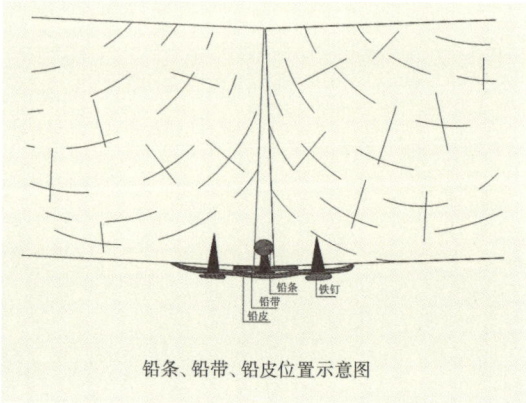

铅条、铅带、铅皮位置示意图

图六　奥美尼角沉船遗址船壳板之间填塞铅条情况

（2）肋骨用材较粗大，一般厚15～26、高15～33、长190厘米以上，大多数肋骨为尽量利用木材，仅在两侧和需要支撑垫板的顶部略加修整成平面，以致形状不太规整，粗细不均，但大部分排列较紧密，揭露完整的肋骨间距多为2～12厘米，肋骨以并排或交错排列的方式与船壳板相连，并使用铁钉固定在船壳板之上（图七）。

图七　奥美尼角沉船遗址肋骨排列情况

（3）垫板铺设于肋骨之上，用于放置船货等，分厚、薄二种（图八）。

一种垫板较薄，厚1～2、宽10～20厘米，这种垫板一般直接纵向铺设于肋骨之上，未见铁钉相连，相邻垫板之间均为平接，薄垫板上保存的船货主要有木桶、原木、象牙、金属盘、铜锭等（图九）。

另一种垫板较厚，约6～10厘米，均为单层铺设于肋骨之上，并以方形铁钉与肋骨相连。这种厚的垫板除个别与薄的垫板混用，主要用于船体中西部。厚垫板上保存的遗物主要为凝结成块状的灰黄色、黑灰色物质以及一些凝结物（图一〇）。

图八　奥美尼角沉船遗址垫板排列情况

图九　奥美尼角沉船遗址薄垫板及文物堆积情况

图一〇　奥美尼角沉船遗址厚垫板及文物堆积情况

（4）奥美尼角沉船遗址发掘过程中没有发现中国传统造船意义上的隔舱板，没有水密舱的设计，船舱或船货之间仅仅使用榫卯结构的隔板相互隔开（图一一）。

 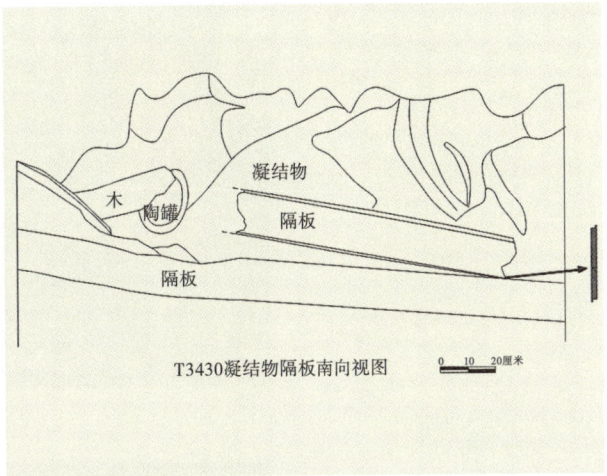

图一一 奥美尼角沉船遗址隔板及文物堆积情况

三

出水文物

2013年度奥美尼角沉船遗址水下考古发掘出水文物标本680余件（片），包括有象牙、铜锭、铜盘、铜范、硫化汞、水银、绿釉陶器、木桶、木质滑轮、石球、圆形穿孔石器、动物骨骼、船钉以及大量带钉孔的铅条、铅带、铅皮等，其中既有船员生活用品，更有运输货物，类型多样且特色鲜明。

1. 铜锭

2013年度奥美尼角沉船遗址水下考古发掘共计出水8件铜锭，除1件采集于遗址西南部边缘外，其余7件皆出自于遗址第②层内。

分布在遗址周边并直接暴露于海床表面上的铜锭外表有一层很薄的绿色铜锈，经过初步检测，这层绿色铜锈的主要成分是碳酸铜（图一二）。

出自于遗址第②层（②层为夹杂有大量黑沙的小石块）的7件铜锭周围分布有大量的原木和船板，铜锭外部皆包裹有一层黑色外壳，黑色外壳壁厚5～7、底厚2～8毫米，外壳内包裹的铜锭皆呈现红铜的本色（图一三）。经过初步检测，黑色外壳的主要成分是含硫的铜氧化物，因此这种黑色外壳应是铜锭在特定埋藏环境下（周围有大量木材，埋藏于夹杂有大量黑沙的小石块内），铜锭本体与大量木材通过分解或受到海洋生物蛀蚀释放出的硫相结合锈蚀而成。

图一二　直接暴露于海床表面的铜锭

图一三　遗址②层内铜锭堆积情况

　　有着相同埋藏环境的铜盘也存在相似的保存现状，铜盘外部有一层黑色外壳，经过初步检测这种黑色外壳的主要成分也是含硫的铜氧化物，其成因应为特定埋藏环境下锈蚀而成（图一四）。

图一四 遗址②层内铜盘堆积情况

2. 硫化汞及水银

从16世纪中叶到19世纪初，欧洲与中国在长达两个半世纪的贸易中一直处于贸易逆差地位，同时16、17世纪中国社会内部对白银有着巨大的需求，而中国的金银比价一直高于欧洲金银市场的比价，欧洲白银的低价和中国的白银高价带来了套汇获利的机会，受利益驱使和贸易逆差的共同影响，欧洲白银被大量运往中国[4]。

欧洲在16世纪50年代之前使用熔炼法生产和提炼白银，产量和纯度较低，无法满足日益增加的白银需求，为了保证流通领域的供需平衡，欧洲开始寻找更多的途径生产和提炼贵金属尤其是白银[5]。

16世纪50年代中期，随着白银提炼过程中汞齐化法的发明和白银生产过程中新的粉碎机、炼炉的使用，欧洲的白银冶炼技术达到空前的工业化水平[6]。

汞齐化法不仅可以提高白银的纯度，还可以大大提高产量，水银作为汞齐化法提炼白银过程中必不可少的一种重要介质，其产量和供应直接影响到白银的生产[7]。

发掘过程中在奥美尼角沉船遗址北部发现有大量块状的硫化汞和液态状的水银（图一五）。固体状的硫化汞不溶于水，物理特性相对比较稳定和安全。硫化汞加热达到580°后快速冷凝可以形成液态状的水银，而直接暴露于空气中的液态状水银在常温下很容易挥发成剧毒的汞蒸汽，但水银在水中状态比较稳定，液态状水银易挥发、有剧毒且不溶于水的特性要求液态状水银必须存储于密闭的容器中或盛水的容器中。

[4] 〔德〕贡德·弗兰克著、刘北成译：《白银资本——重视经济全球化中的东方》，北京：中央编译出版社，2000年，页203～208。李隆生：《晚明海外贸易数量研究——兼论江南丝绸产业与白银流入的影响》，台北：秀威资讯科技股份有限公司，2005年，页101～115。陈昆：《明朝中后期世界白银为何大量流入中国》，中国经济史论坛，http://economy.guoxue.com/?p=7414，2012年10月9日发布。

[5] 曹洁：《论西属美洲殖民地的白银生产》，河北大学历史学硕士学位论文，2010年，页5～10。

[6] 谢乾丰：《16～17世纪世界银冶技术比较研究——以明朝、日本和西属拉丁美洲为对象》，《自然辩证法通讯》第三十一卷，2009年第2期，页75～80。〔英〕莱斯利·贝瑟尔著、中国社科院拉美所组译：《剑桥拉丁美洲史》第二卷，北京：经济管理出版社，1997年，页113～152。

[7] 姜恒尧：《墨西哥殖民地时期白银生产及影响》，北京大学历史学硕士学位论文，2009年，页11～19。

图一五　硫化汞和水银水下分布情况

图一六　船体及原木火烧痕迹

液态状水银及其原料硫化汞同时出现于奥美尼角沉船遗址有两种可能性：

（1）硫化汞和水银都是奥美尼角沉船沉没前装载的物品，在沉没前水银储存于密闭的容器内，沉没后盛于容器内的水银四散分布到船体之上；

（2）只有硫化汞是奥美尼角沉船沉没前装载的物品，奥美尼角沉船北部部分船体及部分原木表面有火烧的痕迹（图一六），大量液态状水银的存在极有可能是船体在沉没前发生过火灾使得部分固体状的硫化汞转化为液态状水银后随船体沉没于海底。

四

沉船遗址时代及性质

奥美尼角沉船遗址2013年度水下考古发掘仅揭露了整个遗址范围的四分之一，但是从已经清理出来的部分船体结构看，奥美尼角沉船遗址船体近底部的船壳板、肋骨、垫板、隔板等主要构件保存较好，船壳板单层、厚实，肋骨排列密集、粗壮，舱底垫板单层、轻薄，不见连续的隔舱板和水密舱设计，船体外包铅皮、中缝填塞铅条，造船工艺较为独特，船体结构与1977～1980年在蒙巴萨发掘的17世纪葡萄牙圣安东尼奥唐纳沉船（Santo Antonio de Tanna）[8]、1999～2000年在葡萄牙里斯本发掘的17世纪葡萄牙胡椒沉船（The Pepper Wreck）[9] 以及2008年在纳米比亚发掘的16世纪葡萄牙奥兰治蒙德沉船（The Oranjemund Shipwreck）[10] 具有一定相似性（图一七），与16～17世纪中国的船型结构有明显的区别[11]。

16～17世纪葡萄牙在造船过程中多采用欧洲橡木建造龙骨和船体框架，使用松木建造船壳板，船壳板外部包裹铅皮以防水，使用铅条和麻絮填塞船壳板之间的缝隙，肋骨排列紧密，没有连续的隔舱板和水密舱设计，在肋骨上部有承梁结构以放置甲板[12]。

而同时期中国造船多使用中国自产的松木、杉木、樟木、楠木等木材，船体横向结构是以排列有一定距离的肋骨和隔舱板构成，纵向结构以龙骨和一层或多层船壳板构成，船壳板外部没有包裹物，船舱内沿用唐代开始的水密舱设计，船板之间多用石灰、桐油混合而成的捻料填塞缝隙[13]。

奥美尼角沉船遗址水下考古发掘出水有铜锭、象牙、原木、石球、铅条、铅皮等文物，与纳米比亚奥兰治蒙德沉船遗址以及里斯本胡椒沉船遗址出水的同类遗物基本一致，尤其是奥美尼角沉船遗址与纳米比亚奥兰治蒙德沉船遗址出水的铜锭底部三叉戟徽章完全相同，这种三叉戟徽章属于16世纪德国著名的富格尔家族[14]（图一八）。

出水文物中数量较多的有铜锭、原木、象牙等。目前通过水下考古工作发现的最早作为船货的铜锭见于1984～1994年在土耳其发掘的前14世纪乌鲁·布鲁恩沉船遗址[15]，纳米比亚发掘的16世纪奥兰治蒙德沉船遗址也发现有大量作为船货的铜锭[16]，由此可见这种铜锭一直是海上贸易中的一种重要商品[17]。

[8] Piercy Robin. Mombassa Wreck Excavation: Preliminary Report, 1977, *International Journal of Nautical Archaeology* 6(4), p.331–347. Piercy Robin, Mombassa Wreck Excavation: Second Preliminary Report, 1978, *International Journal of Nautical Archaeology* 7(4), p.301–319. Piercy Robin. Mombassa Wreck Excavation: Third Preliminary Report, 1979, *International Journal of Nautical Archaeology* 8(4), p.303–309. Piercy Robin. Mombassa Wreck Excavation: Fourth Preliminary Report, 1980, *International Journal of Nautical Archaeology* 10(2), p109–118.

[9] Filipe Vieira de Castro. *The Pepper Wreck: A Portuguese Indiaman at the Mouth of the Tagus River*, Texas A&M University Press, 2005.

[10] Francisco J.Alves. The 16th century Portuguese shipwreck of Oranjemund, Namibia—Report on the missions carried out by the Portuguese team in 2008 and 2009, Trabalhos da DANS, 45, Lisbon, April 2011. Shadreck Chirikure &Ashton Sinamai &Esther Goagoses &Marina Mubusisi &W.Ndoro. Maritime Archaeology and Trans-Oceanic Trade: A Case Study of the Oranjemund Shipwreck Cargo, Namibia, *Journal of Maritime Archaeology*, 2012, Volume 5, Issue 1.

[11] 王冠倬：《中国古船图谱》，北京：生活·读书·新知三联书店，2000年，页167～279。

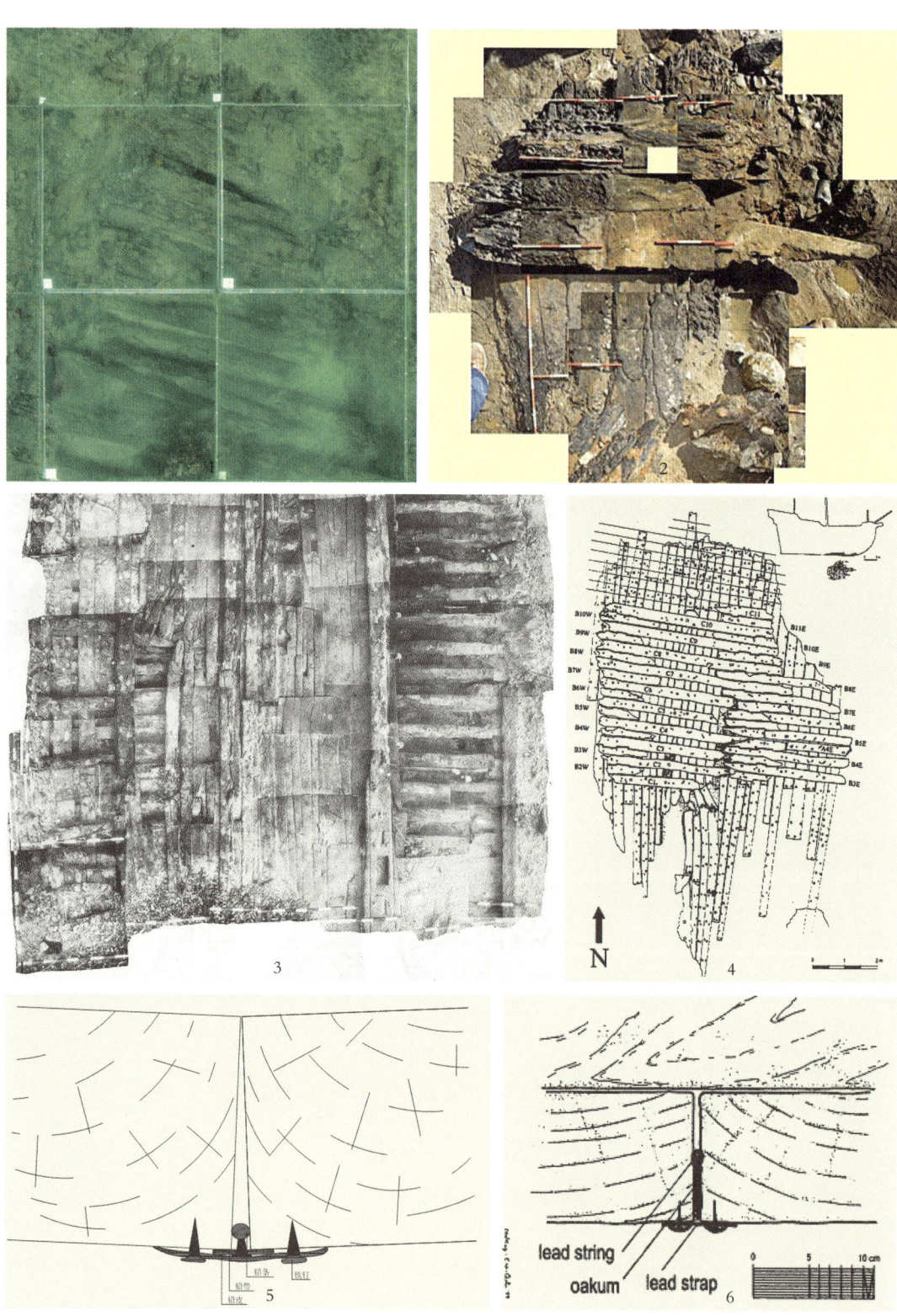

图一七　船体结构对比图

1. 马林迪奥美尼角沉船船体　2. 纳米比亚奥兰治蒙德沉船船体　3. 蒙巴萨圣安东尼奥唐纳沉船船体　4. 里斯本胡椒沉船船体
5. 奥美尼角沉船铅条、铅皮填缝方式　6. 里斯本胡椒沉船铅条、铅皮填缝方式

图一八 出水文物对比图

1. 马林迪奥美尼角沉船遗址铜锭徽章 2. 纳米比亚奥兰治蒙德沉船遗址铜锭徽章 3. 马林迪奥美尼角沉船遗址象牙水下堆积 4. 纳米比亚奥兰治蒙德沉船遗址出水象牙 5. 马林迪奥美尼角沉船遗址铅条与铅皮 6. 纳米比亚奥兰治蒙德沉船遗址铅条与铅皮 7. 马林迪奥美尼角沉船遗址铅条与铅皮 8. 里斯本胡椒沉船遗址铅条与铅皮 9. 马林迪奥美尼角沉船遗址出水石球 10. 纳米比亚奥兰治蒙德沉船遗址出水铜炮与炮弹

图一九　水下原木堆积情况对比图

1. 马林迪奥美尼角沉船遗址　2. 蒙巴萨圣安东尼奥唐纳沉船遗址

[12] Filipe Vieira de Castro. *The Pepper Wreck: A Portuguese Indiaman at the Mouth of the Tagus River*, Texas A&M University Press, 2005, p.147–179.

[13] 王冠倬：《中国古船图谱》，页98～99；金秋鹏：《中国古代的造船和航海》，北京：中国青年出版社，1985年，页112～123。

[14] Francisco J.Alves. *The 16th century Portuguese shipwreck of Oranjemund, Namibia-Report on the missions carried out by the Portuguese team in 2008 and 2009*, Trabalhos da DANS, 45, Lisbon, April 2011, p.19–26.

[15] Bass, George F. A Bronze Age Shipwreck at Ulu Burun (Kas): 1984 Campaign. *American Journal of Archaeology*, Vol. 90, No. 3 (Jul. 1986), p.269–296.

奥美尼角沉船遗址船体内堆放有大量的原木，原木树种尚待进一步检测，船上装载大量原木的现象在蒙巴萨圣安东尼奥唐纳沉船遗址也有发现，是当时船载的一种重要船货[18]（图一九）。

奥美尼角沉船遗址还出水有相当数量的绿釉陶器，器类包括盆、罐、盘、碗等，该类型陶器在肯尼亚陆地考古中有较多发现，肯尼亚考古学者将其定名为"Monochromes"，是阿拉伯风格的陶器，从13世纪一直沿用到17世纪[19]。

这些绿釉陶器的性质有以下两种可能性：

第一，阿拉伯风格的绿釉陶器是船上装载的一种货物。

第二，阿拉伯风格的绿釉陶器是船上阿拉伯船员的生活用品。

这些阿拉伯风格的绿釉陶器出现在葡萄牙船上反映了16～17世纪时期葡萄牙人和马林迪地区阿拉伯统治者的亲密关系。

研究表明，15世纪末葡萄牙人达伽玛进入东非海岸后在蒙巴萨与当地阿拉伯统治者发生冲突并战败，转而退向马林迪，而同时期马林迪与蒙巴萨处于敌对状态，马林迪与葡萄牙人自然结成了对抗蒙巴萨的同盟。整个16世纪马林迪地区阿拉伯统治者和葡萄牙人之间的关系比较友好，马林迪一直是葡萄牙人在莫桑比克以北政治和经济活动的中心。随着16世纪末葡萄牙人重点经营蒙巴萨，将行政、海关以及军队从马林迪迁移到蒙巴萨，同时索马里南部的盖拉族也开始侵扰马林迪等肯尼亚北部地区，失去了葡萄牙人保护的马林迪逐步走向衰弱[20]。

综上所述，马林迪奥美尼角沉船应为16～17世纪运输铜锭、象牙和原木等货物的葡萄牙商贸运输船，其航行路线为从非洲西海岸绕过好望角经非洲东海岸最后抵达亚洲的循环路线，这条航线是16～17世纪葡萄牙的传统贸易路线，而马林迪为该航线上的一处重要贸易点和补给点。

[16] Francisco J.Alves. *The 16th century Portuguese shipwreck of Oranjemund, Namibia-Report on the missions carried out by the Portuguese team in 2008 and 2009*. Trabalhos da DANS, 45, Lisbon, April 2011, p.15-17. Shadreck Chirikure &Ashton Sinamai &Esther Goagoses &Marina Mubusisi &W.Ndoro. Maritime Archaeology and Trans-Oceanic Trade: A Case Study of the Oranjemund Shipwreck Cargo, Namibia. *Journal of Maritime Archaeology*, 04/2012, Volume 5, Issue 1.

[17] 〔英〕理查德·A·古尔德主编,张威、王芳、王东英译:《考古学与船舶社会史》,济南:山东画报出版社,2011年,页120～127。

[18] Christine A. Powell. Ebony and Empire: The Logs from the Mombasa Wreck. *Bulletin of the Regional Centre for the Study of Archaeology in Eastern Africa*, Issue NO. 8 1999, p.15-19.

[19] Neville Chitick. *Manda-Excavation at an Island Port on the Kenya Coast*, The Oxford University Press, 1984. Francisco Siravo and Ann Pulver. *Planning Lamu—Conservation of an East African Seaport*, National Museums of Kenya, p.65-104.

[20] Esmond Bradley Martin. *The History of Malindi—A Geographical Analysis of an East African Town from the Portuguese to the Present*, East African Literature Bureau, 1973, p.17-45.

引用书目

近人论著

曹洁:《论西属美洲殖民地的白银生产》,河北大学历史学硕士学位论文,2010年。

陈昆:《明朝中后期世界白银为何大量流入中国》,中国经济史论坛,http://economy.guoxue.com/?p=7414,2012年10月9日。

姜恒尧:《墨西哥殖民地时期白银生产及影响》,北京大学历史学硕士学位论文,2009年。

金秋鹏:《中国古代的造船和航海》,北京:中国青年出版社,1985年。

李隆生:《晚明海外贸易数量研究——兼论江南丝绸产业与白银流入的影响》,台北:秀威资讯科技股份有限公司,2005年。

王冠倬:《中国古船图谱》,北京:生活·读书·新知三联书店,2000年。

谢乾丰:《16～17世纪世界银冶技术比较研究——以明朝、日本和西属拉丁美洲为对象》,《自然辩证法通讯》第三十一卷,2009年第2期,页75～80。

中国国家博物馆水下考古研究中心、肯尼亚国家博物馆滨海考古部:《肯尼亚马林迪奥美尼角沉船遗址2013年度水下考古发掘简报》,《中国国家博物馆馆刊》2014年第9期,页6～23。

〔英〕莱斯利·贝瑟尔、中国社科院拉美所组译:《剑桥拉丁美洲史》第二卷,北京:经济管理出版社,1997年。

〔德〕贡德·弗兰克著、刘北成译:《白银资本——重视经济全球化中的东方》,北京:中央编译出版社,2000年。

〔英〕理查德·A·古尔德主编,张威、王芳、王东英译:《考古学与船舶社会史》,济南:山东画报出版社,2011年,页120～127。

Francisco J. Alves. *The 16th century Portuguese shipwreck of Oranjemund,Namibia-Report on the missions carried out by the Portuguese team in 2008 and 2009*, Trabalhos da DANS, 45, Lisbon, April 2011.

George F. Bass, A Bronze Age Shipwreck at Ulu Burun (Kas): 1984 Campaign. *American Journal of Archaeology*, Vol. 90, No. 3 (Jul. 1986), p.269–296.

Filipe Vieira de Castro. *The Pepper Wreck: A Portuguese Indiaman at the Mouth of the Tagus River*, Texas A&M University Press, 2005, p.147–179.

Felix A. Chami. *Zanzibar And The Swahili Coast From c30, 000 Years Ago*, E&D Vision Publishing Limited, 2009, p.31–37.

Felix Chami. *The Tanzanian Coast in the First Millennium AD*, Societas Archaeologica Upsaliensis. Uppsala, 1994, p.34–42.

Shadreck Chirikure &Ashton Sinamai &Esther Goagoses &Marina Mubusisi &W. Ndoro. Maritime Archaeology and Trans-Oceanic Trade: A Case Study of the Oranjemund Shipwreck Cargo, Namibia, *Journal of Maritime Archaeology*, 2012, Volume 5, Issue 1.

Neville Chitick. *Manda—Excavation at an Island Port on the Kenya Coast*, The Oxford University Press, 1984.

Esmond Bradley Martin. *The History of Malindi—A Geographical Analysis of an East African Town from the Portuguese to the Present*, East African Literature Bureau, 1973, p.17–45.

Christine A. Powell. Ebony and Empire: The Logs from the Mombasa Wreck. *Bulletin of the Regional Centre for the Study of Archaeology in Eastern Africa*, Issue NO.8, 1999, p.15–19.

Piercy Robin. Mombassa Wreck Excavation: Preliminary Report, 1977, *International Journal of Nautical Archaeology* 6(4), p.331–347.

Piercy Robin, Mombassa Wreck Excavation: Second Preliminary Report, 1978, *International Journal of Nautical Archaeology* 7(4), p.301–319.

Piercy Robin. Mombassa Wreck Excavation: Third Preliminary Report, 1979, *International Journal of Nautical Archaeology* 8(4), p.303–309.

Piercy Robin. Mombassa Wreck Excavation: Fourth Preliminary Report, 1980, *International Journal of Nautical Archaeology* 10(2), p.109–118.

Francisco Siravo and Ann Pulver. *Planning Lamu—Conservation of an East African Seaport*, National Museums of Kenya, p.65–104.

景德镇旸府山明代窑址瓷器之考察*

Study of Porcelains from Kiln Site of Yangfushan in Jingdezhen of Ming Dynasty

陈 冲[1] 刘 未[2]

（1. 北京大学考古文博学院；2.中国人民大学历史学院）

CHEN Chong[1] LIU Wei[2]

(1. School of Archaeology and Museology, Peking University; 2. School of History, Renmin University of China)

内容摘要 /

目前为止，景德镇经正式考古发掘的明代民窑青花瓷窑址，缺乏比较集中的明代中期材料，而见诸报道的明代中期民窑青花瓷窑址调查资料的披露都颇为简略。2007年，在景德镇北郊观音阁窑址发掘期间，我们对与其隔昌江相对的旸府山窑址进行了初步调查，发现这是一处保存较好的明代中期以生产民窑青花瓷为主的窑址。本文对在旸府山窑址采集瓷器标本予以介绍，并结合遗址、窖藏、沉船材料对瓷器年代加以讨论，认为其年代整体上集中在明代中期，其中少部分内底文字、结带宝杵纹碗可能早到成化至弘治时期，其余大部分属于正德至嘉靖早期。以往讨论明代民窑青花瓷的年代，多试图将某些有代表性的纹饰局限于较短的一段时期内，实际上忽略了瓷窑手工业生产在同一时期存在精粗产品之别、同类纹饰跨时期退化延续的特点。而这不但是考察旸府山材料时需要特别注意的，对于其他一些遗址，如竹篙湾、南澳一号出土青花瓷的年代判断也具有启示意义。

关键词 /

景德镇 旸府山 明代 民窑 青花 窑址

ABSTRACT / So far, civilian kilns of blue and white of Ming dynasty in Jingdezhen by formal archaeological excavation, lack of more concentrated in the middle of Ming Dynasty materials, and disclosure of reports in the mid Ming civilian blue and white porcelain kilns survey are quite simple. In 2007, during the excavation of Guanyinge kiln site northern of Jingdezhen, we conducted a preliminary investigation on Yangfushan kiln to and across the Changjiang, found that this is a well preserved mid-Ming blue and white porcelain kiln to produce mainly civilian porcelain. In this paper, collected specimens from the kiln of Yangfushan to be introduced, combined with the sites, cellars, shipwreck materials discussed porcelain years

*本文为教育部人文社会科学研究2013年度青年基金项目《沉船所见景德镇明代青花瓷的考古学研究》成果，项目批准号13YJC780001。

that it's concentrated in the mid-Ming as a whole, in which a small portion of the bottom inside with text and vajra of the bowls earliest possible to Chenghua and Hongzhi period, most of the rest belong to the early Zhengde and Jiajing. Previous discussions of blue and white porcelain of Ming Dynasty, limited some representative decoration within a short period of time, ignored the fact porcelain as handicraft production there are coarse and fine products in the same period, similar ornamentation degenerated and continued cross period. While this is not only investigate Yangfushan materials need to be paid special attention to, for some other sites, such as in the judgment of the blue and white porcelains from Penny's Bay and Nan'ao I ancient ship also has implications.

KEY WORDS / Jingdezhen; Yangfushan; Ming dynasty; civilian kiln; blue and white; kiln site

一

引言

目前为止，景德镇经正式考古发掘的明代民窑青花瓷窑址有湖田[1]、御窑厂[2]、丽阳瓷器山[3]、观音阁[4]和落马桥（红光瓷厂）[5]等处。其中湖田及观音阁所出多为明代中晚期，御窑厂所出以明代晚期为主，丽阳瓷器山所出则属明代早期，落马桥资料尚在整理中。这些窑址均缺乏比较集中的明代中期材料。而见诸报道的明代中期民窑青花瓷窑址虽有景德镇市郊瑶里、内瑶、饶南[6]，昌江西岸十八渡，东郊南河北岸水泥厂，市中心珠山之南陈家街（新光瓷厂），以及市区珠山路西段、四图里、韦陀桥等多处[7]，但调查资料披露都颇为简略。

2007年，在景德镇北郊观音阁窑址发掘期间，我们对与其隔昌江相对的旸府山窑址（东经117°11′45.85″、北纬29°19′37.95″）进行了初步调查，发现这是一处保存较好的明代中期以生产民窑青花瓷为主的窑址（图一）。现将采集瓷器标本予以介绍，并结合遗址、窖藏、沉船材料对瓷器年代加以讨论。

二

标本介绍

采集到的瓷器标本器型全部为碗，以青花为主，少量白釉。

[1] 江西省文物考古研究所、景德镇民窑博物馆：《景德镇湖田窑址1988~1999年考古发掘报告》，北京：文物出版社，2007年。

[2] 北京大学考古文博学院、江西省文物考古研究所、景德镇市陶瓷考古研究所：《江西景德镇明清御窑遗址发掘简报》，《文物》2007年第5期，页4~47。

[3] 故宫博物院、江西省文物考古研究所、景德镇市陶瓷考古研究所：《江西景德镇丽阳瓷器山明代窑址发掘简报》，《文物》2007年第3期，页17~33。

[4] 北京大学考古文博学院、江西省文物考古研究所、景德镇市陶瓷考古研究所：《江西景德镇观音阁明代窑址发掘简报》，《文物》2009年第12期，页39~58。

[5] 翁彦俊：《2012~2013年度景德镇市红光瓷厂窑址考古发掘成果》，《陶瓷考古通讯》2013年第1期，页11、12。

[6] 江建新：《景德镇窑业遗存的考察与研究》，《陈昌蔚纪念论文集》第3辑，台北：台北市陈昌蔚文教基金会，2006年，页77~130。

[7] 黄云鹏：《明代民间青花瓷的断代》，《景德镇陶瓷》1986年第3期，页28~45。江建新：《景德镇窑业遗存的考察与研究》，《陈昌蔚纪念论文集》第3辑，台北：台北市陈昌蔚文教基金会，2006年，页77~130。

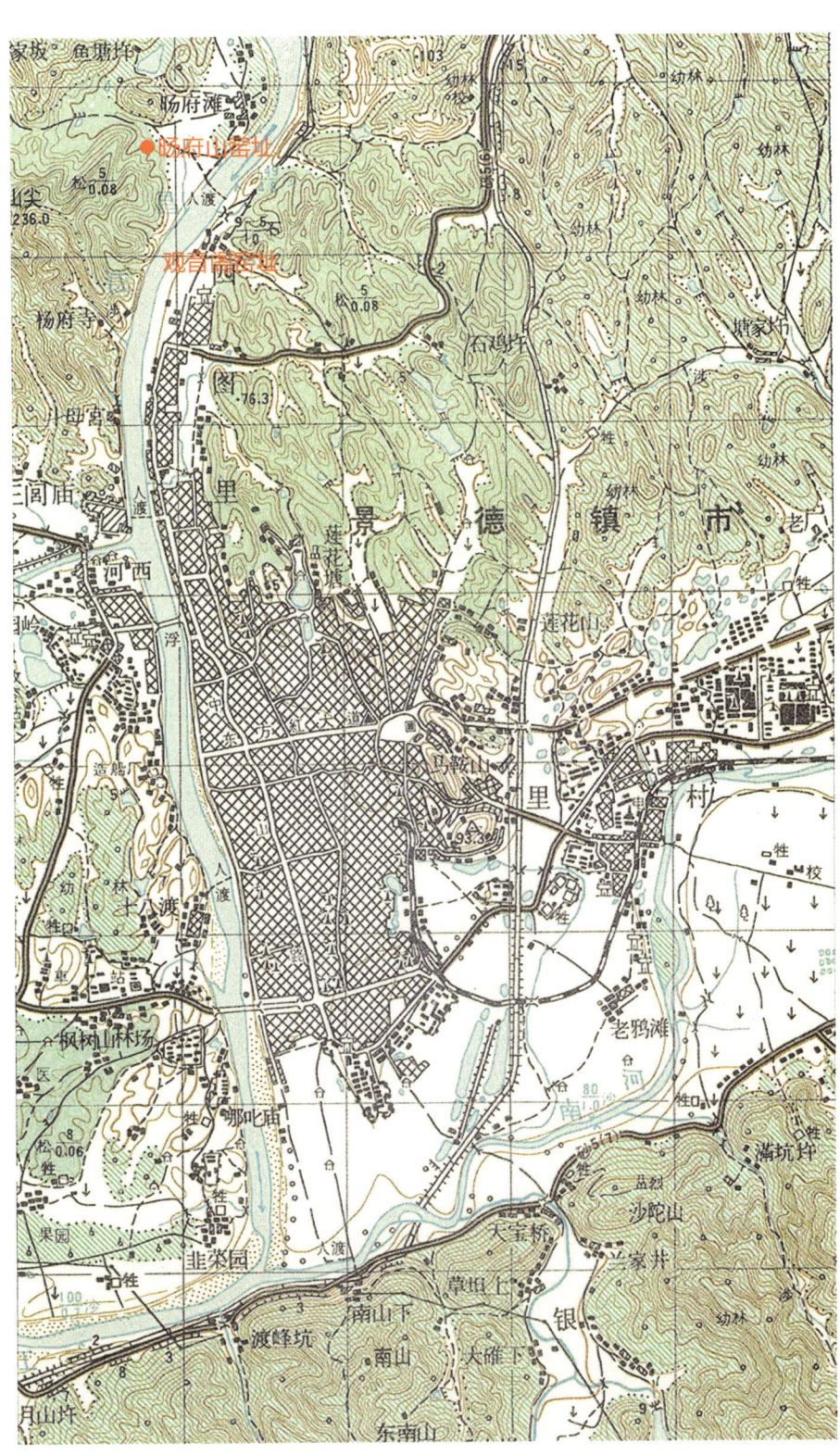

图一　旸府山窑址位置图

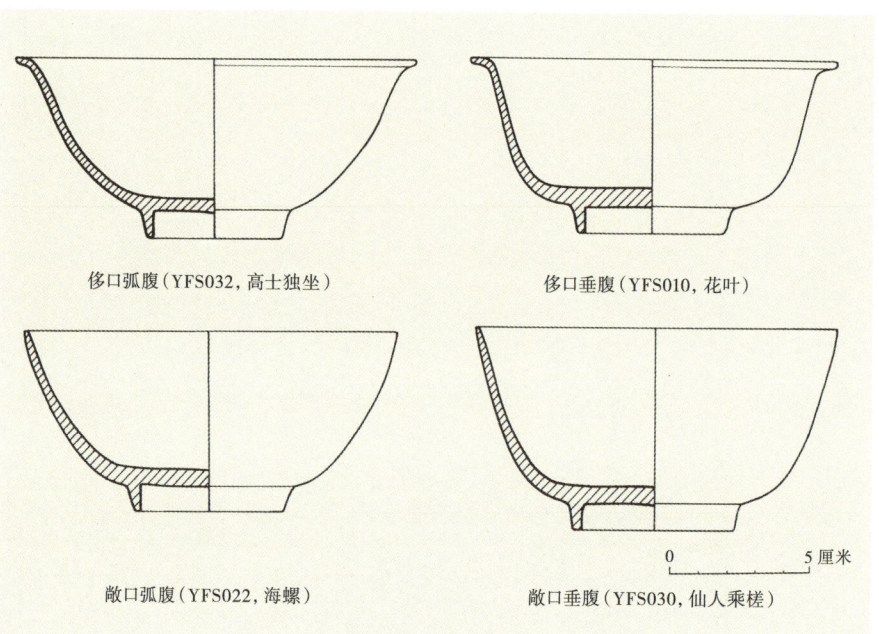

图二 器物形制图

（一）青花碗

器形分为侈口弧腹、侈口垂腹、敞口弧腹和敞口垂腹四类（图二），内底纹饰有器物、文字、植物、动物、人物等，可分为以下十四类：

1.结带宝杵

YFS001：可复原，侈口，垂腹。釉色米黄，釉面有细碎开片，足端刮釉，青花蓝黑。内底绘双弦纹、结带宝杵，口沿内绘梵文，口沿外绘折线纹，外壁绘缠枝花卉托八宝，圈足绘单弦纹（图三，下同）。

YFS002：残底。釉色青白，釉面有细碎开片，足端刮釉，青花蓝色。内底绘双弦纹、结带宝杵，内外壁纹饰残缺，外壁下部绘宽幅莲瓣纹，圈足绘单弦纹。

YFS003：可复原，敞口，垂腹。釉色青白，足端刮釉，青花蓝色。内底绘双弦纹、结带宝杵，口沿内绘双弦纹，口沿外绘留白花叶，外壁绘缠枝宝相花，圈足绘双弦纹。

YFS004：残底。釉色青白，釉面有开片，足端刮釉，青花蓝色。内底绘双弦纹、结带宝杵，外壁绘四组团花，下部绘双弦纹。

YFS005：残底。釉色灰白，釉面有开片，足端刮釉，青花深蓝。内底绘双弦纹、结带宝杵，外壁纹饰残缺，下部绘蕉叶纹。

YFS001

YFS003

YFS004

YFS002

YFS005

图三 青花结带宝杵纹碗

图四 青花文字纹碗

2.文字

YFS006：残底。釉色青白，釉面有开片，圈足内无釉，青花蓝黑。内底绘双弦纹、隶书"福"字，外壁纹饰残缺，似为云气（图四，下同）。

YFS007：残底。釉色青白，釉面有开片，足端刮釉，圈足内局部无釉，青花蓝色。内底绘双弦纹、草书一字，外壁纹饰残缺，似为云气。

YFS008：残底。釉色青白，釉面有开片，足端刮釉，圈足内局部无釉，青花蓝色。足端刮釉露胎，修足不规则。内底绘双弦纹、草书"寿"字，外壁纹饰残缺，似为云气。

图五　青花莱菔纹碗

3. 莱菔

YFS009：可复原。侈口，垂腹。釉色青白，足端刮釉，圈足内局部无釉，青花深蓝。内底绘双弦纹、莱菔，口沿内绘双弦纹，外壁绘四组莱菔纹（图五）。

4. 花叶

YFS010：可复原。侈口，垂腹。釉色青白，足端刮釉，圈足内局部无釉，青花蓝色。内底绘双弦纹、四出花叶，口沿内外分绘单双弦纹，外壁绘缠枝花卉，下部绘水波纹，圈足绘单弦纹（图六，下同）。

YFS011：可复原。敞口，垂腹。釉色青白，足端刮釉，圈足外局部无釉，青花蓝色。内底绘双弦纹、四出花叶，口沿内绘单弦纹，口沿绘外抽象水波纹，外壁绘缠枝花卉，下部及圈足各绘双弦纹。

YFS012：可复原。敞口，垂腹。釉色青白，足端刮釉，青花蓝色。内底绘双弦纹、四出花叶，口沿内绘单弦纹，口沿外绘抽象水波纹，外壁绘花枝，下部及圈足各绘双弦纹。

YFS013：可复原。侈口，垂腹。釉色青白，足端刮釉，青花蓝色。内底绘双弦纹、四出花叶，口沿内外绘单弦纹，外壁绘乳虎、蕉叶、湖石，下部及圈足各绘单双弦纹。

YFS014：可复原。敞口，垂腹。釉色青白，足端刮釉，青花蓝色。内底绘双弦纹、四出花叶，口沿内绘单弦纹，口沿外绘抽象水波纹，外壁绘缠枝宝相花，下部及圈足各绘单双弦纹。

YFS015：可复原。侈口，垂腹。釉色青白，足端刮釉，青花蓝色。内底绘双弦纹、四出花叶，纹饰大部被粘连匣钵覆盖，口沿内绘单弦纹，外壁绘缠枝菊花，下部绘如意，近足部及圈足各绘单双弦纹。

5. 小团花

YFS016：残底。釉色青白，釉面有开片，足端刮釉，青花蓝色。内底绘双弦纹、六瓣小团花，外壁纹饰残缺，下部绘草叶，近足部及圈足绘双弦纹（图七）。

图六 青花花叶纹碗

图七　青花小团花纹碗　　　　图八　青花大团花纹碗　　　　图九　青花如意花纹碗

6.大团花

YFS017：可复原。敞口，垂腹。釉色青白，足端刮釉，青花深蓝。内底绘双弦纹、双层大团花，口沿内绘单弦纹，口沿外绘抽象水波纹，外壁绘缠枝宝相花，下部及圈足各绘单双弦纹（图八）。

7.如意花

YFS018：可复原。敞口，垂腹。釉色青白，足端刮釉，青花蓝色。内底绘双弦纹、四出如意式花卉，口沿内绘单弦纹，口沿外绘留白花叶，外壁绘缠枝宝相花，圈足绘单弦纹（图九）。

8.壬字云

YFS019：残底。釉色青白，足端刮釉，青花蓝色。内底绘双弦纹、壬字云，四周绕以云气，外壁纹饰残缺，下部绘水波纹及四组浪头（图一〇）。

9.海螺

YFS020：残底。釉色青白，足端刮釉，青花蓝色。内底绘双弦纹、海螺，外壁绘缠枝宝相花，下部绘双弦纹（图一一，下同）。

YFS021：可复原。敞口，垂腹。釉色青白，足端刮釉，青花蓝色。内底绘双弦纹、海螺，口沿内绘双弦纹，口沿外绘留白花叶，外壁绘缠枝宝相花，下部及圈足绘双弦纹。

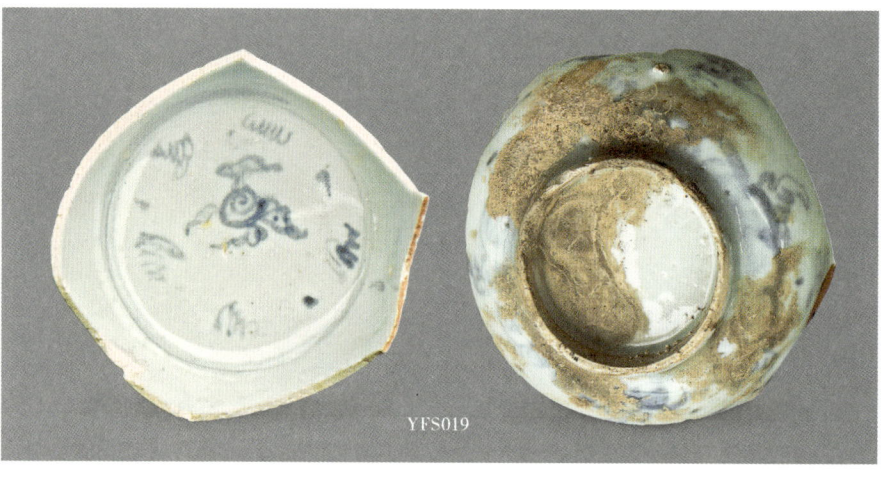

图一〇 青花壬字云纹碗

图一一 青花海螺纹碗

图一二　青花海马纹碗

YFS022：可复原。敞口，弧腹。釉色青白，足端刮釉，青花蓝色。内底绘双弦纹、海螺，口沿内绘双弦纹，口沿外绘抽象水波纹，外壁绘海马四组，下部绘水波纹及四组浪头，圈足绘双弦纹。

YFS023：可复原。敞口，弧腹。釉色青白，釉面有开片，足端刮釉，青花蓝色。内底绘双弦纹、海螺，口沿内绘双弦纹，外口沿绘留白花叶，外壁绘蕉叶，下部及圈足绘双弦纹。

YFS024：可复原。敞口，垂腹。釉色灰白，足端刮釉，青花蓝色。内底绘双弦纹、海螺，口沿内绘双弦纹，外口沿绘留白花叶，外壁绘缠枝宝相花。

10.海马

YFS025：残底。釉色青白，足端刮釉，青花蓝色。内底绘双弦纹、海马及四组浪头，外壁纹饰残缺，下部绘水波纹及四组浪头，近足部与圈足各绘单双弦纹（图一二）。

11.鱼纹

YFS026：残底。釉色灰白，足端刮釉，青花灰蓝。内底绘双弦纹、鱼纹及四组浪头，外壁纹饰残缺，下部绘水波纹及四组浪头（图一三）。

12.乳虎

YFS027：可复原。侈口，垂腹。釉色青白，足端刮釉，青花浅蓝。内底绘双弦纹、乳虎，口沿内外绘双弦纹，外壁纹饰残存乳虎、蕉叶，近足部与圈足分绘单双弦纹（图一四，下同）。

YFS028：残底。釉色青白，足端刮釉，青花深蓝。内底绘双弦纹、乳虎，外壁纹饰残缺，可辨乳虎、蕉叶、湖石，下部与圈足绘双弦纹。

图一三 青花鱼纹碗

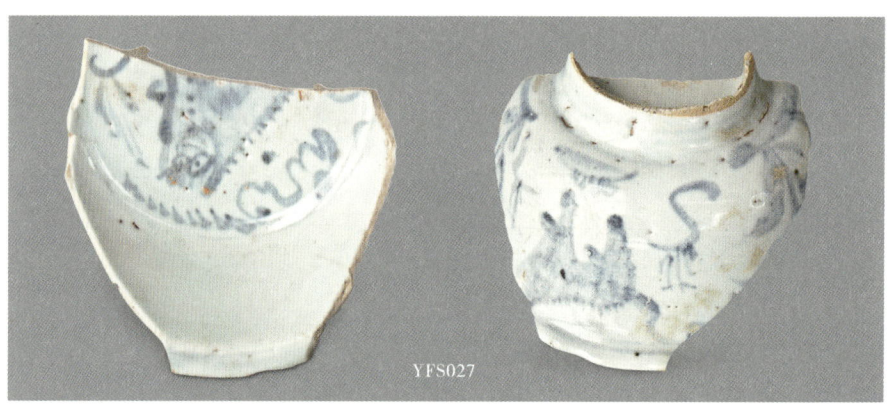

图一四 青花乳虎纹碗

13. 仙人乘槎

YFS029：残底。釉色青白，足端刮釉，青花蓝色。内底绘双弦纹、仙人乘槎及星斗，外壁纹饰残缺，圈足绘双弦纹（图一五，下同）。

YFS030：可复原。敞口，垂腹。釉色米黄，釉面有细碎开片，足端刮釉，青花蓝黑。内底绘双弦纹、仙人乘槎及星斗，口沿外绘回纹，外壁绘仙人乘船及景物，下部绘四组浪头，近足部及圈足分绘单双弦纹。

YFS031：可复原。敞口，垂腹。釉色青白，足端刮釉，青花蓝色。内底绘双弦纹、仙人乘槎，口沿外绘回纹，外壁绘仙人乘船及景物，下部绘四组浪头，近足部及圈足绘双弦纹。

14.高士独坐

YFS032：可复原。侈口，弧腹。釉色青白，足端刮釉，青花深蓝。圈足刮釉露胎，修足规则。内底绘双弦纹、高士独坐，口沿内外绘双弦纹，外壁绘高士乘船及景物，下部及圈足分绘单双弦纹（图一六，下同）。

YFS033：可复原。敞口，弧腹。釉色青白，足端刮釉，青花蓝色。内底绘双弦纹、高士独坐，口沿内绘单弦纹，口沿外绘回文，外壁纹饰残缺，可辨高士乘马，下部及圈足绘弦纹。

（二）白釉碗

器形分为侈口垂腹与敞口垂腹两类（图一七）。

YFS034：可复原。敞口，垂腹。釉色纯白，足端刮釉。

YFS035：可复原。侈口，垂腹。釉色纯白，足端刮釉。

图一五　青花仙人乘槎纹碗

图一六 青花高士独坐纹碗

图一七 白釉碗

三

年代讨论

景德镇明代民窑青花瓷的编年体系尚未完善建立，已有的年代结论大多系根据窑址调查材料推测而来。随着窑址以外各类型遗迹出土资料的逐渐累积，为我们重新考虑窑址出土瓷器的年代提供了新的线索。与旸府山窑址年代讨论有关的材料主要有：

成都下东大街遗址[8]，第四期遗存所出青花瓷与本文有关者：内福寿外缠枝西番莲纹碗，同出其他碗盘内底多见兰草、月梅、莲叶，外壁多见缠枝西番莲、草叶、卷云。

北京毛家湾瓷器坑[9]，所出青花瓷与本文有关者：内草书文字外云气纹碗、内结带宝杵外缠枝宝相花纹碗、内结带宝杵纹"甲辰年造"（成化二十年）款盘、内四出花叶外乳虎蕉叶湖石纹碗、内四出花叶外缠枝花卉纹"甲辰年造"款碗、内乳虎纹碗、内鱼纹碗、内海螺外缠枝宝相花纹碗、内海螺外蕉叶纹碗、内外海马纹碗、内仙人乘槎外高士乘马纹碗、"甲寅年造"（弘治七年）款白釉盘、"丙辰年造"（弘治九年）款白釉碗等。

香港竹篙湾（Penny's Bay）遗址[10]，所出青花瓷与本文有关者：内福字外缠枝西番莲纹碗、内结带宝杵纹碗、外云气纹碗、内麒麟纹盘、内如意云头纹碗、外龟背锦纹碗、内山石缠枝菊纹盘、内海螺外莲荷纹碗，另外同出龙泉窑"顾氏"款碗。

菲律宾利纳浅滩（Lena Shoal）沉船[11]，所出青花瓷多数为窑址所未见，与本文有关者：内福字外缠枝西番莲纹碗、内结带宝杵外缠枝西番莲及宽莲瓣纹碗、内海螺外海马纹盘、内海螺外海马纹碗、内海螺外莲荷纹碗、内麒麟纹盘、内松鹿纹盘、外龟背锦纹碗，另外同出龙泉窑"顾氏"款花口盘。

日本新卷本村窖藏[12]，所出青花瓷有：内福字外缠枝西番莲纹碗、内寿字外云气纹碗、内结带宝杵外缠枝西番莲纹盘、内狮子绣球外缠枝西番莲纹盘，另外同出龙泉窑"顾氏"款菊瓣纹碗。

西沙盘石屿1号沉船[13]，所出青花瓷主要有：内结带宝杵外缠枝西番莲纹碗、内山石缠枝菊纹盘、内四出花叶外缠枝花卉及如意纹盘、内团花外缠枝花卉纹碗、内外山石竹梅纹碗、内仙鹤纹碗、内海螺外蕉叶纹碗、内高士独坐纹

[8] 成都市文物考古研究所：《成都市下东大街遗址考古发掘报告》，《成都考古发现（2007）》，北京：科学出版社，2009年，页452～539。成都文物考古研究所：《成都下东大街遗址明代早期遗存发掘简报》，《文物》2011年第7期，页22～38。

[9] 北京市文物研究所：《毛家湾明代瓷器坑考古发掘报告》，北京：科学出版社，2007年；北京市文物研究所：《北京毛家湾出土瓷器》，北京：科学出版社，2008年。

[10] James Hayes, "Archaeological Site at Penny's Bay, Lantau", *Journal of the Hong Kong Archaeological Society*, Vol. 11, 1984-1985, pp. 95-97. William Meacham, "A Ming Trading Site at Penny's Bay, Lantau", *Journal of the Hong Kong Archaeological Society*, Vol. 12, 1986-1988, pp. 100-115. Peter Y. K. Lam, "Late 15th to Early 16th Century Blue and White Porcelain from Penny's Bay, Hong Kong", *Journal of the Hong Kong Archaeological Society*, Vol. 12, 1986-1988, pp. 146-162. Peter Y. K. Lam, "Ceramic Finds of the Ming Period from Penny's Bay, An Addendum", *Journal of the Hong Kong Archaeological Society*, Vol. 13, 1989-1992, pp. 79-90. Peter Y. K. Lam, "Ceramic Types from Penny's Bay, Hong Kong", *Oriental Art*, No. 2, 2001, pp. 36-42. 竹篙湾出土瓷器除以上文献介绍外，大部分标本展示于香港文物探知馆，笔者于2012年12月考察观摩。

碗、内仙人乘槎纹碗、内寿星纹卧足盘等。

通过以上几处遗迹所出瓷器的共存关系对比，发现器物类型存在互有交错的情况，除北京毛家湾瓷器坑年代跨度较大外（下限为正德），其余遗迹可据此划分为年代早晚相继的三组：

第一组：成都下东大街遗址。与本组相类的材料还见于丽阳瓷器山窑址、景德镇观音阁窑址、菲律宾潘达南（Pandanan）沉船[14]、越南会安（Hoi An）沉船[15]。年代推定在正统至天顺前后[16]，日本出土"染付碗B群"[17]多属于此[18]。

第二组：香港竹篙湾遗址、菲律宾利纳浅滩沉船、日本新卷本村窖藏。与本组相类的纪年材料多见于成化晚期至弘治时期[19]，日本出土"染付碗D群""染付皿B1群"多属于此。

第三组：西沙盘石屿1号沉船。与本组相类的纪年材料多见于正德至嘉靖早期[20]，日本出土"染付碗C群""染付皿C群"[21]部分属于此。

综合以上认识，旸府山窑址所见瓷器与第三组遗存有较多重合，与第二组遗存有部分重合，其年代整体上集中在明代中期。其中少部分内底文字、结带宝杵纹碗可能早到成化至弘治时期，其余大部分属于正德至嘉靖早期。

四

结语

以往讨论明代民窑青花瓷的年代，多试图将某些有代表性的纹饰局限于较短的一段时期内，实际上忽略了瓷窑手工业生产在同一时期存在精粗产品之别、同类纹饰跨时期退化延续的特点。如福寿文字、结带宝杵、云气、缠枝西番莲，尽管是明代早中期流行的纹饰，但仍可延续至明代中期乃至明代中晚期，唯绘画趋于潦草简化，青料不佳。这种产品的退化现象同样表现在形制方面，明代早中期的侈口垂腹碗通常下部厚重，圈足内斜，外底往往无釉，而至明代中期则上下部厚度较为均衡，圈足竖直，外底大多施釉。无独有偶，菜葙、花叶、小团花、四出如意、山石竹梅、乳虎、海螺等明代中期流行的纹饰亦可延续至明代中晚期，并且在形制、釉色、青料、装烧等方面均以该时期粗制产品的面貌而出现[22]。这不但是考察旸府山材料时需要特别注意的，对于其他一些遗址，如竹篙湾、南澳一号出土青花瓷的年代判断也有启示意义。

---

[11] Franck Goddio, Stacey Pierson, Monique Crick, *Sunken Treasure: Fifteenth Century Chinese Ceramics from the Lena Cargo*, London: Periplus Publishing London Ltd, 2000. Frank Goddio, Monique Crick, Peter Lam, Stacey Pierson, Rosemary Scott, *Lost at Sea: The Strange Route of the Lena Shoal Junk*, London: Periplus Publishing London Ltd, 2002.

[12] 〔日〕小野正敏：《山梨県東八代郡一宮町新卷本村出土の陶磁器》，《貿易陶磁研究》1，1981年，页47~55。

[13] 中国国家博物馆水下考古研究中心2010、2011年调查资料，由孟原召先生提供，谨此致谢。

[14] 江西省博物馆等：《江西元明青花瓷》，香港：香港中文大学，2002年，页211~213。

[15] 又名占婆岛（Cu Lao Cham）沉船。Mensun Bound, "Aspects of the Hoi An Wreck: Dishes Bottles, Statuettes and Chronology", *Taoci: Revue Annuelle de la Société Française d'Étude de la Céramique Orientale*, No. 2, 2001, pp. 95-103. Nguyen Dinh Chien & Pham Quoc Quan, *Ceramics on Five Shipwrecks off the Coast of Viet Nam*, Ha Noi: National Museum of Vietnamese History, 2008, pp. 196-199. 广西壮族自治区博物馆等：《越南出水陶瓷》，北京：科学出版社，2009年。

[16] 欧阳世彬、黄云鹏：《介绍两座明景泰墓出土的青花、釉里红瓷器》，《文物》1981年第2期，页46～50。广东省博物馆、东莞市博物馆：《广东东莞明罗亨信家族墓清理简报》，《文物》1991年第11期，页43～50。四川省文管会、绵阳市文化局、平武县文保所：《四川平武明王玺家族墓》，《文物》1989年第7期，页1～42页（M5：16，外壁缠枝莲纹，天顺八年墓）。

[17] 〔日〕小野正敏：《15、16世纪の染付碗、皿の分類とその年代》，《貿易陶磁研究》2，1982年，页71～87。作者将青花碗B群的年代推定为14世纪晚期至15世纪，青花碗C群、D群、青花盘B1群、C群的年代推定为15世纪后期至16世纪晚期。

[18] 青花碗B群中有少部分属于明代中期。

[19] 北京大学考古文博学院、江西省文物考古研究所、景德镇市陶瓷考古研究所：《江西景德镇观音阁明代窑址发掘简报》，《文物》2009年第12期，页55、56（外浪头碗，"壬子年造"弘治五年；白釉碗，"壬子年造"、"甲寅年造"）。曲永健：《北京出土瓷片断代与鉴赏》，北京：文物出版社，2011年，页166～189（内带宝杵盘，"甲辰年造"；内结带宝杵碗，"壬子年造""甲寅年造"；内海马外浪头碗，"壬子年造"；内高士独坐碗，"丙辰年造"；外团花碗，"丙辰年造"）。中国陶瓷编辑委员会：《中国陶瓷·景德镇民间青花瓷》，上海：上海人民美术出版社，1993年，图版65、67（内海螺外莲荷敛口碗，弘治四年墓；外松鹿鹤碗，弘治九年）。中山大学华南文化遗产保护研究与教学中心：《丹江口七里沟墓群2008年发掘报告》，湖北省文物局等《湖北南水北调工程考古报告集》第2卷，北京：科学出版社，2013年，页192、193（M12，内外乳虎碗，弘治通宝）。

[20] 刘新园、白焜：《景德镇湖田窑考察纪要》，《文物》1980年第11期，页46（内底心海螺碗，"大明正德秋月吉日造"）。四川省文管会等：《四川平武明王玺家族墓》，《文物》1989年第7期，图版4-1（M6，外蕉叶碗，正德七年）。湖北省文物考古研究所：《张懋夫妇合葬墓》，北京：科学出版社，2007年，图版28-1（外人物水波浪头碗，正德十五年）。湖北省文物事业管理局等：《秭归庙坪》，北京：科学出版社，2002年，图版83-3、4（M11，外蕉叶碗，嘉靖四年；M28，外海马碗，嘉靖四年）。

[21] 青花碗C群、青花盘C群中另一部分属于明代中晚期。

[22] 北京大学考古文博学院、江西省文物考古研究所、景德镇市陶瓷考古研究所：《江西景德镇观音阁明代窑址发掘简报》，《文物》2009年第12期，页55、56。遗址中此类器物可参见国务院三峡工程建设委员会办公室、国家文物局：《秭归官庄坪》，北京：科学出版社，2005年，页504～589。

引用书目

近人论著

北京大学考古文博学院、江西省文物考古研究所、景德镇市陶瓷考古研究所：《江西景德镇明清御窑遗址发掘简报》，《文物》2007年第5期，页4～47。

北京大学考古文博学院、江西省文物考古研究所、景德镇市陶瓷考古研究所：《江西景德镇观音阁明代窑址发掘简报》，《文物》2009年第12期，页39～58。

北京市文物研究所：《毛家湾明代瓷器坑考古发掘报告》，北京：科学出版社，2007年。

北京市文物研究所：《北京毛家湾出土瓷器》，北京：科学出版社，2008年。

成都市文物考古研究所：《成都市下东大街遗址考古发掘报告》，《成都考古发现（2007）》，北京：科学出版社，2009年，页452～539。

成都文物考古研究所：《成都下东大街遗址明代早期遗存发掘简报》，《文物》2011年第7期，页22～38。

故宫博物院、江西省文物考古研究所、景德镇市陶瓷考古研究所:《江西景德镇丽阳瓷器山明代窑址发掘简报》,《文物》2007年第3期,页17~33。

广东省博物馆、东莞市博物馆:《广东东莞明罗亨信家族墓清理简报》,《文物》1991年第11期,页43~50。

广西壮族自治区博物馆等:《越南出水陶瓷》,北京:科学出版社,2009年。

国务院三峡工程建设委员会办公室、国家文物局:《秭归官庄坪》,北京:科学出版社,2005年。

湖北省文物事业管理局等:《秭归庙坪》,北京:科学出版社,2002年。

湖北省文物考古研究所:《张懋夫妇合葬墓》,北京:科学出版社,2007年。

黄云鹏:《明代民间青花瓷的断代》,《景德镇陶瓷》1986年第3期,页28~45。

江西省博物馆等:《江西元明青花瓷》,香港:香港中文大学,2002年。

江建新:《景德镇窑业遗存的考察与研究》,《陈昌蔚纪念论文集》第3辑,台北:陈昌蔚文教基金会,2006年,页77~130。

江西省文物考古研究所、景德镇民窑博物馆:《景德镇湖田窑址1988~1999年考古发掘报告》,北京:文物出版社,2007年。

刘新园、白焜:《景德镇湖田窑考察纪要》,《文物》1980年第11期,页39~49。

欧阳世彬、黄云鹏:《介绍两座明景泰墓出土的青花、釉里红瓷器》,《文物》1981年第2期,页46~50。

曲永健:《北京出土瓷片断代与鉴赏》,北京:文物出版社,2011年。

四川省文管会、绵阳市文化局、平武县文保所:《四川平武明王玺家族墓》,《文物》1989年第7期,页1~42。

翁彦俊:《2012~2013年度景德镇市红光瓷厂窑址考古发掘成果》,《陶瓷考古通讯》2013年第1期,页11、12。

中国陶瓷编辑委员会:《中国陶瓷·景德镇民间青花瓷》,上海:上海人民美术出版社,1993年。

中山大学华南文化遗产保护研究与教学中心:《丹江口七里沟墓群2008年发掘报告》,《湖北南水北调工程考古报告集》第2卷,北京:科学出版社,2013年,页170~207。

〔日〕小野正敏:《山梨県東八代郡一宫町新卷本村出土の陶磁器》,《貿易陶磁研究》1,1981年,页47~55。

〔日〕小野正敏:《15、16世紀の染付碗、皿の分類とその年代》,《貿易陶磁研究》2,1982年,页71~87。

Franck Goddio, Stacey Pierson, Monique Crick, *Sunken Treasure: Fifteenth Century Chinese Ceramics from the Lena Cargo*, London: Periplus Publishing London Ltd, 2000.

Frank Goddio, Monique Crick, Peter Lam, Stacey Pierson, Rosemary Scott, *Lost at Sea: The Strange Route of the Lena Shoal Junk*, London: Periplus Publishing London Ltd, 2002.

James Hayes, "Archaeological Site at Penny's Bay, Lantau", *Journal of the Hong Kong Archaeological Society*, Vol. 11, 1984-1985, pp. 95-97.

Mensun Bound, "Aspects of the Hoi An Wreck: Dishes Bottles, Statuettes and Chronology", *Taoci: Revue Annuelle de la Société Française d'Étude de la Céramique Orientale*, No. 2, 2001, pp. 95-103.

Nguyen Dinh Chien & Pham Quoc Quan, *Ceramics on Five Shipwrecks off the Coast of Viet Nam*, Ha Noi: National Museum of Vietnamese History, 2008.

Peter Y. K. Lam, "Late 15th to Early 16th Century Blue and White Porcelain from Penny's Bay, Hong Kong", *Journal of the Hong Kong Archaeological Society*, Vol. 12, 1986−1988, pp. 146−162.

Peter Y. K. Lam, "Ceramic Finds of the Ming Period from Penny's Bay, An Addendum", *Journal of the Hong Kong Archaeological Society*, Vol. 13, 1989−1992, pp. 79−90.

Peter Y. K. Lam, "Ceramic Types from Penny's Bay, Hong Kong", *Oriental Art*, No. 2, 2001, pp. 36−42.

William Meacham, "A Ming Trading Site at Penny's Bay, Lantau", *Journal of the Hong Kong Archaeological Society*, Vol. 12, 1986−1988, pp. 100−115.

肯尼亚蒙巴萨耶稣堡出土克拉克瓷的便携式XRF产地研究

Provenance Study Using Portable XRF Analysis of Kraak Porcelains Found in Fort Jesus, Mombasa, Kenya

崔剑锋[1]　徐华烽[2]　秦大树[1]　丁 雨[1]

（1.北京大学考古文博学院；2.故宫博物院）

CUI Jian-feng[1]　XU Hua-feng[2]　QIN Da-shu[1]　DING Yu[1]

(1.School of Archaeology and Museology, Peking University; 2.The Palace Museum)

内容摘要 /

使用便携式XRF分析了肯尼亚蒙巴萨耶稣堡出土的部分克拉克瓷。结果表明使用便携式XRF分析瓷釉的化学组成，可以较为准确地对瓷器的窑口进行区分，这使得瓷器产地研究的原位无损分析成为可能。耶稣堡出土克拉克瓷主要有三个来源，与考古类型学的研究结果基本相符，同时又对窑口判断失误的样品进行了纠正。通过分析结果还对不同组别的瓷片的釉料配方进行了讨论。认为第一组和第四组样品使用了釉灰，因此应该来自景德镇。而第二组和第三组样品配釉时可能采用了草木灰。

关 键 词 /

蒙巴萨耶稣堡　克拉克瓷　产地研究　便携式XRF

ABSTRACT / Chemical compositions of glazes of over 60 Kraak porcelains shards unearthed from Fort Jesus, Mombasa, Kenya were analyzed using portable X-ray Fluorescence (p-XRF). The results indicate that it is practical to source ceramics by their glazes' chemical compositions using p-XRF, which makes non-destructive and in situ provenance-analysis of glazed ceramic possible. The Kraak porcelains found in Fort Jesus can be divided into three groups by the statistical results of their chemical compositions, which confirm the primary conclusions drawn by the archaeological observations. The chemical results may also correct some mistakes of clustering by archaeological observation. According to the results, the flux materials used in the glazes of these Kraak porcelains are also discussed. It is concluded that the flux of Group 1 and Group 4 are likely to have been glaze-ash, which is a unique flux material only used at Jingdezhen. The flux used to make the glazes of Group 2 and Group 3 was wood ash.

KEY WORDS /　Kraak porcelains; Fort Jesus in Mombasa; provenance study; p-XRF

一

简介

1. 耶稣堡（Fort Jesus）出土的"克拉克瓷"

肯尼亚蒙巴萨老城的耶稣堡是由葡萄牙殖民者建筑的，始建于1593年，历时4年，于1596年建成，是一座以防御为主的军事城堡。耶稣堡是非洲第一座由欧洲人设计建造的可抵御大炮轰击的欧式城堡，2011年成为了世界文化遗产[1]。20世纪70年代，肯尼亚考古学者对耶稣堡进行了正式的考古发掘，在所获遗物当中，出土了大量的青花瓷片。绝大多数青花瓷属于所谓的克拉克瓷器，即从明代万历到清代康熙年间主要由景德镇出口到当时世界各地的具有开光纹饰的外销瓷，可能主要为当时的葡萄牙东印度公司所带入[2]。

[1] UNESCO, 2011. http://whc.unesco.org/en/list/1295.

[2] Kirkman, J. 1974. *Fort Jesus: A Portuguese Fortress on the East African Coast.* Clarendon Press: Oxford.

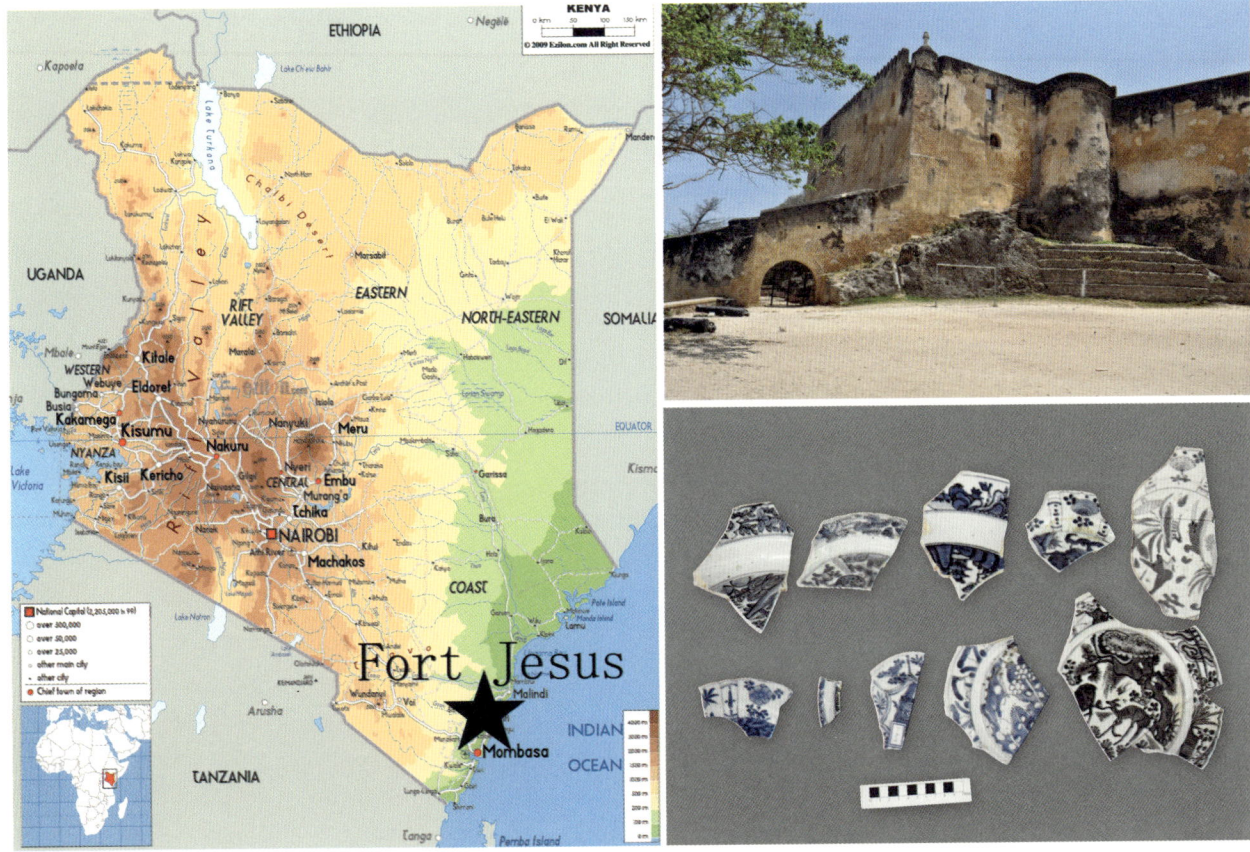

图一　蒙巴萨耶稣堡的位置以及部分其中出土的克拉克瓷残片

关于克拉克瓷的产地研究，之前的研究以考古类型学分析为主。学术界普遍认为克拉克瓷可能主要有3个来源，即中国的景德镇窑、漳州窑以及日本的有田窑（Arita）[3]。有田窑生产的瓷器由于主要从伊万里（Imari）港口运出，因此又被称为伊万里瓷。一般认为，三个窑所生产的克拉克瓷中，以景德镇所产质量最为优良。而釉色较暗、底部有粘砂的质量一般的器物则来自漳州或者有田。这种考古学观察成为判断克拉克瓷窑口的主要方法。但最近曹建文在调查景德镇一处克拉克瓷生产窑址时指出，景德镇实际上也曾经生产过质量较低的底部有粘砂的克拉克瓷[4]。

最近，有学者开始利用科技测试手段来研究克拉克瓷的产地。如Ma（马洪蛟）等使用ICP-MS技术分析了部分景德镇和漳州窑址采集的克拉克瓷片的瓷胎，结果表明两个窑址的制胎黏土成分差别显著，同时他们还研究了不同窑址所产瓷器瓷胎的微痕量元素特征，这样可以为以后分析外销瓷的来源提供参考数据[5]。Dias等使用中子活化技术分析了葡萄牙国内发现的部分克拉克瓷的胎的微量元素，结果表明根据对元素含量的统计结果，葡萄牙发现的克拉克瓷可以分为3组，通过和已经发表的数据进行比较，他们认为大多数克拉克瓷器来自中国南部的窑址，而仅有少量的样品来自景德镇和漳州[6]。

以上的分析由于以分析胎的化学成分为主，同时无论ICP-MS还是INAA都需要取样分析，这使得其对于出土遗址散布世界各地，且大部分都是完整器的克拉克瓷的产地研究实际上意义并不是很大。

2012年夏天，北京大学考古文博学院和肯尼亚国家博物馆组成的联合考古队对耶稣堡所出的克拉克瓷进行了重新整理，在整理过程中，我们使用了便携式XRF对所出瓷器的釉层部分进行了分析，试图通过这种原位、无损的分析手段解决外销瓷产地探索的问题。

2. 便携式XRF应用于陶瓷产地分析

通常来说，瓷器胎的化学成分更具有产地代表性。这是由于古代瓷器的胎通常都是一元配方的，微量元素特征只是指征了作为制胎原料的黏土的来源。但是对于经常为满釉的克拉克瓷来说，分析胎的化学成分就意味着必须通过取样获得少量的胎的样品，这对于完整的器物来说是无法接受的，因此很多博物馆所珍藏的完整瓷器通常只能通过考古学方法来进行判源。

而瓷釉则至少有两种配方：黏土和助熔剂（中国古瓷通常为灰料）。因此通过成分分析可能会引起不确定性，即不能知道所分析的元素哪些代表黏土的来源，哪些又代表助熔剂的来源。因此目前很少有利用釉的成分分析来研究瓷

---

[3] Rinaldi, Maura. *Kraak Porcelain: A Moment in the History of Trade*. London: Bamboo Pub, 1989.

[4] 曹建文：《寻觅已久的景德镇克拉克瓷器窑址被发现》，《中国文物报》2002年4月17日第5版。

[5] Ma, H.J., Zhu, J., Henderson, J., Li, N.S., 2012. Provenance of Zhangzhou export blue-and-white and its clay source. *Journal of Archaeological Science*, Vol.39, 1221-1226.

[6] Dias, I., Prudêncio, I., De Matos, P., Rodrigues, L., 2013. Tracing the origin of blue and white Chinese Porcelain ordered for the Portuguese market during the Ming dynasty using INAA. *Journal of Archaeological Science*, Vol.40, 3046-3057.

器产地的例子[7]。但是由于釉其实是覆盖在陶瓷表面的一层玻璃，玻璃与瓷釉一样，其配方通常有2～3种矿物，而目前古代玻璃的产地研究则主要依靠成分分析来进行，类似的研究都比较成功，所以我们认为用瓷釉的成分来研究瓷器的来源也未尝不可。如之前我们曾经分析了定窑白瓷釉的化学组成，结果发现瓷釉的化学组成可以用来作为定窑的时代特征[8]。如果同一窑口的时代特征都可以用瓷釉化学成分表征，理论上说不同窑口瓷釉的化学成分应该差异更大。因此我们尝试结合考古学观察结果，使用便携式XRF对耶稣堡出土的克拉克瓷的产地进行了探索性分析。

便携式XRF技术是一种无损、原位的化学分析技术，这种仪器体积小，重量轻，可以随身携带，同时XRF技术本身是无损分析，因此特别适合于考古现场分析。这一优点对于我们来说，是其他分析方法无法取代的。因为这些瓷片属于肯尼亚国家博物馆所有，无法带回中国，也无法进行取样分析，只能依靠这种技术进行研究。

不过到目前为止，越来越多的考古学研究开始依赖这种仪器进行。目前这类仪器已经介入到包括黑曜石[9]、玻璃[10]以及陶器等很多考古遗物的产地研究当中。尽管由于仪器本身的准确性问题，其适用性曾遭到质疑。但是对于只是区分产地来说，由于仪器自身所获数据稳定性很好，因此只是用来进行产地分析的，该仪器并不会存在问题。

我们使用仪器为美国赛默费舍尔公司生产的NITON XL3t型便携式XRF，使用内建于该设备的土壤模式，对所有瓷片的白釉部分进行了分析。所分析的元素包括Zr、Rb、Sr、Th、Zn、Fe、Mn、Ti、Ca、K。

[7] Pollard, A.M., Heron, C., 1996. *Archaeological Chemistry*. The Royal Society of Chemistry.

[8] Cui J.F., Wood N., Qin D.S., Zhou L.J., Ko M.K., Li X., 2012, Chemical analysis of white porcelains from the Ding kiln site, Hebei Province, China, *Journal of archaeological Science*, vol.39(4), 818-827.

[9] Nazaroff, A.J., Prufer, K., M., Drake, B.L., 2010.Assessing the applicability of portable X-ray fluorescence spectrometry for obsidian provenance research in the Maya lowlands. *Journal of Archaeological Science*, Vol.37, 885-895.

[10] Goren, Y., Mommsen., H., Klinger., J., 2011. Non-destructive provenance study of cuneiform tablets using portable X-ray fluorescence (pXRF). *Journal of Archaeological Science*, Vol.38, 684-696.

二

样品和分析结果

根据考古类型学研究，耶稣堡所出克拉克瓷被分为三个组，其中第一组（G.1）制作最为精细，可能来自景德镇；第二组（G.2）被认为来自漳州窑；第三组（G.3）则可能来自有田窑。还有部分釉面质量较高的器物，从风格上看，可能来自景德镇，但是由于底部都有粘砂，和第一组相比又有所逊色，不能够确定到底来自哪一处窑址，将这部分瓷器定为第四组（G.4）。表一为分析样品的简单的汇总。这四组典型器物的照片如图二所示。

图二 耶稣堡出土四组典型克拉克瓷
1. 第一组，来自景德镇　2. 第二组，来自漳州　3. 第三组，来自有田　4. 第四组，不确定

表一 耶稣堡出土克拉克瓷分析总表

样品编号	分组	可能来源
131-141, 184-199	第一组(G.1)	景德镇
215-231	第二组(G.2)	漳州
47-57, 200-214	第三组(G.3)	有田
142-151	第四组(G.4)	不确定

表二为分析的克拉克瓷的白釉部分的成分结果。

我们使用社会统计学软件SPSS（软件版本18.0）对以上数据进行了主成分分析(principle components analysis)。共获得三个主成分，用这三个主成分绘制了样品散点图，参见图三。

从统计图上可以看出，除个别样品外，一、二、三组样品区分明显。这说明考古类型学的分析结果基本正确，三个组样品的来源是不同的。第四组样品

表二 肯尼亚出土克拉克瓷的便携式XRF分析结果

(Zr~Ti单位为ppm, Ca和K为质量百分比wt.%)

Sample ID		Zr	Sr	Rb	Th	Zn	Fe	Mn	Ti	Ca	K
47#	Group 3	85	292	150	20	23	2124	839	106	6.49	3.19
48#	Group 3	64	346	132	19	27	2143	693	68	5.18	3.04
49#	Group 3	76	326	160	19	31	2709	1492	137	5.34	3.83
50#	Group 3	82	247	160	20	16	2815	902	68	7.14	3.37
51#	Group 3	70	250	145	18	37	2755	473	69	4.93	2.78
52#	Group 3	76	191	139	17	35	2649	795	88	3.05	1.95
53#	Group 3	82	337	145	17	31	1743	777	107	6.61	3.30
54#	Group 3	77	294	135	16	19	1742	757	92	5.44	2.64
55#	Group 3	70	422	151	18	27	2397	628	135	5.26	3.32
56#	Group 3	80	234	156	22	30	3632	1095	174	5.44	3.86
57#	Group 3	66	477	143	17	12	2428	909	68	8.26	3.61
131#	Group 1	56	56	251	11	81	3256	293	143	4.41	1.77
132#	Group 1	43	68	368	13	50	3147	272	126	5.58	2.31
133#	Group 1	51	61	240	11	73	3675	536	60	5.07	2.78
134#	Group 1	45	67	362	7	47	3237	349	157	3.69	2.41
135#	Group 1	45	54	373	8	54	2696	250	238	4.48	3.00
136#	Group 1	48	58	535	6	138	4069	393	178	3.03	3.47
137#	Group 1	40	74	355	13	31	2928	371	139	1.42	1.16
138#	Group 1	40	46	556	5	54	3686	386	105	2.11	2.77
139#	Group 1	46	70	268	9	68	3000	240	148	4.77	2.33
141#	Group 1	40	52	330	8	49	2815	387	97	3.37	2.75
142#	Group 4	43	64	314	10	46	2986	294	138	5.01	2.48
143#	Group 4	51	67	333	7	78	3781	324	143	4.18	1.51
144#	Group 4	52	53	266	9	54	3437	224	125	9.52	1.12
145#	Group 4	46	115	216	9	61	2608	328	148	6.38	1.86
146#	Group 4	53	55	229	5	73	2926	280	132	3.72	1.45
147#	Group 4	41	61	337	6	57	3388	229	50	4.28	2.00
148#	Group 4	49	65	274	6	22	3882	400	128	6.50	2.56
149#	Group 4	53	59	358	8	62	3288	400	132	6.44	2.21
150#	Group 4	48	65	236	7	54	2886	387	177	5.81	2.40
151#	Group 4	40	54	348	5	40	2343	312	102	4.60	2.64
184#	Group 1	38	53	296	10	35	2165	240	777	4.14	2.08
185#	Group 1	35	57	344	9	44	3548	417	206	3.26	2.79
186#	Group 1	47	54	450	7	69	3815	492	263	4.21	2.83
187#	Group 1	38	50	292	5	38	2832	497	60	3.11	1.71
188#	Group 1	47	53	375	5	37	3187	317	258	4.00	2.73
189#	Group 1	42	44	462	9	53	4014	364	160	1.82	4.39
190#	Group 1	40	82	283	13	29	2000	200	111	3.23	2.00

续表

Sample ID		Zr	Sr	Rb	Th	Zn	Fe	Mn	Ti	Ca	K
191#	Group 1	32	43	400	6	33	3300	522	76	2.00	2.30
192#	Group 1	35	51	300	8	27	1900	286	100	3.34	1.82
193#	Group 1	40	50	263	10	60	3533	308	100	3.00	1.43
194#	Group 1	51	85	415	9	64	4400	462	225	4.84	2.40
195#	Group 1	36	53	250	7	60	2976	383	50	2.35	1.13
196#	Group 1	40	54	435	9	60	4999	631	129	3.25	2.41
197#	Group 1	38	51	413	10	50	2617	382	124	2.50	2.88
199#	Group 1	35	47	400	7	36	3316	358	62	2.28	2.29
200#	Group 3	80	166	163	16	19	2125	631	60	5.10	3.63
201#	Group 3	73	330	159	20	26	2190	922	60	5.50	3.20
202#	Group 3	68	375	152	19	20	2468	900	60	6.92	4.14
203#	Group 3	77	279	165	18	24	2013	480	158	5.28	3.92
204#	Group 3	77	172	168	22	21	2111	612	136	5.33	3.80
205#	Group 3	74	256	164	20	36	2759	1100	151	4.63	3.50
206#	Group 3	73	200	143	21	30	3130	921	161	5.54	3.63
207#	Group 3	70	358	157	18	33	2618	1460	190	5.60	4.10
208#	Group 3	74	200	150	18	16	2000	600	60	4.30	2.90
209#	Group 3	80	344	153	19	15	3240	618	86	8.66	3.87
210#	Group 3	78	283	150	17	36	2500	734	97	6.20	3.38
211#	Group 3	67	476	145	18	14	2513	871	94	5.81	3.73
214#	Group 3	76	274	151	22	21	2944	600	107	5.00	3.50
215#	Group 2	131	186	190	34	80	3300	1500	490	2.22	3.35
216#	Group 2	133	186	165	39	63	4748	1527	348	2.93	2.33
217#	Group 2	140	100	216	36	34	5370	1800	320	1.91	3.79
218#	Group 2	154	218	139	37	162	4342	1268	345	2.83	2.54
219#	Group 2	145	134	163	34	70	3220	555	517	2.08	2.85
220#	Group 2	45	80	300	9	42	2600	321	566	4.70	2.45
221#	Group 2	133	137	176	33	59	3083	1500	360	2.55	3.37
222#	Group 2	80	107	200	10	42	3732	247	453	3.47	2.42
223#	Group 2	130	200	132	30	69	4139	950	200	4.50	2.20
224#	Group 2	78	270	160	20	11	2201	936	110	7.33	3.73
225#	Group 2	53	67	444	11	54	3551	349	120	3.00	2.90
226#	Group 2	142	130	165	35	67	4900	1420	500	2.70	2.73
227#	Group 2	123	100	226	35	37	2437	891	392	3.80	3.38
228#	Group 2	50	74	244	10	38	1827	376	153	5.70	1.92
229#	Group 2	126	240	177	33	47	2712	1577	300	3.15	3.70
230#	Group 2	143	148	177	33	55	3469	1539	382	2.78	3.62
231#	Group 2	122	100	231	36	39	2439	859	482	3.81	3.66

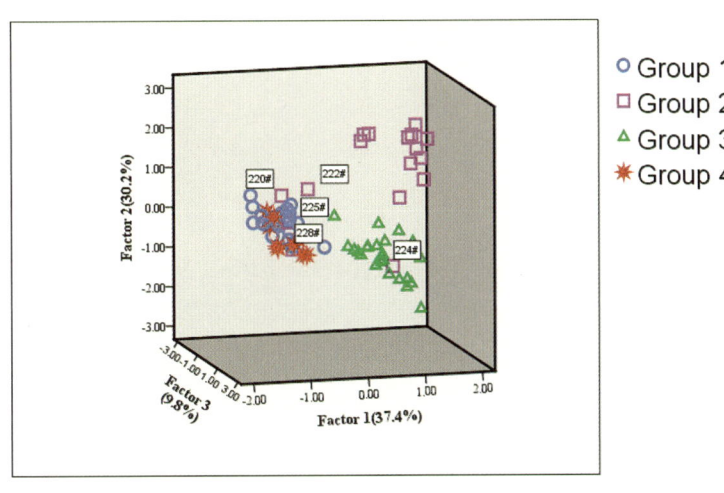

图三　主成分分析结果三维散点图

和第一组样品聚在一起，则表明这两组样品的来源相近。而部分考古学观察属于第二组的样品落入别的组范围内，则由于这些样品本身都为极小的残片，观察比较困难，从而产生了误判。

三

讨论

上述的分析结果显示，通过便携式XRF分析瓷器釉层的化学成分来判断瓷器的窑口是完全可行的。同时分析结果也表明考古类型学的判断大体上是正确的。其中第一组和第三组的聚类程度较第二组更加好，则说明第二组的样品可能并不来自同一窑口，而有可能是地理位置相近的不同窑口。另外大多数第二组的样品都是很小的残片，其风格和纹饰很难判断，大大增加了肉眼观察判断窑口的难度。其中有四件样品落入了第一组的分布范围，一件样品落入第三组的范围。说明这些样品可能分别来自相应组别的窑口。令人感兴趣的是，落入第三组的一件224号样品，仔细观察其青花绘制部分为一个日本女人的形象（参见图四），而根据考古学观察，第三组很可能是日本有田窑烧的伊万里瓷。分析结果既找对了瓷片的窑口，也为考古学判断提供了证据。

前曾述及，第四组样品和第一组样品的纹饰相近，二者唯一的差别是第四组样品底部有大量粘砂，同时釉色也较第一组为深，整体质量不如第一组（图五）。

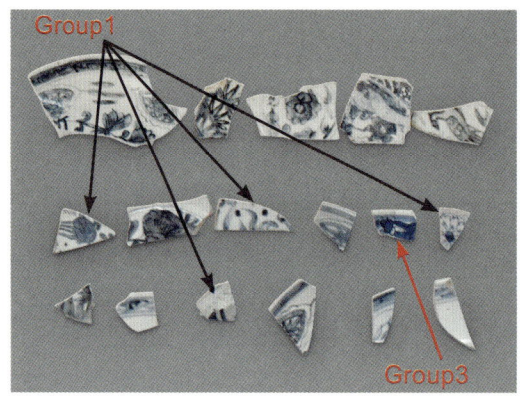 

图四　落入其他组的第二组样品

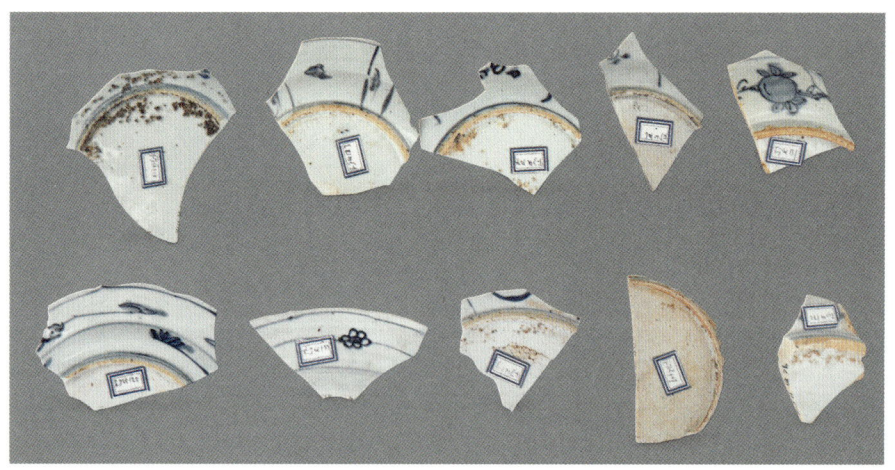

图五　部分底部粘砂的第四组样品

根据其烧造质量最初被认为可能来自漳州,但是其纹饰和第一组的又非常类似,因此我们将其定在未知产地组。而根据成分分析的统计结果,现在可以肯定这一组的确和第一组的产地相同,都可能来自景德镇。

曹建文报道了在景德镇一处窑址也发现有和第四组一样的质量较低的克拉克瓷的生产,这意味着景德镇生产的外销瓷并不都是高质量的,同样为了追逐利益,也会出口质量一般的瓷器。我们的分析证实了他的报道,并为以后克拉克瓷的分类及窑口判断提供了新的思路。

图六为一组使用两个元素作的二元散点图。所有的图都可以看出,除个别瓷器外,三个组别的瓷片成分差别都很明显,另外第四组和第一组的瓷片聚在一起。图六-1显示出三个组别的Ca(钙)元素和Sr(锶)元素都呈现出正比关系。这是由于钙和锶都是碱土金属元素,都位于元素周期表中的第二主族,因此具有很强的地球化学相关性。我国古代瓷器的瓷釉大多以CaO作为助熔剂,

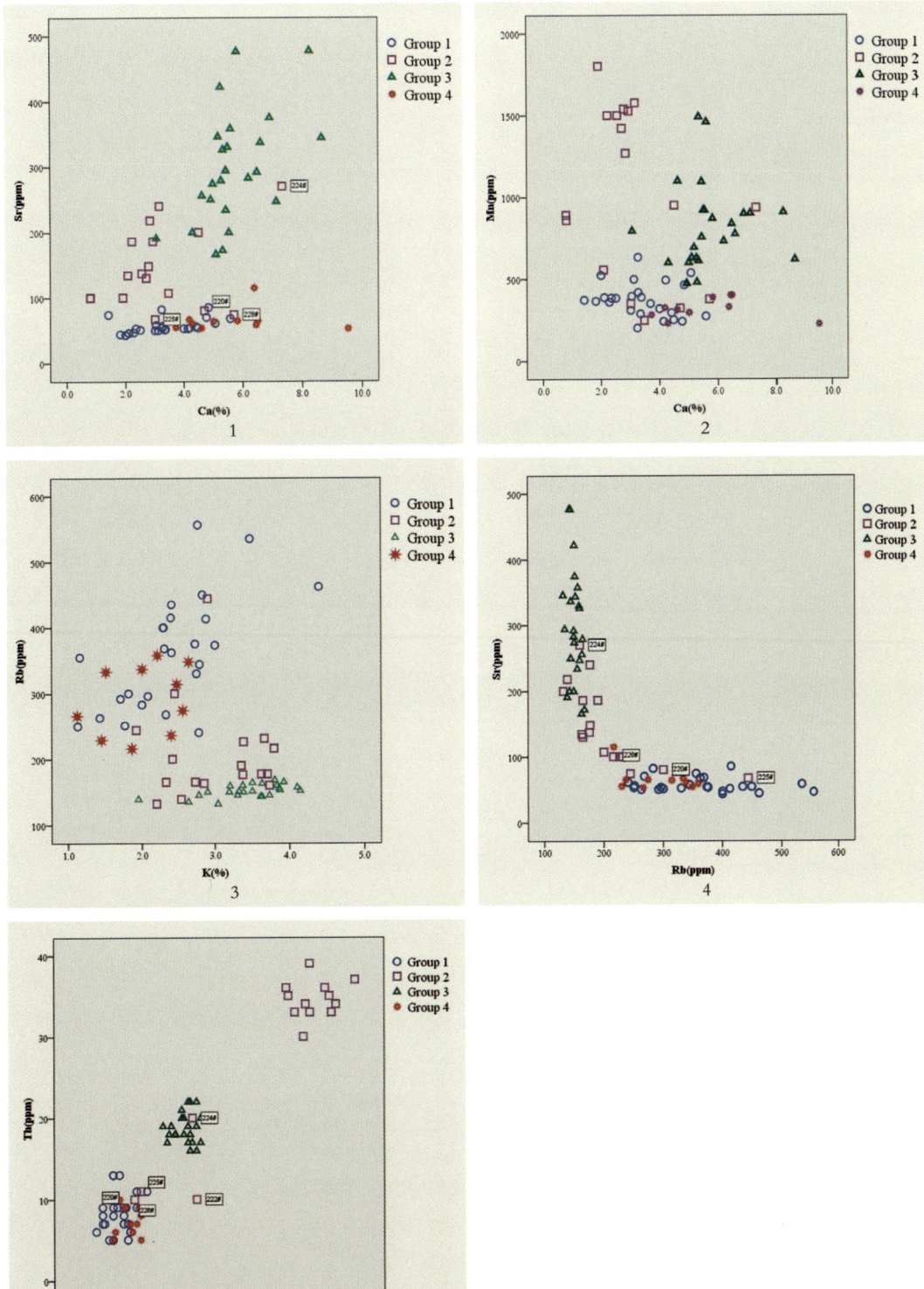

图六 部分元素对比图
1. Ca-Sr 2. Ca-Mn 3. K-Rb 4. Rb-Sr 5. Zr-Th

[11] 李家治:《中国科学技术史·陶瓷卷》,北京:科学出版社,1998年。

[12] Wood, N., 1999., *Chinese glazes: their origins, chemistry, and recreation*. London: A&C Black (Publishers) Limited:263-272.

草木灰和石灰（二者的主要矿物都为碳酸钙）为CaO的主要来源[11]。这两种原料中的Ca和Sr都会呈现正相关的关系。这种关系在第二组和第三组样品中看得尤其明显，因此第二组和第三组的产地使用的是草木灰或者石灰这种单一灰料。但景德镇从元代开始使用草木灰煅烧石灰的方法生产釉灰，釉灰的生产涉及较为复杂的物理化学变化，通过这种方法可以得到非常纯净的CaO，而使得其他杂质元素降低到较低的水平[12]，因此我们可以看到第一组和第四组的Sr的含量水平基本接近，而且较第二组、第三组低得多。因此Sr含量水平对于判断第一组和第四组都来自景德镇提供了重要的化学证据。

图六-2显示出第二组和第三组的元素Mn（锰）含量较第一组高得多，同时和Ca也呈现出正相关的趋势。这一点说明第二组和第三组的CaO很有可能主要来自草木灰，由于石灰中Mn的含量非常低，而草木灰则富含P、Mn等元素。第一组和第四组的Mn含量水平接近，且非常低，应该也和其使用釉灰作为灰料密切相关。

图六-5是Zr（锆）-Th（钍）散点图，三组样品的这两个元素含量彼此差异明显，因此实际上这两个元素就可以作为区分三组样品的特征元素。其中第一组和第三组样品这两个元素的含量非常集中，而第二组样品则较为分散，说明第二组样品可能是来自大窑区的不同小窑址。

四

结论

我们的研究表明利用瓷釉的化学成分来进行瓷器的产源研究是完全可行的。之前瓷器产地分析工作主要依靠瓷胎的成分分析进行，但这种分析需要进行破坏性取样，同时分析必须在实验室内进行，限制了分析样品的种类。而瓷釉的化学分析用于产地研究，使得非破坏分析研究瓷器的产源成为可能。同时我们的研究还证实便携式XRF无损分析可以非常有效地应用于瓷器的产地研究当中。其无损原位的优点使得分析所有古代瓷器的产地研究成为可能，尤其是对于外销瓷以及一些博物馆收藏的精美的完整瓷器。

分析结果显示，依据化学元素特征划分，蒙巴萨耶稣堡出土的克拉克瓷可以分为三组，而这三组分别与考古学研究所定义的景德镇窑、漳州窑以及有田窑相对应。但对部分考古学观察比较困难的小碎片的窑口判断，化学分析则较为轻易地找到了相应的组别。同时，化学分析还校正了类型学观察判断失误的瓷片的窑口。

通过统计分析，我们发现景德镇窑除了生产质量优良的克拉克瓷外，还生产一类质量较为粗糙的外销瓷，这为以后克拉克瓷窑口判断提供了新的思路。根据成分分析，可以看到漳州窑和有田窑以草木灰作为主要的助熔剂，而景德镇则由于发明了釉灰技术，可以生产出杂质含量很低的优质釉。同时，在以后的分析中，可以将Zr和Th作为判断克拉克瓷产地的主要指纹元素，从而使得成分分析判断窑口更加简单。

致谢：本研究受到国家高层次人才特殊支持计划（万人计划）、国家文物局指南针计划《东非地区出土中国古代外销瓷的综合研究》、北京市高等学校"青年人才计划"、国家社会科学基金重大项目《非洲出土中国古代外销瓷与海上丝绸之路研究》（项目批准号：15ZDB057）支持，作者感谢肯尼亚国家博物馆准许对耶稣堡出土古陶瓷进行科技分析。

引用书目

近人论著

曹建文：《寻觅已久的景德镇克拉克瓷器窑址被发现》，《中国文物报》2002年4月17日第5版。

李家治：《中国科学技术史·陶瓷卷》，北京：科学出版社，1998年。

Cui J.F., Wood N., Qin D.S., Zhou L.J., Ko M.K., Li X., 2012, Chemical analysis of white porcelains from the Ding kiln site, Hebei Province, China, *Journal of archaeological Science*, vol.39(4), 818–827.

Dias, I., Prudêncio, I., De Matos, P., Rodrigues, L., 2013.Tracing the origin of blue and white Chinese Porcelain ordered for the Portuguese market during the Ming dynasty using INAA. *Journal of Archaeological Science*, Vol.40, 3046–3057.

Goren, Y., Mommsen., H., Klinger., J., 2011.Non-destructive provenance study of cuneiform tablets using portable X-ray fluorescence (pXRF). *Journal of Archaeological Science*, Vol.38, 684–696.

Kirkman, J.1974.*Fort Jesus:A Portuguese Fortress on the East African Coast* .Clarendon Press:Oxford.

Ma, H.J., Zhu, J., Henderson, J., Li, N.S., 2012.Provenance of Zhangzhou export blue-and-white and its clay source.*Journal of Archaeological Science*, Vol.39, 1221–1226.

Nazaroff, A.J., Prufer, K., M., Drake, B.L., 2010.Assessing the applicability of portable X-ray fluorescence spectrometry for obsidian provenance research in the Maya lowlands.*Journal of Archaeological Science*, Vol.37, 885~895.

Pollard, A.M., Heron, C., 1996.*Archaeological Chemistry*.The Royal Society of Chemistry.

Rinaldi, Maura. *Kraak Porcelain: A Moment in the History of Trade*. London:Bamboo Pub, 1989.

Wood, N., 1999., *Chinese glazes:their origins, chemistry, and recreation*.London:A&C Black(Publishers) Limited:263–272.

UNESCO, 2011.http://whc.unesco.org/en/list/1295.

从玲珑瓷看中国与伊斯兰世界的
文化交流

Cultural Interaction between China and Islamic World: a Perspective of *Linglong* Porcelain

林梅村　马丽亚·艾海提　沈 勰

（北京大学考古文博学院）

LIN Mei-cun　Maliya AIHAITI　SHEN Xie

(School of Archaeology and Museology, Peking University)

内容摘要 /

　　玲珑瓷是一种镂花瓷器，主要流行于清代。从目前考古资料看，景德镇窑烧造玲珑瓷不早于元代，其起源说法不一。通过与大英博物馆藏品及杜伦大学所藏"威廉姆森收集品"中12~13世纪伊朗玲珑陶碗等比较，可知景德镇玲珑瓷工艺一定程度上受到伊斯兰制陶技术的影响，体现了当时中国与伊斯兰世界的文化交流。

关 键 词 /

　　玲珑瓷　玲珑陶碗　伊斯兰制陶技术　文化交流

ABSTRACT / *Linglong* Porcerlain, literally means porcelain with cutout design, was mainly popular in Qing Dynasty. Relevant archaeological discovery shows that the manufacture of *Linglong* Porcelain in Jingdezhen did not begin until Yuan Dynasty, while its origin still remains mysterious. Through a comparative study with Iranian cutout design ceramic bowls of 12-13th century in the British Museum and Williamson Collection at Durham University, we conclude that the technique and design of cutout porcelain in Jingdezhen had been influenced by Islamic technology in some extent, which demonstrates the cultural contact between China and Islamic world.

KEY WORDS / *Linglong* porcelain; *Linglong* ceramic bowl; Islamic pottery technology; cultural interaction

2013年7月，应英国中东考古学家德雷克·康耐特博士（Dr. Derek Kennet）的邀请，我们到英国进行了为期两周的学术考察[1]。走访了大英博物馆、维多利亚和艾伯特博物馆、大英图书馆、牛津大学阿什莫林博物馆、牛津大学自然史图书馆、剑桥大学菲茨威廉博物馆、杜伦大学东方博物馆。这次考察的重点是牛津大学威廉姆森博士（Dr. Andrew G. Williamson）在伊朗各地采集的中国陶瓷，今称"威廉姆森收集品"（Williamson Collection），现藏杜伦大学考古系[2]。此次英国之行收获巨大，在许多方面取得研究新成果。本文将介绍我们对玲珑瓷来龙去脉的研究成果。

玲珑瓷是清代流行的一种镂花瓷器，如东莞市博物馆藏清光绪款青花暗八仙纹玲珑碗、首都博物馆藏清乾隆玲珑白瓷碗（图一）。民国学者许之衡《饮流斋说瓷》评述说："素瓷，甚薄，雕花纹而映出青色者谓之影青镂花，而两面洞透者谓之玲珑瓷。"[3]玲珑瓷制作工艺是：器物成型后，在生坯上按照图案设计镂雕透空花纹，再用釉汁将透雕花纹填平，烧后镂花处得以墁平的花纹清晰可见，具有玲珑剔透、精巧细腻的特色，故名"玲珑瓷"。其上透光小孔叫做"米花"，日本人称为"米通瓷"或"萤手"[4]。

清康熙年间，法国传教士殷弘绪（Père Francois Xavier d'Entrecolles）神父来华传教，并在江西景德镇居住了七年之久。1712年（康熙五十一年）9月1日，他在饶州（今景德镇）写信给耶稣会奥日神父，介绍中国人如何烧造陶瓷。信中提到"当地产的瓷器中，有一种我还未见过。整个瓷胎镂有透明的空洞，中间有可盛利久酒的盏形器物——玲珑瓷。盏与镂空的瓷胎构成完整的一体。"[5]这是西方学人对景德镇烧造玲珑瓷的最早报道。

图一　首都博物馆藏清乾隆玲珑白瓷碗

[1] 这次英国考察得到中国文化遗产研究院水下考古研究所大力支持，由北京大学林梅村教授带队，成员有北大考古文博学院研究生沈翾、马丽亚、杜伦大学考古系研究生张然。考察期间，我们先后得到杜伦大学考古系师生、牛津大学默顿学院教授杰西卡·罗森女爵（Dame Jessica Rosem）、牛津大学博德利图书馆中文部主任赫利维尔博士（Dr. David Helliwell）、大英图书馆中文部主任葛汉博士（Dr. Graham Hutt）的热情帮助，在此一并表示我们由衷的感谢。

[2] 关于威廉姆森生平事迹及其收集品，参Seth M.N. Priestman, *Settlement & Ceramics in Southern Iran: An Analysis of the Sasanian & Islamic Periods in the Williamson Collection*, M.A. Thesis, 2005, p.134.〔英〕德雷克·康耐特、塞斯·普利斯曼、张然：《近东地区考古遗址发现的龙泉窑瓷器——英国威廉姆森藏品及斯拉夫遗址调查藏品中的龙泉窑青瓷简介》，《龙泉窑研究》，北京：紫禁城出版社，2011年，页447～449。

[3] （民国）许之衡撰、杜斌校注：《饮流斋说瓷》，济南：山东画报出版社，2010年。

[4] 冯先铭等：《中国陶瓷史》，北京：文物出版社，1982年。

[5] 〔法〕殷弘绪撰、王景圣译：《给中国和印度传教会计奥日神父的信》，《陶瓷资料》1978年第1期。此信从矢泽利彦（Yazawa Toshihiko）日译本转译。关于殷弘绪书信的日译本，参见矢泽利彦撰、艾廉莹译：《日文本〈耶稣会士中国书简集〉解说》，《中国史研究动态》1980年第6期。

图二　景德镇湖田窑元代地层出土影青玲珑瓷残片
（景德镇陶瓷考古研究所藏）

关于玲珑瓷的起源，有研究者认为："在景德镇湖田窑的宋代遗物中，可见到这种透明的影青釉填满了孔眼的镂空器残片，可惜至今尚未发现可靠的实物证明景德镇在宋代已经生产了'玲珑瓷'。"[6]南京博物院王志敏在《学瓷琐记》提到："玲珑青釉瓷始于北朝末至隋初，唐、宋、元未见，至明初永乐年间有景德镇窑玲珑瓷烧造，此后复见于清代乾隆年间。"[7]可惜王先生没有提供这个假说的立论根据。

据目前考古发现，景德镇烧造玲珑瓷不早于元代。景德镇陶瓷考古研究所在湖田窑南河南岸元代扰土层发现过一片影青（青白釉）玲珑瓷片，残长4.9厘米（图二，右）。据发掘者考证："宋代景德镇经常生产香薰等镂空器，而影青釉又极易流淌，其积釉处产生的艺术效果自然会启迪陶工制作玲珑瓷。但要有意识地生产玲珑瓷，却需要釉具有一定的高温黏度，否则，孔洞中的釉汁会淌光。元代影青釉的高温黏度较宋代增大，具有生产玲珑瓷的工艺基础。该残片似为一直壁香炉近口沿的部位，垂流的釉汁有限，所以镂空中应认为填入釉料，以烧成玲珑剔透的效果。该残片似为景德镇窑最早的玲珑瓷。"[8]

近年还有学者提出，玲珑瓷的诞生源于产品缺陷，"宋代景德镇瓷器中有一种叫熏炉的产品，炉盖采用镂空装饰，在烧成过程中，由于釉料的高温流动性好，加之烧成温度往往控制不严，常使窑内温度过高，从而使釉料熔融后流动而将炉盖上的孔洞填平，出窑后对光一照，光亮透明。这种偶然的产品缺陷却使工匠们大受启发，终于在明代永乐年间成功烧制出晶莹剔透的玲珑瓷器。到明中期成化年间，景德镇把晶莹剔透的玲珑与青翠幽雅的青花结合组成图案，烧造出闻名于世的青花玲珑瓷器。"[9]

[6] 欧阳世彬：《浅谈青花玲珑瓷》，《景德镇陶瓷》1981年第2期，页30。

[7] 王志敏：《学瓷琐记》（油印本初刊于1978年），上海：文汇出版社，2002年。

[8] 香港大学冯平山博物馆、景德镇市陶瓷考古研究所：《景德镇出土五代至清初瓷展》，香港：香港大学冯平山博物馆，1992年，页122～124，图版107。

[9] 郭晓昊：《小清新玲珑瓷源自缺陷美》，《广州日报》2012年5月13日。

殊不知，伊朗陶工早就烧造出玲珑陶碗。2013年7月，我们在英国维多利亚与阿尔伯特博物馆中东展厅中见到一件采用镂空施釉技术烧造的白陶樽，器形为西亚、埃及常见，但是雕刻纹样却模仿景德镇青白瓷。此种镂空施釉技术传入中国后，被称为"玲珑瓷"。后来，我们又在杜伦大学东方博物馆见到12世纪波斯陶工烧造的玲珑陶碗，并在剑桥大学菲茨威廉博物馆见到两件伊朗古尔干出土的12~13世纪玲珑陶碗（图三）。

众所周知，景德镇陶瓷艺术在许多方面受到中东陶器艺术的强烈影响。元青花就是在伊斯兰艺术影响下创烧的，而景德镇青白瓷模制印花工艺亦模仿伊斯兰制陶术。伦敦维多利亚与艾伯特博物馆藏有一件伊朗喀尚出土的伊斯兰印花陶碗模具，为我们研究12世纪伊斯兰模制印花技术提供了重要考古学依据（图四）。

伊斯兰文化起源于阿拉伯荒漠，许多伊斯兰工艺技术实际上源于美索不达米亚文化或古波斯文化，而模制印花技术则来自古波斯艺术。1992年，新疆喀什亚吾鲁克遗址发现一件萨珊波斯风格的三耳陶壶[10]（图五）。这件陶壶上的人物浮雕图案就采用波斯模制印花工艺。20世纪初，德国考察队在新疆和田亦发现一件类似的人物浮雕陶壶，现藏柏林东亚艺术博物馆。

在中东伊斯兰艺术的影响下，景德镇浮梁瓷局窑工还烧造过伊斯兰风格的孔雀翠蓝釉瓷器。1988年5月，景德镇市铺设地下电缆，景德镇陶瓷考古研究所为配合基建工程，在珠山北麓风景路马路中心宽约1.5、长约11、深1.5~1.8米的

[10] 新疆维吾尔自治区文物局、新疆文物考古所、新疆维吾尔自治区博物馆：《新疆文物古迹大观》，乌鲁木齐：新疆美术摄影出版社，1999年，页267，图0728。

图三　12~13世纪伊朗古尔干出土玲珑陶碗
（剑桥大学菲茨威廉博物馆藏）

图四　伊朗喀尚出土12世纪伊斯兰印花陶碗模具
（维多利亚与艾伯特博物馆藏）

图五　公元5世纪萨珊波斯风格的三耳陶壶
（新疆喀什亚吾鲁克遗址出土）

[11] 刘新园:《元文宗——图帖睦尔时代之官窑瓷器考》,《文物》2001年第11期,页58,图10、图27。

[12] 汪勃:《再谈中国出土唐代中晚期至五代的西亚伊斯兰孔雀翠蓝釉陶器》,《考古》2012年第3期,页85～96。

[13] 北京大学考古学系、河北省文物研究所、邯郸地区文物保管所:《观台磁州窑址》,北京:文物出版社,1997年,页312～314。

沟道中,发现了一批形制特异,十分引人注目的瓷器残片,其品类有卵白瓷、青花、蓝地白花、蓝地金彩、孔雀绿地青花、孔雀绿地金彩等。经对合复原,其器型有鼓形平顶盖罐、盖盒、桶式盖罐、小底鼓腹盖罐等。不能复原的尚有青花葫芦瓶与孔雀绿地青花盒之类。以上器皿多饰双角五爪龙纹、变形莲花瓣、杂宝、十字杵、姜牙海水、凤穿牡丹等。但以双角五爪龙纹为多,约占总量90%以上。

值得注意的是,该遗址出土了一件孔雀翠蓝釉金龙纹砚台盖盒和一片孔雀蓝釉五爪金龙纹盖合残片(图六)。孔雀翠蓝釉,又称"孔雀绿釉"。据刘新园先生考证,此类砚台盒是为元文宗烧造的文具。元人烧造孔雀蓝釉瓷器往往在釉下施化妆土。元人为什么要在白瓷胎上覆盖化妆土呢?因为波斯陶器都有一层白色的化妆土,波斯人使用化妆土是因孔雀绿釉透明度高,波斯陶胎粗黑或粗褐,如果不用化妆土,瓷釉颜色便会暗而不鲜;而使用白色的化妆土掩盖粗糙色重的陶胎之后,透明的孔雀绿釉才会亮丽鲜艳。而景德镇瓷器由于瓷胎洁白细密,挂孔雀绿釉时根本就没有必要用化妆土;而元代陶工多此一举地使用化妆土,显然是在亦步亦趋地模仿波斯制陶术[11]。

早在唐代中晚期至五代,中东伊斯兰孔雀翠蓝釉陶器就传入中国[12]。孔雀蓝釉,是以氧化铜和氧化铁为着色剂的低温铅釉陶器,与唐三彩中蓝釉的根本区别在于后者是用氧化钴作着色剂。目前所见最早的孔雀蓝釉器是宋金时期山西制作的磁州窑系产品[13]。如前所述,元代景德镇窑也开始烧造这种伊斯兰艺

图六　元代孔雀翠蓝釉五爪金龙纹瓷片
（景德镇风景路出土）

图七　忽鲁谟斯旧港出土13世纪孔雀翠蓝釉陶片
（威廉姆森收集品）

[14] Andrew G. Williamson, "Hormuz and the trade of Gulf in the 14th-15th centuries A.D.," *Proceedings of the Seminar for Arabian Studies*, 6, 1972, pp. 52-68; Peter Morgan: "New Thoughts on Old Hormuz: Chinese Ceramics in the Hormuz Region in the Thirteenth and Fourteenth Centuries," *Iran* 29, 1991, pp.67-83.

[15] Andrew G. Williamson, "Regional distribution of medieval Persian pottery in the light of recent investigations," *Oxford Studies in Islamic Art*, 4, 1988, pp. 11-22.

术风格的陶瓷。既然元代景德镇青白瓷模制印花工艺、孔雀翠蓝釉工艺皆受到伊斯兰制陶术的影响，那么，元代景德镇窑烧造玲珑瓷的工艺同样在伊斯兰制陶术影响下应运而生。

随着伊利汗国的建立，中国与伊斯兰世界的文化交流，尤其是海上丝绸之路上的国际交流更加频繁。元代早期波斯湾主要国际贸易港在忽鲁谟斯港（今伊朗米纳布）。牛津大学威廉姆森博士在这个古港口遗址发现许多宋元瓷片，包括景德镇青白瓷、德化窑青白瓷和龙泉窑青瓷、景德镇元末民窑青花瓷残片[14]。与之同出的还有大批伊斯兰陶片，如模制印花陶片、孔雀翠蓝釉陶片[15]（图七）。这些伊斯兰陶器当为从事海上国际贸易的穆斯林商人的日常生活用品，而伊斯兰制陶术正是随海上丝绸之路国际贸易，由穆斯林商人传入中国陶瓷的制造中心景德镇的。

2013年8月4日

引用书目

1. 古代文献

〔法〕殷弘绪撰、王景圣译：《给中国和印度传教会会计奥日神父的信》，《陶瓷资料》1978年第1期。

2. 近人论著

北京大学考古学系、河北省文物研究所、邯郸地区文物保管所：《观台磁州窑址》，北京：文物出版社，1997年，页312～314。

郭晓昊：《小清新玲珑瓷源自缺陷美》，《广州日报》2012年5月13日。

〔英〕德雷克·康耐特、塞斯·普利斯曼、张然：《近东地区考古遗址发现的龙泉窑瓷器——英国威廉姆森藏品及斯拉夫遗址调查藏品中的龙泉窑青瓷简介》，《龙泉窑研究》，北京：紫禁城出版社，2011年，页447～449。

刘新园：《元文宗——图帖睦尔时代之官窑瓷器考》，《文物》2001年第11期，页58，图10、图27。

欧阳世彬：《浅谈青花玲珑瓷》，《景德镇陶瓷》1981年第2期，页30。

汪勃：《再谈中国出土唐代中晚期至五代的西亚伊斯兰孔雀翠兰釉陶器》，《考古》2012年第3期，页85～96。

王志敏：《学瓷琐记》（油印本初刊于1978年），上海：文汇出版社，2002年。

香港大学冯平山博物馆、景德镇市陶瓷考古研究所：《景德镇出土五代至清初瓷展》，香港：香港大学冯平山博物馆，1992年，页122～124，图版107。

新疆维吾尔自治区文物局、新疆文物考古所、新疆维吾尔自治区博物馆：《新疆文物古迹大观》，乌鲁木齐：新疆美术摄影出版社，1999年。

许之衡撰、杜斌校注：《饮流斋说瓷》，济南：山东画报出版社，2010年。

中国硅酸盐学会：《中国陶瓷史》，北京：文物出版社，1982年。

〔日〕矢泽利彦（Yazawa Toshihiko）撰、艾廉莹译：《日文本〈耶稣会士中国书简集〉解说》，《中国史研究动态》1980年第6期。

Andrew G. Williamson, "Hormuz and the trade of Gulf in the 14th-15th centuries A.D.," *Proceedings of the Seminar for Arabian Studies*, 6, 1972, pp. 52-68.

Andrew G. Williamson, "Regional distribution of medieval Persian pottery in the light of recent investigations," *Oxford Studies in Islamic Art*, 4, 1988, pp. 11-22.

Peter Morgan: "New Thoughts on Old Hormuz: Chinese Ceramics in the Hormuz Region in the Thirteenth and Fourteenth Centuries," *Iran* 29, 1991, pp.67-83.

Seth M.N. Priestman, *Settlement & Ceramics in Southern Iran: An Analysis of the Sasanian & Islamic Periods in the Williamson Collection*, M.A. Thesis, 2005, p.134.

赐赉抑或贩卖？
——关于海外留存元代青花瓷输出性质的一个思考
Gift or Exported Porcelain?
—A Study on How Blue and White Spread Overseas in Yuan Dynasty

黄 珊

（中国社会科学院考古研究所）

HUANG Shan

(The Institute of Archaeology, Chinese Academy of Social Sciences)

内容摘要 /

关于目前海外留存元代青花瓷的性质，通常有"外销瓷"和"赐赉瓷"两种说法，本文拟从考古发现的元代青花瓷入手，考察其流布及其市场取向，同时结合文献记载，考量元人航海路线及主要活动内容，确定转运贸易在元代航海活动中的重要地位，并对阿拉伯人在元代海外贸易中发挥的重要作用进行了强调。

关键词 /

赐赉瓷　外销瓷　元青花

ABSTRACT / Generally there are two ways of explanation on blue and white porcelain in Yuan Dynasty, one of which is exported porcelain, while the other one is porcelain sent out as gift or reward from the Mongolian court. In this article, my discussion will be developed based on archaeological study to blue and white porcelain, and try to figure out its distribution and market orientation all over the world. Also I will examine the maritime routes and activities in Yuan dynasty and emphasize the importance of transferring trade and Arabian in the maritime activity at that time.

KEY WORDS / Gift porcelain; export porcelain; blue and white porcelain of the Yuan Dynasty

作为元代制瓷业新成就的青花瓷，甫一烧制成功，旋即扩散到亚非各地，在蒙元时期的东西方文化交流方面具有特殊的意义：不仅反映了"混一声教，无远弗届"的超级帝国框架下空前规模的人口流动与文化互惠，更说明了当时不同地理单元之间频繁高效的往来沟通。通过研究我们可以认知到，不特海外元青花瓷的流布存在鲜明的市场取向，仅就目前国内的考古发现来看，也存在数个不同层次的消费空间。如果我们承认这种鲜明的差别在当时就已经存在的话，是什么原因造成了这种局面呢？学者们关于这个问题已经提出过许多设想，尤其是那些最为人津津乐道的气势恢弘的大型元代青花瓷，到底是元政府为获取经济利益而生产的外销瓷，还是与诸汗国政府之间的贡赋赐赉往来有关？

许多学者都认同青花瓷的烧造与伊斯兰世界的审美诉求和实用功能密切相关，波普（J.A.Pope）认为，鉴于7世纪以来，阿拉伯商人一直致力于将中国商品提供给整个阿拉伯世界，阿拉伯世界应该是中国瓷器通往伊朗高原和安纳托利亚高原的重要中转地。根据波普的研究，土耳其托普卡普宫瓷器的迅速增加是1762年至1792年之间的事，其中有许多14～15世纪的中国陶瓷，但这应该不是靠商业贸易和进贡等自然增加的，而是从当时它的从属地叙利亚、埃及向伊斯坦布尔频繁地运来珍贵的商品[1]。三上次男先生也认为这些古代珍品也许就是从收藏很多优质中国瓷器的开罗运来的[2]。从14世纪初合赞汗开始，位于伊朗高原的伊儿汗国信奉伊斯兰教为国教，刘新园先生进一步提出"赐赉瓷"的概念，认为在元青花的烧造过程中，元朝政府起到了较大的主导作用，这类瓷器是专门为伊儿汗国烧造的官窑产品。刘先生的观点将海外分布的元青花从以往单纯的"销售"的视线框架中抽离出来，提出了更为明确的导向性，对元代青花瓷的研究思路具有极大的启发。从伊本·白图泰等旅行家、使节、行商的游记中，我们了解到，元顺帝时期，元朝政府与德里苏丹之间也颇有往来并顺致赠礼，其中就包括瓷器。那么，似亦可推知出德里图格拉克宫殿遗址(Tughlaq)出土的元代青花瓷也是元廷赠送给图格拉克苏丹的国礼。

元代使臣、航海家和旅行家的笔记让我们认识到，有元一代，航海技术得到极大发展，通往波斯湾甚或北非的航线已趋成熟，但印度西南海岸可能是宋元时代中国船只所能够到达的最远处，此处以西再到波斯湾和红海地区，都需要在故临（Quilon，今奎隆）和喀里古特（Calicut，今卡利卡特）换乘阿拉伯或波斯人的船只。通过数篇游记的比对研究，我们认为，绝大多数船只，即便身负元廷重托，仍然在沿途不断参与商业贸易活动，而且由于回回人的参与，面向广大伊斯兰地区的海外贸易得以顺利开展，这种商业行为伴随着贡赋和赐赉，成为陶瓷流向海外的几种方式中不可或缺的一环。

[1] Pope, J.A., *Fourteenth-Century Blue-and-White, a Group of Chinese Porcelians in the Topkapu Sarayi Muzesi*, Istanbul. Washington:The Lord Baltimore Press, 1952.

[2] 〔日〕三上次男著、李锡经译：《陶瓷之路》，北京：文物出版社，1984年，页62。

一

元代青花瓷输出线路与市场取向

元代景德镇瓷器生产的主流是青白瓷和卵白釉瓷，相比而言，青花瓷创烧既

[3] 黄珊：《元青花与中外文化交流》附表一、二，2009年北京大学硕士研究生学位论文。

[4] 陈克伦：《略论元代青花瓷器中的伊斯兰文化因素》，《上海博物馆集刊》第六期，上海古籍出版社，1992年。

[5] Pope, J.A., *Fourteenth-Century Blue-and-White, a Group of Chinese Porcelians in the Topkapu Sarayi Muzesi, Istanbul*. Washington: The Lord Baltimore Press, 1952.

[6] Pope, J.A., *Chinese Porcelains from the Ardebil Shrine*. Washington: The Lord Baltimore Press, 1956.

[7] Smart, E.S., Fourteenth Century Chinese Porcelain from a Tughlaq Palace in Delhi, *T.O.C.S*, Vol.41(1976–1977), p.230.

晚，产量亦小，国内发现的元青花存世量并不丰富，完整器不到两百件[3]，而国外收藏的元青花整器据估计近三百件[4]。考古发现证明，元代青花瓷输出的范围很广，从东南亚、南亚、西亚直到北非和东非等地的沿海城市和重要内地城市都有发现。这些地区的元青花有传世藏品和出土物两类，其中传世藏品主要集中于土耳其托普卡普宫博物馆（Topkapu Sarayi）[5]和伊朗德黑兰考古博物馆[原藏于伊朗阿尔德比神庙（Ardebil Shrine）][6]，出土数量最大的是印度德里图格拉克宫殿遗址（Tughlaq）[7]。这三地收藏或出土的都是体型巨硕、青色鲜丽和绘制精美的大型

图一　国外收藏或出土的元青花瓷器

1. 托普卡普宫博物馆藏梅瓶　2. 托普卡普宫藏八方葫芦瓶　3. 阿尔德比神庙藏盘　4. 图格拉克遗址出土盘

青花瓷器（图一）。此外，东南亚地区也出土或传世不少元代青花瓷器或残片，例如中爪哇发现的"麻诺巴歇（Madjapahit）王都遗址"等[8]。在波斯湾和红海附近的许多城市都发现不少元青花碎片，最具有代表性的例子是埃及开罗北部的福斯塔特遗址（Al-Fustat），据统计，20世纪以来，在福斯塔特出土的中国瓷片的数量，约有12,000余片，包括了由9世纪的晚唐至18世纪初的清早期中国南北方各大窑口产品，其过程延绵千年，而且质量均属上乘[9]。叙利亚位于从港口城市到伊朗高原的交通要冲，那里也发现许多珍藏了数个世纪的元青花[10]。

总而言之，海路沿线发现的元青花构成了一条连贯完整的营销路线[11]。对于陶瓷运输和销售而言，海运无疑也是更合适的选择。陶瓷沉重且易碎，陆路运输显然成本高难度大，但是海船不仅容载量大，而且装载陶瓷还能起到压舱的作用，是陶瓷外销的主要途径。而陆路上目前只有数个城址有相关发现，彼此之间关系并不紧密，至中西亚地区甚至会失去线索，无法构架出一条有始有终的销售路线，更深入的研究尚有待于考古材料的进一步丰富。

相比于境外的发现来看，国内发现的元青花器型多种多样，品相差异较大，不见于国外的类型包括饮具（例如高足杯、匜、盏、劝盘、执壶、凤首壶、梨形壶等）、生活用器（例如笔架、粉盒、鸟食罐等）、礼器（香炉、净瓶、觚、蒜头瓶等）和明器（塔式罐、塑像等）[12]（图二）。土耳其和伊朗以及印度最常见的碗、盘、瓶、罐在国内出土品种中比例较小，许多蓝地白花的器物，以及绘制有庭院景观和动物纹样的盘，都不见于国内窑址以外其他地方的出土，应该是专供这些海外国家使用的。而且同类器物相比较而言，国内的体量不及国外的大，例如伊、土两国收藏的直径达40～50厘米的盘，在国内仅

[8] 朱裕平：《元代青花瓷》，上海：文汇出版社，2000年，页280、281，图版5。

[9] Yuba Tadanori, Chinese Porcelain from Fustat Based on Research from 1998-2001, *Transaction of the Oriental Ceramic Society*, Volume 76, 2011-2012, The Oriental Ceramic Society, pp. 1–17.

[10] Carswell, J., "China and Islam in Maldive Island", *T.O.C.S.*, 1975-1977, p.121.

[11] 黄珊：《〈陶瓷之路〉与元代外销青花瓷研究》，《卡乐B日本研究基金2007～2008年度研究课题成果汇编》，2008年，页104～120。

[12] 前揭《元青花与中外文化交流》。

图二　国内出土的元青花瓷器

1. 内蒙古集宁路窖藏出土高足杯　2. 浙江杭州窖藏出土笔架水盂　3. 江西萍乡市福田乡窖藏出土带座香炉

图三　国内出土的元青花盘

1、2.湖南常德市出土　3、4.内蒙古林西窖藏出土　5.景德镇落马桥出土

[13] 古湘：《介绍几件元、明青花瓷器》，《文物》1973年第12期，页64～66。

[14] 林西县文物管理所：《内蒙古林西县元代瓷器窖藏》，《文物》2001年第8期。

[15] 香港冯平山博物馆、景德镇陶瓷考古研究所：《景德镇出土陶瓷》，香港：香港大学冯平山博物馆，1992年，图版158。

见于湖南常德市出土两件鱼藻纹盘（口径45厘米左右）[13]，内蒙古林西窖藏出土的莲池鸳鸯纹盘口径仅13.6厘米，龙纹盘口径仅15.9厘米[14]，景德镇落马桥出土淡描龙纹盘口径仅27.7厘米[15]（图三）。我们试将国内出土元青花和国外（伊朗、土耳其和印度三地）的器物类型和数量做一简单统计，列表如下：

表一　国内外元青花种类统计对比表

用途	器类	国内（总计164件）		伊土印（总计138件）	
餐具	大盘	7	4.3%	82	59.4%
	大碗	6	3.7%	29	21.0%
储藏器	罐	15	9.1%	7	5.1%
	梅瓶	14	8.5%	10	7.3%
	玉壶春瓶	14	8.5%	1	0.7%
	葫芦瓶	0	0	4	2.9%
	盘口瓶	0	0	1	0.7%
	扁壶	0	0	3	2.2%
饮具	高足杯	47	28.7%	0	0
	匜	5	3.0%	0	0
	盏	9	5.5%	0	0
	劝盘	2	1.2%	0	0
	托盏	2	1.2%	0	0

续表

用途	器类	国内（总计164件）		伊土印（总计138件）	
饮具	执壶	3	1.8%	0	0
	凤首壶	2	1.2%	0	0
	梨形壶	2	1.2%	0	0
生活用器	盒	2	1.4%	0	0
	鸟食罐	2	1.2%	0	0
礼器	净瓶	4	2.4%	0	0
	蒜头瓶	3	1.8%	0	0
	觚	3	1.8%	0	0
	香炉	4	2.4%	0	0
明器	塔式罐	1	0.6%	0	0
	塑像	1	0.6%	0	0

从表一可以看出，元青花的销售有鲜明的市场取向，供应给国内市场和国外市场的元青花在种类和质量上都存在一定差异。可资参考的是，国内在元代统治中心和富庶地区发现的元青花，质量比景德镇周边地区要好得多，还有一些元代的窖藏，保存了大量青花瓷，例如保定和高安窖藏[16]（图四）。窖藏此物，说明元青花在当时也是比较新奇和珍贵的品种，那么在海外发现的大量高质量元青花，应该与国内一样，不是一般平民阶层所能够消费的。当然，这一时期也有频繁的民间贸易，《岛夷志略》的作者汪大渊就是一名附商舶出海的平民[17]，从他的描述中，我们可以窥见当时海运贸易的盛况，故而我们也能在东南亚和北非地区发现一些民间烧制的元青花瓷器及碎片。相比较而言，这些

[16] 河北省博物馆：《保定市发现一批元代瓷器》，《文物》1965年第2期。刘金成：《高安元代窖藏瓷器》，北京：朝华出版社，2006年。

[17] （元）汪大渊著、苏继庼校释：《岛夷志略校释》，北京：中华书局，1981年。

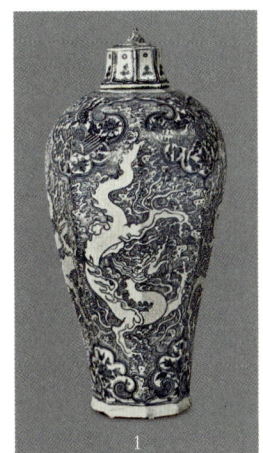   

图四　国内窖藏出土的元青花瓷器
1、2. 河北保定窖藏出土　3、4. 江西高安窖藏出土

小件青花瓷器要绝少于大件器物，在中东地区几乎没有完整器留存下来。这仍然表明大件元青花销售的对象主要是中东和南亚等地区。

元青花的市场取向，关系到其营销背景和市场角色，如果我们承认这种鲜明的差别在当时就已经存在的话，是什么原因造成了这种局面呢？学者们关于这个问题已经提出过许多设想，大件元青花到底是元政府为获得经济利益而生产的外销瓷，还是与政府间的政治活动有关？

二

元伊关系与青花瓷的烧造

作为蒙古帝国的一部分，位于伊朗高原的伊儿汗国长期与元朝中央保持密切联系。公元1252年（宪宗蒙哥汗三年），拖雷之子旭烈兀挥师西征，西征军的主力于1256年抵达呼罗珊，之后迅速席卷西亚，先后击溃亦思马因人固守的伊朗西北部、阿拔斯哈里发王朝的首府报达以及伊拉克和伊朗西部的一些中等城市。1259年，旭烈兀在西亚牢固地建立起了拖雷系蒙古人的统治，即所知的伊儿汗国[18]。由于伊儿汗国与元朝的统治者同出于拖雷一系，双边关系一直比较亲密，伊儿汗承认大汗是他们的君主。对比起曾经困扰忽必烈一朝将近半个世纪之久的窝阔台后汗海都和察合台后汗笃哇之乱，伊儿汗国不仅没有与元朝政府之间有过任何不睦，相反一直有频繁的使团往来。相互之间交通的便利，不难想象。据《元史》记载，伊儿汗所遣来元使节，一年中往往有两三次，大德年间（1297~1307年）合赞汗遣使来贡一次；泰定年间（1324~1328年），元朝遣使两次，不赛因遣使献贡多达十一次；至顺年间（1330~1333年），不赛因遣使六次，元朝政府遣使一次[19]。

从14世纪初合赞汗开始，伊儿汗国转而奉伊斯兰教为国教，一直以来，关于元青花与伊斯兰文化的关系的探讨颇多，许多学者都认同这种瓷器的烧造可能与伊斯兰世界的需要相关。尤其值得注意的是，云南玉溪窑也能烧制青花瓷，而云南地区在元代也是穆斯林的集中地之一，这应该不只是巧合。刘新园先生已经就此问题提出过"赐赉瓷"的概念，认为在元青花的烧造过程中，元朝政府起到了较大的主导作用，是专门为伊儿汗国烧造的官窑产品[20]。刘先生的观点对我们的研究很有启发性，将元青花的外销从以往的"销售"的眼光中解脱了出来。但是这又向我们提出了一个问题：既然是专供伊儿汗国的官方礼

---

[18] （明）宋濂等撰：《元史》，北京：中华书局，1976年。卷三《宪宗本纪》，页46、47、51；卷一百四十九《郭侃传》，页3523、3524。

[19] 前揭《元史》，卷二一《成宗本纪》，页460。卷二九、三〇《泰定帝本纪》，页643~678。卷三四、三五、三六《文宗本纪》，页760~805；卷三七《宁宗本纪》，页812。

[20] 刘新园：《元文宗——图帖睦尔时代之官帖瓷器考》，《文物》2001年第11期。

物，为什么在东南亚和南亚，以及非洲各处都有发现呢？从伊本·白图泰的游记中，我们了解到，顺帝时期，元朝政府与德里苏丹之间尚有往来[21]。那么，也不能排除元廷将青花瓷作为礼物赠送给图格拉克苏丹的可能性。至于其他零星遍布于各地的元青花，我们认为，应该从元朝海路运营方式的角度来解释。

三

元代海上交通盛况与青花瓷外销性质

从13世纪早期开始，成吉思汗及其子孙的铁蹄席卷旧大陆，迅速建立起"混一声教，无远弗届"的超级帝国。其版图东起太平洋，西达地中海，超过了地理大发现以前人类历史上的任何世界帝国，极大地促进了这个地理单元内的人群活动与文化交流。自五代十国以来，由于内地政治局面步入长期的分裂对峙阶段，以及西北地区政权的崛起，汉唐时期往来络绎不绝的丝绸之路一度归于沉寂，转而发展海路交通。进入蒙元时期以后，不特陆上通道重新得到恢复，航海贸易也臻于极盛。但是，由于元朝与西北诸王海都、笃哇的长期战争，以及察合台汗国与伊儿汗国不时发生争夺领地的战争，使得蒙元时期的陆上交通时断时续。而海路则相对畅通许多。

元朝政府重视海外贸易，采用了许多具体政策，广开海路。元世祖至元十四年（1277年）取浙、闽等地后，就沿袭南宋制度，在泉州、庆元（宁波）、上海、澉浦四地设立市舶司，重用南宋时期管理泉州市舶的官员蒲寿庚[22]。从忽必烈时期到英宗至治二年（1322年）的46年间，元代的航海政策经历了前后"四禁四开"，但四次海禁加起来不过十年时间[23]。至治二年"复置市舶提举司于泉州、庆元、广东三路。"[24]之后直到元代灭亡，没有再发生过变动。在政府扶持和商业利益驱动下，元代海外贸易得到空前大发展，当时的史籍和笔记中记录的海路贸易的国家、地区的名称在200个以上，这些国家和地区，遍布中南半岛、马来半岛、菲律宾群岛、印度尼西亚群岛、印度次大陆及其周围地区、波斯湾和阿拉伯半岛、东非和北非。其中相当一部分是以前不见于记载的[25]（图五）。

有元一代涌现出大批著名的使臣、航海家和旅行家，关于海路交通的记载大量丰富，这些都使我们相信，元代航海技术得到极大发展，通往波斯湾甚或北非的航线已趋成熟。

[21]〔摩洛哥〕伊本·白图泰著、马金鹏译：《伊本·白图泰游记》，银川：宁夏人民出版社，1985年，页485~491。

[22] 前揭《元史》，卷九、十《世祖本纪》，页175~219。

[23] 陈高华：《元代的海外贸易》，《历史研究》1978年第3期，页61~69。

[24] 前揭《元史》，卷二十八《英宗本纪》，页621。

[25] 陈高华、陈尚胜：《中国海外交通史》，台北：文津出版社，1997年，页94。

[26] 孛罗名见《元史》卷九《世祖本纪》，只提到他在世祖年间的任职："至元十四年二月，以大司农、御史大夫、宣慰使兼领侍仪司事孛罗为枢密副使兼宣徽使、领侍仪司事"，据余大钧先生考证，孛罗是蒙古朵儿边部人，1283年夏，奉旨出使波斯伊利汗国，于1284年末或1285年初到达，从此一去不返。见余大钧：《蒙古朵儿边氏孛罗事辑》，《元史论丛》第1辑，北京：中华书局，1982年，页179~199。

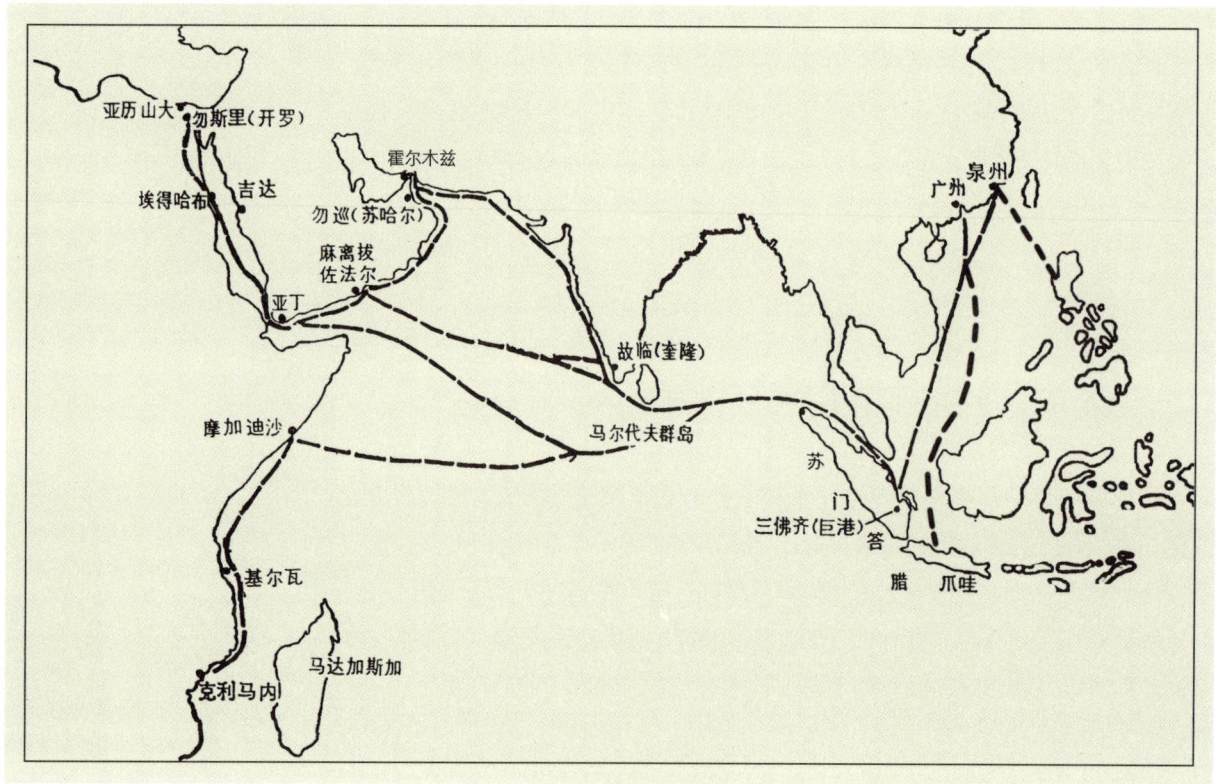

图五　元代航海范围示意图

[27]〔法〕沙海昂注，冯承钧译：《马可波罗行纪》，北京：中华书局，2004年，第一卷第十七、十八章。

[28] 该使者回泉州之后，立碑记出使事。此碑现存泉州市海外交通史博物馆。

[29]（元）黄溍：《松江嘉定等处海运千户杨君墓志铭》，《四部丛刊·金华黄先生文集》三十五卷。

世祖至元二十年（1283年），蒙古朵儿边氏贵族孛罗奉命出使伊儿汗国，当时正值海都叛乱，陆路不通，孛罗一行遂取海道，在忽鲁谟子（霍尔木兹）登陆[26]。至元二十八年（1289年），伊儿汗阿鲁浑遣使者兀剌台、阿卜思哈、火者等三人入朝世祖，请求从其已故王妃卜鲁罕之族部伯牙乌氏中选女子为续弦，次年此三使者即奉旨与马可·波罗一家一同护送所选女子阔阔真，取海道回波斯。他们从泉州启程，经过苏门答腊和印度，最后从忽里模子（今霍尔木兹）登陆[27]。成宗大德三年（1299年），成宗遣使者悬带金字海青牌前往伊儿汗国火鲁没思（霍尔木兹），其往返皆由海道[28]。大德八年（1304年），成宗派杨枢护送伊儿汗国合赞汗的使臣那怀归国复命，他们同样经过海路，抵达忽鲁谟斯[29]。虽然元朝与伊儿汗国之间的使臣往来的路线并没有附记于其中，但是我们参考上述出使伊儿汗国的记录，可以猜测，其中走海路者必不在少数。这些政府派遣的使者各自都身负重任，但是他们选择海路，并且基本上都是冬季从泉州出发，在霍尔木兹港登陆伊儿汗国，说明当时这条路线已经相当成熟。不过值得一提的是，由此并不能得出元代已经能够直航航波斯湾的结论。

印度西南海岸可能是宋元时代中国船只所能够到达的最远处，此处以西再到波斯湾和红海地区，都需要换乘阿拉伯或波斯人的船只，这里最重要的港口城市是故临（Quilon，今奎隆）和喀里古特（Calicut，今卡利卡特）。宋人周去非在《岭外代答》中介绍从中国到阿拉伯半岛的海路为："中国舶商欲往大食，必自故临易小舟而往，虽以一月南风至之，然往返经二年矣。"[30]相反方向亦然："大食之来也，以小舟运而南行，至故临国，易大舟而东行。"[31]元世祖曾经遣畏兀儿人亦黑迷失两次出使招谕八罗孛，即印度西南部马拉巴尔海岸，即今奎隆所在；稍后还有四次出使俱蓝（亦为奎隆）的杨庭璧[32]。世祖时期政府派遣的大规模的出使活动范围主要限于东南亚和印度半岛南端，说明当时的航海技术仍然与宋代相去不远，中国船只行动的范围仅止于此。同时期的西方旅行家行记也向我们透露了这一点。1342年，摩洛哥旅行家伊本·白图泰（Ibn Battuta）奉德里苏丹之命，与中国使团一起回访中国。他们从喀里古特出发，当时港口内停泊有十三艘中国船只，起航后不久遇险，生还者逃到奎隆，中国使臣就此乘船归国[33]。值得一提的是，印度市场在中国的陶瓷外销中扮演着重要的角色。《岛夷志略》中记载小唄喃（奎隆）、古里佛（喀里古特）、朋加剌（恒河口）和天竺（印度河口）都消费中国瓷器[34]。

考查上述人士的出海历程可知，农历十二月从泉州出发，次年三月正好到达印度西南的俱蓝（Quilon），全程耗时仅四个月而已[35]。此时基本上离霍尔木兹港已不算遥远，基本已经走完了一半的路程。马可·波罗、孛罗、杨枢、成宗使者等人的目的地都是伊儿汗国，大都是冬季出发，登陆的港口都是霍尔木兹港。其中航行时间最长的是杨枢，大德八年（1304年）出发，十一年到达，来回共五年。马可·波罗与其接近，全程两年零两个月。比照杨庭璧的速度，我们很难相信，横渡印度洋北部的时间竟然会是从泉州到印度的五倍，而这一点也很难用等候季风来解释。在这种情况下，再看孛罗，至元二十年冬（1283年）出发，次年就登陆之后沿波斯法尔斯北上，于二十一年十月就到达了阿兰（阿塞拜疆），加上陆路行程，全程不到一年。

要了解杨枢和马可·波罗速度如此缓慢的原因，需要仔细审查他们途中的经历。杨枢的航海事迹见于其墓志铭[36]。从文中我们可以得知，杨枢远航至霍尔木兹港是他的第二次航海，他于第一次航海归国时结识了伊儿汗国合赞汗的使臣那怀，并以商船载其至中国。后来那怀归国时要求杨枢同行，得到了元朝政府的同意。杨枢第一次出海是为了经营官本船，第二次出海身负政治任务，元朝政府对杨枢也有所封诰，但是杨枢在这个过程中"又用其私钱市其土物、白马、黑犬、琥珀、葡萄酒、蕃盐之属以进"。即是说，他同时仍然在从事商

[30]（宋）周去非著、杨武泉校注：《岭外代答校注》，北京：中华书局，1999年，卷二"故临国"条。

[31] 前揭《岭外代答校注》，卷三"航海外夷"条。

[32] 前揭《元史》，卷一三一《亦黑迷失传》，第3198页；卷十二《世祖本纪》，页250。

[33] 前揭《伊本·白图泰游记》。

[34] 前揭《岛夷志略校释》。

[35] 杨庭璧至元十六年十二月出发至元十七年三月（1280年）顺利到达俱蓝，次年他再次出使，正月出发，舟行三月到达至僧伽耶山（斯里兰卡）时，北风已经停止，只能滞留在印度东南海岸。

[36]《松江嘉定等处海运千户杨君墓志铭》：

杨氏之先，世有显人，宋之盛时，有自闽而越而吴居澉浦者，累世以材武取贵仕。入国朝，仕益显，最号钜族。今以占籍为嘉兴人，君讳枢，字伯机，赠中宪大夫、松江府知府、上骑都尉，追封弘农郡伯春之曾孙，福建安抚使赠怀遂大将军、池州路总管、轻车都尉、追封弘农郡侯发之孙，嘉议大夫、杭州路总管致仕梓之第二子。母陆氏，所生母徐氏，陆以封，徐以赠，并为弘农郡夫人。徐夫人，温之宦家女，生君甫数岁而殁，陆夫人抚君不啻如己出。君幼警敏，长而喜学，一不以他嗜好接于心目，刮摩豪习，谨厚自将，未尝有绮纨子弟态，其处家虽米盐细务皆有法仪，隶辈无敢以其年少而易之，诸公贵人多称其能。大德五年，君年甫十九，致仕院俾以官本船浮海。至西洋，遇亲王合赞所遣使臣那怀等如京师，遂载之以来。那怀等朝贡事毕，请仍以君护送西还。丞相哈剌哈孙答

业活动。

陈得芝先生曾经总结过元代海外贸易空前兴盛的三个原因：其一，元朝统治者，尤其是世祖忽必烈，采取了积极进取的海外政策。其二，元朝政府重视海运贸易所带来的盈利，官方以及贵族都参与这一商业活动，这也与元朝政府取用回回人理财相关。其三，元朝与伊儿汗国的统治者同是拖雷后裔，两家关系至为密切[37]。第二点是元代海外贸易中尤其突出的一个特点，阿拉伯人历来就是活跃在南海贸易上的重要角色，到了元朝，位居第二等公民之列的回回人在元朝航海事业和经济活动中更是发挥着举足轻重的作用，例如宋末降元的泉州市舶使司蒲寿庚，关于蒲寿庚及阿拉伯人与宋元时代海外贸易的关系，日本学者桑原骘藏的著作《蒲寿庚考》已广为人知[38]。陈高华先生则从杨枢入手，讨论元代著名的航海世家，除蒲寿庚以外，还有掌管泉府司和市舶司的回回人沙不丁和合不失[39]。泉府司"掌领御位下及皇太子、皇太后、诸王出纳金银事"[40]，即为皇族理财。除此以外，这个机构还一度专领海运。我们不难想象，正是因为回回人的参与和说明，面向广大伊斯兰地区的海外贸易才能顺利开展，元朝政府依赖他们为自己谋取利益。

《经世大典》中记载了同马可·波罗一起护送阔阔真到伊儿汗国的使团归国时乘船的情况："平章沙不丁上言：今年三月奉旨，遣兀剌台、阿卜思哈、火者取道马八儿，往阿鲁浑大王位下。同行一百六十人，内九十人已支分例，余七十人，闻其诸王所赠遗及买得者，乞不给分例口粮。奉旨：勿与之。"[41]从这一条记录我们可以看出，这个使团中只有九十人领有经费的，其余七十人将以赠与诸王的岁赐（或礼物）和货物为自己的经费。这些岁赐和货物如何支付这七十人航海期间的支出呢？那当然是要将其投入到海路贸易中赢得利润了。

关于岁赐的性质，学者们已经作过一系列研究。根据波斯文献记载，1298年合赞汗派使节前往中国，向元成宗贡献珍宝异物。使臣留中国四年，回国时元成宗厚赐之，"并以答书及蒙哥汗时代以来旭烈兀应得之岁赐付使者，遣官一人送使者回国"[42]。前文提到的与杨枢同行的那怀，于大德八年（1304年）来到中国，同年，元朝政府设立了"管领本投下大都等路打捕鹰房诸色人匠都总管府，秩正三品，掌哈赞大王位下事……"[43]。蒙古制度，宗王在中原各有分地、封户，旭烈兀于蒙哥汗七年（1257年）分封时，他的名下"分拨彰德路二万五千五十六户"[44]。他应得的贡赋由元政府代为收存，前文提到的1298年使团带回的岁赐，可能就是四十年来积攒的从彰德路收得的贡赋。一般岁赐的形式为封户贡的丝、钞以及皇帝每年赏赐的定额银币，狭义的仅指后者[45]。最近林梅村先生提出针对伊儿汗国的岁赐，可能用以订烧青花瓷。

刺罕如其请，秦授君忠显校尉、海运副千户、佩金符，与俱行。以八年发京师，十一年乃至其登陆处曰忽鲁模思云。是役也，君往来长风巨浪中历五星霜，凡舟楫糇粮物器之须，一出于君，不以烦有司，既又用私钱市其土物白马、黑犬、琥珀、葡萄酒、番盐之属以进，平章政事察那等引见宸庆殿而退。方议旌擢以酬其劳，而君以前在海上感瘴毒疾作而归。至大二年也，阅七寒暑，疾乃间。寻丁陆夫人忧，家食者二十载，益练达于世，故绝圭角，破崖岸，因自号默默道人。泰定四年，始用荐者起家为昭信校尉、常熟江阴等处海运副千户。居官以廉称，被省檄，给庆绍温台漕挽之直，力划宿蠹掊克之弊，绝无所容，天历二年部运抵直沽仓，适疾复作，在告满百日，归就医于杭之私廨，疾愈剧，不可为，俄升松江嘉定等处海运千户，命下，君已卒。至顺二年八月十四日其卒之日，也享年四十有九……

[37] 陈得芝：《元代海外交通的发展与明初郑和下西洋》，收入《蒙元史研究丛稿》，北京：人民出版社，2005年，页414～418。

[38] 〔日〕桑原骘藏著、陈裕菁译：《蒲寿庚考》，上海：中华书局，1929年。

[39] 陈高华：《元代的航海世家澉浦杨氏》，见《元史研究新论》，上海社会科学出版社，2005年，页238～261。

[40] 前揭《元史》，卷十一《世祖纪八》，页227页。

[41] 《经世大典·站赤》，见《永乐大典》卷19418，页15。

[42] 《瓦撒夫书》，见：（瑞典）多桑著，冯承钧译：《多桑蒙古史》下册，北京：中华书局，1962年，页319。

综上，元代船只不具备直航能力，除了不时靠岸补给并买卖货物之外，到印度西海岸时还需要换乘阿拉伯或波斯人的商船。在这种条件下，显然不可能有专门的供使臣使用的非营利性船只，与明初郑和下西洋的情况是完全不同的，使臣必须搭载商船完成政治使命，伊儿汗国的使臣那怀搭载海商杨枢的商船来到中国就是例证之一。元朝所谓官方经营的"官本船"是营利性的商船[46]，常常委托给商人（其中不乏回回商人）进行，为皇室和贵族谋取利润。在这种前提下，就算有作为国礼的青花瓷，在长途跋涉以及流转贸易中也会被转卖到其他地区。印度的许多地方都消费中国瓷器，顺帝时期，元朝政府与德里苏丹之间尚有往来。可以说，纯粹的"馈赠瓷器"或许存在，但即便真的有携带元青花作为礼物的使团，这个使团在行进过程中难免被商业活动所影响，部分青花瓷器不可避免地要进入市场流通。

[43] 前揭《元史》，卷八十五《百官志一》，页2141。

[44] 前揭《元史》，卷九十五《食货志三》，页2417。

[45] 前揭《元代的航海世家澉浦杨氏》。

[46] 政府给本让商人出海舶易，回国后政府得七，商人得三。见《元史》，卷九十四《食货志·市舶》，第2417页："二十一年，设市舶都转运司于杭、泉二州，官自具船、给本，选人入蕃，贸易诸货。其所获之息，以十分为率，官取其七，所易人得其三。"

引用书目

1. 古代文献

（宋）周去非著、杨武泉校注：《岭外代答校注》，北京：中华书局，1999年。

（元）《经世大典·站赤》，见《永乐大典》卷19418。

（元）黄溍：《松江嘉定等处海运千户杨君墓志铭》，《四部丛刊·金华黄先生文集》卷三十五。

（元）汪大渊著、苏继庼校释：《岛夷志略校释》，北京：中华书局，1981年。

（明）宋濂等撰：《元史》，北京：中华书局，1976年。

〔法〕沙海昂注、冯承钧译：《马可波罗行纪》，北京：中华书局，2004年。

〔摩洛哥〕伊本·白图泰著、马金鹏译：《伊本·白图泰游记》，银川：宁夏人民出版社，1985年。

〔瑞典〕多桑著、冯承钧译：《多桑蒙古史》下册，《瓦撒夫书》，北京：中华书局，1962年。

2. 近人论著

陈得芝：《元代海外交通的发展与明初郑和下西洋》，收入《蒙元史研究丛稿》，北京：人民出版社，2005年，页414～418。

陈高华：《元代的海外贸易》，《历史研究》1978年第3期，页61～69。

陈高华：《元代的航海世家澉浦杨氏》，《元史研究新论》，上海社会科学出版社，2005年，页238～261。

陈高华、陈尚胜：《中国海外交通史》，台北：文津出版社，1997年，页94。

陈克伦：《略论元代青花瓷器中的伊斯兰文化因素》，《上海博物馆集刊》第六期，上海古籍出版社，1992年。

古湘：《介绍几件元、明青花瓷器》，《文物》1973年第12期，页64～66。

河北省博物馆：《保定市发现一批元代瓷器》，《文物》1965年第2期。

黄珊：《元青花与中外文化交流》，北京大学硕士研究生学位论文，2009年6月。

黄珊：《〈陶瓷之路〉与元代外销青花瓷研究》，《卡乐B日本研究基金2007～2008年度研究课题成果汇编》，2008年6月，页104～120。

林西县文物管理所：《内蒙古林西县元代瓷器窖藏》，《文物》2001年第8期。

刘金成编：《高安元代窖藏瓷器》，北京：朝华出版社，2006年。

刘新园：《元文宗——图帖睦尔时代之官窑瓷器考》，《文物》2001年第11期。

香港冯平山博物馆、景德镇陶瓷考古研究所：《景德镇出土陶瓷》，香港大学冯平山博物馆，1992年，图版158。

余大钧：《蒙古朵儿边氏孛罗事辑》，《元史论丛》第1辑，北京：中华书局，1982年，页179～199。

朱裕平：《元代青花瓷》，上海：文汇出版社，2000年，页280、281，图版5。

〔日〕三上次男著、李锡经译：《陶瓷之路》，北京：文物出版社，1984年。

〔日〕桑原骘藏著、陈裕菁译：《蒲寿庚考》，上海：中华书局，1929年。

Carswell, J., "China and Islam in Maldive Island", *T.O.C.S.*, 1975-1977, p.121.

Pope, J.A., *Fourteenth-Century Blue-and-White, a Group of Chinese Porcelians in the Topkapu Sarayi Muzesi, Istanbul*, Washington: The Lord Baltimore Press, 1952.

Pope, J.A., *Chinese Porcelains from the Ardebil Shrine*. Washington: The Lord Baltimore Press, 1956.

Smart, E.S., Fourteenth Century Chinese Porcelain from a Tughlaq Palace in Delhi, *T.O.C.S*, Vol.41(1976-1977), p.230.

Yuba Tadanori, Chinese Porcelain from Fustat Based on Research from 1998-2001, *Transaction of the Oriental Ceramic Society*, Volume 76, 2011-2012, The Oriental Ceramic Society, pp.1-17.

澳门出土明代青花瓷器研究

Research on Chinese Ming Dynasty Blue and White Porcelains Found at Macau

马锦强

（澳门特别行政区民政总署）

MA Kam-keong

(IACM, Macau)

内容摘要 /

20世纪90年代位于澳门南湾附近龙嵩街的一幅护土墙因大雨影响而垮塌，从倒塌的泥土中发现混集着大量陶瓷瓦片、海沙及贝壳，南湾是澳门当年货物起卸的一个重要海湾；另一批瓷片收集于北湾，该湾因城市发展所需，现已填海成为内陆，北湾亦是澳门当年另一个货船的重要进出港。

这两批瓷片现在分别收藏于澳门博物馆及澳门艺术博物馆，总数大约有4000多片，本文的主要研究对象是从澳门艺术博物馆收藏的千余片从北湾收集的青花瓷片中选取具代表性及较大件的作为研究，研究方法是从考古学角度来对每件瓷片作详细的分析，如在器型、纹饰及款识等方面作分类、排比等。同时，亦与国内外出土及世界各地博物馆收藏的晚明青花器作对比，从而得出澳门出土瓷片准确的生产年代、生产地点及当年货物的去向等。借澳门这些遗留下来的瓷片，研究中国瓷器在晚明期间外销的情况，了解葡萄牙人在16世纪东来的缘由及在澳门贸易的过程、如何从她的辉煌时代走至没落，以及个中的原由等。

关键词 /

澳门 瓷片 转口贸易 影响

ABSTRACT / At late 20th century a number of porcelain fragments were unearthed near South Bay in Macau. These fragments were found at the Rua Central from a retaining wall which was collapsed due to heavy rains. A large number of mixed porcelain fragments sands and shell from the sea were collected from the collapsed cement, South Bay was an important port of Macao for massive activities of cargo ships at early stage. Another large quantity of porcelain fragments were collected at North Bay, which was later transformed into interior land in result of reclamation. North Bay was also another important cargo ships loading point. These two collections of porcelain fragments are now stored at the Macau Museum and Macau

Museum of Art, with a total number around four thousand pieces. This article is to make a study on analysis from the perspective of archaeological point of view unpon these collections according to their shapes, patterns and marks, then make classification and comparison with the unearthed porcelains from inland China and abroad as well as from the collection of late Ming Dynasty from other museums around the world. After all these multi-angle study and research, we may have a more accurate assumption of when and where the Macau unearthed porcelains were produced and the destination of trading, etc., and how the Portuguese became rich by means of the monopolized trading and how their business declined at later stage.

KEY WORDS / Macao; porcelain fragments; export trading; influence

1994年夏天，一场大雨过后，位于龙嵩正街、冈顶附近的一段约20米的小山坡垮塌，其中一位瓷器爱好者在塌方现场附近居住，有一天经过时，工作人员正清理塌方的沙泥，他发现清理倒塌的泥土中夹杂着大量陶瓷碎片及建筑废料。该名爱好者同几位朋友连夜在塌方现场收集这些瓷片，经过一两天的时间，所收集的瓷片数量达数千片之多，其中大部分是青花瓷片。

在这过后，收集瓷片的其中一位朋友，继续关注从澳门一些工地出土的瓷片及进行收集，特别是当遇上在澳门半岛老区，因工程需要翻土时，每当发现有瓷片便会在下班后或在空余时间来进行收集，收集后的瓷片经清洗后便立刻贴上标记，注明收集的地点及日期。他这样的收集持续了十多年，在这十多年间收集的瓷片达千件以上，而这些瓷片绝大部分都是青花瓷器。

从冈顶及老区出土的瓷器，现分别收藏于澳门博物馆及澳门艺术博物馆之内。在澳门博物馆的瓷片，馆方作了小部分的整理，并于1998年博物馆正式对外开放时展示了极小的一部分；而在澳门艺术博物馆的那些瓷片，收集者于2010年才送交艺术博物馆。

澳门出土的瓷片，一部分收集于龙嵩正街，龙嵩正街位于南湾的斜坡上，南湾是澳门早期货物起卸的其中一个重要港口。另一批瓷片收集于草堆街、关前街、营地大街、大街等地方，这一带正好是在澳门填海之前，北湾的海岸线的地方，是澳门当年另一个货物进出口的地方。在屈大均著的《广东新语·澳门编》中有如下的记载：

"凡番船停泊，必以海滨之湾环者为澳，澳者，舶口也。香山故有澳，名曰浪白，广百余里，诸番互市其中。嘉靖间，诸番以浪白辽远，重贿当事求蚝镜为澳，蚝镜在虎跳门外，去香山东南百二十里，有南北二湾，海水环之，番人于二湾中聚众筑城。"[1]

文中提及的"南北二湾"的北湾就是指已填土的草堆街、关前街、营地大

---

[1] （清）屈大均撰：《广东新语》，北京：中华书局，1985年，页36。

街、大街等一带的地方。在龙嵩正街出土以青花为主的瓷片大约有3000多片，当中包含一些陶器、建筑废料及瓦片等。发现瓷片的爱好者表示，当时在塌方现场边缘一段地方瓷片较多，表层多为晚清至近代的瓷片，中层为石块并没有瓷片，下层的土壤中则夹杂着明末清初的瓷片，当中更有大量海沙、大型贝壳等，并在数天内收集了数千件的瓷片。

一

澳门出土瓷器的情况

明万历十四年(1586年)意大利天主教奥斯定修会在冈顶(龙嵩正街的山坡上)兴建教堂，名为奥斯定教堂，三年后教堂归葡萄牙人所有，此教堂是澳门最古老的教堂之一。教堂于1825年重修。1994年教堂旁的花园部分因大雨而坍塌。而在这里所收集的瓷片，相信是当时大量船只运载货物沿珠江南下，到达澳门后再在澳门装卸，如遇有在途中损破的器物时，会就地抛于海中。当时为兴建或重修奥斯定教堂需要大量沙泥作填土，相信施工者当时就地取材，从就近的海岸抽取沙泥作为地基填土之用。因此，在塌方土壤中发现大量海沙及贝壳夹杂瓷片在其中。

这一大批瓷片的发现当时在报章上亦作出了广泛的报导及谈论，但最终并未能引起当时学者的反应及兴趣。1995年澳门博物馆正式开始筹建；当时筹建及收集博物馆展品及资料主要由一位葡萄牙的建筑师来主理，他表示，对这批瓷片有兴趣，愿意接收及作为博物馆日后展出之用。当时这几位收集瓷片爱好者便把这批瓷片捐赠给筹建中的澳门博物馆。在1997年12月《澳门杂志》第二期曾经以《明清古瓷片冈顶出土始末》为题并配图作为封面，内文以八版的篇幅来做报导，文中只对瓷片的出处、来源作描述，并没有任何的分析与研究。澳门是一个高度资本主义商业化的社会，因这些瓷片并没有任何市场的价值，所以当年并没得到应有的重视。澳门博物馆于1998年正式对外开放，在开馆前对这批瓷片作了小部分的整理及复原，并于开馆后在馆内作小量的展出；同时发表了一些简单的文章，但并没有对这些瓷片作出任何详细及深入的研究分析，十多年来这批瓷片都是闲置在储藏库之中。

而在北湾一带所收集的瓷器亦是以青花瓷为主，瓷器收集的地方正好是19世澳门填海前的海岸、船只上落货的地方，此区为旧日澳门繁盛的商业之处。在收集者十多年间的努力搜集下，数量亦达上千件。2010年收集者愿意把瓷片交到澳门艺术博物馆，博物馆根据瓷片上的原始资料对瓷片作了编码，以作为日后研究的依据。该批瓷片在2011年6月在澳门艺术博物馆作了为期一个多月的展出，但整体对瓷片未作任何的整理及研究。

香港城市大学亦注意到在澳门老区所收集的瓷片，曾与收集者进行了对话及拣选了约100件的瓷片于2010年在香港举办了一个小型出口瓷的展览；同时在不同的时段举行了多次小型的内部有关出口瓷的研讨会，并出版相关研讨会的论文集《陶瓷下西洋——早期中葡贸易中的外销瓷》[2]，在该论文集中，复旦大学的刘朝晖以《澳门发现的克拉克瓷》为题撰文作了描述，文中主要依里纳尔蒂(Maura Rinaldi)撰写的《克拉克瓷贸易史》(*Kraak Porcelain: A Moment in the History of Trade*)一书，把在港展出约100件的"克拉克"瓷片的图案作分类。该文集还包括了一些不同种类出口瓷的文章，如江建新的《景德镇考古发现的克拉克瓷》，黄薇、黄清华的《上川岛与十六世纪中葡早期贸易》等，但文集中的文章对澳门出土的瓷器并没有详尽深入的研究与论述，只是作了简单及表面的描述而已。因此，从总体来说，除了展览及零碎的文章解说外，对澳门出土瓷器的研究是较为薄弱的。

[2] 香港城市大学中国文化心、陶瓷下西洋研究小组：《陶瓷下西洋——早期中葡贸易中的外销瓷》，香港城市大学出版，2010年。

二

澳门的地理环境及历史背景

在研究澳门出土的瓷器之前，我们必须了解澳门的地理环境及历史背景，这样才能进一步了解澳门这些出土瓷片的背后原因。

（一）地理环境

澳门位于东经113°33′、北纬22°12′的位置，在广东珠江的出口处南端的西岸，是一个向南延伸的长条形的半岛，澳门地形南高北低，是由丘陵与平地所组成，而丘陵比平地的面积为多，丘陵最高处也只不过91.6米。澳门的地域主要是由澳门半岛和氹仔、路环两个岛屿所组成，但这只是在1851年以后才有这样的定义，因葡人分别在1847年和1851年才占有上述两岛。在这之前澳门的含义就是单指澳门半岛。

澳门位于珠江口西岸，其形成主要是由珠江所夹杂的沙土堆积而成，地质以花岗岩为主。澳门的地形变化主要是从两方面进行，一是大自然的力量，就是从珠江水流所带来大量沙泥自然冲积所造成。二是人工填海。澳门处于珠江河口，珠江水分别在澳门的东及西面两侧流经澳门，再流出大海，但当流至澳门地域时水流已减至很慢，河水中所夹杂的沙泥长期堆积在河口处，以至澳门的河床浅，河道狭窄，海岸形成大量浅滩，较大船只并不能进出自如，失去船只停靠的作用，最终需作大规模的人工填土，把浅滩填成陆地。据英国海军在1865年所绘测澳门地域的水位在潮退时有8～10米，但在1881年再测量时则只有5.5米，在按照如此的增长率计算，澳门的港口将会在40年之内在潮退时见底。在1883年的另一次勘测时表明，澳门的港口在25年内吸纳的淤积沙泥达6900万吨[3]。

16世纪澳门半岛面积约为2.74平方千米，17世纪增至2.83平方千米，从16世纪到21世纪初澳门半岛的陆地面积扩大至9.3平方千米，增幅达3.4倍之多。

如前述澳门半岛陆地面积的扩大主要是自然形成及人工填海所构成。而人工造地是澳门增加土地的主要来源，葡萄牙人在澳门定居后于不同的时间进行了数次大面积的填海，主要是位于澳门东、西两侧，不同程度地大规模填海使当年临海的商业地区，逐渐变成内陆。葡人在定居澳门后注意到从珠江冲下来的沙泥使澳门的河床逐渐变浅，为保持澳门作为海上运输的重镇，整治河道的方案成了葡人的重要议程，更派员由葡萄牙来到澳门作出河道整治的研究[4]。在整治河道的同时澳门的陆地面积亦相对扩大，据下环街福德祠在同治十二年(1873年)的碑志记载称：

"……前人尝拟建祠，碍难择地，为形势所拘，故延宕至今。幸而神人感召，境土加辟，同治七年(1868年)，会海傍新筑基岸，绰然宽展可图……"[5]

该碑立于同治十二年，填海的地方是沿沙栏仔街(即澳门中部向西近海的地方)对开的海岸延伸至南面的妈祖庙，把海岸线填土弄直，其中包括十月初五街、草堆街、关前街、营地大街、大街等地方，这些地方原为近海之地，后继而成为内陆。

1557年葡萄牙人定居澳门，所居住的地方主要是以澳门半岛的南半部为主，并以大三巴炮台为分隔线，筑建城墙把澳门划分为两部分，城墙东至加思栏炮台，西至白鸽巢石墙街附近。南部为葡人聚居的地方，北面为华人居住及耕地。城墙在明万历丁未年(1607年)之前已建成。在明代沈德符撰《万历野获编》卷三十"香山嶴"有如下的记载：

"丁未年，广东番禺举人卢廷龙，请尽逐香山屿夷，仍归濠镜故地，时朝

[3]〔葡〕徐萨斯（Montalto de Jesus）：《历史上的澳门》，澳门基金会，2000年，页266。

[4]〔葡〕徐萨斯（Montalto de Jesus）：《历史上的澳门》，澳门基金会，2000年，页266。

[5] 陈炜恒：《澳门庙宇丛考》下卷，澳门传媒工作者协会，2009年，页283。

[6] （明）沈德符：《万历野获编》，北京：中华书局，1959年，页785。

[7] （清）印光任、张汝霖著，赵春晨校注：《澳门纪略校注》，澳门文化司署，1992年，页147。

[8] 〔葡〕徐萨斯（Montalto de Jesus）：《历史上的澳门》，澳门基金会，2000年，页59。

[9] （明）王临亨：《粤剑编》，北京：中华书局，页91、92。

[10] （清）印光任、张汝霖著，赵春晨校注：《澳门记略校注》，澳门文化司署，1992年，页65。

议以事多窒碍，寝阁不行，盖其时屿夷擅立城垣，聚集海外杂沓住居，吏其土者皆莫敢诘，甚有利其宝货，佯禁而阴许之者，时督两广者戴燿也，又七年甲寅（1614年），则督臣为张鸣冈，疏言嶴夷近状，谓嶴中私畜倭奴，且私筑墙垣，抗杀官兵，倭已有妻子庐舍，今不亡一矢，逐名取船，押送出境，数十年嶴中之患，一旦祛除，惟倭去而夷留。议事者有谓必尽驱逐……"[6]

葡人在澳定居后的几十年便开始私筑城墙，葡人曾请求明政府准其修缮垣墉[7]，但在明、清政府不同时间相继的反对下拆毁，后来又再建起，但最终因城市的扩展，葡人亦把城墙拆毁。当时葡人称城墙兴建的主要目的是作为军事上的防御工程[8]。1622年葡萄牙人曾利用兴建的炮台把欲夺取澳门的荷兰人击退。

葡萄牙人早期主要生活在澳门半岛以南的地域，而该部分主要是平地及小丘，当中包括两个海湾："南湾"及"北湾"，这两个海湾是早期澳门对外海上贸易的主要上落货点，大量货物从广州南下运至澳门，而从外洋来的货物亦经这两个海湾停泊，再转运进中国大陆，所以这两个海湾是当年货物的重要上落货点。

在明人王临亨撰的《粤剑编》中有如此的描述：

"西洋古里，其国乃西洋诸番之会。三四月间入中国市杂物，转市日本诸国以觅利，满载皆阿堵物也。余驻省时，见有三舟至，舟各赍白金三十万投税司纳税，听其入城与百姓交易。

西洋人之往来中国者，向以香山澳中为舣舟之所，入市毕，则驱之以去。日久法弛，其人渐蚁聚蜂结，巢穴澳中矣。当事者利其入市，不能尽法绳之，姑从其便，而严通澳之令，俾中国不得输之米谷种种，盖欲坐而困之，令自不能久居耳。然夷人金钱甚伙，一往而利数十倍，法虽严，不能禁也。今聚澳中者，闻可万家，已十余万众矣。此亦南方一痈也，未审溃时何如耳！"[9]

从上文中可以知悉西洋人带备大量的现金来华做买卖，澳门是船只停泊之所。而货物会由国内运到澳门再作分流，分配到不同的船只，转运至不同的地方。

（二）历史背景

据《澳门记略》记载："三十二年，蕃舶托言舟触风涛，愿借濠镜地暴诸水渍贡物，海道副使汪柏许之。"[10]明嘉靖三十二年即1553年，开始时葡萄牙人在澳门只是"搭茅暂住"，经过几年，1557年明朝嘉靖晚年葡萄牙人定居澳门，开始大规模进行贸易，垄断了中国对外以至东南亚一带的贸易市场。初期到澳定居的葡萄牙人只有约500人，到1563年增至900人。这些人主要是由浪白滘过来定居，同时还有数千的满剌加人、印度和非洲人，他们主要是充当劳工及奴隶[11]。船只初期只有两三艘，但到约1564年时增至二十多艘，而且更有倍增的趋势[12]。葡萄牙人在澳门停留下来，数百年来澳门是中国唯一可以让外国人长期停留的地方，而且亦是中国当时唯一对外的通商口岸。葡萄牙人利用澳门，把大量中国的货物运往日本、东南亚以至欧洲各地，获取丰厚的利润。同时，在16世纪期间欧洲正掀起一片"中国热"，大量中国货物经澳门输往欧洲，其中以丝绸、茶叶及瓷器为最大宗。直至荷兰人在1602年成立东印度公司，步葡萄牙人后尘打入东方市场，至约1647年完全夺取葡萄牙人在东南亚的市场。

葡萄牙人通过澳门大量从中国购入欧洲人所需的物资如丝、茶及瓷器等，这时间约90年，是葡萄牙人在澳门最辉煌的日子，大量货物从广州经澳门运往世界各地。在澳门出土的这些瓷器估计是葡萄牙人来澳定居后，瓷器运抵澳门后打破，而所遗留下来的一鳞半爪。从瓷器采集的地理环境分析，南北二湾正好是货物来澳的上落点，货物运送期间每当有瓷器破损时就就地遗弃，所以遗留大量的瓷器残片。

本文主要是对这些残留下来的瓷器作分析与研究，而其中更以在"北湾"一带所收集的，现收藏在澳门艺术博物馆的瓷器作为主要的研究对象，当中亦有少部分为澳门博物馆的收藏品。

需要特别说明一点，文中的所有瓷片，无论是在南湾或北湾出土的，皆不是出自正式田野考古发掘所得，而是由一些非考古专业人士所采集得来，所以在收集期间可能因环境或个人喜好而作出个别选择与取舍，这样会对研究有一定的影响，但有一个可取之处，采集者对每一件瓷器作了明确的采集地点及日期的记录，这对研究起着一个重要的作用。

（三）瓷器的类型

在北湾出土的瓷器是出自草堆街、营地大街等不同路段的地方，但这些地方基本上在未进行填海之前是同属一个海湾，出土的瓷器大多数为日常生活用瓷，并以青花为主，器型种类繁多，主要有盘、碗、杯、罐、壶、盒、器盖、军持等；其中以盘和碗的数量最多，出土的瓷器全部是残瓷，没有完整的器物，有少部分可以复原。出土瓷器的表面一般并没有使用过的痕迹，瓷器中有一个共同之处就是大部分是有相对时间特征的民窑出口瓷。现把出土青花瓷器的类型作如下分析：

[11]〔葡〕徐萨斯（Montalto de Jesus）：《历史上的澳门》，澳门基金会出版，2000年，页32。

[12] 陈乐民：《16世纪葡萄牙通华系年》，沈阳：辽宁教育出版社，2000年，页29。

1. 器型

（1）碗。大部分皆残破，只有约20多件可以复原，同时根据碗的口沿、圈足及腹部形状，大体可以分为四型。

A型 2件。侈口，弧腹，圈足（图一）。

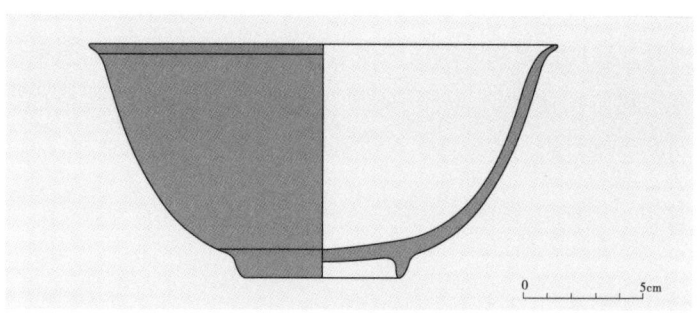

图一　A型碗

B型 共计18件。直口，弧腹，圈足。分二亚型。

Ba型 斜腹略弧，圈足（图二）。

Bb型 弧腹，圈足（图三）。

C型 八方，侈口，弧腹，圈足（图四）。

D型 弧腹，卧足（图五）。

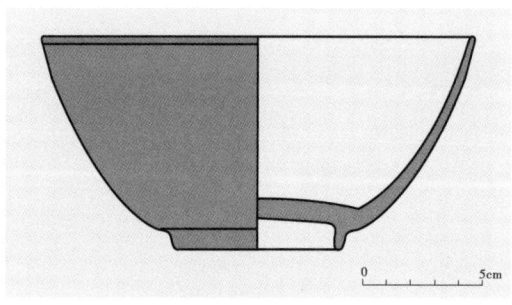

图二　Ba型碗

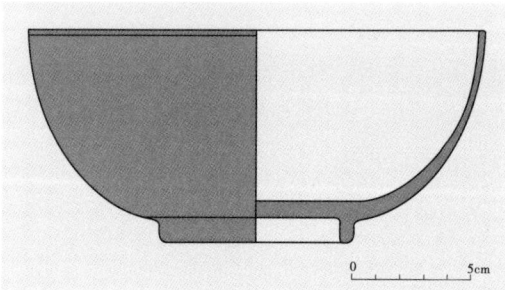

图三　Bb型碗

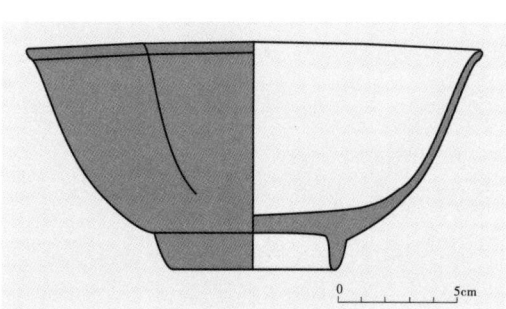

图四　C型碗

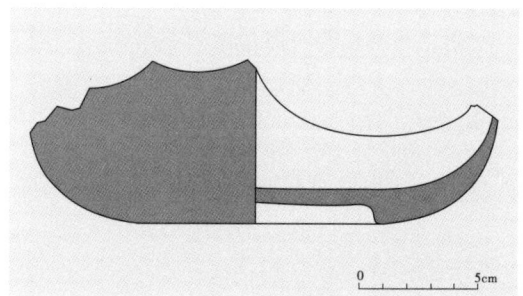

图五　D型碗

（2）盘。在这批出土瓷器之中以盘的数量为数最多，约有70多件可以复原，现按盘的口沿、腹、底足形状各异可分为四型。

A型 青花印模菊花瓣纹，瓜棱，弧腹，圈足。从众多的瓷器中只有1件如此的盘（图六）。

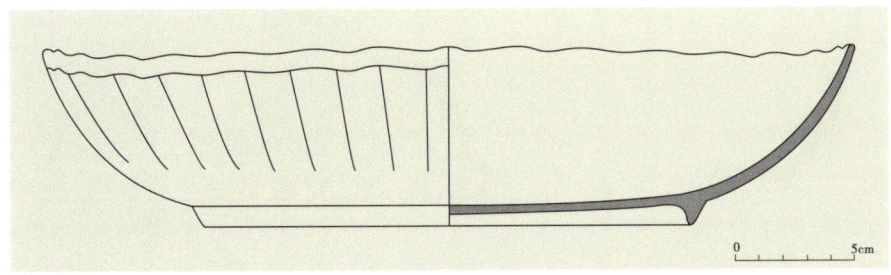

图六 A型盘

B型 菱口、折沿，圈足，可复原的有16件（图七）。

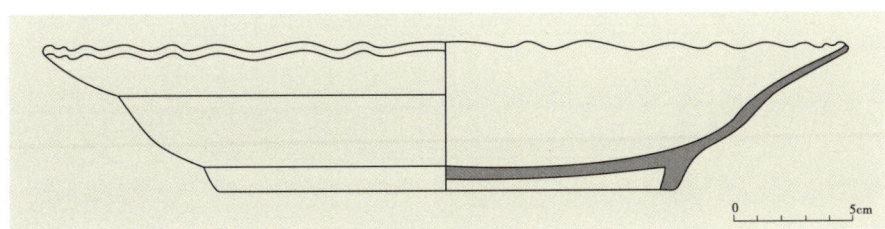

图七 B型盘

C型 敞口，折沿，圈足，可复原的有33件（图八）。

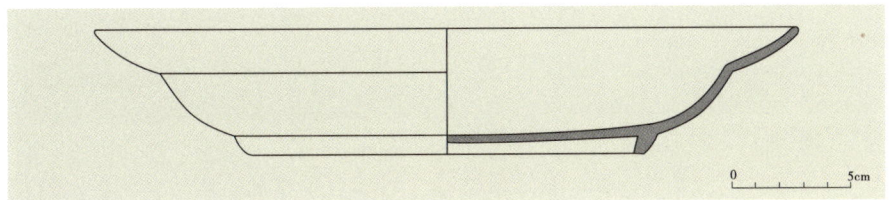

图八 C型盘

D型 敞口、弧腹，圈足。可复原的有23件（图九）。

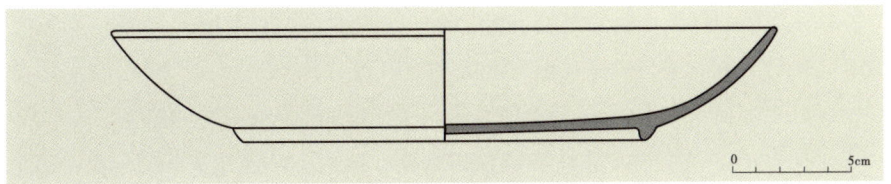

图九 D型盘

（3）杯。分可复原者、不可复原和杯底。可复原者均直口，弧腹，圈足（图一〇）。

（4）器盖。器盖共有9件，1件可复原，其余皆不能复原（图一一）。

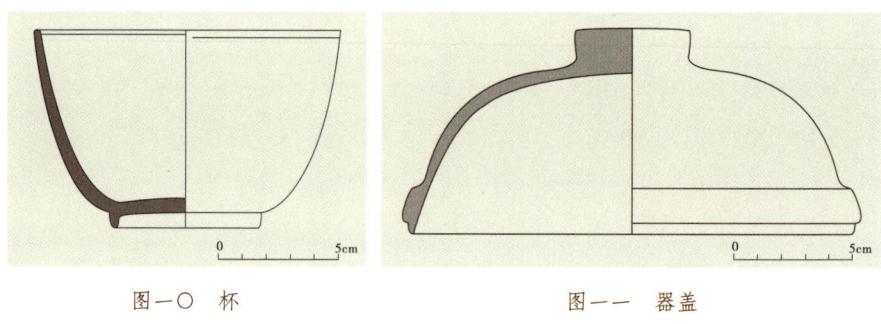

图一〇　杯　　　　　　　　图一一　器盖

（5）盒。只有1件（图一二）。

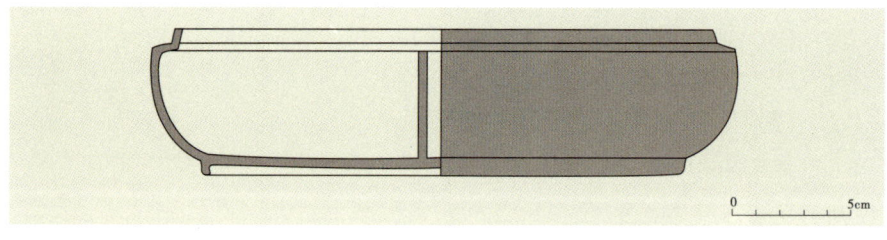

图一二　盒

（6）方碟。数量不多，只有2件，皆不能复原。敞口，弧腹，方足。青花发色蓝黑，白釉泛青，胎白，足沿有沙粒。碟沿绘青花叶纹，碟心绘卷草螭龙纹。

（7）炉。只有1件，青花三足炉，扁圆腹，残，不能复原。青花发色明亮，白釉泛青，胎白。炉身绘折枝花卉纹及云纹。

（8）花瓶。共有12件，皆不能复原。有的只余颈部、肩部者。颈部附有残耳，大部分青花发色明亮，白釉泛青，胎白，有瓶内附沙粒。纹饰有绘青花花草飞蝶纹、山石竹叶花卉纹、松叶白鹭纹、飞凤云纹等。底款有书青花方框款、青花双圈楷书款、青花兔纹图记款等。

（9）壶。数量不多，共有3件，仅存流及把，皆不能复原。青花发色明亮，白釉泛青灰，胎白。绘青花花草纹。

（10）军持。共有6件，皆不能复原。以壶口的形状可以分为二型。

A型　1件。壶口成帽形。只存壶口残件，胎白，绘青花花草纹，釉面钙化严重。

B型　1件。长颈，直口。只存颈、肩及流。胎白，白釉泛青，青花发色明亮。颈部一组相对三角内绘青花地反白纹，肩部绘缠技花纹，流成长形乳状，绘折技花卉纹。

其余4件皆只余部分残件，不能分型，青花发色明亮至蓝紫，胎灰，釉泛青灰。

（11）垫饼。在澳门出土的瓷器之中发现有垫饼，共有9个，胎皆白黄，无釉。垫饼包括有残及完整者，直径4.1～9厘米。

2. 纹饰

在澳门出土的瓷器纹饰多样，其中绘花草、植物纹饰为大多数，雀鸟、动物类次之。

纹饰种类有花鸟、虫鱼、走兽、人物、高士、小桥、湖石、海水纹及纹章等。画法绝大部分以青花双勾轮廓，混水和晕染技法。只有一两件以白描或没骨的画法来表现，画工手法有写意及工整两种，现就各类分列如下。

（1）人物纹。合共有四种，包括寿星纹、高官厚禄纹、仕女及婴戏纹、人物故事。

（2）山水、城池宝塔纹。共有两种，分别为山水纹和城池宝塔纹。

（3）植物花卉、草虫纹。出土的瓷器多双勾绘松树花果、菊花、折技花卉、荷花、水仙花及花草纹，而盘有绘荷塘及不同形态的花草小虫，画工有精细、工整与写意，共九种，包括：①花草、小虫纹，②兰草纹，③水仙花，④竹子纹，⑤荷花纹，⑥缠枝花卉纹，⑦团花纹，⑧折枝花卉纹，⑨花篮纹。

（4）动物纹。绘以动物为题的种类多样，所绘方式亦以青花双钩轮廓，以混水和晕染技法为主，其中狮子纹的为数最多。鹿纹画工有细腻及粗糙者，细腻的有清晰绘出鹿身的皮毛。出土的瓷器中所绘的动物有活泼可爱的枝头小鸟，寓意吉祥的祥云飞凤、三羊开泰、爵禄封侯等，合共19种，包括：①鹿纹，②猴子纹，③羊纹，④锦鸡纹，⑤鹤纹，⑥凤纹，⑦鹭鸟纹，⑧花鸟纹，⑨宝鸭纹，⑩雄鹰纹，⑪草猛纹，⑫白兔纹，⑬蟹纹(铁甲军)，⑭鱼藻纹，⑮云龙纹，⑯奔马纹，⑰黄牛纹，⑱狮子纹，⑲螭龙纹。

（5）云纹。

（6）吉祥字纹。吉祥文字有单一个福字及寿字，当中亦有以寿字重复字体作为装饰性的底纹，此纹饰有强烈的晚明风格。

（7）八卦纹。

澳门出土的瓷器云纹、吉祥文字纹、八卦纹等较少。所绘方式亦以青花双勾轮廓。混水和晕染技法,画工有写意及精细等,手法流畅。

(8)纹章。在澳门出土众多瓷片之中发现一件纹章瓷片,这纹章较为特别,青花发色淡雅,双钩轮廓,以青花混水和晕染技法绘"七头龙"怪物,五首为动物,一首为女性(另一首应为男性,瓷片未能见到),身长翅膀。这瓷片是在冈顶出土,现收藏在澳门博物馆(图一三)。现在所知存世同样纹饰的瓷器只有3件,分别收藏在大英博物馆、美国皮博迪·埃塞克斯博物馆及葡萄牙里斯本桑托斯宫。这纹章为何人所订制?至今尚未有结论。

图一三　澳门博物馆藏"七头龙"瓷片
(照片由澳门博物馆提供)

3. 款识

在澳门出土,现收藏在澳门艺术博物馆约1200件瓷片之中,有款识的约180件,占总数的15%。款识在万历中期的瓷器出现特别多。究其原因,主要是瓷器的外需量大增,因17世纪欧洲人对中国瓷器特别钟爱,其中器皿有款识的为甚,他们认为这是"皇家的象征"。1605年荷兰东印度公司一位高级主管由印度的默苏利珀德姆(Masulipatnam)发函,要求采购中国瓷器时需要有底款的,他说:"要牢记,瓷器底部书有蓝色好像文字的底款是最受欢迎的。"[13]

澳门艺术博物馆、澳门博物所收藏的瓷片,绝大部分的底款皆出现在碗或盘的底部,只有一件在碗内,并全部以青花书写。其中有一件纪年款书"隆庆元年"四字两行楷书款,现收藏在澳门艺术博物馆,这件瓷片的发现对澳门出土瓷器年代的断定,有着重大的意义。

180件有款识的瓷片可以分为以下几大类。

[13] S. Sjostrand, *The Wanli Shipwreck and its Ceramic Cargo*, Department of Museums Malaysia, p. 261。

（1）纪年款。共有14件，包括有："大明嘉靖年制"5件、"隆庆元年"1件、"大明万历年制"3件、"大明年造"5件。这14件纪年款之中包括有官款及年代款，字体一般皆工整，书写有力。

（2）寄托款。合共有27件，包括"宣德年造"2件、"大明宣德年制"14件、"大明宣德年造"1件、"成化年制"1件、"大明成化年造"1件、"大明成化年制"8件。字体方面与前者相类，书写工整有力。

（3）吉语款。共有31件，包括"万福攸同"11件、"福寿康宁"1件、"长命富贵"3件、"福"11件、"永保长春"5件。字体书写有工整及潦草的。

（4）赞颂款。共有6种59件，包括"富贵佳器"34件、"天禄富贵佳器"6件、"上品佳器"3件、"上上佳器"1件、"长春佳器"3件、"精制"12件。其中"天禄富贵佳器"款识多出现于一些大盘的底部，而底部大多有塌底现象。

（5）堂名款。只有2件，其中1件较为少见的款识"怀赤新造"，以楷书在青花双圈内书写，这款识在著录中亦不甚多见。其余的有"玉堂佳器"。

（6）图记款。有1件白鹭款及5件白兔款。在国外收藏的出口瓷之中，白鹭款是较为常见的款识，在澳门出土的瓷器中亦发现有1件。而白兔款多绘白兔俯卧伏回首状，此两种动物底款在晚明出口瓷中是常见的款识。

（7）花押款。主要是一些像文字或以横直线条造成的底款为主。可分为三大类：

①像文字款，17件，主要是由一些不能辨认的文字所组成，大部分书写于方框内。

②横直线条款，9件，主要是由一些横及直线所组成的方格或一些断续的横及直线所组成，大部分绘于方框内。

③花押款，5件，主要是绘一些不规则的图案。

（8）其他。这些瓷片主要是只余一小点字迹或只绘青花双或单圈的底款。共12件。

三

澳门出土瓷器的分期、年代与特点

（一）分期、年代

15～17世纪葡萄牙人的地理大发现是指船队通过非洲南部好望角到达印度以至亚洲的旅程，这旅程对人类的文明史及贸易史起着重大的影响。在贸易方面，传统的陆上丝绸之路贸易路线起了巨大的变化，取而代之的是新兴的海上丝绸之路，这海上贸易路线为葡萄牙人带来巨大的财富。在中国早期并没有与国外自由贸易的概念，只有传统的"朝贡贸易"，外国人的到来让这传统的"朝贡贸易"乱了阵脚，并受到了严峻的考验。为了禁止外国人的任意进出，明政府实行海禁，但走私活动屡禁不绝，外国人的非法贸易活动不断地在中国沿岸进行，明政府对"开"或"禁"海来防范海盗及外夷有着不同的意见，在沈德符[14]撰的《万历野获编·户部》中对海禁有以下的记录：

"今广东市舶，公家尚收其羡以助饷，若闽中海禁日严，而滨海势豪，全以通番致素封，频年闽南士大夫，亦有两种议论，福、兴二府主绝，漳、泉二府主通，各不相下……"[15]

明人叶权乙丑年(嘉靖四十四年，1565年)撰的《贤博编》附"游岭南记"中有如下的记载：

"广城人家大小俱有生意，……广城人得一二分息成市矣。以故商贾骤集，兼有夷市，……。广东军饷资番舶。开海市，华、夷交易，夷利货物，无他志，固不为害。乃今数千夷团聚一澳，雄然巨镇，……。是年春，东莞兵变，……汤总兵克宽与战，连败衄，乃使诱濠镜澳夷人，约以免其抽分，令助攻之，然非出巡抚意。已夷平贼，汤剿为己功，海道抽分如故。夷遂不服，拥货不肯输税，省城官谋困之，遂阻道不许运米麰下澳。夷饥甚，乃听抽分，因谓中国人无信，不知实汤总兵为之也。中国亦谓夷难驭，不知汤固许之免也。天下事变每生于两情不通。岛中夷屋居者，皆佛郎机人，乃大西洋之一国……"[16]

成书于万历二十一年(1593年)张瀚撰的《松窗梦语》也有这样的说法：

"尝谓两粤之盗如深秋落叶，扫尽复聚。"[17]

直至隆庆年间明政府才局部开放海禁，海上贸易进入了新的年代。从历史上我们可以知道，葡萄牙人是在1557年定居澳门并开始大量采购丝绸、茶叶及瓷器

---

[14] 沈德符（1578～1642年），明朝文学家，字景倩、虎臣，浙江嘉兴人，万历四十六年（1618年）举人。万历三十四年撰《万历野获编》，多记万历以前国事。

[15] （明）沈德符：《万历野获编》，卷十二，页317。

[16] （明）叶权：《贤博编》，北京：中华书局，1987年，页43、44。

[17] （明）张瀚：《松窗梦语》，北京：中华书局，1985年，页161。

等物品经澳门运往外地，隆庆元年（1567年）福建巡抚都御史涂泽民奏请开海获批，史称"隆庆开海"。在福建月港只准许船只出海，与澳门的特殊处不一样。

澳门大量货物是从广州到澳及由海外输入的大量货物，但货物与澳门总是擦身而过，其中只有打破的瓷器能在澳门"保存"下来。通过对这些瓷片的形制、胎釉、纹饰、款识和青花用料等方面的对比及在一件器物上的共存关系结果，可得出如下结论：

澳门出土的瓷器按前文的分析成果及器物底款所记顺序，最早为明朝的嘉靖、隆庆，最晚为万历至崇祯。嘉靖至崇祯时间跨度达120多年。参考澳门出土器物的类型、纹饰等异同处，可将澳门出土的瓷器分为两期，并以"隆庆元年"（1567年）作为分界线，因明政府于隆庆年间作局部开放海禁及在澳门出土瓷片中含该底款，所以以此作为一个分界。

第一期包括嘉靖及隆庆这两朝，共51年的时间。以盘与碗为主，标本数量较少，含官窑及民窑，所绘纹饰精细，绝大部分瓷片基本都是绘青花为主，青花发色明亮，白釉泛青，胎白。标本包括：无编号1，俗称"海碗"的大碗。碗内绘五爪云龙纹，外沿绘山石海水游龙纹，碗外底书青花"大明嘉靖□□"楷书六字两行款。字体书写工整有力，从其形制及纹饰来判断，这碗肯定为官窑。另一件标本2002BWCD1-041，青花碗。胎体厚重，外沿绘八宝纹，足外沿绘水波纹，外底双圈内书青花"大明嘉靖年制"六字两行楷书款，字体书写工整有力。标本2006BWDG2-053，青花碗。碗心单圈内绘青花螭龙纹，螭龙纹在澳门出土的瓷片中在万历中后期大量出现，这纹饰两朝与之相比，前朝的画工较为细致，此碗外底书"大明嘉靖年制"六字两行楷书款，字体书写有力。2006BWDG2-059，青花花草纹碗，花草画工细致，外底书青花"大明嘉靖年制"六字两行楷书款，字体书写工整有力。1998BWDG1-019，青花瓷片，此片只余一小部分，瓷片绘羊纹，羊身上绒毛画工细致，底只余一个"靖"字，字体有力。编号2006BWDG2-015，青花盘，盘心以明确线条双钩飞虫、山石、花卉纹，青花发色灰蓝，白釉泛青，胎白。盘外底书青花双圈"隆庆元年"四字两行款，字体书写工整有力。

第二期是"隆庆"以下的瓷器，包括万历至崇祯(1573～1644年)合共73年。第二期出土的瓷器亦包含有官窑及民窑，其中无编号2的青花盘，盘内绘青花双圈内五爪正面行龙纹，该纹绘于盘心，青花发色浓重泛紫，龙身张牙舞爪，龙眼炯炯有神，笔触有力，盘外底青花双圈内书"大明万历年制"六字两行楷书款，字体书写工整有力，是标准的官窑器。此外，底款书"大明万历年制"有标本2002BWCD2-106、1998BWDG1-084，"大明年造"及一些"宣德""成化"寄托款、堂名及花押款等的青花器,这些亦是以盘与碗占绝大多数,这些器物大部分青花发色明亮,釉色多以白中泛青、胎白为主。绘画多工整但亦有潦草。纹饰种类繁多,有"高官厚禄""山水城池宝塔""折枝花卉""缠枝花""螭龙""云龙""鹿""奔马""狮子"纹等。器物底款多样,有"大明万历年制""大明年制""宣德年制""大明宣德年制""大明成化年制""万福攸同""长命富贵""永保长春""富贵佳器""天禄富贵佳器""上品佳器""上上佳器""长春佳器""福""怀赤新造""玉堂佳器""精制"及花押款等。

澳门出土的青花器与景德镇观音阁出土的晚明瓷器无论在器型、色釉、胎体、纹饰及底款等多方面均有着很多相同之处。同时,在马来西亚及菲律宾出水的"万历号"与"圣迭戈号"沉船,船上的青花器与澳门出土的同样在器型、纹饰、底款等的均有着很多共同的特征。

(二) 与观音阁出土瓷器之比较

观音阁窑址位于景德镇市北郊3千米处的昌江东岸,景德镇遗留下的窑址遗存分布范围非常广,北起观音阁,南达董家坞,西至昌江东岸,东到田坞山坡。观音阁是景德镇众多具代表性的明代民窑窑场其中的重要生产地,也是17世纪景德镇外销瓷的主要产地之一。早在明代中期,景德镇已有大量瓷器输往东南亚以至欧洲各地。

2007年9月25日至12月30日,北京大学文博学院、江西省文物考古研究所、景德镇陶瓷考古研究所组成联合考古队,在景德镇北面观音阁一带民窑窑场遗址进行了为期三个多月的发掘,发掘面积约600平方米,揭露的虽只是这个遗址的冰山一角,但出土遗物却十分丰富[18]:发现一大批明代晚期作坊遗迹、制瓷工具和明代中后期重要瓷器标本数万件,这批遗迹、遗物对研究景德镇明代制瓷、经济形态和陶瓷作坊内部的具体分工形式,以及17世纪景德镇"转变期"瓷器和外销瓷烧造情况提供了一个很有力的科学数据;出土的大批有纪年且有地层关系的瓷器标本,为研究景德镇明代晚期瓷器的具体烧造年代提供了科学断代的标尺;而这些题材丰富的晚明青花标本,对研究中国晚明瓷器装饰技艺及中国艺术史有重要参考价值;根据遗物显示,观音阁窑场是明中后期最有代表性的民窑窑场之一,亦可能是明嘉靖时期所谓"官搭民烧"的民窑优秀窑场之一。同时,在堆积层中夹杂着大量的残瓷及垫饼,说明这些残瓷堆积物是出窑时的次品,出土的瓷器中发现有纪年的瓷片,其中发现有"癸

[18] 北京大学考古文博学院、江西省文物考古研究所、景德镇市陶瓷考古研究所:《江西景德镇观音阁明代窑址发掘简报》,《文物》2009年第12期,页39~58。

丑年制"的瓷片，"癸丑年"为嘉靖三十二年(1553年)，这瓷片的发现对遗址的断代起着一个重要的作用。在澳门出土的瓷器与观音阁出土的瓷器无论在形制、釉色、青花发色等方面都有着很多相同之处，现列举部分作比较（图一四）。

从上述的对比，可以清楚看到，澳门出土的瓷器与景德镇出土的瓷器无论是形制、纹饰及釉色等都有着很多相同之处，有些甚至完全一样，从这可以推断在澳门出土的瓷器是出自景德镇的产品。

在澳门出土的瓷片就是商人把景德镇的瓷器运来澳门后，在装船或搬运期间如有破碎的便会遗弃在澳门。在景德镇观音阁出土的晚明瓷与澳门出土的瓷属同样的性质，景德镇的瓷器是出窑时破损不能装运而抛弃，而澳门的瓷器是在景德镇出窑时完好，但在运输时破损，在澳门被抛弃。

在澳门出土的青花瓷器年代跨度由嘉靖至崇祯年间，在嘉靖至万历中期这一段期间，澳门出土的瓷器主要是以传统的风格为主，直到万历中期（约1600年）以后，因瓷器外销量大增，同时指定的样式亦有所增加，特别是在纹饰上的要求，因此出现了所谓的"克拉克"瓷的瓷种，"克拉克"瓷是指器物本身特定的开光纹饰的青花瓷。其主要成因是在17世纪欧洲正流行着一股强烈的"中国风"，当时大量中国的物品运往欧洲，其中瓷器被视为一种新事物，受到欧洲上流社会的推崇，特别是一些皇室、贵族与教会的青睐，而一些更在瓷器上要求写上特定的名字或徽章。在澳门出土的瓷片主要是以民窑为绝大部分，只有一两件相信是官窑的瓷器，而民窑主要是为民间所用，但当经商人采购后经澳门运往国外，这些瓷器便成了外销瓷。所以从澳门出土的瓷器可以发现，瓷器无论在形制、纹饰等方面都是有强烈的中国民间用瓷的味道，而早期特订纹饰来烧制的瓷器还是极少的一部分。

据统计，从1970年到2000年的30多年间，单在暹罗湾附近的东南亚海域发现的沉船约有120艘，而这些船只在海底数百年甚至上千年，而伴随出水的绝大多数为陶瓷器[19]。1610年，一艘船便载运了9227件瓷器到荷兰；1612年，上升为38,641件；1614年上升至69,057件；1636年为259,380件；1637年21万件及至1639年达到36.6万件[20]。每年有大量的商船往来欧亚两地，由明末到清初从中国出口到欧洲的瓷器每年达300万件[21]，由此可估算中国陶瓷出口量之庞大。

[19] 施静菲：《陶瓷数据库的拼图——布朗博士的东南亚沉船研究》，《故宫文物月刊》264期，2005年，页92。

[20] 中国硅酸盐学会：《中国陶瓷史》，北京：文物出版社，1982年，页410。

[21] 故宫博物院：《瑞典藏中国陶瓷》，北京：紫禁城出版社，2005年，页43。

1. 仕女及婴戏纹碗

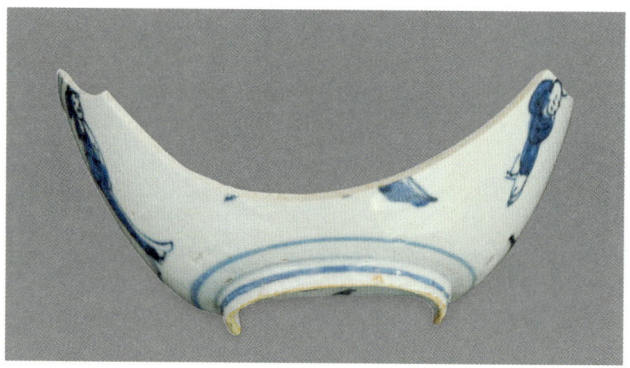
2. 2006BWDG2-076 仕女及婴戏纹碗

3. 高官厚禄纹

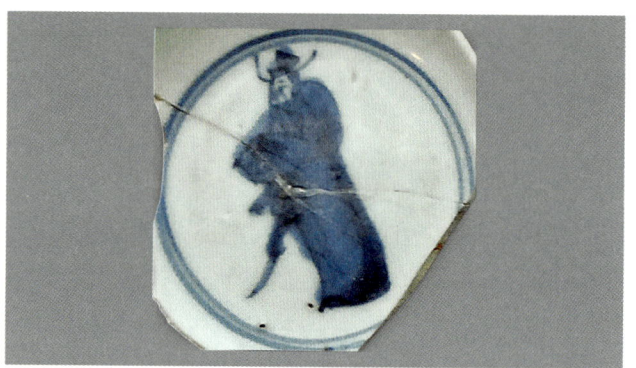
4. 2006BWDG2-096-2-1/2 高官厚禄纹

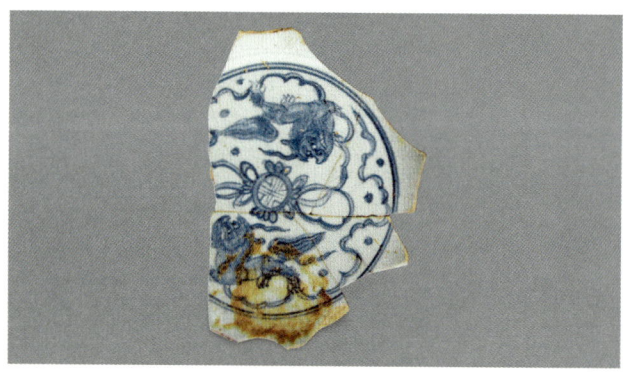
5. 狮子戏球纹

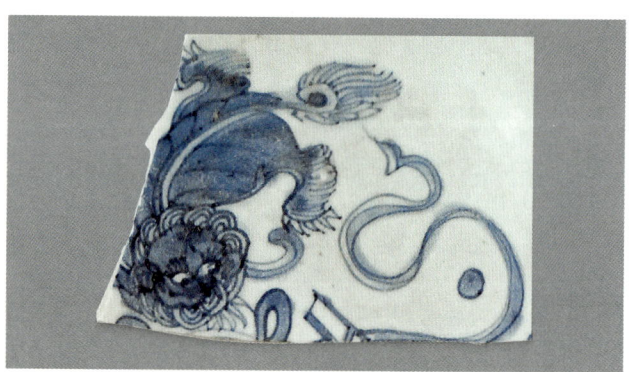
6. 1998BWDG1-017 狮子戏球纹

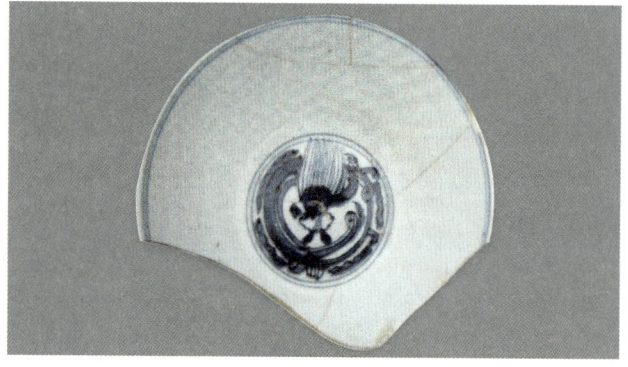
7. 螭龙纹

8. 2002BWCD2-088 螭龙纹

图一四　景德镇观音阁与澳门出土瓷器的比较图
1、3、5、7. 景德镇观音阁窑址出土　余. 澳门出土

四

晚明中国外销瓷在东南亚海域的发现

（一）马来西亚"万历号"出水的瓷器[22]

1997年一位渔民在海上作业时，意外地捞起一件满布蚝壳的青花瓷罐，瑞典籍海洋考古学者史垣（Mr. Sten Sjostrand）在1999年得知这消息后，开始有打捞这艘沉船的意念，但因沉船的资料不足而搁置。一年后，即2000年，另一艘装备有卫星导航定位的渔船，在海上作业时亦捞获大量青花瓷片，史垣先生得到这些消息后，开始向马来西亚政府申请打捞的许可证。申请最终在2004年得到批准，同年4月开始打捞的工作，直至2006年4月，所有出水物品完成编号及整理。期间出水的瓷器达9083千克，瓷片占了80%，而破损程度小于50%的瓷器共有7434件，以瓷器的形状分类与较好及完整的作比较来计算，该船瓷器最少有37,300件。

发现沉船的位置是在马来西亚东岸的丹绒加拉（Tanjong Jara）离岸约60海里处位置，水深约40米。因沉船位于数条河流的出口处，水流多变及混浊，对水下考古工作有一定程度的影响及困难（图一五）。

"万历号"沉船的遗物整体可以分为两大类，除上述瓷器的数量外，非瓷器类的物品发现并不多，总共只有54件，包括一些青铜与黄铜的器物，并且已变形。其中有两台长1.75米的小型火炮，每台约重200千克，而火炮并非欧洲的形制。还有几枚炮弹、一枝火绳枪、一箱爆竹、5件残铜盘、10件挂锁、3件残破银烛台、1件很重的铜盖、1件有把柄的残黄铜壶、1件残缺的象牙耶稣像、一把马来西亚传统刀等。非瓷器类有一个共同之处，就是全部都是价值不高的东西，船上并没有发现金、银器或任何货币。根据船体的破坏情况来估计，船只是曾经发生火警及爆炸而导致下沉。

船上发现的瓷器以青花器为主，种类包括粗瓷及精瓷，并以日用器为多，器物包括碗、碟、盖罐、盖盒、军持、花瓶、罐等，而碗及盘的数量为最大宗。其中盘最大的直径为51.5厘米，在粗瓷中以绘青花双鹿纹的为数最多，达2674件。

出水的瓷器纹饰多样，而部分瓷器绘开光图纹是晚明欧洲流行的所谓"克拉克"瓷，纹样有八吉祥纹、虫鱼、蚱蜢、宝鸭、花鸟走兽、松鹿、山石、龙、凤纹等。出水瓷器有底款的共有2187个，占已登记较好的瓷器总数

[22] 有关资料是根据 *The Wanli Shipwreck and its Ceramic Cargo* 的打捞报告而撰写。

图一五 万历号沉船的位置

[23] 这纹章一直误传为Alvaro Vilas Boas所有,实为Saldanha Bobadilha的族徽,参看*Portugal Encontra a China*, Fundacao Oriente, 2005, p. 63。

的29%。底款的种类繁多,纪年款及寄托款的有双圈"大明成化年制""大明成化年造""大明嘉靖年制",单圈的有"大明宣德年制"及"成化年制";堂名款有"莲亿""兼亿""丹桂""德化""玉器""清雅""满制""何""源""金""玉"等;吉语款有"福""寿""善""雅"等,兔纹款图记有两个,出现在军持的底部。全部瓷器中"成化年制"及"大明成化年制"款共有1991个。

有几点很重要,就是船在下沉时的方位,船只是由北向南躺在海床上,即船头向南;船尾向北,其次是在船上发现了一件象牙制成的耶稣像,这是西班牙人或葡萄牙人天主教的信物,在船上大量瓷器之中发现了一件画有葡萄牙贵族"Alvaro Vilas Boas"[23]纹章的方瓶。从以上三种现象可以推断,这艘船是葡萄牙人所有,并且很可能由澳门开出。

在"万历号"沉船中的一些器皿上还粘有垫饼。史垣在2005年3月曾赴景德镇与刘新园共同研究"万历号"出水的瓷器,并到观音阁古窑址做考察,在观音阁古窑址发现"万历号"相同的瓷片及垫饼。可以推论"万历号"船上的瓷器是明万历年期间在景德镇所生产的经澳门的外销产物。

（二）菲律宾"圣迭戈号"出水的瓷器[24]

1600年10月，菲律宾总督唐·弗朗西斯古·特洛(Don Francisco Tello)及副总督唐·安东尼奥·达·穆尔加(Don Antonio de Morga)下令把"圣迭戈号"(San Diego)货船改装为商、战两用船，以便对进入菲律宾水域的敌人作反击，这次行动主要是针对荷兰的船只而设。

两个月后，在12月14日，圣迭戈号在菲律宾东北海面约900米吕宋岛八打省的幸运岛与荷兰的"毛里求斯号"(Mauritius)相遇，双方进行6小时的激战，最终"圣迭戈号"被"毛里求斯号"打沉，因船上的火炮及弹药超载，船只很快便沉到海底，而"毛里求斯号"则开回印度尼西亚进行维修。

经过研究及探查，"圣迭戈号"在1991年被发现，船只平躺在水下50米深处的土丘中，菲律宾政府与法国一家水下考古公司——弗兰克·歌殿农(Franck Goddio)公司在1992年合作打捞了这艘沉船。

"圣迭戈号"出水约34,000件物品，当中包括瓷器及非瓷器两大类，其中有500多件是出产自江西景德镇明万历年间的青花瓷，器型有盘、碗、瓶、军持和盒等；而纹饰有花草、动物纹等，瓷器中亦包括一些漳州窑的瓷器。还有超过750件中国、泰国、缅甸、西班牙及墨西哥的大陶缸，这些陶缸主要是用作盛水之用。大部分出水的瓷器皆完好无缺。而非瓷器类有14枚葡萄牙制造的铜火炮、欧洲步枪、石和铅制弹药、日本剑、松脂、墨西哥银币、金属导航罗盘及海洋星盘等。

明万历二十八年（1600年）为该船明确的沉船年期，船上出水的物品对研究晚明景德镇出口瓷及海上运输路线起着一个很重要的作用。"圣迭戈号"出水的瓷器及物品现收藏在菲律宾国家博物馆作长期的展出。

[24] 有关资料是根据 *Kraak Porcelain* 78页、《江西元明青花瓷》221页及网上资料编写而成。

（三）澳门出土瓷片与"万历号"出水瓷器的比较

"万历号"出水的瓷器与澳门发现的瓷片两者有着很多相同之处，如形制、纹饰、胎釉等多方面都相若，同时，两者均发现相同的垫饼，而瓷器都是输往欧洲及东南亚的出口日用瓷。船上的瓷器，相信是经澳门运往外地的。"万历号"的发现对研究澳门作为16、17世纪外销瓷的重要出口港有着重要的意义。通过澳门出土的瓷器与"万历号"出水的瓷器作比较，可以清楚看到两者是同出一辙，对证明船上的货物是经由澳门运出的说法有着强而有力的说服力，反过来亦可以证明澳门出土的瓷器是运往世界各地，因破损而被"遗弃"在澳门。

澳门出土的瓷器与"万历号"出水的瓷器作如下的比较（图一六）。

1. 青花兰草纹格盒　　　　　　　　2. 1995LS1-081青花兰草纹格盒

3. 青花狮子纹　　　　　　　　　　4. 2006BWDG2-023青花狮子纹

5. 青花双鹿纹盘　　　　　　　　　6. 1998LS1-029青花双鹿纹盘

 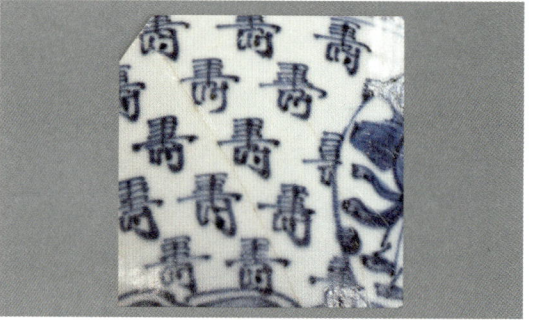

7. 青花行书寿字纹碗　　　　　　　8. SA/95385青花行书寿字纹

图一六（1）"万历号"出水瓷器与澳门出土瓷器的比较图

1、3、5、7."万历号"沉船出水　余.澳门出土

9. 青花蚱蜢纹盘

10. 2002BWCD1-032青花蚱蜢纹

11. 青花石上小鸟纹碗

12. 2002BWCD3-017青花石上小鸟纹

13. 青花白兔纹款

14. 2002BWCD2-150青花白兔纹款

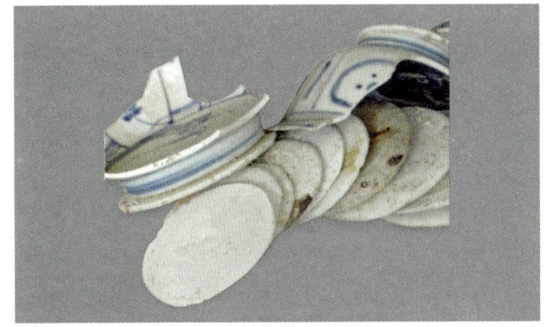
15. 垫饼

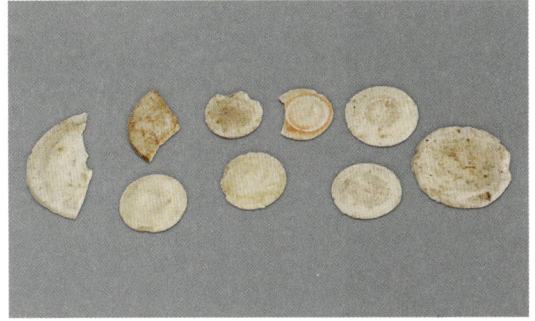
16. 垫饼

图一六（2）"万历号"出水瓷器与澳门出土瓷器的比较图
9、11、13、15."万历号"沉船出水　余.澳门出土

(四)澳门出土瓷片与"圣迭戈号"出水瓷器的比较

"圣迭戈号"有着明确的沉船日期,出水的瓷器与澳门发现的瓷片不论在形制、纹饰、胎釉等方面皆有很多相同之处。这样可以证明澳门出土瓷器的年代与"圣迭戈号"出水的瓷器相近,即1600年,明万历年间。同时,船上除了发现景德镇的瓷器外,还有漳州及大量东南亚国家和地区所出产的大缸及粗瓷。这对研究晚明海上贸易船只所经路线的研究起着重大的作用。

澳门出土的瓷器与"圣迭戈号"出土的瓷器作如下的比较(图一七)。

(五)西方博物馆收藏品与澳门出土瓷器的比较

现收藏于西方博物馆的中国出口瓷数量庞大,特别是在土耳其、葡萄牙、荷兰及英国等地。每个国家所收藏的瓷器都不尽相同,土耳其所收藏的主要是由元至明代,葡萄牙及荷兰所收藏的主要是由明至清早期,而英国的则主要是以清早期的为主。澳门出土的瓷器,大部分与西方博物馆的藏品无论在造型、纹饰等都有着很多相同之处。

在土耳其托普卡帕萨拉伊博物馆(Topkapi Saray Museum)收藏有大量中国的出口瓷。其主要原因是,土耳其即15世纪的奥斯曼帝国(Ottoman Empire),所在的地理位置正好处于东方通往西方的要塞,大量物资必须首先通过这里。因此直至现在,土耳其博物馆仍收藏着大量中国的出口瓷。经查阅及对比,托普卡帕萨拉伊博物馆所收藏的瓷器部分与澳门出土的有着很多相近或完全相同之处,现将两者比较如下(图一八)。

1. 青花鹿纹菱口盘　　　　　　　　　　　　2. 1995LS1-026青花鹿纹盘

图一七(1) "圣迭戈号"出水瓷器与澳门出土瓷器的比较图

1. "圣迭戈号"沉船出水　　2. 澳门出土

3. 青花鹿纹菱口盘

4. 2002BWCD1-001青花鹿纹盘

5. 青花军持

6. 1998BWDG1-298青花军持

7. 青花鹿纹碗

8. 2002BWCD1-053青花鹿纹碗

9. 青花盒

10. 1995LS1-081青花盒

图一七（2）"圣迭戈号"出水瓷器与澳门出土瓷器的比较图
3、5、7、9."圣迭戈号"沉船出水　余.澳门出土

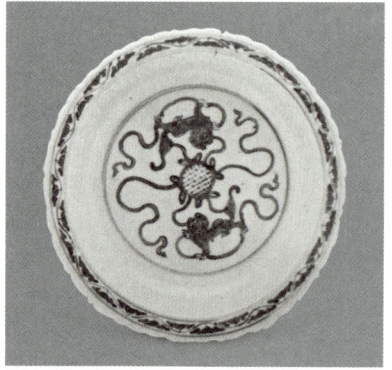 

1. 16世纪早至中期的青花狮子纹盘[25]　　2. 2006BWDG2-023青花狮子纹盘

3. 16世纪中期的青花猴子纹盘[26]　　4. 1998BWDG1-068青花猴子纹盘

 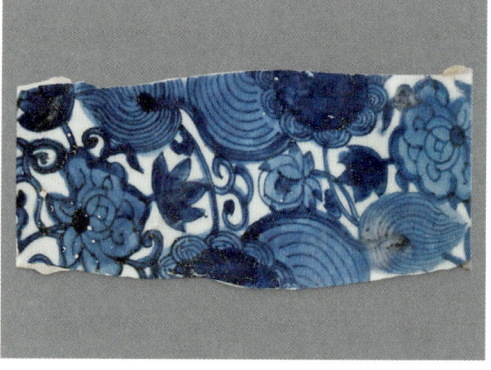

5. 16世纪中期的青花狮子纹盘[27]　　6. 2002BWCD1-024青花狮子纹盘

7. 16世纪中期的青花锦鸡纹盘[28]　　8. 1998BWDG1-087青花锦鸡纹盘

图一八（1） 土耳其托普卡帕萨拉伊博物馆藏瓷器与澳门出土瓷器的比较图

1、3、5、7. 土耳其托普卡帕萨拉伊博物馆藏品　余. 澳门出土

[25] Regina Krahl, Chinese Ceramics in the Topkapi Saray Museum Istanbul, Sotheby's. p. 583.

[26] Regina Krahl, Chinese Ceramics in the Topkapi Saray Museum Istanbul, Sotheby's. p. 617.

[27] Regina Krahl, Chinese Ceramics in the Topkapi Saray Museum Istanbul, Sotheby's. p. 618.

[28] Regina Krahl, Chinese Ceramics in the Topkapi Saray Museum Istanbul, Sotheby's. p. 621.

9. 16世纪中期的青花白兔回首纹底款盘[29]　　10. 2006BWDG2-054青花白兔回首纹底款

11. 16世纪中期的青花白兔纹碗[30]　　12. 2006BW DG2-026青花白兔纹盘

13. 16世纪中至后期的青花石上小鸟纹碗[31]　　14. 1995LS1-071青花石上小鸟纹碗

 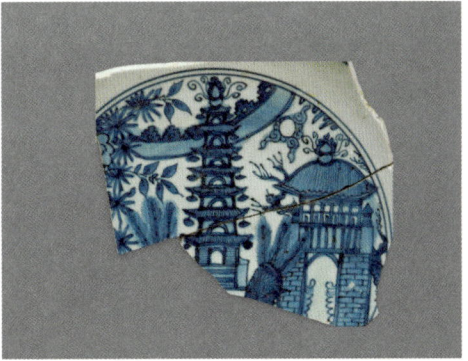

15. 16世纪中至后期的青花宝塔楼阁纹大盘[32]　　16. 2002BWCD1-005青花宝塔楼阁大盘

图一八（2） 土耳其托普卡帕萨拉伊博物馆藏瓷器与澳门出土瓷器的比较图
9、11、13、15. 土耳其托普卡帕萨拉伊博物馆藏品　余. 澳门出土

[29] Regina Krahl, Chinese Ceramics in the Topkapi Saray Museum Istanbul, Sotheby's. p. 625.

[30] Regina Krahl, Chinese Ceramics in the Topkapi Saray Museum Istanbul, Sotheby's. p. 640.

[31] Regina Krahl, Chinese Ceramics in the Topkapi Saray Museum Istanbul, Sotheby's. p. 682.

[32] Regina Krahl, Chinese Ceramics in the Topkapi Saray Museum Istanbul, Sotheby's. p. 698.

 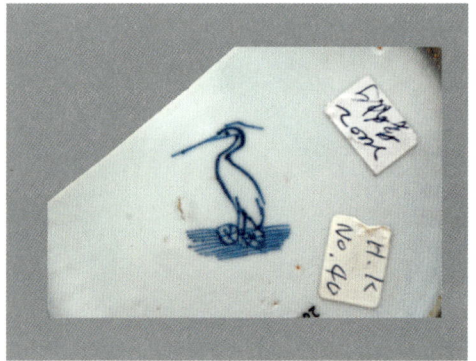

17. 16世纪中至后期的青花白鹭纹底款盘[33]　　18. 2002BW CD1-055青花白鹭纹底款

19. 16世纪中至后期青花青花三凤朝阳盘[34]　　20. 2006BWDG2-012青花三凤朝阳盘

 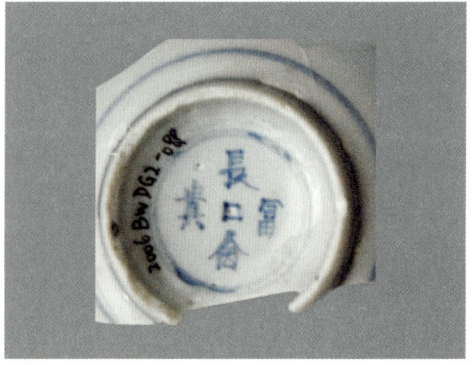

21. 16世纪中至后期的青花碗，底书"长命富贵"四字金钱型楷书款[35]　　22. 2006BWDG2-089青花碗，底书"长命富贵"四字金钱型楷书款

23. 17世纪早至中期的青花团花纹杯[36]　　24. 1988BWDG1-278青花团花纹杯

图一八（3）　土耳其托普卡帕萨拉伊博物馆藏瓷器与澳门出土瓷器的比较图
17、19、21、23. 土耳其托普卡帕萨拉伊博物馆藏品　余. 澳门出土

[33] Regina Krahl, Chinese Ceramics in the Topkapi Saray Museum Istanbul, Sotheby's. p. 702.

[34] Regina Krahl, Chinese Ceramics in the Topkapi Saray Museum Istanbul, Sotheby's. p.707.

[35] Regina Krahl, Chinese Ceramics in the Topkapi Saray Museum Istanbul, Sotheby's. p.708.

[36] Regina Krahl, Chinese Ceramics in the Topkapi Saray Museum Istanbul, Sotheby's. p. 791.

在葡萄牙里斯本Anastacio Goncalves博物馆亦收藏有大量中国晚明青花瓷。现就该馆部分晚明瓷器与澳门出土的瓷器作比较（图一九）。

[37] Philip Wilson, Chinese Export Porcelain from the Museum of Anastacio Goncalves, p. 61.

[38] Philip Wilson, Chinese Export Porcelain from the Museum of Anastacio Goncalves, p. 77

[39] Philip Wilson, Chinese Export Porcelain from the Museum of Anastacio Goncalves, p. 91.

1. 16世纪中叶的青花丹凤朝阳纹盘[37]

2. 2002BWCD2-004青花丹凤朝阳纹盘

3. 16世纪中至后期的青花猴子纹瓷罐[38]

4. 1998BWDG1-068青花猴子纹盘

5. 16世纪后半叶的青花山水人物纹盘[39]

6. 2002BWCD2-021青花山水人物纹盘

图一九（1） 葡萄牙Anastacio Goncalves博物馆藏瓷器与澳门出土瓷器的比较图

1、3、5. 葡萄牙Anastacio Goncalves博物馆藏品 余. 澳门出土

[40] Philip Wilson, Chinese Export Porcelain from the Museum of Anastacio Goncalves, p. 108.

7. 明万历期间的青花缠枝花卉纹碗[40]   8. 2002BW CD1-049青花缠枝花卉纹碗

图一九（2）　葡萄牙 Anastacio Goncalves 博物馆藏瓷器与澳门出土瓷器的比较图

7. 葡萄牙Anastacio Goncalves博物馆藏品　8. 澳门出土

在荷兰阿姆斯特丹Rijhs博物馆所收藏的16世纪末的青花碗[41]与澳门出土的相比。

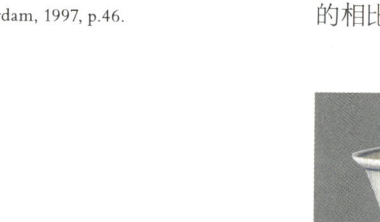

[41] Philip Wilson, Chinese Ceramics in the Collection of the Rijksmuseum Amsterdam, 1997, p.46.

 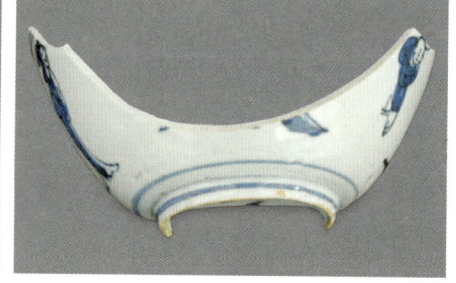

1. 16世纪末的青花仕女婴戏纹碗　　　　2. 2006BWDG2-076青花仕女婴戏纹碗

图二〇　荷兰阿姆斯特丹 Rijhs 博物馆藏瓷器与澳门出土瓷器的比较图

1. 荷兰阿姆斯特丹Rijhs博物馆藏品　2. 澳门出土

五

总结

将田野考古发掘、海底沉船出水的瓷器及欧洲各大博物的藏品与澳门出土的瓷器作对比后，对澳门出土的瓷器得出一个较清晰的概念，澳门出土的瓷器是生产自江西的景德镇，生产年代应是在16世纪中叶至17世纪初，即晚明嘉靖至崇祯年间，年代横跨120多年。而葡萄牙人在澳门与中国进行贸易的黄金时期正好是在这期间的90年间。澳门出土的这批瓷器就是葡萄牙人在澳门这一段历史的强而有力的证据；同时，欧洲各大博物馆所收藏的晚明瓷器很有可能是经澳门出口的。

澳门地处南中国珠江口西岸，地理位置及海上交通便捷，16世纪中叶葡萄牙人租借澳门作为贸易的据点，把澳门从一个小渔村变成各国虎视眈眈的一个贸易重镇。澳门从繁荣到衰落都与贸易分不开，其中陶瓷贸易更占了重要的部分。澳门出土的瓷器揭示了大量货物曾经通过澳门输往世界各地，同时更展示了晚明时期出口瓷的造型与纹饰的基本情况。通过与田野考古发掘出土、东南亚海上出水及现存世界各大博物馆藏品的对比，对澳门出土的瓷器得出一个清晰而明确的时代分类，同时，对景德镇晚明出口瓷有一个较清晰的脉络，特别是一般人认为"克拉克"瓷有专属的窑场，而其实这只是陶瓷贸易发展中的一小部分而已。澳门这批出土瓷片虽然不是以正式考古方法所得，但有明确的采集地点及时间，这批瓷器的发现对研究中国瓷器外销的路线，了解外国人对中国瓷器的喜好、对中国文化热爱的程度及生活的影响，以及对研究早期中葡贸易史及中国外销瓷，特别是研究"克拉克"瓷的来由有着重要的作用。通过对这些瓷片的研究，可以了解到当时欧洲人来中国采购大量的货物如丝、茶叶及瓷器经澳门运往世界各地的情况。同时澳门这批瓷器的发现对研究景德镇、澳门至海外这条"海上陶瓷之路"起着重要的作用及深远的影响。

澳门这个弹丸之地，在16世纪开始成为西方来华的重地，曾经是各国贸易的兵家必争之地。数百年来，澳门经历了无数的风雨，在贸易史上留下了不少文字的记载。但今天在这方面遗留下来的实物则甚少，特别是丝及茶叶，这些东西不能作长时间的保留，只有打破的瓷器才会在澳门留下，这些残留下来的瓷器主要是在装船或搬运时打碎并被"遗弃"在澳门。通过对这批瓷片的整理，包括对器型、纹饰及款识的分类及排比，对瓷器的产地来源、销售去处等得出明确的源流及方向，从而补充了澳门作为中西文化、贸易交流上的重镇在历史文献记载上的不足之处，从瓷器中的形制及纹饰可以窥见陶瓷贸易在中西文化、历史交流中所扮演的角色。

1557年葡萄牙人大量东来定居澳门，期间把西方的宗教、思想等不同文化及事物引进到澳门并带到中国。葡萄牙人的到来使澳门这个小镇起了重大的变化。葡人是为贸易而东来，希望赚取更大的利润，从澳门出土的这批瓷器可以得知当时贸易的繁盛情况，1655年荷兰东印度公司大班对澳门有以下精简的描述："过了这岛(大屿山)再航行两天，将会经过澳门，一个出名而富庶的地方……。"[42]当时的澳门可以说是富甲一方，其致富的原因很简单，就是贸易

[42] James Orange, The Charter Collection, p. 276.

的中转出口，大量货物经澳门运往世界各地，葡人就是从这一买、一卖的过程中抽取利润。葡人在澳门的辉煌时光只是短短的约一百年，其衰落的主要原因是经济的单一化，这是葡人在澳门从富庶走向一贫如洗的主要原因。当荷兰人加入东方海上贸易的竞争，逐渐把葡人驱逐出东南亚，葡人只能苟延残喘地据守澳门这个小半岛上。其后英国人加入竞争，更使葡人在澳门的出口贸易完全走至低谷，经济一落千丈。葡人为了挽回澳门的疲弱经济，想尽种种方案，如宣布澳门为自由港[43]，修建新海港等[44]，但都不能使澳门恢复昔日的光辉。

前车可鉴，当年澳门一贫如洗的主要原因是贸易的单一化，当外来竞争者介入时则导致完全失败。澳门自回归祖国后，赌权开放，引进外资投入大量资金，改变了澳门的面貌，以博彩旅游业为龙头带动澳门走向兴旺，赌场的收入现在已成为澳门经济的主要收入来源。单一收入来源，亦是危机之所在，居安思危，要吸收历史的教训，使澳门不再重蹈覆辙，澳门需要增加多元化经济发展，增加收入来源，以为澳门的未来早作准备。

[43] 〔葡〕徐萨斯（Montalto de Jesus）：《历史上的澳门》，澳门基金会，205页。

[44] 〔葡〕徐萨斯（Montalto de Jesus）：《历史上的澳门》，澳门基金会，283页。

引用书目

1. 古代文献

（明）叶权：《贤博编》，北京：中华书局，1987年。

（明）王临亨：《粤剑编》，北京：中华书局，1987年。

（明）沈德符：《万历野获编》，北京：中华书局，1959年。

（清）印光任、张汝霖：《澳门记略》，赵春晨校注本，澳门文化司署，1992年。

（清）屈大均：《广东新语》，北京：中华书局，1985年。

（清）梁廷枏：《海国四说》，北京：中华书局，1993年。

〔葡〕曾德昭著、何高济译、李申校：《大中国志》，上海：上海古籍出版社，1998年。

〔葡〕费尔南·门德斯·平托等：《葡萄牙人在华见闻录》，澳门文化司署、东方葡萄牙学会，海口：海南出版社、三环出版社，1998年。

〔瑞典〕龙思泰：《早期澳门史》，北京：东方出版社，1997年。

Elibron Classic, *The Chinese Repository*, Vols. I to XX, from May 1832 to December 1851, 2005 reprinted.

James Orange, *The Chater Collection pictures relating to China Hong Kong Macao* 1655–1860, by Thornton Butterworth Limited, 1924.

Hosea Ballou Morse, *The Chronicles of the East India Company Trading to China* 1635–1834, Clarendon Press Oxford, 1926.

2. 近人论著

澳门杂志编辑部：《明清古瓷片岗顶出土始末》，《澳门杂志》1997年第3期，页7～14。

白焜：《晚明至清乾隆时期景德镇外销瓷研究》，《福建文博》1995年第1期，页27～35。

北京大学考古文博学院、江西省文物考古研究所、景德镇市陶瓷考古研究所：《江西景德镇明清御窑遗址发掘简报》，《文物》2007年第5期，页4～47。

北京大学考古文博学院、江西省文物考古研究所、景德镇市陶瓷考古研究所：《江西景德镇观音阁明代窑址发掘简报》，《文物》2009年第12期，页39～58。

冯先铭、冯小琦：《荷兰东印度公司与中国明清瓷》，《江西文物》1990年第2期，页101～104、117。

傅宋良、朱高健、彭景元：《漳州窑青花与景德镇民窑青花》，《福建文博》中国古陶瓷研究会1999年年会专辑，页29～33、123。

故宫博物院：《瑞典藏中国瓷》，北京：紫禁城出版社，2005年。

广东省文物考古研究所、国家水下文化遗产保护中心、广东省博物馆：《广东汕头市"南澳Ⅰ号"明代沉船》，《考古》2011年第7期，页39～46。

郭学雷：《崇祯、顺治年间的景德镇青花瓷器研究》，《福建文博》中国古陶瓷研究会1999年年会专辑，页7、168～181。

胡雁溪、曹俭：《它曾经征服了世界：中国清代外销瓷集锦》，北京：中国大百科全书出版社，2010年。

黄薇、黄清华：《广东台山上川岛花碗坪遗址出土瓷器及相关问题》，《文物》2007年第5期，页78～88。

江西省轻工业厅陶瓷研究所：《景德镇陶瓷史稿》，北京：生活·读书·新知三联书店，1959年。

江滢河：《清代洋画与广州口岸》，北京：中华书局，2007年。

金国平：《中葡关系史地考证》，澳门基金会，2000年。

李家治：《中国科学技术史·陶瓷卷》，北京：科学出版社，1998年。

李靖堃：《列国志——葡萄牙》，北京：社会科学文献出版社，2006年。

林发钦：《澳门史稿》，澳门近代文学学会，2005年。

林梅村：《广东上川岛访古——葡萄牙舰队首次来华登陆地的发现》，《嘉模讲谈录》，澳门民政总署，2009年，页15～24。

林梅村：《澳门开埠以前葡萄牙人的东方贸易》，《文物》2011年第12期，页61～71。

刘芳辑：《葡萄牙东波塔档案馆藏清代澳门中文档案汇编》，澳门基金会，1999年。

马锦强：《从澳门搜集的瓷片看中国出口瓷》，《文化杂志》2011年春季刊，澳门特别行政区政府文化局，页143～162。

裴光辉：《克拉克瓷源流》，《福建文博》1999年增刊，页79～84。

彭适凡、林业强：《江西元明清瓷器》，江西省博物馆、香港中文大学文物馆，2002年。

上海博物馆：《海帆留踪》，上海辞书出版社，2009年。

施静菲：《陶瓷资料库的拼图——布朗博士的东南亚沉船研究》，《故宫文物月刊》，台北故宫博物院，264期，2005年3月，页90～99。

汤开建：《澳门开埠初期史研究》，北京：中华书局，1999年。

碗礁Ⅰ号水下考古队：《东海平潭碗礁Ⅰ号出水瓷器》，北京：科学出版社，2006年。

王健华：《明末清初中国瓷器在欧洲的外销》，《中国古陶瓷研究》第八辑，北京：紫禁城出版社，2002年，页191～197。

王孝通：《中国商业史》，上海：商务印书馆，1936年。

香港城市大学中国文化心、陶瓷下西洋研究小组：《陶瓷下西洋——早期中葡贸易中的外销瓷》，香港城市大学，2010年。

香港艺术馆：《中国外销瓷——布鲁塞尔皇家艺术历史博物馆藏品展》，香港市政局，1989年。

香港艺术馆：《珠江风貌——澳门，广州及香港》，香港市政局，1996年。

肖发标：《中葡早期贸易与漳州窑的兴烧》，《福建文博》中国古陶瓷研究会1999年年会专辑，页50～53。

薛翅、刘劲峰：《明末清初景德镇陶瓷外销路线的变迁与福建平和县窑址的发现》，《福建文博》1995年第1期，页22～26。

叶农、吴忠明：《澳门古地图——从地图看澳门城市在16至20世纪初的发展》，《澳门历史研究》第六期，2007年，页17。

张海钢：《15～16世纪葡萄牙人在东非的征服与贸易》，《文化杂志》2011年春季刊，澳门特别行政区政府文化局，页192～200。

张健雄：《列国志——荷兰》，北京：社会科学文献出版社，2006年。

中国古陶瓷学会：《中国古陶瓷研究》（第十三辑），北京：紫禁城出版社，2007年。

中国古陶瓷学会：《中国古陶瓷研究》（第十四辑），北京：紫禁城出版社，2008年。

中国硅酸盐学会：《中国陶瓷史》，北京：文物出版社，1982年。

〔葡〕徐萨斯著，黄鸿钊、李保平译：《历史上的澳门》，澳门基金会，2000年。

〔葡〕J.H.萨拉依瓦：《葡萄牙简史》，澳门文化司署，1994年。

Maria Alexandra da Costa Gomes, *Do Neolitico ao Ultimo Imperador*, Governo de Macau, 1994.

Museum of Anastacio Goncalves, *Chinese Export porcelain*, Published by Philip Wilson Publishers Limited, Lisbon, 1996.

John Carswell, *Chinese Ceramic in the Sadberk Hanim Museum*, Istanbul, 1995.

John Carswell, *Blue & White Chinese Porcelain Around the World*, British Museum Press, 2000.

Raffaella D'lntino, *Portugal Encontra a China*, Fundacao Oriente, 2005.

David Sanctuary Howard, *Chinese Armorial Porcelain*, Faber and Faber Limited, 1974.

David Sanctuary Howard, *Chinese Armorial Porcelain*, Volume II, Heirloom & Howard Limited, 2003.

Jessica Harrison-Hall, *Ancient Chinese Trade Ceramics from The British Museum*, London, National Museum of History, R.O.C.1994.

Jessica Harrison-Hall, *Ming Ceramics in the British Museum*, British Museum Press, 2001.

Christian J.A.Jorg, *Chinese Ceramics in the Collection of the Rijksmuseum Amsterdam*, Philip Wilson Publishers Limited, 1997.

Regina Krahl, *Chinese Ceramics in the Topkapi Saray Museum Istanbul*, Sotheby's, 1996.

Carol Michaelson & Jane Portal, *Chinese Art in Detail*, British Museum Press, 2006.

Maura Rinaldi, *Kraak Porcelain a moment in the history of trade*, Bamboo Publishing Ltd.1989.

Sten Sjostrand & Sharipah Lok Lok bt. Syed Idrus, *The Wanli Shipwreck and its Ceramic Cargo*, Department of Museums Malaysia, 2007.

Luisa Vinhais and Jorge Welsh, *Kraak Porcelain*, Jorge Welsh books, 2008.

Wang Gungwu, *The Nanhai Trade, The early history of Chinese trade in the south China sea*, Times Academin Press, 1958, reprinted 1998.

Jorge Welsh, *Important Collection of Chinese Export Porcelain*, Jorge Welsh book, 1999.

海洋出水有机质文物的保护
——以木材和谷物为例

Conservation of Waterlogged Archaeological Organic Objects Excavated Underwater
—Focused on Woods and Grains

〔韩〕车美永

（韩国国立海洋文化财研究所）

CHA Mi-young

(National Research Institute of Maritime Cultural Heritage, Republic of Korea)

范佳楠　〔韩〕高美京　译

（北京大学考古文博学院）

Translation / FAN Jia-nan & KO Mi-kyung

(School of Archaeology and Museology, Peking University)

内容摘要 /

　　近5年，韩国国立海洋文化财研究所主持发掘了木制品、竹制品、谷物类和骨质类等大量有机质出水遗物。本文介绍了针对海洋出水木材和谷物的保存处理方法。

　　水浸木材大部分主成分已被分解并被水替代，所以必须在水浸状态中进行保管。保存处理按脱盐—处理前状态调查—洗涤—尺寸稳定化—干燥—拼合与复原—处理后的状态记录—保管和管理的顺序进行。目前海洋出水古木材的保存处理最常用的方法是低浓度PEG含浸后真空冷冻干燥法、高浓度PEG含浸后调节干燥法及高级醇法。海洋出水的谷物有稻、荞麦、粟和稗等。水浸谷物呈现内核（大米等）分解无存，仅留下糠皮的状态。谷物的保存处理顺序和水浸木材相同，仅在尺寸稳定化过程中使用实验结果最良好的高级醇，在高级醇法中采用十六醇。

关键词 /

　　水浸古木材　水浸谷物类　低浓度PEG含浸后真空冷冻干燥法　高浓度PEG含浸后调节干燥法　高级醇法

ABSTRACT / For the past 5 years, massive amount of organic objects have been excavated by National Research Institute of Maritime Cultural Heritage in Korea, such as wooden objects, bamboo objects, grains, herbaceous kinds, bones and so on. This study suggests conservation methods of waterlogged archaeological woods and grains excavated underwater.

Waterlogged archaeological woods were filled with water instead of their original ingredients due to degradation, which is why they must be stored in water. Conservation of waterlogged archaeological woods have to be processed as below : desalination—examination—cleaning—consolidation—drying—bonding and loss compensation—documentation—storage. The most common conservation method for waterlogged archaeological woods is low concentration PEG treatment and vacuum freezing-dry, high concentration PEG treatment and controlled drying and high alcohol treatment.

Excavated grains include rice, buckwheat and millet. The starch, the main ingredient of these grains, was decomposed and disappeared, leaving their bran only. High alcohol treatment was applied using cetyl alcohol for conservation of grains.

KEY WORDS / Waterlogged archaeological wood; waterlogged archaeological grains; low concentration PEG treatment and vacuum freezing-dry; high concentration PEG treatment and controlled drying; higher alcohol treatment

一

序言

海洋中出水有机质文物的科学保存处理伴随着水下考古一起发展。韩国首次水下考古发掘是新安沉船的发掘调查。从1976年10月至1984年9月，新安沉船的发掘中除打捞陶瓷器、金属、木材、石材、骨材、琉璃、植物和果实等各类文物共22,040件之外，还发现铜钱28吨、紫檀木1017根，船只一艘[1]。为了安全地保存和管理出水文物，随即开展了对水浸有机质文物的保护工作。

韩国所开展的水浸古木材保护以1975年出水于庆州雁鸭池的木船的处理为最早实例，这次采用PEG（聚乙二醇/polyethylene glycol）浸泡法，进行了长达9年的处理[2]。几年后，随着新安船的发现与打捞，学界开展了水浸古木材特性及保存处理法等方面的研究，为古船舶及水浸古木材的保护打下了学术基础。此外，通过对新安船上打捞出来的大量木制品、食物和果实类、紫檀木等的保护工作，使韩国文物保护的领域不仅限于古船舶，而扩展到经验尚不充足的多种水浸有机质文物的研究和保护。韩国文物保护获得了发展的契机。

新安船发现以后，水下考古工作的发现以古船舶和陶瓷器为主，因此海洋

[1]〔韩〕文化公报部、文化财管理局：《新安海底遗物（综合篇）》，1998年。

[2]〔韩〕金炳虎、郑亨均：《雁鸭池出土木船의保存处理》，《保存科学研究》第5集，1985年，页109～127。

文物的保护也集中在古船舶和陶瓷器上。但是，从2009年起，在先后发掘的马岛1号船（2009年）、马岛2号船（2010年）、马岛3号船（2011年）中，除古船舶和陶瓷器以外，还有包含木简在内的木制品、竹制品、谷物类、草本类、骨制品等有机质文物的大量出水。以此为契机，以往几乎停滞不前的海洋水浸有机质遗物的保护如火如荼地发展起来。

最近5年，水浸有机质遗物的相关研究和保护产生了如下的较大变化：第一，水浸竹材的保存处理正以对其微视形态上的化学特征的基础研究[3]和正在实验的保存处理方法为依据进行着；第二，也开展了水浸谷物类、草本类的研究及保护；第三，将木制品保存处理中最常用的经PEG浸泡后再进行真空冷冻干燥法时使用的溶媒，从有机溶剂叔丁醇（tert-butyl alcohol）换为了水，使文物的安全性更有保障。

本文将重点介绍目前韩国国立海洋文化财研究所采用的海洋出水木材类和谷物类遗物的保存处理法。本文选取2013年韩国国立海洋文化财研究所出版的《海洋出水遗物保存处理指南书》中的"有机遗物"部分进行了修改和补充，并加入了水浸稻实验的内容[4]。

二

水浸木材的保存处理

（一）水浸古木材的特征

古木材指的是人类因特殊目的所使用的、保留着过去文化活动痕迹的年代较古老的木材[5]。据古木材含水率的不同，可分为干燥古木材和水浸古木材，水下考古发现的古木材应归为水浸古木材，主要从海洋、湿地和泥炭层中出水或出土，在水浸状态下木材的主成分已分解并被水分所代替。

海洋环境中出水的水浸古木材因为被海洋穿孔虫等微生物所劣化，即使同一遗址的出水遗物，由于遗物的分布和所处海洋环境不同，肉眼观察到的遗物状态也存在差异（图一、图二）。

存活木材的最大含水率在100%上下，也就是说每1千克的木质含有约1千克的水分。但是，水浸古木材的含水率如下：针叶树为100%～500%，阔叶树在300%～800%[6]，微生物劣化现象严重的阔叶树材的最大含水率甚至可以达到1200%。最大含水率增加是木材的成分分解引起的现象，因此通过最大含水率的

[3] M. Y. Cha, K. H. Lee, Y. S. Kim, Micromorphological and chemical aspects of archaeological bamboos under long-term waterlogged condition, *International Biodeterioration & Biodegradation* 86(B), pp.115–121, 2014.

[4] 〔韩〕车美永、尹容熙：《海洋出水遗物保存处理指南书》，"3.有机遗物"，国立海洋文化财研究所学术丛书第31集，2013年，页22～55。

[5] Florian, M-L.E., Scope and history of archaeological wood, *Archaeological Wood, Properties, Chemistry, and Preservation*, Washington, D.C., pp.3-32, 1990.

[6] 〔日〕澤田正昭、〔韩〕金圣范著，郑光龙译：《文化财保存科学概说》，"第3章·木材遗物保存处理"，首尔：书经文化史，2000年，页90。

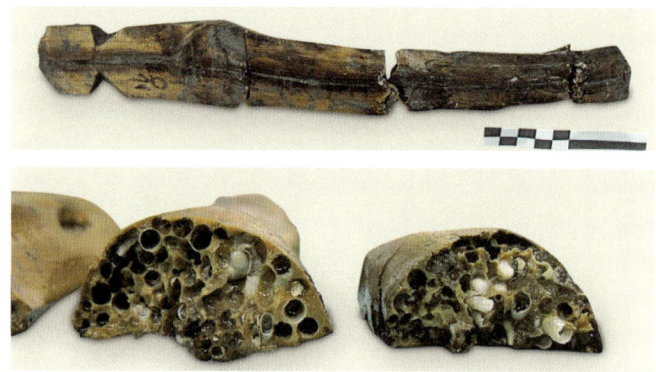

图一 木简中的海洋穿孔虫（马岛1号船出水）

图二 木简中的微生物（马岛1号船出水）

测定，可以诊断水浸古木材的分解程度。

图三是在透射电子显微镜（TEM/Transmission electron microscopy）下观察最大含水率达到600%的橡树的图像。最大含水率为600%意味着水分的含量是木质的6倍，随着水分含量的增加，木材也不断分解。将未经分解的正常橡树的细胞（图三）与最大含水率600%的水浸橡树的细胞（图四）相比，可以看到图四中的细胞被分解，已分解的细胞壁的孔隙被水分置换。如果将此状态的水浸古木材放到空气中而水分蒸发的话，木材会产生收缩变形失去原状。为了对其安全地保存管理，保存处理工作是必然要进行的。

（二）水浸古木材的保存处理

水浸古木材保存的基本原则是保持遗物大小和形态的稳定，通过尺寸稳定化

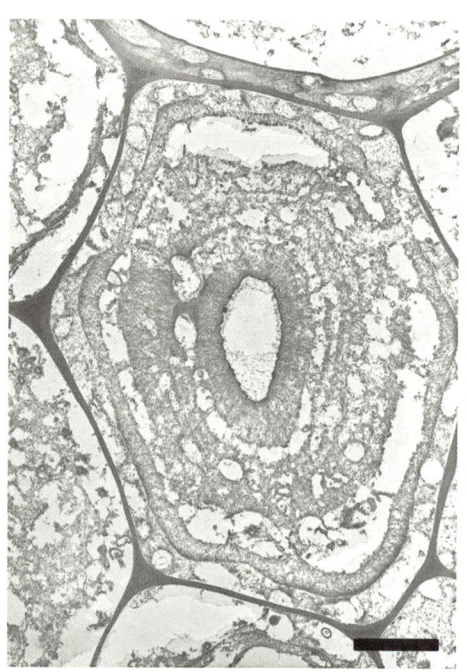

图三 橡树的木纤维（$KMnO_4$, bar=2.7 μm）

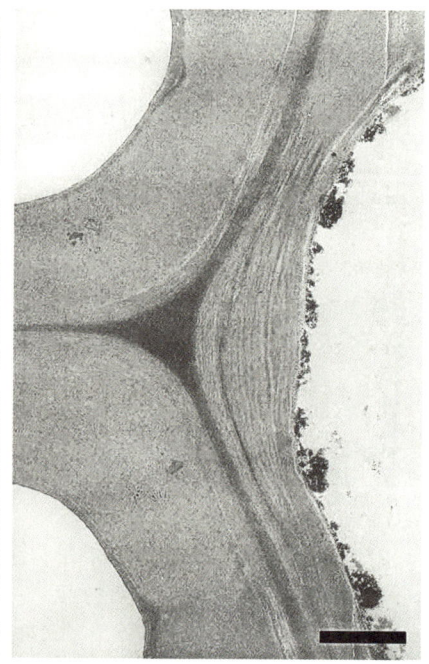

图四 水浸橡树的木纤维（$KMnO_4$, bar=1.9 μm）

处理（consolidation）加强遗物的强度，将木材材质的损伤降到最低，并注意以下事项[7]：①考虑美观性；②不要改变遗物的形态；③不要损坏其历史、考古方面的任何信息；④赋予其耐久性；⑤所有遗物都不是以展览为目的来进行保存处理的，还要对保存处理对象水浸古木材的劣化状态、要使用的处理试剂的浸透性、与树种有关的特点等方面充分探讨和调查，再计划与遗物的状态相符的保存处理法。

水浸古木材的保存处理过程如表一所示，只是因遗物的状态和尺寸不同，细节操作方法有所差异，但保护处理程序是相同的。

[7] Grattan D.W., R.W. Clarke, 9. Conservation of waterlogged wood, *Conservation of marine archaeological objects*, Edit. Colin Pearson, Butterworths Series in Conservation and Museology, p. 164, 1987.

表一　水浸古木材的保存处理过程

脱盐	• 用淡水浸润去除海洋盐 • 尺寸稳定化处理前对水浸木材的保管要保证其未受干燥损坏
处理前的状态调查	• 处理前状态的记录和拍照 • 树种识别、测定含水率、成分分析、组织的分解状况调查 • 决定与遗物状态相符的保存处理方法
洗涤	• 物理法：用各种小工具去除异物质；超声波洗涤 • 化学法：利用螯合物(chelating compound)去除异物质
尺寸稳定化处理	• 将水浸木材内水分用尺寸稳定化剂（药品）置换，增加遗物强度
干燥	• 调节干燥 • 冷冻干燥
拼合与复原	• 用氰基丙烯酸酯（cyanoacrylate）拼合 • 需要加固和充填时，用环氧树脂（epoxy），将树脂HV427, SV427和无机颜料混合后使用
处理后状态的记录	• 处理后状态的记录和拍照
保管和管理	• 在20±2℃，50±5%的环境内保管

1. 脱盐

为了保存处理水下发掘出的遗物，在实验室内首先拍摄遗物照片，进行状态观察并做好记录。之后在装有淡水（自来水、电离子水、蒸馏水）的密封容器里对遗物进行浸润保管，从而消除海盐。对于上面附着铁化合物（iron compound）的水浸古木材，在脱盐和保管时绝对要区别对待。如果未对水浸古木材上附着的铁化合物进行消除，随着时间的推移，会对遗物的其他部分产生污染，因此需要特别注意（图五、图六）。

2. 保存处理前的状态调查

在保存处理前做好对遗物的状态调查，对决定其适合何种保存处理法十分重要。对处理对象遗物的各种信息进行收集、状态观察、大小尺寸、测定重

图五 局部被铁化合物污染的水浸古木材（脱盐处理前）

图六 局部被铁化合物污染的水浸古木材（脱盐处理后的状态变化）

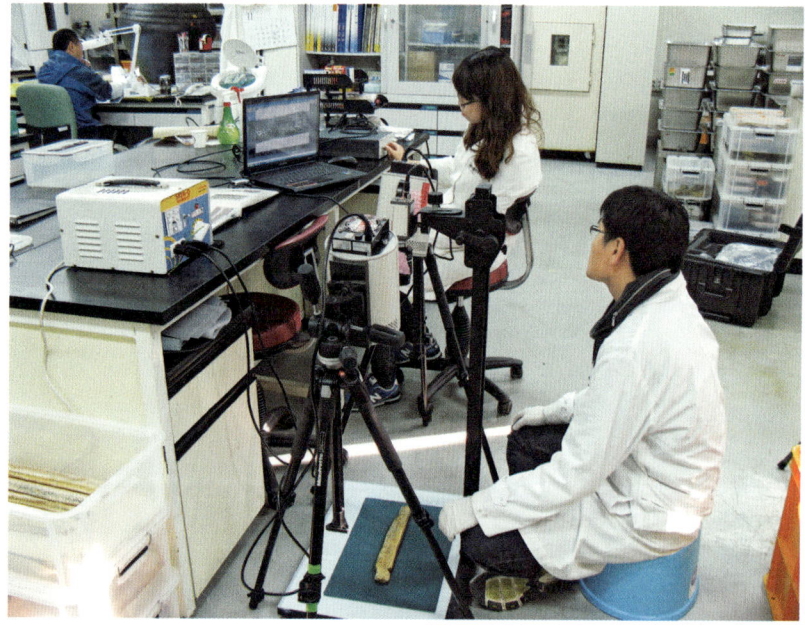

图七 红外线摄影

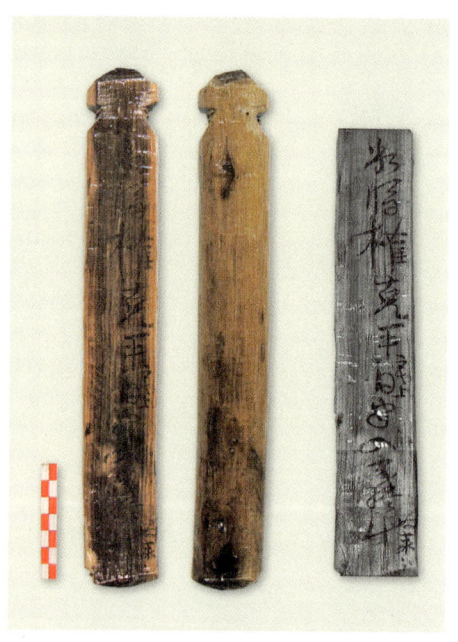

图八 木简与其红外线摄影照片

[8] Cha M.Y., K. H. Lee, Y. S. Kim, Alteration of Physical and chemical characteristics of waterlogged archaeological woods after cleaning, Printed in Republic of Korea, *Journal of Conservation Science* 19: 19–30, 2006.

[9] 〔韩〕金润受、金奎赫、金荣淑：《木材保存科学》，光州：全南大学校出版部，2004年，页362。

[10] 〔韩〕曹性权：《堆积学》，祐成，1995年。

量、记录并拍照，即处理前做好状态记录。另外，如果发现墨书或可能会存在墨书时，要在遗物的洗涤前对其进行红外线摄影，确定是否存在墨书（图七、图八）。对其进行树种分析或放射性碳素年代测定提取标本时要格外当心，必须在需要的情况下才提取标本。

3. 洗涤

对水浸木材的洗涤是保存处理过程中的重要一环。木材有多孔性，长期的埋藏使水浸木材的表面和内部都掺杂了无机物等各种各样的异物[8]。对水浸木材的化学组成进行分析便可明确其灰分量增加了，这是因为周边环境中的无机物等堆积到木材分解形成的孔隙中所致[9]。

学界一般定义土壤的粒度组成为：2000-50μm的沙，50-2μm的淤泥和2μm以下的黏土[10]。占出水水浸木材大部分的松树的假导管直径在40μm左右，橡树种的春材（或称早材）的导管直径为250μm，木纤维的直径则在20μm左右[11]。因此，大部分的土壤颗粒易向木材中渗透，土壤中颗粒的直径越小，向水浸木材内部渗透得越深。

这些异物会对尺寸稳定剂的渗透和扩散进行阻碍[12]，如未完全消除，保存处理后木材表面仍会附着异物，这是产生异质感的原因。此为问题的焦点，通过精密地洗涤能相当程度地解决这一问题，这也说明了洗涤对遗物保存处理的重要性。

水浸木材保存处理的洗涤方法有四种（表二）。洗涤对尺寸稳定的效果有着直接的影响，因此要进行精密的洗涤。根据不同的遗物状态在（表二）中选择不同的洗涤方法。物理洗涤过后（图九、图一〇），化学洗涤也要并举，一般来说对所有的水浸古木材用2%（w/v）的EDTA-2Na(乙二胺四乙酸二钠/EDTA Disodium Salt)进行72小时浸泡的方式进行化学洗涤（图一一、图一二）。经化学洗涤后，再用淡水浸泡，去除化学洗涤的残留药品。EDTA会与

[11]〔韩〕朴相珍、李元用、李华珩：《木材组织识别》，乡文社，1987年。

[12] Kang A. K., S. J. Park, Micromorphological changes of waterlogged archaeological wood in PEG 4000 and Sucrose Treatment, Printed in Republic of Korea, *Journal of Conservation Science* 5(2): 3-14. 1996.

表二　水浸古木材的洗涤方法

分类	洗涤法	比较
物理法	使用工具	• 毛笔，牙签，洒水器等各种小工具
	脱气	• 制作真空状态下的饱水材料
化学法		• EDTA 处理：2%(w/v) EDTA-2Na, 72小时 • P.C.D处理：5%PEG400，5%连二亚硫酸钠（Sodium dithionite），2%柠檬酸二铵水（Diammonium citrate in water）
物理法	超声波洗涤	40KHz, 30分钟

图九　洗涤——使用工具（毛笔）　　　　图一〇　洗涤——使用工具（洒水器）

木材内的金属阳离子形成螯合物（chelating compound），对去除水浸木材内的无机成分效果很好，处理后木材的颜色也会变亮。

测定pH后决定停止洗涤的时间。木材表面固定有铁腐蚀化合物时，单用EDTA处理没法完成洗涤。这种情况下，只能用5%（w/v）PEG400，5%（w/v）的连二亚硫酸钠（Sodium dithionite），2%（w/v）的柠檬酸二铵水（Diammonium citrate in water）溶液进行浸润清洗[13]（图一三、图一四）。

4. 尺寸稳定化

尺寸稳定化旨在增强水浸古木材的硬度，并不是去除当中的水分，而是指将样品的水分置换出来的过程。要根据遗物状况的不同采取与之适应的尺寸稳

[13] Richards V., K. Kasi, I. Godfrey, Iron removal from waterlogged wood and the effects on wood chemistry, *Proceedings of the 11th ICOM-CC WOAM conference*, Greenville, North Carloina, USA, 24–28 May 2010, Edit. K. Strætkvern & E. Williams, pp.383–400, 2012.

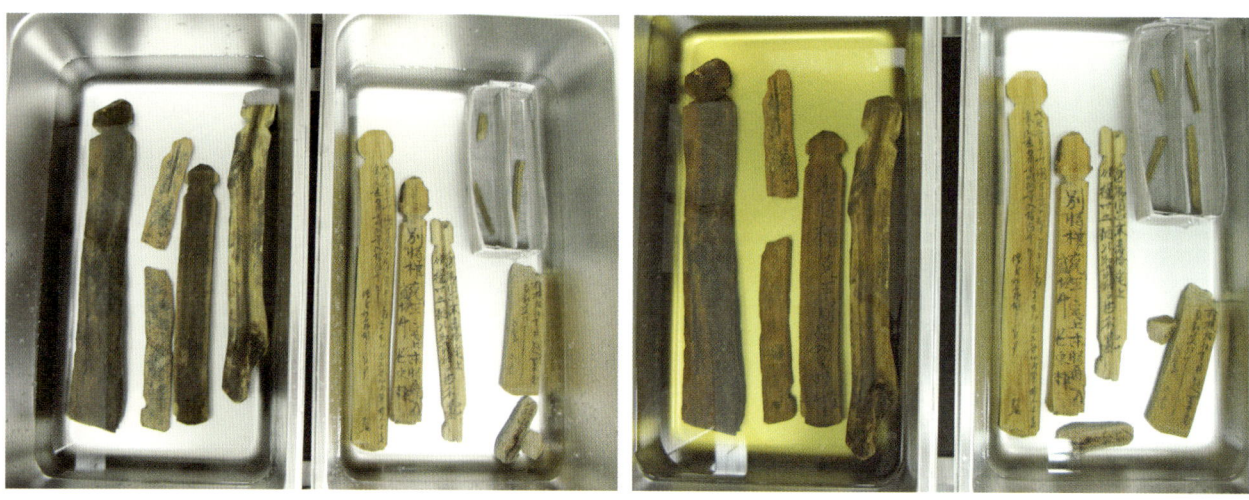

图一一　洗涤——EDTA处理前　　　　　　图一二　洗涤——EDTA处理后

 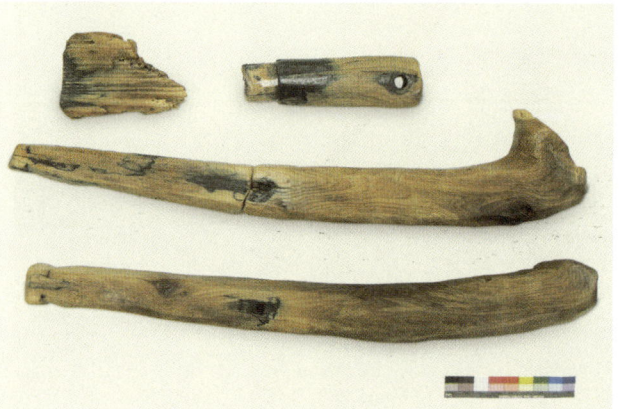

图一三　洗涤——P.C.D处理前　　　　　　图一四　洗涤——P.C.D处理后

定化处理法。最常使用的有低浓度或高浓度的PEG4000含浸法与高级醇(higher alcohol)含浸法。

根据遗物尺寸、状态的不同以及稳定化后是否有使用真空冷冻干燥器的可能性，尺寸稳定化的方法也有差异。低浓度PEG4000含浸适用于使用真空冷冻干燥器干燥时。用低浓度PEG4000含浸时，使其溶解的溶媒要用叔丁醇和水。

低浓度PEG（溶于水）含浸法主要使用平均分子量为3900g/mol的PEG4000。在40℃的加温含浸试管中使PEG4000(溶于水)的浓度按照10%→20%→30%→40%（w/w）逐渐上升。每个阶段的含浸期均为一个月，并根据遗物的大小调整含浸时间。

使用低浓度PEG(溶于叔丁醇)是为了安全地以叔丁醇去置换，首先按50%→70%→90%→95%→100%→100%（v/v）的顺序实施醇置换，再在50℃的加温含浸试管中按照50%→70%→90%→95%→100%→100%（v/v）的方式使叔丁醇去置换。之后，在50℃的含浸试管内以10%→20%→30%→40%的PEG4000（溶于叔丁醇）含浸。当水分没有完全被置换为醇时，叔丁醇的置换会遇到阻力，并且PEG4000的含浸环节可能发生问题，处理后遗物上也可能出现割裂或收缩的现象，所以醇（alcohol）的置换过程十分重要。并且，在含浸过程要注意避免水分的影响。

目前木制品的保存处理最常用的方法是真空冷冻干燥法。进行真空冷冻干燥法前将叔丁醇或水当做PEG4000的溶媒，这两种方法的特点见表三。用叔丁醇作尺寸稳定剂的溶媒，在高真空下不进行液化直接升华，因此能在干燥中防止木材的收缩和变形。由于叔丁醇的蒸气压比水要高，所以缩短了干燥时间，还具备尺寸稳定化时PEG的浸透量和浸透速度都很高的优点。但叔丁醇有易燃性强、对人体有毒、尺寸稳定化时间长，其过程中一定要加热的缺点。然而，用水作溶媒具备整个保存处理时间短、处理后的尺寸稳定性佳、对人体无害、能在室温下进行处理的优点。因此目前常以水来代替叔丁醇作尺寸稳定化剂。

高浓度PEG含浸法的平均分子量是3900，将PEG4000放入在40℃的加温含浸试管中，按10%→20%→30%→40%→50%→60%→70%（w/v）的顺序增加浓度。每个阶段的含浸期为1个月，但当遗物的厚度在10厘米以上时，含浸期需增至2~3个月。

高级醇处理法是使用高级醇进行尺寸稳定化的方法，即以有机溶剂去置换水分的方法。使用高级醇中的十六醇（鲸脂醇/cetyl alcohol, fw=242.4g/mol）和十八醇（硬脂醇/stearyl alcohol, fw=270.5g/mol）作为尺寸稳定化

[14] Yi Y. H., Conservation of Waterlogged Wooden Finds Excavated in Wet-Site, Printed in Republic of Korea, *Journal of Conservation Science* 6(2) : 120-140, 1997. Kim S. C., W. K. Park, Y. H. Yi, Dimensional Change of PEG-Freeze Dried Waterlogged Woods Exposed at Various Humidity Conditions, Printed in Republic of Korea, *Journal of Conservation Science* 16: 110-118, 2004.

[15] Yi Y. H., Conservation Status and Challenges of Excavated Wooden Artifacts, *Present and Future of Conservation for Organic Artifacts, 2013 Intnational Conservation Symposium*, Printed in Republic of Korea, Cultural Heritage Conservation Science Center, p.19, 2013.

表三 尺寸稳定化剂的溶媒：叔丁醇与水对比[14]

溶媒	
叔丁醇（Tert-buthyl alcohol）	水
• 高真空下的不进行液化过程而是升华——防止木材在干燥中收缩变形	
• 蒸气压比水高，缩短干燥时间	
• PEG的渗透量和渗透速度高	
	• 保存处理后的尺寸稳定性优秀
• 易燃性强	• 安全
• 人体有毒	• 人体无毒
• 尺寸稳定化过程长且复杂，加温（40～50℃）：alcohol置换→叔丁醇置换→PEG(溶于叔丁醇)含浸	• 尺寸稳定化过程短，室温或加温处理：PEG(in D.W)含浸
• 醇置换完美 • 当醇置换不完全，木材内水分残留时，保存处理过程中遗物的损坏概率就高	

剂，与常用的PEG4000相比，分子量远少于后者，因此应用于分解不厉害的水浸木材的保存处理。并且高级醇是非水溶性含浸溶剂，不用担心木材吸湿性增加，也不受环境的影响，多被运用于木材和金属组成的复合状遗物的保存处理[15]。水浸古木材的保存处理常用高级醇中的十六醇。高级醇法操作方式如下：在室温中，按"50%→70%→90%→95%→100%→100%（w/v）"的顺序置换乙醇（ethyl alcohol）后，在50℃的加温含浸试管中，按"10%→20%→30%→40%→50%→60%→70%（w/v）"顺序进行十六醇（溶于乙醇）（cethyl alcohol/ethanol）含浸。为了水分的完全置换要进行充分的含浸，按照遗物的状态可调整含浸处理时间。

5. 干燥

干燥可分调节干燥和真空冷冻干燥两大类。

在水溶性高浓度PEG含浸处理时或水浸木材没有受到分解还很健康的情况下，为了使干燥应力最小化，要对木材周边进行保湿，从高湿向低湿缓缓进行干燥。最好使用恒温恒湿机，但如果无法准备此设备，则要注意防止水分急剧蒸发以及收缩和割裂现象的产生。开始调节干燥之初，要防止水分急剧蒸发，

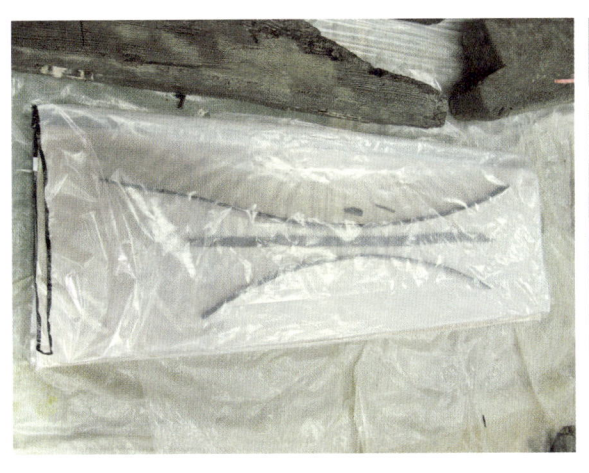
图一五　调节干燥中已包装的木材

图一六　真空冷冻干燥后的木简

应将调节干燥的对象以封闭塑料布盖好或放在箱子内，内置湿度计测定水分的实时变化，保持一定的高湿环境。待处理对象在高湿环境下变得稳定后，才将封闭塑料或箱子盖打开，将湿度调低，再次用盖子或塑料布封好保湿，利用湿度稳定化的方式来进行干燥（图一五）。

真空冷冻干燥法是使木材内的水分在高真空下升华的方法。用水溶性药品或在有机溶媒内溶解的药品进行尺寸稳定化处理后，把表面残留的过量PEG去除，再放入-40℃的急速冷冻温度机内进行预备冷冻，预备冷冻期持续约3日到1周。把遗物转移到车床，温度设定为-40℃，电容器设定为-80℃的真空冷冻干燥机的机床上，将2个温度传感器放在遗物的表面（如果木材有缝隙或裂痕则放入其内），剩下的一个置入干燥室的空间内，再把冷冻干燥机的门关上，开始创造真空环境。此时把真空维持到5mm真空度(Torr)的程度。先将附着在遗物上的温度传感器设为-40℃，开始温度稳定化。干燥初期，在-40℃的机床温度下，遗物上附着的传感器一旦显示温度稳定就可以继续在-30℃的条件下干燥，此时要维持下去直到遗物上附着的传感器显示温度达到平衡。运用真空冷冻干燥法进行保存处理时，PEG4000的溶解温度是-17℃，所以在此温度以上不应该进行干燥。完成真空冷冻干燥的遗物要放入密闭的箱子中，在室温下变得稳定化（图一六）。

6. 表面处理

干燥后的木材表面局部残留的药品要用棉签蘸90%（v/v）的乙醇（溶于水）擦拭掉或者用加热枪将残留的尺寸稳定化剂热溶后擦拭。经过低浓度PEG（溶于水）含浸处理后，如果真空冷冻干燥过的遗物颜色变得过亮而有异质感时，则用设定为60℃的加热枪对表面进行热处理，便能克服异质感（图一七）。

7. 拼合与复原

遗物需要拼合时使用氰基丙烯酸酯（cyanoacrylate）系列的拼合剂。拼合

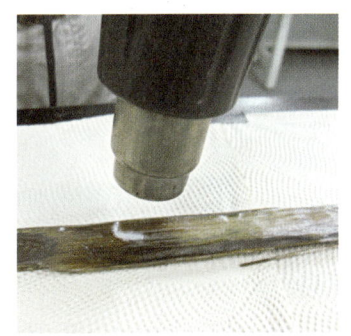
图一七　表面处理——使用加热枪

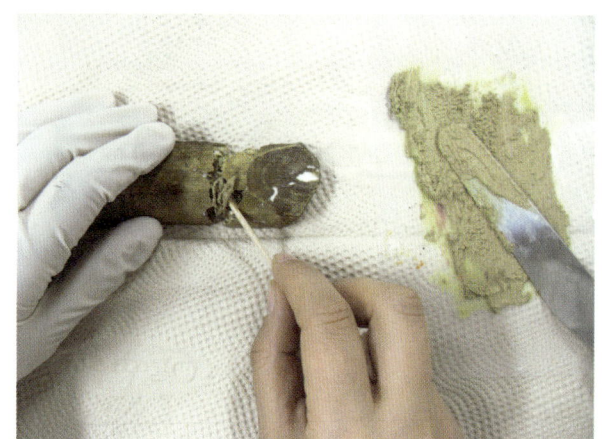

图一八　拼合与复原

图一九　调整色彩

后如果需要增加木材遗物硬度或者复原，将环氧树脂（epoxy）系列的HV427、SV427与无机颜料混合后使用（图一八、图一九）。

8. 处理后状态的记录

在保存处理卡上详细记录保存处理的过程，利用摄影对处理后的状态进行详细记录，并开具保存处理结果报告书。

9. 保管和管理

木材遗物放在20±2℃，50%±5%的环境里进行展示与保管，并且要周期性地检查遗物的状态（图二〇～图二三）。

图二〇　木制器盖——保存处理前后对比［使用低浓度PEG(溶于水)进行真空冷冻干燥］

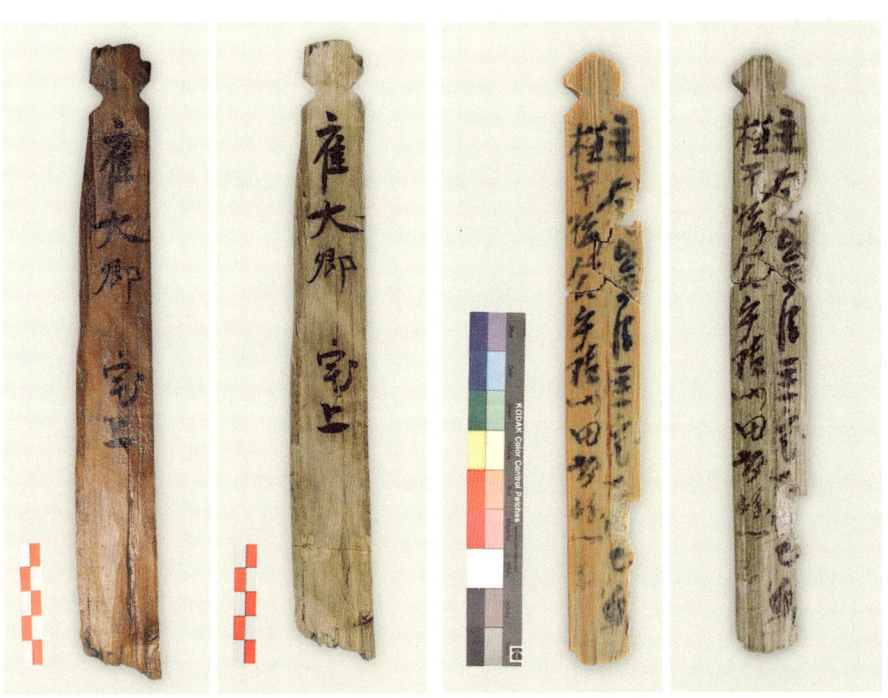

图二一　木简保存处理前后对比［使用低浓度PEG4000(溶于叔丁醇)进行真空冷冻干燥］

图二二　木简保存处理前后对比［使用低浓度PEG（溶于水）进行真空冷冻干燥］

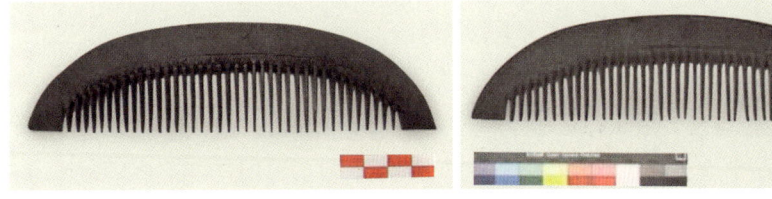

图二三　木梳保存处理前后对比（高级醇法）

三

水浸谷物类遗物的保存处理

韩国遗址中出土的谷物有大米、大麦、黍、粟、大豆等。按照出土遗物的状态可分为碳化谷物和水浸谷物两类。碳化谷物要么是被火烧过，要么在地层中被碳化，完整保存的例子不多。由于碳化谷物的出土状态相对完整，不必进行尺寸稳定化处理等保存处理，只是为了避免露出在急剧的环境变化中坏损，要在适合的环境内保管，保证安全管理。然而，水浸谷物从湿地或海洋环境中出水，谷物的内核（大米等）已分解消失，只会留下外部的糠皮。在高丽时代的船舶马岛1号船中发现的稻、谷、粟、稗虽然保存着其外部形状，但仅有糠皮存留。特别是稻和植物的根部吸收了硅酸，体内形成结硬的游离子组织，如此形成的细胞被称为"植物硅酸体"。与此同样是硅酸体很小的游离子变成细胞组织的原因，是因为它在海洋和陆上的湿地中长期埋藏期间没被分解而存留下来。可一旦除掉水浸谷物中的水分，就无法维持其原来的形态，与此同时遗物的价值也将失去，因此必须要运用适合的方法来保存处理。

马岛1号船中谷物类遗物出水之前，曾在韩国光州新昌洞等遗址也发现过水浸稻。但是目前对水浸谷物的保存处理的相关研究几乎未进行。为了做好水浸稻安全保存和管理，我们以马岛1号船中出水的水浸稻为对象进行了保存处理实验。以此实验结果为据，对水浸谷物类遗物进行保存处理。

（一）水浸稻的保存处理实验

1. 材料与方法

实验对象是2009年在马岛1号船中出水的稻。水浸稻包含在淤泥中出水，因此首先要用筛把稻表面附着的淤泥去除。之后用淡水浸泡去除海洋盐，再用2%的EDTA-2Na(溶于水)洗涤后作为实验试料。

选用的保存处理法和药品与水浸木材试料相同。经过第一次实验结果，保存处理后无法维持其形态的处理方法有：十八醇（Stearyl alcohol）法、达马树脂（Dammer）法、低浓度PEG4000（溶于水）含浸后再用真空冷冻干燥法。因此这些方法在第二次实验中都被排除，并未采用。

将准备好的试料经蔗糖（Sucrose）法、高浓度PEG含浸法、低浓度PEG4000（溶于叔丁醇）含浸后进行真空冷冻干燥PEG（溶于叔丁醇）[PEG（T）]、高级醇法中选用十六醇[Cetyl alcohol(CE)]。并且，因十八醇[Stearyl alcohol（ST）]的溶融点为60℃，在室内容易凝固，这是使用上的难处。为了弥补这些缺点，要将十六醇(CE)和十八醇(ST)的比例调和为1∶1或者2∶1。实验后通过肉眼观察各试料的形态维持和色相变化，再在体式显微镜内观察表面，并通过测量处理前后尺寸的数值变化来得出尺寸变化率。

2. 结果与考察

肉眼及显微镜观察结果如表四及图二四~图二六所示。

经肉眼观察，没有进行保存处理而只是经干燥控制后的遗物的表面出现下陷，不能维持其形态。蔗糖法虽然可以维持遗物形态，但会使保存处理后的稻的表面向白色变化。蔗糖虽然能维持很好的形态，但使试料的表面看上去闪烁并变得透明。PEG(T)也能维持形态，但和保存处理前的水浸稻相比，表面脆弱，这是因为过度干燥的缘故。和蔗糖法一样，在表面也会留下白化现象。高级醇法对所有的处理试料来说都能维持良好的形态和色相。只有使用100%的CE

表四　对水浸稻运用各种保存处理法的结果对比

		肉眼观察		显微镜观察
		形态维持	表面状态	
选用的处理方法		X	下陷	皮层分离
含浸法	Sucrose	O	白化现象	良好
	PEG	O	闪烁	良好
真空冷冻干燥法	PEG(T)	O	过度干燥	细微坏裂
高级醇法	CE	O	良好 (100%CE-白化现象)	良好
	1:1=CE:ST*	O	良好	药品附着于表面
	2:1=CE:ST*	O	良好	药品附着于表面

*十八醇[Stearyl alcohol（ST）]在表面处理时容易凝固

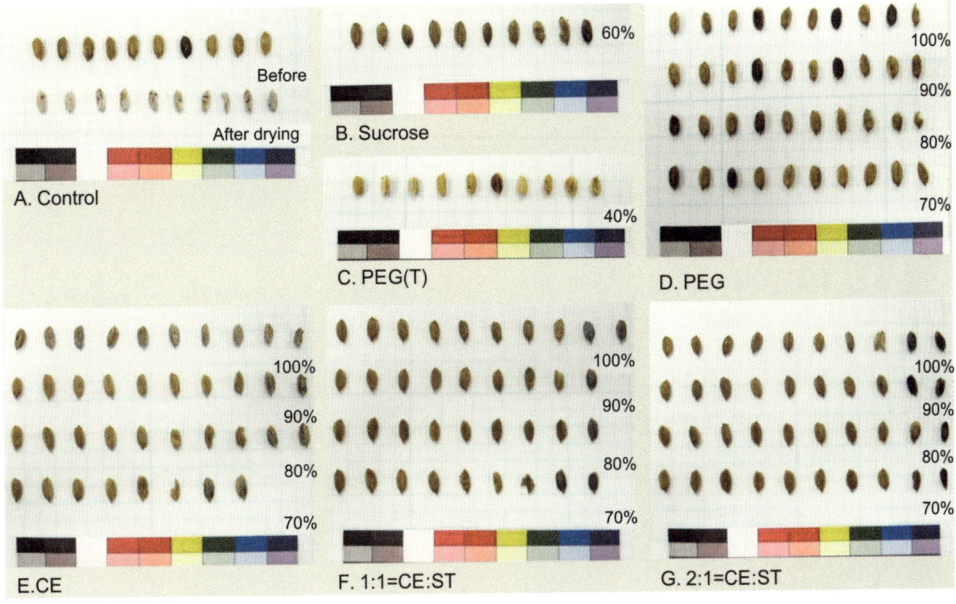

图二四　保存处理后的稻

图二五　保存处理前后的稻

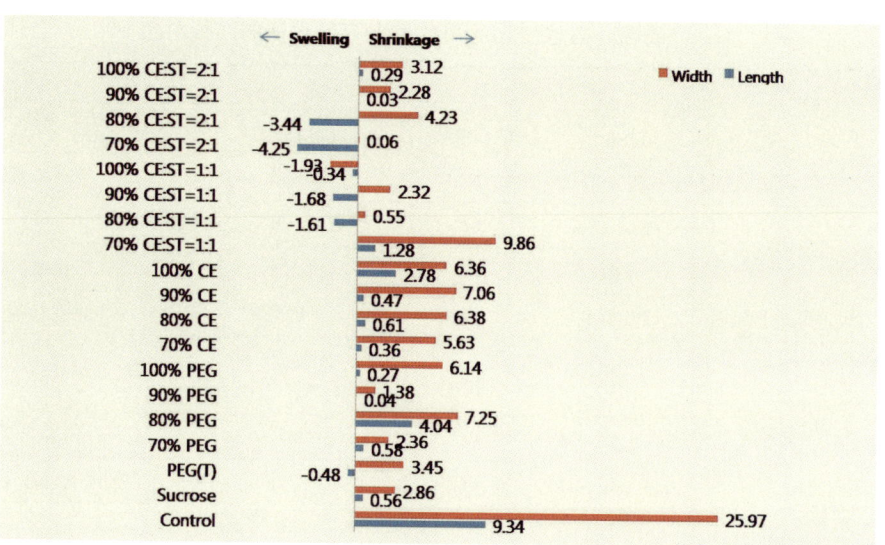

图二六　保存处理前后稻的尺寸变化率(%)

时，在试料表面观察出白化现象。

通过体式显微镜观察得知Sucrose法、PEG法处理后的稻表面状态良好。使用PEG(T)时，表面可以观察到细微的割裂现象。高级醇法处理中的CE法会使遗物形成比较良好的表面，则选用1:1=CE:ST法和2:1=CE:ST法处理时，药品会凝结在试料的表面上。

保存处理前后测量稻的最大宽度和长度得到尺寸变化率，这一结果见表四。不进行保存处理而是自然干燥的试料的尺寸变化率为长度9.34%、宽度25.97%，可见其形态会收缩而无法维持，再次证明对水浸稻保存处理的必要性。在所有的试料中都测定到收缩或膨胀的尺寸变化率，其中宽度变化率比长度更高。高级醇法中用70%、80%、90%、100%的CE:ST=1:1和70%、80%的CE:ST=2:1来处理稻的长度会发生膨胀，体式显微镜中观察时如果在表面看见药品凝结，推断与尺寸变化有关。

水浸稻的保存处理结果显示，采用CE法在肉眼和显微镜下观察都有良好结果。尺寸变化方面，经所有实验过的处理群中收缩或膨胀的尺寸变化率的测定，可知使用90%CE:ST=2:1时尺寸变化最小。

但是，如果要保存处理大量的谷物类，综合考虑肉眼和显微镜下的形态观察结果及尺寸变化率，我们认为高级醇法应该是最适合的选择。用CE和ST一起处理时，虽然尺寸稳定化率很高，但在通过表面处理去除过量药品之后，稻的表面依然会有药品附着。另外，用70%～100%的CE去处理时，设定为70%的CE使稻在形态上的变化最小，所以如果要处理大量的谷物类的话，不妨用70%的CE。

（二）水浸谷物类遗物的保存处理

2009年泰安马岛1号船的水下调查发掘发现了大量的稻、荞麦、粟和稗，马岛2号船和3号船中则没有稻出水。海洋出水的谷物类遗物因为埋藏了约800余年时间，谷物的主成分淀粉已经分解无存，被其他的成分填满，是有机化的形态。为了水浸谷物类遗物的安全保存和管理，一定要对其进行保存处理。

谷物类遗物的保存处理过程见表五。

表五　谷物类遗物的保存处理过程

收集试料	• 移入密闭容器内保管
脱盐	• 淡水浸泡去除海盐
处理前的形态观察	• 保存处理前形态的记录与拍照 • 专家分析种属(species)
洗涤	• 物理方法：用筛子过滤异物质 • 化学方法：2% w/v EDTA-2Na处理
尺寸稳定化	• 醇脱水，室温 （50%→70%→90%→95%→100%→100% v/v乙醇） • 十六醇含浸，50℃有机溶媒含浸剂 10%→30%→50% v/v 十六醇（溶于乙醇）
表面处理	• 去除过量的十六醇 (加温处理) 分离原形和残片
处理后状态的记录	• 处理后的形态记录并拍照
保管和管理	20±2℃，50±5%内展示和保管

为了对水下出水的谷物类遗物安全的管理和保存处理，在运入实验室时，有的保持水浸状态放入密闭容器中（图二七），还有的大量出水遗物为了运送的便利用袋子运入（图二八），此时要立刻将它们移到密闭容器内，在密闭容器内装水，防止遗物干燥使其保持原状。

图二七　进入实验室后的荞麦

图二八　发掘后进入实验室后之稻的状态

1. 脱盐

谷物的脱盐处理要和洗涤一同进行。脱盐溶液用蒸馏水或自来水，测量使用的蒸馏水或自来水的原有盐度，当谷物的盐分达到与脱盐溶液一致时便可停止。

2. 处理前的状态调查

处理前的状态调查在保存处理之前进行，首先要请专家对谷物的种属（species）进行分析。种属分析前是否洗涤以及采样法要在与专家商议后再进行。还要在保存处理之前，对谷物的状态进行文字和拍照记录。

3. 洗涤

海洋出水的谷物往往是和淤泥等异物混合在一起进入实验室的。还有单一种类的谷物或和其他种类混合在一起的情况。多种谷物混合时，要用孔最细的筛来筛除异物，对谷物进行分离及洗涤（图二九）。筛除异物质后，用2%的EDTA-2Na(溶于水)浸泡谷物3日，用来去除谷物内的异物（图三〇、图三一）。之后用自来水（或用蒸馏水）的溶液交替浸泡谷物的方法去谷物内的残留药品，直到去除残留药品所使用的自来水和蒸馏水具备相同的pH值时才停止。

4. 尺寸稳定化

尺寸稳定化处理时，需要经常移动遗物。因此要将保存处理的谷物类对象放入比其尺寸小的不锈钢筛里，并且只能将谷物薄薄地放入一层，在进行各项处理时，要将移动筛子时可能发生的损伤降到最低。

谷物类遗物的尺寸稳定化处理采用十六醇法。为了用十六醇含浸，要按照50%→70%→90%→95%→100%→100%（v/v）的浓度顺序置换乙醇。根据用乙醇置换的谷物的大小和量的不同，各阶段需进行3~7日（图三二）。

图二九　用筛对水浸稻进行分类和洗涤

图三〇　用2% EDTA-2Na 处理前

图三一　用2% EDTA-2Na 处理后

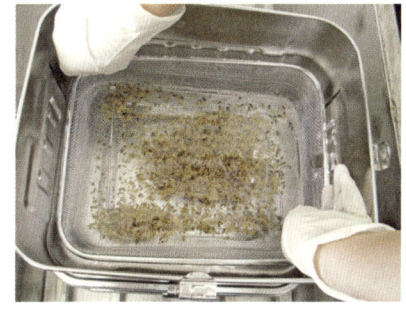  

图三二　乙醇（Ethyl alcohol）置换　　图三三　十六醇（Cethyl alcohol）含浸　　图三四　尺寸稳定化处理后

　　之后放入50℃的有机溶媒含浸机中，按10%→30%→50%（w/v）的浓度顺序用十六醇（溶于乙醇）溶液浸泡的方法进行含浸处理，处理期间各阶段要持续7日以上的时间（图三三）。

　　尺寸稳定化处理完成的遗物要放在网兜内，进行残留药品的蒸发和干燥。那时干燥后的试料如（图三四）一样，谷物的表面会变白色，这是因为使用了过量的十六醇，在谷物的表面顽固地留存下来。

5. 表面处理

　　谷物的表面处理操作如下：在加热到65～70℃的热板上，将装着经尺寸稳定化处理后固结有谷的筛倒过来，用60℃的加热枪加热筛的底部，将谷物和筛分离开。之后要在热板上将谷物表面过量的十六醇去除掉（图三五）。那时将热板上铺垫的报纸或过滤纸更换，谷物表面的药品便可消除。

　　将表面处理完的谷物用镊子和手术刀将其完整形和残形小心翼翼地区分出来（图三六）。

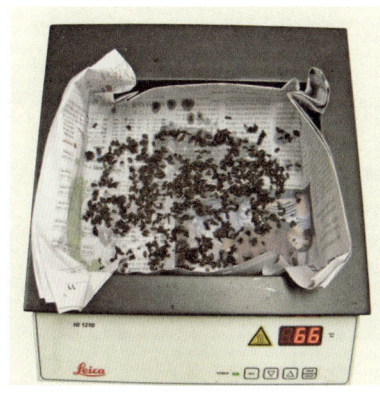 

图三五　稻的表面处理　　　　　　图三六　保存处理后区分完整形和残形

6. 处理后状态的记录

记录下保存处理的过程和状态,并以拍照来结束保存处理的过程(图三七～图四二)。

图三七　保存处理前的稻

图三八　保存处理后的稻

图三九　保存处理前的荞麦

图四〇　保存处理后的荞麦

图四一　保存处理前的粟和稗

图四二　保存处理后的粟和稗

7. 保管和管理

用十六醇处理过的稻要放在国际博物馆学会提倡的20±2℃，50%±5%的条件下保管与展示，并且周期性地检查其状态。

四

结论

海洋出水有机质遗物与水下发掘出水的遗物的保存像是同树之枝叶般共同发展着。新安沉船发掘之后韩国的水下考古主要出水遗物是古木材和陶瓷器，然而，在马岛1、2、3号船的发掘中出水了大量的木简、竹制品、谷物类、草本类、骨制类等多种材质的遗物，与其相关的研究和保存处理工作正值繁荣，最佳保存处理法的探索也从未停止。其中，水浸古木材的特性和保存处理法、水浸谷物的保存处理实验及保存处理法较具代表性，既相似又有区别，且过程复杂。希望以上内容对韩国的水浸古木材和谷物类遗物的保存提供参考。

引用书目

近人论著

〔韩〕曹性权：《堆积学》，祐成，1995年。

〔韩〕车美永、尹容熙：《海洋出水遗物保存处理指南书》，第3章《有机遗物》，国立海洋文化财研究所学术丛书第31集，2013年，页22~55。

〔日〕澤田正昭著，〔韩〕金圣范、郑光龙译：《文化财保存科学概说》，第3章《木材遗物保存处理》，首尔：书经文化史，2000年。

〔韩〕金炳虎、郑亨均：《雁鸭池出土木船의保存处理》，《保存科学研究》第5集，1985年，页109~127。

〔韩〕金润受、金奎赫、金荣淑：《木材保存科學》，光州：全南大学校出版部，2004年。

〔韩〕朴相珍、李元用、李华珩：《木材组织识别》，乡文社，1987年。

〔韩〕文化公报部、文化财管理局：《新安海底遗物（综合篇）》，1998年。

Cha M.Y., K. H. Lee, Y. S. Kim, Micromorphological and chemical aspects of archaeological bamboos under long-term waterlogged condition, *International Biodeterioration & Biodegradation* 86(B), pp.115-121, 2014.

Cha M.Y., K.H.Lee, Y.S.Kim, Alteration of Physical and chemical characteristics of waterlogged archaeological woods after cleaning, Printed in Republic of Korea, *Journal of Conservation Science* 19:19-30, 2006.

Florian, M-L.E., Scope and history of archaeological wood, *Archaeological Wood, Properties, Chemistry, and Preservation*, Washington, D.C., pp.3-32, 1990.

Grattan D.W., R.W.Clarke, 9.Conservation of waterlogged wood, *Conservation of marine archaeological objects*, Edit.Colin Pearson, Butterworths Series in Conservation and Museology, p.164, 1987.

Kang A.K., S.J.Park, Micromorphological changes of waterlogged archaeological wood in PEG 4000 and Sucrose Treatment, Printed in Republic of Korea, *Journal of Conservation Science* 5(2): 3-14.1996.

Kim S.C., W.K.Park, Y.H.Yi, Dimensional Change of PEG-Freeze Dried Waterlogged Woods Exposed at Various Humidity Conditions, Printed in Republic of Korea, *Journal of Conservation Science* 16:110-118, 2004.

Richards V., K.Kasi, I.Godfrey, Iron removal from waterlogged wood and the effects on wood chemistry, *Proceedings of the 11th ICOM-CC WOAM conference*, Greenville, North Carloina, USA, 24-28 May 2010, Edit.K.Strætkvern & E. Williams, pp.383-400, 2012.

Yi Y.H., Conservation of Waterlogged Wooden Finds Excavated in Wet-Site, Printed in Republic of Korea, *Journal of Conservation Science* 6(2):120-140, 1997.

Yi Y.H., Conservation Status and Challenges of Excavated Wooden Artifacts, *Present and Future of Conservation for Organic Artifacts, 2013 International Conservation Symposium*, Printed in Republic of Korea, Cultural Heritage Conservation Science Center, p.19, 2013.

The Naval Architecture of Ancient Fujian Style Sailing Junks, an Overview

福建古代造船技术略论

XU Lu

(Chinese Sailing Junk Expedition Society)

许　路

（福龙中国帆船发展中心）

ABSTRACT / As the most important qualities of ancient Chinese sailing junks, the square bows and sterns with transverse watertight bulkhead and the lugsails with bamboo mat and strip remained the same over thousands of years. Of which, the traditional Fujian style sea going junks is one of the major vessel forms for the ocean and oversea route in ancient China. This paper make an interpretation of Fujian style sea going junks through ship form and structure, principle of design, models, choice of material, sequence of construction, painting and decoration, tools, ship-builders, and ship component remains. This study is combined with the interpretation of Chinese historical documents and drawings, foreign historical drawings, ethnographical field work on main traditional shipbuilding centers along the Fujian coast, reconstruction of traditional shipbuilding, land archaeology evidence, and especially gathers information from a newly discovered illustrated manuscript for shipbuilding[1]. This manuscript at present is the most detailed manuscript found pertaining to the principle of design, modulus system, main unit data, measures and amounts materials used for each ship form. The purpose of this paper is to recover the historical archetypes of ancient Fujian Style Sea going sailing junks, then providing one set of helpful method to explain and identify relevant ship remains excavated in future shipwreck underwater archaeological projects.

KEY WORDS / Fujian style sea going junks; traditional shipbuilding; ship remains; naval architecture; manuscript

[1] Chen Guo Zai(?-1949). *The Naval Architecture Manual of Chen's Family*, manuscript, private collection, Xiamen.

内容摘要 /

在古代的福建，西北部的武夷山和戴云山阻隔了古代闽人与中原内陆的交往，而穿梭于山地丘陵独流入海的丰富水网则让闽人的视线随着河流的方向通达大海，这成为闽人造船出海谋生的最大动因。福建境内物产丰富，盛产造船所需的木材和铁、桐油、蛎灰、藤、棕、麻、生漆等物料，这为建造大量、大型的帆船提供了便宜的物质条件；而福建海岸线曲折，岛屿星罗棋布，既潮差大，海流急，涌浪多，又有每年把帆船送出去又带回来的季风和洋流，这为航海提供了适合的自然条件。

独特的环境，足具的资源条件造就了闽地相对独立的生产方式和生活方式，形成了异于中原农耕文化的海洋性区域文化，福建人成为世界上最早探索海洋的古老族群之一，福船则代表着中国古代最具远洋能力的木质帆船船型。

福建东南沿海处于寒暖流交错的海区，夏季常有台风登陆，地理因素构成了复杂的港湾、航道和渔场情况，也决定了适合这一海区的船型具有如下共同的构造特征：尖削的船底，加装压舱石，以最大限度地提高船只的稳性；突出明显的龙骨，以减缓船只横漂，尽可能地保持航向；可升降深插舵，也能减缓船只横漂，还能使船只操纵灵活，适合浅水和深水的航道；首尾舷弧大，避免海浪拍上船甲板；甲板梁拱大，容易迅速排水；船舷多为平板状，上宽下窄，当船舷下陷水中时，舷部产生较大的瞬间浮力，避免船头入水；船艉多为马蹄形的内凹槽艉封，以增加阻尼，减小纵摇；尽量放低和简化的甲板舱室，可减少受风面积，并且降低重心。独特的外界条件和内在动因，使福建帆船逐渐成为航海木帆船的主要船型。

从技术层面考察，不同历史时期、航行于不同航区、各种用途的福建海船千姿百态，但离不开横向舱壁式结构的重要特征，使之成为具有中国文化区特色的一项发明，而水密隔舱与方首、方尾正是这种结构的主要特征和表现。福船体系的大型海船独特的桅座结构，巧妙地承载和固定了重量巨大的桅杆和船帆，桅杆的前方加装单根撑材，更高效地把受风的推力传递到船体，福船的桅杆有别于世界其他文化区，不需要用任何侧支索固定。

此外，近代福建帆船的黑舷、红艕、白底、头狮、鳅鱼和船眼睛。其中头狮、鳅鱼和船眼睛等涂装画饰特征，蕴含着丰富的海洋社会人文内涵。

进入19世纪下半叶，在世界海洋载具体系中，以蒸汽机为动力的铁壳船的运量逐渐超过了木质帆船。中式传统帆船随后在中国也进入衰落期，但福建帆船仍然凭借其优异的经济性能和在近海复杂水域的灵活航行能力，占领一定的市场。一些精明的西方商人或对中国帆船情有独钟的西方人士，更是将福建帆船驶过大洋，展现到西方国家的民众面前。

同期，西方人开始采用民族志的研究方法，对以福船帆船为主的中式帆船进行细致的观察和分类研究，留下一批较有权威性的测绘和论著，其中福州运木船成为最受西方学者关注的大型海船船型。

本论文针对福建传统帆船的船型、设计、选料、建造工艺、涂装、造船工具、造船工匠，采用文献学挖掘与民族志调查的二重法进行考察，并特别介绍新近在厦门港沙坡尾造船传统田野调查发现的陈氏公司屋造船图谱。这本迄今为止最详尽记录福建海船尺度与设计模数的图谱，记录了清末至民国初年以惠安大牌为主的14种船型，其中大牌经考察与惠安峰尾著名的黑舷五枪眼、峰尾船为同一种船型，是为晚近福建帆船的典型船型之一。

关键词 /

福船　传统造船技艺　船舶遗存　造船技术　造船谱牒

1. Preface

The traditional Fujian style sea going junks is one of the major vessel forms in ancient China.But, what did that ancient junks look like?How were they made? How were they operated and maneuvered?

China's navigation and ship-building constitute the history of a production technology with its root in the common people. Extant historical data is rather limited and therefore regrettably slight when contrasted with the art and expertise accumulated over time and the ancient and magnificent culture that it represents.

The emergence of sea-faring wooden vessels, their development, transformation and eventual disappearance had a lot to do with the political and economic conditions, and the available natural resources at any specific time.Without question, changes in available resources as well as in sea routes entailed modifications to form, size, function, names, and even the mode of operation of these vessels. Equally, technological development and improvement in ship design had its effects on society and the subsequent trajectory of social history.

As one of the most important instruments of production in ancient time, ship itself is a complicated and systematic carrier which involves naval architecture and art of seamanship, fishing production, social function of trade and navy, and anthropology meaning as a special settlement[2].With respect to naval architecture, studies divided it into parts like ship form, structure and principle of design.

Before, domesticated shipwreck archaeology remained in matching and displaying of wrecks, and never goes further to carry out an experiment on replica and reconstruction according to ancient navigation environment perspectives.

Even after researching into the history of naval architecture and ancient writings and searching through relics from different dynasties, focusing mainly on general conditions of ship-building and the wide variety of methods of manufacturing through every historical period, we are unable to reconstruct history in its entirety. What could be done was to set up a systematic way of collecting data; then to summarize, understand and subsequently experiment with them. With these data as the foundation, the project became to produce a series of replicas using methods of construction that had been passed down from generation to generation, so that

[2] Eric Rieth, 2006. Epaves, Archeologie Sous-Marine Et Histoire De L'architecture Navale. *Histoire, Archeologie Et Societe Confererces Academiques Franco-Chinoises*, Ecole francaise d'Extreme-Orient Centre, Beijing, Cabier No 13:1-20.

people today can see and experience them, and which replicas might allow later generations to reconstruct actual history.Only by doing so can we answer the three questions pertaining to ship-building and sea-faring history listed above; only then can the value of research be made clear.

2. Ship form and structure of Fujian style junks

Facing Taiwan across the strait, Fujian has 3324 kilometers of coastline and 1404 small islands off the coast.The way of life of the ancient Yue people, Fujian's early inhabitants, was sea orientated with sea travel their main means of communication. So despite the hilly landscape and the mountain ranges in Fujian's hinterland, these proved no barrier to its economic interaction with other provinces and places overseas.The inland, inshore and offshore sea-faring networks linked Fujian with the outside world thereby ensuring that Fujian's shipping and fishing industries continuously developed.In addition, Fujian was rich in natural resources such as wood, iron, tong oil(Vernicia fordii seeds oil), lihui (lime obtained by burning oyster shells), rattan, hemp and lacquer. With such handy materials that could be used to build ships, ship-building prospered across the province.

Viewed from a different perspective, Fujian's coastline was full of creeks and inlets, and facing the Strait of Taiwan, it was positioned where warm and cold air currents mingled.Not only was the wind strength very inconsistent, it was also where typhoons move inland from the sea during summer and autumn. Due to this complicated natural environment, certain demands had to be met with regard to form, function and structure of ships, and to the choice of materials and skills employed in their manufacture.It is such circumstances that gave birth to vessels with V-shaped bottoms, raised flat bows, indented sterns, flaring bulwarks, framing, stern-hung, lifting rudders lowering deeply below the keel line, and wide cambered decks that eased the drainage of water.These unique environmental and cultural factors together made the Fujian style junks one of the major vessel forms in ancient China.

Building Fujian style junks required standard procedures in the choice of form, design, materials and construction strategy, and involved manufacturing processes such as wood and metal work, sewing, painting and smelting.

The Southern Song dynasty seagoing ship unearthed in Houzhu in Quanzhou in 1974, the mid-Yuan dynasty Fujian merchant ship discovered in Xin'an of Korea in 1976, the late-Yuan dynasty warship found in the water at Penglai in Shandong in 1984, and the many ships found in the sea-beds in Lianjiang, Pingtan, Putien and Dongshan in Fujian province consist only of those parts of the ships that were below the waterline. They, therefore, provide no information on the complete form and design of these vessels. These remains, however, do prove that during the Song and Yuan dynasties the necessary skills developed to build the three-sectioned keel, the water-tight cabins and the stern-hung rudders that could be hoisted and lowered.

3. Historical evidence

Official history writers were used to recording history – fundamentally an account of the emperors and their generals and ministers – using the written language. Apart from Han Yu, Su Shi and their likes who experienced demotion and made their way to the south, then a region outside of the centre of civilization, the literati of the ancient times preferred to stay in the capital or big cities and showed no interest in the lives, customs and practices of the common people. On the contrary, Europe, under the influence of the ancient civilization that developed around the Mediterranean, was more accustomed to recording history with images. Historical data that survive through images are generally not found in written history, particularly when issues such as the lives of the ordinary people and production technologies were considered too menial therefore unworthy of documenting in official archives and annals.

Within the period of three hundred and fifty years from the sixteenth century, group after group of Westerners made their way to China. Some went as tourists, others to spread their religion, to trade or to fight in wars. While there, many sketched down or painted what they saw-the lives and practices of the people as well as the natural scenery of the different places. These works were done with pen, in water color or oil. Upon returning home, some published their sketches, reproduced as prints, to avail those who never set foot on China a chance to catch a glimpse of this mysterious ancient nation of the East.

The Yuan Dynasty came to an end in 1368. China closed its doors to the outside world once again.Foreigners were banned from entering the country, and those already there were forbidden to travel inland beyond the coastal ports.From this time up to in the sixteenth century, China remained a mystery to Europe.Scene after scene of ordinary life in our country in the old days.

The Sixteenth Century

In 1509, the Portuguese oceangoing freighter Diego Lopes de Sequira sailed eastward, taking the east-west route that had just been opened up as a result of the "big geographical discovery". For the first time, it came across a Chinese junk in Malacca.In 1514, Afonso de Albuquerque (1453-1515), Governor of Portuguese Malacca, sent another oceangoing freighter to the Island of Tunmen in Dongguan of Guangdong province.The delegation was headed by Jorge Álvares who became the first Western force to reach China by sea with the hope of opening up trade relations.Frei Tomé Pires, a Portuguese official stationed in Malacca, wrote a book titled *Suma Oriental* Soma Horiemtall based on reports provided by the oceangoing freighter and his own experience in the East, in places such as India and Malacca, and presented it to King Manuel I of Portugal.For many years this book was obscured and was rediscovered only in the twentieth century[3].It is now considered another important book written by a Westerner, after Travels of Marco Polo, that contains geographical information on nations in the East and descriptions of their customs and practices.

In 1517, Fernao Peres d'Andrade arrived Guangzhou as Portugal's first special ambassador.The delegation was made up of eight junks including the 800-ton ship and three Chinese junks which belonged to merchants in He headed the mission that sailed from Malacca from where the delegation set sail, with the purpose of reaching the Chinese capital, befriend the Ming government and promote trade.They were finally able to meet the Ming Emperor in 1520. Before this time, the fleet sent Jorge de Mascarenhas to Quanzhou; he became the first Portuguese to set foot on the place.The mission, however, was a failure.The Portuguese turned to Zhejiang and Fujian where they traded secretly for over twenty years.It was only after the Ming government lifted entry and exit restrictions at seaports that the Portuguese built settlements in Macau in 1553.

Spain took occupation of Luzon in 1565.The route of Chinese junks that used to run between China and Manila was extended with the opening of a new route

[3] On this occasion to the great Armando Cortesao's edition and translation of Pires in 1944 and his discovery of the previous publication of an extract, though of unknown authorship, in the 16th century by Giovanni Battista Ramusio.

between Fujian and Mexico via Manila. Looking for trade opportunities, the Spanish Governor of the Philippines sent Martin de Rada and Jeronimo Marin (one source mentions that they were priests who accompanied the mission; the envoys were Miguel de Loarca and Pedro de Sarmiento) as envoys to China in 1575. Their fleet is known to have been in Xiamen and Quanzhou.

From this time on, the West developed an immense interest in Chinese products and Chinese culture, stimulated by cargoes brought by Portuguese and Spanish ships, of goods such as porcelain, silk and tea. At the same time, Macau became a greatly coveted target of European maritime powers. Under the command of Don Junade Zamudio and Don Luiz Dasmarinas, Spanish battleships sailed to Macau in 1598 where they came into conflict with Portuguese battleships at sea.

With the opening of a trade route between Macau, Goa and Lisbon, a number of priests of the Sociedade de Jesus who lived in Macau, and others like Gregorio Gonzales, M. Ruggieri, F. Passio and Matteo Ricci, were able to find their way inland in China during the second half of the sixteenth century, irrespective of restrictions imposed by the Ming government. Before this, the Christian religion had died out in China for two hundred years. Reports and letters they sent to Europe helped to unveil the mask covering this mysterious empire of the East.

Throughout the sixteenth century, apart from *Suma Orienta*, a hand-painted navigation route-map of 1554 which included "Formosa", and *Spieghel der Zeevaart of* 1592 written by Lucas Waeghenaer[4], we do not know how many more images remain of China and Chinese junks among the large volume of navigation logbooks, travel guides, reports and accounts of travel experiences.

The Seventeenth Century

The seventeenth century can be regarded as the age of Holland (the Netherlands) at sea, for it was then owner of the world's largest fleet. In 1594, a group of nine businessmen started a company, the "Compagnie van Verre" (the long distance company), and sent a fleet to Java under the command of Jacob van Neck. This was the first fleet ever to consist of three armed merchant ships. A typhoon caused the ships to hit on the mouth of the Pearl River in Guangdong. The following year, the newly founded Vereenigde Oostindische Compagnie (Dutch East India Company) promptly sent a fleet to China, headed by Wjbrant Van Warwick. Van

[4] Dirck Gerritszoon Pomp was the first Dutch who traveled to China as passenger onboard a Portuguese merchant ship. Pomp is not recorded as having written anything, but to have contributed by way of oral description to Linschoten's well known *Itinerario*. He did contribute in the same way to Lucas Waghenaer's *Threesor der Zeevaert* (1592), on which see CE Kroese, *Dutch Trade with the People's Republic of China*, Law and Contemporary Problems, Vol.38, No.2, Trade with China (Summer-Autumn, 1973):230-239.

Warwick's name is recorded in Chinese history and he is known to have participated in Captain van Neck's expedition to China a little earlier. In December 1604, he arrived at the port of Ping'an in Taiwan after traveling through many places.

In 1622, the Dutch East India Company sent a fleet of oceangoing freighters to Xiamen.The vessels set off from Batavia (Jakarta) and sailed via Penghu, Liu'ao and Wuyu, traveled against the currents on the Jiulongjiang River, and through places such as Yuegang along the shore.Its Dutch captain Willem Ysbrantsz Bontekoe recorded in his *Memorable Description of the East Indian Voyage 1618-1625*[5]trade activities and raids that his fleet engaged in.The following year, Jan Pieterzoon Coen, an appointed envoy of Holland, traveled to Beijing via Xiamen and Fuzhou but failed to open China's doors to trade.The Dutch turned their attention to Taiwan where there was no real government and took occupation in 1624. A base was set up in Dayuan (present-day Tainan).It was only in 1662 that the Dutch were driven out of Taiwan by Zheng Chenggong and his men.On the lower right corner of a painting done by an anonymous Dutch painter in 1644 of the port of Dayuan is a colored image of a Fujian-built Chinese junk, the earliest portrayal discovered so far.This important painting is currently in the collection of the Nederlands Scheepvaartmuseum.Castle-style architectures that stood in Dayuan at that time – Fort Zeelandia and Fort Provintia – have been preserved.It is likely that more information on Chinese junks exist in the documents of the Dutch East India Company.These remain to be discovered.

Looking for extra benefits, Holland sent a diplomatic mission to China in 1655, with Pieter de Goyer and Jacon de Keyser as envoy and vice-envoy respectively. This was the first diplomatic mission sent to China by a Western nation.It landed at the port of Humen, and after reaching Guangzhou, cruised along inland waterways in southern China and through canals in the north.A greater part of the journey was conducted on water. The mission was summoned to meet the Emperor Shunzi after reaching Beijing, then backtracked to return.The trip lasted for more than nineteen months and took the delegates through the provinces of Guangdong, Jiangxi, Jiangsu, Anhui, Shangdong and Hebei, and the cities of Tianjin and Beijing.After reaching home, one of the members named Johan Nieuhof published *Voyages and Travels to the East Indies 1653-1670* which is an illustrated record of his experiences[6]. The volume contains a hundred and fifty copperplate etchings of topography, scenery,

[5] Willem Ysbrantsz Bontekoe, 1982. *Memorable Description Of The East Indian Voyage 1618-1625*, Chinese translation, Chinese Publishing House, Beijing.

[6] Johan Nieuhof, 1665. *Voyages and travels to the East Indies 1653-1670*, Jacob Van Meurs, Amsterdam.

Fig. 1　The Fujian style junk printed by Cornelis Matelief de Jonghes armada,1607

Fig. 2　The earliest meticulous color image of Fujian style junks in middle 17th century

architecture junks and lively scenes of everyday life of the common people. These early realistic portrayals of China opened the eyes of the West.Many renditions exist of Nieuhof's book which can be regarded as a milestone in the western understanding of China and the Chinese culture.The original manuscript is now in the collection of the German National Library.

The earliest records from extant historical writings that contain information on different types of ship from the Fujian style junk series were written around the late 16th to the mid 17th century. The earliest realistic pictorial representation was printed by Netherlandish armada commanded by Cornelis Matelief de Jonghes[7](Fig.1). A middle 17th century, collection of Berlin Etnologisches Museum was the earliest meticulous color image of Fujian style junks[8](Fig.2).

A mass of Drawings of Chinese ship anchored around Matsuura and recorded by local Japanese painters since last decade of 17th century[9] were of great value for study.

The Navy Abstract (*Shui Shi Ji Yao*) written in the year of the emperor Kangxi by the regional commander Chen Liangshi contained an iconography for Fujian style warship[10].

The Eighteenth Century

During the eighteenth century, merchant ships from Western countries including Austria, Belgium, Prussia, Denmark and Sweden proceeded to China. In 1715 three Swedish ships arrived at Guangzhou; in 1739 the Gotheborg of the Swedish East India Company sailed into Guangzhou for the first time;and in 1784

[7]　This printing was cited by Isaac Commelin, 1646. *Beginning and Ending of the Dutch-East Company*, Amsterdam.

[8]　Anonymous, middle 17th century. *The Island of Formosa*, painted on parchment, collection of Berlin Ethnologisches Museum.

[9]　Oba Osamu, *About Drawings of Chinese ship Kept in Matsuura Hirato History Museum—The Referential Material of Chinese Merchant ship in the Era of Edo*, Memo 5 of Research Institute of East and West Academical studies of Kansai Uiversity. 1972.

[10]　Chen Liangshi, 2002. *The Navy Abstract* (*Shui Shi Ji Yao*), later 17th century, reprint Shanghai Ancient Books Publishing House, Shanghai.

the American ship Empress of China brought to Guangzhou fur, ginseng, cotton, pepper, wine, tar and resin oil.

In 1740, the British government set up a naval task force that aimed at the retaliation and pillaging of Spanish ships. Headed by George Anson, the British vessels sailed through the Atlantic to reach the Pacific where they intercepted a fleet of Spanish merchant ships. After a lengthy period of affliction, the only British flagship that remained – the Centurion – intercepted a large Spanish junk off the Philippines. In 1742 and 1743, the Centurion twice sailed to Humen of Guangdong province to try to sell the cargo looted from the Spanish ships. It was the first British warship permitted entry into China. A big fire broke out in Guangzhou when the Centurion was there. The British navy helped to put out the fire thereby leaving a good impression on the Chinese people. George Anson was invited to meet with the Governor General of Liangguang (the two "guang", i.e., Guangdong and Guangxi) in Guangdong. During this time, Piercey Brett, a man on board the British ship, sketched down the image of a Chinese junk he saw somewhere near Macau[11]. Another man on board, Lieutenant Philip Saumarez, too left a number of sketches he made of Chinese junks.

James Cook, a famous British explorer, navigator and cartographer, is well-known for the three journeys he made on sea. Members of his fleet included painters John Webber and William Hodges both of whom made a considerable number of sketches of Chinese junks in 1777 when they stopped over in Macau[12]. Most of John Webber's drawings are in the collections of the British Library and the Auckland Museum. Those related to Chinese junks have been reproduced in *Art of Captain Cook's Voyages*[13].

Many years went by before the British government sent another diplomatic mission to China in 1792, with George Macartney and George Staunton as envoy and vice-envoy respectively. The justification this time was to extend greetings to the Emperor Qianlong on his birthday but the real intention was to look for special trade privileges. The fleet sailed north on the China Sea to the port of Tianjin where passengers changed to smaller boats that took them inland via the river before they continued on land to reach first the city of Tianjin and then Beijing. They were received by Emperor Qianlong in Chengde. After the meeting they sailed south by way of the canal linking Beijing and Hangzhou. The rest of their journey to

[11] There are 70 or so references to work by Piercey Brett in the National Archive and these are all administrative stuff to do with Brett was Master Attendant at Chatham Dockyard, captain of the Lyon, Yarmouth, Sunderland, etc., or to do with his promotion-nothing of his time in the Centurion. This can only be a reference to the Centurion's log (ADM 51/175) for the period of the voyage much of which was the responsibility of Brett.

[12] All of these drawings were made after Cook's death when the Resolution, under the command of William Broughton after Charles Clerke's death, called in Macau on her way back to Britain.

[13] Rudiger Joppien, Bernard Smith, 1988. *The Art of Captain Cook's Voyages*, Volume 3, *The Voyage of the Resolution and the Discovery, 1776-1780*, Paul Mellon Center, BA.

The Naval Architecture of Ancient Fujian Style Sailing Junks, an Overview

Fig. 3　William Alexander's colour images of Fujian style war junk, 1796

Guangzhou was completed on land until they reach Huangpu where they joined a fleet of home-bound ships to return. Their trip to China lasted over two hundred days in all. When home, many of the delegates wrote books that recount their experiences in China. Among these is an authentic account of an embassy from the King of Great Britain to the Emperor of China authored by George Staunton which had thirty illustrations. These new writings provoked and caused the revival of the interest of the Western world to better understand China. Important publications of this time include *Views of Eighteenth Century China:costumes, history and Customs*[14], an album of paintings by William Alexander, the mission's painter, and John Barrow's *Travels in China*[15] which has a lot of illustrations.

William Alexander's colour images are the earliest and the best realistic portrayals of Fujian style junks available to us today(Fig. 3). One will be impressed by their photographic qualities and the extent of details shown. And with beautiful colors added, they are almost perfect. William Alexander's oeuvre numbers a few hundred. A greater part of these have been donated by his family to the British Museum;others are scattered and in the collections of other museums and private collectors. The Hong Kong Museum of Art has about forty colored copperplate and woodblock prints. It is a pity that in spite of the fact that the afore-mentioned British painters were among

[14] William Alexander and George Henry Mason, 1988. *Views of 18th Century China Costumes, History, Custom*.1796, reprint Portland House, New York.

[15] John Barrow, 1804. *Travels in China*. Cadell & Davis, London.

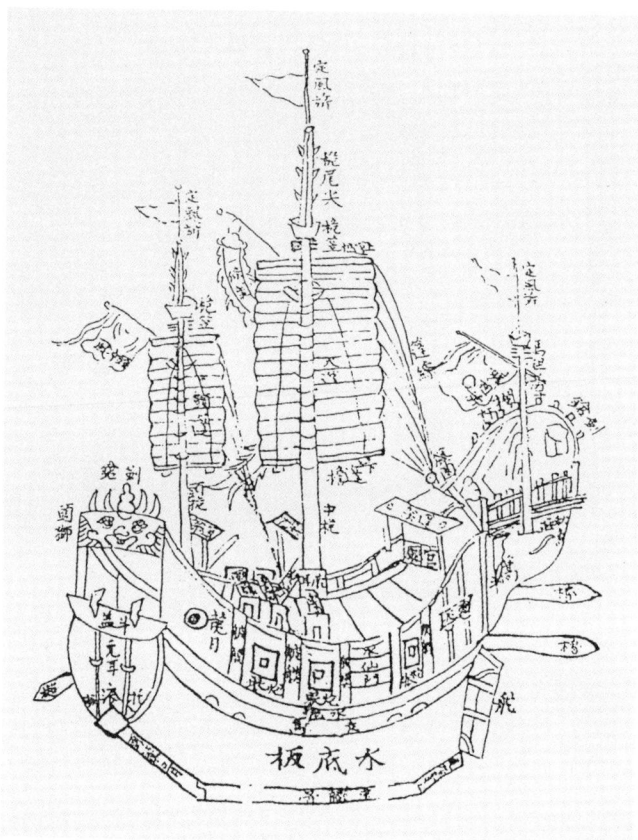

Fig. 4　Ganzeng style warship recorded in the middle of 18th century

the earliest painters allowed entry into China, and having twice sailed pass the sea off Fujian, they never went on-shore and therefore left no images of their travel there.

Interiorly, *The Taiwan Conversation by Writing* (*Chi Kan Bi Tan*) was written between the years of the emperor Kangxi to Yongzheng by Huang Shujing, the first imperial senior government official in Taiwan in Qing Dynasty.Recorded parts of materials, quantities and specifications needed to build the Ganzeng types of Fujian warship[16].

The Illustrated Manual Of Instruction In Shipbuilding For The Navy Of Fujian Province (*Min Sheng Shui Shi Ge Biao Zhen Xie Ying Zhan Shao Chuan Zhi Tu Ji*), a manuscript between the year of the emperor Yongzheng to Qianlong by anonymous writer recorded by the order of the Admiralty[17].The manuscript had four chapters: Figures, Register of ships, Name of ships, Construction and Classification.It listed the kinds of warships are Ganzeng, Shuangpeng, Pingdi, Fazhuo, Bajiang, and their peculiarities and used for different areas and condition. The first page of text was a figure for Ganzeng style warship(Fig.4), with 52 terms descriptive of the details of ships, followed the key dimensions of seventeen sizes of Ganzeng, the largest was 80 chi in length.It contained 10 figures and explanation for details of construction, 50 figures and specifications of main components. These

[16] Huang Shujing, 1957. *The Taiwan Conversation by Writing* (*Chi Kan Bi Tan*), early 18th century, reprint Economic Academe of Taiwan Business Bank, Taibei.

[17] Anonymous, middle 18th century. *The Illustrated Manual Of Instruction In Shipbuilding For The Navy of Fujian Province* (*Min Sheng Shui Shi Ge Biao Zhen Xie Ying Zhan Shao Chuan Zhi Tu Ji*), manuscript.

figures offered a reliable evidence for what did ancient Fujian junk looks like. For instance, Fore "bridle-wood" and main "bridle-wood", apparently the nearest English equivalent would be mast-beam, the cross-pieces in it are called "bridle-wood-shoes" to fix up on deck;and the tenons inside the middle part were used to engage "deer's ears", the partners to hold the mast.

The Regius Formula of Fujian Sea Going Warships (*Qin Ding Fu Jian Sheng Wai Hai Zhan Chuan Ze Li*), a woodblock edition was Written in 1768 by the order of the emperor Qianlong[18].Fore chapter 1 *The Pandect of Sea Going War Junks for All Provinces* outlines the official formula for building and repairing the war junks and their evolution.Fore chapter 2 *The Pandect of Sea Going Warships for Fujian Provinces* outlines the key dimensions of all sizes of Ganzeng and Shuangpeng constructed by Fuzhou, Quanzhou, Zhangzhou, Taiwan warship shipyards and their evolution;the quantities and numbering of these war junks in every battalions(Table1).The primary chapter with 15 041 Chinese characters provided the specification and detailed list of the amounts and costs of materials used for the construction of Ganzeng that might serve in Jinzhou Navy battalion, also a list of the number of work-units required for each task in building. Chapter 1 to 16 provided 16 types and sizes of Ganzeng the specification and required. Chapter 1 (Table 2) the length of deck 13.8 metre, it was the small one in Ganzeng series, designed to cross stormy waters and open seas of Taiwan Straits.

[18] Anonymous, 2002. *The Regius Formula of Fujian Sea Going Warships* (*Qin Ding Fu Jian Sheng Wai Hai Zhan Chuan Ze Li*), 1768, woodblock edition.reprint Shanghai Ancient Books Publishing House, Shanghai.

Table 1 The key dimensions of all sizes of Fujian Ganzeng warships

Number	Qty	Length of deck	Beam	Deep of hold	Cabin
Liminary	3	22.2 m	5.61 m		21
Chap.1	5	13.8 m	3.96 m	1.29 m	15
Chap.2	2	16.2 m	4.71 m	1.60 m	16
Chap.3	4	15.0 m	4.38 m	1.46 m	16
Chap.4	9	16.5 m	4.71 m	1.60 m	16
Chap.5	14	17.1 m	4.86 m	1.60 m	16
Chap.6	8	18.6 m	5.01 m	1.66 m	17
Chap.7	3	19.5 m	5.52 m	1.84 m	18
		……			
Chap.16	3	25.8 m	6.39 m	2.37 m	22
Chap.17	9	24 m	6.24 m	2.18 m	22

Table 2 The specification of Chapter 1 Fujian Ganzeng warship

Main measurement			
Length of deck	13.80 m	Beam of middle bottom	3.06 m
High sheer forward	1.20 m	Length of tail	3.60 m
High sheer tail	0.9 m	Beam of tail deck	3.78 m
Length of fore ship	5.40 m	Beam of tail bottom	2.82 m
Beam of forship deck	2.64 m	Length of top-side plank	15.78 m
Beam of forship bottom	2.40 m	Height of top-sideplank	1.20m
Length of middle	4.80 m	Cabin	15
Beam of middle deck	3.96 m	Deep of hold	1.29 m

This subject takes these drawing materials as the research object, and focuses on their development of technical logic, which can lead to a deeper analysis through the methods of experimental archaeology.

The Nineteenth Century

For the hundred years from the mid eighteenth to the early nineteenth century, European countries such as Britain and Russia sent diplomatic missions repeatedly to China, hoping to open up this closed market. They tried to persuade the Qing emperors to open China to trade but all efforts proved futile. The Qing government ultimately decided to seal off all its doors and caused the West to force them open once again with gunboats.

From 1830 to 1832, the French government sent the battleship La Favorite on a trip around the world. Captain François-Edmond Pâris used paintings and sketches to portray, analyze and record his observations and study of the distinctive ship forms used by different countries and places. Twenty-five of these are realistic water-color representations of warships, passenger ships and fishing boats he saw along the shore of Guangdong[19]. The National Maritime Museum (Musee de la Marine) of France published an album of his works in 1992[20].

From this time on, the number of British warships that sailed to China was continuously on the increase. In April 1840, the "gunboat diplomacy" turned into a war. At the close of the Opium War, Guangzhou, Fuzhou, Xiamen, Ningbo and Shanghai were named as trade ports.

[19] The whole was first published as *Essai sur la construction navale des peuples Extra-Europeens* in Paris in 2 volumes between 1841–1843 at the order of the Navy Minister.

[20] Musee de la Marine, 1992. Le voyage de la Favorite. Paris.

Thomas Allom was the founder of the Royal Institute of British Architects and a painter proficient in realistic landscape paintings[21].He collected more than two hundred works by painters who had been in China, such as Johan Nieuhof of the Dutch mission, William Alexander of Macartney's British mission, the French painter Auguste Borget, and British navy painters Lieutenant White and Captain R.N.Stoddart.Allom created his own style of painting upon a foundation based on the different styles and themes used by the earlier painters.His works, accompanied by captions written by Knight, were compiled into *China: in a series of views, displaying the scenery, architecture, and social habits of that ancient empire* and published in 1843[22].Within a short time, the album became the most popular pictorial textbook on Chinese history across Britain and throughout Europe.Among those painters whom Allom emulated, Auguste Borget, in his round-the-world journey that took him four years to complete, traveled along the Chinese coast from 1838 to 1839 and is known to have lived briefly in Hong Kong, Guangzhou and Macau.In his *Sketches of China and (the) Chinese*[23] published in Paris in 1842 are a bunch of letters and thirty-two illustrations in two-colored lithoprints.

These are sketches and records he made while traveling in China.Many are scenes of ship-related activities on the Pearl River.

Lieutenant White and Captain James Stoddart RN are British Navy painters who participated in the Opium War.They left many realistic portrayals when they traveled north from Hong Kong, Guangzhou, Macau and Xiamen to Ningbo. Some of their works are in the collection of the Hong Kong Museum of Art.

The Early Twentiety Century

Since the later nineteenth century, a group of sinologists and navigators with keen interest in Chinese junks conducted an in-depth field-study on junk-building technologies along the coast and the rivers of China.The result was the publication of books such as *Les Jonques Chinoises*[24], *Lorchas, Juncos E outros Barcos no sul da China*[25], *Chinese Junks and Other Native Craft*[26] which included a detailed survey and illustration of the major shapes of vessels, *The Junks and Sampans of the Yangtze*[27] and *Mariner's Mirror* journal, while another significant recorder Etienne Sigaut's manuscript is expected to publish in coming year[28]. These publications regarding Chinese junks document the results of researches conducted from the end

[21] In general Allom drew and had the drawings engraved.Most of his China drawings based on the work of others first appeared as engravings illustrating pieces in his China Illustrated, published in instalments 1843-1847 which had 91 engravings illustrating every day scenes, in an exaggeratedly gothic revival style.

[22] Thomas Allom, 1843. *China, In A Series Of Views Displaying, The scenery, architecture and social habits of that ancient empire*. Drawings, Fisher, Son & CO.London.

[23] Auguste Borget, 1842. *Sketches of China and the Chinese*. Drawings, Tilt and Bogue, London.

[24] L.Audemard, 1957, 1959, 1960, 1962, 1963, 1965, 1969, 1970a, 1970b.*Les Jonques Chinoises*, (10 volumes), Museum voor Land-en Volkenkund en Maritiem Museum Prins Hendrik, Rptterdam.

[25] Artur Leonel Barbosa Carmona, 1990. *Lorchas, Juncos E outros Barcos no sul da China*, repaint Museu e Centro de Estudos Maritimos de Macau.

[26] Donnelly Ivon A, 1925, *Chinese Junks and Other Native Craft*, Kelly & Walsh, Shanghai.

[27] G.R.G.Worcester, 1947.*The Junks & Sampans of The Yangtze*, Statistical Department of The Inspectorate General of Customs, Shanghai.

[28] Etienne Sigaut (887-1983) spent more than thirty years in China to investigate South Chinese junks since 1911, his manuscript and sketch

of the nineteenth to the early twentieth century.

Through putting together mostly-forgotten information that have been scattered all over the world, the appearance and design of fu ships traceable to the Song and Yuan dynasties are displayed before our eyes.This is how ancient Fujian style sea-going junks probably looked.

4. Crossed the Pacific voyages

In Donnelly's *Chinese Junks and Other Native Craft*, He listed three most important crossed the Pacific voyages have been taken by type of Fuzhou pole junk and another one was make by Xiamen fishing junk.

- "Keying" : length of 48.7 meter, Hong Kong to London, 1848.
- "Whangho" : length of 30 meter, Shanghai to San Pedro, 1906.
- "Ningbo" : length of 42 meter, Shanghai to San Pedro, 1912.
- "Amoy" : length of 21.03 meter, Xiamen to Victoria, 1922.

From 1932 to 1935, Captain Eric de Bisschop sailed a Xiamen built about 12 tons gross junk Fou Po II with Tatibouet in the southwestern Pacific Ocean and east Indian Ocean.The voyage is under the patronage of the French Geographical Society to study the direction and the limit of the counter equatorial current, about which very little is known at that time.During the voyage they also fixed definitely the location of three islands, whose positions on the narine maps are doubtful.

In 1955, a Fuzhou style cargo junk of length 23 meter Free China sailed from Taiwan to San Francisco.

5. Models

As early as 1851 World Fair in London, Chinese junk models had been shown by Hewett & Cie and Sichait & Cie.In 1904 St.Louis World Fair, 125 models of merchant junks and war junks included Fujian style was collected by the Customs of Xiamen, Fuzhou and other cities then exhibited in St.Louis and later on also in Liege World Fair in 1905.The models vary widely in quality and some are minutely finished. In 1993, whole collection have been presented again in National Maritime museum of Antwerp[29].

---

however, have never been published and remain in National Maritime Museum of France.

[29] Ed. W. Johnson, 1993. *Shaky Ships:The formal richness of Chinese shipbuilding*.Exhibition Catalogue, May 8-december 1993, National Maritime museum of Antwerp.

The British Science Museum collection of models was put together by the 1930s Inspector General of the Chinese Maritime Customs, Sir Frederick Maze was mainly gathered in Shanghai. The Science Museum catalogue print out gives the date of one Fujian style merchant junk model as 1936.

A middle 18th century model of a Fujian merchant junk collected by Hong Kong Maritime Museum probably of the second class in the measurement classification.

The building process started with making a model. Measurements would then be proportionately enlarged for making the ship. This was a method recorded in documents from the Song dynasty onward and continues to be used even in the present. Currently, scholars take the making of models as the means by which to conserve and record the technology used to make a particular ship, but the shipbuilding industry knows well that components are difficult to reduce and reproduce to scale. Hence details that scaled down would be too small to show are often omitted. Furthermore, to build a ship requires totally different skills to those required for making a model. When detailed plans and descriptions are lacking, models can at times be misleading.

Model offered the possibility of experimenting with various solutions before the replica in full scale was begun.

6. Ethnographical Field Investigation and Manuscripts

From 2004, we began to visit the main traditional shipbuilding centers along the Fujian coast and carried out the field investigation of wooden sailing junks. We found 7 manuscripts recorded and inherited by 4 shipwright families. The Sha Po Wei inside Xiamen Gang (Old Amoy Port) is a famous traditional shipbuilding center up to the first half of the 20th century(Fig.5). It was comprised of more than 15 private dockyards around 3 hectares of shoreline (Fig.6). The Chen family in one of largest and oldest dockyards in the region, the family migrating from Huian country to Xiamen Gang at least five generations ago. An illustrated manuscript of naval architecture was archived by Mr.Chen Yan Ning of this family. It is 51 pages of paper, 22.5 cm in length and 11cm wide, 6 vertical red lines to a page, badly written in the end of 1910s. The manuscript was drawn by Chen Yan Ning's uncle, Chen Guo Zai (died in 1949),

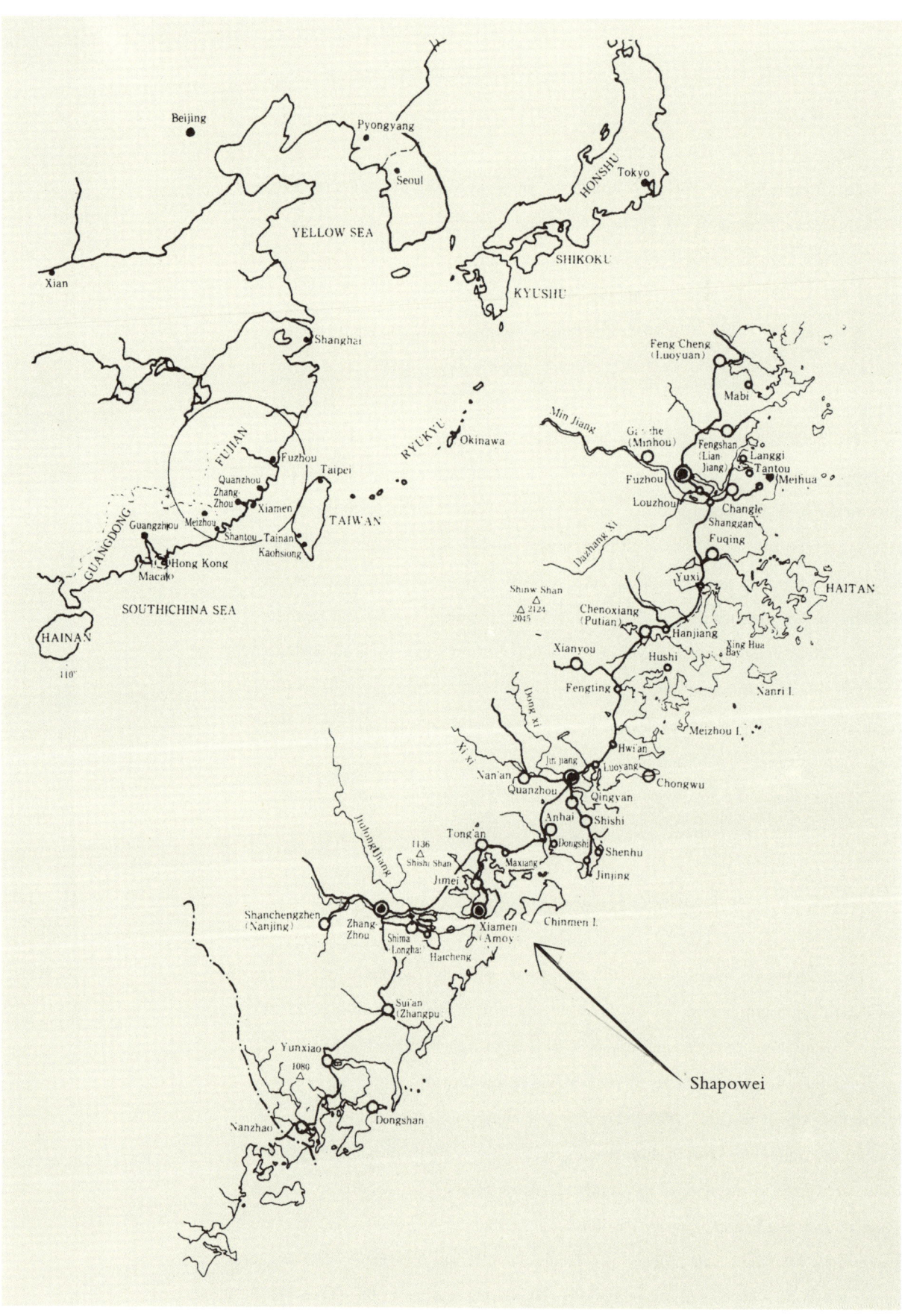

Fig. 5 The Coast of Fujian Province and The Location of Sha Po Wei

The Naval Architecture of Ancient Fujian Style Sailing Junks, an Overview

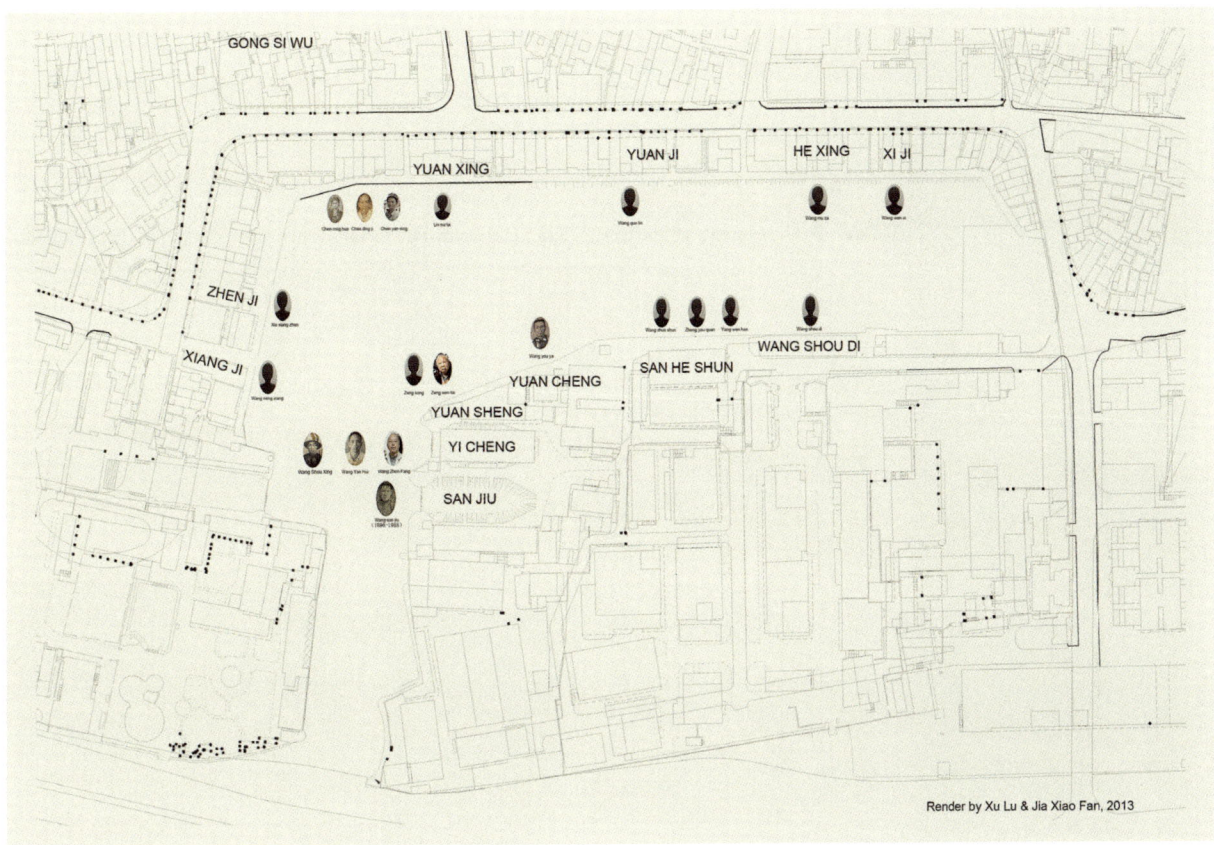

Fig. 6 The old dockyard in Sha Po Wei inside Xiamen Gang

then his son gave it to Chen Yan Ning. It contents size and cost of fourteen Fujian sea-going sailing junks, all the numbers expressed in Suzhou numerals (Table 3).It is the most detailed record so far pertaining to the principle of design, modulus system, main unit data, measures and the amount of materials used for different ship forms.One of those is Da Pa, a junk that each side of hull is printed five gun ports (Fig.7), it is the only civil junk with gun ports in the period of the Republic of China, alias Hei Bo or Feng Wei Chuan by recorded of G.R.G.Worcester[30] (Fig.8).

[30] G.R.G.Worcester., 1948. *A Classification of the Principal Chinese Sea-going Junks (south of the Yangtze).*Shanghai Statistical Department of the Inspectorate General of Customs.

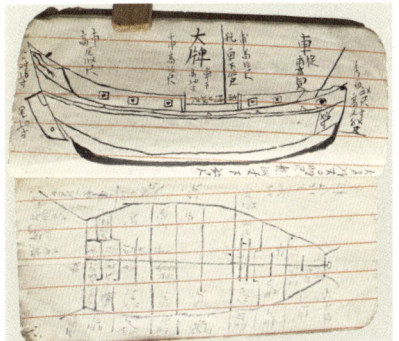

Fig. 7 The Manual of Da Pai in The Naval Architecture Manual of Chen's Family

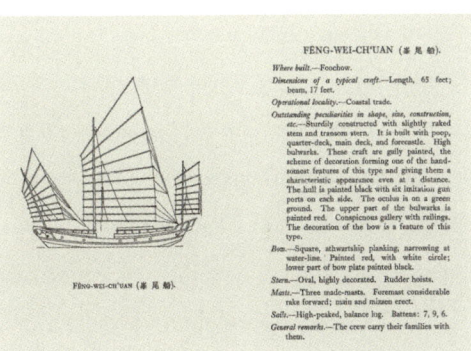

Fig. 8 Feng Wei Chuan(G. R. G. WORCESTER, 1948)

Table 3 The contents of fourteen Fujian junks from The Naval Architecture Manual of Chen's Family

	Launched	Type	Owner	Length of keel (chi/meter)	Cost (Silver Dollar)
1		Da Shuang Zhang (Jiang)	Qiu Xiong	28.4/8.72	500
2		Da Gu		22.7/6.81	
3		Da Gu		28/8.4	
4		Da Gu	Jin Mu Chuan	21/6.3	
5			Chong Wu Changshun hang	35/ 10.5	
6	1915	Da Pai	Chong Wu Cheng Chuan	31.5/9.45	500
7	1914	Da Pai	Chong Wu Chang Shun	21/6.3	
8		Da Pai	Xiu Chuan	30.5/9.15	
9		口 Cao (Diao Cao?)	Jiu Zhi	22/6.6	
10	1906		He Shang	30.5/9.15	
11			Tou Chuan	30.5/9.15	
12			De Bao	27/8.1	
13				31/9.3	
14		Shui Chuan		20/6	230

7. Design

In ancient times, master ship-builders relied on their individual experience and the knowledge passed down from previous generations. They would make patterns on the spot rather than prepare drawings with precise dimensions in advance. Traditional ship-building was a conservative, physically demanding profession. Apprentices were people from the lower end of society who could not afford education. Being mostly illiterate, ship-builders held their experience and knowledge as an oral tradition, passing it down to apprentices as they worked. In those days livelihoods very much depended on such skills, so what they learned was kept to them and seldom disclosed. For these reasons, illustrated construction manuals were rare.

When designing a new ship, Fujian shipwright would decide on the measurements:

- The length of the keel(longgu) and the rise at both ends based on the intended use of the particular ship;
- The location of the four main transverses—those at the front and back, behind the mast and that which defines the main cabin;
- The width and depth of the ship in proportion to the length of the keel (longgu), for example, the measurement of the transverse behind the mast should be 4/10 the measurement of the keel;
- All other measurements such as the bottom-width of the transverse behind the mast, the top and bottom widths and locations of other transverses were then defined based on experience and according to the type, usage and other requirements of the vessel;
- The height of the mast depended on the top-measurement of the transverse immediately behind. So was the size of the major sail;
- Finally, measurements of width and the size and shape of the rudder post and tiller were determined.

The earliest historical document about design of Fujian style junk that has been discovered up to now is a document from the early Qing dynasty. The design of the Ganzeng warship it contains is an exquisite drawing of a Fujian junks. The employment of outlines to illustrate the design, and the terminology used are very similar to illustrated manuals from the early Republican Period discovered in Quanzhou and Zhangzhou[31].

8. Choice of material

As far as the choice of wood is concerned, a kind of natural fir tree Cunninghamia lanceolata (Lamb.)Hook from Fujian a mountainous area was normally used for the parts of a ship's shell that have direct contact with the sea, such as the keel (longgu), bottom, shuishe (literally water snake), and zouma (literally running horse), the deck and transverses (gecangban, literally cabin-separating boards), and natural small-leaf camphor for other parts of the body such as cangliang

[31] Xu Lu, 2007. An Analysis of the Manuscript on Junk-building of the Zheng Family of Haicheng in Zhangzhou. *Maritime History Studies*, Vol.2007 (1):119-128.

zhuo (base of cabin beams) liangtou (beam-end) and gecang fuqiang (cabin-separating strengtheners).For the rudder and anchor which required harder material, kundian wood, which was grown in Guangdong and Southeast Asia was used.Wood for the mast was the most carefully selected, natural fir trees from Fujian aged 80 or more were generally used.

Extant historical documents prove that tight rules governing the selection and quantity of materials to be used for ships built in imperial shipyards existed from the mid Ming.The allowances, however, seem overly lavish.With experienced folk ship-builders, measurements of all the parts would be clear in their minds as they searched for materials.Any piece of wood was to them an assembly of some parts.

Ship-building uses a lot of wood, but the availability of wood is subject to specific growth cycles.A shortage of supply appeared in Fujian from the early Ming Dynasty, and with it, the cost of ships went up and wood was imported in large quantities from Southeast Asia.At the same time, some folk-shipyards moved out of Fujian.Some relocated abroad where a few expanded to substantial size.With them Fujian ship-building technology spread overseas.

9. Sequence of construction

Traditional production start with establishing the keel(longgu), fixing transverses(longgu yiban, literally dragon bone wing-boards), parts of bottom planking, gecangban, biban (bilge Keel), wen (stabilizer), lianggung (upper ribs), then the intermediate ribs between the transverses, and finally, the remaining bottom planking.After these, work on the weather deck begins.First the boards along the bulwarks, followed with shishe on the exterior of the bulwarks, shuixianmen (literally narcissus door) and then the bulwarks.The dragon-eye is usually installed on an auspicious day chosen by the boatman.When the making of the ship's hull is finished, the filling or Lihui(Caulking) and all sewing work too come to completion(Fig. 9).Before the new ship is launched, the exterior of the shell is first covered with a mixture of rice soup and lihui to protect against shipworm.The owner selects a date and time for the launching after which the mast is set up and the sails bent on.This pattern of ship-building is traditional for many areas along China's coastline and continues to be used even up to the present. Scholars named it "chuanke fa",

Fig. 9 Sewing material: tong oil mix round lihui and rattan

Fig. 10　The sequence of construction

literally the Chinese frame first system(Fig. 10).

The modern Chinese building techniques for large wooden ships begins with the keel, then erects the frames or ribs and the bottom planking before completing the side planking. This method of ship-building first appeared in *Shi Ryukyu Lu (Diplomatic Mission to Ryukyu)*[32] written by the Ming dynasty diplomat Xia Ziyang in 1606, the 30th year of the reign of Emperor Wanli. It is generally believed that European wooden shipbuilding technology was a source for this process, which is known as "jiegou fa", literally the structure first method.

10. Painting and decoration

That part of any ship below water is usually covered with baikehui (lime from white shells). The flares (tuolang ban, wave-lifting boards near the bow) are also first covered with lime before painting the figure that characterizes fu ships with a solution made of glue, tung oil and natural color pigments. Some fu ships even come with a carved head of a lion at the bow. Dragon eyes on the bulwarks near the bow are usually made of camphorwood. Particular rules govern the size and shape of these eyes: the ratio between the keel length and eye should be 110:4; eyes for

[32] Xia Ziyang, 1970. *Shi Ryukyu Lu (Diplomatic Mission to Ryukyu)*, The Taiwan Conversation by Writing (Chi Kan Bi Tan), 1606, reprint Economic Academe of Taiwan Business Bank, Taibei.

Fig. 11 Decoration of stern

fishing boats should look downwards to signal the search for catches while eyes for merchant ships should look ahead, at the route ahead. Mulong (wooden dragon), i.e., loach poles (qiuyuji) are painted on the bulwarks near the stern, a seabird (muyi) on the yingban (eagle board) beneath the after peak (weilou, compartment at the stern) (Fig. 11), and at the bottom of the yingban is the board which carries the ship's registration number. According to legend, qiuyuji, muyi bird and Matsu (Goddess of the Sea) are the three treasures that watch over the safety of ships. A statue of Matsu may be placed in a sanctuary in the after peak, or a paper charm as its substitute.

11. Tools

Confucius says, "Good tools are a prerequisite to the successful completion of a job." For the execution of specific tasks, special tools are required, such as axes, chisels, saws, files, tweezers, awls, knives, rulers and modou(ink markers) used by carpenters, and hammers, large tweezers, sickles, paint-brushes, truncheons for working with lime etc. used by other workers.

Axe: triangular in shape, 7 cun (approximately 1/10 foot) in length and 3 cun in width. The handle is made of hard wood and measures about 2 chi (approximately 1.1 foot). The axe is the most important tool in ship-building. In traditional ship-building, the qualification of ship-building masters is measured by the number of years he has used an axe.

Fig. 12　Adze

　　Adze: shaped like a hoe, 7 cun in length and 3 cun in width. It is also named guangfu (smooth-out, or faying axe) meaning that it is used for smoothing out or faying in parts(Fig. 12).

　　Saw: 5 to 6 chi long, for cutting raw materials into boards.

　　Plane: 8 cun in length and 2 cun in width, for smoothening out wood surfaces.

　　Lu Ban ruler: also known as "wengong ruler", which, according to legend, was a system of measurement invented by Lu Ban following Daoist truth and the laws of the Eight Diagrams. The ruler measures 1 chi and 4.4 cun, which is roughly 0.46 meter. With birth, aging, sickness, death and suffering as the basis, the ruler is divided into 8 parts named cai, beng, yi, li, guan, li, hai and ben. When using the ruler, cai is the top and beng the end, and it is important also to avoid the inauspicious and adopt what is auspicious.

　　Modou: 7 cun in length and 3 cun in width. That part which serves as a container of ink is called mochi (ink-well) which holds cotton wool soaked in ink. There is a line reel at the end. Cotton thread comes through from the modou and is also soaked with ink. To use the modou, the cotton thread is first fastened to the piece of wood which requires marking at each end, and by gently pulling the thread outwards near the centre and then letting it go, a clear and distinct ink line appears on a raw piece of wood or boards measuring several meters.

　　Caulking iron: made of wrought iron and steel for the teeth. An iron loop forms part of the wooden handle and is used for mixing hemp, rattan and lime and inserting the mixture into crevices.

12. Ship–Builders

According to legend, ship-building in Fujian started with Jiang Liuli of the village of Nanqing, Jiangxi Province, in ancient times.Over the centuries, ship-builders from Fuzhou, Quanzhou and Zhangzhou gathered here.Apprenticeship generally started at the age of 11 or 12.Those who joined the profession were mostly members of ship-builders'families;their children, cousins or relatives. No less than 3 years of training were necessary.In the beginning, apprentices were not allowed to handle the axe and helped only in menial duties such as mending or minor repair work.Only after a number of years of training, when students had picked up sufficient knowledge and skills from their masters, were they allowed to work on important components such as keels, weijin (sternposts?), helms and masts before they became masters. There is a common saying, "Master of a particular shipyard builds ships exclusive to that shipyard." Each shipyard had its unique ship form. Generation after generation of ship-builders inherited the skills, expertise and experience passed to them by their predecessors, which over time established a given set of practices and forms.

13. Experimental archaeology apply in the reconstructions of ship remains

The reconstruction of Ganzeng warship in early Qing dynasty was based on the historical documental evidences, integrated with methods of ship design and building acquired from the ethnographical field work on main traditional shipbuilding centre of Fujian province, according to method of experimental anthropology, being the first full scale reconstructed project in China.Based on the reconstruction and research on Ganzeng warship, and the quantity study on the features of the transverse watertight bulkhead, mast base structure, the axis helm that can lift and swing and bamboo strip sail, and the preliminary sorting of the modular system of construction which was the design principle and design method of ancient ships.

The original ship was Qing 8 of Taiwan Navy recorded in Chapter 1 of above woodblock edition *The Regius Formula of Fujian Sea Going Warships* with 15041 Chinese characters.The length of deck 13.8 metre, it was the small one in Ganzeng series, designed to cross stormy waters and open seas of Taiwan Straits.

Fig. 13 No.4 model for Ganzeng reconstruction experimen

Fig. 14 Princess Taiping (photo by Qiao Yang)

Eight models were made Since Nov 2005 by two individual teams accomplished by master junk builder(Fig.13).

Our experimental setup was that the replica is to make voyages, with original tools and building materials 300 years ago, under the conditions that the original ship was built for.Thus the sailing potentials of the original ship can be realistically tested and assessed.

The replica of 15.8 length overall was constructed by folk master junk builders from Quanzhou and Zhangzhou under the direction of Chinese Sailing Junk Expedition Society.The project was commenced in Jan 2007, launched in Oct and named Princess Taiping, and culminated in a Trial Voyage from Quanzhou to Xiamen in Feb 2008(Fig. 14).

To sail at a speed of 6 knots when downwind and fair current, it reached the fastest when in "beat". Good metacentric stability but bad athwart ships drift.

14. Conclusions

The voyage of Fujian's wooden junks came to an end in the 1990's when builders proficient in traditional skills were mostly over fifty years of age.Today, even though the age of junks is over, and the brilliance of the 2000-year-old Fujian ship-building industry has died out, we should not forget the benefits it brought to this coast.It stands as history's witness of an age past, and represents the technical achievements of our forefathers.

Although shipwreck archaeology has very few cases of Chinese sea-going junks, many clues can be found in kinds of historical documents.Furthermore majority kinds of the sailing junk were still on their voyages at the middle of 20th century, and the last traditional shipbuilding craftsmen are still alive.So when we applied

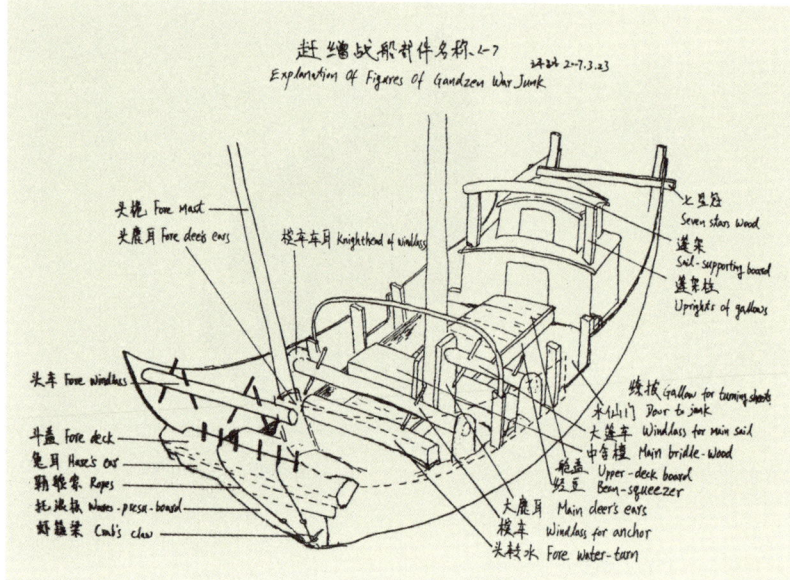

Fig. 15 Figure of Fujian Ganzeng warship

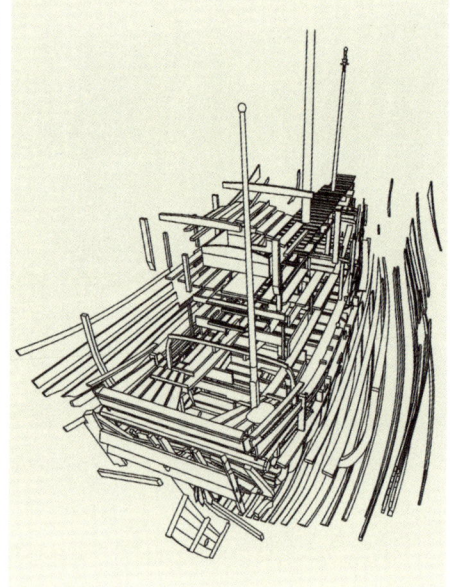

Fig. 16 Components of Fujian Ganzeng warship

experimental archaeology methods to ship remains study, distinctive prototype could be selected and masts of craftsmen could be found for traditional design, building and trial voyage. Compared to other reconstruction experiments of different culture area, Ganzeng reconstruction totally applied traditional technology, and every steps all traced back to the old building procedures.

Reconstruction experiment is effective study method to revert to the history. The replica will be on the trial voyage in same circumstance, and the safety of the voyage is the precondition of the reconstruction. So any baseless conjecture must be expelled, quantitative investigations and tangible evidences must be applied. This kind of history study on production instruments should based on concrete practice rather than document studies, and should avoid in mechanically piecing out a result like previous Zhenghe treasure ship study.

To decode two official criterion in shipbuilding for Qing Dynasty naval warship, to build a replica of one of these series in full scale, to discover the history of naval architecture of Fujian Ganzeng warship. So that people today can have answer of the three questions listed above.

The terms descriptive of the components of Ganzeng Fujian style junk within early Qing's historical materials combined the terminology and local dialects used in Fuzhou, Quanzhou and Zhangzhou. About 80% of them continue to use in today(Fig. 15). About 5% of terms descriptive of the components of Ganzeng are still uncertainty, and we changed rigging from bamboo strip sail to cotton sail. It can be seen as an experimental setup that reached about 80% with the original ship(Fig. 16).

Designing, building and sailing replica is a very effective way of researching and understanding the technical system of ancient Chinese junks, maritime archaeology should contribute to such projects, make these experience as authentic as possible, and these activities are also open to visitors, and given them the option to work with craftsmen and sailing.

We are waiting for related excavation of underwater archaeology, while looking for copartner and sponsor to the plan to reconstruct second replica sample.

We get a conclusion that constantly experimental reconstruction of the ship remains is the only effective means to preserve the Chinese junk heritage. Furthermore, we give an introduction on the use of modern technology and research tools of the ship remains' reconstruction experiment.

15. Discussions

Reconstruction of ship remains needs to based on archaeology evidences and historical documental evidences, integrated with methods of ship design and building acquired from the ethnographical field work on main traditional shipbuilding centre.How to organize all the findings of the studies above is the important part of reconstruction experiments.Some study academes began to collect and sort domestic navigation documents of Chinese history, however the documents scattered in libraries and museums aboard have been neglected.To improve the effectiveness of retrievers and studies, a visual database of documents organized by database technique, image technique and the internet technique need to be created, to classify according to uses time, region and usage then sort of warships, traders, ambassador ships, fishing and other carriers.The three-dimension database of shipwreck archaeology could be set up on the same way.

Unlike shipbuilding of other indigenous areas, Chinese shipbuilding tradition changed a little through all the time, and the last successors of traditional shipbuilding are alive.Western classifying studies of Chinese sailboats in the early twentieth century just based on the field investigations and the interviews with the successors of traditional naval architecture.Projects need to be invested promptly on these field investigation, and the investigation case of Manchuria railway is a precise and standard model of these studies.

The jargons of traditional shipbuilding and navigation usually passed on from mouth to mouth.The verbal jargons haven't totally recorded in old documents, and some of them had no equivalent norms of words.Furthermore the meanings of the norms changed along with the time and place.Those puzzled domestic scholars, and the westerns besides.Although the interviews in field investigations, distinguishing the dialect jargon will be the first step to make the synopsis between the traditional jargons and standard norms.And the glossary of Chinese terms relevant to traditional Fujian junk should be authorized and translated to Englishi and other languages for better communication.

Besides the basic works mentioned above, the index of abroad drawings, photos and models of traditional Chinese sailing junks need to be done, and the documents aboard need to be copied and sorted. For example the neglected series drawings made in Guangzhou in the 19th century collected by Victoria & Albert Museum have been the best illustrations of western scholar's classification.The scripts of François-Edmond Pâris, Louis Audemard, Etienne Sigaut, Barbosa Carmona still have no Chinese versions, and some of them even have no English versions.For the convenience, these translation works are urgent to be done professionally.

My current experimental reconstruction project is the replica a 10 meter length later 19th century to early 20th century Fujian style sea-goning sailing junk. The original ship came from the manuscript on Junk-building of the Zheng Family of Haicheng in Zhangzhou in early Republican Period.The detailed redesign was made by a 88 year-old-master named Zheng Liangzhao in his life end. We aimed to reconstruct this double-masts sailing junk fort the trial voyage, and to grasp the sail manipulation methods and the navigation techniques which haven't quantizing recorded in any documents.

Acknowledgements

Thanks are due to all members of CSJES, the last craftsmen of traditional Fujian naval architecture and seamanship, who provided their invaluable experience and knowledge. Also, I must express my sincere thanks to Dr. Jia Hao whom helped me to search relevant historical materials and revised the article format.

附记：本文系作者2011年投递于 *Maritime Contacts of The Past* 论文集的修订稿（Xu Lu, "The Naval Architecture of Ancient Fujian Style Sea Going Sailing Junks: An overview," in Sila T. (eds) *Maritime Contacts of The Past*, New Delhi, Delta Book World, 2014, pp. 429-456）。

References

Chen Guo Zai(?-1949).The Naval Architecture Manual of Chen's Family, manuscript, private collection, Xiamen. 陈国仔：《陈氏家族造船图谱》，手抄本，私人收藏，厦门。

Chen Liangshi, 2002.*The Navy Abstract(Shui Shi Ji Yao)*, later 17th century, reprint Shanghai Ancient Books Publishing House, Shanghai.（清）陈良弼：《水师辑要》，《续修四库全书》，史部·政书类，第860册，上海古籍出版社，2002年。

Huang Shujing, 1957.*The Taiwan Conversation by Writing (Chi Kan Bi Tan)*, early 18th century, reprint Economic Academe of Taiwan Business Bank, Taibei.（清）黄叔璥：《赤嵌笔谈》《台海使槎录》，《台湾文献丛刊》第4种，台北：台湾银行经济研究室，1957年。

Anonymous, middle 18th century. *The Illustrated Manual of Instruction In Shipbuilding For The Navy of Fujian Province (Min Sheng Shui Shi Ge Biao Zhen Xie Ying Zhan Shao Chuan Zhi Tu Ji)*, manuscript.（清）佚名：《闽省水师各标镇协营战哨船只图说》，手抄本，18世纪中叶。

Anonymous, 2002.*The Regius Formula of Fujian Sea Going Warships (Qin Ding Fu Jian Sheng Wai Hai Zhan Chuan Ze Li)*, 1768, woodblock edition.reprint Shanghai Ancient Books Publishing House, Shanghai.（清）佚名：《钦定福建省外海战船则例》，乾隆三十三年（1768年）木刻本，《续修四库全书》，史部·政书类，第858册，上海古籍出版社，2002年。

Xia Ziyang, 1970. *Shi Ryukyu Lu (Diplomatic Mission to Ryukyu)*, The Taiwan Conversation by Writing (Chi Kan Bi Tan), 1606, reprint Economic Academe of Taiwan Business Bank, Taibei.（明）夏子阳：《使琉球录》，万历三十四年（1606年），《台湾文献丛刊》第287种，台北：台湾银行经济研究室，1970年。

Xu Lu, 2007. An Analysis of the Manuscript on Junk-building of the Zheng Family of Haicheng in Zhangzhou. *Maritime History Studies*, Vol. 2007 (1): 119-128. 许路：《<漳洲海澄郑氏造船图谱>的解读》，《海交史研究》2007年第1期，页119～128。

Willem Ysbrantsz Bontekoe, *Memorable Description Of The East Indian Voyage 1618-1625*, Chinese translation.〔荷〕威·伊·邦特库著、姚楠译：《东印度航海记》，北京：中华书局，1982年。

Isaac Commelin, 1646. *Beginning and Ending of the Dutch-East Company*, Amsterdam.

Johan Nieuhof, 1665. *Voyages and travels to the East Indies 1653-1670*, Jacob Van Meurs, Amsterdam.

Anonymous, middle 17th century.*The Island of Formosa*, painted on parchment, collection of Berlin Ethnologisches Museum.

John Barrow, 1804. *Travels in China*.Cadell & Davis, London.

Thomas Allom, 1843. *China, In A Series Of Views Displaying, The scenery, architecture and social habits of that ancient empire*. Drawings, Fisher, Son & CO.London.

Auguste Borget, 1842. *Sketches of China and the Chinese*. Drawings, Tilt and Bogue, London.

William Alexander and George Henry Mason, 1988.*Views of 18th Century China Costumes, History,*

Custom. 1796, reprint Portland House, New York.

L.Audemard, 1957, 1959, 1960, 1962, 1963, 1965, 1969, 1970a, 1970b. *Les Jonques Chinoises*, (10 volumes), Museum voor Land-en Volkenkund en Maritiem Museum Prins Hendrik, Rptterdam.

Artur Leonel Barbosa Carmona, 1990. *Lorchas, Juncos E outros Barcos no sul da China*, repaint Museu e Centro de Estudos Maritimos de Macau.

Ivon A Donnelly, 1925, *Chinese Junks and Other Native Craft*, Kelly & Walsh, Shanghai.

Ed.W.Johnson, 1993. *Shaky Ships:The formal richness of Chinese shipbuilding*. Exhibition Catalogue, May 8-December 1993, National Maritime museum of Antwerp.

Rudiger Joppien, Bernard Smith, 1988. *The Art of Captain Cook's Voyages*, Volume 3, *The Voyage of the Resolution and the Discovery, 1776-1780*, Paul Mellon Center, BA.

CE Kroese, *Dutch Trade with the People's Republic of China*, Law and Contemporary Problems, Vol.38, No.2, Trade with China(Summer-Autumn, 1973):230-239.

Musee de la Marine, 1992. Le voyage de la Favorite. Paris.

Oba Osamu, *About Drawings of Chinese ship Kept in Matsuura Hirato History Museum—The Referential Material of Chinese Merchant ship in the Era of Edo*, Memo 5 of Research Institute of East and West Academical studies of Kansai Uiversity.1972.

Eric Rieth, 2006. Epaves, Archeologie Sous-Marine Et Histoire De L'architecture Navale.*Histoire, Archeologie Et Societe Confererces Academiques Franco-Chinoises*, Ecole francaise d'Extreme-Orient Centre, Beijing, Cabier No 13: 1-20.

G.R.G.Worcester, 1947. *The Junks & Sampans of The Yangtze*, Statistical Department of The Inspectorate General of Customs, Shanghai.

G.R.G.Worcester, 1948. *A Classification of the Principal Chinese Sea-going Junks (south of the Yangtze)*. Shanghai Statistical Department of the Inspectorate General of Customs.

Introduction: Of Ships and Men

"船与人·欧洲船舶考古与历史"专题论文导言

Paola CALANCA[1] Pierre-Yves MANGUIN[1] Eric RIETH[2]

(1. EFEO; 2.CNRS / LAMOP)

柯兰[1] 莽甘[1] 李特[2]

(1. 法国远东学院；2. 法国国家科学研究中心 / 巴黎西方中世纪文化实验室)

In memory of Ole Crumlin-Pedersen (1935–2011)

The international conference "Of Ships and Men", which took place in Beijing on November 9 to 11, 2009, aimed to present a summary of research on the maritime history and archaeology of Asia's nautical spaces. Indeed, this is one of the regions of the world that has seen, over the course of the last few decades, a marked development in the excavation of shipwrecks (in wet and underwater contexts). From a comparative perspective, we also aimed to blend the approaches of these "new territories of archaeological research" with those of the "ancient research domains" of Europe, which are linked to a secular tradition of maritime historical and archaeological studies.

The ships and boats of Asia's nautical spaces – at sea, but also along rivers and lakes – were at the centre of communication and exchange, during an extended period that stretches out from prehistory to the present day. From single-log canoes for close range river navigation to ocean going sailing vessels, the boats and ships were privileged by the contributors as the subject of technical history and archaeology. Other facets of the history and the archaeology of the boats and ships, relating to environmental, social, economic, and cultural subjects, were nevertheless not neglected. As Jean Poujade very correctly pointed out in the middle of the twentieth century: "We can say that a boat represents, at the moment of its construction, the synthesis of a culture." To this, he added: "A boat encapsulates a society."[1] The study of boats, of their architecture, their rigging, their navigational devices, their apparel, teaches us about revealing technical choices, but equally

[1] J. Poujade, *La Route des Indes et ses navires [The Passage to India and Its Ships]*, Éditions Payot, Paris, 1946, p. 13 and 16. Additionally, Poujade dedicated a book to the traditional ships of what was then called Indochina (*Bateaux en Indochine [Boats in Indochina]*, Saigon, 1940).

exposes the economic, social, and cultural choices of the societies that are thus investigated. The title of this conference, "Of Ships and Men," took into account this broad spectrum of history and architecture of ships.

For this line of questioning, the contribution of research conducted in Europe, born in the nineteenth century from ship archaeology, has been important[2]. Within this domain, two approaches – indeed, two scientific schools – came into being, the French and the Scandinavian schools of nautical archaeology. The former is characterized by its privileged recourse to written and iconographic sources, principally ancient and medieval, of which the standard reference is that of historian Augustin Jal, *Archéologie navale [Ship Archaeology]* (Paris, 1840, 2 volumes). This classical historical perspective of the study of boats and ships, the origins of which, in France, go back to the Renaissance[3], had a much more original and innovative approach superimposed on it with the first experimental endeavours of ship archaeology: the reconstruction of a Roman trireme, based on Jal's historical studies, and its construction in 1860-1861 under the supervision of the famous maritime engineer, Dupuy de Lôme[4]. Today, we might call this reconstruction "a floating hypothesis."

Simultaneously, and apparently unrelated to this "French school", these same years in the middle of the nineteenth century saw the definition, in France, of the scientific and methodological foundations of what is currently known as nautical ethnography. The manifesto of this discipline of social sciences is *L'Essai sur la construction navale des peuples Extra-européens [Essay on the Naval Construction of Extra-European Peoples]* (Paris, 1843, 2 volumes); the author, then a young officer in the navy, was later appointed as the director of the Louvre's naval museum, the predecessor of the Musée National de la Marine [National Maritime Museum]. This book is important not only for the body of documents with which it provides the scientific community, but also for its thematics, which address certain contemporary questions of nautical archaeology[5].

As for the contemporary "Scandinavian school of ship archaeology", it was of an entirely different nature. It rested entirely on archaeological data and called upon the techniques and methods of archaeology, of which the primary scientific act was excavation. Two archaeological programmes marked its beginnings. The first was that of the exploration (1859–1863) of the boats at Nydam, including that of the great oak ship Nydam 1, dating from the fourth century C.E., probably deposited as

[2] It was only in the 1970s that the field of ship archaeology began to accept the field of maritime archaeology, which takes into account the totality of characteristics that define a boat: technical criteria, functional criteria, environmental criteria, etc. One of the seminal works is that of Keath Muckelroy, *Maritime Archaeology*, Cambridge, Cambridge University Press, 1978. Many other works have since been added to the field, including: Seán McGrail, *Boats of the World: From the Stone Age to Medieval Times*, Oxford, Oxford University Press, 2001; Ole Crumlin-Pedersen (ed.), *Aspects of Maritime Scandinavia AD 200–1200*. Roskilde, Viking Ship Museum, 1991.

[3] E. Rieth, *L'archéologie Navale: des ouvrages de la Renaissance à l'archéologie expérimentale*, Neptunia, 1982, n° 148, p. 5–16.

[4] P. Pomey et E. Rieth, *L'Archéologie navale [Ship Archaeology]*, Paris, Errance, 2005.

[5] E. Rieth, *Voiliers et pirogues du monde au début du XIXe siècle: Essai sur la construction navale des peuples Extra-européens, de l'amiral Pàris [Sailboats and Canoes of the World at the Beginning of the 19th Century: the Essay on the Naval Construction of Extra-European Peoples, by Admiral Pàris]* (1843), Paris, Le Layeur Editions, 2012.

a votive act in a swamp (that was at the time located in Danish territory). The second was that of the exploration of the burial ship from Gokstad (Norway), dating from the middle of the ninth century C.E.

From the beginning, three principal elements characterized ship archaeology in northern Europe: an excellent mastery of the methodology of and techniques for the exploration of non-submerged wrecks; the choice of an experimental ship archaeology stemming directly from archaeological vestiges, as in the 1892 construction of a sailing replica (The Viking) of the ship from Gokstad (followed by a North Atlantic crossing); and attention paid to conservation, and to the museum development of wreck displays (the two ships, the Gokstad and the Nydam 1 were exhibited in two museums, one in Oslo, Norway, and the other in Gottorf, Germany). These three elements still remain at the centre of scientific and patrimonial issues of nautical archaeology.

In terms of this already-long history of a discipline born in Europe, it seemed interesting and stimulating to introduce a dialogue between these ways of "thinking and making" research, after more than a century of European experiences, and those experiences, more recent and often quite different, from Asian countries. Such was the spirit we aimed for at the Beijing conference. And this spirit of exchange, of discussion, of confronting ideas and projects, of points of view at once scientific, technical, and patrimonial, were well and truly present at the Beijing symposium.

We have nevertheless chosen to publish the papers relating to European nautical archaeology and history separately from those that especially pertain to researchers working on Asia. The former are the texts published here. Texts concerning the maritime archaeology and history of Asia, being more numerous, will be published in Paris in the *Études thématiques* [Thematic Studies] collection of the École française d'Extrême-Orient, the Co-organizer of the Beijing conference.

This collection thus contains seven contributions that cover a significant share of current trends in European nautical archaeology. Three articles particularly address questions relevant to the issues and methodologies of archaeology. Christer Westerdahl presents the concept, rich in its interpretive perspectives of archaeological data, of "cultural maritime landscape," and Seán McGrail defends the central role of ethno-archaeology in the study of constructive systems. Tinna Damgård-Sørensen and Ole Crumlin-Pedersen present the historical trajectory of Danish maritime archaeology around the Museum of the Viking Ship in Roskilde and, in particular, the programs of experimental ship archaeology that have made Roskilde the world leader in research in this area. Three other contributions illustrate archaeological themes more specifically developed in France: that of Patrice Pomey, on the evolution of an architectural family of ancient Mediterranean boats, namely sewn boats in the Greek manner; that of Eric Rieth, on the specifics of nautical archaeology in inland waters, illustrated by the case of a sea/river coastal wreck in the middle of the fifteenth century C.E.; that of Elisabeth Veyrat, dedicated to a general reflection on the contribution of archaeological data to the knowledge of the history of material culture in maritime societies. Michel L'Hour revives the tradition of French maritime historiography by presenting, on the basis of a manuscript report, the expedition to China organised by Michel Dubocage (1706–1716) aboard the *Découverte*, for purposes of both exploration,land economical benefits and commercial exploitation.

"船与人：亚洲古船历史学与考古学比较研究的新视角"国际学术研讨会于2009年11月9～11日在北京召开。此次研讨会的主旨在于展现亚洲水域的航海史与考古研究成果。近几十年来，这一区域是水下和湿地环境中的沉船考古发掘发展最显著的地区之一。从比较研究的角度出发，本次会议还致力于将欧洲"考古学研究新领域"与"传统研究领域"的方法论相结合。欧洲传统研究方法则与航海史和考古学研究的学术传统紧密联系。

从史前至今的漫长发展时期，亚洲的航运船舶包括海船和河船都是交流与交易的中心。从近距离内河航行的独木舟到远距离的远洋海船，都是本次研讨会参会者进行航海技术史或考古学研究的首选对象。此外，与船舶史和船舶考古主题相关的环境、社会、经济、文化也颇受研究者重视。琼·布嘉德（Jean Poujade）在20世纪中期已准确无误地指出："我们可以说一艘船在建造之时即为一个文化的综合体。"对此，他还补充说："一艘船就是一个社会的缩影。"[1]船舶结构、帆索具、航行设备和船具的研究不仅能为我们揭示其技术选择的缘由，同时还可反映其所属社会的经济、社会、文化方面的深层原因。上述诸方面在参会学者的研究中均有体现。本次研讨会以"船与人"为题，也是基于船舶史和船舶结构方面的广泛研究。

在这一系列问题上，源自19世纪的欧洲船舶考古学研究贡献颇为重要[2]。这一领域有着两种不同的研究方法，准确地说是两个学术传统，即法国和斯堪的纳维亚船舶考古学派。法国学派以利用古籍和图像资料，特别是古典时期和中世纪的图像文字资料为主要特征，如奥古斯汀·雅尔（Augustin Jal）的《船舶考古学》[Archéologie navale (Ship Archaeology)，Paris, 1840] 两册。这种以传统历史学视角进行船舶研究的方法，在法国究其根源可追溯到文艺复兴时期[3]。在最初船舶考古的试验性努力中，这一研究视角赋予了更多的原创性和革新性方法。例如，1860～1861年，在著名航海工程师迪皮伊·德·洛梅（Dupuy de Lôme）的主持下，建造了以雅尔的历史研究为基础复原的罗马时期三列桨座战船[4]。今天，我们可将这种重建称为"一种漂浮的假设"。

19世纪中期，在法国还有一类与"法国学派"同时产生却又毫无关联的科学方法论体系，即如今被我们称作航海民族志的学科。这一学科的宣言是阿德米拉尔·帕里斯（Admiral Pâris）的关于欧洲以外船舶制造的论文（巴黎，1843年，两册，有关19世纪早期的帆船与独木舟）（L'Essai sur la construction navale des peuples extra-européens [Essay on the Naval Construction of Extra-European Peoples], Paris, 1843）。该书作者曾是法国海军的年轻军官，后来被任命为卢浮宫海事博物馆（法国国家海事博物馆的前身）馆长。这本著作不仅为研究者提

[1] J. Poujade, *La Route des Indes et ses navires [The Passage to India and Its Ships]*, Éditions Payot, Paris, 1946, p. 13, 16. 另外，布嘉德的另一本书中则是研究曾被认为是中南半岛传统的木船（*Bateaux en Indochine [Boats in Indochina]*, Saigon, 1940）。

[2] 直到20世纪70年代，船舶考古学才开始接受航海考古学进入其研究领域，将船舶的所有特征纳入船舶的定义中，如技术标准、功能标准、环境标志等。这方面的代表作有：Keath Muckelroy, *Maritime Archaeology*, Cambridge: Cambridge University Press, 1978。其他著作有：Seán McGrail, *Boats of the World: From the Stone Age to Medieval Times*, Oxford: Oxford University Press, 2001及Ole Crumlin-Pedersen (ed.), *Aspects of Maritime Scandinavia AD 200-1200*. Roskilde: Viking Ship Museum, 1991。

[3] E. Rieth, *L'archéologie Navale: des ouvrages de la Renaissance à l'archéologie expérimentale*, Neptunia, 1982, n° 148, p. 5-16.

[4] P. Pomey, E. Rieth, *L'Archéologie navale [Ship Archaeology]*, Paris, Errance, 2005.

供了丰富的资料，更重要的是其引入了一些当代船舶考古学的问题[5]。

至于同一时期的"斯堪的纳维船舶考古学派"，则是全然不同的类型，它完全依靠考古数据，并要求运用考古学技术与方法进行基本的科学发掘。两项考古发掘工作标志了这一学派的开端。一是1859~1863年尼丹姆（Nydam）沉船的发掘，包括最大的橡木船尼丹姆一号（Nydam 1），年代为公元4世纪，这艘船很可能是在一次祝祷活动中被沉入沼泽的（当时该地区属于丹麦领土）。二是在挪威科克斯塔德（Gokstad）发掘出土的船葬用船，其年代约为公元9世纪中期。

北欧的船舶考古学从一开始便具有以下三个基本要素的特征：一是针对非水下沉船发掘有着一套完善的技术与方法论；二是实验船舶考古学的选择直接来自考古发掘遗物，如1892年根据科克斯塔德沉船而复原建造的维京号（The Viking）在北大西洋航线进行了试航；三是注重文物保护及博物馆的沉船展示（科克斯塔德号和尼丹姆一号分别在挪威奥斯陆博物馆和德国戈特奥夫博物馆展出）。这三大要素至今仍是船舶考古学研究和文化遗产保护的核心。

就一门产生于欧洲已有很长历史的学科而言，我们发现将存在一个多世纪的欧洲"思考与实践"研究方法论与亚洲国家新近的而不同的学术经验引入一场对话，是一项极有意义和颇具促进作用的工作。在这一想法驱动下，我们在北京举办了这次研讨会。本着交流与讨论的精神，与会者针对这一领域内科学、技术与传统的不同想法和议程、观点进行了充分的讨论。

我们最终选择将有关欧洲船舶考古与历史方面的论文和亚洲区域的研究文章分册出版。本书所收录文章即为前者。亚洲航海考古与历史的文章数量更多，我们整理之后将由法国远东学院（EFEO，本次北京研讨会主办方之一）的《专题研究》（Études thématiques [Thematic Studies]）丛刊出版。

本书所收录的七篇文章代表了当代欧洲船舶考古学研究的趋势。其中三篇文章着重针对考古学方法论：克里斯特·维斯特道尔（Christer Westerdahl）阐述了"海洋文化景观"概念，而其有着丰富考古资料的解释分析；肖恩·麦克格雷（Seán McGrail）则在其文章中重点强调了民族志考古学者在复原研究中所扮演的关键角色；奥勒·克拉姆林-佩德森（Ole Crumlin-Pedersen）和汀娜·达姆加德-索伦森（Tinna Damgård-Sørensen）的论文围绕罗斯基勒维京船博物馆阐述了丹麦船舶考古学的发展轨迹并着重介绍了他们的实验船舶考古项目，这一项目使罗斯基勒博物馆成为了该研究领域的带头人。另外三篇文章则是以法国考古为主题的典型研究案例：帕特里斯·帕米（Patrice Pomey）探讨了古代地中海造船体系中被称为缝制船的希腊造船技术的演化；埃里克·李特（Eric

[5] E. Rieth, *Voiliers et pirogues du monde au début du XIXe siècle : Essai sur la construction navale des peuples extra-européens, de l'amiral Pâris* [*Sailboats and Canoes of the World at the Beginning of the 19th Century: the Essay on the Naval Construction of Extra-European Peoples, by Admiral Pâris*] (1843), Paris, Le Layeur Editions, 2012.

Rieth）则以河海交汇处15世纪中期沉船为例重点讨论了内陆水域船舶考古学的特殊性；伊丽莎白·维拉（Elisabeth Veyrat）的论文则总体考察了考古资料对海洋社会物质文化史研究的作用。最后，米歇尔·劳尔（Michel L'Hour）的文章通过介绍米歇尔·杜波卡基（Michel Dubocage）在"发现号"（la Découverte，1706~1716）上的日志手稿，展示了当时以探险和贸易为目的的航路开发，以此尝试恢复法国海洋学术史研究的传统。

谨以此组"船与人"文章纪念奥勒·克拉姆林–佩德森（1935~2011）。

2015年9月30日于巴黎

邱丹丹 译；柯兰 审校

The Maritime Cultural Landscape: An Introduction to an International Perspective on Coastal Cultures

海洋文化景观：国际视野下的海岸文化导论

Christer WESTERDAHL

(Institute of Archaeology and Religious Studies, Norwegian University of Science and Technology)

克里斯特·维斯特道尔

（挪威科技大学考古与宗教研究所）

ABSTRACT / The concept of the maritime cultural landscape dates from the middle of the 1970s. The starting position is the cultural landscape, a term originally used to summarize the material remains and structures of the agrarian economies inland, irrespective of period. In 1978 the contents of the term was defined as the network of sea routes and harbours, indicated both above and under water. From its very inception it meant cross-disciplinary ways of research and the obliteration of the archaeological border between sea and land, while recognising the overriding importance of the position of this border in the past in order to analyse and interpret remains and their meaning. Two other concepts were introduced in the analysis of primarily Early Modern times: the maritime cultural areas and centres of maritime culture.

The networks of the landscape thus mainly consisted of: principal sailing routes/destinations (main towns/ports), older sailing routes, older sailing marks and beacons, early lighthouses, pilot stations, harbours for shipping, fishing harbours, ship yards, ballast sites. Special features are ancient boathouses and pile, shipwrecks and stone blockages. Maritime culture would then generally be defined as "human utilization (economy) of maritime space by boat: settlement, fishing, hunting, shipping and in historical times, its attendant subcultures, such as pilotage, lighthouse and sea mark maintenance. It should include any hermeneutic kind of human relationship to the sea."

KEY WORDS / Maritime culture (remains of); place names; cognitive landscapes; habitus; liminality

内容摘要 /

　　海洋文化景观的概念始见于20世纪70年代中期，它是源于最初用来概括各种时期物质遗存及内陆农耕经济结构的"文化景观"一词。1978年，"海洋文化景观"一词被定义为海上航线与港口形成的水上及水下网络。从一开始,这一概念就意味着一种摒除海洋与陆地考古学界线的跨学科研究思路;同时,为了分析和解释遗存及其含义,它也认识到这一界线在过去有着极为重要的地位。"海洋文化区域"与"海洋文化中心"是分析近代早期景观引入的两个概念。因而,景观网络主要包括:主要航路与目的地(主要城镇与港口)、古航路、古航标及信号灯、早期灯塔、引航站、航运港、渔港、造船厂、压舱物遗址等。特殊的还有古船屋与木桩、沉船与石堵等。因而,海洋文化可定义为"人类通过船舶利用海洋空间(经济)进行定居、渔猎、航运活动,以及历史时期随之产生的亚文化,诸如领航、灯塔和航标维护,也应包含任何人类与海洋关系的解释。"

关键词 /

海洋文化(遗存)　地点名称　认知景观　习惯　界限

Introduction

Evidently, it is important to know what is meant here by *landscape*. This term is still very much part of a lively scientific discourse, performed by representatives of various disciplines, geography, anthropology etc. In archaeology landscape has not at least been of recent interest to *phenomenology*. Here an effort is made to use and to move inside historic and prehistoric cultural landscapes marked by ancient monuments and other traces of land use in order to understand the physical experiences of the past. It is mainly a visual fieldwork but it could include other senses as well, hearing and smelling, and the vistas of openness, contrasted by others of seclusion and isolation. Sometimes it could preferably involve experiencing and mapping a bird's eye-view as well as movements in tiny miniatures of a part of the terrain. The starting point in archaeology would always be the intimate involvement with the precise location of a site, and its relationship to other relevant sites. The problems of too much subjectivity are apparent but experiences could in fact – at least to certain extent – be quantified (Tilley 1994, Tilley 1996, esp. Hamilton & Whitehouse 2006). Another fairly recent variety of archaeology is *visual landscape analysis*, where the physical landscape, settlement space and grave-fields are integrated (Gansum *et al.* 1997, Keller 1997). It seems that this has always been a part, albeit not systematically, of the study of the maritime cultural landscape or what it may have been called in the past. Cognition in this landscape is extremely dependent on the senses. It is no coincidence that this new idea of Seascapes is referred to as "*seeing* [my italics] land from the sea" (Cooney,

2003). But at sea, on mobile shipboard, the main occupation is location in relationship to various stable or constant features in the process of moving all the time.

My principal version of sources is very simply the orally transmitted experiences of people living a lifetime in their maritime landscape. How could a few days spent by an outsider possibly make up for that (in any landscape)? Other methods and sources are based on cross disciplinary considerations, on the combination of oral tradition and descriptions, local history, field observations, archaeological investigations and linguistic material, above all place names.

In this short presentation a definition will be tried step by step for the specific purpose of explaining the rise of and the applications of the term used in the title above, in a way *ad hoc*. A maritime cultural landscape would appear to be *the landscape of maritime culture* (Westerdahl, 2007a). Thus, its delimitations would appear to be set only in terms of human culture.

Still, research only concerns fragments of the geographies of maritime culture. However, human use of this landscape is based on its topography and natural resources, *i.e. the physical landscape*. This may to a certain extent be transformed and changed by human action, but would then basically still be a considered physical unit. All the relict features, ancient monuments and other left-overs from cultural land and sea uses would reasonably belong to it.

But from its imprint on living people emerges the remembered or memorized landscape, even more a part of an ever-changing array of cultural aspects. To use phenomenology as an example, it cannot escape what already belongs to its own performers, or the accumulated effect of experiences from the lives of people still living in the studied section of landscape. This landscape exists in human minds even detached from its physical basis. As a general characterisation this could be called *the cognitive landscape*. So *Man in Landscape* becomes *Landscape in Man* (a quotation of a chapter title from the ethnologist Orvar Löfgren; Honko & Löfgren 1981). Thus, a first elementary definition of a maritime cultural landscape would be *the combination of the physical and the cognitive landscape*.

But this does not necessarily mean that this definition could not be used for other landscapes than the maritime cultural landscape. The traditional use of the term cultural landscape pertains to agrarian landscapes inland, those created for cultivation and the keeping of livestock. Like the maritime cultural landscape they usually display relict features, which could be investigated in order to understand the prehistory and economy of societies. In fact, the term of the title grew out of this application explicitly to introduce a worthy parallel in maritime environments. This means also a challenge to broaden the maritime perspective as far as that of other ecologies and economies. And maybe the MCL could contribute in its own way to the others.

The maritime landscapes are still alive and this fact gives the impetus of any study: its topography and nature, its intricacies of maritime life: fishing, hunting, seafaring, and agrarian pursuits using the coast, the islands and the sea. It is imperative to acquire an intimate knowledge of this living landscape and its people. Preferably this could by made by means of a survey of oral traditions and of archaeological remains, perhaps with some elements of participant observation (Westerdahl, 2006c). It is not always advantageous to the investigator to be too much a part of this life from the start. Paradoxically, that *could* in fact impede a deeper understanding. Structures, especially their discrete sides are perhaps best perceived from the outside.

The maritime cultural landscape provides both a perspective and a method. And it is not only that. The term implies that this landscape has to be taken into account in any analysis of prehistory or early history, even inland. Human existence presupposes land and sea. At land the sea is a constant metaphoric reference. The perspective that is going to be introduced here emphasizes the unity of various human spheres expressing maritime culture. As mentioned, maritime cultural landscape implies both the physical landscapes and the cognitive, the experienced, remembered and mythologized landscapes.

If analyzed thoroughly it might be practical to discern different landscapes, or aspects of the whole. It seems that they were once – or are still – mobilized in the human mind for different purposes and at different times. In a certain sense these aspects are equal to what Tim Ingold has called *taskscapes*.

This perspective is maybe at its best confronting the study effort of a certain geographical area, using ethnology, history, topography and cartography etc to delimit it in a meaningful way. At least this is how the term was born and developed during the first twenty years of its existence. However, the challenges of any local area presupposes a coherent cultural context of much larger area to compare and test indications and hypotheses. Part of this is going (destined) to be local, but a sizeable part belongs to an international maritime culture or to common traits inherent in such cultures along the entire globe. To discover those traits is the fundamental challenge of any study. Thus, there are at least two landscape perspectives, apart from cognitive and physical presences, one for the local or regional orbit and one for the global scene of generalisations.

I have recently tried to characterise some of the peculiarities of maritime culture in general (Westerdahl, 2007a). They comprise the particular habitus of the maritime sphere, its outward identity, its international character, its archetypes, its cultural landscape, and not least its cognitive landscape, and then including its ritual negotiation of the antagonistic relationship between sea and land (below), its cosmology and finally its peculiar economic and social world. Although debatable, insubstantial and imprecise categories, they show the potential of a study in fact never undertaken.

Categories to be studied are e.g. the social and thereby the symbolic role of the boat within maritime culture, its gender perspective (which seems to be more variable than imagined), its mental habitus of fatalism and at the same time profound solidarity, its role of reserve and safety valve of societies inland, where a mutual dependence almost never has been acknowledged. Instead this dependence of "landlubbers" on coastal culture often turned into indifference to the vagaries and dangers of maritime life. The only situation where the maritime experience was valued highly inland seems to conform to powers empire-building at sea, when coastal people were recruited as cannon-fodder, galley rowers and pilots.

Fig.1   The maritime cultural landscape is a living landscape: the largest log boats of the world are found on the shores of Ghana, West Africa. Photo: Morten Sylvester, Trondheim

Fig.2　Interviews with fishermen at their boatsheds is an important source to the use of the landscape at sea.
Photo: Christer Westerdahl

Fig.3　The coastal landscape of South Norway is still followed primarily in the traditional way in small vessels, by way of natural land contours, not by way of sea marks, nor by GPS.
Photo: Christer Westerdahl

Fig.4　Wrecks are a most important part of the maritime cultural landscape. In many cases they could be analyzed and used as dating instruments of its use. In this case the ship type, archaeologically called a cog, dated c. AD 1250, was indicated by the place name Kuggmaren.
Photo: Johan Rönnby

Fig.5　Exploitation of isolated islands far from the coasts in the archipelagoes started early. This is in fact a rather late example, a stone quarry for axes and other implements of about 5000 BC in Southwestern Norway, Hespriholmen, Bømlo. Photo: Christer Westerdahl

The applicability of the perspective offered by the maritime cultural landscape today would very likely be mainly the last centuries, roughly 500 years, depending on context. To reconstruct a past landscape further back in time only archaeology creates new sources. But the perspective applied would then have recourse to the reflections of the living landscape and the analysis of the fairly recent totality of combinations.

Fig.6　The coastal zone appears often to have been understood in the past as a liminal area, between two worlds or elements, and thus suitable for the disposal of the dead. Burial cairns at the seaboard, Later Iron Age (c AD 600-800). Mølen, Vestfold, South Norway. Photo: Christer Westerdahl

Fig.7　Another ritual element in the liminal position of the shore are panels of rock carvings, which are dated from c. 7-8000 BC to about the year 0. Quite a number of figures are maritime in nature, such as vessels, but also land animals and humans occur. Photo: Christer Westerdahl

Fig. 8 During the Middle Ages, in this case ca AD 1300−1550, the first stone mazes (labyrinths) were constructed close to the sea shores, predominantly on islands. This is also an indication of a liminal element at the seaboard. They are distributed in almost all of Northern Europe, especially Sweden and Finland on the Baltic. The pattern is that of the maze of Classical Antiquity of the Mediterranean, but the location and materials are different. Rataskär, N. Sweden. Photo: Christer Westerdahl

History and applications

The concept of the maritime cultural landscape dates from the middle of the 1970s. The field area to which it was applied was northern Scandinavia. It is an area deeply influenced by the Last Ice Age. It has since then, the greatest land uplift in the world (highest point once covered by water is found today at 286m above sea level) and was not colonized by human beings until 10.000−8.000 BC. Prominent among the first immigrants were maritime hunters and fishermen who settled the coasts. But successively their settlements had to adjust to the land upheaval which was very rapid at the outset. This means that a series of maritime cultural landscapes could be envisaged in a very dynamic way and fairly well dated all along.

But this is not enough. In the southern part of Scandinavia the land sunk down to at least 17m below sea level as of today. Here the remains of the past landscapes are under water and have to be documented that way. These are elementary facts and a number of topographic models have been devised to predict settlement sites according to recent economic experience, of favourable sites for fishing and for a settlement nearby.

In a global perspective changes of the physical landscape and its relationship to the seaboard has numerous other causes, although much less in terms of the inexorable processes of eustatic and isostatic land rise or sinking, where dating and coherence is comparatively easy to record. Tectonic and volcanic factors lend dramatic features to such change. Erosion and sediment deposition by rivers, currents and wave action would appear to be the most important complex of geology for slow but profound changes over time. Still at any moment in history, the maritime cultural landscapes are physically attached to the location of the beaches and rocks of the water-line.

Basically, the same principles pertain to great inland lakes and to the rivers. Some of them have been strongly influenced by several of the processes mentioned above, not least the unevenness of post-glacial rebound of the earth's crust, but also by damming by way of sedimentation and tectonic activities. Some examples are the Great Lakes of the United States and Canada, like Lake Ontario (Ford, 2009 & in prep.). A smaller one is Lake Vänern in Sweden, where I myself made my first experiences of maritime culture, both under and above water (Westerdahl, 2003, in press. 2).

Returning to the starting position *the cultural landscape* is a term originally used to summarize the material remains and structures of the *agrarian economies* inland irrespective of period (*cf.* for prehistory *e.g.* Fabech & Ringtved, 1999).

This was the creation of above all German cultural geographers during last century (August Maitzen, Wilhelm Müller-Wille, etc.). In Sweden it had a more profound influence that in the rest of the North. Part of this was absorbed into archaeological thinking. Thus agriculture was at the basis of this definition. On the other hand a coherent cultural landscape of hunting, fishing and gathering at the sea or in the lakes, in forests and mountains, had early been observed by e.g. the Swedish ethnologist Åke Campbell (Campbell, 1936). In so far as a *maritime culture* existed parallel to the agrarian mainstream, as was exposed by the prominent maritime ethnologist, Olof Hasslöf, a fisherman's son of Bohuslän, West Sweden (*cf.* Hasslöf, 1949; Hasslöf *et al.*, 1972), the potential of a cultural landscape of comparable range based on this could be inferred. What was needed was tangible proof.

My first systematic surveys were made in Sweden 1975-1982, a coastal stretch of approximately 1250km. In 1978 the contents of the term was defined as *the network of sea routes and harbours, indicated both above and under water*. The scope of the concept was later published by me in German in 1986, in English in 1992. Before the last publication the term was known only in Northern Europe.

From the beginning the concept refers to a "fossil" or "relict" archaeological landscape, a landscape of survivals, but could as well subsume landscapes of today. From its very inception it meant cross disciplinary ways of research and the obliteration of the archaeological border between sea and land, while recognising the overriding importance of the position of this border in the past in order to analyse and interpret remains and their meaning.

By way of this perspective the ship wreck sites underwater have been reduced to a more reasonable role in the subject matter of maritime archaeology. In most cases, they can also in a most meaningful way be analysed as an integral part of the maritime cultural landscape. It cannot be denied that maritime archaeology so far has got most of its material from such sites, a fact willingly and thankfully admitted. Ship technology is still seminal in the discipline, not the least as a fairly independent dating instrument.

It was stressed already in my first report papers that "a holistic study and interpretation of maritime remains in their own cultural landscape presuppose *cross disciplinary* insights," which meant that even the surveyor himself/herself had personally to obtain such insights. Sources should include interviews, archaeological surveys, archival material of various kinds, place names, historical sources, cartographic material, iconographic sources etc. The need for source criticism would require considerable versatility of the observer.

Two other concepts were introduced in the analysis of primarily early modern times: *the maritime cultural areas and centers of maritime culture*. The latter term worked partly as an application of *central place theory* in a maritime setting (for this term, applied first in geography by Walter Christaller (*cf.* Christaller, 1966; Hodder & Orton 1976; and Smith, 1976).

So far most of the related studies in Scandinavia concerned Iron Age harbours (Denmark, Gotland in the Baltic Sea). A pioneering holistic study for a waterway, the fiord landscape of Roskilde was Crumlin-Pedersen 1978. Another for larger area based on archaeological material but without the oral traditions was Crumlin-Pedersen *et al.* 1996 (*cf.* comments by Crumlin-Pedersen, 1996a & 1996b). Other elements of the landscape studied in Denmark were defensive route blockages under water. As pointed out above, in some areas in the south the ancient shorelines have sunk considerably, at present there are ancient coastal landscapes at a depth of down to ca. 17m. The potential of Stone Age cultural landscapes underwater is staggering, settlement sites could apparently be counted in thousands.

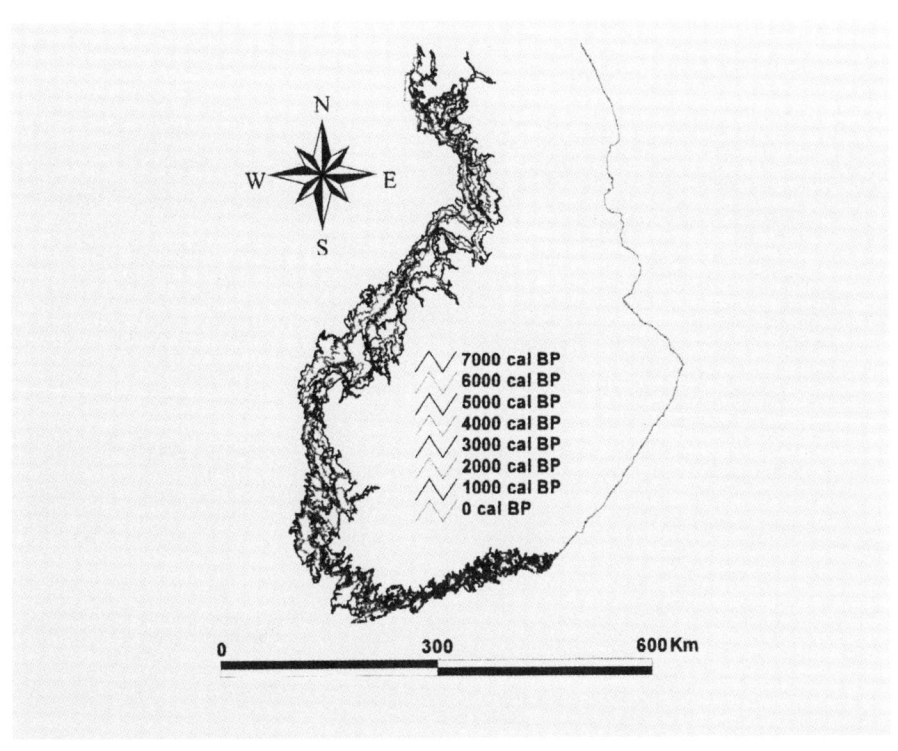

Fig.9　The coastline of Finland changing its position during millennia, due to the land up-lift after the Ice Age, which ended ca 10.000 BP. Along this zone are found the elements interpreted as luminal in figs 6,7, 8, although no rock carvings have been found in this, Finnish, case. Courtesy of the Regional Museum of Pori, Finland.

In 1987 and 1989 were published the results of my survey as *Norrlandsleden I-II, The Norrland Sailing Route I-II*, with extensive English summaries and inserted parts, the title true to the original definition of the maritime cultural landscape as mainly a network of routes and harbours. The explicit intention was later to distil an outline of the maritime cultural landscape of the (Nordic) Middle Ages (c. AD 1050-1550). As an example of numbers I refer here to the naked facts of the original catalogue of findings in oral material. Within brackets is found the approximate present stage of field research:

Oral tales not associated directly with wrecks: 307 (400)

Known shipwrecks: 745 (1000)

Founderings: 729 (900)

Unknown foundering sites: 9 (2)

Net fastenings: 376 (400)

Indications on sonar: 23 (50)

Loose finds (indicating wrecks): 95 (100)

Undetermined positions / localities in general: 59 (62)

Harbours, havens, anchorages, seasonal fishing harbours: 538 (600)

Ballast sites: 56 (100)

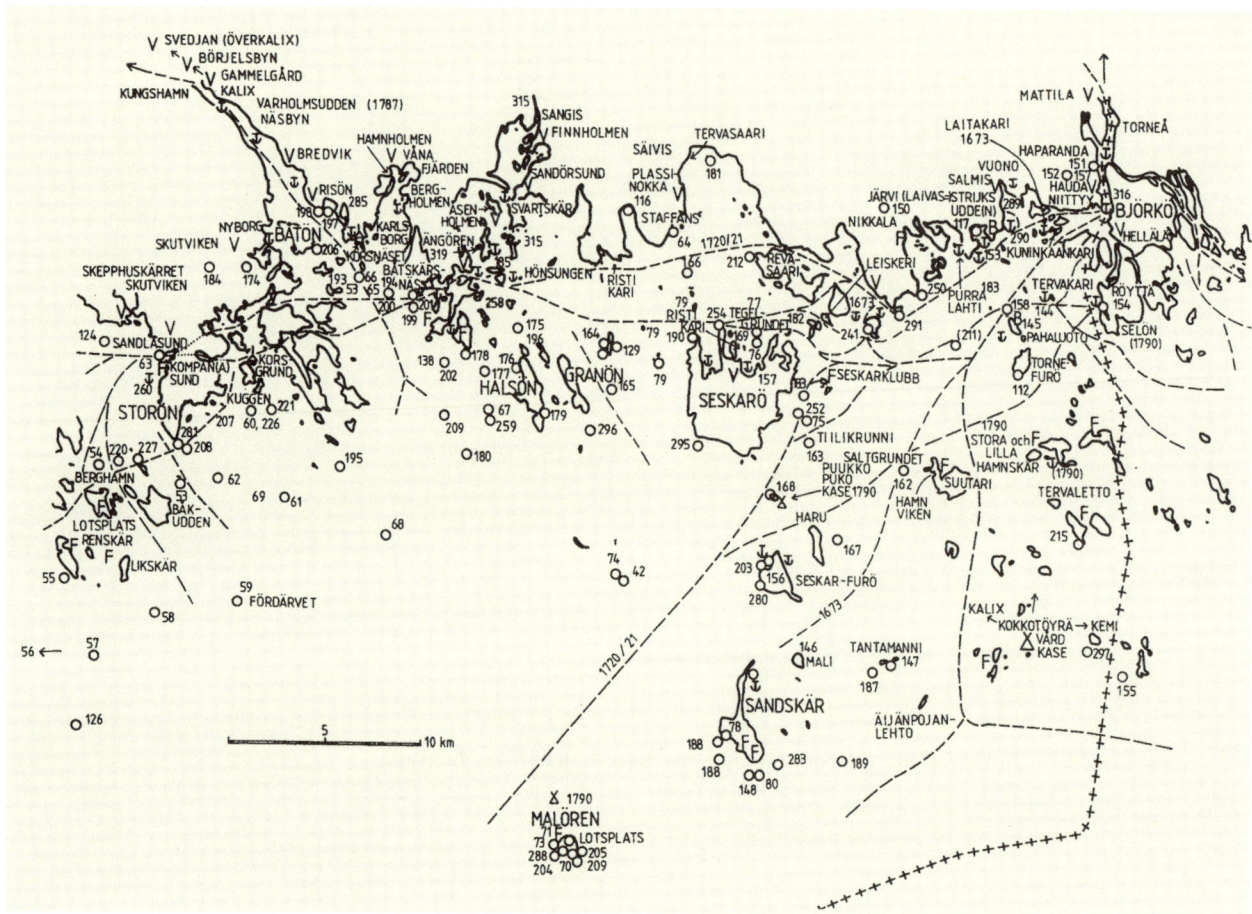

Fig.10 Survey map of northernmost Sweden at the border to Finland (right). Ship wrecks, indications of such, traditions of foundering, harbours (included those for fishing=marked with an F) and ship yards (=V) are marked together with ancient ship routes, some of dated according to information on dated maps. Production: Christer Westerdahl.

Place names of relevance (in this stage): 131 (200)

Shipyards: 234 (300)

Route blockages: 6 (7)

Canals: 1 (2)

The networks of the landscape thus mainly consisted of: principal sailing routes/destinations (main towns/ports), older sailing routes, older sailing marks and beacons, early lighthouses, pilot stations, harbours for shipping, fishing harbours, shipyards, ballast sites. Special features are ancient boathouses and piles, shipwrecks and stone blockages (Westerdahl, 1987; 1989).

Maritime culture would then generally be defined as "human utilization (economy) of maritime space by boat: settlement, fishing, hunting, shipping and in historical times, its attendant subcultures, such as pilotage, lighthouse and sea mark maintenance. It should include any hermeneutic kind of human relationship to the sea."

In general it is possible to talk – processualist style – of "aquatic adaptations" (Erlandson, 2001). Island and coastal settlements are there almost by definition.

Rivers and lakes would be considered as well, not only as part of the transport landscape. A natural and necessary way of discovering the material, environmental as well as the cognitive facets of this landscape, would be by way of local traditions.

Aspects

A rigorous scrutiny of the elements of the maritime cultural landscape produced a number of *aspects*, a kind of headings where they could be subsumed. They are still valid, but further comments are given here (*cf.* for similar transformations, power and cognitive elements in the agrarian landscape see Fabech & Ringtved, 1999). These aspects are briefly enumerated here with some relevant comments:

1) *The economic landscape*, or the landscape of sustenance, of fishing, hunting (traps, sheds) & gathering but also including elements of coastal agriculture. It is thus an astoundingly versatile part of the maritime world, a fact somewhat underestimated, passed over or even misunderstood by land-oriented students of the past.

2) *The landscape of transport & communications* (communicative landscape): routes, sea marks, pilotage, harbours, roads, portages, urban features. The arteries of movement could be summarised as corridors, rather than fixed routes. The only narrowing of a water lane is that of channels and blockages, in particular in an elongated bay or fiord where seldom alternatives are given (e.g. Crumlin-Pedersen, 1978). The sea route is never fixed: it must be covered by indirect means, such as the application of place names or historical documents. Even the names of sea marks may reflects restrictions and reactions against it, a truly surprising social story.

3) *The power landscape*, that of mansions of great chieftains, as administrative & central places; would as well include the landscape of defence, a *territorial landscape* (on defensive measures, such as warning systems by way of fire beacons, barrages underwater and place names denoting these complexes, reflected in various aspects, *cf.* Westerdahl, 2002). The study of power in all its forms is currently almost an obsession amongst archaeologists, as it seems mainly due to the impressive character of its remains. Accordingly they can easier be documented, mapped and interpreted or analysed. It should, however, always be remembered that landed power does not control and has never ever been able to control all economic or other activities. There has always existed a *landscape of resistance*. Its remains, if meagre in

comparison, would rather present a more qualified challenge to archaeology than the obvious ones.

4) *The outer resource landscape*, more specifically for supplying material & resources for ship building. This aspect covers social mechanisms, not only the lure of a potential freedom in a vessel on the seas to small-holders and the control of forests and ships by power and ownership but also the effects of dearth of resources due to over-exploitation. It is astounding how much not only the shore but also the forest terrain is "encultured" by the memories of specific timber supplies (Westerdahl, 2010b).

5) *The inner resource landscape*, emphasizing the necessary surplus for ship expeditions & trade. Any sea expedition would be a considerable investment, conforming to the scale of the number of people involved. Only by a study of this background the prerequisites for maritime life at the coast could be sketched. However, this landscape aspect interacts directly with maritime culture, since what the sea produces is often a necessary reserve inland, not only in connection with failures of crops, but without which inland agrarian cultures may not have been able to survive.

6) *The cognitive landscape*, the mental map, as expressed e.g. in oral traditions, place names, including the *ritual & symbolic landscape*. This includes the locations of temples, chapels, generally religious buildings, burial sites, etc. Possibly this is the most promising aspect for new and innovative studies within the disciplines implied in the pursuit of maritime studies in general.

7) *Re-creative (leisure) landscape*. To remind us of an only recent landscape aspect, all the same producing a new kind of maritime cultural landscape.

Place name types

Place names do not only indicate maritime activities but could also be a seminal source to the cognitive landscape. In many ways they encultured the landscape long before any physical remains were added by humans. They are in fact the most prolific source pertaining to maritime culture, since they cover aspects not inherent or not possible to find in any other categories of remains. But during the pioneering years of the term maritime cultural landscape this extraordinary quality was not realised to its full extent. Rather, the primary categories were still very much related to shipping (Westerdahl, 1992):

Sailing route names include harbour, wreck and foundering indicators, such as:

Names of individual ships.

Names of ship types.

Nationality names (names of origin).

Names of a person or profession/title.

Harbour names: It should be pointed out that the main cargo type is often named at loading places and anchorages (iron, wood, etc).

The other name types in fairways are primarily:

Names of beacons (often only with a faint, indirect relationship to the sailing routes). This concerns sites of warning fires (Westerdahl, in press. 3)

Names of sailing marks (at a dangerous spot, later sometimes marked by a modern seamark or a lighthouse (Westerdahl, op.cit).

Names of warning (danger names). As an example, there is a place names denoting the spit of land in the extreme southwest of the Scandinavian peninsula which once gave its warning name to the whole of it. This old Germanic name apparently is at least 2000 years old, probably considerably more (Svennung, 1963).

Names denoting the sailing route itself or navigation in it, emphasizing determination of reference points on land.

Names at ferry routes or fords.

Authority names with power or religious connotations.

Migrant names, showing maritime cultural, particularly commercial, contacts.

In a much wider sense the markings along the routes, for recognition and memorisation as well as for the obvious needs of navigation has been studied recently by me (Westerdahl, in press 3).

As I have observed elsewhere maritime culture in a general sense is preoccupied with directions, and combinations of time, direction and distance. This preoccupation pertains both to its cognitive world and to its remains. Knowledge and experience of navigation pervades life and is transmitted to the children. The transit lines for alignment with sighting points and their crossing sites in the sea was elementary learning stuff by tactile and oral means from Scandinavia, where it was called *me(d)* (Hovda, 1961) to its Antipodes, the *maori* culture in New Zealand, where it went under the name *tohu* (for the later see Barber, 2004: 445). These sighting points were most important, economically as well as ritually; in fact they assumed an almost sacred significance, even on land, partly because they were kept secret to outsiders.

It is obvious and not very surprising that maritime culture is characterised by such a wealth of linguistic and mental concepts relating to boats, winds, navigation and the weather in general, but the degree to which the perception is trained and engages all senses is altogether exceptional. At the outset I have already pointed to the relevance of phenomenology to understand this world.

Of course, another preoccupation worth mentioning is that of the natural landscapes, including the sea itself and its obvious combination with and extension to the life and the landscape topography underwater. A Norwegian fisherman during last century knew the landforms underwater as well as those above. This goes as well for his Australian counterpart.

All these preoccupations are reflected by place names, but in a much wider selection than what is possible to apply here.

As indicated, the cognitive landscape at the seaboard displays a huge potential for the study of a lot of other aspects of maritime culture. Apparently, it includes almost all maritime place name types (Westerdahl, 1987; 1989).

Transport zones

Stemming from the study of the cultural landscape at the sea, although also including land roads and rivers is the concept *traditional zones of transport geography*, for short *transport zones*. Transport zones consist of route corridors in elongated and easily recognizable *socio-cultural space*, but not identical with any single route or only following coasts. The zones are influenced by and influencing cultural borders and border zones. The concept transport zones purports to contribute to explain differences in ship and boat types.

The transitions between two zones could mean the change of boat or vessel type or means of transport (e.g. portage, land transport in general), sometimes with seasonal implications. *Transit points* or areas were found at the sites for transshipment such as at the neck of an isthmus/headland or at the estuaries of important and navigable rivers. The rivers are main arteries for the transport landscape inland, supplying the maritime area at the coast. The same goes for systems of lands roads and paths (Westerdahl, 2007c).

In a sense the riverine landscapes form a close counterpart to the maritime cultural landscape. Therefore, to understand the latter the studies of conditions of the river valleys would be natural and necessary, especially in an environment as that of China. Portages of cargoes and boats overland usually extend the availability of water arteries considerably, at the coast as well along rapids or between river systems, sometimes across a watershed (Sherratt, 2006; Westerdahl [ed.], 2006 & 2006d). In a later stage many of these portages or overland passages devolve into canals dug between the natural waterways.

The phenomenon of *transport enclaves* or *niches*, meaning concentrated all-year settlements of maritime people serving as transporters, skippers & crews, assisting sea transport in various ways, including harbour functions, change of vessel, portage and pilotage, can sometimes be related directly to the intensive use of such a zone. The heyday of their existence and their intensity may be time-bound (e.g. Sherratt, 1996), but they usually stay where they once were, albeit sometimes in a heavily reduced capacity.

Apart from seasonal variations, we find among the transport zones, extending to land corridors, mainly the following types (Westerdahl, 1995):

a) Trans-isthmian zones (cross-ridge/cross-watershed) land zones (Sherratt 1996).

b) Ferry corridors or routes of regular transportation across waters.

c) Zones based on river valleys or other far-reaching water courses.

d) Estuary lagoon zones protected by extensive sand spits or barriers.

e) Lake zones (*e.g.* on Lake Vänern; Westerdahl, in press 2).

f) Zones of the open sea.

The cognitive ritual landscape

The ritual landscape among North European sailors and fishermen in early modern times has recently been studied. The basic feature appears to be the contrast between the sea and the land, leading to ritual acts. This means that another behaviour is required at sea, onboard the boat. A whole range of phenomena are suddenly taboo, forbidden. A general taboo concerns females, but also certain males, such as priests. Place names on land, words for any kind of boat equipment, species of fish, sea mammals change. A kind of sea language, or rather vocabulary is thus applied with extraordinarily evocative associations.

Its expressions are normally in recent times called superstition but it seems originally to have been a consistent system of belief.

In the current sphere of meanings I am finally drawing together ethno-archaeology, place names and some *major prehistoric shore-aligned monumental categories* of the Nordic area. This pertains to burials, esp. cairns, rock carvings from the Mesolithic and the Bronze Age and to medieval stone mazes. A particular interest concerns burials. According to age-old traditional lore the dead cannot pass water. In order to prevent them walking the earth island and generally edges of water were preferred.

But the principal idea is the notion that *the beach is a liminal area*, an ambiguous zone, where anything could happen. It is a space in-between, loaded with serious and dangerous meanings. If a fisherman went down to his boathouse to put out the boat and go fishing and on the path met a woman, or a priest, or generally heard something that was taboo he might return to his home. Even more so is the space of the boat at sea. Its liminality is absolute. As we have seen this is where things become forbidden. However, what is taboo on board could be used to inflict strong magic at sea. Among these are the incarnations of land, above all males. In rock carvings this concerns the large animals, the kings of nature, like the bear, the stag and the elk, later the horse, but also – surprisingly perhaps – females. The mistress of the sea is usually the Mermaid. I assume that they all bring luck at sea. These I have called *liminal agents*.

Presumably what is taboo on land has worked the reverse way. The boat, the seals and the whales, are all potentially the liminal agents of land. Accordingly, they bring luck on land. This might mean the boat physically (*e.g.* in boat graves) or parts and pictures of it, whale bones or crania of seals etc.

The specific roles assigned in this scheme could have been the reverse. What is important is that the dualism of the two elements, the opposites, remains.

I am thus trying to interpret in this light the location of various such monuments as a part of the maritime cultural landscape and its culture. Some components may be primary in the maritime environment and later adopted inland, but also vice versa. Comparisons have been made with the Inuit (and partly historic

Thule) culture of Greenland and Northern Canada and could be extended further. I have indicated that this notion of opposition sea-land might be at its strongest in the Arctic and the Subarctic (Westerdahl, 2007b; in press. 1).

In my hypothesis on the north other major monument groups indicate various aspects of what I have called *hydroliminality*. I believe that the same basic structure of a "cosmological" contrast, dualism, dichotomy or opposition between fresh water and land appears to be there, also in wetland offerings (Bradley, 1998/1990).

Final remarks for the future

Thus, the term maritime cultural landscape emerged in northern Scandinavia in its particular context of land rise, a comparatively young cultural area. However, it appears that its conceptual contents can be used universally, even though some may prefer to vary its name (culture landscape, seascape, waterscape, island archaeology, etc.).

They have simply to be adjusted to any specific context. A most important step was the publication dedicated to *Seascapes* by World Archaeology (2003). In recent years Brad Duncan has made significant contributions to the perspectives of the maritime cultural landscapes and not only in Australia which is his empirical material (Duncan, 2006; 2011).

The potential even back into Palaeolithic times is huge (Erlandson, 2001; 2010). The study of maritime culture and its landscape ought to mean the exploration of all kinds of human relationships to the sea, very plausibly to any large body of water. The scope will always be the leaps from physically major to minor, even tiny, features.

Classifications of elements or aspects as those made above are not an end in themselves. I am definitely not the person who ought to review all the positive efforts that are currently made across the globe to make the concept even more meaningful and enrich our appreciation of the maritime heritage. It was pointed out in 1993 by Marek Jasinski at the University of Trondheim, Norway (Jasinski, 1993), that maritime (as opposed to marine or underwater) archaeology had been given a new direction by the concept maritime cultural landscape. It has now been recognized as a new direction within archaeology, in particular its maritime variety. In the old days an encyclopaedia of maritime archaeology (Delgado 1997) would only mention ship wreck sites, but the Oxford Handbook in 2011 will contain several articles on the maritime cultural landscape and its aspects (Westerdahl, 2011a; 2011b)

I would like to suggest that the maritime cultures of the Chinese orbit and those of South East Asia would be perfect for comparative studies. In fact I once tried to introduce it in India for a survey of the Indian Ocean (Westerdahl, 2006b). A truly international perspective could be applied, A pioneering comparative study, precisely between Scandinavia and Southeast Asia was that of Ballard *et al.* (2003).

I prefer myself to use the term maritime cultural landscape to *seascapes*, which sometimes seems to mean the same. Seascapes was originally a term for the kind of painting which either only depicts the sea or a ship in the sea, often in dangerous situations. The intention was then to illustrate the ocean wilderness and how man is helpless confronted with its potentially tremendous forces. Most seascapes do not depict the coast but, if they do, only the forbidding cliffs are emphasized. In essence this term has been mainly devoted to the physical landscape, monotonous or wild as it may be, in a mere passage by human beings in a ship.

As contrasted with seascape, the term maritime cultural landscape refers to a particular human experience and culture, worthy of being a parallel to the dominant interpretation of cultural landscape as only referring to agrarian pursuits inland. Basically the cultural landscape on the seas is in sight of land, the home of humans. The primary issue is that of resources for human uses in the landscape in question. The coast, archipelagos and islands constitute a versatile and dynamic environment. The history of it is a part of any social history.

References

Ballard, C., Bradley, R., Nordenborg Myhre, L., Wilson, M., 2003, "The ship as symbol in the prehistory of Scandinavia and Southeast Asia", in *World Archaeology (Seascapes)* Vol. 35 (3): 385–403.

Barber, Ian, 2004, "Sea, land and fish: spatial relationships and the archaeology of South Island Maori fishing", in *World Archaeology (Seascapes)* Vol 35 (3): 434–448.

Bradley, Richard, 1998 (1990), *The Passage of Arms. An archaeological analysis of prehistoric hoard and votive deposits*. Oxford, Oxbow Books.

Campbell, Åke, 1936, *Kulturlandskapet. En etnologisk beskrivning med särskild hänsyn till äldre svenska landskapstyper* (The cultural landscape. An ethnological description with particular respect to older Swedish landscape types). Stockholm, Verdandis småskrifter 387.

Christaller, Walter, 1966, *Central places in southern Germany*, transl. by C.W. Baskin. Englewood Cliffs.

Cooney, Gabriel, 2003, "Introduction: seeing land from the sea", in *World Archaeology (Seascapes)*, 35.3, December 2003: 323−328.

Crumlin-Pedersen, Ole, 1978, "Søvejen til Roskilde", (The sea route to Roskilde) in *Historisk årbog for Roskilde amt*. Roskilde.

Crumlin-Pedersen, Ole, 1996a, "Studiet af det maritime kulturlandskab" (The study of the maritime cultural landscape), in Crumlin-Pedersen, O., E. Porsmose & H. Thrane (eds), *Atlas over Fyns kyst i jernalder, vikingetid og middelalder* (Atlas of the coast of Funen in the Iron Age, the Viking Age and the Middle Ages), Odense, Odense universitetsforlag: 10−20.

Crumlin-Pedersen, Ole, 1996b. "Undersøgelsens perspektiver" (The perspectives of the investigation), in Crumlin-Pedersen, O., E. Porsmose & H.Thrane (eds), *Atlas over Fyns kyst i jernalder, vikingetid og middelalder* (Atlas of the coast of Funen in the Iron Age, the Viking Age and the Middle Ages), Odense, Odense universitetsforlag: 204−206.

Crumlin-Pedersen, Ole, E. Porsmose & H.Thrane (eds), 1996, *Atlas over Fyns kyst i jernalder, vikingetid og middelalder* (Atlas of the coast of Funen in the Iron Age, the Viking Age and the Middle Ages). Odense, Odense universitetsforlag.

Delgado, James (ed.), 1997, *Encyclopedia of Underwater and Maritime Archaeology*. London, British Museum.

Duncan, Brad G., 2006, "The Maritime Archaeology and Maritime Cultural Landscape of Queenscliffe: A Nineteenth Century Australian Community", School of Anthropology, Archaeology & Sociology, James Cook University. Doctoral diss., web public.

Duncan, Brad, 2011, "'What Do You Want to Catch?': Exploring the Maritime Cultural Landscapes of the Queenscliffe Fishing Community", in B. Ford (ed.), *The Archaeology of Maritime Landscapes*. New York, Springer Press.

Erlandson, Jon M., 2001, "The Archaeology of Aquatic Adaptations: Paradigms for a New Millennium", in *Journal of Archaeological Research* Vol. 9, No. 4, December 2001: 287−350.

Erlandson, Jon McVey, 2010, "Neptune's Children: The Evolution of Human Seafaring", in A.Anderson, J. H. Barrett & K.V. Boyle, eds, 2010, *The global origins and development of seafaring*, Cambridge, McDonald Institute Monographs: 19−27.

Fabech, Charlotte & J. Ringtved (eds), 1999, *Settlement and Landscape*. Højbjerg/ Aarhus, Jutland Archaeological Society.

Ford, Benjamin L., 2009, *Lake Ontario Maritime Cultural landscape*. Texas A & M University, College Station. Doctoral diss. Web public.

Ford, Benjamin L., 2011, "The Shoreline as a Bridge, not a Boundary: Creating a More Complete History of Lake Ontario", in Ford, B.(ed.), *The Archaeology of Maritime Landscapes*. Society of Historical Archaeology & Springer Press.

Ford, Benjamin L. (ed.), 2011, *The Archaeology of Maritime Landscapes*. Society of Historical Archaeology & Springer Press.

Gansum, Terje/ Gro B. Jerpåsen & Christian Keller, 1997, *Arkeologisk landskapsanalyse med visuelle metoder* (Archaeological analysis of landscape by way of visual methods). AmS-Varia 298. Stavanger, Arkeologisk museum i Stavanger.

Hamilton, Sue & R. Whitehouse, 2006, "Phenomenology in Practice: Towards a methodology for a 'subjective' approach," in *European Journal of Archaeology* vol. 9: 31−71.

Hasslöf, Olof, 1949, *Svenska västkustfiskarna* (Fishermen on the Swedish west coast). Göteborg. Diss.

Hasslöf, Olof (*et al.*), 1972, *Ships and shipyards, sailors and fishermen. Introduction to maritime ethnology*. The Scandinavian Maritime History Working Group, with a Preface by Basil Greenhill. Copenhagen, Rosenkilde and Bagger.

Hodder, Ian & C. Orton (eds), 1976, *Spatial analysis in archaeology*. Cambridge.

Honko, Lauri & Orvar Löfgren, 1981, *Tradition och miljö. Ett kulturekologiskt perspektiv* (Tradition and environment. A culture-ecological perspective). Lund, Skrifter utg. av Etnologiska sällskapet.

Hovda, Per, 1961, *Norske fiskeméd. Landsoversyn og to gamle médbøker* (Norwegian transit lines for fishing. National survey and two note books). Oslo/ Bergen, Skrifter fra Norsk Stadnamnarkiv 2.

Ingold, Tim, 1993, "The temporality of landscapes", in *World Archaeology 1993, 25*: 152–74. Also in: Thomas, J.(ed.), *Interpretive Archaeology*. Leicester U.P.

Jasinski, Marek E., 1993, "The maritime cultural landscape-an archaeological perspective", in *Archeologia Polski* XXXVIII, 1993, Zeszyt 1: 7–21.

Keller, Christian, 1993, "Visuelle landskapsanalyser i arkeologien" (Visual landscape analyses in archaeology), in *Årbok 1991/1992. Universitetets Oldsaksamling*, Oslo: 59–80.

Sherratt, Andrew, 1996, "Why Wessex? The Avon Route in later British prehistory", in *Oxford Journal of Archaeology 15 (2)*: 211–234.

Sherratt, Andrew, 2006, "Portages: a simple but powerful idea in understanding human history", in Westerdahl, C. (ed.), *The Significance of Portages*. Oxford, BAR Intern. Series 1499: 1–13.

Smith, C.A., 1976, *Regional analysis*. London & New York.

Svennung, J., 1963, *Scadinavia und Scandia. Lateinisch-nordische Namenstudien*. Uppsala, Skrifter K. Humanistiska Vetenskapssamfundet.

Tilley, Christopher, 1994, *A Phenomenology of Landscape: Places, Paths and Monuments*. Berg, Oxford.

Tilley, Christopher, 1996, "The Power of Rocks: landscape and Topography on Bodmin Moor", in *World Archaeology* 28: 151–176.

Westerdahl, Christer, 1987, *Norrlandsleden II. Beskrivning av det maritima kulturlandskapet. Rapport från en inventering i Norrland och norra Roslagen 1975–1980. The Norrland Sailing Route II. Description of the maritime cultural landscape. Report from a survey in Norrland and northern Roslagen, Sweden, in 1975–1980,* Arkiv för norrländsk hembygdsforskning XXIII 1987. Härnösand.

Westerdahl, Christer, 1989, *Norrlandsleden I. Källor till det maritima kulturlandskapet. En handbok i marinarkeologisk inventering. The Norrland Sailing Route I. Sources of the maritime cultural landscape. A handbook of maritime archaeological survey*. Arkiv för norrländsk hembygdsforskning XXIV. Härnösand.

Westerdahl, Christer, 1992, "The maritime cultural landscape", in *The International Journal of Nautical Archaeology* 21/1 1992: 5–14.

Westerdahl, Christer, 1995, "Traditional zones of transport geography in relation to ship types", in Olsen, O., Skamby Madsen, J. (eds), *Shipshape. Essays for Ole Crumlin-Pedersen*. Roskilde, Vikingeskibshallen: 213–230

Westerdahl, Christer, 2002, "The cognitive landscape of naval warfare and defence. Toponymic and archaeological aspects", in A. Nørgård Jørgensen, J. Pind, L. Jørgensen & B. Clausen (eds), *Maritime Warfare in Northern Europe. Technology, organisation, logistics and administration 500*

BC-1500 AD. Copenhagen, Publications of the National Museum, Studies in Arch. & History vol 6: 169-190.

Westerdahl, Christer, 2006b, "From River to Sea Catching the Monsoon. Concepts of the Maritime Cultural Landscape", in L. Varadarajan (ed.), *Indo-Portuguese Encounters. Journey in Science, Technology and Culture part I*. New Delhi/ Lisbon, Manohar: 334-350.

Westerdahl, Christer, 2006c, "Finding and asking the right people the right questions. On the use of oral tradition in archaeology", in J. Urtans, J.(ed.), *Kultūras krustpunkti 3. Laidiens*. Riga, Latvian Academy of Culture: 131-150.

Westerdahl, Christer, 2006d, "On the Significance of Portages. A survey of a new research theme", in Westerdahl, C. (ed.), *The Significance of Portages Proceedings of the First International Conference on the Significance of Portages, 29th Sept-2nd Oct. 2004: 15-51*. Oxford, British Archaeological Reports (BAR) International Series 1499: 15-51.

Westerdahl, Christer (ed.), 2006, *The Significance of Portages. Proceedings of the First International Conference on the Significance of Portages, 29th Sept-2nd Oct. 2004*. Oxford, British Archaeological Reports (BAR). International Series 1499.

Westerdahl, Christer, 2007a, "Fish and Ships. Towards a Theory of Maritime Culture", in *Deutsches Schiffahrtsarchiv* 30, 2007: 191-236.

Westerdahl, Christer, 2007b, "Bonden, Kråkan och Jungfrun (The Farmer, the Crow and the Virgin)", in *Oknytt. Tidskrift för Johan Nordlander-sällskapet* 1-2 2007, Umeå: 9-33.

Westerdahl, Christer, 2007c, "The Relationship between Land Roads and Sea Routes in the Past- Some Reflections", in *Deutsches Schiffahrtsarchiv* 29, 2006: 59-114.

Westerdahl, Christer, 2010a, "Horses are strong at sea. The liminal aspect of the maritime cultural landscape", in Anderson, A., J.H. Barrett & K.V. Boyle (eds), *The Global Origins of Seafaring*. Cambridge, McDonald Institute Monographs: 275-287.

Westerdahl, Christer, 2010b, "Ship yards and boatbuilding. Features of the maritime cultural landscapes of the North", in *Deutsches Schiffahrtsarchiv* 32, 2009: 267-344.

Westerdahl, Christer, 2011a, "The Maritime Cultural Landscape Revisited", in B. Ford, B. (ed.), *The Archaeology of Maritime Landscapes*. Society of Historical Archaeology & Springer Press.

Westerdahl, Christer, 2011b, "The maritime cultural landscape", in Alexis Catsambis, Ben Ford, Donny L. Hamilton (eds), *The Oxford Handbook of Maritime Archaeology*, Oxford University Press: 733-762.

Westerdahl, Christer, (in press 1), "Sea versus Land. An Arctic and Subarctic Cosmology?", in C. Westerdahl (ed.), *A Circumpolar Reappraisal*. Oxford, British Archaeological Reports (BAR), International Series 2154: 301-327.

Westerdahl, Christer, (in press 2), "Lake Vänern. Reflections on dynamic continuity and changing shore-lines", in *Scyllis*, DEGUWA.

Westerdahl, Christer, (in press 3), "Ancient seamarks, A Social History in a North European perspective", in *Deutsches Schiffahrtsarchiv* 33. 2010, October.

Nautical Ethnography as an Aid to Understanding the Maritime Past

航海民族志对理解海洋史的作用

Seán McGrail

(University of Oxford)

肖恩·麦克格雷

（牛津大学）

ABSTRACT / Nautical ethnography may be defined as "the description and analysis of recent or present-day water transport built by hand and used in non-industrial, small-scale societies". Such boats, rafts and floats are made from natural materials – hides, reeds, bark of wood – and propelled by human muscles or by wind, tidal flow or current. The ethnographic documentation of such water transport presents archaeologists with a range of possible solutions to reconstruction problems encountered when attempting to deduce the original form, structure and use of excavated evidence which is always incomplete. During the twentieth century, James Hornell, Basil Greenhill and Jean Deloche published much about transport of South Asia, nevertheless vast regions of that sub-Continent remained un-investigated. Between 1994 and 2000, a team documented several boat types in Bangladesh and along India's Bay of Bengal coast. There were two aspects of that fieldwork in which the links between ethnography and archaeology featured: the traditional plank boat built in frame-first sequence; and the boats with reverse-clinker planking.

KEY WORDS / Nautical ethnography, South Asian fieldwork, reverse-clinker, frame-first, Chinese ship building

内容摘要 /

航海民族志可以被定义为"描述和分析近代或现今由手工建造并被非工业社会、小规模所使用的水路运输"。这些用于运输的小船、木筏、浮子是由皮革、芦苇、树皮等天然原料建造，并依靠人力或风、潮流或水流前进。在推断沉船的原始形状与结构时，考古资料总是不够全面的，而民族志所记载的水路运输资料则可为考古学家提供了一系列可能的解决方案。虽然20世纪詹姆斯·霍内尔、巴泽尔·格林希尔和珍·德罗查发表了很多有关南亚的论著，但是还有一些次大陆的广阔区域至今还没有研究。1994年至2000年间，一队民族志学者记录了孟加拉和印度湾孟加拉沿岸的几种船型。此次田野工作在传统骨架结构木板船和反向搭接壳板船两个方面凸显了民族志与考古学之间的联系。

关 键 词 /

航海民族志　南亚田野工作　反向搭接壳板　骨架结构　中国造船

Excavated evidence is always incomplete. Moreover, excavated artifacts and structures may prove to be of a type never previously encountered. We can, however, draw on ethnography to help us interpret such evidence and thus increase our understanding of former times. "Ethnography" may be defined as: "the description and analysis of the material aspects of recent or present-day, non-industrial, generally illiterate, small-scale societies".

In our case, such "material aspects" are principally floats, rafts and boats that have been built from natural materials, such as hides, reeds, bark or wood, and are propelled by wind, tide or current, or by muscle power. Ethnographic documentation of such craft enables archaeologists to escape the bounds of their own culture and to become aware of other technologies, thereby widening their understanding of what is practicable in boatbuilding and in boat-usage.

Where there is cultural continuity between prehistory and the recent past – as there appears to have been in Norway (Christensen, 1977: 112) – ethnographic evidence can be especially useful. The problems are greater when analogies are used crossculturally, but the more similar in environmental, technological and economic terms the two cultures can be shown to be, the greater is the likelihood that ethnographic studies will be relevant to archaeological problems. By such means, archaeologists are helped in the technological interpretation of excavated material and may also be guided when formulating hypotheses and making deductions about the economic life of ancient communities.

Although similarities of raw materials, form and constructional techniques may be demonstrated in a particular comparison of excavated and ethnographic evidence, a simple 1 to 1 relationship between artifact and function cannot be assumed. Even within one culture an artifact may have several different functions: thus a paddle may be used to propel or to steer a boat or to avoid an underwater obstacle – with the added complication that, in certain parts of the world, paddle-shaped objects are also used to dig, to shovel, to beat washing, to move loaves into and out of an oven, and to stir butter or beer. Conversely, a single function may be satisfied in several ways: thus stitches, wooden treenails or iron nails may be used to fasten boat planking. Moreover, there is no certainty that knowledge of the

Fig. 1 Bronze Age, sewn-plank boat Ferriby 1 exposed in the early-twentieth century, on the northern foreshore of the Humber Estuary in eastern England. The ruler is 2 feet (60cm) in length (Photo. E.V. Wright).

original use of an excavated artifact will have survived: the precise, prehistoric use may not be included in any of the ethnographic data it is now possible to record.

It can be seen, therefore, that ethnographic analogues do not provide one, certain identification, rather a range of possibilities for the archaeologist to combine with information about the context of the excavated object or structure, its spatial and temporal relationships to other artifacts, signs of wear or of use, and conclusions drawn from the natural sciences, ergonomics, documentary evidence and the like. As Professor Grahame Clark (1953: 357) said some sixty years ago, "comparative ethnography can prompt the right questions, only archaeology, in conjunction with the various natural sciences, can give the right answers". To which we should now add that, in the present state of knowledge, no answers may be possible and any answer will be probabilistic rather than definitive.

Three ancient boats, now in Hull Museum, formerly in the reserve collection of the National Maritime Museum at Greenwich, are the world's oldest planked boats after those in Egypt. Between 1946 and 1963, the remains of these sewn-plank boats were excavated by E.V. Wright at North Ferriby on the northern shores of the

Fig. 2 A *masula* sewn-plank boat on the foreshore of the Bay of Bengal near Madras in the early-20th century (Photo : J. Hornell).

Humber estuary, on England's eastern coast (Fig. 1). They were subsequently dated to the period 1,900 to 1,700 BC (Wright, 1990; Wright *et al.* 2001). Their oak planking had been lashed together by ropes made from twisted yew withies, with a caulking of moss to make the joints watertight. In those days there were no comparable archaeological finds, and the interpretation and reconstruction of the original form of these boats proved difficult. Ethnography, however, came to the aid of archaeology.

The *masula* (Fig.2.), an Indian seagoing, oared boat, used today off the coasts of Tamil Nadu, is also a sewn-plank boat (Kentley, 2003: 120-166). Ted Wright used his knowledge of these 20th century boats in his published discussion of the structure and the uses of the Ferriby boats. Subsequently, after I had seen how those Indian boats were built and how they were used through the surf, I felt that I too had a much better understanding of the prehistoric builders and crew of the prehistoric Ferriby boats. Moreover, I became more confident in my attempts to interpret these, and other, excavated boat timbers that had survived from the British Bronze Age (McGrail, 2004: 184-191).

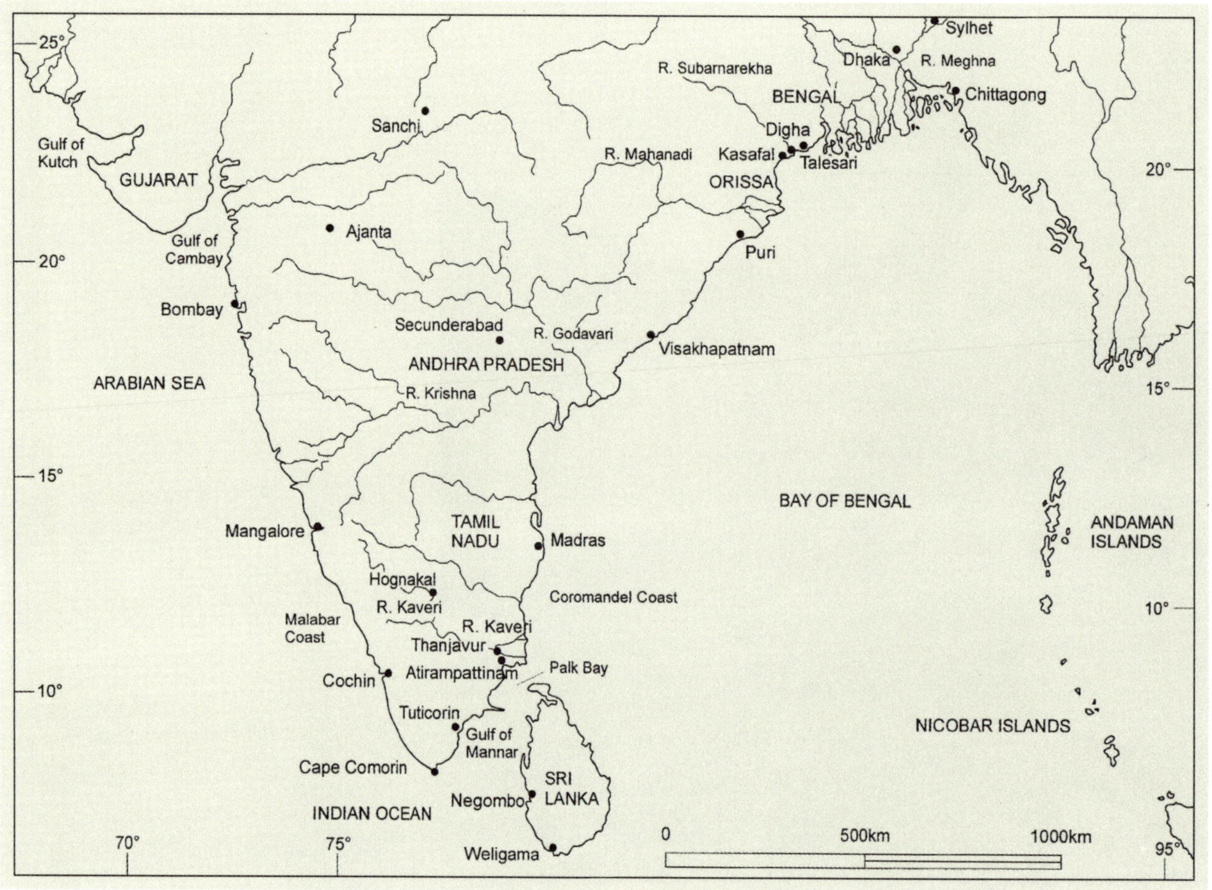

Fig. 3　Map of South Asia showing sites in Tamil Nadu, Orissa, West Bengal & Bangladesh　(Map: author).

Fieldwork in South Asia

During fieldwork in the Indian sub-Continent between 1994 and 2000, a team of two archaeologists, an ethnographer and a naval architect, examined and recorded some of the indigenous boats in Bangladesh and on India's Bay of Bengal coast (McGrail, 2003). From Cape Comorin (Kanyakumari) in the far south of Tamil Nadu to the headwaters of rivers in the foothills of the Himalayas, more than 1,000 miles further north (Fig. 3), we surveyed several boat types during six winter seasons of fieldwork. Although much had been learnt, earlier in the 20th century, about indigenous boats in parts of South Asia – see publications by James Hornell (1946), by Basil Greenhill (1971) and by Jean Deloche (1994) – there had been little attempt to investigate the water transport of vast regions of that sub-Continent. It seemed to me that not only was boat ethnographic fieldwork required to fill those gaps, but also that such research might become the first stage in establishing boat archaeology in India. By documenting today's water transport, Indian scholars would learn recording methods and develop related skills that could, in due course, lead to the

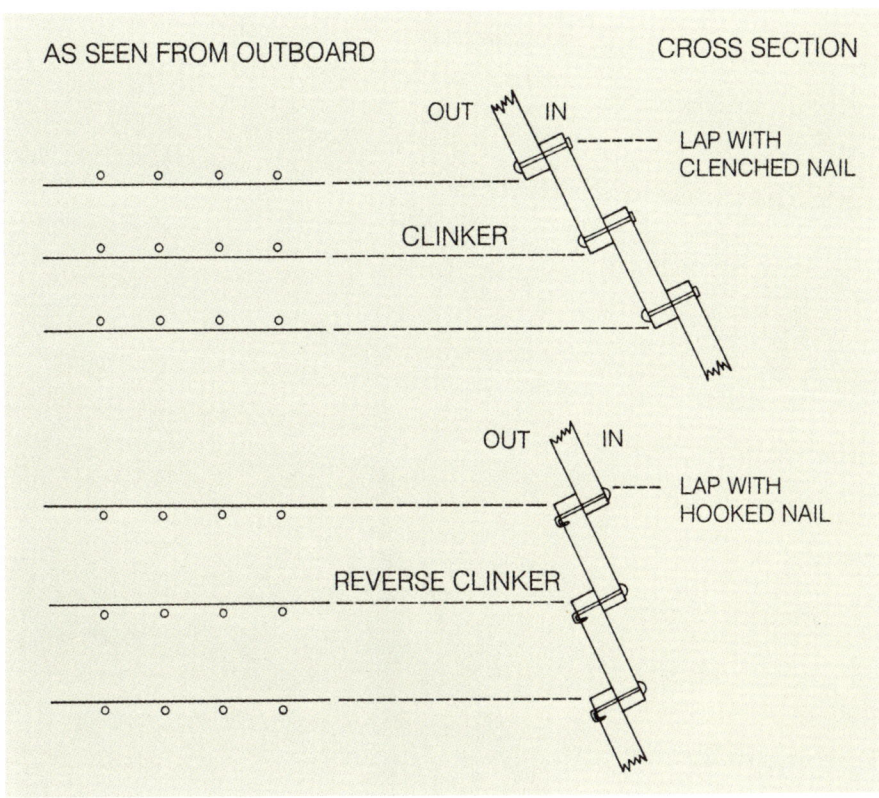

Fig. 4 Diagram showing two methods of fastening planking: European clinker (upper); South Asian reverse-clinker (lower). Not to scale (Drawing: author).

planned location, excavation, conservation and public display of early Indian rafts and boats. To a limited degree, boat ethnography has now been established in India as a practical topic; boat archaeology, on the other hand, remains in the future.

There are two aspects of our fieldwork in South Asia which illustrate the links between ethnography and archaeology: first, work on boats with reverse-clinker planking; and second, investigations of traditional vessels built in the frame-first sequence.

Reverse-clinker planking (Fig.4)

Unlike most frame-first boats, the planks of plank-first, clinker-built boats are fastened together through their overlapping edges. In European clinker planking, as seen in medieval Viking ships, each succeeding strake of planking overlaps outboard the strake below, and the two strakes are fastened together by nails driven from outboard and clenched inboard, usually by deforming the tip of the nail over a metal rove. In reverse-clinker work (as used in India), on the other hand, the upper strake overlaps the lower strake inboard, and the fastening nails are driven from inboard through the lap and clenched outboard, often by turning the nail tip through 180° back into the wood.

Reverse-clinker planking is depicted in at least one of the drawings of Indian

Fig. 5 A "pettoo-a": a late-18th century South Asian reverse-clinker boat depicted by the Antwerp artist, Balthazar Solvyns [Photo: The Bodleian Libraries, University of Oxford: Ind.Inst. FC 4(10) section 9 No. 5].

boats published in the late 18th century by the Antwerp artist Frans Balthazar Solvyns: this drawing is of a "pettoo-a from Balassor on the coast of Palmira" (Fig.5). In his text, Solvyns (1799) noted that, in such boats, "the overlaps were reversed, that is, the upper edge of the lower plank is outside the lower edge of the upper plank".

In the late-1950s the existence of reverse-clinker planking in the Indian sub-Continent was confirmed during fieldwork undertaken in East Bengal (now Bangladesh) by Basil Greenhill. Dr Greenhill subsequently became Director of the National

Fig. 6   Reverse-clinker boats used in the extraction of stone from the near-dry bed of the River Surma in the Sylhet region of Bangladesh during the winter 1997–8 (Photo: author).

Maritime Museum at Greenwich and, in December 1997, with his encouragement, Dr Lucy Blue (University of Southampton) and I followed in his footsteps to the Sylhet region of Bangladesh where, in sight of the foothills of the Himalayas, we found a veritable fleet of reverse-clinker boats engaged in the "quarrying" of stone and its derivatives from the nearly-dry bed of a tributary of the River Surma (McGrail, 2003: 25–66) (Fig.6). During the Bangladesh dry season, hundreds of such boats are used, and thousands of people employed, in the extraction and transport of this stone which is used to repair and replace roads and bridges damaged during the annual floods. There are similar reverse-clinker boats in other parts of Bangladesh, and also further south at Indian coastal sites in West Bengal and Orissa.

We found that Indian & Bangladeshi boats with reverse-clinker planking often had a planking pattern with high rise at both ends. Furthermore, this planking ended, not at a post or stem, but on a near-horizontal line. In a few cases this feature was pronounced; in most it was vestigial. A similar planking pattern may also be seen on a number of late-medieval depictions of a type of North West European cargo ship named as a *hulc* (Fig. 7). Moreover, on a number of those depictions the planking

Fig. 7   The late-12th century font in Winchester Cathedral. To the left, a *hulc* (with curving, reverse-clinker planking) is depicted in a scene from the life of St Nicholas (Photo: B 5988, National Maritime Museum, Greenwich).

is shown as reverse-clinker. To-date, no vessel excavated in North West Europe has been found to have reverse-clinker planking or to have that *hulc* planking pattern. Nevertheless, the practicality of reverse-clinker has been ethnographically documented in Bangladesh, West Bengal and Orissa, and we are now in a better position to interpret any future European excavated remains that may have been part of a reverse-clinker vessel or one with a *hulc* planking pattern.

We have tried to work out how two similar, but fundamentally different, techniques using overlapping planking might have originated. One theory is that South Asian reverse-clinker evolved when a flat-bottomed boat was needed, and so a thin ("low height") keel was selected-we would now call it a "plank-keel". The garboards would naturally be fitted on top of this squat keel. Subsequent strakes would similarly be fitted overlapping inboard, thus producing reverse-clinker. The European version of clinker, on the other hand, was possibly devised when building a vessel with a more rounded section and with a keel that would protrude well below the planking. In this case it would have been natural to fasten the garboard strakes to the sides (i.e. outboard) of the relatively-tall keel, where they would have a better landing.

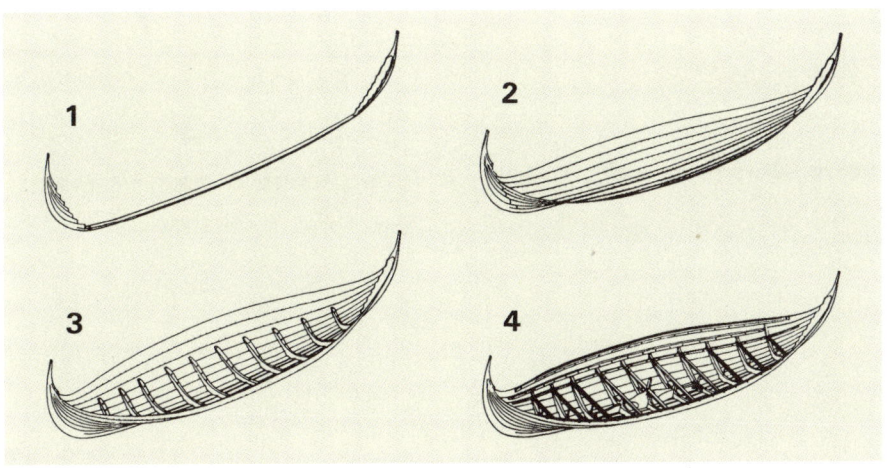

Fig. 8 The "plank-first" sequence of building a boat of the Viking tradition (Diagram: author-after Crumlin-Pedersen, 1986: fig 3).

Building Sequences

Present studies suggest that, possibly throughout the world, the earliest planked boats were built "plank-first" (Fig. 8). In this building sequence, the hull shape is first defined by fastening shaped planks together and to keel and posts: planking determines hull shape. The framing is then fashioned and fastened inside that hull form. The oldest planked vessels in the world – those from Egypt of the early-3rd millennium BC – were built in this sequence.

An alternative way of building is "frame-first" (Fig. 9). In this method the frames are first designed; fashioned to the required shape; and then fastened to the keel or to the central bottom ("foundation") plank, so that, with the posts, the hull's three dimensional shape is outlined. In this case, framing determines hull shape and individual planks are then fastened to it. It is also relevant to note that, apart from the smallest examples, hide boats (sometimes known as "skin boats") are built frame-first.

An early form of the use of the frame-first sequence to build planked boats first appears in the archaeological record in the $1^{st}/2^{nd}$ century AD, in the Celtic parts of coastal North West Europe (McGrail. 2013). A similar sequence of construction, but different in detail, subsequently appeared in the eastern Mediterranean in the $5^{th}/6^{th}$ century AD (Pomey et al. 2012). There is then a period when there is little, if any, trace of this distinctive building sequence until the $12^{th}-13^{th}$ century AD when it was used in southern European shipyards. This technique spread from there to coastal Atlantic Europe as far as the Baltic, to become the style of shipbuilding that produced the European sailing vessels that sailed the seas of the world from the 15th century AD.

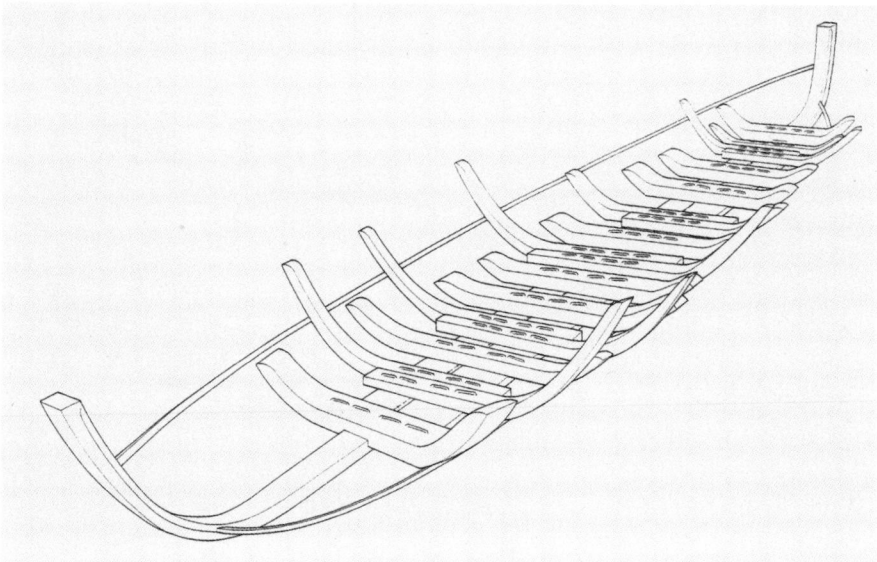

Fig. 9 Stage 4 in building a Romano-Celtic boat of the early centuries AD. Hull shape has been defined by plank-keel, stems and several framing timbers. The curved timber running along the far side of this set-up is a hypothetical ribband that could have been used to check the fair run of the frames before planking was fastened to them (Diagram: copyright Glamorgan-Gwent Archaeological Trust).

Whether there was continuity with the earlier Celtic or Levant frame-first building methods is not, at present, clear (McGrail, 2004: 163-165, 196-206, 245-247).

In Tamil Nadu we found that, although most traditional boats and ships were built in the plank-first sequence, certain specific types of traditional vessels were built in the frame-first sequence, in particular the *vattai* boat (Fig. 10) and the thoni ship. A feature of these two types is that they are formally designed (McGrail, 2003: 202-213). A mould-loft floor, two large moulds and a prescribed procedure are used to design a ship's framing; a master frame template and a scrieve board are used to design a boat's framing (Fig. 11). Over the central part of these vessels, where cargo is to be carried, several frames are fashioned to the shape of the master frame thus giving this length of hull a constant transverse section. Towards the ends, where the transverse section is to vary, pairs of frames are individually designed on the scrieve board or on the mould loft floor to give the required hull form.

This Tamil design method has similarities with the procedure used in 15th century Venice to design galleys using a wooden tablet known as a *mezza luna* (a "half moon"). As it now stands, the evidence suggests that the 16th century Portuguese, or the 17th century French, brought a version of these European design methods to Tamil Nadu. Nevertheless, this must remain a hypothesis for the present, since it is not yet proven that the Tamil tradition goes back that far. From the European viewpoint, this knowledge of the Tamil method of frame-first design should lead to greater understanding of how, in late-medieval/post-medieval Europe, a shift evidently took place, from a predominately plank-first building sequence to a

Fig. 10 An early stage in the building of a *vattai* fishing boat at Atirampattinam, Tamil Nadu. The framing defines the hull shape (Photo: author).

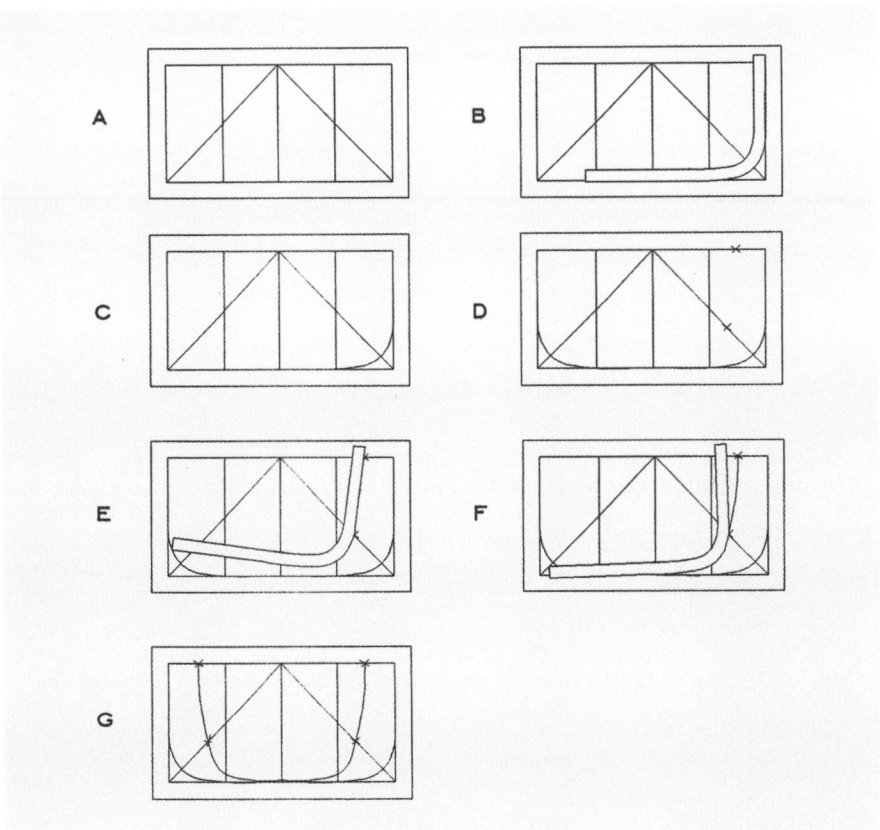

Fig. 11 Diagram to illustrate the design of *vattai* frames using a scrieve board and a single mould: A, B, C. The shape of the mould is transferred to the scrieve board-this becomes the shape of all "equal" frames; D. Points (X) calculated & marked to give the rising (along diagonal) and the narrowing (along top edge) of a pair of "unequal" frames; E, F. Mould positioned on these two points and then rotated to give the shape of an "unequal" frame (Diagram: E. Kentley).

frame-first sequence, with consequent changes from informal ways of obtaining the required hull shape to the formal design methods that were to dominate European shipbuilding for the next 300 years.

Medieval Chinese ships built frame-first?

It may be that, at about the same time as in Europe, there was also a shift to building frame-first in China. This possibility came to mind as I read reports, in translation, of several excavated early-medieval Chinese merchant ships (see, for example, Xi & Xin, 1991). These vessels appear to have been built frame-first or possibly one should say "bulkhead-first". In the descriptions and drawings studied it is possible to see that, although the strakes of both Quanzhou 1 and Penglai 1 ships were fastened together ("edge-fastened"), most (possibly all) plank scarfs were at bulkhead stations (Fig.12).

Moreover, these two vessels had *ju* nails or similar fastenings between planking and bulkheads which were so positioned that, in Penglai 1, the bulkheads were almost certainly in place before the planking was fitted and fastened. Furthermore, Penglai's planking is 120-280 mm thick (significantly thicker than the planking of ships of comparable size) and capable of holding inserted caulking. If these conjectures prove to be true, the lower hull, at least, of Penglai 1 was built bulkhead-first, a variant of the frame-first sequence. In other words, the hull shape of late-14th century Penglai 1 (and possibly also Quanzhou 1) was determined by her framework of bulkheads, not by her planking: these two ships appear to have been built "frame-first" rather than "plank-first" (McGrail, 2004: 372-3, 375-6).

Generally speaking, edge-fastened planking indicates that a hull was built "plank-first". However, it is possible to fasten planking together using angled nails or treenails after strakes have been individually fastened to a bulkhead framework. I understand that 20th century Chinese junks were indeed built in this manner: bulkhead-first, yet with edge-fastened planking.

Questions that need to be asked about those two excavated ships (Penglai 1 and Quanzhou 1) include: Were the bulkheads of those medieval Chinese ships fastened to the keel? Were plank scarfs fastened together or merely to bulkheads? What was the spacing, centre to centre, of bulkheads? Were any strakes fastenings immediately

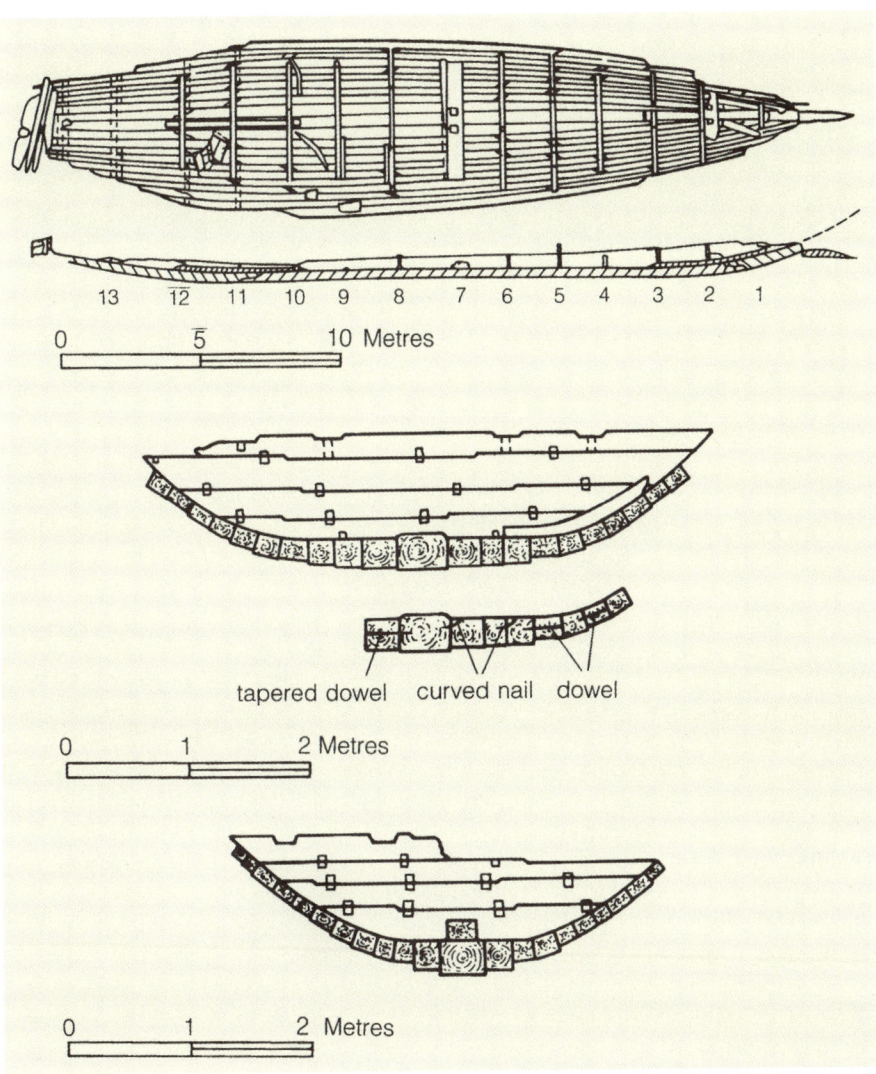

Fig. 12 Plan and sections of the 14th century wreck Penglai 1. Plank scarfs within strakes are marked by an angled line: all appear to be associated with bulkheads (Drawing after Xi & Xin, 1991: figs 1-3).

outboard of bulkheads? Was caulking inserted before or after planking was fastened together? The measured drawings published in the English language articles about Penglai 1 and Quanzhou 1 are too small-scale to give answers to such questions.

It is notable that this shift from plank-first to frame-first shipbuilding, possibly at about the same time in China and in Atlantic Europe, was followed, in both cases, by long-range, ocean-going voyages: into the Atlantic Ocean by Portuguese and Spanish ships; and into the Indian Ocean by the Chinese ships of Admiral Zheng Ho's seven fleets.

Concluding remarks

This paper has dealt with the building and use of water transport made of natural materials such as wood, hide, bark and reed. These are rafts and boats that are built by hand, without mechanical or electrical power. When in use they are propelled by human muscles, by wind-power, or by tidal flows and river currents. Of the unique importance to mankind of such simple forms of water transport, there can be no doubt. But that importance is not reflected in the knowledge we now have of early nautical capabilities and achievements. Nor is it fully reflected in our knowledge and understanding of recent and, indeed, today's water transport. The skills and knowledge embodied in the traditional forms of water transport that are still built and used were inherited from our predecessors. In the living tradition of these vessels, there is immense potential for learning more about our maritime past. Traditionally built craft are disappearing fast. In some countries fibreglass copies have been made and used-the Indian *oruwa*; the Irish *currach*; and the Yorkshire *coble* are examples. These retain the traditional shape but little else, making those genuine boats that survive in museums especially important.

Nautical ethnography is the academic topic that seeks to record and understand those traditional floats, rafts, boats and ships that are still used today. It has a vital part to play not only in recording, before it is too late, the "boating world" that has survived from earlier times, but also in providing evidence that can be used to increase our understanding of the material remains that archaeologists excavate. The archaeological record is undoubtedly biased in that evidence for early water transport is overwhelmingly about log boats and plank boats. Furthermore, it is biased towards Egypt and Europe: this bias would be reduced by the worldwide documentation of ethnographic examples of water transport. In such ethnographic studies of floats, rafts and boats, priority should be given to log rafts, buoyed rafts, bundle rafts, bundle boats, basket boats and hide ("skin") boats: these are seldom, if ever, excavated. I believe that some of these craft types continue to be used on the rivers and in the coastal waters, of China. Ethnographic studies of the building and use of these craft would not only be valuable in themselves, but also would enable archaeologists to visualise how such ephemeral types of water transport could have played an important part in early man's use of the waters of the world.

References

Christensen, Arne-Emil. 1977, "Comment", in S. McGrail (ed.) *Sources and Techniques in Boat Archaeology,* National Maritime Museum Archaeological Series 1. Oxford: British Archaeological Reports S.29: 112.

Clark, J.D.G. 1953, "Archaeological theories & interpretation: Old World", in A.L. Kroeber (ed.), *Anthropology Today*, Chicago: Chicago University Press: 343−60.

Crumlin-Pedersen, O . 1986, "The 'Roar' project", in O. Crumlin-Pedersen, O. and M. Vinner (eds.). *Sailing into the Past*, Roskilde: Viking Ship Museum: 94−103.

Deloche, Jean. 1994, *Transport & Communications in India prior to Steam locomotion*, Vol. 2. *Water Transport*. Delhi: Oxford University Press.

Greenhill, Basil. 1971, *Boats & Boatmen of Pakistan*. Newton Abbot: David & Charles.

Hornell, Jarnes. 1946, *Water Transport: Origins & Early Evolution*, Cambridge: Cambridge University Press (repr. 1970 Newton Abbot: David & Charles).

Kentley, Eric. 2003, "Masula - a sewn plank surfboat of India's eastern coast", in S. McGrail (ed.), *Boats of South Asia*, London: RoutledgeCurzon, 2003: 120−166.

McGrail, Sean. 2003 (ed.), *Boats of South Asia*, London: RoutledgeCurzon for the Society of South Asian Studies.

McGrail, Sean. 2004, *Boats of the World*, Oxford: Oxford University Press, 2nd (paperback) edition.

McGrail, Sean. 2013, "Transition from Shell to Skeleton in the Mediterranean & in North-West European Waters", *International Journal of Nautical Archaeology* 42: 188−189.

Pomey, P., Y. Kahanov, Y. & E. Rieth. 2012, "Transition from Shell to Skeleton in Ancient Mediterranean Ship-construction: analysis, problems & future research", *International Journal of Nautical Archaeology*, 41: 235−314.

Solvyns, F.B.. 1799, *Les Hindoos*, Calcutta.

Wright, E. V. 1990, *Ferriby* Boats, London: Routledge.

Wright, E.V., R.E.M. Hedges, A. Bayliss & R. van de Noort, 2001, "New AMS radiocarbon dates for the North Ferriby boats", *Antiquity*, 75: 726−734.

Xi, Longfei. & Xin, Yuanou. 1991, "Preliminary research on the historical period and restoration design of the ancient ship unearthed in Penglai", in S. Zhang (ed.), *Proceedings of the International Sailing Ship History Conference*. Shanghai: Society of Naval Architecture & Marine Engineering: 225−236.

Widening the Scope and Refining the Methods of Maritime and Experimental Archaeology: The Roskilde Case - Viking Ships from Excavation to Full-size Sea Trials

海洋和实验考古学的视野拓展与方法改进：以罗斯基勒维京船的发掘到原尺寸复原试航为例

Ole CRUMLIN-PEDERSEN[†] Tinna DAMGÅRD-SØRENSEN

(The Viking Ship Museum, Roskilde, Denmark)

奥勒·克拉姆林-佩德森 汀娜·达姆加德-索伦森

（丹麦罗斯基勒维京船博物馆）

ABSTRACT / A holistic approach to maritime archaeology has been developed in Roskilde since the early 1990s with a strong emphasis on the archaeological study of prehistoric and medieval maritime societies in northern Europe, especially in Scandinavia. During the years 1993–2003, the National Museum and the Viking Ship Museum have conducted intensive interdisciplinary research within the themes *Seafaring and Society*, *Ships and Boats and Development of Processes and Tools*. Since 2003 the Viking Ship Museum has continued a long-term programme of experimental archaeology as an all-important means for the scholarly study of ships of the past, their impact on contemporary society, their role as technological innovators, etc. The culmination of this large programme came in 2007–08 with the experimental voyage of the reconstructed 11th-century longship *The Sea Stallion* from Roskilde to Dublin and back, with a crew of 62 persons, recording all aspects of the voyage in the waters for which the original ship was constructed.

KEY WORDS / Experimental archaeology; roskilde; the Viking Ship; reconstructed ship; experimental voyage

内容摘要 /

自上世纪九十年代初罗斯基勒就建立起一整套海洋考古方法，其重点是对北欧地区特别是斯堪的纳维亚半岛史前及中世纪海洋文化社会的考古学研究。1993年至2003年间，丹麦国家博物馆及维京船博物馆已集中组织了"航海与社会"、"海船与河船"与"工序与工具的发展"等跨学科研究。自2003年起，维京船博物馆还持续开展了一项长期的实验考古学研究，研究重点是古代船舶对当时社会的影响及其在技术变革中的作用等。此项研究的最大成果是2007～2008年复原的11世纪长维京船"海上种马号"的首次航行。这艘复原船搭载着62人从罗斯基勒出发到爱尔兰的都柏林，而后返航。航行期间，船上人员记录下了此次航行的所有细节以期了解原船的航行状况。

关键词 /

实验考古学　罗斯基勒　维京船　复原船　试航

Introduction: The environmental conditions

The presentation of a case study from the small North-European country of Denmark may seem far-fetched here, but we hope to be able to show that the methods applied and the results achieved in the Danish study of Maritime Archaeology may be relevant at a more general level for the community of maritime archaeologists in Asia.

Throughout millennia, the Danish waters have served as crossroads for international sea-routes between the Baltic and the North Sea, for contacts between the Scandinavian Peninsula and the rivers of Central Europe, and for communication between the local islands (Fig. 1). Such a geographical and hydrographical setting is characteristic for other maritime centres in the world as well, and several locations along the coasts and rivers of Asia offer similar potentials as those described here for Denmark.

Due to isostatic changes since the latest Ice Age, the present Danish seabed has a large potential for well-preserved submarine Stone Age finds, and during other periods the many reefs and shallows of the Danish waters caused the loss of thousands of ships. Thus the shallow waters and the many silted-up areas along the coasts provide optimal conditions for retrieving archaeological finds from all periods of the past. Consequently, Denmark has an obligation to focus on research in maritime archaeological aspects of the prehistory and early history of northern Europe, and to safeguard the underwater cultural heritage against damage and looting.

A special focus in our early research has been on ships and shipping of the period 800-1100 AD, the period called the Viking Age. During those centuries, Scandinavians ventured out from their homelands in Denmark, Norway and Sweden to all parts of coastal Europe and along the Russian rivers to the Caspian and Black Seas. They even

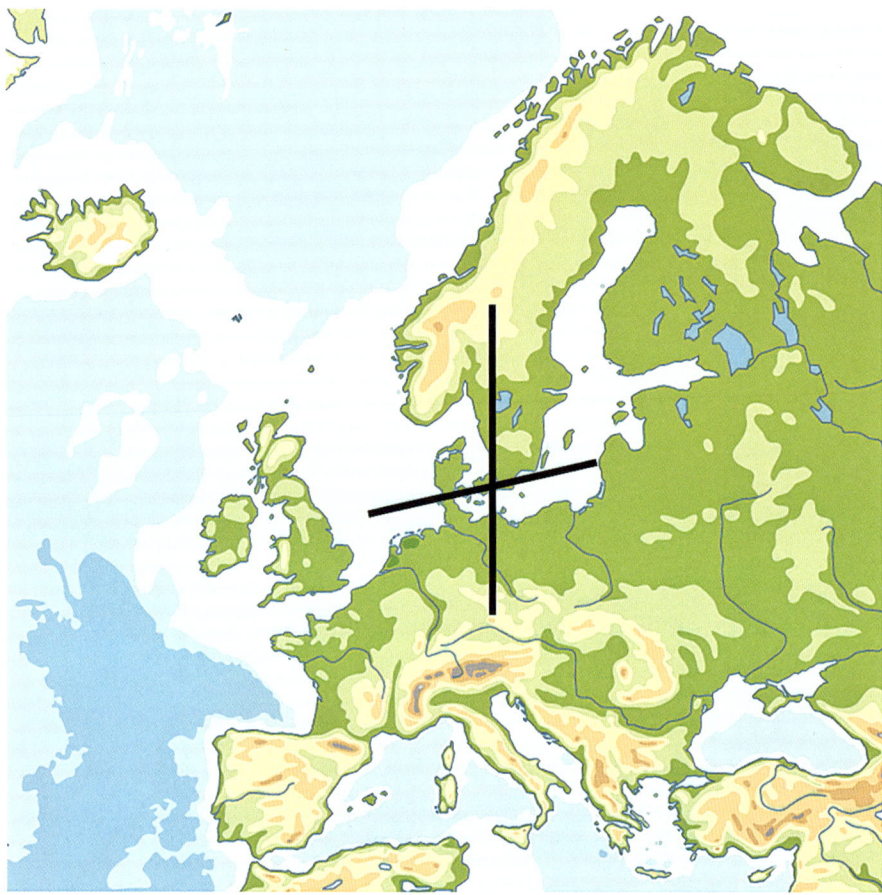

Fig. 1 Denmark is situated at the centre of important maritime crossroads of Northern Europe.

crossed the North Atlantic to Iceland, Greenland and North America (Fig. 2). The history of these centuries can not be fully understood without a profound knowledge of the ships which enabled them to undertake those daring voyages.

The Skuldelev excavations

In 1957, the first underwater investigation was initiated by the Danish National Museum at Skuldelev in Roskilde Fjord close to Copenhagen. During three years of diving, a stone barrier with five 11th-century ships was mapped and partly excavated. In 1962 the full excavation of the site followed within a cofferdam[1] (Fig. 2). This was the starting point of a deliberate Danish effort to study and promote the preservation of the Danish maritime archaeological heritage.

In order to cope with the documentation of the timbers of the Skuldelev ships, as well as their analysis and conservation, a maritime archaeology unit was formed at the National Museum, and the new Viking Ship Museum was built in the town of Roskilde for the restoration and exhibition of the ships, opened to the public in 1969. The first phase was the analysis on the basis of the recovered parts of the ships

---

[1] Crumlin-Pedersen et al., 2002.

Widening the Scope and Refining the Methods of Maritime and Experimental Archaeology: The Roskilde Case - Viking Ships from Excavation to Full-size Sea Trials

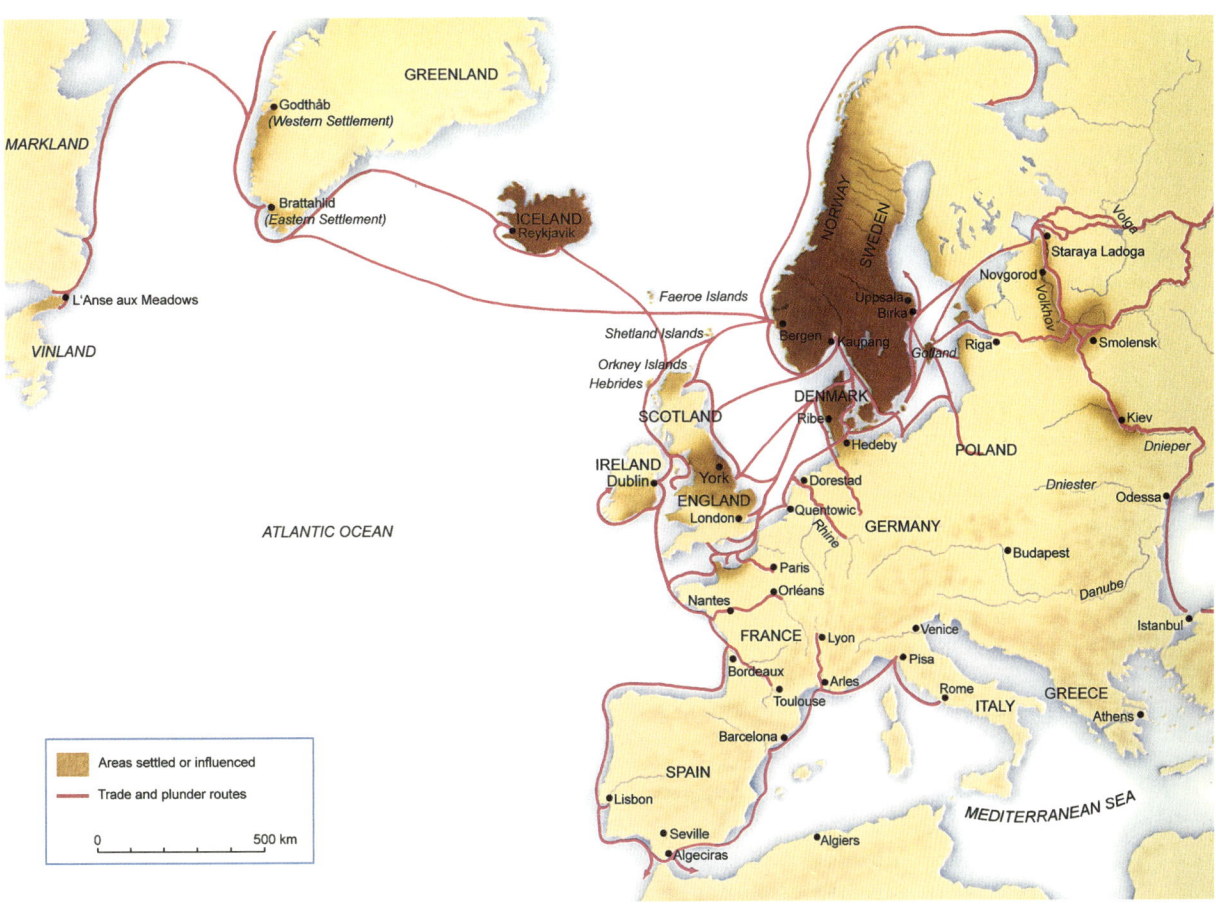

Fig. 2 Scandinavian voyages and expansions during the Viking Age, ca 800–1100 AD.

Fig. 3 Excavation of the Skuldelev Viking ships in Roskilde Fjord in 1962. After Crumlin-Pedersen & Olsen (eds) 2002.

Table 1 Boats and ships surveyed and excavated during the period 1962–1993
(by the Danish National Museum and the Viking Ship Museum.)

Skuldelev	5 shipwrecks	11th cent.	1962–1964
Slusegård	boatgraves	2nd cent.	1965
Ellingå	shipwreck	12th cent.	1968
Lynæs	shipwreck	12th cent.	1975
Vejby	shipwreck	14th cent.	1976–1977
Kyholm	shipwreck	13th cent.	1978
Kollerup	shipwreck	13th cent.	1978
Hedeby	shipwrecks	10th cent.	1979
Fotevik	5 shipwrecks	11th cent.	1981–1982
Fribrødre	shipyard	11th cent.	1982–1986
Uggerby	shipwreck	c. 1800	1984
Stinesminde	shipwreck	17th cent.	1987–1989
Gedesby	shipwreck	14th cent.	1988–1990
Nydam	3 ships	3rd–4th cent.	1989–1993
Ll. Kregme	shipwreck	14th cent.	1992
Gislinge	boat wreck	12th cent.	1993

of the construction principles, capacities and seaworthiness of the five Skuldelev ships, representing two warships, two cargo carriers and a fishing vessel. An important second step of this study was the building of reconstructions at full scale and sea trials with all five ships, as described below.

The dendro analysis provided evidence for the date, origin and repairs of the ships. Two of these were from Western Norway, one from Viking settlements in Ireland and two were local Danish ships. They were all built around AD 1030–1040, and thus the Skuldelev find gave a broad representation of the ship-types of the Late Viking Age.

But work did not end with these Viking ships, since there were several other challenges to Danish maritime archaeology. During the years 1962–1993, and even later, we have carried out intense fieldwork activities under water as well as on land at sites where ancient ships or boats were found. Some of these were chosen to be excavated for their source value for the history of shipbuilding, whereas others had to be rescued as they were threatened by human activities or soil erosion.

Table 1 gives a survey of the 1962–93 finds ranging in date over two millennia, but with a concentration in the 10th to 14th centuries AD. The reconstruction sketches (Fig. 4) indicate the variation in sizes and shapes from the early paddled and rowed boats over single-masted sailing ships to the multi-masted ships of the Late Middle Ages and later.

Fig. 4 Reconstructions of some of the vessels surveyed and excavated during the period 1962–1993. Drawing Morten Gøthche.

The clinker tradition (lapstrake construction)

This comprehensive body of archaeological evidence resulted in the identification of different basic building concepts, reflected primarily in the bottom structure of medieval ships as well as in local boats. In the first instance, our studies focused on the clinker tradition and its origins in the expanded logboat.[2] By carving a log to a thin shell and expanding the sides, a broad, gently curved and

[2] Crumlin-Pedersen, 2004.

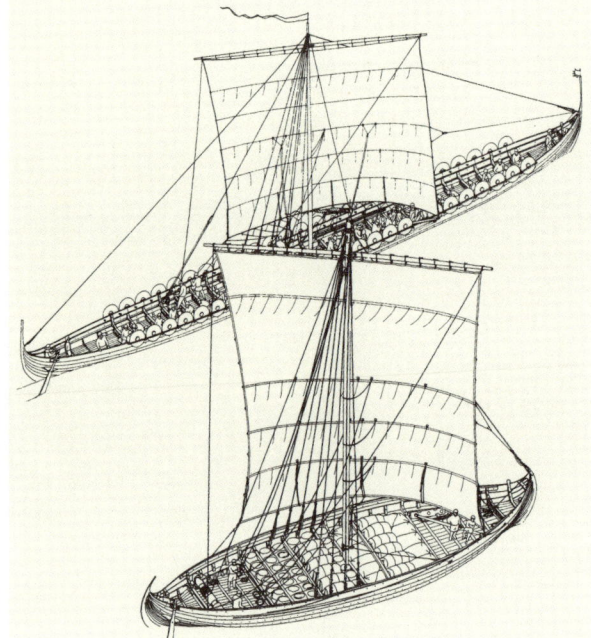

Fig. 5 Expanded logboat from Finland (ca 1930), shown before and after the expansion of the logboat base and compared with boat from ca 700 AD found at Kvalsund, Norway. After Crumlin-Pedersen 2004.

Fig. 6 Reconstruction sketches of two of the ships from ca 1000 AD, found in the Viking harbour of Hedeby, the longship of royal standard Hedeby 1 above and the cargo carrier Hedeby 3 below. After Crumlin-Pedersen 1999a.

seaworthy boat-shaped vessel emerged, and this is seen as a clue to the origin of the shape and internal structure of the Scandinavian Iron-Age boats (Fig. 5). Such expanded boats were found locally in Iron-Age finds as well as among later traditional boat types in various parts of Northern Europe and elsewhere, and the basic shape and framing system has been maintained until today among traditional clinker-boat builders.

During many centuries, the ships in the North were built on the basis of the clinker tradition. Around AD 1000, specialisation had taken place among these ships, with long, narrow and low warships, built for speed and manoeuvrability and manned with many rowers to supplement sail propulsion[3]. An extremely slender 31-m long warship of excellent quality has been excavated in the Viking harbour at Hedeby, and several other longships have been found as well, including another one of a royal quality, found in 1996 in Roskilde, originally c. 36m in length. In this group, differences in the quality of the building materials and craftsmanship clearly indicate that they represent three different status levels, a royal, a standard and a discount level[4].

In contrast, the cargo ships were broader, higher and more solidly built to carry their load under sail alone[5] (Fig. 6). Among the numerous cargo ships from the period AD 1000-1500 found around the coasts of Denmark, Norway and Sweden are seven cargo ships that were excavated in Roskilde's medieval harbour when it was

[3] Crumlin-Pedersen, 1997b.

[4] Crumlin-Pedersen, 1997a; 2002; Gøthche, 2006.

[5] Crumlin-Pedersen, 1999a; 2003a; Englert, 2009.

dredged out for a new boat harbour for the Viking Ship Museum in 1996-97. This is a striking illustration of the importance of having archaeological control with all kinds of construction work involving dredging in old harbour areas and along the coastline.

These finds include a number of large cargo ships of clinker construction of the 11th and 12th centuries, with Skuldelev 1 representing the lower end of this series[6]. This ship represents the medium-sized cargo ships; it was built in western Norway for trade with the Baltic region. The hull is well preserved, and trials with full-size reconstructions have demonstrated the ship's seaworthiness under extreme conditions, with one of the reconstructions even having circumnavigated the Globe. Several of the smaller cargo vessels found in Denmark and elsewhere in Scandinavia are also so well preserved that reliable reconstructions have been made of them.

These finds demonstrate the capacity of Scandinavian shipbuilders to build seaworthy ships large enough to provide bulk tonnage for the new towns being founded during this period. The largest of these ships, built 1180 in Bergen, Norway, with a beam of over 9m, and a cargo capacity of at least 120 metric tons would have been one of the largest ships of its time in northern Europe[7].

This group of ships illustrates a change from relatively prestigious craftsmanship with graceful shapes during the 11th century, to more simple standards with a business-minded approach after c. 1200, giving maximum tonnage at minimal cost[8]. These anonymous ships provide important information on the impact on forestry of the need for high-quality timber for shipbuilding, and even on the organisation in society in response to the rise of towns and trading networks.

Cogs and hulcs

Medieval historians have focused on the *cog* type during the 13th and 14th centuries as the main ship-type of the trade network of the Hanseatic League[9]. Evidently the type developed from a flat-bottomed craft of the tidal and fluvial south-coast of the North Sea. According to the finds, especially the Kollerup *cog* from c.1150, the early stages in the conversion to sea-going vessels took place during the 12th century. This probably resulted from interaction between Frisian and Danish shipbuilders in the southern part of Jutland, from where the timber for the earliest known sea-going *cogs* came[10].

[6] Crumlin-Pedersen *et al.*, 2002: 97-140; Englert, 2003; 2009.

[7] Christensen, 1985; Englert, 2001.

[8] Bill 1995.

[9] See for example Heinsius, 1956. Ellmers, 1994.

[10] Crumlin-Pedersen, 2000; Daly, 2009.

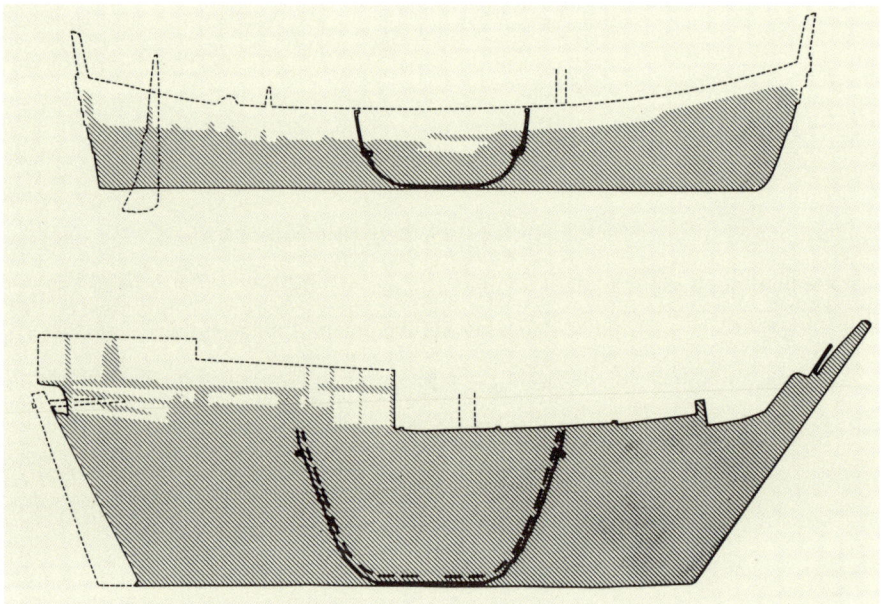

Fig. 7 The earliest known seagoing *cog*, from Kollerup, Denmark, ca 1150 AD, compared to the high-medieval Bremen cog of 1380. The shading represents the preserved parts of the ships. After Crumlin-Pedersen 1991.

[11] Hoffmann & Schnall (eds), 2003.
[12] Bonde & Jensen, 1995.
[13] Greenhill, 2000.
[14] Van de Moortel, 2009.

From this early start, the *cogs* gradually grew in size and cargo capacity, into large bulk-cargo transporters as the Bremen *Cog* from 1380, exhibited in Bremerhaven, Germany[11] (Fig. 7). The *cogs* all have flush bottom planking and an angular transition to the straight stems. Except for the earliest ones, they are built from heavy sawn planks in contrast to contemporary clinker-built ships built from radially split planks. Some of these later *cogs*, including one which was built in 1372 in Poland and wrecked on the Danish coast a few years later have also been excavated. This ship was returning in ballast from a voyage to Western Europe, and with the wreck, 110 English gold nobles and other valuables were found, the outcome of a trading mission that failed to return to the home port in the Baltic[12].

According to the written sources the *hulc* ship type took over from the *cog* as the main ship type in the North Sea region in the late 14th and early 15th centuries. No high-medieval finds of this ship type have yet been identified, but its characteristics are known from contemporary town seals and coins, as well as earlier images, showing its crescent-shaped lines with all planks carried up to the extreme ends and held there, sometimes with a rope lashing[13].

There are, however, Dutch finds of vessels of this nature from the 11th century, with the Utrecht ship as the main example (Fig. 8). The 14m-long and 2m-wide bottom element of this vessel was made in the expanded logboat technique, thus indicating a common origin in that technique for the *hulc* as well as for the Nordic clinker-built ships[14].

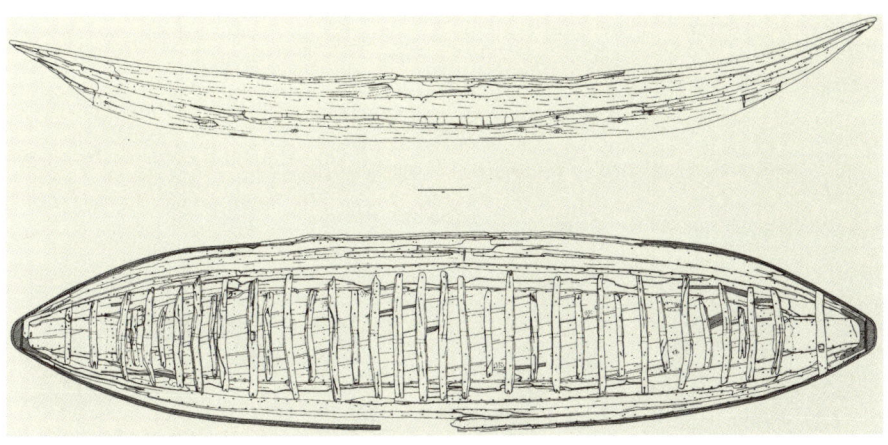

Fig. 8 The Utrecht vessel from 11th century AD, based on a 14-metre-long expanded bottom element, and a probable ancestor to the high-medieval *hulc* type. After Crumlin-Pedersen 2010.

Maritime Archaeology Research Centre in Roskilde, 1993–2003

During the period 1993–2003, a major grant from the Danish National Research Foundation enabled us to engage research teams including members from several countries in Europe, USA and India, and to focus our research within three thematic groups:

1. *The archaeology of watercraft,*
2. *Development of tools and techniques in Maritime Archaeology*
3. *Maritime aspects of archaeology* [15]

The ship archaeological studies have primarily been published in our monograph series *Ships and Boats of the North* [16]. Five archaeological volumes have been published till now, and several more volumes are in preparation, in order to make this important archaeological evidence available in context for the international research community.

In the second sector, pioneer work has been carried out within several fields, including new methods of archaeological recording, such as the use of the Faro-Arm digital registration of complex elements. This technique is now being applied for ship-archaeological recording in several other countries.

The coastal zone has been searched for traces of structures and settlements indicating human activities in the past in the interface between the dry land and the sea. Such studies greatly benefit from an approach where the landscape is seen with the eyes of the seafarer. Studies in coastal morphology and place-names also supplement traditional land-based reconnaissance along the coast.

The integration of this maritime archaeological approach into mainstream archaeology has been furthered with the publication of several scholarly books

[15] Crumlin-Pedersen (ed.), 2003.

[16] Crumlin-Pedersen, 1997; Sørensen, 2001; Crumlin-Pedersen & Olsen (eds), 2002; Crumlin-Pedersen & Trakadas (eds), 2003; Lemeé, 2006.

Fig. 9 Launching of a reconstruction of the Pearyland *umiaq* hide boat from Greenland, ca 1500 AD, built 1980 in the Viking Ship Museum (in the background). Photo: Viking Ship Museum, Denmark.

on maritime aspects of settlement, warfare and cult, many of these resulting from international research seminars organised from Roskilde. Most recently, the Viking Ship Museum has issued a new series, *Maritime Culture of the North* with reports of Ohthere and Wulfstan, two 9th-century travellers, studied and commented upon by international scholars in the light of the most recent results of archaeological and historical investigations[17]. The third volume in the series is a personal account of Ole Crumlin-Pedersen's fifty years of studies of maritime archaeology in Scandinavia and Britain[18].

Ethnographic boats

Over the years, the Viking Ship Museum has also organised ethnographical studies of pre-industrial boat building traditions from around the World. Native craftsmen still mastering these skills have been brought to Roskilde to teach us the essence of their crafts in public demonstrations in the museum (Fig. 9). These activities are also relevant for the study of Scandinavia's prehistory, as similar boat building methods may have been in use there, although they are very difficult to trace archaeologically, such as with skin or bark boats.

[17] Bately & Englert (eds), 2007; Englert & Trakadas (eds), 2009.

[18] Crumlin-Pedersen, 2010.

Fig. 10 As part of the Viking Ship Museum's outreach programmes, school groups are taken to sea to experience the challenges of seafaring in the past. Photo: Werner Karrasch. Copyright: The Viking Ship Museum, Denmark.

Another example is the expanded boat technique which has been practised around the globe until recently. Some of our projects have focused on examples of such boats still being built in Finland and Canada, and on Borneo[19]. As already explained, they serve as an eye-opener for the understanding of the basics of ancient boat and ship types.

Outreach

Finally it is important to stress the museum's outreach programmes to the visitors and the local community. A collection of traditional Scandinavian boats serve the double purpose of offering the visitors realistic sailing trips (Fig. 10), and the challenge for the boat-builders of the museum of repairing them, and even building new boats to the same traditions.

Some larger traditional wooden ships have also been preserved, restored and engaged in various activities. Since 1970, a restored three-masted schooner *Fulton*, built 1915 as one of the last cargo ships to cross the Atlantic under sail without an engine, has served during the summer months as a sailing museum ship taking teams

[19] Nicolaisen & Damgård-Sørensen, 1991; Petersen, 2000.

of youngsters to sea for one-week trips in Danish waters. This ship has also been used as a base for an annual course in underwater archaeology for sport divers. They are sailed to various underwater archaeological sites and are taught how to record such sites without causing damage, thus creating a sense of mutual responsibility for the underwater heritage among amateurs and professionals alike [20].

The Skuldelev ships as a reflection of Viking society

As briefly stated above, the Skuldelev Viking ships belong to a renowned period in Scandinavian history. The written sources are sparse and the archaeological evidence therefore plays a major role in the investigation of this dynamic period when the three Scandinavian Kingdoms were established, the old pagan gods were replaced by Christianity, towns were founded and Scandinavia became part of European history [21].

The cultural unity of Scandinavia was furthered by the waterways, and seafaring was crucial for the development. Advances in politics, economy and culture stimulated progress and specialisation in shipbuilding, leading to sailing vessels that could face the new demands.

As already demonstrated, the five Skuldelev Viking ships reflect this development, and offer a rich and complex approach to the study of Viking ships and society. However, their capacities and limitations can only realistically be established through working with full-scale reconstructions.

The ship as an archaeological source of information

A shipwreck is a complex and valuable source of information to the study of contemporary society, as ship design and construction reflects the owner's specific requirements on function, capacity and speed, and not the least the image he wants to display.

A careful analysis of the building materials, supported by natural science analyses, of an ancient ship provides information on:

Date and origin of the ship

Woodland management

---

[20] Crumlin-Pedersen, 2003b.

[21] Sawyer (ed.), 1997.

Materials technology

Craftsmanship

The ship's activities

The archaeological experiment

The archaeological experiment provides the tools for a multi-disciplinary approach to the reconstruction of ancient ships, since no single person – not even a maritime archaeologist – is able to see or to interpret all this information alone.

Therefore, in 1980 the Viking Ship Museum established a multi-disciplinary team of academics, craftsmen and sailors using their various areas of expertise and experience to interpret and decipher archaeological shipwrecks. The objective was and still is to gain an overall understanding of the original ship's design, function and qualities, and its importance for Viking society.

The first full-scale project of the museum was the *Roar Ege* reconstruction of Skuldelev 3, built 1980–1982 by a team of young people who gradually became experts in Viking Age craftsmanship (Fig. 11). Most members of this group are still associated with the museum today, 30 years later, reflecting the high degree of continuity in

Fig. 11   The Skuldelev 3 reconstruction *Roar Ege* during construction in Roskilde 1981.
Photo: Bo Jørgen Nielsen, The Viking Ship Museum, Denmark.

Fig. 12 Reconstructions of all five Skuldelev ships, sailing on the Roskilde Fjord in 2008.
Photo: Werner Karrasch. Copyright: The Viking Ship Museum, Denmark.

building up the expertise. During this long period we have been able to build and test full-size reconstructions of all five Skuldelev ships as an eye-opener for us in studying each ship find as a fully functional unit serving the purpose for which it was originally built [22] (Fig. 12).

The longship project

The longship project *Thoroughbred of the Sea* is a research project based on the reconstruction of the 30-meter-long Skuldelev 2 warship. The project was started in 1996, and after launching in 2004, it culminated in a trial voyage from Roskilde in Denmark to Dublin in Ireland and back in 2007–2008. This project is the most complex and ambitious ship archaeological experiment accomplished by the Viking Ship Museum, and it is probably also the most ambitious experiment of its kind ever undertaken in the field of maritime archaeology.

According to the dendro-analysis, the original ship was built in 1042 in Dublin, Ireland. The historical setting for Skuldelev 2's original voyage to Roskilde was probably in the aftermath of the Norman invasion in England in 1066 [23]. The vessel was designed for the stormy waters of the Irish Sea and the North Atlantic. It represented generations of accumulated experience with materials, design, building methods and sailing characteristics. It originally had ca. 60 oars and a sail of ca. 120 square metres.

After the excavation in 1962, all parts of the original planks and timbers of the

[22] Crumlin-Pedersen, 1986a; 1986b; 1995; 1996; 1999b; 2006; Nielsen, 2006; Bill et al., 2007.

[23] Crumlin-Pedersen & Olsen (eds), 2002: 326–30.

Fig. 13 The preserved remains of the Skuldelev 2 longship exhibited in the Viking Ship Museum, Roskilde. Photo: Werner Karrasch. Copyright: The Viking Ship Museum, Denmark.

ship were carefully drawn at full scale before the wood was conserved and assembled in the museum (Fig. 13). The drawings were subsequently reduced to the scale of 1:10, transferred onto cardboard, cut out and fitted together by pins through the original nail holes into a model which gave guidelines to the shape and to the original length of the ship. The bottom structure was well documented but there was some uncertainty about the construction of the upper parts of the ship, not to mention the rigging. However, elements from some of the other ship finds of the period could guide us, not the least the many rigging details found in the Viking harbour of Hedeby.

Then a one-tenth scale wooden model of the ship was built with proposals for the missing parts of hull and rig. The model offered the possibility of experimenting with various solutions before work at full scale was begun.

In 2000 the building of the reconstruction in full scale began at the Museum Boatyard (Fig. 14). The ship was built of the same materials and with the same tools and techniques as the original ship, including cleaving the planks instead of using saws. These principles have been observed during the continuous reconstruction work carried out at the museum, and all recorded original details were carefully copied.

The resources needed for the building of a Viking longship was investigated, as well as the necessary organisation for the job. A record of all materials brought into the boatyard was kept, and all working processes were trained well in order to give a realistic basis for time taking. Processes carried out elsewhere, as tar burning and

Fig. 14 A fish-eye view of the Skuldelev 2 longship reconstruction on the stocks in front of the Viking Ship Museum in 2003. Photo: Werner Karrasch. Copyright: The Viking Ship Museum.

the forging of iron nails, were recorded at the production site, while the resources needed for sail and cordage were estimated on the basis of previous experiments.

The calculation of the working hours needed to build the ship using Viking-Age technology showed a total of ca. 44,000 man-hours for craftsmen, rope-makers and weavers, but not including unskilled labourers. Thus it would have been possible originally to build Skuldelev 2 in seven months with one master boat builder and 10 ordinary boat builders, provided the materials needed were at hand.

In 2004, our reconstruction was launched and named *The Sea Stallion of Glendalough* to commemorate the Irish origin of the Skuldelev 2 longship; Glendalough being a valley close to Dublin from where the original timber probably came[24].

Trial voyages

The first years after launching were used to test the longship under oars and sail in Danish waters and on a passage to southern Norway. However, the ultimate test was the trial voyages 2007–2008 from Roskilde to Dublin and back across the North Sea (Fig. 15). These voyages were performed with documentation of the behaviour of the ship as well as weather conditions around the clock under the constantly changing forces of Nature. In this environment, it is impossible to isolate and analyse single factors and compare the results with measurements obtained from experimental setups like tank tests, which in principle can be repeated indefinitely under controlled conditions.

[24] Bill *et al.*, 2007.

Fig. 15 *The Sea Stallion of Glendalough* en route for Dublin 2007.
Photo: Dougie Petrie, Viking Ship Museum, Denmark.

Instead, the *Sea Stallion* can be seen as a hypothesis reflecting our interpretation of the original ship and its missing parts. To test the hypothesis it is necessary to use the ship under the conditions for which it was originally built. The basic idea behind the test is that the original ship was a fully functioning unit since it had survived many years of active service before being scuttled. If we had added parts which did not fit into the entirety of the ship, they might have fail. If the ship and the many individual parts functioned as intended, our interpretations would be made probable, and the reconstruction and the results of the sailing tests be considered representative of the original vessel – and of Viking longships in general.

It is indeed a challenge to achieve authenticity in an archaeological experiment of this nature (Fig. 16). With 65 persons onboard we could not accept the same safety risks as our forefathers had to live with a thousand years ago. We endeavoured to reach modern standards for safety, navigation and communication, food and clothing, and to do so without compromising the principles of the experiment. During the entire voyage a modern support vessel followed as a safety backup. A full set of life-saving equipment and modern navigational means was carried onboard the longship. During the entire voyage close contact was kept with the home base, and daily reports, including video footage, appeared at the homepage of the SeaStalion project (www.seastallion.dk) which was visited by a large audience from all over the World, stirred by programmes in national and international TV media.

Fig. 16 *The Sea Stallion* in rough weather in the Irish Sea in 2007. Photo: Werner Karrasch. Copyright: The Viking Ship Museum, Denmark.

Fig. 17 The route sailed 2007−08 by *The Sea Stallion*. Illustration: Mette Kryger. Copyright: The Viking Ship Museum, Denmark.

The Trial Voyage from Roskilde to Dublin and back followed the routes employed in the Viking Age for journeys between Denmark and Ireland around the British Isles. In total 2.482 nautical miles were covered (Fig. 17).

The purpose of the Trial Voyage was to test the reconstruction, to examine the seaworthiness, sailing qualities and travelling speed and to investigate the functions, organisation and logistics of the ship and her crew. The crew, 65 men and women from 8 nations, consisted mostly of volunteers who had sailed in long periods of initial tests. Captain, mates, boatswains, communication officer and photographer were museum employees.

The various functions onboard have been investigated in detail. Consumption of food and water has been documented. The figures reached here, indicating a need for 5-6 landfalls along the route, is probably too high since it reflects modern standards of food rather than those of the Viking Age. The health situation of the crew has been good in general in spite of the extremely uncomfortable conditions onboard. Day and night there was nowhere to seek shelter from rain and wind, and everybody slept in the open on 4-hour shifts with less than one square-metre deck space pr. person.

Documentation

A ship under sail is a complex mechanism, as the vessel and the crew interact with the weather, the waves and the currents. In order to record the trial voyage, the *Sea Stallion* was equipped with electronic equipment continuously recording the position of the ship and the course steered, the speed through the water, wind and temperature (Fig. 18).

Skipper and mate kept the official logbook with notes on navigation and the situation on board. The boatswain recorded wear and tear and any damage to the hull, rudder and rigging. The five foremen took notes about experiences within the section of the ship for which they were responsible. The steward kept an account of food and water consumed on board, and the nurse recorded the state of health. In addition the museum photographer documented the voyage on video and photos, while a journalist wrote a personal account of the travel.

Establishing the displacement and standard draft of the ship was no problem. But the flexibility of the ship was one of the most challenging issues. It is closely linked to the principles of construction, and also influenced by the rigging, strengthening the entire structure. Since the longitudinal reinforcing elements were not fully preserved in the original ship, it was important to note that the solution chosen in the reconstruction was fully functional.

Fig. 18　Skipper and mate with the electronic data logging and communication unit of the *Sea Stallion*. Photo: Werner Karrasch. Copyright: The Viking Ship Museum, Denmark.

The steering system was based on other finds and experience from previous experiments. During the trial voyage there were severe problems with the hemp cordage and the leather strap fastening the side rudder to the side of the ship. The materials could not endure the pressure on the rudder, and they broke several times during the voyage from Roskilde to Dublin. In contrast, the rudder functioned perfectly on the voyage home with a strong birch withy fastening. Then the ship proved to be very seaworthy and well balanced even in rough seas.

The trial voyage has focussed on seaworthiness, manoeuvrability and speed of the ship under realistic conditions, such as along the Scottish coast and in the very turbulent Irish Sea. How interesting top speed may be, it does not throw much light on the ship as a transport tool under everyday conditions in these waters. However, the ship's peak performance and technical qualities have also been recorded, such as the greatest speed under sail and oars, the closest possible angle to the wind, the time

Fig. 19 Preliminary results of the experiment: The longship can carry full sail up to 12 m/s and can beat against the wind at an angle of 59° to the wind. The top speed recorded is 11 knots.
Photo: Werner Karrasch. Copyright: The Viking Ship Museum, Denmark.

it takes to turn the ship, etc. (Fig. 19) The results of these experiments provide an insight into the strategic decisions facing the Viking naval commander who had to bring ship and crew from one place to the next under given conditions.

The crew found the ship relatively heavy to row. It could be rowed against the wind up to a wind velocity of 10–12 m/s. The rowing technique was tested, showing that at short distances it is best to use all oars, while at long distances every second oar is used with half of the crew resting at any time.

Conclusion

Summing up for the longship project, it is possible to state that the reconstruction in general seems to be reliable, and that the ship is seaworthy and well balanced at sea. The ship is primarily for sailing – the oars are of secondary importance. The ship can cover long distances within a short time if the wind is favourable, and it would therefore often be sensible to wait for the wind. Thus the *Sea Stallion* represents, together with the other full scale reconstructions, a unique sum of experience and data based on many years of research.

When the experimental method was introduced in Roskilde in 1980, the know-how of Viking Age boat building and sailing was long lost and forgotten. Since then our research team of craftsmen and sailors have developed the specialised skills necessary for refining the methods of experimental archaeology, and for widening the perspective from the study of ship technology into a broader analysis of the relationship between ship and man.

The experimental method is not yet fully approved as a scientific method in European archaeology. As many newborn disciplines it has not yet developed a common standard, and the field is full of all kinds of people and projects-out of which only some contribute to our understanding of the past.

Based on the Roskilde experience, the experimental method can contribute significantly to the academic study of the complex information embedded in an archaeological ship find. To exploit the full potential of the method it is necessary to have a team of researchers with professional backgrounds within crafts and sailing in parallel to the well established academic structures. Our ambition has been to widen the perspective into a broader field – and to reach a level of competence from where it is possible to focus on problems and questions that were also relevant for the people of the past [25].

[25] The experimental methods and results of the building and sea trials of the Skuldelev reconstructions are being prepared for publication in the *Ships and Boats of the North series*, edited by Tinna Damgård-Sørensen.

References

Bately, J., & A. Englert (eds), 2007, Ohthere's Voyages. *A late 9th-century account of voyages along the coasts of Norway and Denmark and its cultural context*, Maritime Culture of the North 1, The Viking Ship Museum, Roskilde.

Bill, J. 1995, "Getting into business-Reflections of a market economy in medieval Scandinavian shipbuilding", in O. Olsen et al. (eds), *Shipshape. Essays for Ole Crumlin-Pedersen*: 195-202. Roskilde.

Bill, J., S. Nielsen, E. Andersen & T. Damgård-Sørensen 2007, *Welcome on board! The Sea Stallion from Glendalough. A Viking longship recreated*, The Viking Ship Museum, Roskilde.

Bonde, N. & Jensen, J.S. 1995, "The dating of a Hanseatic cog-find in Denmark". *Shipshape, Essays for Ole Crumlin-Pedersen*, eds. Olsen et al: 103-121. Roskilde.

Christensen, A. E., 1985, "Boat Finds from Bryggen". *The Bryggen Papers*, Main Series 1: 47-278. Bergen.

Crumlin-Pedersen, O. & A. Trakadas (eds), 2003, *Hjortspring. A Pre-Roman Iron-Age Warship in Context*, Ships and Boats of the North 5. Roskilde.

Crumlin-Pedersen, O., & Olaf Olsen (eds), 2002, *The Skuldelev Ships I. Topography, Archaeology, History, Conservation and Display*, Ships and Boats of the North 4.1. Roskilde.

Crumlin-Pedersen, O., (ed.), 2003, "Centre for Maritime Archaeology, 1993-2003". *Maritime Archaeology Newsletter from Roskilde*, No. 20. Roskilde.

Crumlin-Pedersen, O., 1986a, The "Roar"-Project. *Sailing into the Past*. Proceedings of the International Seminar on Replicas of Ancient and Medieval Vessels, Roskilde, 1984: 94–103. Roskilde.

Crumlin-Pedersen, O., 1986b, "Aspects of Viking-Age Shipbuilding in the Light of the Construction and Trials of the Skuldelev Ship-Replicas *Saga Siglar and Roar Ege*", *Journal of Danish Archaeology* 5: 209–228. Odense.

Crumlin-Pedersen, O., 1991, "Ship types and sizes AD 800–1400", in O. Crumlin-Pedersen (ed.), *Aspects of Maritime Scandinavia AD 200–1200*, 659–82. Viking Ship Museum. Roskilde.

Crumlin-Pedersen, O., 1995, "Experimental archaeology and ships-bridging the arts and the sciences", *The International Journal of Nautical Archaeology* 24/4: 303–06.

Crumlin-Pedersen, O., 1996, "Problems of Reconstruction and the Estimation of Performance", *The Earliest Ships. Conway's History of Ships*: 110–19. London.

Crumlin-Pedersen, O., 1997a, *Viking-Age ships and shipbuilding in Hedeby/Haithabu and Schleswig*. Ships and Boats of the North 2. Schleswig & Roskilde.Gøthche, M., 2006, The Roskilde ships, in L. Blue *et al.* (eds), *Connected by the Sea*. Proceedings of the Tenth International Symposium on Boat and Ship Archaeology, Roskilde 2003: 252–258. Oxford.

Crumlin-Pedersen, O., 1997b, "Large and small warships of the North", in A.N. Jørgensen & B.L. Clausen (eds) 1997: *Military Aspects of Scandinavian Society in a European Perspective AD 1–1300*. PNM Studies 2: 184–94. Copenhagen.

Crumlin-Pedersen, O., 1999a, "Ships as indicators of trade in Northern Europe 600–1200", in *Maritime topography and the Medieval Town* (eds. J. Bill & B.L.Clausen). PNM Studies 4: 11–20. Copenhagen.

Crumlin-Pedersen, O., 1999b," Experimental Ship Archaeology in Denmark", in: *Experiment and Design. Archaeological Studies in Honour of John Coles* (ed. A. F. Harding): 139–47. Oxbow Books, Oxford.

Crumlin-Pedersen, O., 2000, "To be or not to be a cog. The Bremen cog in perspective". *The International Journal of Nautical Archaeology*, 29.2: 230–46.

Crumlin-Pedersen, O., 2002, "Splendour versus duty. 11th-century warships in the light of history and technology", in Jørgensen, Pind, Jørgensen & Clausen (eds), *Maritime Warfare in Northern Europe. Technology, organisation, logistics and administration 500 BC – 1500 AD*. PNM Studies 6: 257–70.

Crumlin-Pedersen, O., 2003a, "Variations on a Theme: 11th century Ship Types of the North", in: Beltrame, Carlo (ed.), *Boats, Ships and Shipyards*. Proceedings of the Ninth International Symposium on Boat and Ship Archaeology. Venice 2000. Oxford: 253–260.

Crumlin-Pedersen, O., 2003b, "FULTON aus Marstal. Ein dänischer Schoner in Vergangenheit und Gegenwart", *Deutsches Schiffahrtsarchiv* 25–2002: 97–116.

Crumlin-Pedersen, O., 2004, "Nordic clinker construction", in F.M. Hocker & C.A. Ward (eds), *The philosophy of shipbuilding. Conceptual approaches to the study of wooden ships*: 37–63. College Station.

Crumlin-Pedersen, O., 2006, "Experimental archaeology and ships-principles, problems and examples", in Blue, L. *et al.* (eds), *Connected by the Sea. Proceedings of the Tenth International Symposium on Boat and Ship Archaeology Roskilde 2003*: 1–7. Oxford.

Daly, A., 2009, "The Chronology of Cogs and their Timber Origin", in Ronald Bockius (ed.),

Between the Seas. Transfer and Exchange in Nautical Technology. Proceedings of the Eleventh International Symposium on Boat and Ship Archaeology, Mainz 2006: 237-248. Verlag des Römisch-Germanischen Zentralmuseums, Mainz.

Ellmers, D., 1994, "The Cog as Cargo Carrier", *Cogs, Caravels and Galleons: The Sailing Ship 1000-1650* (eds. Gardiner, R. & Unger, R.W.). Conway's History of the Ship: 29-46. London.

Englert, A., & A. Trakadas (eds), 2009, *Wulfstan's Voyage. The Baltic Sea region in the early Viking Age as seen from shipboard*. Maritime Culture of the North 2, The Viking Ship Museum, Roskilde.

Englert, A., 2001, "The Dating and Origin of the 'Big Ship' from Bergen", *Ships and Commodities*. The Bryggen Papers Supplementary Series No 7: 43-49. Bergen.

Englert, A., 2003, "Large Cargo Vessels in Danish Waters 1000-1250. Archaeological Evidence for Professional Merchant Seafaring before the Hanseatic Period", in: Beltrame, Carlo (ed.), *Boats, Ships and Shipyards*. Proceedings of the Ninth International Symposium on Boat and Ship Archaeology. Venice 2000. Oxford: 273-280.

Englert, A., 2009, "Cargo Ships as Indicators of Commerce and Urbanisation in medieval Denmark 1000-1250", in Engberg, N. et al. (eds), *Archaeology of Medieval Towns in the Baltic and North Sea Area*. Publications of the National Museum Studies in Archaeology & History 17: 119-131. Copenhagen.

Greenhill, B., 2000, "The mysterious hulc", *The Mariner's Mirror* 86,1: 3-18.

Heinsius, Paul, 1956, *Das Schiff der hansischen Frühzeit*. Quellen und Darstellungen zur hansischen Geschichte, N.F.12. Weimar.

Hoffmann, G., & U. Schnall (eds), 2003, *Die Kogge. Sternstunde der deutschen Schiffsarchäologie*. Schriften des Deutschen Schiffahrtsmuseums 60. Bremerhaven.

Lemée, C.P.P., 2006, *The Renaissance Shipwrecks from Christianshavn*, Ships and Boats of the North 6. Roskilde.

Nielsen, Søren, 2006, "Experimental archaeology at the Viking Ship Museum in Roskilde", in Blue, L. et al. (eds), *Connected by the Sea. Proceedings of the Tenth International Symposium on Boat and Ship Archaeology Roskilde 2003*: 16-20. Oxford.

Nicolaisen, I. & T. Damgård-Sørensen, 1991, *Building a Longboat. An essay on the culture and history of a Bornean people*, The Viking Ship Museum, Roskilde.

Petersen, E., 2000, *Jukung-Boats from the Barito Basin, Borneo*, The Viking Ship Museum, Roskilde.

Sawyer, P., (ed.) 1997, The *Oxford Illustrated History of the Vikings*, Oxford University Press. Oxford, New York.

Sørensen, A.C., 2001, *Ladby. A Danish Ship-Grave from the Viking Age*, Ships and Boats of the North 3. Roskilde.

Van de Moortel, A., 2009, "The Utrecht Ship Type: an Expanded Logboat Tradition in its Historical Context", in Ronald Bockius (ed.), *Between the Seas. Transfer and Exchange in Nautical Technology*. Proceedings of the Eleventh International Symposium on Boat and Ship Archaeology, Mainz 2006: 329-336. Verlag des Römisch-Germanischen Zentralmuseums, Mainz.

Determining an Architectural Family and Its Evolution: The Example of the Greek Tradition of Sewn Shipbuilding in the Ancient Mediterranean

古代地中海希腊缝接造船传统：一种造船体系的确认及其演化的例证

Patrice POMEY

(CNRS, Centre d'Études Alexandrines)

帕特里斯·帕米

（法国国家科学研究中心-亚历山大城研究中心）

ABSTRACT / The technique of ship assembly by sewing in the ancient Mediterranean has long been considered, solely on the basis of literary evidence, as an archaic, and long outdated-model, a technique with no well-defined context and referring to a legendary past. Recently, however, numerous ancient shipwrecks, constructed either partially, or entirely using this sewing technique, have been discovered, and have conferred a material reality to these literary testimonies. The ensemble, covering the greater part of Antiquity from the Archaic era up until the Early Middle Ages, exceeds the framework of archaic and legendary times. But it appears, as a whole, to be rather heterogeneous and springs from very different architectural systems and contexts.

KEY WORDS / Antiquity; architectural tradition; Mediterranean; nautical archaeology; sewn boat

内容摘要 /

　　古代地中海以缝制连接船板的技术在很长一段时间都被认为仅是基于文献证据，完全是一种古老而长期过时的技术，它也无明确的背景仅是来自传说中的过去。然而，最近发掘的一些古代沉船，有建造时部分或全部使用了缝制技术的痕迹，从而为那些文学记载提供了实物证据。这种技术存在于古典时期的绝大部分阶段，从古风时代直到中世纪早期，超越了上古及传说时代。总体而言，这种技术也是相当复杂的，其源自不同的造船体系与背景。

关键词 /

　　古典时期　造船传统　地中海　航海考古学　缝接船

The technique of ship assembly by sewing in the ancient Mediterranean has long been considered, solely on the basis of literary evidence, as an archaic, and long out-moded, technique without any well-defined context and referring to a legendary past (Casson, 1963; Pomey, 1985).

Recently however, numerous ancient shipwrecks, constructed either partially or entirely using this sewing technique, have been discovered and have conferred a material reality on these literary testimonies. The ensemble, covering the greater part of Antiquity from the Archaic era up until the Early Middle Ages, exceeds the framework of archaic and legendary times. But it appears, as a whole, to be rather heterogeneous and springs from very different architectural systems and contexts [1].

An architectural family of Greek tradition

Nevertheless, within this ensemble one can distinguish no less than a dozen shipwrecks that belong to a well-defined Greek context dating from the sixth to fourth centuries BC. Their characteristics allow for the definition of a true architectural family growing out of a shared tradition of naval construction, the evolution of which can be followed over several centuries until the final disappearance of sewn shipbuilding to the advantage of construction using mortise-and-tenon joints. Such a processes is rather rare and could be undertaken only in this single case for all the history of the naval construction of the ancient Mediterranean. The fact deserves to be underlined and retained as example on the methodological level.

It is on the ancient wreck *Bon-Porté 1* (Saint-Tropez, France) that this particular tradition of sewn boats was identified for the first time in 1981, in particular thanks to ethnographic comparisons coming from the Indian Ocean (Pomey, 1981). This technique was further clarified by the exceptional discovery of the shipwrecks *Jules-Verne 7* and *9* that led not only to a more precise definition of the characteristics but also to an understanding of the tradition's evolution (Pomey, 1995; 1997) (Fig. 1).

Discovered in Marseilles (France) in 1993, *Jules-Verne 7* and *9* are exceptional in that they simultaneously present, within a shared historical and chronological context, a remarkable example of the original technique of sewn assembly, represented by the wreck *Jules-Verne 9*, and the beginnings of the evolution of this

[1] For an overall study of the various traditions of sewn boats of Mediterranean Antiquity (Egypt included), one will refer to Marlier 2003 which is the only complete study on this subject.

Fig. 1 Overall picture of the wrecks *Jules-Verne 7* and *9* during excavation. In the foreground, on the right, the wreck *Jules-Verne 9*.
Photograph CCJ, CNRS, Aix-en-Provence.

technique with the introduction of elements of construction by mortise-and-tenon, illustrated by the wreck *Jules-Verne 7* (Pomey, 1998; 2001). Abandoned at the end of the sixth century BC, the ships were built at the beginning of the second half of that same century, certainly at Marseilles for the *Jules-Verne 9*, a largish coastal craft for local navigation, and probably also for *Jules-Verne 7*, a small trading ship that displayed the same construction marks (Pomey, 2003). Built by the second generation of the Greeks coming from Phocaea in Asia Minor to found Marseilles c. 600 BC, the two boats illustrated the ship construction techniques of Greek tradition as used in the Aegean Sea and especially in Phocaea.

From the characteristics of these two shipwrecks, it is possible to define an architectural family of Greek tradition and, within this tradition, several phases of evolution (Kahanov, Pomey, 2004; Pomey, 2010).

Phase 1 – Origins

Besides the shipwreck *Jules-Verne 9*, this "origins phase" is also represented by the *Giglio* (Bound, 1985; 1991), *Bon-Porté 1* (Joncheray, 1976; Pomey, 1981), *Pabuç Burnu* (Polzer, 2010) et *Cala Sant Vicenç* (Nieto, Santos, 2008) wrecks. All are dated to the sixth century BC. These wrecks, as a whole and in a complementary way, have a certain number of fundamental characteristics – referred to as architectural signatures or fingerprints (Pomey, Rieth, 2005) – which define a particular architectural system. This system refers in its turn to an architectural family whose filiations will be established through these signatures and their evolution. Starting from these wrecks, one can thus define a family of origin such as it appears

Fig. 2 Transversal section with a round bottom of the wreck *Jules-Verne 9*. Drawing by M. Rival, CCJ, CNRS, Aix-en-Provence.

in the sixth century BC[2].

This phase is mainly characterised by:

— a hull with rounded transversal section (Fig. 2);

— a keel without rabbet (found only at the extremities of the stem-and sternposts); the various elements of the axial timber (keel, stem-and sternposts) are assembled by a hook scarf with vertical key;

— a planking assembled by stitches running through oblique holes beginning from tetrahedral cavities, along with pre-assembly treenails (or tenons) (Fig. 3, 4);

— a watertightness of the assembling realized by fabric rollers coated with resin placed over the joints before the binding.

— widely spaced frames composed of floor timbers with futtocks, and alternating with top timbers;

— frame timbers lashed to the planking, showing a particular morphology characterised by a trapezoidal section whose narrow underside is regularly notched,

[2] We call "origin family", the oldest state which we can establish through the documentation we have. It is certain that this family, already elaborated at the architectural level, has much older origins; however, we are, for the moment, unaware of their characteristics.

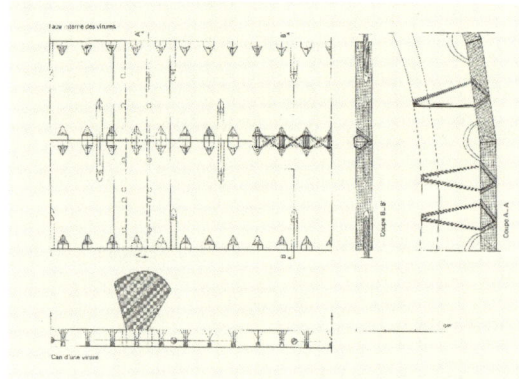

Fig. 3 Diagram of the assembly system by sewing and lashing of the wreck *Jules-Verne 9*. Drawing by M. Rival, CCJ, CNRS, Aix-en-Provence.

Fig. 4 Study model of the assembly system by sewing and lashing of the wreck *Jules-Verne 9*. Realization and photograph CCJ, CNRS, Aix-en-Provence.

allowing space for the planking seams, with flared flanks and a rounded upper side for a better tightening of the bonds;

— a mast step timber with multiple cavities fitted into the floor timbers;

— a hull covered with a resinous coating, inside and outside, for its protection and its watertightness.

Phase 2 – Transition

It is through the characteristics of the wreck *Jules-Verne 7*, compared to the wreck *Jules-Verne 9*, that this phase called "transition phase" could be identified and dated to the end of the sixth and the beginning of the fifth centuries BC. This can also be observed in the *Villeneuve-Bargemont/César 1* (Pomey, 2001), *Grand Ribaud F* (Long, Gantes, Rival, 2006; Pomey, 2006) and *Gela 1* (Panvini, 2001) wrecks. We now notice the appearance of construction with mortise-and-tenon joint within the tradition of sewn assembly. The morphological and technical characteristics of the original system are still clearly present and allow to firmly establish a filiation between these two groups of wrecks.

This phase is characterised by:

— a hull with rounded transversal section (Fig. 5);

— a keel with rabbets at either end and stem-and sternposts fully rabbeted; assemblies by a hook scarf with vertical key;

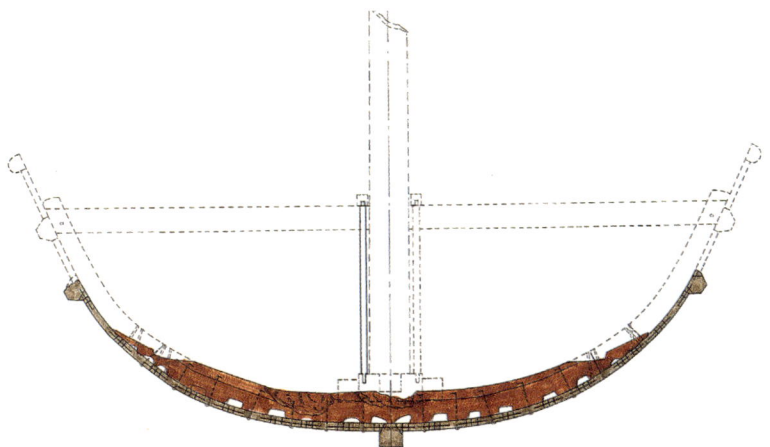

Fig. 5 Transversal section with a round bottom of the wreck *Jules-Verne 7*. Drawing by M. Rival, CCJ, CNRS, Aix-en-Provence.

Fig. 6 Detail of a tenon of assembly of the wreck *Jules-Verne 7*. Photograph CCJ, CNRS, Aix-en-Provence.

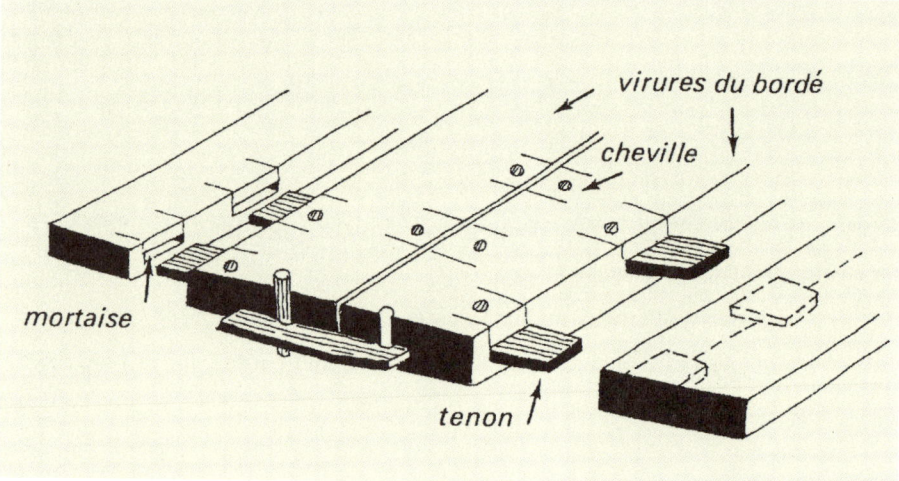

Fig. 7 Diagram of the mortise-and-tenon assembly system. Drawing by M. Rival, CCJ, CNRS, Aix-en-Provence.

— a planking principally assembled using mortise-and-tenon joints, where the use of sewing, similar to the former system, is limited to the ends of the strakes and to repairs (*Jules-Verne 9, Grand Ribaud F*) (Fig. 6, 7);

— a widely spaced frame of the same composition and morphology as before;

— frame timbers now nailed (clenched nails);

— beams attached to the ends of the floor timber futtocks;

— a mast step timber with multiple cavities fitted into the floor timbers and extended by keelsons at both ends;

— a hull covered with a resinous coating, inside and outside, for its protection and its watertightness.

In addition to the assemblies by sewing, the similarity of the section of hull and the architectural system confirms the membership of this group of wrecks to the family previously defined. It will be noted that the morphology of the frames, whose characteristics are due to the assembling by lashings, is preserved, whereas they are henceforth nailed. This is a matter of particularly strong architectural signature which confirms the force of the family tradition.

Phase 3 – Evolution

Dated to the second half of the fifth century BC, this "evolution phase" is essentially exemplified by the *Gela 2* (Panvini, 2001) and *Ma'agan Mikhael* wrecks (Linder, Kahanov, 2003; 2004). The evolution is most notably seen in the morphology, and the use of sewing is merely residual. Nevertheless, the relationship with the past is clearly evident in the survival of certain characteristics which, though not very distinct, are still present.

With reference to the Ma'agan Mikhael wreck, this phase is characterised by:

— a transversal section evolving to a sharp bottom, shaped like a wine glass, with a curving garboard strakes (Fig. 8);

— a keel with no rabbets except at the extremities and stem-and sternposts fully rabbeted;

— a planking assembled essentially by mortise-and-tenon joint;

— residual sewing, of the same principle as before, only on the deadwood extremities and on repairs;

— a frame as before, widely spaced, nailed to the planking (clenched nails), the morphology of which is moving towards a rectangular section, and where the notches of the foot disappear;

— beams attached to the ends of the floor timber futtocks;

— deadwood reinforcement of the extremities;

— a mast step timber with multiple cavities fitted into the floor timbers and extended by keelsons at both ends.

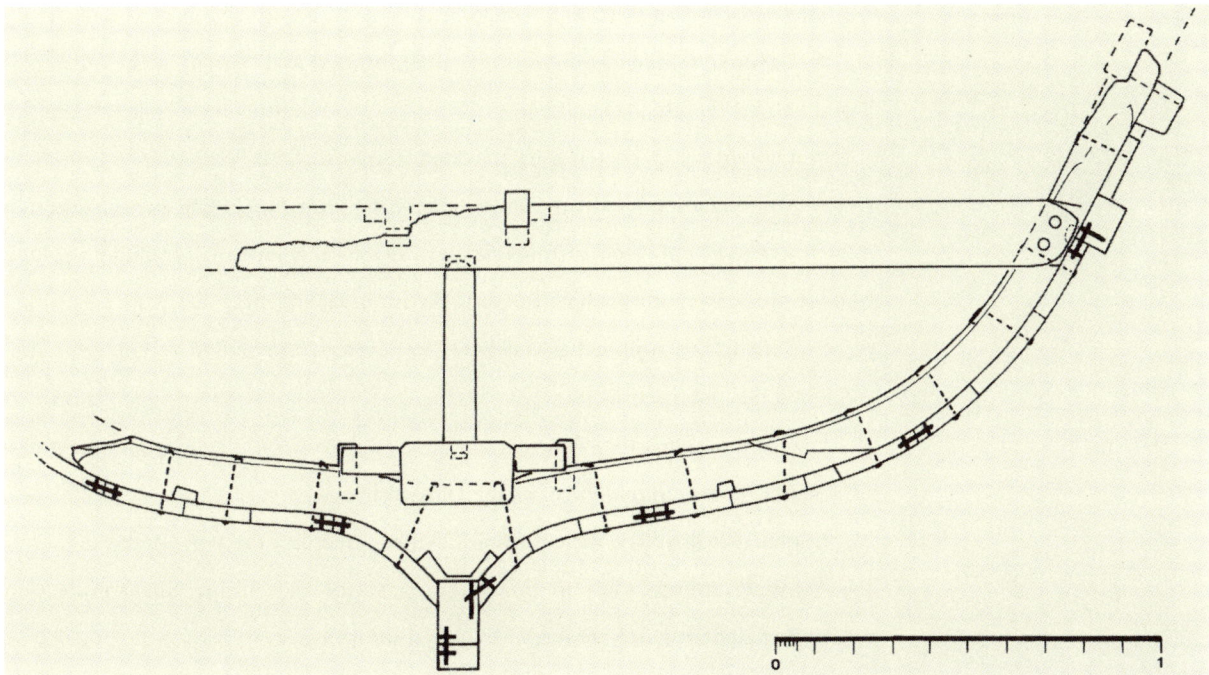

Fig. 8 Transversal section with a sharp bottom (wine glass section) of the wreck *Ma'agan Michael*. Drawing by J. Roslof-Y. Kahanov (Linder, Kahanov, 2003).

— a hull covered with a resinous coating, inside and outside, for its protection and its watertightness.

If the sewing decreases and if the morphology of the hull and the frame has evolved, the characteristics of the sewing system, with tetrahedral cavities, and of the architectural system, in particular of the frame, always confirms the filiation of this group and its membership of the same family.

Phase 4 – Final phase

This "final phase", represented by the *Kyrenia* shipwreck from the end of the fourth century BC (Steffy 1985, 1994), appears as the final outcome of an evolution within the architectural family of Greek sewn boats that sees the introduction of a mortise-and-tenon assembly technique. At the end of this evolution of two centuries, the principal original characteristics have finally disappeared to be replaced by new characteristics; however, the connecting thread is evident thanks to the different intermediary stages. It is noteworthy that the presence of a ceiling plank re-used from a hull plank that had originally been sewn confirms the connection.[3]

The new characteristics are:

— a transversal section displaying a sharp bottom and curving garboard strakes shaped like a wine glass (Fig. 9);

— a completely rabbeted keel, stem-and sternposts;

— planking assembled with mortise-and-tenon joints, including any repairs;

— a frame composed of floor timbers alternating with half-frames – evolved from top timbers – and of which the futtocks are independent.

— The frame timbers, rectangular in section, are nailed (clenched nails, hammered through treenails);

— beams attached to wales;

— deadwood reinforcement of the extremities;

— a mast step timber with multiple cavities fitted into the floor timbers;

— a hull covered with a resinous coating, inside and outside, for its protection and its watertightness and reinforced by a lead sheathing.

The evolution of the hull shape, of the architectural system (half-frames evolved from the top timbers), and of the components morphology is the direct result of

---

[3] Personal communication of J.R. Steffy. On the re-employments in the hull, see also Steffy 1985, p. 95.

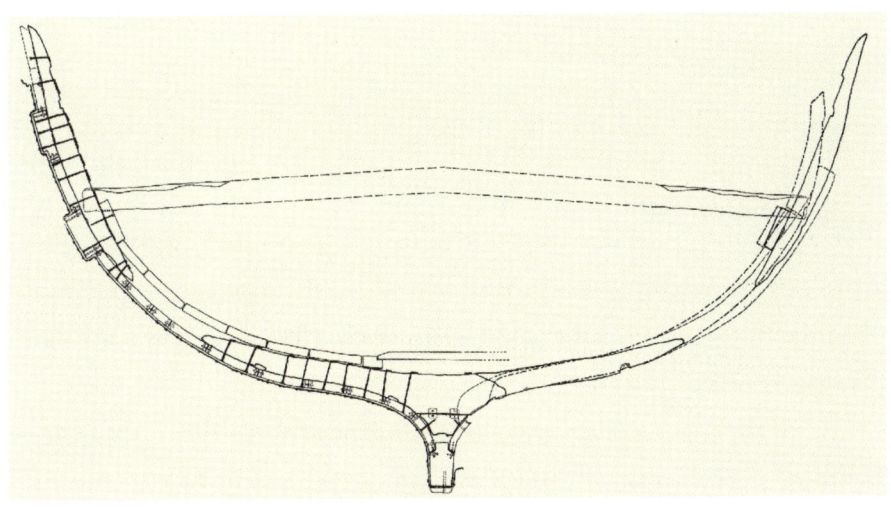

Fig. 9   Transversal section with a sharp bottom (wine glass section) of the wreck *Kyrenia*. Drawing by J. R. Steffy (1994)

the previous evolution. Without the intermediate stages, and the evolution of the architectural signatures followed in the previous phases, the filiation of the *Kyrenia* wreck with the family of the sewn boats would have been difficult to establish. This lineage is nevertheless assured.

At the same time, this evolution led to a new logic of construction that allows us to consider the *Kyrenia* ship as the beginnings of a new architectural system based upon assembling using mortise-and-tenon joints, that would be successfully adopted throughout the Mediterranean. Indeed, this new system which one can qualify, according to the expression of J.R. Steffy (1995), of "mortise-and-tenon" construction, will become a characteristic of Punic and Greco-Roman ship construction until the end of Antiquity.

A family with a long future

This architectural family that we have been able to follow over almost three centuries, from the beginning of the sixth to the end of the fourth century BC, is part of a well-established Greek, and notably Aegean, context. Moreover, given the increasing number of discoveries, this architectural family today appears as the dominant example of Greek naval architecture in the Archaic and Classical periods.

Its final evolution will be rich in possibilities. By increasing the solidity and longevity of the construction by replacing fragile sewing with tenons, it became possible to increase considerably the dimensions and tonnage of ships, to conceive hulls of more elaborate shape and to build new and more diversified types of shipping better adapted to different functions. It is probable that the development of the Greek trieres and their introduction into the Greek fleets, towards the end of the sixth century BC, is due to this evolution. In the same way, the formidable expansion of the ancient naval construction of the Hellenistic time is the direct consequence of the use of the "mortise-and-tenon" construction (Pomey, 2009).

As for the origins of this evolution, is to be found in the influence exerted by Phoenician naval construction, which seems to be where the technique of mortise-and-tenon assembly began. The latter point is attested, starting in the Bronze Age, by the *Ulu Burun* shipwreck from the end of the fourteenth century BC, of very probable Near Eastern provenance (Pomey, 1997; Kahanov, Pomey, 2004; Pomey, Rieth, 2005: 157-163).

One sees how much the analysis of specific architectural signatures, that reveal the fundamental characteristics of ship architecture, is important to define the architectural families. If they evolve with the time and under various influences, all these signatures do not evolve at the same speed, which makes it possible to follow the general evolution. At the same time, it is necessary to be able to have sufficient wrecks distributed in time to follow these evolutions. For the moment the possibilities are still limited in the field of Mediterranean Antiquity and are illustrated primarily by this Greek boat family. It remains to be hoped, in the future, that this Greek model can be applied to other families.

References

Bound, Mensun, 1985, "Early observation on the Construction of the Pre-Classical Wreck at Campese Bay, Island of Giglio: Clues to the Vessel's Nationality", in S. McGrail, E. Kentley(eds.), *Sewn Plank Boats*, Oxford (BAR Int. Series 276): 49-65.

Bound, Mensun, 1991, *The Giglio Wreck: A Wreck of the Archaic period (c. 600 BC) off the Tuscan Island of Giglio. An Acount of its Discovery and excavation: A review of the Main Finds*, Athens, (Enalia Supplement 1).

Casson, Lionel, 1963, "Sewn boats", *The Classical Review* III: 257-259.

Joncheray, Jean-Pierre, 1976, "L' épave grecque ou étrusque de Bon Porté", *Cahiers d'Archéologie Subaquatique* V: 5-36.

Kahanov, Yaakovand Pomey, Patrice, 2004, "The Greek Sewn Shipbuilding Tradition and the *Ma'agan Mikhael* Ship: A Comparison with Mediterranean parallels from the Sixth to the Fourth Centuries BC", *The Mariner's Mirror* 90/1: 6-28.

Linder, Elisha and Kahanov Yaakov, 2003, *The Ma'agan Mikhael ship. The Recovery of a 2400-Year-Old Merchantman. Final Report*, Haifa, vol. I.

Linder, Elisha and Kahanov Yaakov, 2004, *The Ma'agan Mikhael ship. The Recovery of a 2400-Year-Old Merchantman. Final Report*, Haifa, vol. II,

Long, Luc, Gantes, Lucien-François and Rival, Michel, 2006, "L'épave Grand Ribaud F. Un chargement de produits étrusques du début du Ve siècle avant J.-C.", *Gli Etruschi da Genova ad Ampurias, Atti del XXIV Convegno di Studi Etruschi ad Italici, Marseille-Lattes 2002*, Pise, Rome: 455−495.

Marlier, Sabrina, 2003, *Systèmes et techniques d'assemblage par ligatures dans la construction navale antique méditerranéenne*, thèse de doctorat sous la direction de P. Pomey, Université de Provence, Aix-Marseille I, (inédit).

Nieto, Xavier and Santos, Maria, 2008, *El Vaixell grec arcaic de cala Sant Vicenç*, Girona (Monografies del Centre d'Arqueologia Subaquàtica de Catalunya 7).

Panvini, Rosalba, 2001, *La nave greca arcaica di Gela (e primi dati sul secondo relitto greco)*, Palermo.

Polzer, Mark, 2010, "The VIth-Century B.C. Shipwreck at Pabuç Burnu, Turkey. Evidence for Transition from Lacing to Mortise-and-Tenon Joinery in Late Archaic Greek Shipbuilding", in P. Pomey (ed.), *Transferts technologiques en architecture navale méditerranéenne de l'Antiquité aux temps modernes: identité technique et identité culturelle, Actes de la Table Ronde d'Istanbul, mai 2007*, Varia Anatolica XX, Institut Français d'Etudes Anatoliennes, Istanbul: 27−44.

Pomey, Patrice, 1981, "L'épave de Bon Porté et les bateaux cousus de Méditerranée", *The Mariner's Mirror* 67/3: 225−243.

Pomey, Patrice, 1985, "Mediterranean sewn boats in Antiquity", S. McGrail, E. Kentley (eds.) *Sewn Plank Boats*, Oxford (BAR Int. Series 276): 35−48.

Pomey, Patrice, 1995, "Les épaves grecques et romaines de la place Jules-Verne à Marseille", *Compte rendu Académie Inscriptions et Belles-Lettres*, avril-juin: 459−484.

Pomey, Patrice, 1997, "Un exemple d'évolution des techniques de construction navale antique: de l'assemblage par ligatures à l'assemblage par tenons et mortaises", in D. Garcia, D. Meeks (eds.), *Techniques et économie antiques et médiévales. Le Temps de l'innovation. Colloque d'Aix-en-Provence (mai 1996)*, Paris: 195−203.

Pomey, Patrice, 1998, "Les épaves grecques du VIe siècle av. J.-C. de la place Jules-Verne à Marseille", in P. Pomey, E. Rieth (eds.), *Construction navale maritime et fluviale. Approches archéologique, historique et ethnographique. Actes du 7e Colloque International d'Archéologie navale (7th ISBSA), île Tatihou 1994*, (Archaeonautica, 14, 1998), Paris: 147-154.

Pomey, Patrice, 2001, "Les épaves grecques archaïques du VIe s. av. J.-C. de Marseille: épaves Jules-Verne 7 et 9 et César 1", in H. Tzalas (ed.), *Tropis VI, 6th International Symposium on Ship Construction in Antiquity, Lamia 1996 proceedings*, Athens: 425−437.

Pomey, Patrice, 2003, "Reconstruction of Marseilles 6th century BC Greek ships", in C. Beltrame (ed.), *Boats, Ships and Shipyards. Proceedings of the IXth International Symposium on Boat and Ship Archaeology, Venice 2000*, Oxford, Oxbow Books: 57−65.

Pomey, Patrice, 2009, "L'influence des techniques navales sur le contexte économique de la Grèce à la fin de l'époque archaïque", in M. Wissa (ed.), *The Knowledge Economy and Technological Capabilitie. Egypt, the Near East ans the Mediterranean 2nd millennium B.C.-1st millenium A.D.*, Barcelone, (Aula Orientalis, Supplementa, 26), 2009: 123−140.

Pomey, Patrice, 2010, "De l'assemblage par ligatures à l'assemblage par tenons et mortaises. Introduction", in P. Pomey (ed.), *Transferts technologiques en architecture navale* méditerranéenne de l'Antiquité aux temps modernes: identité technique et identité culturelle, Actes de la Table Ronde d'Istanbul, mai 2007, Varia Anatolica XX, Institut Français d'Etudes Anatoliennes, Istanbul:15−26.

Pomey, Patrice and Rieth, Eric, 2005, *L'Archéologie navale*, Paris (Errance).

Steffy, J. Richard, 1985, "The Kyrenia Ship: An Interim Report on its Hull Construction", *American Journal of Archaeology* 89: 71−101.

Steffy, J. Richard, 1994, *Wooden Ship Building and the Interpretation of Shipwrecks*, College Station, Texas A&M University Press.

Steffy, J. Richard, 1995, "Ancient scantlings: The projection and control of Mediterranean hull shapes", in H. Tzalas (ed.), *Tropis III, 3rd International Symposium on Ship Construction in Antiquity, Athens 1989 proceedings*, Athens: 417−428.

Wrecks and Nautical Archaeology of Inland Waters: New Perspectives of Research. The Example of the 15th Century Wreck EP1-Canche (Pas-de-Calais, France)

内陆水域的沉船与船舶考古学研究新视角：
以法国加莱海峡省15世纪沉船康什河EP1为例

Eric RIETH

(CNRS-LAMOP; Musée national de la Marine, France)

埃里克·李特

（法国国家科学研究中心–巴黎西方中世纪文化实验室；法国国家海事博物馆）

Translation / Richard BARKER

理查德·巴克 译

ABSTRACT / The excavation of wrecks in inland waters, and in particular in rivers, has advanced in Europe since the years 1970s. It arises from a field of research somewhat different from that of the underwater excavation of sea-going shipwrecks. The particularities of archaeological problems, of methods of excavation and of the study of wrecks situated in inland waters are connected to the importance of the role of the environment. All the dimensions constituting the functional realities of these spaces as natural and managed environments – axes of communication and of exchange, sites of exploitation of the halieutic riches of fisheries, and for the utilisation of hydraulic energy – need to be taken into account, and envisaged in relation to the whole "nautical functional system". The fifteenth century wreck EP1-Canche (Pas-de-Calais, France) will be presented as an example of such inland excavations.

KEY WORDS / Nautical archaeology; underwater archaeology; inland shipbuilding; cultural maritime landscape; North France

内容摘要 /

20世纪70年代以来，欧洲内陆水域特别是在河流水域的沉船考古发掘，有了长足的发展。它起源于田野研究，与海底沉船水下考古发掘略有不同。内陆水域沉船的考古学问题以及发掘和研究方法，其特殊性在于与周边环境有着密不可分的关系。所有与自然或人为环境相关的功能性空间都需要纳入考虑范围并设想其与整个"船舶功能体系"存在联系，诸如交流与交易中心、渔场开发区域、水力资源利用点等。在法国加莱海峡省发现的15世纪沉船康什河EP1就是内水发掘的一个典型案例。

关键词：

船舶考古　水下考古　内陆造船　海洋文化景观　法国北部

Introduction

The excavation of wrecks of inland vessels, both underwater and in a wet environment, has been progressively developed in France from the years 1975–1985, and arises from a field of research somewhat different from that of the underwater excavation of the wrecks of sea-going ships envisaged principally, even exclusively, as "closed" archaeological sites. These latter are studied, classically, according to three principal historical perspectives defined by Keith Muckelroy from 1978 (Muckelroy, 1978: 215–225): as "machines", at the same time architectural structures and technical systems, as "functional assemblages" in relationship with the activities of commerce, of war, of fisheries, and as "living space" for a population of several hundreds of individuals in the case of a warship of the modern era. According to these three historical perspectives, the excavation is carried on within the limits of a "closed" site, on the architectural vestiges of the hull, on the preserved elements of the rigging, on the cargo, on the artillery, on the ballast, or even on the furniture on board...

The wrecks of boats of inland navigations, even the smallest vessels, and also of sea-going vessels found in rivers, are studied in the same way, but at a very different scale however, from that of a Chinese war junk of the 15th century, of a Portuguese carrack of the 16th century or of a vessel of the VOC of the 18th century, as a "machine" and a "functional system". From these points of view, wrecks of sea-going ships and of inland navigations do not constitute fundamentally distinct objects of study. The wrecks of boats from inland navigations are however more rarely studied as "living space", the time spent aboard a boat in the course of inland navigation offering much more reduced evidence than that arising from the time passed on a ship during a maritime, and especially an oceanic, navigation, without any contact with the land for revictualling of food and water, in particular.

There is another difference, much more fundamental from the scientific point of view, between wrecks located at sea and those situated in inland waters. Indeed, these latter present a certain number of particularities at the level of archaeological problems arising, and principally of the methods of excavation, connected to the importance of the role and the influence of the environment – river bed and banks – on the boats, which puts these wrecks, unlike those situated at sea, into a "continental" context, of "open" archaeological sites.

1. State of the problem

Some few French researchers, essentially pre-historians, have since the 19th century been interested in logboats. In 1867 for example, Gabriel de Mortillet published in Paris a small book entitled *Origine de la navigation et de la pêche* [Origin of navigation and of fishing] in which he described a certain number of logboats found in France and elsewhere. Such studies remained, however, exceptions.

Nevertheless, discoveries of logboats were very numerous in France. An effort to make an inventory (Cordier, 1963; 1972), published in 1963 and completed in 1973, listed 98 of them. Since then this number has increased greatly. A precise number is difficult to propose to the extent that either certain discoveries have only resulted in brief mention in regional journals, or that numerous discoveries have remained unstudied or unpublished (and in some cases there is doubt as to whether finds were in fact boats). The most recent inventory established in 2004 identified 314 logboats discovered on French territory (Laurent, 2004). Today, the real number of these wrecks of vessels, of all sizes and states of preservation, is without doubt around 350.

Until recently these logboats constituted the sole archaeological vestiges holding the attention of researchers concerned with fluvial archaeology. Most often, the wrecks were studied from a strictly technical point of view. The functional aspects, in relation to a particular economic context, but equally in connection with a specific natural environment, were rarely taken into account[1].

It is from the years 1975–1980 that a definition of fluvial archaeology as a field of research wholly set apart has been elaborated. This development has occurred in parallel with the development of *Waterfront Archaeology* (a first colloquium held in London, 1979), and its archaeological problems centred around the vestiges

[1] See, for example: Rieth 2003.

(quays, jetties, wrecks...) and the environmental context connecting, positively or negatively, the activities of the waterborne populations to those of the urban and rural populations.

It was no longer only the means of water transport and the management of the banks of watercourses in urban and rural contexts that were studied, but the entirety of the archaeological and paleo-environmental material evidence, connected to the fluvial environment as much as it is to nautical spaces. Thus all the dimensions constituting the functional realities of these spaces as natural and managed environments, as axes of communication and of exchange, sites of exploitation of the halieutic riches of fisheries, and for the utilisation of hydraulic energy were taken into account. Besides, each of these functions was hereafter envisaged in relation to the whole "functional system". No longer was it, for example, only the isolated vestiges of a fluvial fishery that were the subject of an analysis, but the integrality of the identifiable data associated with that fishery – the geomorphological modifications of the river to the consequences, from the point of view of the conditions of navigation, resulting from the driving of stakes and piles in the river bed – that ought to be taken into consideration.

This evolution of the definition of fluvial archaeology[2] has been interpreted by a double mutation, from the thematic and methodological point of view, leading from an archaeology of structures (wrecks, jetties, fisheries, groynes, fords, dams...) to an archaeology of the relationships between structures and fluvial spaces (the river bed and the banks) (Rieth, 1998; 2006).

2. Boats and the fluvial environment

Unlike the maritime space, the fluvial environment is one limited in the longitudinal sense (upstream, downstream), transverse (left bank, right bank), and vertical (depth of water). These different limitations of the fluvial environment are translated into severe constraints on the architecture (dimensions, proportions, morphology, structure) of boats. Three important facts may be noted: these constraints, and notably those resulting from the depth and from the breadth of the river bed, are not stable. They evolve along the length of a watercourse, creating, as a function of the succession of shallows and deeps, with currents running at variable

---

[2] Ole Crumlin-Pedersen and Seán McGrail have greatly influenced our understanding of nautical archaeology of inland waters (or fluvial archaeology). See: Crumlin-Pedersen, 1996, 2010; McGrail, 1997.

speed, a succession of sectors of navigation, individual and more or less continuous, endowed with different navigabilities (Serna, 1996). Besides, these constraints also vary according to the accidents of climate: low water, high water and floods. All these constraints are similarly modified in the short term at the annual scale and in the long term at the scale of centuries.

The waterway as much as the natural environment thus has a complex history. The morphological, structural, and dimensional characteristics of the boats, adapted to the conditions of navigability, are the privileged indicators of that complex environmental history which archaeology tries to recover.

But the waterway is also an environment managed by man in conjunction with the two major functions of the stream and river: those of communication on the one hand and of exploitation of its energy and of its fisheries on the other.

Certain of these managements (groynes, dams...) are intended to improve the conditions of navigability by controlling the fluvial regime. Others (jetties, quays, slipways...) are carried out to the end of adapting the banks and beaches to rural and urban port activities. Still others are conceived to utilise the hydraulic power. These are the mills that multiplied from the Middle Ages. Finally, others serve as fish-traps, which were very important in feeding the western populations of the Middle Ages and the modern era because of the high number of fast (fish) days.

It is evident that that series of very varied managements of nature, similarly exercise a marked influence on the boats, be it in facilitating their navigation, or in hindering it.

In what manner is that organic relationship between the boats and the fluvial environment translated in terms of fluvial archaeology ?

3. Wrecks, fluvial environment and underwater archaeology

In the case of an isolated wreck, stranded or abandoned along a river bank, as in that of a group of wrecks, taking the environmental context into account leads to passing from an archaeology of the wreck or wrecks to an archaeology of a site or of a fluvial excavation. One again finds there this so important step leading from an archaeology of the structures to an archaeology of the relationships between structures and fluvial space underlined above.

Besides this extended position of the wrecks in the construction of the historical discourse on the knowledge of a fluvial territory and in the strategy of excavation it ought not to be forgotten that the wrecks of fluvial vessels, like the wrecks of sea-going vessels, ships for pilotage or for the high seas, fishing boats or cargo vessels are also bearers of a singular history which arises from the fields of the archaeology of techniques and of the history of naval architecture. We recall briefly here that every wreck, whether of logboat, extended logboat or plank-built architecture, once dated by measurements of radio-carbon age and dendrochronological analyses, is inscribed in a specific process of research, with its methods and problems arising, taking into account both its structure and its morphology as well as its functions. It is the whole of the operative chain leading to the conception of the boat, from both its architectural structure and technical system, to its use as a machine in relation with a defined environmental context and techno-economic environment, that one tries to define through the examination of archaeological data.

The broad approach to wrecks, both from the fluvial setting and from nautical archaeology corresponds to the methods of land archaeology. It is a matter of studying the vestiges, its hull, and perhaps its cargo. But it is also a question of associating with it a study of its geomorphological context inscribed within the topography, the alluvial deposits, the composition of the sediments, the distribution of the stratigraphic layers; knowledge of which is essential for the comprehension of the archaeological vestiges of the wreck. Besides, the archaeological vestiges, consisting to a great extent of elements of wood, are susceptible to permitting dendrochronological analyses in a double perspective: that, clearly, of specifying the dating of the remains; and that of reconstructing, at a technical and economic level (the supply economy of the shipyard), the utilisation of the materials, passing from the raw material to the wrought and transformed materiel.

In this perspective, such research can only be effected, before, during, and after the fieldwork phase, within the body of a multi-disciplinary team associating immediately, from the beginning of the programme, archaeologists specialising in the study of boats of inland navigations, and those for river management, but equally historians, dendrochronologists, geomorphologists, palynologists (pollen studies, etc). But questions arise. If this scientific course is taken to develop a nautical archaeology without interdisciplinary boundaries, does it not bring with it a confusion of disciplines?

Is there a risk that the introduction of too many diverse topics of research could lead to a superficial treatment, within the limitations of time-scale or of the costs of the project and its publication - even if the knowledge made available to all the participants is increased.

In reality, wishing to consider the archaeological facts globally does not signify effacing the differences at all. Each object of research involves its own knowledge and demands a specialisation on the part of the researcher. The history of the techniques of naval architecture, with its methods, its problems, its references, constitutes one of these specialisations - as equally are those of the fixed systems of fishing, of hydraulic equipments, of riparian landscape. Furthermore, each necessary specialism ought not to be involved as a closed scientific field, but rather, on the contrary, broadly open in respect of the other specialisms. Again, the dialogue with the other relevant specialisms of nautical archaeology ought to be established in advance of the research, even at the moment when the objectives of the programme of study are determined, and not after, when the excavation has been completed, at the stage of the analysis and interpretation of the archaeological data. The result of such a course, certainly difficult to conduct, imposes one demand: that of multidisciplinarity understood not as a tendency to dilute the knowledge, but rather the opposite, as a movement of convergence of knowledge within the framework of the shared perspectives of research.

It is in this corpus of nautical archaeology that the programme of underwater excavation of the wreck of the 15th Century EP1-Canche, chosen as the example, has been defined. It is certain, however, that the problems, methods and techniques applied in the case of this wreck and of this site in the north of France are transferable and adaptable, as a function of their historical and environmental specificities, to the rivers and streams of China and of South-East Asia.

4. The 15th-Century EP1-Canche Wreck (Pas-de-Calais, France)[3]

The wreck was discovered in 1989 by a local sports divers in the vicinity of the villages of Beutin and la Calotterie, around 5 kms upstream of the fishing port of Etaples-sur-Mer (Pas-de-Calais) (fig. 1). In the course of the summer of 1991, the site

[3] Rieth 2009, 2010, 2013; Rieth, Gaucher 2010; Rieth, Texier 2009.

Fig.1. Cartographic location of the wreck in the Canche, Beutin, Pas-de-Calais (France). (Credit: map IGN)

was the subject of pillage leading to the degradation of one extremity of the wreck and to a definitive loss of archaeological data, the nature and significance of which it is unhappily difficult to know precisely. It was necessary to wait a further ten years – until 2001 – for the first archaeological observations to begin, and to wait patiently for some years more – until 2005 – for the first of two campaigns of excavation for archaeological evaluation to begin, organised under my direction, with the limited purpose of evaluating the state of conservation of the remains, and of defining the overall characteristics of the wreck, and of collecting again archaeological samples intended to define the first radiocarbon dating, which placed the wreck chronologically between the middle of the 15th and the beginning of the 17th century. At the end of the second evaluation campaign a multi-year programme (2006–2010) had been elaborated, for research carried out with the technical and logistical collaboration of the Département des Recherches Archéologiques Subaquatiques et Sous-Marines (Ministry of Culture).

Description of the fluvial terrain of the Canche

Today, the wreck is situated in a 25m wide meander of the Canche (fig. 2). It is disposed across the bed, at a depth reckoned, according to the state of the river and the tides, as between 2.5 and 3.5m, between a relatively steep right bank, and a left bank of shallower slope (fig. 3). To the always strong current of the Canche is superposed the very noticeable alternating currents of the tide, which, at spring tides, is of more than a metre range, rendering the waters turbid. This contemporary landscape of the river corresponds to a relatively recent evolution of the Canche, connected, notably, to the modifications of the estuary and to its silting up on the one hand and to management of the river on the other (fig. 4). This river management, mostly dated to the modern era (17th–19th centuries), consists in particular of flood-banks on the land (2–3m broad and at least a metre high) intended

Fig.2. Aerial view of the site of the wreck in the Canche. The base for the excavation is located on the right bank, to the left of the image.
(Photo: Marine Nationale 35F/SP Le Touquet).

Fig.3. View of the whole site from the right bank. (Photo: E. Champelovier, Drassm/Ministère de la Culture).

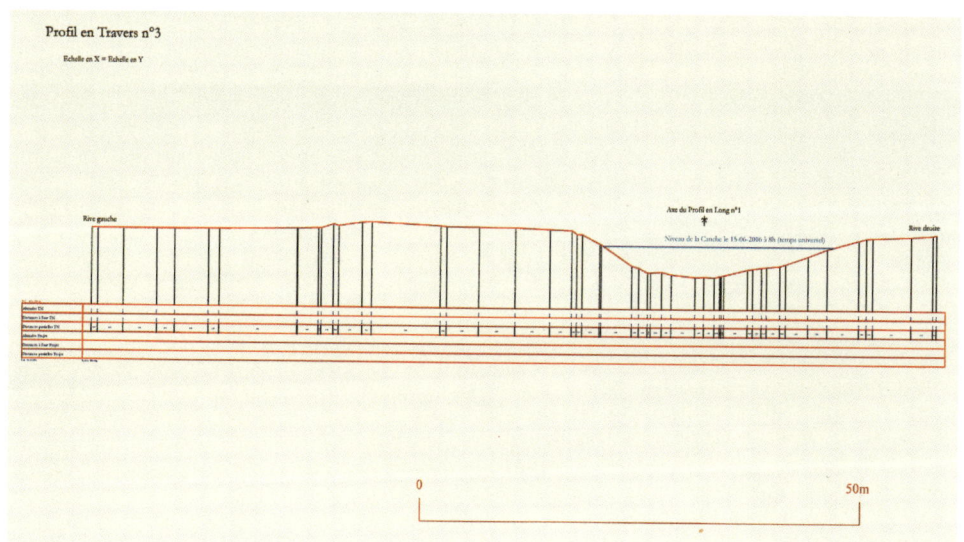

Fig.4. Transverse topographic section 3 at the position of the wreck(Topography and CAD: P. Texier, Inrap).

[4] Professor Alain Trentesaux, Adjunct Professor Eric Armynot du Châtelet (Laboratoire Géosystèmes, Université des Sciences et Technologies Lille 1, Lille).

for the creation of "polders" for agricultural purposes (cultivation and livestock). These flood-banks, still very discernible, have been one of the principal anthropological factors for modification of the fluvial landscape of the Canche.

Besides, the results of the analyses of the geological boreholes[4] have made apparent a succession of sedimentary beds indicative of the filling up of a vast estuary, transformed into a delta, threaded through by many channels, which would seem to have been much more open and maritime in the past than it has been since the modern era at least. It is doubtless in one of these channels that the wreck was originally situated, resting on a sand bank, of geologically marine formation. In the event, the conclusions of archival studies confirm that estuarial and maritime dimension of this lower reach of the Canche, the port of Montreuil-sur-Mer upstream of the site of the wreck having been, in the later Middle Ages contemporaneous with the wreck, a site qualifiable as an "interior sea-port", according to the topographic typology of maritime towns established by Jan Bill, or, in terms of transport geography, a fluvio-maritime port (Bill, 1999: 254).

It is as a function of this environmental approach (Serna, 2009) that the study of the EP1-Canche wreck has been developed, in a strict nautical archaeological perspective.

Description of the naval architecture

One fundamental preliminary datum is that of the dating of the wreck. The dendrochronological analyses[5] of the samples first lifted from the wreck and representative of the major structural elements (bottom, frames, side planking) of the hull have tended to date the felling of the oaks (*Quercus* sp.) between late 1425 and early 1426, with, in all probability, a setting to work on the wood in the course of 1426. The region of origin of the oaks remains unknown at present, as also is the date of abandonment or wrecking of the boat.

It is thus in the light of that dating that the architectural characteristics of the wreck are to be envisaged (fig. 5).

As regards the body of the hull (the central part), the flat bottom consists of five carvel strakes (fig. 6). While the three central strakes of 4 to 4.5cm thickness form a strictly horizontal plane, the two side strakes, in summary, are raised and their thickness increases up to 6cm. The absence of any keel, even of a proto-keel in the form of a thicker central strake (plank-keel), corresponds, at the structural and morphological level, to the characteristics of the flat-bottomed architecture of fluvial tradition. The rising of the outer strakes of the bottom on the other hand, can be interpreted as an adaptation of fluvial architecture to a fluvio-maritime nautical context, corresponding to the mode of use of the cargo boat on the Canche.

The floor timbers of 14-15cm moulded height and of 10-12cm sided thickness are connected with the flat bottom, provided with several quadrangular limber holes (fig. 7). In other quadrangular notches likewise worked in the floor timbers, laths are

[5] Catherine Lavier (Laboratoire d'Archéologie Moléculaire et Structurale —LAMS—, université Pierreet et Marie Curie, Paris), with the collaboration of Victoria Asensi Amoros (Société Xylodata, Paris).

Studies of Underwater Archaeology (Volume 2)

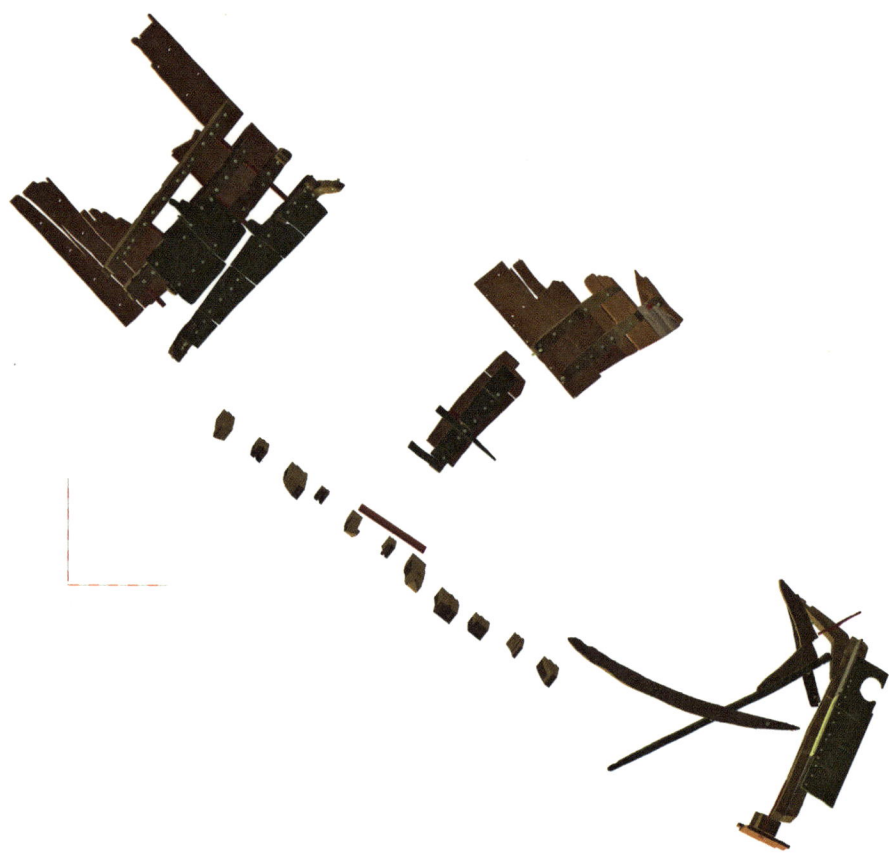

Fig. 5. Plan of the wreck. In the central zone of the wreck, only a part of the excavated remains is represented (Topography and CAD: P. Texier, Inrap).

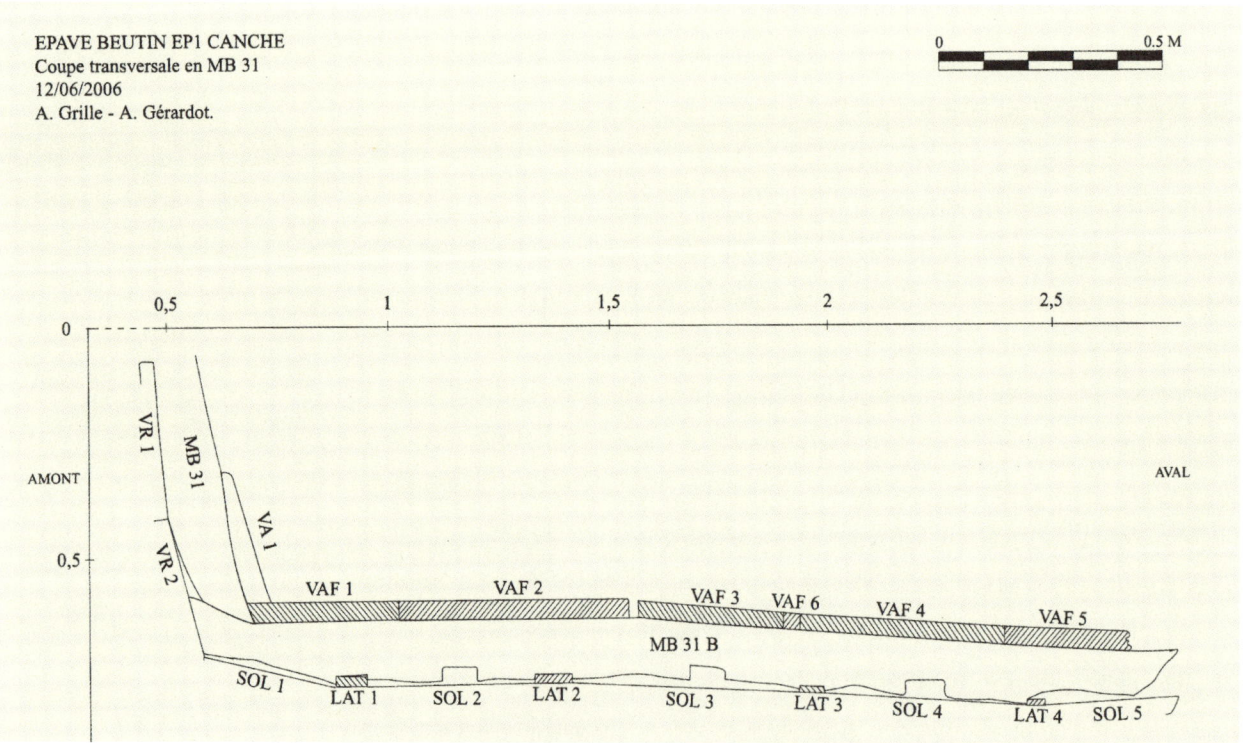

Fig.6. Transverse section in situ adjacent frame MB 31.

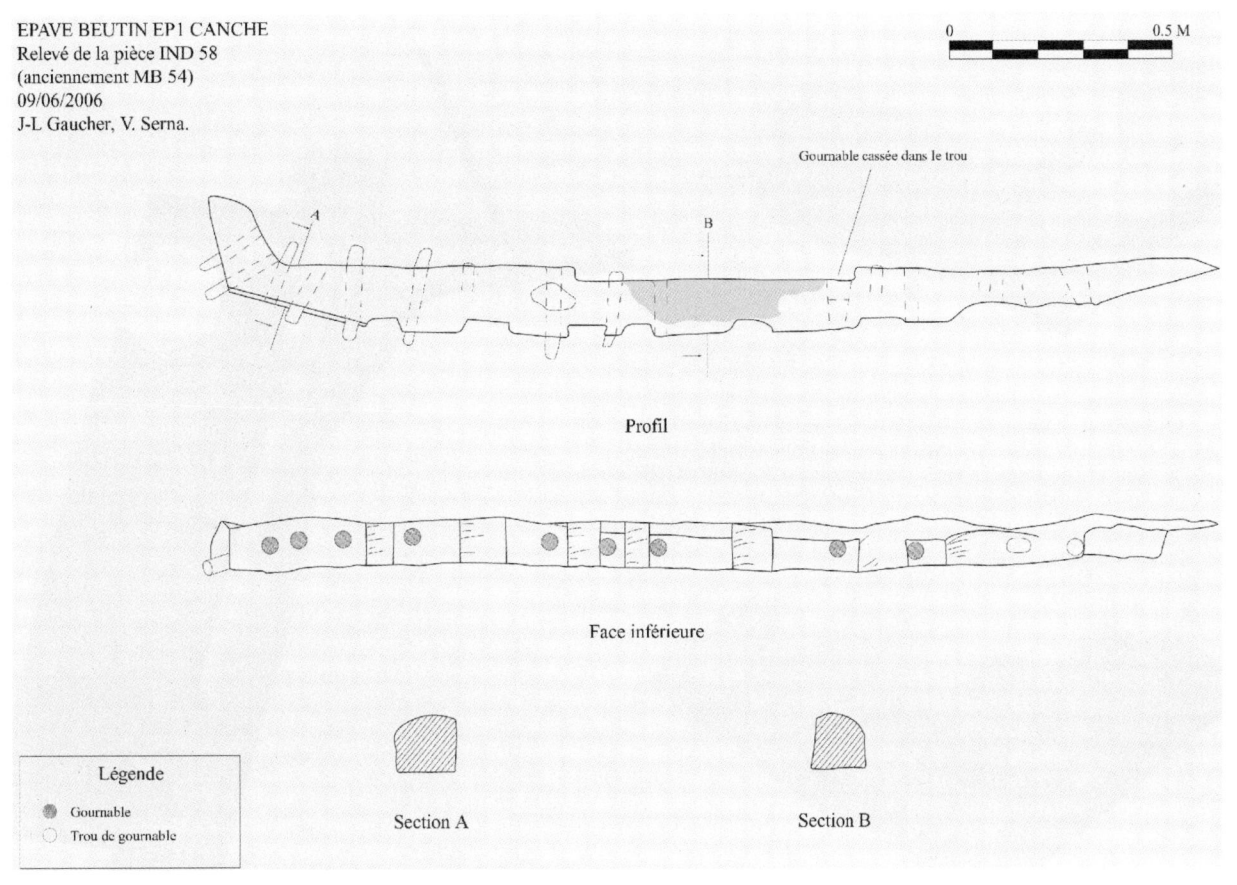

Fig.7. Drawing of floor timber IND 58.

nailed, covering fibres of flax (*Linum usitatissimum*) or of hemp (*Cannabis sativa*), serving to ensure, within the hull, the watertightness of the joints of the bottom strakes (fig. 8). We note that this method of making the joints watertight, called in French *palatrâge*, is characteristic of fluvial shipbuilding.

The connection between the bottom and the sides is made with a hard chine. In the body of the hull, the sides comprise four lifts of strakes, two lower rectilinear strakes disposed as carvel of 3.5cm average thickness, and two upper strakes, curved and re-entrant, disposed as overlapping clinker, of 4cm average thickness (fig. 9). The clinker assembly is secured by iron nails driven from the outside, whose points are clenched by turning over 90 degrees twice on the inside. The carvel and clinker planks are fixed to the frames principally by treenails. Towards the preserved extremity, corresponding in all probability to the stern of the boat, the nature of the side planking is modified, the whole of the planking being clinker thereafter.

Towards that same extremity of the hull which is terminated at a point on what in all likelihood is a sternpost, a beam (BX 2) is preserved in place, connected to the sides (fig. 10). This beam, 2.12m long, 18cm broad and 26cm deep, serves as a support to the end of a deck at the stern (fig. 11).

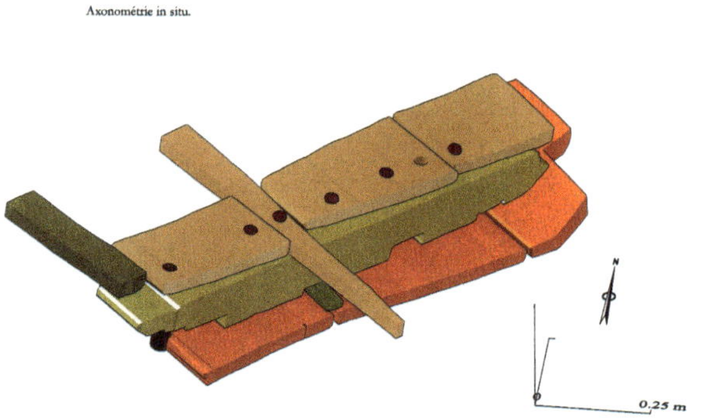

Studies of Underwater Archaeology (Volume 2)

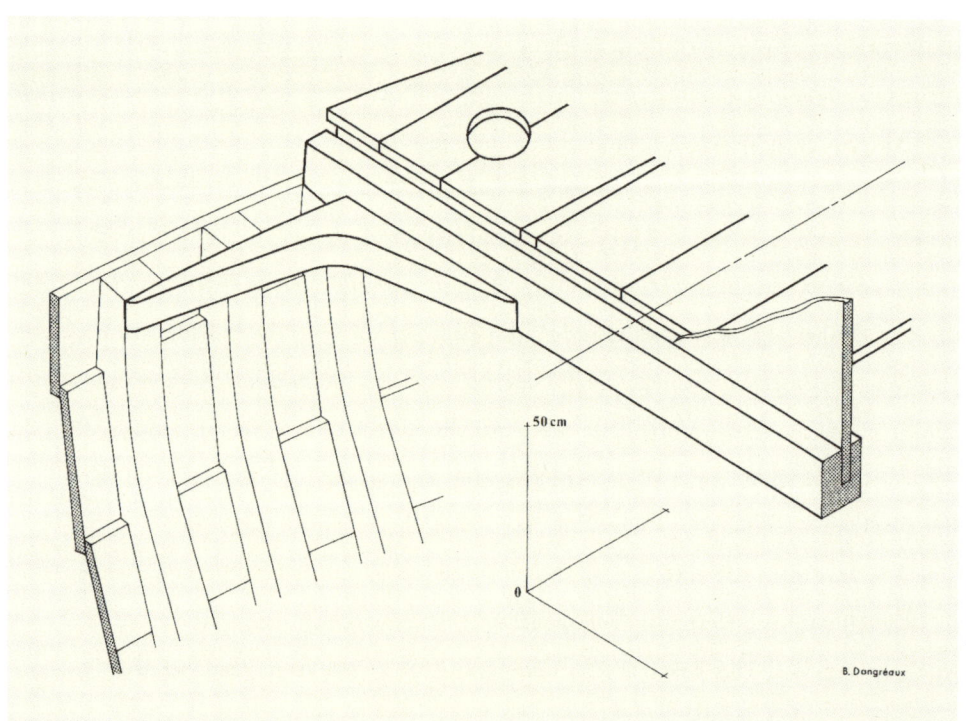

Fig.8. Orthogonal drawing from the fragment made adjacent frame MB 30. The seam lath (palâtre) of the flat bottom (sole) is visible at the left, at the right of the seam between the bottom strakes SOL 4 and SOL 3 (Survey and CAD: P. Texier, Inrap)

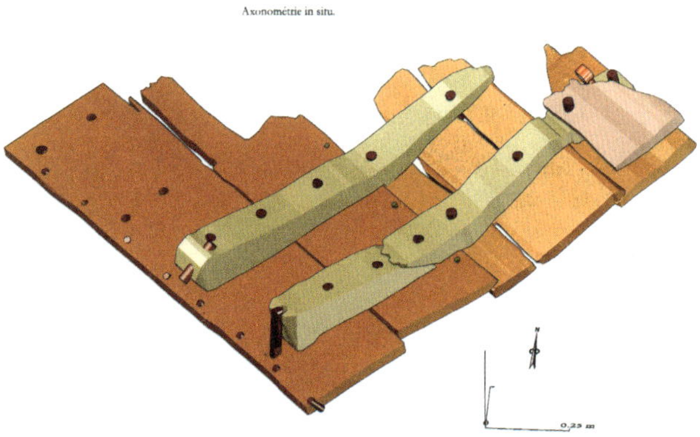

Fig.9. Fragment of the side planking forward in the vicinity of the futtocks MB31 and MB 30. (Survey and CAD: P. Texier, Inrap).

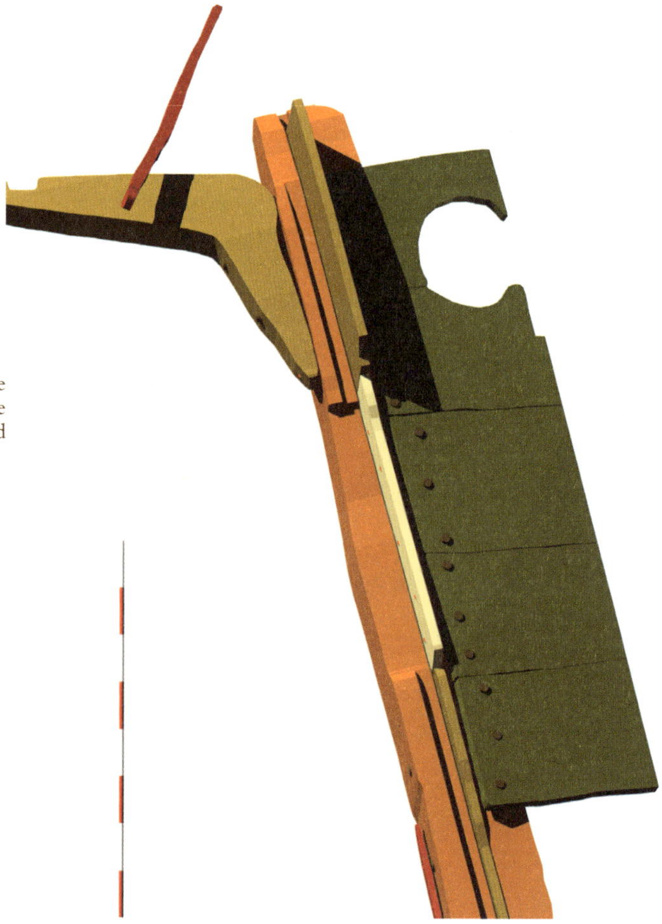

Fig.10. Isometric drawing of beam BX 2 (Survey and CAD: P. Texier, Inrap).

Fig. 11. Isometric reconstruction of the beam BX 2 and of the start of the decking at the stern by B.Dangréaux

Internally the hull includes bottom ceiling planking whose strakes are tree-nailed to the floor timbers, a single ceiling plank nailed to the futtocks above the bilge, a rounded fillet covering the lower corner of the ceiling planks, filling pieces pushed into the spaces between the futtocks at the top of the ceiling plank and a clamp built-in at the head of the futtocks.

Associated with the connected remains are disjointed and displaced elements, very likely the result of the pillage of the site. These pieces comprise floor timbers, futtocks and a beam (IND 62), fully preserved for a length of 2.3m and still possessing a connecting hanging knee, and a cleat on the upper part, a thwart 2.48m long (probably a mast partner), and a fragment of stem 1.33m long. Amongst the pieces situated towards the destroyed end of the hull (probably the bow of the boat), those corresponding to the floor timbers (especially floor timber IND 57) present several important characteristics, notably a diminution of the length and a rising of the outer ends of their horizontal part, which constitute the starting point of the futtocks of the sides (fig. 12).

This double morphological evolution is accompanied by another notable modification. The number of carvel strakes in the bottom is reduced in correlation with an increase in the number of clinker strakes in the sides. This increase in the number of clinker strakes in the sides is confirmed by other isolated pieces of carpentry of which two futtocks (notably futtock IND 69) are provided with 4 lands to fit against 5 clinker strakes (fig. 13).

A first approach to the restitution of the forms and dimensions of the hull has been achieved by making use, notably, of the construction of a series of study-models – five at the present stage of research – at a scale of 1:15 (Rieth, Gaucher 2010). One of the models using moulds and ribbands has thus represented the general evolution of the forms from the central zone of the hull, close to the master section, and the necessary closure of the sides on a stem and sternpost at the extremities (fig. 14-15).

At the position of the master-frame, the principal dimensions reconstructed for the hull are of the order 2.25m for the internal breadth of the flat bottom, 2.65m for the upper breadth, 1.15m for the depth to the ceiling, and 1.4m for the external height (fig. 16-18). As a function of the data presently collected, the first hypotheses advanced place the original total length of the hull around 14m, with a significant

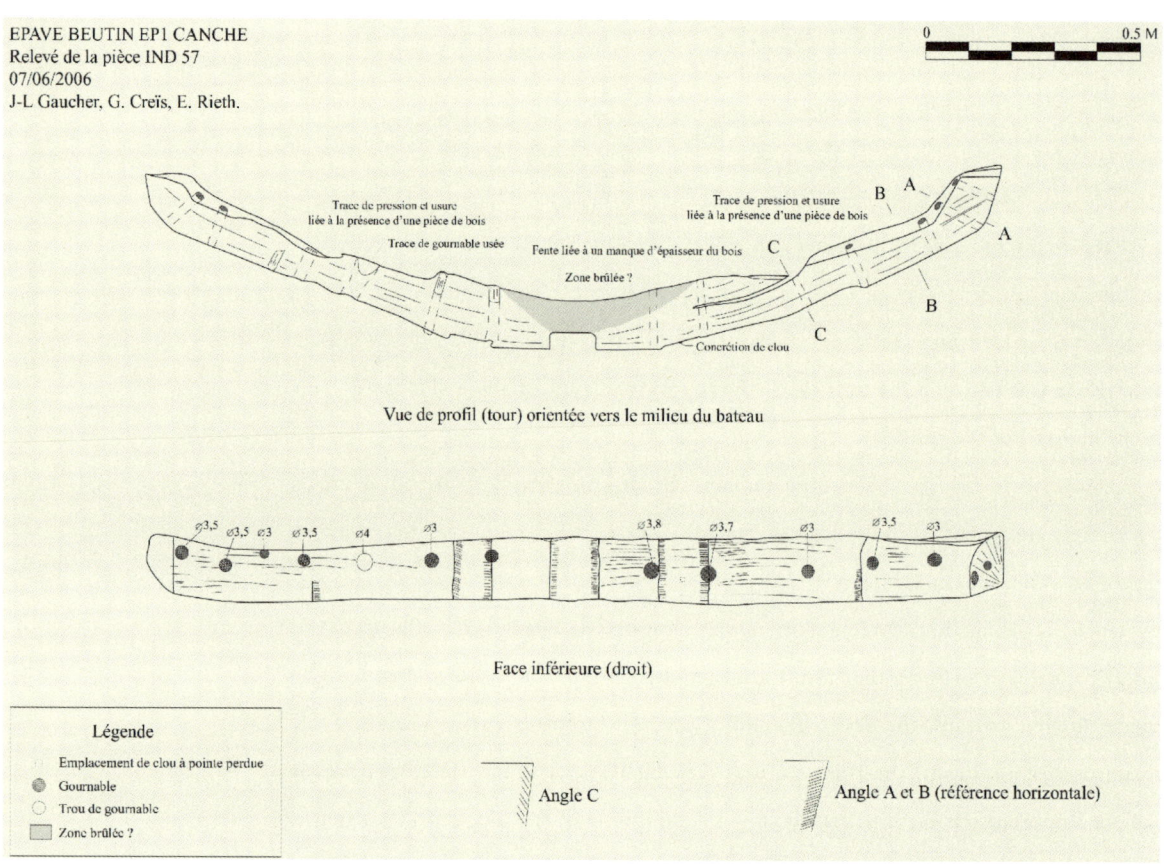

Fig.12. Drawing of the displaced rising floor timber IND 57.

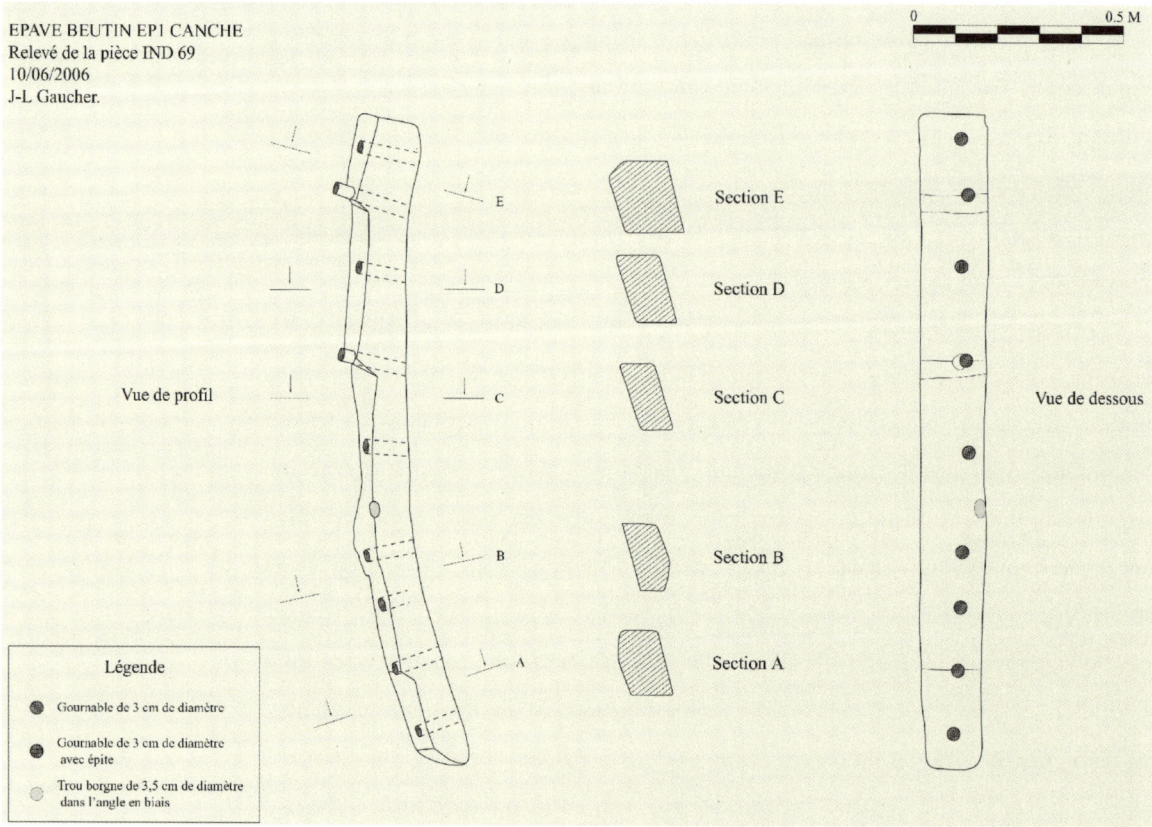

Fig.13. Drawing of the displaced futtock IND 69.

Fig. 14. Model (scale 1: 15) with moulds and ribbands by J.-L. Gaucher (Photo: J.-L. Gaucher).

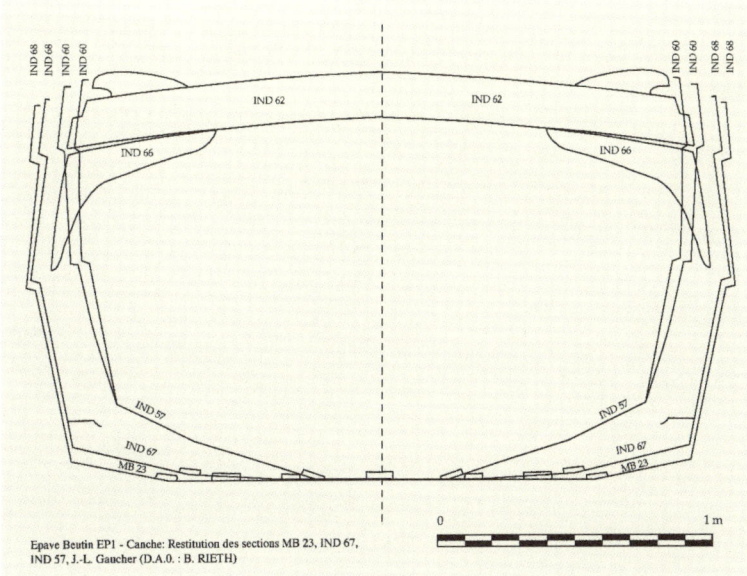

Fig. 15. Reconstruction of several transverse sections showing the rising and the reduction of the breadth of the floor timbers (Credit: drawing J.-L. Gaucher).

length/breadth ratio of 5.3, which appears to be indicative of a geometry of forms more fluvial than maritime in conception.

Several hypotheses of reconstruction are possible for the processes of flat-bottom construction of the hull, in relation to the central part. It is possible that a few straight floor timbers were first added to the assembled bottom strakes, but it is not known how the ends would be prepared to be compatible with the garboards. The procedural differences are then situated at the start of construction of the sides. The garboard strakes, in two pieces scarphed together, show some evidence of temporary fastenings to the outer bottom strakes. Temporary chocks and props were presumably used during the adjustments, but leave no evidence. In the present state of advance of the research, it cannot be determined whether one or more L-shaped floor-futtock timbers (with straight side-arms just long enough to be connected to the second strakes) were in place as moulds while the garboards were adjusted, or were only added after the garboards. The second carvel strakes of the sides would be placed after a number of the floor-futtock timbers were securely fastened to the garboards, in the central part. The introduction of curvature in the rising ends of the carvel strakes, and throughout the clinker strakes, was probably done with temporary props, tongs and fastenings, with timbers only fitted to the result.

A coaster of the cog family

The reconstructed length of the EP1-Canche wreck, and its moderate breadth and depth in relation to its length, would place the boat from the Canche within a

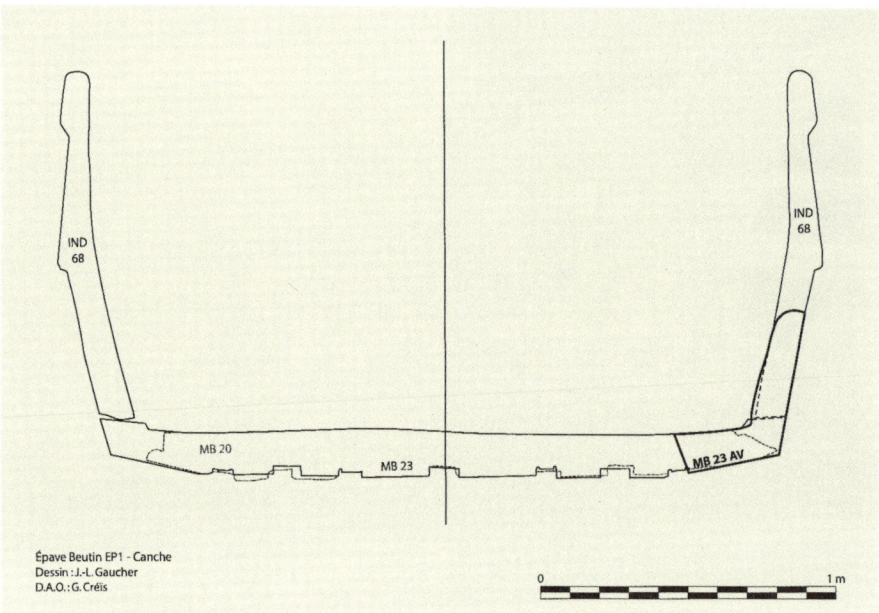

Fig. 16. Reconstruction of the midship section in the vicinity of frame MB 23 (Credit: drawing J.-L. Gaucher).

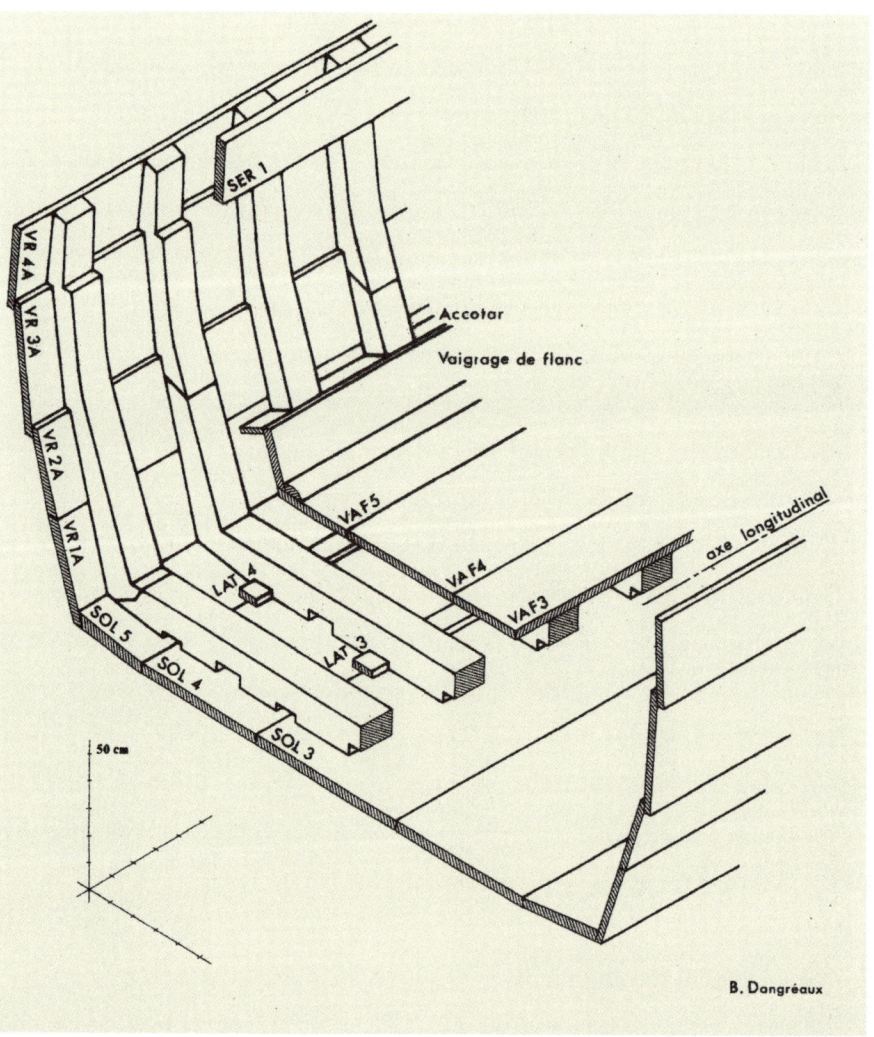

Fig.17. Isometric reconstruction of the central part of the hull by B.Dangréaux.

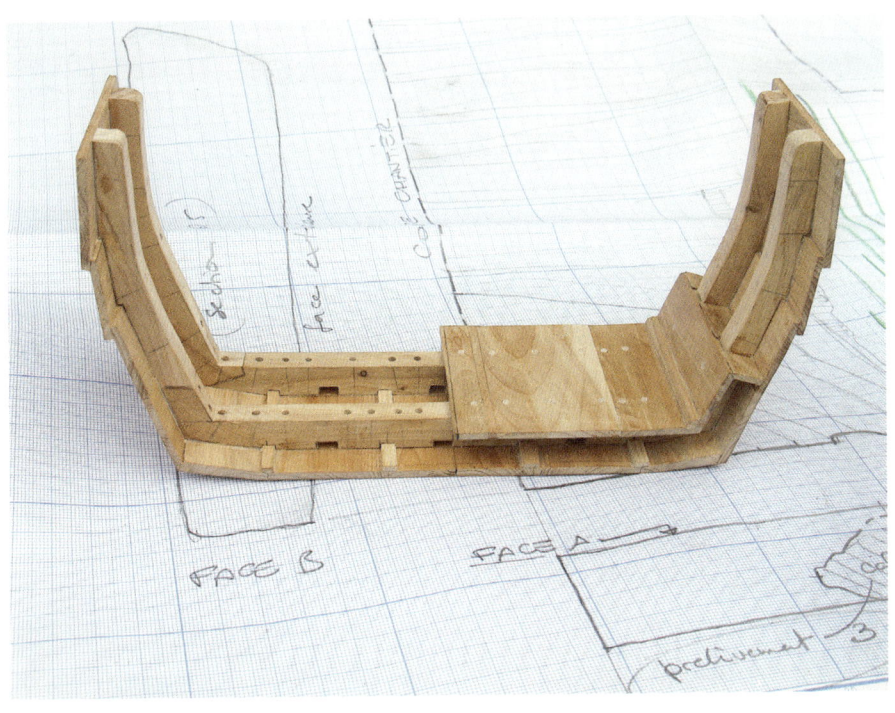

Fig. 18. Model (scale 1: 15) of the central part of the wreck by J.-L. Gaucher
(Photo: E. Champelovier, Drassm/Ministère de la Culture).

sub-group of small vessels adapted, from the point of view of nautical capabilities, to a mixed navigation, both fluvial and maritime, and intended to function in a transport activity. In this hypothesis, it would seem that the fluvio-maritime character of the boat ought rather to be considered as an adaptation of an architecture of the fluvial tradition to the particular constraints of a coastal environment.

In the absence of regional models for comparison, one of the closest models to the EP1-Canche wreck, as much from the architectural, functional point of view as chronological, seems to be that of the early 15th century wreck from Almere Wijk 13 (Flevoland, Netherlands), identified as that of a cargo boat of the cog family ("cog-like vessels"), adapted to navigation in the closed and protected maritime waters of the Zuyderzee and on its waterways (Hocker, Vlierman, 1996).

Construction and use

The dendrochronological analyses of the samples taken from various elements of the hull have shown that all the pieces were of oak (*Quercus* sp.) and presented similar characteristics connected to that of "[…] trees of strong to very strong annual growth typical of open and very open spaces, at low altitude and without real competition between them"[6]. The environment with the statistically nearest biogeographic comparison corresponds to the regions of the western edge of present-day Holland. However, this biogeographic approach connected to the protocol of

[6] According to Catherine Lavier.

dendrochronological studies (a problem notably of the available dendrochronological reference sequences), ought not to be confused with the origin of the wood supply for the shipyard. Indeed, other sectors of the Channel and of the North Sea between the estuary of the Seine in the south and that of the Scheldt in the north present an analogous biotope to that of the western coast of Holland.

On the subject of the construction and use of the boat, we establish that only one material – oak – is attested and present, and is also besides, from the similar characteristics, indicative in all likelihood, of a single supply zone for the shipyard. It can be shown that there was probably only a short interval between the moment of cutting the oaks and the beginning of construction which would seem to indicate a relative geographic proximity between the supply zone and the shipyard. This same short interval could also signify that the shipyard had a method of business of acquiring materials all at one time as a function of the rhythm of orders, without any capacity of holding stock, following a rhythm of production more in accord with a small shipyard, rural or urban, than a great urban shipyard.

The whole question is to locate, in a historical perspective and as a function of its characteristics, the place of the EP1-Canche boat in the regional context. What was the place of construction? What was the port of fitting out? What was the port for loading? What was the destination? What type of cargo was transported? The question is also posed of the presence of this fluvio-maritime coaster in the Canche between the sea-port of Etaples and the fluvio-maritime port of Montreuil-sur-Mer. How do we interpret that fluvio-maritime navigation, in the regional economy of water transport at the end of the Middle Ages? Would it represent a situation of regular exchanges? Which? Equally, it remains to understand the origin of the presence of the wreck lying across the Canche, of the causes of its loss or its abandonment, of the reasons for the absence of any re-floating, or of dismantling, more or less important, to recover the good quality timbers. Such are some of the questions which are at the centre of the researches in hand.

At the end of that presentation of the results of the excavation of the 15th century wreck EP1-Canche, one of the questions, amongst others, that is posed, is that of the relationship between this fluvio-maritime coaster of the cog family with the regional types of boat attested in the written sources from the end of the Middle Ages and the beginning of the modern era.

A particular type of boat is distinguished in the written sources, in the framework of what one could call, according to the model of historical interpretation elaborated by Christer Westerdahl (Westerdahl, 1995), a micro "traditional zone of transport geography in relation to ship types", that is in our regional context of northern France a fluvio-maritime nautical zone extending from the river Somme in the south to the river Canche in the north, at which point the character of the coast changes. This is the "gribane, gribanne, gribenne", characterised in the documents as "flat bottomed vessel" or again as a "vessel without a keel", expressions indicative of a very probable construction on a flat bottom. These "gribanes" frequently appear constructed in shipyards situated on the banks of the Somme, or of its estuaries, in Picardy. These coasters, whose dimensions and proportions mentioned in the documents seem very comparable to those reconstructed for the EP1-Canche boat, navigated along the shoreline towards Calais and also as various archive documents attest went up the Canche as far as to Montreuil-sur-Mer.

If too many unknowns still remain to make that identification with certitude, the wreck from the Canche has contributed notably to a new, more complete and precise reading of the history of the mediaeval naval architecture of the north of France.

One last question concerns the possible relationships of architectural descendance with a family of vernacular vessels from the marshes of Saint-Omer (Pas-de-Calais), the "bâcove" (Gaucher, 2008). Indeed, this traditional boat, constructed on a flat bottom, and double-ended, is characterised, notably, by an evolution of the flat bottom and a transition from carvel side planking in the central part of its hull to clinker side planking at its ends.

Conclusion

At the end of that reflection on the problems arising and the methods of fluvial archaeology, through the case of a wreck from the north of France, but which could very well be that of a wreck in the centre of China, we are conscious that numerous aspects have not been developed. In the space limited to a few pages, it was effectively necessary to make drastic choices. Those choices have been worked out in a double perspective: to show that this field of archaeological research of wrecks in interior waters, much more recent than that of the archaeology of wrecks in the sea, immediately mastered its problems and its methodological tools; to make apparent, through the particularities of underwater excavation of wrecks in inland waters, the complexity and the scientific interest of fluvial archaeology; and that that archaeology is inscribed within the limits of French fluvial territory through the example of the 15th century EP1-Canche wreck, or within the framework of the fluvial territory of China, albeit, from its immensity and diversity, on an incomparably greater scale.

Acknowledgements

We thank Richard Barker for his valued collaboration and commentary.

References

Bill, Jan,1999, "Port topography in medieval Denmark", in J. Bill, B. L. Clausen (eds), *Maritime Topography and the Medieval Town*, Studies in Archaeology and History, vol. 4. Copenhagen, Publications from The National Museum: 251–261.

Cordier, Gérard, 1963, "Quelques mots sur les pirogues monoxyles de France", *Bulletin de la Société Préhistorique Française*, 60 (5/6): 306–315.

Cordier, Gérard, 1972, "Pirogues monoxyles de France (Premier supplément)", *Bulletin de la Société Préhistorique Française*, 69: 206–21.

Crumlin-Pedersen, Ole, 2010, *Archaeology and the Sea in Scandinavia and Britain. A personal account*, Maritime Culture of the North, 3, The Viking Ship Museum in collaboration with The Society of Antiquaries of Scotland. Roskilde, 2010.

Crumlin-Pedersen, Ole, 1996, *Archaeology and the Sea*, Achttiende Kroon-Voordracht, Nederlands Museum voor Anthropologie en Praehistorie. Amsterdam, 1996.

Gaucher, Jean-Louis, 2008, "Barquette, escute et bacôve du marais audomarois", *Le Chasse-Marée*, 202, 2008: 31–37.

Hocker, Frederick M., Vlierman, Karel, *A small cog wrecked on the Zuiderzee in the early fifteenth century*. Excavation report 19, Flevobericht 408, Nederlands Instituut voor Scheeps-en Onderwater Archaeologie, ROB (NISA). Ketelhaven/Lelystad, 1996.

Laurent, Fabrice, 2004, *Inventaire des pirogues monoxyles découvertes en France, des plus anciennes au 18ᵉ siècle*, mémoire de DEA sous la direction d'Etienne Hubert, EHESS-Université de Lyon II. Lyon, 2004.

McGrail, Seán, *Studies in Maritime Archaeology*, British Archaeological Reports, British Series, 256. Oxford, 1997.

Muckelroy, Keith, 1978, *Maritime Archaeology*, Cambridge University Press. London, 1978.

Rieth, Eric (dir), 2013, *L'épave de la première moitié du XVᵉ siècle de la Canche à Beutin (Pas-de-Calais). Archéologie nautique d'un caboteur fluvio-maritime et d'un territoire fluvial*, Revue du Nord. Hors Série. Collection Art et Archéologie. 20, Lille, 2013.

Rieth, Eric (dir.), 2010, *L'épave du XVe siècle de Beutin, Canche (Pas-de-Calais)*, Archéologie en Nord-Pas-de-Calais 23, Service régional de l'archéologie, Lille, 2010.

Rieth, Eric, 2009, "L'épave du XVe siècle EP1-Canche, Beutin (Pas-de-Calais): un premier bilan archéologique (2005-2008)", *Revue du Nord. Archéologie de la Picardie et du Nord de la France*, 91 (383): 203-242.

Rieth, Eric, 2006, *Archéologie de la Batellerie. Architecture nautique fluviale*, Cahiers du Musée de la Batellerie (45). Conflans-Sainte-Honorine, 2006.

Rieth, Eric, 2003, "La pirogue 2 de Mortefon (Charente-Maritime): remarques sur l'architecture monoxyle et le «système nautique» du bassin de la Charente au Moyen Age", *Mer et Monde : questions d'archéologie Maritime. Archéologiques* (Québec), collection Hors Série 1: 43-61.

Rieth, Eric, 1998, "A propos de l'archéologie nautique", in E. Rieth, V. Serna (eds), *Du manuscrit à l'épave. Archéologie fluviale*, Cahiers du Musée de la Batellerie (39). Conflans-Sainte-Honorine, 1998: 4-7.

Rieth, Eric, Jean-Louis. Gaucher, 2010, "Archéologie nautique et modélisme de recherche: l'épave de la première partie du XVe siècle de Beutin, Canche (Pas-de-Calais)", *Cahiers d'Archéologie Subaquatique*, XVIII: 171-204.

Rieth Eric, Texier Pierre, 2009, "L'épave médiévale de la Canche", *Archéologia*, 463, 2009, p. 40-47.

Serna, Virginie, 2009, "Milieu nautique, espace navigant : approche archéologique du paysage fluvial de l'épave de Beutin (Pas-de-Calais)", 11e Rencontres internationales de Liessies. Lit mineur, lit majeur, lit voyageur, *Revue du Nord, hors série, Collection Art et Archéologie*, 14: 63-80.

Serna, Virginie, 1996, "Quelques réflexions à propos du concept de navigabilité des rivières au Moyen Age en France", in F. Ciciliot,(ed.), *Navalia Archeologia e Storia*. Savona: 105-115.

Westerdahl, Christer, 1995, "Traditional zones of transport geography in relation to ship types", in O. Olsen, J. Skamby Madsen, F. Rieck, (Eds.), *Shipshape. Essays for Ole Crumlin-Pedersen*. Roskilde The Viking Ship Museum: 213-230.

Crews' Material Culture from the Study of Artefacts Recovered off Historic French Shipwrecks: Gathering Data, Processing and New Evidence

从法国历史时期沉船文物看船员物质文化：资料收集、整理与新证据

Elisabeth VEYRAT

[Département des Recherches Archéologiques Subaquatiques et Sous-marines (DRASSM), Ministry of Culture and Communication, France]

伊丽莎白·维拉

（法国文化与交流部水下考古研究中心）

ABSTRACT / Often tenuous, always precious, traces of material culture found on shipwrecks are used to restore the environment, and the daily lives of crews aboard. Despite the difficulty at times in recognizing historical artefacts from fragmentary elements, the significant presence of identical objects on various shipwrecks of similar contexts allows the identification of some of the main elements of life onboard, and the portraying of some objects cited by archival documents. Thanks to the anaerobic environment that allows the preservation of organic material, and through shipwreck archaeology, our knowledge of Modern material culture has changed and enlarged. In a context of underwater and land archaeological excavations, the differential conservation of materials brings about an inversely proportional representation of everyday wood, ceramic or tin-based items. Thanks to the data produced by recent archaeological excavations of Modern shipwrecks, researchers are now able to build up new reference series that could identify and date, together with the chrono-typologies based on traditional ceramic studies, the context and the provenance of the excavated shipwrecks. These different aspects will be presented through artefacts taken from archaeological excavations of several French wrecks of the modern times: the Royal vessels of the Hougue (1692), the frigates of la Natière – *Dauphine* and *Aimable Grenot* (1704 and 1749), and the frigates *Boussole* and *Astrolabe* of the Lapérouse expedition (1788).

KEY WORDS / Post Medieval shipwrecks material culture; crew's utensils; ship's daily life objects; inventory and identification of artefacts; archives

内容摘要 /

作为能够复原环境及船员海上日常生活的沉船物质文化遗痕通常是极为少见又尤为珍贵的。通过碎片来鉴别历史时期的人工制品还存在着较大困难，但是，在相似背景下

不同沉船中发现的同类物品却可帮助我们识别出一些船上生活的主要元素，并可判别出一些文献记载中的器物。厌氧环境有助于有机物的保存，而沉船考古发现则改变并扩大了我们对近代物质文化的认识。在水下与陆地两种不同的物质保存环境下，考古发掘中发现的日常木制品、陶制品和锡制品等文物呈现出了反比例存在现象。根据近来一些近代沉船考古发掘所获取的资料与传统陶器研究的年代类型学，研究人员已可建立起新的参照序列。这些新的数据可使我们识别与断定沉船年代和背景及其来源地。本文将通过对乌盖皇家战舰（1692）、拉那题埃尔的Dauphine号和Aimable Grenot号护卫舰（1704、1749）及拉佩鲁斯探险活动中的Boussole号和Astrolabe号护卫舰（1788）等几艘已发掘的法国近代时期沉船中发现的人工制品来探讨以上几个方面的问题。

关键词 /

后中世纪沉船物质文化　船员器具　船上日常生活用品　物品登记及识别　档案

On a shipwreck, the tools and utensils, related to the ship itself or not, and the distribution of these artefacts leave many archaeological traces that allow the archaeologist to get a better understanding of the shipboard material culture. Nevertheless, despite archaeology's main mission to study ways of life of past populations, testimonies of daily life are curiously still too often neglected by maritime searchers. They are left far behind others remains, such as hull structure, cargo or ordnance for example. Organic material, especially wooden objects, are numerous on a well preserved shipwreck and compose one of the most fantastic series of items to understand daily life aboard. The fact that these objects need, most of the time, great attention to be understood, and expensive lab treatment to be preserved, may partly explain the lateness to consider them.

The aim of this paper is to underline some of the archaeological evidences of daily life aboard ships that deserve way more attention from archaeologists. Reference data considered is mainly provided by wrecksites of late 17th and 18th century French ships: the five ships of the line of La Hougue (1692), the two frigates of La Natière – *Dauphine*, and *Aimable Grenot* (1704 and 1749), the Frigate *Machault* (1760), two Lapérouse research expedition frigates *Boussole* and *Astrolabe* (1788) and the man-of-war *Séduisant* (1796). This paper will also considers other shipwrecks of the period: Dutch VOC ship *Mauritius* (1609) and *Hollandia* (1743), English ships *Maidstone* (1747), *HMS Swift* (1770) and *HMS Pandora* (1779), an English unidentified shipwreck at Porspoder (Brittany, France) and the Swedish merchant ship *Jeanne Elizabeth* (1755)(Fig. 1).

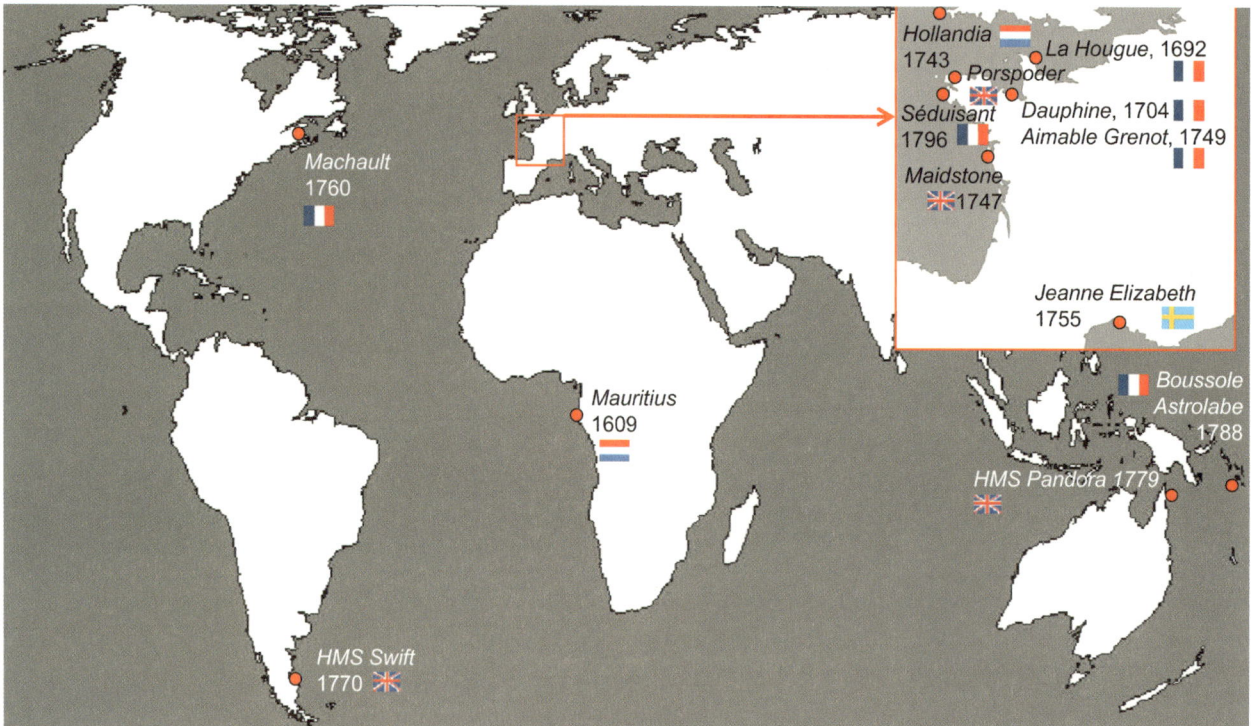

Fig.1 Localization map of shipwrecks quoted in this paper: Late 17th and 18th century French ships: the five ships of the line of La Hougue (1692), the two Frigates of La Natière Dauphine and Aimable Grenot (1704 and 1749), the Man-of-war Machault (1760), two Lapérouse Frigates Boussole and Astrolabe (1788) and the Man-of-war Séduisant (1796). Other European ships quoted: Dutch VOC ship Mauritius (1609) and Hollandia (1743), English Man-of-war Maidstone (1747), HMS Swift (1770) and HMS Pandora (1779), an English unidentified shipwreck at Porspoder (Brittany, France) and Swedish merchant ship Jeanne-Elizabeth (1755)
(map by Élisabeth Veyrat, from Daniel Dalet, © histgeo.ac-aix-marseille.fr)

Processing and cataloguing archaeological finds

The first difficulty when studying shipboard material culture is to understand the function from only fragments of complex items that have been shattered and scattered on a wrecked ship. On the *Aimable Grenot* shipwreck (1749), a small rectangular beech wood item, fastened with a sheet of lead on one side and a layer of leather on the other side, was first identified in 2001 as a shoe heel with a lead protection underneath. But the answer laid elsewhere… The research conducted by Thierry Boyer on ship's bilge pumps (Boyer, 2008) brought to light a similar item, found indeed inside one of the pump tubes of the *Machault* shipwreck (1760) (Fig. 2). So, years later, the true identification of this component was revealed: a part of a pump leather valve clapper, weighted up by the lead sheathing fastened to the wooden part!

Even if shipwrecks are often seen as time capsules, it is highly unusual, virtually miraculous, to find all tools of a craftsmanship, still stored together in their chest. Most of the time, the wreckage caused some objects to be shuffled around the site and the shipwreck looks more like a battlefield (Fig. 3). For the understanding of the

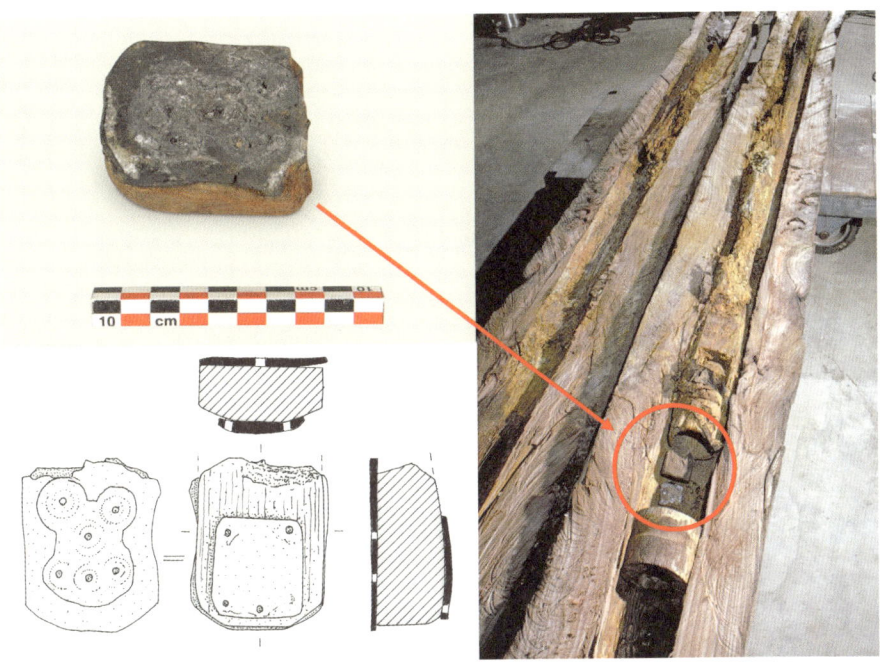

Fig. 2 Misunderstanding of a dismantled artefact: The example of a pump foot valve of Aimable Grenot shipwreck (1749, Nat 870) first identified as a shoe heel. Location of a similar item found inside one of the pump tubes of Machault shipwreck (1760). Photos Teddy Seguin (Adramar) and Thierry Boyer (Parcs Canada)

Fig. 3 Two wooden monkeys are lying close to a pewter dish and to rigging components in the forepart of the French Frigate Aimable Grenot shipwreck (1749). Photo Teddy Seguin (Adramar)

site, the maritime archaeologist is helped by the great diversity of materials that can be found on a submerged site: metal, ceramics, glass, lithic and organic material.

As a matter of fact and thanks to the anaerobic environment of a submerged and well buried site, organic material (wood, leather, rope, textile, wicker...) can represent up to 60% of the artefacts. But these organic remains require to be carefully excavated and meticulously protected before being removed from the site, to avoid loss of information or even of the artefact itself. This procedure is the price to pay to bring up to light new evidence and data and to develop tremendous new fields of research for archaeologists.

Help from archives and documentary sources

Analysis of artefacts from post-medieval shipwrecks is undeniably linked to the complementary study of archival sources. Cross-referencing information can bring light on an item that was solely known by its archival name. Written sources sometimes allow the identification of the function of some artefacts discovered on a wreck, but it is only from excavating that its size and true shape can be revealed, since it brings a tangible testimony instead of a simple reference in an historical account.

If archives are greatly helpful to reassign their historic name to the archaeological finds, they also play a major role to place back artefacts in their conjuncture and their historic context, in order to avoid overemphasis or misinterpretations. In this regard, the case of the rigging block sheaves at La Hougue is exemplary. During the excavation of five French royal men-of-war shipwrecks sunk in La Hougue (1692), a very scarce use of *lignum vitae* wood (*Guaiacum* sp) was observed for the working of block sheaves: only 1 out of 24 sheaves was made of *lignum vitae*, the others were made of various European species, as ash, elm, walnut, beech, green oak or maple. Despite later written sources clearly affirming the preference of royal dockyards for this hard, heavy and greasy exotic wood, the La Hougue shipwrecks did not show at all such an evidence. This could be easily accepted as an archaeological evidence that *Guaiacum* was not used for the navy of King Louis the XIV. Nevertheless, this interpretation would be a major misunderstanding, as the study of written archives of Brest royal dockyard, where the five ships were prepared for their campaign at sea, gave us the clue: Desclouzeaux, the administrator of the harbour, complains in 1691/1692 about a shortage of *lignum vitae*'s supply in the warehouses of Brest (Service Historique de la Marine, Brest: "[…] *I beg your Excellency to order some to be brought from America, 50 ro 60 thousand of 10 to 15 inches diameter, and if any other ports have unused one that they could be send here…*" (1E459, f° 118); "*I learned that in the King's stores […] of dunquerque, there is a considerable number of lignum vitae wood to make pulley sheaves, I beg your Excellency to order some to be sent to us by all possible means, and that they should not be less than 12 to 15 inches in diameter...*" (1E462, f° 64). So, far less than a preference for others species, the archaeological absence of *lignum vitae* in the La Hougue block sheaves shows a significant shortage of it.

The discovery of 25 beech wood shovels stored in the forepart of the hold the Natière 1 shipwreck gives another case of the necessity to intersect written archives with archaeological finds. With regard to the former identification of the shipwreck, believed to be the remains of the French ship *St. Jean-Baptiste* returning from Newfoundland, it was obviously tempting to identify those shovels without iron components as a serious evidence of salt shovels used to prepare cods on Newfoundland banks. However, the reading of archives and ship's inventories of the period points out a common practise to bring numerous wooden shovels aboard ships. In 1785, the French frigate *Boussole* left Brest for a planetary journey, with 24 wooden shovels placed under the responsibility of the ship's master. Only four of them were bound with iron (Archives Nationales de France, Mar, B/4/319, f° 1-54, 14/5/1785). Nowadays, the Natière 1 shipwreck has been identified with certainty as the *Dauphine*, a royal privateer frigate intended for rather short and local privateering trips along Normandy and Brittany. We still ignore why such a ship had so many shovels on-board...

It appears more and more obvious than the knowledge of written sources should be a necessary condition for the archaeology of historic shipwrecks, in order to understand the remains and to analyse the site. This should be not only a later confrontation of archaeological data to archives, but an on-going process during the excavation and the study of shipwrecks.

More generally, and in order to understand proper identification of dismantled artefacts, no information source should be discarded by the underwater archaeologist. Other disciplines, such as models, ethnology and traditional architecture, are precious to understand archaeological remains. For example, some small scattered and dismantled wooden items often found on French shipwrecks have been understood by the observation of vernacular Canadian barns: indeed, several simple locking devices, preserved on various doors of houses and barns from Newfoundland and New Brunswick have explained the use of some dismantled items frequently

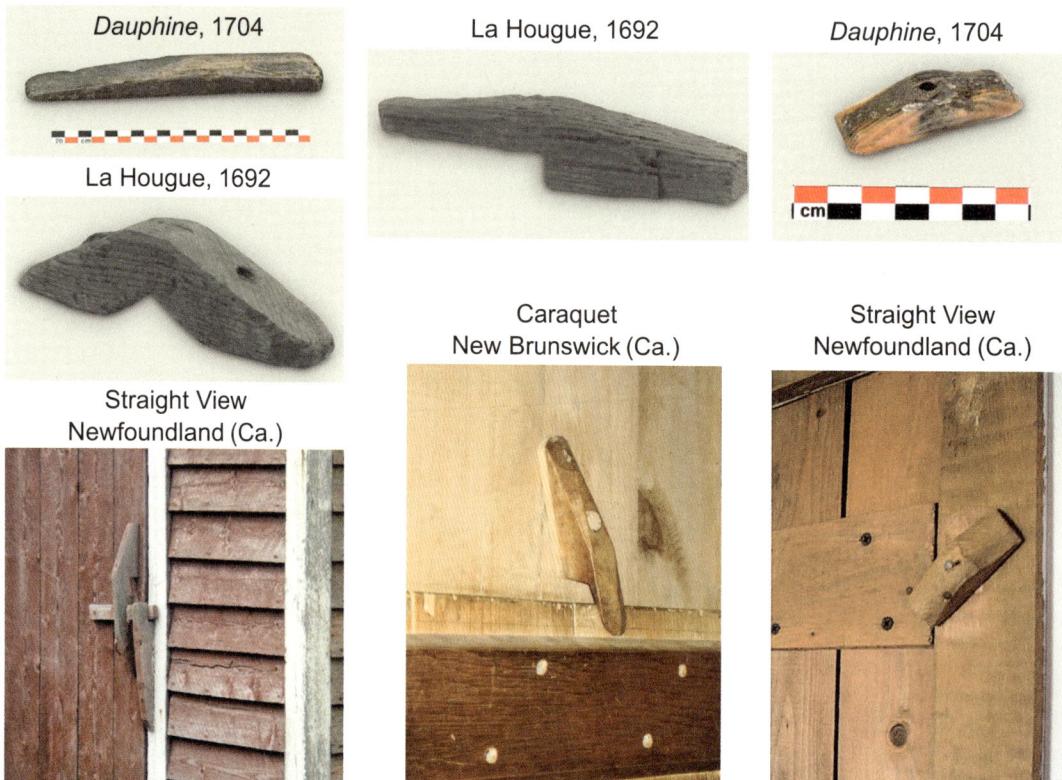

Fig. 4 Left: Numerous vernacular door locks in Newfoundland and New Brunswick old buildings show the use of similar items recovered on French shipwrecks of La Hougue (1692, STVH 308 & 309) and Dauphine (1704, Nat 1759). Right: Even a tiny artefact from Dauphine shipwreck (1704, Nat 1274) can reveal inner fitting device of the ship. Photos Philippe Foliot (CNRS-CCJ), Teddy Seguin (Adramar) and Élisabeth Veyrat (DRASSM)

recovered on French shipwrecks, as those of La Hougue (1692) & the *Dauphine* (1704)(Fig. 4).

A specific vade-mecum for identifying the historical function of artefacts

During the cataloguing process, it is essential to study artefacts according to their supposed functional attribution aboard. At this stage, a specific vade-mecum for cataloguing, dedicated to post-medieval maritime material culture, is of great help. It includes pictures and documentation, and a lexicon with ancient terms, measurements and a list of items of each craftsman aboard. An historical terminology should be preferred to name artefacts and to classify them: items of the caulker, the carpenter, the surgeon, the cook, etc. This consideration allows the archaeologist to track back the whole kit of items that were dedicated aboard to the same craft.

Meanwhile, cataloguing should pay a special attention to ancient measures, such as feet and inches, pounds and ounces. This may be of great help to specify the chronology of artefacts (transition between pounds and metric system in late 18th century France, for example) or to recognize the kind of standard in use (French or English foot, for example), and, more generally, to understand the historical context of artefacts.

The choice of specific feet and inches, pounds and ounces can express the origin of items and their purposes. The use of the medicinal pound, or of the French, English or Amsterdam feet, offers some excellent examples of this gratifying approach. The simple recognition of inches or metric system can provide a good, quick and simple chronological and cultural origin marker to identify an artefact. But one should never forget to keep in mind than all these tools and approaches only give clues upon the original context of artefacts, which is not always the one in use aboard. The archaeology of ship constantly shows evidences of transfers of property and secondary allocation for artefacts, by means of trade, privateering or even by simple reuse on-board.

For the cataloguing process of round artefacts, it is very rewarding to pay attention to the circumference rather than to the diameter or to general width and height. As a matter of fact, French Ancien Régime archives and treatises frequently considered some rigging components, as deadeyes, according to their circumference, "*un cap de mouton de x pouces de tour*" (a deadeye of x inches of loop). During the recording of artefacts, such an approach will help to understand the conception and historic classification of items. By the way, it is important to point out than this measurement is, on a circular object, far simpler to take and far more accurate than any other one.

A specific form for organic artefacts

During the inventory process, specific data on wooden artefacts is carefully registered: wood species, woodworking process, using marks, etc. A particular inventory sheet has also shown its great interest for hemp ropes, in order to facilitate the study of these valuable, soft and fragile items (Sanders, 2010: 16-17). In the future, special cataloguing sheets, dedicated to textiles or wickerwork, should be also created for a better understanding, and further registration, of these fragile and complex items.

In the specific case of waterlogged artefacts, it is of great importance that all the data is carefully collected during fieldwork. As a matter of fact, organic artefacts have to follow a very long conservation process in laboratories after the excavation and will not be available for further study during years. In addition, conservation treatments tend to affect surface of artefacts, and particularly could erase some using or identification marks.

The identification of specific items of post-Medieval material culture of shipwrecks

Among the artefacts recovered from a shipwreck, many of them are related to the material culture of the board. Some come under personal belongings, but most of items materialize the general supply of the ship. In that respect, collective items were chosen according to their function aboard and to economic data, such as purchase price and availability.

However, three specific factors should also be pointed out for selection of shipboard maritime material culture items:

— The limitation of space aboard: interlocking and stackable items were preferred because they were more suitable to be easily packed aboard. It generated a rather standardized lists of tools and crockery which were placed under the supervision of craftsmen aboard;

— The sea corrosion: materials more likely to resist to salt and corrosion are preferred;

— The resistance in front of swell, pitching and rolling: Solid or flexible materials, as metal and wood, are preferred to breakable items, as glass and pottery.

Considering the lack of space aboard and the necessity to have the proper item for the specific function, collective items were therefore carefully elected and the composition of shipboard material culture tends to evolve from the one on land. Archaeological data underlines many common features, and even similar items, among artefacts recovered off post medieval shipwrecks off the two sides of the Atlantic Ocean. This reinforces the idea of an emerging post medieval global maritime material culture, beside of persistent local particularities. The following examples of common items will outline some directions of research.

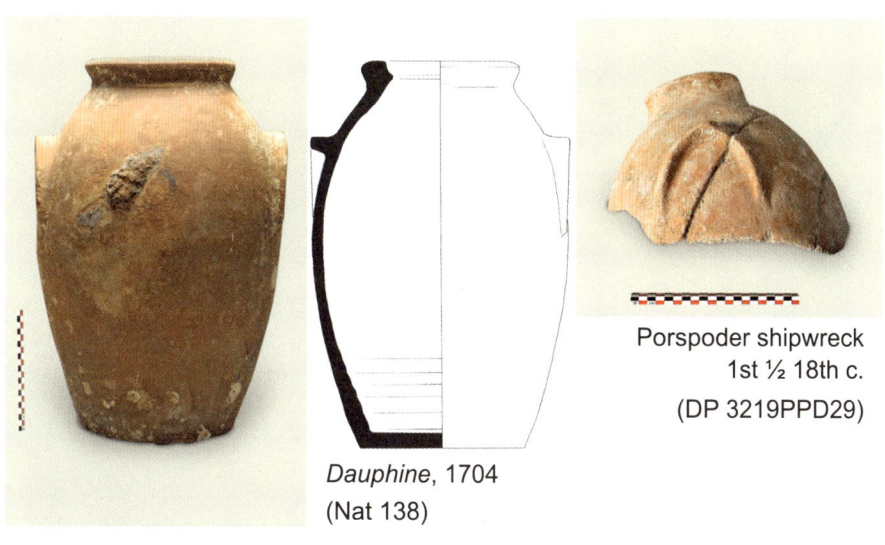

Fig. 5 Large earthenware Tuscan jars from Dauphine (Nat 138) and Porspoder shipwrecks (DP3219PPP29). Photos Teddy Seguin (Adramar), drawing Laurent Gubellini

A collective item familiar to marine archaeologists: the example of earthenware jars

Beside well-known Spanish olive jars recovered from numerous post medieval maritime sites of Atlantic coasts and studied for years (Goggin, 1960), another group of earthenware jars, with an ovoid body, a flat bottom and a round rim fitted up for a lid, becomes more and more relevant. Highly recognizable because of its two horse-shoe or crescent shaped handles on shoulders (Fig. 5), with or without stamp, this model is frequently attested in private gardens (London, Amsterdam, Sartène, St. Servan...) and museums (Ramezay, Toulouse-Lautrec, Borely, Augustines...). Until recently, this group was wrongly thought to be of Spanish origin.

British specialists have recently identified the origin of these jars: they were massively imported by the English Royal Navy from Montelupo in Tuscany (Italia) for the transport of olive oil (Coleman & Porter, 2007). Number of these jars have been found in Jamaica and on English shipwrecks of the 18th century, notably the *HMS Swift* (1770, Elkin *et alii*, 2011: 243-244), the *HMS Pandora* (1779, Illidge, Doyle & Mann, 2014) and one probably English shipwreck at Porspoder (Brittany, France, 1st half of 18th c., unpublished).

The evidence of one of these jars aboard the French privateer frigate *Dauphine* (1704, L'Hour and Veyrat, 2005: 310-313; Veyrat, 2014: 101), and on the *Queen Anne's Revenge* pirate shipwreck (1718, Carnes and McNaughton, 2008, vessel I) evokes some reuse of these jars and may proceed from a possible catch at sea of an English ship.

New research now shows that these Italian jars (wrongly considered as Spanish

Dauphine 1704

Aimable Grenot 1749

Boussole 1788

Séduisant 1796

Fig. 6　Lead rolls from French 18th century shipwrecks. Photos Jean-Michel Kéroullé & Teddy Seguin (Adramar)

in origin) spread over the world by mean of the maritime trade routes of English Empire (Blake & Hughes, to be published). By the recording of the archaeological finds aboard shipwrecks, these jars could be precious markers of contacts and exchanges in the maritime world of 18th century.

The identification of specific items: the example of lead rolls

The discovery of similar items on several shipwrecks allows us to outline some very essential components for daily life aboard and to point out some objects referred to in written archives but totally unknown from historical collections.

This is the case of heavy lead rolls, found on several French shipwrecks of the 18th century: Two on the French royal Frigate *Dauphine* (1704), one on the Norman private Frigate *Aimable Grenot* (1749), French royal Frigates *Boussole* and *Astrolabe* (1788, L'Hour and Veyrat, 2008: 291) and French Man-of-war *Séduisant* (1796, unpublished) (Fig. 6). An earlier archaeological evidence is provided by the Dutch VOC *Mauritius* shipwreck (1609), where one roll has been found (L'Hour, Long and Rieth, 1989: 216). Mentioned by Nicolas Aubin in his *Dictionnaire de Marine* (Amsterdam, 1702), lead rolls are often listed in French ship's inventories of the 18th century, under the name of *"Lead Roll"* or *"Lead sheet"*. One is mentioned by Daniel Defoe in his famous novel, *Robinson Crusoé* (1719), *"May 9: Went to the wreck, and with the crow made way into the body of the wreck, and felt several casks, and loosen'd them with the crow, but could not break them up; I felt also the roll of English lead, and could stir it, but it was too heavy to remove*" (Daniel Defoe, *Robinson Crusoé*, 1719, Dover Publications, 1998: 62).

Lead rolls were essential to the ship and used aboard for various tasks and mendings: re-usable, easily cut and pliable, lead was the perfect solid and waterproof material for protection of specific areas of hull structure and fittings. Archives tell us that these items were placed under the responsibility of the caulker and archaeological data indicates than they were displayed in units of one or two feet wide. At this stage of research, we could cautiously notice than the module of the earliest examples (*Mauritius* and *Dauphine*) is quite smaller than the one of the latest (*Aimable Grenot*, *Boussole*, *Astrolabe* and *Séduisant*), but only the increase of testimonies will bring conviction on the possible evolution of these items. Much neglected for a long while, these artefacts deserve a proper study. In that regard, one can warmly welcome the current thesis carried out since 2013 by Magali Veyrat upon lead objects in the material culture of historic shipwrecks (Veyrat, ongoing).

Definition and Evolution of daily life objects: The case of Monkeys

Data gathered on French shipwrecks of the end of the 17th and 18th centuries shows evidence of typo-chronological evolution for various kinds of artefacts familiar to shipboard material culture, such as small wooden cans used to contain the daily water or wine rations of a mess of seven men. The role of these cans, or monkeys, was important enough to be mentioned aboard Ships of the Line by the French decree of 1689 (*L'Ordonnance de Louis XIV pour les armées navales et arcenaux de marine*). Monkeys are frequently noted as well in French ships' inventories of the period, under the French name of *bidons* and relate to the cooper's items (Archives départementales d'Ille-et-Vilaine, Rennes, 9B225: Saint-Jean-Baptiste inventory-1704, 9B249: the Paix inventory-1713, 9B301: Comte de Maurepas inventory-1747). But historical sources offer very scarce contemporary figurations, such as one drawing by Deslongchamps l'Aîné, in 1763 (fol 152-153: "*bidon a vin et eau*"). Monkey appears there as a truncated cone, with a pouring lip, a round opened lid with a little rope to be handled. This is the way Jean Boudriot draws them in his well-known monograph on the 74 guns ship, and that is also attested on the French *Aimable Grenot shipwreck* (1749, cf. Fig. 3, op. cit.).

Recent archaeological data, however, has shown older variations for this very specific item. Both the royal shipwrecks of La Hougue (1692) and the *Dauphine* shipwreck (1704) have revealed monkeys, but they are smaller than later ones and closed by an ingenious oaken device, intended to seal, to lock and to transport those monkeys (cf. Fig. 7, left below). These devices were complex to make and we can assume it is the reason why they were no longer in use some decades later, having been replaced by a bigger can, with a circular lid held in place by a rope.

More and more, recent archaeological studies pay attention to features of various types of artefacts discovered on shipwrecks, such as tools, wooden crockery, rigging components, etc., in order to understand their role aboard and to determine their permanence, replacement or evolution. It is just the beginning of the process and we can be pretty sure than the increase of data should generate new chronological markers for the future, made of various materials and items, beside traditional typologies based upon pottery and ceramic.

The on-board art of engraving and carving

On a well buried shipwreck, the fantastic preservation of wooden artefacts allows us to discover some rare individual expressions of engraving and carving of post medieval seamen. By the use of a simple knife, a marlinspike or an awl, rope or leather could be also repaired aboard, or reused if they could not. In fact and at the difference of pottery, glass or metal (with the exception of lead), all organic materials could be worked aboard by the crew, to be repaired or to create new items.

If the art of engraving and carving wood could not seem a priority concern for sailors and seamen involved in a hard life at sea, underwater archaeology reveals that woodcarving was a quite popular hobby for the crew members. Indeed, the omnipresence of wood aboard, beginning by the hull structure itself, the disposal of reusable material, and the easiness to mark with a simple knife a wooden surface, probably allowed each man of the crew to develop a particular taste for woodcarving and creation of new items. Post-medieval shipwrecks constantly underline this massive activity aboard and reveal numerous indications of reusing items, and above all, the recycling of oak. This high quality wood came aboard under the form of casks and barrels, but these containers were dismantled when emptied, or broken. Wood was then reused to carve various objects: hammock frames, monkey lids, tobacco rasps or marlinspikes, to quote just a few of them recovered on the French frigate *Dauphine* shipwreck (Fig. 7).

Aimable Grenot French frigate shipwreck (1749) points out a rare example of a dismantled oak barrel the staves of which have been voluntarily cut in two, by means of an axe (Fig. 8). Maybe more than a simple way to get firewood, this could suggest the will to provide raw material for woodworking and to gain some precious place aboard.

Fig. 7 Reusing and carving oak aboard: hammock frame, monkey lid, marlinspike and tobacco rasp, Dauphine shipwreck (1704). Photos Frédéric Osada (Images Explorations) et Teddy Seguin (Adramar)

Fig. 8 Reusing & carving oak aboard: oak staves voluntarily broken in two, Aimable Grenot shipwreck (1749, Nat 2848). Photos Teddy Seguin (Adramar)

Fig. 9 Wooden turned handles from Aimable Grenot (1749, Nat 2896 & 2920, up) and Boussole shipwrecks (1788, FAI 259 & 390, down). Photos Teddy Seguin (Adramar)

A providential source for post medieval material culture knowledge

Comparatively to land archaeological sites, post medieval shipwrecks often offer the opportunity of homogeneous and precisely dated contexts. Furthermore, the proportion of organic material among the preserved artefacts on a shipwreck gives tremendous possibilities to study daily life testimonies. On the contrary, the art of knife carving has left nearly no traces on land archaeological contexts. By showing the blanks, the archaeology of shipwrecks constitutes in this manner a providential data source for land sites studies.

In this regard, numerous wooden turned handles for knifes, found on English man-of-war *Maidstone* (1747, De Maisonneuve, 1992), French frigate *Aimable Grenot* (1749, Veyrat, 2009: 14), Dutch VOC ship *Hollandia* (1743, Gawronski, 1996: 164), Swedish ship *Jeanne Elizabeth* (1755, unpublished) and French frigate *Boussole* (1788, L'Hour and Veyrat, 2008: 267), highlight the great popularity of these items in the 18th century European maritime context (Fig. 9). This helps us suspect an equal diffusion on land, even if the related sources are still lacking on this matter.

Fig. 10 "The tenuous testimony of wood, leather and rope...". Reconstitution of rigging storage by mean of the artefacts found in the hold of French shipwrecks. *La mer pour mémoire*, French travelling exhibition (2005–2009), Buhez / Drassm. Photo Teddy Seguin (Adramar)

Through the growing diversity of artefacts to consider, archaeology of shipwrecks is due to modify our knowledge of post-medieval material culture and to enlarge our vision. During excavation and cataloguing process, the growing importance of organic material deeply modifies our understanding of daily life aboard, and, further, of maritime history. By reaction, the way to present this underwater heritage to public, through large scale exhibitions, is noticeably evolving. By changing the colour and the texture of exhibited artefacts, by substituting, to the bronze majesty, the tenuous testimony of wood, leather and rope, exhibitions are becoming more human and intimate, more accurate in fact (Fig. 10).

References

Blake Hugo, Hughes M.J. [to be published], "Montelupo oil jars: source, contents and diffusion", in *Jarres et grands contenants entre Moyen Age et Époque moderne (Premier Congrès International Thématique de l'AIECM3, Montpellier-Lattes, 19–21 novembre 2014)*, Aix-en-Provence: AIECM3.

Boudriot, Jean, 1986-1988, *Seventy-Four Gun Ship: A Practical Treatise on the Art of Naval Architecture*, 4 volumes, English edition 1986–1988.

Boyer, Thierry, 2008, *Les pompes de cale du Machault*, Mémoire de Maîtrise (unpublished), Université de Paris I, 2008, 225 pages.

Carnes-McNaughton, Linda, 2008, "Ceramic Assemblage Analysis from Shipwreck 31CR314 Queen Anne's Revenge Site", Queen Anne's Revenge Shipwreck Project, research Report and Bulletin Series QAR-R-08-03: 4–6. Underwater Archaeology Branch, Office of State Archaeology, Department of Cultural Resources, State of North Carolina (Vessel I-Large Oil Jar).

Coleman, Ronald & Anthony Porter, 2007, "The so-called 'Spanish Jars' of Jamaica and their Italian connection", *Jamaica Journal* 30.3, 2007, pp. 50–61.

De Maisonneuve, Bernard & Mireille, 1992, *Le Maidstone, miroir d'une mémoire*, édition ARHIMS, 1992, 189 pages.

Deslongchamps l'Aîné, 1763, *Recueil de toutes sortes de machines d'outils et d'ustenciles en usage pour la construction et carenne des vaisseaux et de tout ce qui a raport a leurs armements dans un arsenal de marine*, 1763, fol 152–153 (Brest, Bibl. Munic., MS 54).

Elkin, Dolores, *et alii*, 2011, "El Naufragio de la HMS Swift-1770", *Arqueologia Maritima en la Patagonia*, 2011, pp. 243–244.

Gawronski, Jerzy, 1996, De Equipagie van de Hollandia en de Amsterdam, VOC-bedrijvigheid in 18de-eeuws Amsterdam, De Bataafsche Leeuw, Amsterdam, 317 pages.

Goggin, John M., 1960, "The Spanish Olive Jar: an Introductory Study", in *Papers in Caribbean Anthropology*, Vol.62, Yale University Publications in Anthropology, New Haven.

Illidge, Peter, Coleman Doyle, and Alison Mann, 2014, "The Recovery and Laboratory Excavation of the Contents of a Georgian Olive Oil Jar from the Wreck of HMS Pandora", *Bulletin of the Australasian Institute for Maritime Archaeology* 38: 82–92.

L'Hour, Michel, Long, Luc & Rieth, Éric, 1989, Le Mauritius, la mémoire engloutie, Dossiers archives du temps Casterman, 271 pages.

L'Hour, Michel, Veyrat, Élisabeth, 2005, "À la fortune du pot : L'approvisionnement des navires d'époque moderne", in L'Hour & Veyrat (ed.), *La mer pour mémoire, archéologie sous-marine desépaves atlantiques*, éditions Buhez-Somogy, Paris, p. 310–313.

L'Hour, Michel, Veyrat, Élisabeth, 2008, "Enquête archéologique sous-marine à Vanikoro", in Association Salomon, *Le mystère Lapérouse, ou le rêve inachevé d'un roi*, éditions de Conti, Très Grande Bibliothèque Thalassa, Paris, p. 252–304.

Sanders, Damien, 2010, "Knowing the Ropes: The Need to Record Ropes and Rigging on Wreck-Sites and Some Techniques for Doing So", *International Journal of Nautical Archaeology* 39.1, 2010, p. 2–26.

Veyrat, Élisabeth, 2009, "The Natière 2 Shipwreck: The Remains of the French Frigate L'Aimable Grenot (1747-1749)", in *ACUA Underwater Archaeology Proceedings*, Society for Historical Archaeology Symposium, Toronto 2009, pp. 9–16.

Veyrat, Élisabeth, 2014, "Food Aboard! Eating & Drinking on French Frigates of the Early 18th century, according to the Natière Shipwrecks", in *ACUA Underwater Archaeology Proceedings*, Society for Historical Archaeology Symposium, Québec, 2014, pp. 99–106 : 101.

Veyrat, Magali (ongoing thesis since 2012), Les plombs embarqués. Approche d'un métal du quotidien à bord des navires de la période moderne (XVe–XIXe siècle).

French Seamen and Chinese Commerce at the Beginning of the 18th Century: The Voyage of La Découverte (1707-1716)

十八世纪初期法国海员与中国贸易："发现号"之旅（1707~1716）

Michel L'HOUR

[Département des Recherches Archéologiques Subaquatiques et Sous-marines (DRASSM), Ministry of Culture and Communication, France]

米歇尔·劳尔

（法国文化与交流部水下考古研究中心）

ABSTRACT / Since the Roman Empire and until the Portuguese intrusion in Asia, very few Europeans have established direct links between Europe and China, by land or sea routes. However, towards the end of the sixteenth century, inspired by the Portuguese example and the success of their *Carreira da Índia*, the exploration of sea routes to China motivated the dynamism of Europeans. French merchants were involved with Dutch and English trading companies. Economic issues were in fact important and justified the efforts made by the ship-owners. In the early eighteenth century, some French captains sought to associate to their China trading projects some commercial shipments for the Iberian markets along the Pacific coast of South America. In 1712, one of these intrepid navigators even ratified a commercial agreement with Xiamen merchants. The aims of this article are to recall the example the sea journey of *La Découverte*, the sea-going context of such long-distance commercial undertakings, and to evoke the difficulties of those first direct encounters between French ship-owners/seamen and Chinese traders.

KEY WORDS / Clipperton; commercial treaty; Dubocage; French-Chinese maritime trade; Xiamen, 1712.

内容摘要 /

从罗马帝国到葡萄牙人侵入亚洲之前的漫长时期，鲜有欧洲人在陆地或是海上建立欧亚间的直接联系。然而，自十六世纪末，在葡萄牙人印度贸易航路的刺激和鼓励下，欧洲人开始致力于开拓前往中国的海上通道。法国商人加入了荷兰和英国的贸易公司。对于船主而言，经济问题不仅极为重要，而且也是其成就的标志。在十八世纪早期，一些法国船长尝试将他们的中国贸易计划与南美西海岸与伊比利亚市场贸易一些货物联系起来。1712年，一位勇敢无畏的航行者甚至成功与厦门商人达成了贸易协议。本文通过介绍"发现号"航海日记中所描写的远洋贸易航程，展示了法国船主和海员在与中国商人之间直接贸易初期所遇到的困难。

关键词 /

克利铂顿岛　贸易协议　Dubocage　中法海上贸易　厦门　1712年

As a preamble I think it would be useful to recall how I became interested in the story of Michel Dubocage, an exceptional mariner who is at the centre of this paper.

From the wrecks of the Natière to the trail of Michel Dubocage!

The story began in 1999 when my colleague Elisabeth Veyrat and myself undertook the underwater archaeological excavation of the wrecks of two corsair frigates lost at the beginning of the 18th century at the entrance to St Malo harbour, on the north coast of Brittany in western France (Fig. 1). These two wrecks had been discovered by accident and we had no information to enable us to identify them, so we named them conveniently Natière one and Natière two, from the name of the

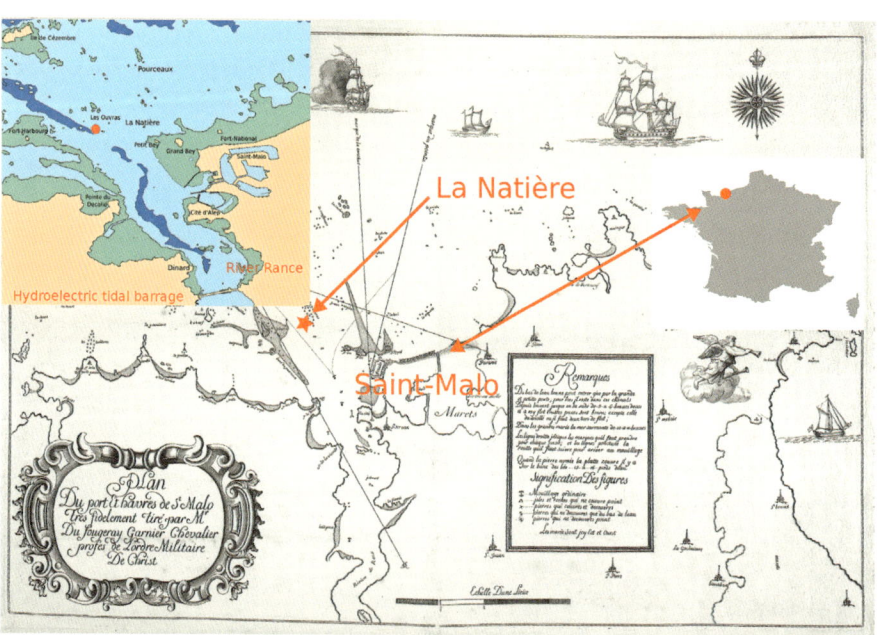

Fig. 1　La Natière: localisation on map

Fig. 2　Architectural plotting of the Natière shipwreck (MLH)

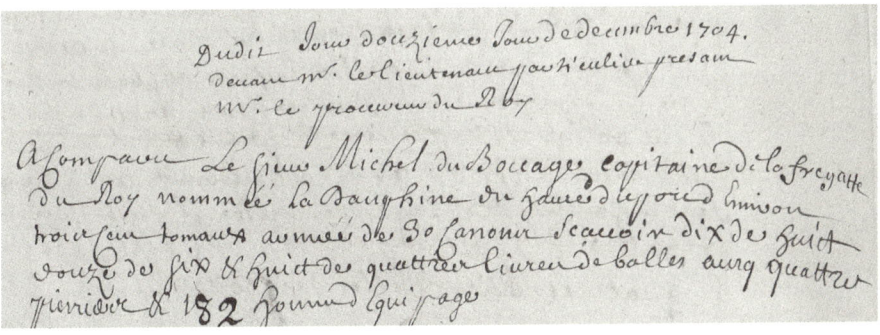

Fig. 3　Extract from the *Rapport de mer* (9 B517, f° 78v°)

rocky islet at whose base they were found (Fig. 2). The archaeological data began to give us approximate dates for them, and we began to trawl systematically through the archives which seemed likely to help us with identification. As a result in November 2001, wreck Natière two was identified as that of the large corsair frigate *L'Aimable Grenot* from Granville which was lost on 6 May 1749 as it left St Malo for Cadiz. However despite all of our research, the Natière one wreck remained anonymous and it was only in June 2006, after eight years of research that we finally found the document which enabled us to definitely identify it. This crucial document is the sea report written by its captain on the day following the wrecking, in order to explain the conditions surrounding the loss of his ship *La Dauphine* on 11 December 1704 (Fig. 3). Courtesy of this same document we also learnt that *La Dauphine* was a Royal frigate from Le Havre and that her captain was Michel Dubocage. Following

Fig. 4   Reconstitution of the *Dauphine*, 1703

this initial information, we began a new and lengthy research into the archives in order to learn more, both about the construction of the frigate *La Dauphine* as well as the story of her captain. We quickly found considerable information regarding *La Dauphine*, notably that she was constructed in 1703 in the Royal Arsenal of Havre by the shipwright Philippe Cauchois (Fig. 4). As for our research into her captain, who in the beginning was almost just anecdotal to our study of the St Malo wrecks, it soon became clear that his story was exceptionally interesting, and over the last four years has become the major focus of our investigation. Apart from the wreck of *La Dauphine*, several dates, some limited information and a major event quickly stimulated our curiosity towards Michel Dubocage. Born in Le Havre on 28 January 1676 (Fig. 5) to a family whose means were modest without actually being poor, Dubocage died a rich man in Havre on 10 May 1727. He probably joined the Navy at an early age and was made lieutenant of a frigate by the King of France on 1 January 1692 when he was only 16 years old. As an experienced sailor he was made captain of a corsair ship at the age of 20 where he excelled sufficiently to be given larger and larger ships. It was thus that at the age of 27 the King entrusted him with the Royal frigate *La Dauphine* on which he was wrecked at St Malo, although he was in no way held responsible for the loss. Although his career was brilliant, it was not an isolated example in the maritime history of France during the 17th and 18th centuries; and on its own would not justify the level of interest we have shown towards him.

Our fascination with this great mariner of Le Havre comes from another major story, which came to light when we realised that Michel Dubocage was also the man who discovered the *Ile de la Passion* in the eastern Pacific, on Good Friday 3 April

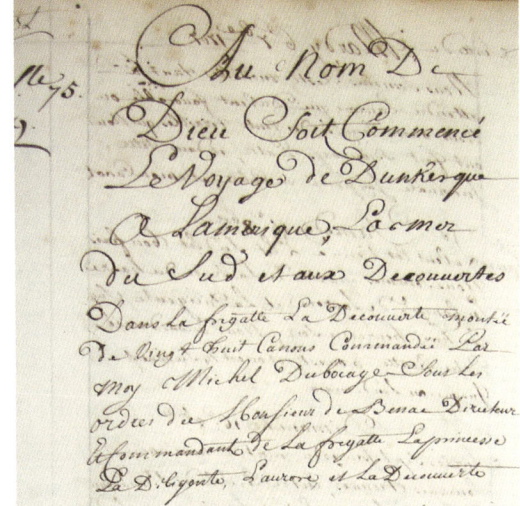

Fig. 5 Birth certificate of Michel Dubocage   Fig. 6 Manuscript by Dubocage (4JJ47)

1711, which is today the French island of Clipperton. Stunned by this information, we continued our investigations and in the French National Archives in Paris discovered a logbook written by Michel Dubocage between 1707 and 1716 (Fig. 6), when he commanded the Dunkirk frigate *La Découverte*. This 400 page manuscript is a very important primary source regarding the voyage made by Michel Dubocage across the Atlantic, then the Pacific as far as China where in 1712 he made what is perhaps the oldest commercial agreement ratified between France and China.

To understand the importance of this testimony, it's necessary at this point to recall the historical context of the maritime relations between France and China.

The voyage 'to China': an unusual undertaking for French Mariners

In contrast to the far eastern maritime preoccupations of Portuguese merchants in the 16th century and in the following century by Dutch merchants, the majority of merchants involved in French maritime trade were, with rare exceptions, disinterested in the commercial attractions of an Asiatic voyage. The distance to Cathay, as well as the failure of attempts made at the beginning of the 16th century by exceptional individuals such as the Verrazani and the Parmentier brothers, probably explains this initial lack of motivation. The founding in 1664 of the *Compagnie française pour le commerce des Indes orientales* (the French East India Company) by Louis XIV and his minister Colbert, which created a 50 year monopoly in this long-distance trade, provides another valid explanation. For a number of decades in the 17th century, the fact that French trade with Asia rested with a monopoly, meant that private merchants had to content themselves with the redistribution in France of goods which had been imported from Asia. A turning point occurred with the *guerre de Hollande* (The Dutch War) of 1672-1678. Naval warfare had drained the French East India Company and forced them to seek alliances with private commerce. Although this opening did not last long, it provided French merchants with the opportunity to test the potential of Asiatic trade. This potential was quickly confirmed in 1695, when French corsairs seized several richly loaded Dutch Indiamen at sea. Almost simultaneously at the end of the 17th and the beginning of the 18th centuries, several French business groups decided to fit out their vessels for China. Two maritime routes were open to the navigators. The first, via the Cape of Good Hope, was the one mostly used by the Portuguese over the previous two centuries. The second was considerably more ambitious, via Cape Horn and traversing the Pacific. This formed a gigantic long-distance triangular trade linking that of "*à la Mer du Sud*" (South Sea trade), along the coast of Chile and Peru, with China. This itinerary was a round trip of 39,000 nautical miles or 72,000 km, and demanded highly competent oceangoing captains and crews. It also required courage and patience. The first attempts began at the beginning of the 18th century and were entrusted to experienced sailors. It's in this context that Noël Piécourt, a shipping merchant from Dunkirk, with Parisian business associates, organised a squadron of four ships in 1707 to undertake an exploration of the commercial route to the South Seas and China.

Placed under the command of Benoît de Bénac, this squadron included a 250 ton frigate (28 guns and 127 crew members) (Fig. 7), *La Découverte*, commanded by Michel Dubocage, a 31 year old captain from Le Havre. By chance, as I have described, his exceptional logbook has survived. It is an extraordinary testimony of life aboard a large commercial exploration frigate of the early 18th century and relates living conditions and events on a daily basis for the nine years that this unusual voyage lasted. The revelations in this document leave the reader with a sole regret; not to have access to the account book where Michel Dubocage noted the results of his commercial negotiations during stopovers, both in South America and in China. The existence of this second document, which has not been found, is not in doubt because Dubocage himself in his logbook makes several references to his "negotiations book". Despite this, the logbook of Michel Dubocage is still very informative.

Fig. 7   Plan of a 28 canon *frégate* by French shipwright Philippe Cauchois (Denmark Royal Archives)

Leaving Dunkirk on 28 August 1707, then Brest on 23 March 1708, *La Découverte* arrived at the mouth of Rio de la Plata on 6 November 1708, after a short stopover in the Canaries. In the intervening period, scurvy had badly affected the crews, with a number of deaths amongst the squadron's ships. Distress and discouragement had spread amongst the men to the point where the leader of the expedition himself, Benoît de Bénac fell into a deep depression from which nothing could lift him. So it was on 1 December 1709, that two officers of Bénac's ship *La Princesse*, came aboard *La Découverte* to inform Michel Dubocage of the death of the squadron's commander. Dubocage's logbook describes that Bénac "*s' était jeté à la mer*" (threw himself overboard), which is a surprise, because confirmed suicides were extremely rare aboard ships and were seldom described as such. The circumstances of this disappearance were troubling at the time, and on the return of the expedition, there was an immediate enquiry to establish whether or not Bénac had simply been murdered. His illness and indecision dangerously compromised the success of the expedition and it is easy to imagine how great the temptation must have been to arrange a premature disappearance...

A new commander, Martin de Chassiron, was immediately nominated to head the expedition and the ships left Rio de la Plata almost immediately, on 11 January 1710, after a stay of more than 14 months on the coasts of what are today Argentina and Uruguay. The Lemaire Strait and then Cape Horn were passed on 31 January 1710 at the cost of a detour which took *La Découverte* to beyond 60° 21 south, placing the mariners amongst the first Frenchmen to round Cape Horn, and also some of the first to head so far towards Antarctica.

After a long 12 months stay on the Pacific coast of South America, where Dubocage stayed successively in Conception Bay, Valparaiso, Arica, Coquimbo and

Pisco, engaging in coastal trade with the Spanish colonists, he refitted in Huacho, north of Lima on March 1711 in preparation for crossing the Pacific to China. *La Princesse*, commanded by Martin de Chassiron, accompanied *La Découverte* on this long crossing and Dubocage's logbook states that Spanish merchants were embarked on his ship and we can guess that Spanish goods were loaded as well. This testimony shows how close relations were between the Spanish colonists and the European ships which supplied them, despite these exchanges being officially forbidden by the Spanish Crown which reserved a monopoly on trade between Europe and its colonies.

Dubocage states in his logbook that three weeks after leaving Huacho, he discovered an island which he called "l'Île de la Passion" (Island of the Passion) and made the first map known of it (Fig. 8). Today, this French island is known as Clipperton Island, and lies in latitude 10° 17 S, longitude 109° 12 W; 1220 km to the west of the Mexican coast.

After Clipperton, the two frigates continued on their route. On 14 May 1711, they reached Guam, to the south of the Marianas Islands, then they followed the north coast of the Philippines and Formosa at the beginning of June before finally anchoring in the Amoy Roads, present day Xiamen, on 15 June 1711. The choice of Amoy, little frequented by Europeans at the time, in preference to Canton where Europeans had customarily headed, is tied to the fact that the French East India Company had granted Noël Piécourt authorisation to go to China, but had not granted him permission to trade at Canton where the Company itself had no right to trade. This is explained by Michel Dubocage in his logbook entry for 3 June 1711.

The French crews were soon authorised to live in the town, and the first commercial transactions were drafted. These would continue for more than a year and would require numerous subterfuges as well as the decisive intervention of a French Jesuit, Father Laureaty, an adviser to the Chinese Emperor, to ensure the success of the negotiations. On 13 July 1712 the French and Chinese merchants ratified what was probably one of the first bilateral commercial agreements between France and China. This important commercial treaty consisted of seven articles and is extensively commented on in the logbook of *La Découverte*, accompanied with Dubocage's interesting observations (Fig. 9).

Fig. 8　Map of the Ile de la Passion (6JJ-39p50a2)

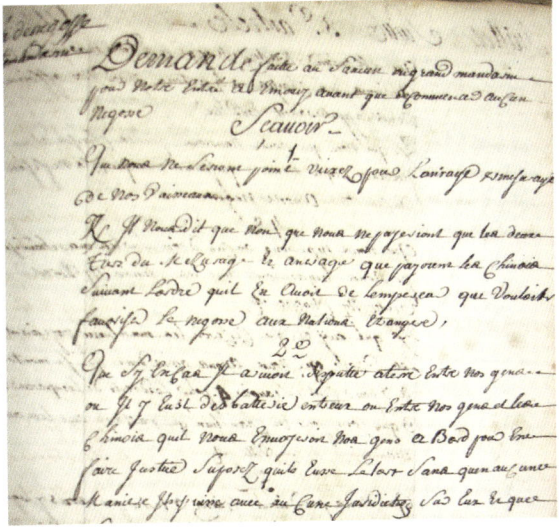

Fig. 9　Commercial agreement by Dubocage (extract)

The Franco Chinese commercial agreement of 1712 and inter ethnic difficulties.

Article 1 states that whilst moored in Amoy, the French ships are not to be surcharged for anchoring or according to their size. On the contrary it states that they will pay only two thirds of what Chinese merchants pay for anchoring at Amoy. The 'Grand Mandarin of Amoy', informs the French that this measure has been decided by the Emperor in order to 'facilitate negotiations with foreign nations'.

Article 2 aims to ease potential difficulties and tensions between the two communities and states the rules of justice applicable in the event of brawls or worse, if a man is killed. If such an event occurs, the Mandarin informs the French that he will not be able to respond strongly to the Chinese population, which would risk the French 'losing everything'.

Article 3 states that the French captains and merchants have right to chairs with two porters but not to four porters as they had asked.

Then, article 4 gets to the point. It states that the French will not pay taxes on products negotiated, but that these taxes, levied at 7% will be paid by the Chinese merchants themselves. This levy will be divided as follows: 4% to the Emperor and 3% shared between the different Mandarins of the town.

Article 5 grants the French merchants the right to use a house in the town as a warehouse with an armed guard doubled by a Chinese guard provided by the houpou or hoppo.

Article 6 says that the French merchants can embark their money without paying tax and Article 7 concedes to the French the right to buy their supplies directly in the town without paying tax. On this subject however, Dubocage states that the Mandarins followed the "Maître d'Hôtel", or accommodation managers, when they went shopping in town and they extorted money from all the Chinese merchants who sold products to the French; to the point where the merchants had to raise their prices to recoup these secret taxes. Dubocage adds that 'wood, resins, nails and oil, which he needed for refitting his vessels' were sold to them 'at twice the price they were sold to the Chinese' and that the Chancun increased the taxes on Chinese merchants and also the men who worked for the French.

The entries made by Michel Dubocage (Fig. 10 et 11) in his logbook throughout his stay in Amoy clearly illustrate the difficulties which accompanied the first contacts between French seamen and the Chinese of Amoy. Dubocage reports that "these people are so malicious that they misrepresent foreigners to the uttermost degree and regard all of us as barbarians with the greatest misrepresentation possible. These rascals vomit at us as they pass in the street, hurling atrocious verbal abuse at us and often actual stones, particularly when we have to pass through the back streets".

Barely tolerated in the town, it's clear that the French did not arouse sympathy

Fig. 10　Portrait of Dubocage　　Fig. 11　Wooden statue of Dubocage, made in China

amongst the population. On several occasions the French captains had to intervene to prevent their crews revolting against the poor treatment to which they were subjected by the locals. Equally, a French sailor was severely punished on 28 October 1711 for having wronged Chinese merchants. The psychological gulf separating the Chinese and European social groups seem to have persisted even after death. Thus, when Nicolas Dautine, a 55 years old sailor died on board *La Découverte* on 25 June 1711, Dubocage requested and received Chinese authorisation to bury him on "*l'île de Columsué*", probably the island of Gulangyu, because this was where all of "*the English were buried*". It would be interesting to find these European sailors' graves on this island, which is almost certainly Gulang Yu, located next to Xiamen, and subject them to anthropological study.

Confidence between the negotiators on both sides was equally fragile, to the point where on 11 July 1711, the mandarins dealing with the two captains demanded that the two vessels' rudders, sails, ships' guns and powder be discharged onto land and handed to the town authorities, which naturally neither Michel Dubocage nor Pierre de Chassiron consented to do.

The long return home

Despite this difficult inter-ethnic apprenticeship, the holds were eventually loaded with Chinese goods in accordance with the treaty signed with Xiamen merchants, and Dubocage finally weighed anchor and left Amoy Roads on 13 July 1712. They passed along the coast of Japan and then the northern edge of the Pacific, before reaching Spanish South America in March 1713. Dubocage remained there for another three years in order to trade the products bought from China with the Spanish.

Now loaded mostly with chests full of silver, *La Découverte* finally left for France on 1 April 1716. After a detour via Brazil, Michel Dubocage finally reached Le Havre on 23 August 1716 after a voyage lasting nine years.

He had become rich as a result of his voyage to China and the South Seas, and established himself permanently as a shipping merchant, buying numerous properties (Fig. 12) and becoming one of the most eminent people of the town of Le Havre. He died on 1727, at the age of 51. His family was ennobled in 1753, and his son

Fig. 12　The house of Dubocage

became Mayor of the town of Le Havre that same year.

　　Thus, in less than two generations, courtesy of long-distance maritime trade, the Dubocage family became one of the most wealthy and famous families in one of the largest maritime ports of the French realm.

约稿启事
Call for Papers

　　本刊为水下考古学及相关研究领域的综合性学术刊物，由国家文物局水下文化遗产保护中心负责编辑出版，拟不定期出版。欢迎海内外学者赐稿，凡有关之学术论文，均所欢迎，并请勿一稿数投。

　　一、本刊刊登与水下考古学及相关研究领域、且未曾以其他文字发表之学术论文。

　　二、来稿中、英文不拘，中文稿以不超过三万字（以二万字论文为宜）、英文稿以不超过五十页为原则，并请附中、英文摘要（500字左右），中、英文篇名及关键词（3~5个）。

　　三、来稿请使用Word或WPS格式处理，并提供文稿电子档（含中英文摘要、关键词、正文）；图片请以JPG或TIFF格式存档，除附于文中相应位置外，还需单独提供图片文件（单色线图600dpi或以上，黑白和彩色图片300dpi或以上）。

　　四、来稿者请附中、英文姓名、工作单位、职称及联系方式（包括地址、电话、传真、E-mail）等信息。

　　五、投稿之论文经评审通过后，将函告之，请勿再将稿件他投。若未通过评审，当尽速退稿。作者请自留底稿，未能采用之稿件，本刊将不负责寄还。

　　六、本刊不负责来稿内容所涉及的版权问题（如引用文献、图版、表格等），请作者自行负责。本刊发表之论文，其著作权属作者，第三者欲刊登，必须取得作者之同意。

　　七、体例及书目引用格式请参照内文，亦可来函索取投稿须知。文中注释采用脚注方式，置于当页下方，每注另起一行；编号以每篇论文为单位，使用阿拉伯数字（如[1]，[36]，加方括号），顺次排列，置于标点符号之前。中日韩文书名、篇名以书名号（《》或<>）标示；西文书刊名以斜体标示，论文篇名使用正体。引用书目分古代文献（以时代为序）、近人论著（以著者姓名拼音或外文字母为序），中日韩与西文文献分排，引用论文请标注全文起始页码。

　　八、惠稿一经刊出，谨致赠作者本刊五本、论文抽印本三十份，酌付稿酬。

　　九、稿件请寄：

　　　　北京市海淀区宝盛南路1号院4号楼（邮编：100192）
　　　　国家文物局水下文化遗产保护中心　《水下考古学研究》编辑组
　　　　电话：+86-10-50972157
　　　　传真：+86-10-50972180
　　　　邮箱：sxkgxyj@163.com或info@uch-china.org

Studies of Underwater Archaeology (*SUA*) is an academic publication edited and published by the National Centre of Underwater Cultural Heritage of China, founded by the Underwater Archaeology Research Centre of the National Museum of China in 2012. *SUA* welcomes the submission of manuscripts in English dealing with underwater archaeology and related research fields. Manuscripts must not exceed 20,000 English words. The form of footnotes and references are available upon request (see guidelines below). We cannot accept manuscripts that do not follow these guidelines. To cite online materials, it is required to include the URL, the name of the database, and an access date. Please specify the following on the manuscript: author's English and Chinese names, affiliated institution, position, and address. The author is required to submit a digital version with the submission as its attachment. The preferred editing programme is a recent version of Word. Please avoid fancy formatting of the text. After a manuscript has been accepted, we will notify the author as soon as possible. Rejected manuscripts are not returned to the author. The author has sole responsibility for obtaining permission from publishers to use copyrighted materials, such as illustrations, charts, or lengthy quotations. Upon publication, authors will receive free of charge thirty offprints of their articles and five copies of the entire issue concerned.

Manuscripts should be addressed as follows:
Editorial Board of *Studies of Underwater Archaeology*
National Center of Underwater Cultural Heritage of China
Buliding 4, No.1 Baosheng Nan Road, Haidian District
Beijing 100192, P. R. China
Tel: +86-10-5097 2157
Fax: +86-10-5097 2180
E-mail: sxkgxyj@163.com
info@uch-china.org

Guidelines for footnotes and references:
Roxanna Maude Brown, *The Ming Gap and Shipwreck Ceramics in Southeast Asia*, Ph.D. dissertation, Los Angeles: University of California, 2004.
Hugh Edwards and Michael Hatcher, *Treasures of the Deep, The Extraordinary Life and Times of Captain Mike Hatcher*, Australia: Harper Collins, 2000.
Michael Flecker, Excavation of an oriental vessel of c. 1690 off Con Dao, Vietnam, *The International Journal of Nautical Archaeology*, Vol.21(3), pp.221-244, 1992.
Ho Chuimei: The Ceramic Boom in Minnan during Song and Yuan Times, Angela Schottenhammer ed. *The Emporium of The World: Maritime Quanzhou, 1000-1400*, Koninklijke Brill NV, Leiden: The Netherlands, 2001, pp.237-282.

编后记
Afterword

经过将近三年的漫长编辑历程，《水下考古学研究》第二卷终于付梓了。这本以水下考古学研究为主的学术论文集刊自2012年由中国国家博物馆水下考古研究中心编辑刊印第一卷以来，颇受学界关注。随后，中国国家博物馆即着手第二卷的约稿和编辑工作，国家文物局水下文化遗产保护中心独立建制后，决定继续编辑、出版此书刊，前后历时三载，至此方得以刊印。在此，我们向热情为本卷惠赐大作的诸位作者深表感谢，也为延至今日出版而向作者致以最诚挚的歉意。同时，我们也就本卷编辑出版中的一些情况向作者和读者作一简要说明。

本书从约稿到编辑、出版，耗时较长。期间，适逢国家水下考古机构整合，2014年6月，经中编办批准，文化部、国家文物局决定中国国家博物馆水下考古研究中心整体划转并入国家文物局水下文化遗产保护中心，并独立建制，负责统筹全国水下文化遗产保护业务工作。因此，本卷的编印单位已由约稿时的中国国家博物馆改为国家文物局水下文化遗产保护中心。

本卷刊发了18篇论文，内容涉及东南亚海域沉船及出水文物、东非水下考古新发现、中国古外销陶瓷与海外贸易史、出水文物保护、传统造船技术、欧洲船舶考古学与历史学研究等方面，反映了水下考古学研究多样化的领域和视角。谢明良关于"黑石号"沉船、陈国栋关于所谓"的惺号"沉船和出水文物研究，以及东南亚海域沉船发现与研究、东非地区肯尼亚水下考古新发现等几篇论文，重点探讨了古代海上丝绸之路上的南海贸易和印度洋贸易网络。有关中国古外销陶瓷的5篇研究文章，分别从窑址考古调查、贸易航线上的沉船发现及其海外地区的消费使用等不同角度，勾勒出了古代陶瓷器的海外贸易状况。出水文物保护方面，车美永以木材和谷物为例探讨了韩国海洋出水有机质文物的保护方法及实践。传统造船技术方面，许路探讨了福建古代造船技术的发展概况。欧洲船舶考古与历史研究的一组共7篇文章，源于2009年11月由法国远东学院（EFEO）、中国国家博物馆、中国社会科学院考古研究所、法国国家科学研究中心（CNRS）等联合举办的"船与人：亚洲古船历史学与考古学比较研究的新视角"（Of Ships and Men: New Comparative Approaches in Asian Maritime History and Archaeology）国际学术研讨会，本次研讨会中的亚洲航海考古与历史的论文将由法国远东学院《专题研究》（*Etudes thématiques* [*Thematic Studies*]）丛刊出版；而关于欧洲船舶考古与历史的文章则以英文收录本卷中，并且文前附有此次会议组织者之一的柯兰（Paola Calanca）、莽甘（Pierre-Yves Manguin）、李特（Eric Rieth）专门为此撰写的《导言》。这些不同领域的研究，围绕水下文化遗存、海外贸易史、舟船航行、船舶社会与生活等一系列问题，运用考古学、历史学、人类学和民族学方法，从不同角度探讨了与之相关的社会生活，也反映了当前水下考古学研究的多元化趋势。

限于编者水平和经验,加之工作繁忙,本书中难免出现讹误,请各位作者和读者及时予以指正。同时,我们再次向支持本刊和提交论文的各位作者,致以深深的谢意,也希望诸位先生以及更多的学者以后继续关注、鼓励、支持我们。

本书编委会各位委员为约集、审定和统筹稿件,花费了不少精力,并时刻关注着本书进度与出版情况,特为致谢。特别是法国远东学院柯兰女士,统筹了欧洲船舶考古与历史方面的七篇论文,协助联络作者,并审校了全文和中文摘要等内容。

法国巴黎第一大学博士候选人邱丹丹女士翻译了欧洲船舶考古与历史文章的中文导言和七篇论文的中文摘要,韩国首尔特别市厅文化本部(首尔工艺博物馆)高美京女士协助联络韩国学者并翻译了其论文和摘要,中国社会科学院考古研究所黄珊女士、中国国家博物馆外事处夏美芳女士承担了书中部分论文英文摘要的翻译与审校,在此一并致谢。

本书的责任编辑李茜女士认真负责、耐心细致、多次联系、商谈出版事宜,并及时督促本书的排版、审校,为本书的编辑工作不辞繁琐,付出了大量辛苦努力,谨此致谢。

"夫学须志也,才须学也。非学无以广才,非志无以成学。"在静心求索中,让我们继续砥砺前行。

编　者

2016年3月12日